THE MOST SOLITARY OF AFFLICTIONS

The Most Solitary of Afflictions

Madness and Society in Britain 1700–1900

ANDREW SCULL

Yale University Press
New Haven and London · 1993

Set in Linotron Bembo by Best-set Typesetter Ltd., Hong Kong

Printed in Great Britain by The Bath Press, Avon

This book is printed on acid-free paper

Library of Congress Cataloging-in-Publication Data

Scull, Andrew T.
    The most solitary of afflictions: madness and society in Britain,
1700–1900 / Andrew Scull.
        p.   cm.
    Includes bibliographical references and index.
    ISBN 0-300-05051-8 (alk. paper)
    1. Psychiatric hospital care—England—History.   2. Mentally ill—Care—
England—History.   3. Mental health laws—England—History.
I. Title.
    [DNLM: 1. Mental Disorders—history—Great Britain.   2. Social
Conditions—history—Great Britain. WM 11 FA1 S4m 1993]
RC450.G7S285   1993
362.2′1′094209034—dc20
DNLM/DLC
for Library of Congress   92-48395
                                                                                      CIP

A catalogue record for this book is available from the British Library

For Nancy, and for Anna, Andrew Edward, and Alexander

CONTENTS

LIST OF TABLES

LIST OF ILLUSTRATIONS

ACKNOWLEDGEMENTS

It is hard to know where to begin, and certainly impossible to know how to end, a list of thanks to all those who have helped me over the years with research for this book. Certainly, I must once again acknowledge the help of my thesis supervisor, Robert Scott, who helped to encourage my fledgling efforts in historical sociology more than two decades ago. In the years since, the American Council of Learned Societies, the Guggenheim Foundation, the Commonwealth Fund, the American Philosophical Society, the Shelby Cullom Davis Center for Historical Studies, and a University of California Presidential research fellowship have all helped to underwrite my further researches. Given my distance from the archives I need to consult, their financial assistance has simply been indispensable. I hope this book is some recompense for their generosity.

Librarians and archivists in many institutions have been enormously helpful over the years, and though it is invidious to mention particular people, the staff at the Wellcome Institute for the History of Medicine in London nonetheless deserve special thanks. It has obviously been vital for me to consult the records of mental hospitals themselves, and I am most grateful to the medical directors who made these available to me. My debt to other historians of psychiatry is acknowledged, formally if inadequately, in my footnotes and bibliography (though William Bynum and Roy Porter deserve special mention for stimulating conversation, and for disagreeing with me often enough to make life interesting).

Introduction

Madness constitutes a right, as it were, to treat people as vermin.
Lord Shaftesbury, *Diaries*, September 5, 1851

There is always much to be done to alleviate and smooth the march to the grave.
H.C. Burdett, *Hospitals and Asylums of the World*

'What an awful condition that of a lunatic! His words are generally disbelieved, and his most innocent peculiarities perverted; it is natural that it should be so; and we place ourselves on guard – that is, we give to every word, look, gesture a value and meaning which oftentimes it cannot bear, and which it would never bear in ordinary life. Thus we too readily get him in, and too sluggishly get him out, and yet what a destiny!'
Lord Shaftesbury, *Diaries* November 18, 1844

Two decades have passed since I first began to try to understand the social organization of insanity in nineteenth-century England. At that time, I most certainly neither expected nor intended to devote so much of my scholarly life to the exploration of the history of madness. Still, the combination of choice and circumstance which first led me to take an interest in what is surely 'the most solitary of afflictions to the people who experience it; but . . . the most social of maladies to those who observe its effects'[1] has never been an occasion for regret. Over the past twenty years, my initial fascination with this subject matter has if anything deepened, as I have continued to find new questions to pursue, new intellectual puzzles to worry over, and new archives to explore.

Of considerable importance in sustaining my interest in the field has been the increasing number of talented historians attracted to it. Their work has greatly expanded the range and depth of our knowledge, and has provided a far richer and more challenging historiographic context within which to work. Yale University Press's invitation to re-explore the

---

1. Michael MacDonald, *Mystical Bedlam: Madness, Anxiety, and Healing in Seventeenth Century England*, Cambridge: Cambridge University Press, 1981, p. 1.

territory I had first surveyed in *Museums of Madness*[2] was thus a welcome development, for it provided me with the incentive and the occasion to re-examine the intractable dilemmas the Victorians confronted in coping with unreason, with the advantages bestowed by much additional research and reflection.

From the outset, once my editor and I had agreed that the project was worth undertaking, I wanted to do more than simply reissue my earlier text in barely modified form. At the risk of immodesty, it seems fair to say that a good deal of the past generation of work on the history of English psychiatry has made explicit or implicit reference to my work, either seeking to elaborate and refine some of the claims I had advanced in *Museums of Madness*, or to engage in more thoroughgoing criticism of its contentions. To ignore this body of scholarship or to fail to undertake a serious and systematic consideration of its implications for my arguments would, I concluded, sharply limit the value of the enterprise. At the same time, my own further researches had broadened and (I hope) deepened my grasp of the field, so that simply adding a chapter of afterthoughts to my existing discussion seemed doubly unsatisfactory, a timorous avoidance of an intellectual challenge and opportunity which I felt fortunate to have been offered.

I have therefore chosen to undertake a more extensive reworking of my original text, one that builds upon the foundation provided by my earlier work but aims to rethink and to add substantially to it. Hence the decision to issue this book under a new title. In revisiting the Victorians' 'museums for the collection of insanity,' I have observed and recorded much that I overlooked or insufficiently emphasized when I first attempted to comprehend the rise of asylumdom. Over the past decade and a half, others have taught me to look at and for aspects of our responses to insanity that I had previously neglected, and to reassess the significance of some of those that I had observed. In a variety of ways, then – both large and small – this is a very different and I hope a better book than its predecessor. It is still, nonetheless, recognizably descended from the account I first offered fifteen years ago – necessarily so, for I remain convinced that most of the central arguments I made then have stood the test of time.

I cannot expect, of course, to have pleased all of my critics, and nor have I sought to. I hope this stance is more than a stubborn persistence in error. In some instances, my critics seem to me to have attacked a caricature of my argument, rather than what I actually wrote; and in others, they have made claims that I believe are not supported by the historical record.[3] Nor am I interested in producing the sort of sanitized

2. *Museums of Madness: The Social Organization of Insanity in Nineteenth Century England*, London: Allen Lane, 1979.
3. See, for example, Gerald Grob, 'Marxian Analysis and Mental Illness', *History of Psychiatry* 1, 1990, pp. 223–32; G.E. Berrios and H. Freeman, Introduction to their edited volume, *150 Years of British Psychiatry 1841–1991*, London: Gaskell, 1991; J.L. Crammer, *Asylum History: Buckinghamshire County Pauper Lunatic Asylum – St John's*, London: Gaskell, 1990.

and 'responsible' history that seems necessary to secure a warm welcome in some quarters. Part of the historian's task ought surely to be to rescue those portions of the past our collective memory seeks to repress, if not to cast into oblivion; and the history of our responses to madness, if far from being an unrelieved parade of horrors and ever-increasing repression, is equally far from being a stirring tale of the progress of humanity and science. My work thus continues to have a critical edge, for I am convinced that there is much to be critical about.

In practice, though I expected to make considerable changes and additions to my original text, it turned out that in certain respects I had underestimated how much rethinking and rewriting would be involved. This book is perhaps twice as long as its predecessor. No chapter has survived unscathed, and much of the original discussion has been modified to some degree or other. Nineteenth-century developments, for instance, cannot be understood in isolation from an earlier history of efforts to grapple with unreason; and yet, fifteen years ago, with the exception of William Parry-Jones's pioneering work on 'the trade in lunacy',[4] and Hunter and MacAlpine's monumental anthology of early writings on insanity and their revisionist reinterpretation of George III's 'madness' as porphyria,[5] the history of madness in early modern England was, to borrow Sir Richard Blackmore's phrase, 'an intellectual Africa'.[6] Much exploration still remains to be done, but our maps of the territory are by now far more detailed and accurate, and in the light of the researches of Michael MacDonald, Roy Porter, and Jonathan Andrews (to name just a handful of major contributors to the expansion of our knowledge), we have moved decisively beyond the period of writing fables about a dark and dimly understood continent. My own discussion of the early modern period could not but benefit from taking this work into account, however much I continue to disagree with some of the arguments that Porter and Andrews, among others, have made. And to cite merely one additional example, at the other end of the temporal spectrum covered in this book, my original discussions of late Victorian psychiatry were similarly handicapped by the underdeveloped state of the existing historiography, a state of affairs numerous scholars have attempted to rectify over the past decade and a half, fortunately with considerable success. In hindsight, I must say that the sections of *Museums of Madness* that dealt with developments in the last third of the nineteenth century now strike me as somewhat cursory and schematic – defects I have sought to remedy here.

4. William L. Parry-Jones, *The Trade in Lunacy: A Study of Private Madhouses in England in the Eighteenth and Nineteenth Centuries*, London: Routledge and Kegan Paul, 1972.
5. Richard Hunter and Ida MacAlpine, *Three Hundred Years of Psychiatry, 1535–1860*, London: Oxford University Press, 1963; Ida MacAlpine and Richard Hunter, *George III and the Mad Business*, London: Allen Lane, 1969.
6. Sir Richard Blackmore, *A Treatise of the Spleen or Vapours*, London: Pemberton, 1724, p. 263.

In modifying and reshaping my own views about English responses to madness, I suspect that my own continued immersion in the relevant primary materials has been at least as important as the growth of a significant secondary literature. If not wiser, I have inevitably become more knowledgeable on a whole range of issues, and I have had the opportunity to explore sources, such as asylum casebooks and patient records, with which I had only the most glancing acquaintance when I wrote the first edition of this book. Then too, one hopes that the passage of the years may bring a little maturity and broadening of intellectual horizons as some slight compensation for the encroachments of middle age. Taking all this together, and with the added advantages that ordinarily flow from gaining some intellectual distance from one's own work, I trust that the result is a more nuanced, thoughtful, and thoroughly grounded treatment of the subject, but one that I have tried to ensure remains lively and compelling reading. The past, as a now infamous social theorist once insisted, may weigh like a nightmare on the brains of the living; the historian ought at least to prevent it smothering us beneath its dead weight.

CHAPTER ONE

The Rise of the Asylum

Men make their own history, but they do not make it just as they please; they do not make it under circumstances chosen by themselves, but under circumstances directly encountered, given and transmitted from the past. The tradition of all the dead generations weighs like a nightmare on the brain of the living.
Karl Marx, *The Eighteenth Brumaire of Louis Bonaparte*

No medical advance, no humanitarian approach was responsible for the fact that the monotony of insanity was divided into rudimentary types. It was the depths of confinement itself that generated the phenomenon; it is from confinement that we must seek an account of this new awareness of madness.
Michel Foucault, *Madness and Civilization*

1. The Social Control of the Mad

The typical response to the deranged underwent dramatic changes between the mid-eighteenth and mid-nineteenth centuries. At the outset of this period, mad people for the most part were not treated even as a separate category or type of deviants. Rather, impoverished madmen were assimilated into the much larger, more amorphous class of the morally disreputable, the poor, and the impotent, a group which also included vagrants, minor criminals, and the physically handicapped; and their richer (though not necessarily more fortunate) counterparts were for the most part coped with by their families. Furthermore, just as in the case of the indigent generally, the societal response to the problems posed by the presence of mentally disturbed individuals did not involve segregating them into separate receptacles designed to keep them apart from the rest of society. The overwhelming majority of the insane were still to be found at large in the community. By the mid-nineteenth century, however, virtually no aspect of this traditional response remained intact. The insane were clearly and sharply distinguished from other 'problem populations'. They found themselves incarcerated in a specialized, bureaucratically organized, state-supported asylum system which isolated them both physically and symbolically from the larger society. And within this segregated environment, now recognized as one of the major varieties of deviance in English society, their condition had been diagnosed as a uniquely and essentially medical problem. Accordingly, they had been delivered into the hands of a new group of professionals, the so-called 'mad-doctors'.[1] This book seeks to provide a critical account and understanding of this major historical shift in the styles and practices of social control, and an assessment of its major consequences.

Conventionally, of course, this transformation is known to historians as the 'reform' of the treatment of the 'mentally ill'. The very language that is used thus reflects the implicit assumptions which for many years marked most historians' treatment of the subject – a naive Whiggish view of history as progress, and a failure to see key elements of the reform process as sociologically highly problematic. For those writing from this perspective, lunacy reform reflects two converging forces. On the one hand, the rise of an urbanized, industrial society is seen as producing a social order whose very complexity forced the adoption of some form of institutional response. On the other, the acceptance of state 'responsibility' for the insane, the advent of the asylum, and the developing link between medicine and insanity are pictured as the 'natural' outcome of the growing civilization of social existence, the rise of a humanitarian concern for one's fellow citizens, and the advances of science and human understanding. For proponents of this viewpoint, the direction of the line of march undertaken in the early nineteenth century and the sources of the impulse to march were essentially unproblematic:

> The obstacles to [reform] had been not vested interest but public ignorance and apathy. For centuries [sic] that apathy had remained unchallenged, but when nineteenth century humanitarianism joined with a more scientific understanding of insanity it diminished. Yet neither humanitarianism nor science would have availed much had not government officials investigated the abuses and had not Commons [sic] placed asylums under the surveillance of government inspectors.[2]

The direction taken by lunacy reform in the nineteenth century is thus presented as at once inevitable and basically benign – both in intent and in consequences – and the whole process crudely reduced to a simplistic

1. The term 'mad-doctor' was widely used throughout the eighteenth and into the nineteenth century. As it steadily acquired negative connotations, the medical men engaged in trading in lunacy increasingly referred to themselves as 'asylum superintendents' and then, borrowing from the French, as 'alienists'. Only in the last third of the nineteenth century did the German term, 'Psychiatrie', begin to enter general usage, though those running the asylums were by then more inclined to call themselves 'medical psychologists'. Similarly, 'insanity' and 'lunacy' were the standard eighteenth-century terms for mental disorder and remained so through the nineteenth century, while the eighteenth-century 'madhouses' gradually became 'asylums' before eventually being transmogrified into 'hospitals for the insane'.
2. David Roberts, *Victorian Origins of the British Welfare State*, New Haven: Yale University Press, 1960, p. 63.

equation: humanitarianism + science + government inspection = the success of what David Roberts terms 'the great nineteenth-century movement for a more humane and intelligent treatment of the insane'.[3]

In this and subsequent chapters, I shall endeavour to show that almost all aspects of this purported 'explanation' are false, or provide a grossly distorted and misleading picture of what lunacy reform was all about. Reform did indeed have deep structural roots in the changing nature of English society, but these roots were embedded to a far greater extent and in far more complex ways in broader transformations of the English political and social structure and especially in the nature of capitalism as a social phenomenon than conventional simplistic references to urbanization and industrialization have managed to grasp. The reformers did indeed profess to be actuated by 'humane' concern with the well-being of the lunatic (I have yet to meet a reformer who conceded that his designs on the object of his attentions were malevolent). But whatever the Victorian *haute bourgeoisie*'s degree of sympathy with the sufferings of the lower orders, and however convinced one may or may not be of the depth of their interest in the latter's welfare, it remains the case that to present the outcome of reform as a triumphant and unproblematic expression of humanitarian concern is to adopt a perspective which is hopelessly biased and inaccurate: one which relies, of necessity, on a systematic neglect and distortion of the available evidence. It is time to transfer our attention away from the rhetoric of intentions and to consider instead what a more searching examination of the historical record reveals about the establishment and operation of the new apparatus for the social control of the mad.

Similarly with the notion that the medical capture of madness reflected and was somehow caused by some mysterious advance in scientific understanding: as an ideological prop for the professional claims of psychiatry, this claim has obvious merits; as an historical analysis of the process itself, it has none. Knowledge (or what passes for knowledge at any given historical juncture)[4] is, of course, a vital weapon in the competition for

3. *Ibid.*, p. 62. The *locus classicus* of this view is, of course, Kathleen Jones's two-volume history, *Lunacy, Law, and Conscience 1744–1845*, London: Routledge and Kegan Paul, 1955; and *Mental Health and Social Policy 1845–1955*, London: Routledge and Kegan Paul, 1960. As Orwell recognized, the ability to rewrite the past to provide an account supportive of the present powers that be is an extraordinarily useful ideological weapon. It thus should come as no surprise that psychiatrists have been unusually attentive to the need to police their own history: often writing it themselves; bestowing praise and whatever expert authority they can muster on writers who write accounts they find congenial; and evincing violent hostility to historians whose work presents the history of psychiatry in a less than flattering light. For examples, see J.K. Wing, 'Review of *Social Order/Mental Disorder*', *Times Literary Supplement* 7 July 1989, pp. 747–8 (praising Kathleen Jones and criticizing my work); and Martin Roth, 'Psychiatry and its Critics', *British Journal of Psychiatry* 122, 1973, pp. 374–402 (denouncing those not endorsing the triumphalist view as callous barbarians, irresponsibly meddling with justified authority and wilfully obstructing the relief of suffering).
4. As should be apparent, one of the central advantages enjoyed by an established profession in the contest for jurisdiction is precisely its ability to define what legitimately *counts* as 'knowledge', just as one of its major tasks is the production of new knowledge.

professional jurisdiction, as well as in the legitimation of professional work.[5] The power of a profession's knowledge – its ability to rationalize, reorganize, and make sense of experience; its value as a systematized source of prescriptions for intervention; and most certainly the practical and perceived efficacy of the interventions it licenses and makes possible – constitutes a crucial foundation for efforts to secure and sustain professional dominance and control over a particular territory. But the fight for turf is nonetheless always and necessarily a political process, in which the mobilization of organizational resources and of various forms of social and cultural capital comes decisively into play – and these dimensions of the struggle must be analysed with care if we are to obtain an adequate understanding of the ultimate outcome.

Among those committed to (or trapped within) the conventional accounts of psychiatric history, central elements of the reform process become 'obvious', taken for granted, insulated from critical scrutiny. And where reality is too insistent and diverges too sharply from their mythical representation of it, the discrepancies between the ideal and the real are dismissed as the predictable outcome of human imperfection or the unintended, 'accidental' consequences of well-intended actions.[6] Mere facts are thus reordered so as to leave the myth intact. Nor should this surprise us. As Gilbert Ryle once pointed out, 'A myth is, of course, not a fairy story. It is the presentation of facts belonging in one category in the idioms belonging to another. To explode a myth is accordingly not to deny the facts but to reallocate them.'[7] My task, indeed, far from being one of denying the facts, must be to re-emphasize them, and to show how they lead to an interpretation of lunacy reform widely at variance with that traditionally offered. I shall suggest that the sources of the movement for lunacy reform are infinitely more complex, the humanitarianism and the science indisputably more ambiguous, and the intelligence and humanity of the regimen in the public museums of the mad built by the Victorians inescapably more dubious than an earlier generation of historians ever imagined.

I want to emphasize at the outset, however, that I see little to be gained from simply turning the old Whiggish history on its head. What Peter Sedgwick has dubbed 'the anti-history of psychiatry'[8] – whether in its

---

5. Cf. Andrew Abbott, *The System of Professions: An Essay on the Division of Expert Labor*, Chicago: University of Chicago Press, 1988, pp. 52–7, 102–3.

6. This is, for example, the strategy Gerald Grob repeatedly adopts in his meliorist accounts of the history of American psychiatry. See *Mental Institutions in America: Social Policy to 1875*, New York: Free Press, 1973; *Mental Illness and American Society, 1875–1940*; and, especially, his historiographic essays, notably 'Rediscovering Asylums: The Unhistorical History of the Mental Hospital', *Hastings Center Report* 7, #4, 1977, pp. 33–41. For a more extended critique of his position, see my *Social Order/Mental Disorder: Anglo-American Psychiatry in Historical Perspective*, London: Routledge, 1989, chapter 2.

7. Gilbert Ryle, *The Concept of Mind*, New York: Harper and Row, 1949 (London: Penguin, 1970).

8. Peter Sedgwick, *Psychopolitics*, London: Pluto Press, 1981.

Szaszian or Foucauldian guise – has exercised a powerful influence over the historiography of the field during the past quarter century, threatening to establish its own counter-orthodoxy. Like the anti-psychiatrists, I am profoundly sceptical of psychiatry's self-proclaimed rationality and disinterested benevolence, a scepticism which is rooted in what is, on the whole, a dismal and depressing historical record. But I cannot accept the Szaszian claim that mental alienation is simply the product of arbitrary social labelling or scapegoating, a social construction *tout court*; nor his vision of psychiatry as merely a malevolent or cynical enterprise, with the psychiatrists themselves no more than concentration camp guards or manufacturers of madness (a caricature as crude and misleading as its obverse, the claim that they are the benevolent and disinterested purveyors of humanity and science). As I hope this book will demonstrate, to examine psychiatry and its ministrations with a critical eye by no means entails the adoption of the romantic idea that the problems it deals with are purely the invention of the professional mind. Nor does it require us to embrace the Manichean notion that all psychiatric interventions are malevolent and ill-conceived.

Foucault is a more complicated case (as befits someone who is a much more sophisticated thinker), and one must acknowledge that heuristically, at least, the intellectual challenges he threw down three decades ago have directly or indirectly been the stimulus for much of the best recent work in the history of psychiatry. Still, his analysis, provocative though it may be, rests on the shakiest of scholarly foundations;[9] and its metaphysical subtleties, its flamboyant romanticism, and its dazzling prose notwithstanding, its reconstruction of the encounter of (Western) civilization and madness remains deeply and fundamentally flawed. For Foucault, the history of psychiatry is anything but the history of the gradual liberation of the insane from their fetters of iron and the shackles of superstition. Quite the contrary: his version of that history first offers us a romantic portrait of the Middle Ages as a Continental equivalent of Merrie Olde England, an era in which folly flourished largely free of pernicious social restraint; and then contrasts this with a picture of the period from the midseventeenth century onwards as marked by a grand internment, a 'great confinement' of the mad and of other social undesirables whose very existence constituted an affront to bourgeois sensibilities; before it finally concludes with an assessment of the dawn of the nineteenth century as corresponding to the imposition of an ever more thoroughgoing 'moral uniformity and social denunciation' – the historical moment at which the medical gaze secures its domination over the mad, launching 'that gigantic

---

9. For further discussion of this point, see Andrew Scull, 'A Failure to Communicate? On the Reception of Foucault's *Histoire de la folie* by Anglo-American Historians', in Arthur Still and Irving Volody (eds), *Rewriting the History of Madness*, London: Routledge, 1992; and my *Social Order/Mental Disorder*, chapter 1.

moral imprisonment which we are in the habit of calling, doubtless by antiphrasis, the liberation of the insane by Pinel and Tuke'.[10]

Neither of the first two claims will withstand scrutiny, and the third, the contention that 'kind' psychiatry is more repressive and worse than 'cruel' confinement, is (as Roy Porter has pointed out)[11] not subject to straightforward empirical confirmation or refutation. Foucault's prose poem opens with some lyrical passages conjuring up the wandering existence of the existentially free medieval madman, roaming 'the open countryside, when not entrusted to a group of merchants and pilgrims'.[12] As he himself summarized his argument, this was a period in which, '[g]enerally speaking, madness was allowed free reign; it circulated throughout society; it formed part of the background and language of everyday life, it was for everyone an everyday experience that sought not to exalt nor to control . . .'.[13] The plastic and literary arts are drawn upon as evidence of the wide-ranging cultural fascination with Folly, and then, most famously of all, Foucault invokes the ship of fools, which captures for him the essence of the medieval response to madness. In its origins, Foucault concedes, the *Narrenschiff* is a literary or an artistic conceit, no different from its fashionable counterparts, the Ship of Princes, the Ship of Virtuous Ladies, or the Ship of Health. But, he insists, 'of all these romantic or satiric vessels,' the Ship of Fools 'is the only one that had a real existence – for they did exist, these boats that conveyed their insane cargo from town to town'.[14] Having made this claim, Foucault then launches on a lengthy discussion of the practical and symbolic significance of these 'real' ships, with their floating cargo of madmen off in search of their reason, parading up and down the Rhine, haunting the imagination of the entire early Renaissance, living symbols of 'the madman's *liminal* position on the horizon of medieval concern'.[15]

Unfortunately for all those enamoured of this romantic and delightfully delineated landscape, reality must be rendered in rather darker hues. As Erik Midelfort has pointed out, the ship of fools (like Foucault's other striking image of the medieval leprosaria, waiting across three centuries, 'soliciting with strange incantations a new incarnation of disease, another grimace of terror, renewed rites of purification and exclusion'[16] till they were populated by the mad) is simply a figment of the latter's overactive

---

10. Michel Foucault, *Madness and Civilization*, New York: Mentor Books, 1965, pp. 259, 278 (London: Tavistock Publications, 1971) (*Histoire de la folie*, new edition, Paris: Gallimard, 1972, pp. 514, 530).
11. Roy Porter, 'Foucault's Great Confinement', *History of the Human Sciences* 3, 1990, p. 51.
12. M. Foucault, *Madness and Civilization*, p. 8.
13. M. Foucault, *Mental Illness and Psychology*, Berkeley: University of California Press, 1987, p. 67.
14. M. Foucault, *Madness and Civilization*, p. 8.
15. *Ibid.*, p. 11, emphasis in the original.
16. *Ibid.*, p. 3.

imagination: 'Occasionally the mad were indeed sent away on boats. But nowhere can one find reference to real boats or ships loaded with mad pilgrims in search of their reason.'[17] Where the mad proved troublesome, as we shall see, they could expect to be beaten or locked up; otherwise, they might roam or rot. Either way, the facile contrast between psychiatric oppression and an earlier, almost anarchic toleration is surely illusory.

Similarly with his view of the Classical Age as the first decisive step in Reason's repression of Unreason: from Foucault's perspective, the period from the founding of the first *Hôpital Général* in Paris in 1656 to the events of 1789 was in essence the age of the Great Confinement, a movement which swept up the idle and insane from the streets, severed their connections with society, and cast them into oblivion – an oblivion in which they were nonetheless compelled, lest they further offend bourgeois sensibilities, to work as a moral duty. Foucault insists on the sudden emergence and the universality of the impulse to confine: the spread of 'an entire network' of places of confinement 'across Europe'; an associated shift in meaning,

> which had so hastily, so spontaneously summoned into being all over Europe the category of classical order we call confinement.... There must have formed, silently and doubtless over the course of many years, a social sensibility common to European culture, that suddenly began to manifest itself in the second half of the seventeenth century; it was this sensibility that suddenly isolated the category destined to populate the places of confinement.... Confinement, that massive phenomenon, the signs of which are found all across eighteenth century Europe....[18]

Here again, we see a cavalier tendency to overgeneralize. Whatever merits this account may have as a portrait of French responses under the *ancien régime*,[19] it corresponds scarcely at all to developments elsewhere. In England, as I shall show, there was no substantial state-led move to confine the mad (or the poor, come to that) during the seventeenth or the eighteenth century. Indeed, the management of the mad on this side of the Channel remained ad hoc and unsystematic, with most madmen kept at

17. Erik H.C. Midelfort, 'Madness and Civilization in Early Modern Europe', in B.C. Malament (ed.), *After the Reformation: Essays in Honor of J.H. Hexter*, Philadelphia: University of Pennsylvania Press, 1980, p. 254; see also W.B. Maher and B. Maher, 'The Ship of Fools: *Stultifera Navis* or *Ignis Fatuus?*' *American Psychologist* 37, pp. 756–761.
18. M. Foucault, *Madness and Civilization*, pp. 44–7.
19. To cite just one major problem, even with the French case: I think that Foucault's account errs in according madness a much more significant place in comprehending the *ancien régime*'s resort to confinement than its quite marginal role actually warrants. The mad formed only a tiny fraction of the total swept up and confined in the *hôpitaux généraux*, and Foucault's attempt to identify 'all forms of social uselessness' with madness, and to see confinement as constituting a grand confrontation between Reason and Unreason, rests on little more than verbal gymnastics and tricks.

home or left to roam the countryside, while that small fraction who were
confined could generally be found in the small madhouses which made
up the newly emerging 'trade in lunacy'. There was, as we shall see,
no English 'exorcism' of madness; no serious attempt to police pauper
madmen (on the contrary, a sizeable fraction of the clientele of the
new madhouses came from the affluent classes, necessarily so if the new
entrepreneurial system was to flourish); and so far from attempting to
inculcate bourgeois work habits, as Roy Porter has commented, 'what
truly characterised [life in the handful of eighteenth-century asylums] was
idleness'.[20]

As for Foucault's final sweeping historical judgement, whether, and in
what respects, one can fairly assess the moral treatment era as marking a
'gigantic moral imprisonment' of the mad is a question with no single
answer. Foucault's ringing denunciations (part of his larger assault on the
Enlightenment and its values) embody a rather complex set of assertions,
some of which I think are defensible and correct, others quite dubious
or wrong. (And on other levels, of course, his furious assault on the
machinations of bourgeois Reason reflects a set of moral choices that lie
beyond the reach of empirical argument.) In my view, to reduce moral
treatment simply to a species of imprisonment, a more thoroughgoing
form of repression, is to mask an important truth behind a screen of
rhetorical excess. Instead, I shall suggest, we do better to view moral
treatment (like the larger reform it spawned) as fundamentally ambiguous:
pace Foucault, it cannot be reduced to 'the irruption of a bureaucratic
rationalism into a preceding Golden Age of permissiveness towards
insanity',[21] and, from my perspective, at least, there are good grounds for
preferring the tactful manipulation and equivocal 'kindness' of Tuke and
Pinel to the more directly brutal coercion, fear, and constraint that marked
the methods of their predecessors. Yet one must also recognize that in the
not-so-long run, it was the other, less benevolent, face of moral treatment
that came to the fore: its strength as a mechanism for inducing conformity. In this wider perspective, it *is* fair to conclude that the major – if
unintended – contribution of those who introduced the techniques of
moral treatment was to make it possible, in a very practical sense, to
manage and clothe with a veil of legitimacy the nineteenth- and twentieth-
century museums for the collection and confinement of the mad.

But this is to anticipate conclusions that can only be established through
a lengthy and detailed analysis. My primary concerns in the chapters
which follow will be to examine the history of the English encounter with
madness to establish how and why insanity came to be exclusively defined

20. Roy Porter, *Mind Forg'd Manacles: A History of Madness in England from the Restoration to
    the Regency*, London: Athlone, 1987, p. 8. On the madhouse business, the standard work
    is William Parry-Jones, *The Trade in Lunacy*, London: Routledge and Kegan Paul, 1972.
21. P. Sedgwick, *Psychopolitics*, p. 138.

as an illness,[22] a condition within the sole jurisdiction of the medical profession; to answer the related question of why the mad-doctors and their reformist mentors opted for the asylum as the domain within which the insane were to receive their 'treatment'; and to delineate the effects of these choices on mad people themselves, and on society at large. Such questions deserve to be raised in the first instance because the adoption of the state-run asylum system, the transformation of madness into mental illness, and the subsequent reverberations of these developments represent the most striking and lasting legacy of the reform movement. Furthermore, it is not at all obvious on the face of things why these changes took the form that they did. Since the initial and continuing costs of making this separate provision for the mentally ill were obviously high, and apparently cheaper means of sustaining them were already in existence (for example, in the general mixed workhouses which the Webbs found to be such a characteristic feature of the nineteenth-century English response to poverty and dependency, or through a system of outdoor relief providing for maintenance in the community), the successful 'capture' of such a group by the medical profession and the large-scale and costly construction of mental hospitals in which to incarcerate them must be seen as inherently problematic phenomena.

Even apart from their historical importance, such questions have an obvious contemporary relevance, not least because, as Paul Rock has put it, 'modes of social control exerted in the past become part of the moral and definitional context [of the present]. . . . This propensity to preserve earlier moral reactions means not only that much contemporary deviance is a fossilized or frozen residue from the past, but that contemporary control is constrained and oriented by the past. Each new generation does not rewrite the social contract.'[23] As it happens, since the mid-1950s, we have been moving away from one aspect of the nineteenth century legacy in the field of mental health – the primary reliance on the asylum. But even here a historical context is vital if we are to grasp what is being abandoned and why.[24] The significance of nineteenth-century approaches is still more incontestable in those areas – state intervention to control

---

22. I must emphasize 'exclusively', since the identification of madness and sickness has a long history in Western culture, dating back at least to the ancient Greeks. But for millennia, this was merely one among many competing interpretations of insanity. In seventeenth-century England, for instance, as Michael MacDonald has recently documented, 'Individual cases of mental disorder might be attributed to divine retribution, diabolical possession, witchcraft, astrological influences, humoural imbalances, or to any combination of these forces . . .' (*Mystical Bedlam: Madness, Anxiety, and Healing in Seventeenth Century England*, Cambridge: Cambridge University Press, 1981, p. 7). What concerns me is the process by which some of these competing accounts became culturally illegitimate, and the medical profession acquired a monopoly over the treatment of the mad.

23. Paul Rock, *Deviant Behaviour*, London: Hutchinson, 1973, pp. 156, 159.

24. See Andrew Scull, *Decarceration: Community Treatment and the Deviant: A Radical View*, 2nd edn, Oxford: Polity Press, 1984.

problem populations and the 'medicalization' of deviance – where the application of nineteenth-century approaches continues to grow in scope and importance.

Sociologically speaking, the answers to these questions possess in addition a potentially much wider significance. For the developments I shall analyse here have obvious parallels with changes occurring almost contemporaneously in other sectors of the social control apparatus. Thus the key elements which distinguish deviance and its control in modern societies from the shapes which such phenomena assume elsewhere likewise grew to maturity in the period stretching from the late eighteenth through the nineteenth century. Of major importance in this respect were: (1) the substantial involvement of the state, and the emergence of a highly rationalized, centrally administered and directed social control apparatus; (2) the treatment of many types of deviance in institutions providing a large measure of segregation from the surrounding community; and (3) the careful differentiation of the different sorts of deviance, and the subsequent consignment of each variety to the ministrations of experts – which last development entails, as an important corollary, (4) the emergence of professional and semi-professional 'helping occupations'. From this perspective, the differentiation of the insane, the rise of a state-supported asylum system, and the emergence of the psychiatric profession can be seen to represent no more than a particular, though very important, example of this much more general series of changes in the social organization of deviance. Accordingly, a more adequate understanding of lunacy reform can be expected to provide us with important clues as to the structural sources of this wider transformation of the mechanisms for the social control of problem populations, and as to the kinds of effects bureaucratic processing, state intervention, and 'expert' involvement have produced.

Before proceeding directly to a discussion of the reform movement and its ramifications, however, I think one must address a logically prior set of issues, namely, what were the social preconditions of elite receptivity to the idea of an asylum system as the primary, almost the sole, response to the problems posed by insanity? How did the changing relationship between the state and civil society contribute to both the possibility and the pressures for state intervention in the control of the mad? And what social and cultural climate had to exist before claims on anyone's part to possess an expertise allowing of the reconstruction and rehabilitation of the deviant would be taken seriously? In the remainder of this chapter, I shall attempt to answer these questions, and in the process to show that the resolution of each of these issues is closely interconnected with the resolution of the others. Ultimately, I shall argue, they can all be seen to rest in one way or another on the same underlying changes in the social structure and intellectual climate of English society.

2. *Changing Responses to Insanity: Their Nature and Sources*

In medieval England, the dependent classes relied principally on a haphazard and often ineffectual tradition of Christian charity and almsgiving. Poverty, particularly if it were voluntarily assumed, was a status invested with considerable religious significance and meaning. But neither the Church nor private individuals made any serious effort to match aid to need or to provide an organized response to specific problems of dependency. On the contrary, such a measured, calculated response was clearly foreign to a society where the impulse to give was governed largely by the desire to ensure one's own salvation.

The insane were affected by this general, unsystematic approach to the deviant. Some were left to their own devices: the deranged beggar was a familiar part of the medieval landscape, wandering from place to place, community to community, in search of alms. Other lunatics relied on their families as a primary means of support. '[Since] the public did not make itself responsible for the custody of the lunatic, his own people were required to guard him and others from harm . . .',[25] sometimes with some temporary or permanent financial assistance from the community. Rich lunatics came under the jurisdiction of the Court of Wards and Liveries, the institution charged with administering the affairs of minors who inherited land as tenants-in-chief, and as Michael MacDonald notes, '[t]he chief concern of the crown's policy toward insane landowners was to preserve the integrity of their estates so that their lineages would not be obliterated by the economic consequences of their madness'.[26] But in only a small minority of cases was any effort made to relieve the family of the burdens the insane imposed by gathering lunatics together in institutions. At least until the seventeenth century, Bethlem remained the only specialized receptacle of this kind, and provision there was on an exceedingly modest scale. (In 1403–4, the inmates consisted of six insane and three sane patients, and this number grew only slowly in the following centuries. In 1632, for example, it was reported to contain twenty-seven patients, and in 1642, forty-four.)[27] In other parts of the country, some of the insane who posed a particularly acute threat to the social order, or who lacked friends or family on whom they could call for support, were likely to find themselves, along with the 'sick, aged, bedridden, diseased, wayfaring men, diseased soldiers and honest folk fallen into poverty', cared and provided for within the walls of one of the many small medieval

25. R.M. Clay, *The Mediaeval Hospitals of England*, London: Methuen, 1909, p. 32.
26. M. MacDonald, *Mystical Bedlam*, p. 6.
27. W.K. Jordan, *The Charities of London 1480–1660*, New York: Russell Sage, 1960, pp. 189–90. As Michael MacDonald aptly puts it, while 'Bedlamites swarmed through the imaginations of Jacobean playwrights and pamphleteers, . . . the famous asylum was in truth a tiny hovel. . . .' *Mystical Bedlam*, p. 4.

'hospitals'.[28] Custody for others who proved too violent or unmanageable to maintain in the community was provided by the local jail.[29]

The first (largely abortive) efforts to break with medieval precedent in dealing with the poor came in the sixteenth century. Throughout Western Europe in this period, the efforts of centralizing monarchs to augment state power produced a series of clashes between Church and state. In England, this conflict led to a decisive subordination of the former to secular political authority, and greatly accelerated the diminution of the Church's role in civil society. The dissolution of the monasteries and the redistribution of monastic lands were both symptoms and causes of this decline, a decline which rendered a Church-based response to the indigent increasingly anachronistic and unworkable. Not only did these developments sharply reduce the funds available to the poor, curtailing the sources of charity to which they could appeal, but they also necessarily and inevitably affected attitudes towards dependence in the society at large. The old charitable and religious ideals did not disappear overnight (indeed, they continued to be invoked, particularly in times of dearth, throughout the sixteenth and seventeenth centuries); but there was a growing sense of the unworthiness of some of the recipients of aid, and with official encouragement, by the last third of the sixteenth century, 'condemnation of the poor was becoming respectable; and the refusal of alms to a substantial proportion of them was widely regarded as legitimate'.[30]

At the same time, however, demands for the maintenance of internal order were if anything still more acutely felt than in the past. Increasing population, coupled with the growing commercialization of agriculture and the spread of enclosures, was spawning a volatile 'army' of vagrants, beggars, and idlers, no longer needed on the land.[31] And the threat these

---

28. The medieval hospital was 'an ecclesiastical, not a medical institution' and, like Bethlem, 'it was for care rather than for cure'. R.M. Clay, *The Mediaeval Hospitals*, pp. xvii–xviii, 13.

29. As this brief discussion should make clear (*pace* naive suggestions that mental disturbance is somehow the invention of the professional mind), the distinction between madness and other conditions creating dependency was clearly recognized both popularly and in the legal system even in medieval times. For most of the mentally disturbed, however, the distinction appears to have been without major practical consequences. Only where serious anxieties arose about a threat to public order (in which case, some sort of confinement was seen to be in order) or in cases where substantial amounts of property were at risk (where idiocy or innate mental incapacity was held to be a permanent bar to the inheritance of property, while the possibly remitting condition of lunacy could prompt a perhaps temporary deprivation of one's inheritance, subject to the supervision of the Court of Wards) does there seem to have been organized social intervention of a limited sort. For surveys of this period, see Basil Clarke, *Mental Disorder in Earlier Britain*, Cardiff: University of Wales Press, 1975; and Richard Neugebauer, 'Treatment of the Mentally Ill in Medieval and Early Modern England: A Reappraisal', *Journal of the History of the Behavioural Sciences* 14, 1978, pp. 158–69.

30. Paul Slack, *Poverty and Policy in Tudor and Stuart England*, London: Longman, 1988, p. 19.

31. On the vagrancy problem, *cf.* A.L. Beier, *Masterless Men: The Vagrancy Problem in England 1560–1640*, London: Methuen, 1985; *idem.*, 'Vagrants and the Social Order in

groups posed to the power of the central royal authorities was heightened by the still precarious nature of the latter's control, both vis-à-vis potential challengers from within, and in the context of the ever-intensifying international rivalries of the emerging European state system. Forced to attend to the demands of internal order, the Tudor monarchs found themselves increasingly compelled to supplement religious with secular control of the poor.[32]

As part of their efforts to cope with this problem, the Tudors and their Stuart successors made tentative efforts to make local administrators responsible and subject to central authority, and to encourage the establishment of institutions in which a portion of the threatening army of idle vagrants and beggars could be confined and kept under surveillance. (The most famous of these places was the Bridewell, or house of correction, established in London in 1555 in an old royal palace.) But the new institutions were often short-lived, and the drive for increased central control ultimately collapsed in the aftermath of the English Civil War.[33]

The contrast with the rest of Western Europe is an instructive one. Here, the same imperatives produced an initially similar response: the primitive beginnings of an institutional approach to the deviant. In Europe, though, these first institutions continued to receive royal encouragement and to grow in size and numbers during the seventeenth century, a process which culminated in the establishment of the French *Hôpitaux Généraux* from 1656 onwards, and the inauguration of what some historians have called the Great Confinement.[34] The difference clearly reflects the divergent path taken by the English state apparatus in this period. In the rest of Western Europe, the ever-present spur of military conflict (actual or threatened) prompted the establishment of large standing armies,[35] which had as their corollary a massive build-up of royal

Elizabethan England', *Past and Present* 64, 1974, pp. 3–29; and Paul Slack, 'Vagrants and Vagrancy in England 1598–1664', *Economic History Review* 2nd series, 27, 1974, pp. 360–79.

32. Paul Slack has noted the heightened emphasis on the dangers of the idle poor which characterized state responses to poverty 'for roughly a century after 1530 . . . [an emphasis which] helped to determine the perception and treatment of the poor as a whole'. P. Slack, *Poverty and Policy in Tudor and Stuart England*, p. 18.

33. Sidney and Beatrice Webb, *English Poor Law History: Part I The Old Poor Law*, London: 1927, pp. 65–100.

34. M. Foucault, *Madness and Civilization*, 1965; Georg Rusche and Otto Kirchheimer, *Punishment and Social Structure*, New York: Russell and Russell, 1968. For discussion of the differences between English and French approaches to the management of the poor in this period, see P. Slack, *Poverty and Policy in Tudor and Stuart England*, pp. 11–14. The evidence presented in C.C. Fairchilds, *Poverty and Charity in Aix-en-Provence 1640–1789*, Baltimore: Johns Hopkins University Press, 1976, undermines some of Foucault's more extreme claims about a continental 'Great Confinement'.

35. In the course of the sixteenth and seventeenth centuries, the size of continental armies increased tenfold. 'By the last quarter of the seventeenth century, the Spanish army consisted of 70,000 troops, the Dutch of an astonishing 110,000, the French 120,000, the Swedish 63,000, and the Russian army of 130,000. In contrast the British army had only 15,000; it was smaller than it had been in 1475.' John Brewer, *The Sinews of Power: War,*

power. Continental Absolutisms, with their ever larger bureaucratic apparatus and their ever greater fiscal exactions, thus possessed the capacity to continue to promote the confinement of the troublesome. They also possessed the incentive to do so, since a volatile mass of half-starved paupers, vagabonds, and minor criminals posed an obvious threat to state stability which, given the persistence and intensity of other internal and external threats, could scarcely be ignored.

While incentive and capacity were far from entirely absent in England, neither was present to anything like the same degree. Largely protected by its island status from the dangers of external assault,[36] the royal adminis-tration could afford to develop a somewhat less repressive policy towards its poor.[37] Moreover, spared the need to extract massive taxes to support a modernized apparatus of war, the English state did not need to exploit its poor as harshly, so that English sovereigns had far less need to fear the periodic explosions of the lower orders, goaded beyond the limits of endurance by the exactions of the tax collectors – rebellions which were so recurrent a feature of the continental monarchies' experience in this period.[38] If the English monarchy was thus spared the political necessity of encouraging confinement as a means of disciplining the poor, this was fortunate, since by and large it lacked the institutional capacity to do so. '[In the absence of] the forcing house of warfare on land which had speeded the development of Absolutism on the Continent . . .', the royal administration, already deprived of a standing army, could develop neither

Money and the English State, 1699–1783, Cambridge, Massachusetts: Harvard University Press, 1990, p. 8; see also the discussion in Geoffrey Parker, 'The "Military Revolution", 1560–1660 – A Myth?' Journal of Modern History 48, 1976, pp. 195–214.

36. Cf. Sir Lewis Namier, England in the Age of the American Revolution, 2nd edn, London: Macmillan, 1961, p. 7; for the comparative perspective, see Felix Gilbert (ed.), The Historical Essays of Otto Hintze, New York: Oxford University Press, 1975, chapter 5, 'Military Organization and the Organization of the State.' In his The Sinews of Power (see esp. pp. 10–4), John Brewer has objected to some aspects of Hintze's argument, particularly the latter's stress on naval strength as a source of England's security. The point is well taken: the English navy did not become a formidable force until the late seventeenth century. But England's insular status nonetheless remains a key factor in understanding its idiosyncratic development. Brewer himself concedes the central point at issue: given the increased size of armies in the early modern era, any attempted military invasion of England was a 'costly and complicated operation . . . beyond the capacity of even the most powerful sixteenth-century [and I would add, seventeenth-century] state'. Reciprocally, the sheer scale of warfare in early modern Europe also rendered 'English invasion of the Continent a matter of exceptional difficulty. . . .' In effect, then, the outcome was precisely to leave the country 'in none-too-splendid isolation', and English monarchs without the need (or capacity) to maintain a standing army. Hintze is indeed correct when he argues (ibid., p. 199) that 'In consequence, [England] developed no absolutism. Absolutism and militarism go together on the Continent just as do self-government and militia in England.'

37. Paul Slack has suggested that this policy difference may also have reflected the distinct possibility that 'the problem of poverty was in important respects less severe in England than in France', Poverty and Policy in Tudor and Stuart England, p. 13.

38. See Gabriel Ardant, 'Financial Policy and Economic Infrastructure of Modern States and Nations', pp. 164–242 in Charles Tilly (ed.), The Formation of National States in Western Europe, Princeton, New Jersey: Princeton University Press, 1975.

the centrally controlled bureaucracy nor the fiscal resources vital to the successful long-run pursuit of such a policy. As a consequence, what limited English experiments there were with a state-directed confinement of the poor fell by the wayside with the collapse of the first two Stuarts' attempts to build an indigenous English Absolutism. For this larger failure necessarily also meant the collapse of efforts by men like Cecil and Laud to extend a greater measure of central control over the treatment of the 'disreputable poor.'[39]

Thus, after a brief flurry of activity in the late sixteenth and early seventeenth centuries, the poor, including the insane poor, continued to be dealt with on a local, parish level[40] – though under the Poor Law Act of 1601 (43 Elizabeth *c*. 20) they were now acknowledged to be a secular rather than a religious responsibility. In consequence, as many as 15,000 separate administrative units were involved in the management of the poor; and the pervasive emphasis on localism was further reinforced by the custom of restricting aid to those belonging to one's own parish, a custom which received statutory recognition in the 1662 Act of Settlement (14 Charles II *c*. 12). Yet despite this wide scope for the exercise of local discretion, most parishes continued to provide for the derelict in essentially similar ways. Of all the funds expended for such purposes during this period, 'by far the largest amounts were dedicated to uses which we may fairly describe as household relief... for the support at a subsistence level of needy and worthy poor, legally resident in the parish'.[41] Lunatics were simply one group among many who received such support. Those who remained permanently insane (unless they happened to come from the propertied classes) did not pose a unique problem, but formed part of the larger class of the really poor and impotent: the senile, the incurably ill, the blind, the crippled, and the maimed. Efforts were made to keep these people in the community, if necessary by providing their relatives or others who were prepared to care for them with permanent pensions for their support.[42]

39. Perry Anderson, *Lineages of the Absolutist State*, London: New Left Books, 1974, p. 129 and passim, for a comparative treatment of European Absolutism. For a provocative collection of essays on European state building in this period, see C. Tilly (ed.), *The Formation of National States in Western Europe*.

40. For discussion of this emphasis on localism, *cf*. P. Slack, *Poverty in Tudor and Stuart England*, esp. pp. 127–31, 148–56; and more generally, for the period from the Restoration onwards, Roy Porter, *English Society in the Eighteenth Century* London: Penguin Books, 1982, chapters 3 and 7.

41. W.K. Jordan, *Philanthropy in England 1480–1660. A Study of the Changing Pattern of English Social Aspirations*, New York: Russell Sage, 1959, p. 256.

42. Samuel Mencher, *Poor Law to Poverty Program: Economic Security Policy in Britain and the United States*, Pittsburgh, Pennsylvania: University of Pittsburgh Press, 1967, p. 39; A. Fessler, 'The Management of Lunacy in Seventeenth Century England', *Proceedings of the Royal Society of Medicine, Historical Section* 49, 1956, pp. 901–7; P. Rushton, 'Lunatics and Idiots: Mental Disability, the Community, and the Poor Law in North-East England, 1600–1800', *Medical History* 32, 1988, pp. 34–50; Akihito Suzuki, 'Lunacy in Seventeenth and Eighteenth Century England: Analysis of Quarter Sessions Records, Part I', *History of Psychiatry* 2, 1991, pp. 437–56.

From the end of the sixteenth century and throughout the seventeenth (perhaps stimulated by the lack of alternative outlets for the investment of capital) this system of household relief was gradually supplemented by 'a steadily mounting attempt to provide for the care of the hopelessly indigent, the permanent casualties of society, in carefully constructed almshouse foundations' created by private charity.[43] At first, these were no more than substitute households, supplementary provision along familiar lines for the care of those in need. No efforts were made to classify inmates according to the (supposed) underlying causes of their pathology, or to impose a new and radically different routine on them. The almshouse was simply one more household among many; its inmates continued to mix indiscriminately with one another and with the community at large. More frankly punitive functions were assumed by the houses of correction or 'Bridewells', modelled on the original London foundation. As well as being for 'vagrants and beggars who could not be convicted of any crime save that of wandering abroad or refusing to work',[44] such places served as houses of confinement for the more dangerous or troublesome lunatics.[45]

More extensive and wide-ranging changes in what was still a policy of placing primary reliance upon non-institutional means for controlling deviance did not begin to be discussed and implemented until the eighteenth century.[46] There then emerged an increased emphasis on providing for the indigent and disreputable in institutions, a trend which was most marked in London. Defoe, listing twenty-seven 'public gaols' and 125 'tolerated prisons' (a general term for all types of institutions for deviants), commented that 'there are in London, notwithstanding we are a nation of liberty, more public and private prisons, and houses of confinement, than in any city in Europe, perhaps as many as in all the capital cities of Europe put together'.[47] Many were long-established institutions, such as Bethlem

43. W.K. Jordan, *Philanthropy in England*, p. 257; Christopher Hill, *Reformation to Industrial Revolution: A Social and Economic History of Britain 1530–1780*, London: Weidenfeld and Nicolson, 1967, p. 47; W.J. Ashley, *An Introduction to English Economic History and Theory Part II: The End of the Middle Ages*, New York: Putnam, 1893, p. 364. Jordan has been criticized for over-emphasizing the role of private charity, and recent scholarship suggests that by the mid-seventeenth century, at least half of the money expended on the poor was raised by taxation rather than charitable contributions. *Cf.* the discussion in P. Slack, *Poverty in Tudor and Stuart England*, pp. 169–73.
44. Kathleen Jones, *Lunacy, Law, and Conscience 1744–1845*, p. 22.
45. *Cf.* Akihito Suzuki, 'Lunacy in Seventeenth and Eighteenth Century England: Analysis of Quarter Sessions Records, Part II', *History of Psychiatry* 3, 1992, pp. 29–44.
46. From the late seventeenth century onwards, as John Brewer has recently demonstrated, the English state acquired steadily greater fiscal and military muscle; yet strong opposition to any drift in the direction of absolutism effectively contained the domestic effects of these developments. '[P]rotected by the well-built fortifications of English constitutionalism, . . . the proponents of small government . . . were able to conduct an effective war of containment' and were largely successful in retarding, though not preventing, the state's 'intrusion into civil society'. See John Brewer, *The Sinews of Power*, pp. xix–xx.
47. Daniel Defoe, *A Tour Through the Whole Island of Great Britain*, London: Penguin edn, 1971, p. 321.

Fig. 1   An anonymous engraving of the second Bethlem, built in 1675–6, prior to the addition of the wings for incurables. By 1815, when the treatment of its inmates provided lunacy reformers with some of their most potent ammunition, it was on the point of physical collapse, and it was replaced by a third asylum in St. George's Fields. The third Bethlem is now the Imperial War Museum.

and Bridewell, but almost all of these were now considerably enlarged. (Bethlem, for instance, had moved to a new site in 1676. It now contained between 130 and 150 inmates and was being extended to provide for a sizeable number of incurables.)[48] These were supplemented by a large number of new institutions, many of them charitable foundations.

Hospitals provide one example of the growing tendency to isolate the indigent from the rest of society. In this period, they were used almost exclusively by the poor. Between 1719 and 1751, seven new hospitals were added to the ancient foundations of St. Bartholomew's, St. Thomas's, and Bethlem in London alone. Others were founded in major provincial

48. By the latter part of the seventeenth century, Bethlem was increasingly aiming to confine its ministrations to 'curable' patients, and although there was 'no particular time limited for the continuance of a patient in the hospital, who is under cure . . . it is generally seen in a twelvemonth, whether the case will admit relief'. Thomas Bowen, *An Historical Account of the Origin, Progress, and Present State of Bethlem Hospital*, London: 1783, p. 14, quoted in Jonathan Andrews, 'The Lot of the "Incurably" Insane in Enlightenment England', *Eighteenth Century Life* 12, 1988, p. 17. Construction of additions to Bethlem to house incurable patients was begun in 1723. The wing for male incurables was completed and opened in 1728, and its counterpart for females in 1736.

cities such as Liverpool, Manchester, and Leicester. Similarly, work-houses, first established on an experimental basis in a few towns in the 1630s, spread rapidly following the more successful example of the Bristol workhouse, founded in 1696. 'By the middle of the eighteenth century the urban community of market town size or above, which had no workhouse, was a rarity . . .', and 'from about 1760 onwards' these institutions were increasingly purpose-built.[49] By modern standards, most of these eighteenth-century institutions possessed a peculiarly mixed character. Workhouses, for example, despite their name and the inten-tions of their founders, became dumping grounds for the decrepit and dependent of all descriptions. Prisons mixed young and old, men and women, debtors and felons, in a single heterogeneous mass. Hospitals, while more and more concentrating on caring for the sick, also made provision for lunatics, orphans, and the aged. The distinctions between the varied categories making up the disreputable classes continued to be very imprecise, but there had begun to emerge a number of institutions specifically concerned with the insane.

Several of these were charitable establishments, similar to (and in some instances forming part of) the recently founded voluntary general hospitals, and like them, primarily intended to serve the poor but respectable segments of the community.[50] The earliest of these were the small receptacle at Norwich, founded in 1713, and the ward for incurable lunatics established at Guy's Hospital in 1728. More important than these, inasmuch as it provided a model for other asylums established later in the century and also (as we shall see) represented a major attempt to assert medical control over the problem of insanity, was the establishment of St. Luke's Hospital in London in 1751. Subsequently, another charity asylum began operations in 1764 at Newcastle upon Tyne, and in 1766 a 'lunatic hospital' with twenty-two cells opened in Manchester, attached to the existing Infirmary. These were followed by similar institutions at York, Liverpool, Leicester, and Exeter. By the standards of the nineteenth century, none of these was a very large institution,[51] and they never contained more than a minor portion of the insane population. Like their ancient rival, Bethlem, most claimed to be in the business of providing cure as well as care. But in reality, they proved the source of 'no . . . innovations – medical, mechanical, moral, or organizational'.[52] Their primary importance lay in the fact that they helped to legitimate the

49. G.W. Oxley, *Poor Relief in England and Wales 1601–1834*, Newton Abbot: David and Charles, 1974, p. 84.
50. Most admitted paying as well as pauper patients, intending to use the former to subsidize the latter. As we shall see, those in charge of these establishments did not always resist the temptation to profit from their paying patients, creating the potential (subsequently realized) for scandal.
51. The asylum at Norwich, for instance, made provision for between twenty and thirty lunatics; that at Manchester had cells for twenty-two.
52. R. Porter, *Mind Forg'd Manacles*, p. 135.

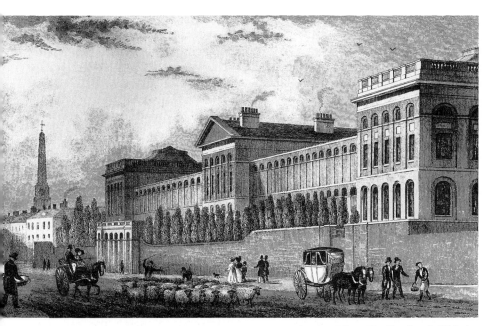

Fig. 2   St. Luke's Hospital from an engraving by J. Gough after Theo H. Shepherd. This is the second building, opened in 1787. The architect, George Dance, also designed Newgate Prison. Neither Bethlem nor St. Luke's possessed a chapel for its inmates. This differentiates them sharply from the general hospitals built in the eighteenth century. Perhaps it is not too fanciful to link this omission to the lunatics' ontological status in this period: deprived of the divine attribute of reason, the God-given quality which distinguished man from the brutes, the insane were presumably incapable of communion with the Deity. By contrast, the prominent place occupied by the chapel in nineteenth-century asylum architecture reflects not just the influence of Evangelical reformers, but also the decreasing emphasis on the loss of reason as the defining characteristic of insanity, and the new insistence that the insane had not lost their essential humanity.

notion of institutionalization as a response to the problems posed by the presence of mentally disturbed individuals in the community.

Alongside these at least nominally charitable foundations, however, a parallel, private, profit-oriented 'trade in lunacy' was emerging, widely viewed from its earliest years as a sordid, disreputable business – albeit frequently a highly lucrative one. Compelled to cope with the most acutely disturbed and refractory lunatics, those the community was least anxious to see at large, the madhouse keeper was usually able to secure a good price for his or her services. Like many of his counterparts at the head of a charity asylum, for instance, the appositely named William Battie, prime mover in the foundation of St. Luke's, owned his own madhouses on the side – in Islington and Clerkenwell – to which he transferred the more well-to-do private patients who came his way. A self-made man, at his death he left an estate valued at the astonishing figure of between one and two hundred thousand pounds.[53] Few could rival this sort of success (though the Monro family at Bethlem, who operated Brooke House for more than a century, may well have done even better).[54] But the entrepreneurially inclined could obviously make a handsome living from speculating in this variety of human misery.

Throughout the century, a major way of drumming up trade and attracting clients was the publication of small books or pamphlets making considerable claims for the author's success in curing lunatics.[55] Despite these claims, for much of the century the methods used to manage the insane were rudimentary at best, the product of practical experience, often passed down (together with the madhouse and its stock of patients) through generations of the same family. Also characteristic was the clustering of madhouses in certain parishes, as former assistants in existing houses left to set up their own rival establishments. In the vicinity of London, for instance, the trade was concentrated in two areas, Hoxton and Chelsea, while in the provinces, such places as Gateshead and Henley-in-Arden became centres of the new service industry.

Partly because of the lack of any legal requirement for licensing or registration, partly because of the ephemeral nature of many of these establishments, and most importantly because one of the major attractions of the madhouse for the well-to-do was the promise it would draw a discreet veil over the madman's very existence, we lack an accurate estimate of even as basic a matter as the number of private madhouses in

53. Richard Hunter and Ida MacAlpine, *Three Hundred Years of Psychiatry*, London: Oxford University Press, 1963, p. 402.

54. James Monro's predecessor, Richard Hale, who was physician at Bethlem from 1708 until his death in 1728, was not entirely a self-made man, but it is significant that he too was able to exploit his position at the hospital to obtain a large private practice, and thereby to acquire a considerable fortune. According to the *Daily Journal*, he 'left an Estate of near £100,000'. See Jonathan Andrews, 'A Respectable Mad-Doctor? Dr Richard Hale, F.R.S. (1670–1728)', *Notes and Records of the Royal Society of London* 44, 1990, pp. 169–203. Hale, the Monros, and Battie were all fully representative, in this respect, of eighteenth-century doctors, who regularly made use of part-time and unpaid hospital appointments as a source of credentials and social connections, and thus as a primary means of securing a lucrative fee-paying clientele. See William F. Bynum, 'Physicians, Hospitals, and Career Structures in Eighteenth Century London', in W.F. Bynum and R. Porter (eds), *William Hunter and the Eighteenth Century Medical World*, Cambridge: Cambridge University Press, 1985, pp. 105–28.

55. Again, Battie furnishes a prime example, his 1758 *Treatise on Madness* (London: Whiston and White) advertising his humanity as well as his skills at curing lunacy. For early eighteenth-century examples, see David Irish, *Levamen Infirmi, or: Cordial Counsel to the Sick and Diseased*, London: for the author, 1700; and Thomas Fallowes, *The Best Method for the Cure of Lunaticks*, London: for the author, 1705. Among a superfluity of late eighteenth-century examples, one might cite William Perfect, *Select Cases in the Different Species of Insanity*, Rochester: Gillman, 1787; Benjamin Faulkner, *Observations on the General and Improper Treatment of Insanity*, London: for the author, 1789; and Thomas Arnold, *Observations on the Nature, Kinds, Causes, and Prevention of Insanity*, 2 vols, Leicester: Robinson and Cadell, 1782–6.

operation during the eighteenth century.[56] Apart from passing references to individual institutions in contemporary books and pamphlets, local evidence of a fragmentary kind sometimes survives; and on this basis, one may surmise that madhouses were created in at least two distinctive ways. One of the origins of the madhouse system, at least so far as pauper lunatics were concerned, was the practice which developed from the mid-seventeenth century onwards of boarding them out 'at the expense of the parish, in private dwelling houses, which gradually acquired the description of "mad" houses'. Among the more affluent classes, insane relatives were most often cared for on an individual basis, for which purpose they were frequently placed 'in the custody of medical men or clergymen'.[57]

In a period which witnessed 'the birth of a consumer society',[58] here was a fertile market ripe for cultivation and expansion by the entrepreneurially inclined. Of course, not all segments of the market grew equally rapidly: the strong demand on the part of the upper classes for some system of private care which would relieve them of the burden of their unmanageable relatives and sequestrate them away from public view, and their ability to provide substantial rewards for those who obliged them in these ways, meant that it was this sector of the private madhouse system which grew most rapidly through much of the eighteenth century. By contrast, though the presence of a few pauper patients, with payment guaranteed by their parishes, could provide a useful source of steady income, confinement of the meaner sort was in general obviously less lucrative and attractive: unless, of course, they could be dealt with in bulk – wholesale, as it were, rather than retail. The few establishments able to adopt the latter strategy were, not surprisingly, located in the metropolis. Sir John Miles's house in Hoxton, for instance, contained as many as 486 patients by 1815, and derived a substantial part of its trade from a contract with the War Office to incarcerate members of the armed forces who were deemed to have taken leave of their senses.

Such mammoth institutions were wholly atypical, however. Most eighteenth-century madhouses were quite small, often containing fewer than ten inmates. Created in accordance with no central scheme or plan, and subject to virtually no legal regulation or restraint, they were, as one would expect, extremely diverse in their orientations and operations. Few were purpose-built, partly because it was obviously cheaper to adapt

56. For a discussion of the paucity of evidence concerning the numbers, distribution, and character of eighteenth-century madhouses, see W. Parry-Jones, *The Trade in Lunacy*, pp. 29ff.
57. W. Parry-Jones, *The Trade in Lunacy*, pp. 7–8. For some details on the use of madhouses by London parishes in the eighteenth century, cf. Jonathan Andrews, 'Bedlam Revisited: A History of Bethlem Hospital c. 1634–c. 1770', unpublished Ph.D. thesis, London University, 1991, pp. 497–9.
58. Neil McKendrick, John Brewer, and J.H. Plumb, *The Birth of a Consumer Society: The Commercialization of Eighteenth Century England*, London: Europa, 1982.

existing buildings to the purpose, but also because little connection was seen in this period between the characteristics of the physical space within which lunatics were confined and the possibilities of curing them. (Thus, even the charity asylums, which *were* built to contain lunatics, were not 'purpose-built' in the nineteenth-century sense of the term, when the asylum was to be transmuted into the moral machinery through which the mind was to be strengthened, and reason restored. Apart from its uses for decorative purposes, for loosening the purse-strings of potential benefactors, or for show – the exterior of Bethlem, for example, was modelled on the Tuileries[59] – the architecture of these places was designed primarily to secure 'the safe confinement and imprisonment of lunatics',[60] an approach that led later generations to comment on 'the prison-mindedness of eighteenth-century insane asylum designers'.)[61]

The resulting structural deficiencies of the buildings, together with the lack of constraints on entry into or conduct of the mad business, undoubtedly played a role in the widespread reliance on chains, manacles, and physical coercion to manage the patients (though, as we shall see, many madhouse keepers argued that in any event, restraints and fear were essential elements in the management and cure of the mad). But such practices were not uniformly endorsed: Lewis Southcomb, for instance, one of a number of country clergymen who dabbled in the practice of 'physick' and found themselves consulted in the cure of the mad, objected to attempts to coerce right-thinking, rejecting 'all those Means which tend to the giving of Pain and Uneasiness . . . such as *Blisters, Seatons, Cupping, Scarifying*, and all other Punishments of the Like kind'. Such 'tormenting Means', he was convinced, often 'rendered a very curable Disease, either incurable or [were] the occasion of protracting the Cure longer than

---

59. In constructing the new Bethlem at Moorfields in the late seventeenth century, 'the Governors had been much more concerned with "the Grace and Ornament of the . . . Building" than with the patients' exercise or any other therapeutic purpose. Patients had actually been forbidden to walk in the front yard and gardens of new Bethlem, as apparently was originally intended, simply because its front wall would have had to be built so high (to prevent escape) that the view of the hospital "towards Moorefields lyeing Northwards" would be spoiled. New Bethlem was constructed pre-eminently as fund-raising rhetoric, to attract the patronage and admiration of the elite, rather than for its present and future inmates, whose interests took a poor second place. Nor did contemporaries fail to perceive and remark upon the ironic antithesis between the sober splendour of the hospital's palatial exterior and the impoverishment and chaos that lurked within.' J. Andrews, 'Bedlam Revisited', pp. 174–5.

60. House of Commons, *Report of the Select Committee on Madhouses*, 1815, p. 76.

61. The words are J.D. Thompson and G. Goldin's, taken from their study of hospital design, *The Hospital: A Social and Architectural History* (New Haven: Yale University Press, 1975), but such sentiments were a commonplace in nineteenth-century reform circles. It is perhaps of interest to recall, therefore, that the architect of St. Luke's Hospital, as we have seen, the most influential of the eighteenth-century charity asylums, was George Dance the Younger, who was also responsible for the design of the new Newgate Prison.

otherwise the Nature of the Case would have required'.[62] In similar fashion, Nathaniel Cotton of St. Albans managed his patients (who included the poet William Cowper) without either violence or restraint.[63] And the lack of uniformity in this regard was matched by variability in other respects: 'in size, opulence, the social rank of their charges, the qualifications and skills of their proprietors, and their notions of treatment.'[64]

Predictably, given that most eighteenth-century madhouses were small, informal, and not infrequently ephemeral family concerns, engaged in the business of peddling discreet silences,[65] the information which survives about their operations is distinctly patchy and incomplete. Certainly, though, enough is known to cast doubt on any claim that they constituted a uniformly benighted and brutal regime. The very existence of a free trade in lunacy,[66] essentially untrammeled by outside intervention, super-vision, or control, created a social space within which therapeutic experi-mentation could proceed; and while neglect may indeed have been the norm, individual madhouses seem to have made genuine efforts to secure their inmates' well-being and comfort.[67]

But the public image of the Georgian madhouse had no room for such nuances. In the rueful words of one of the more ambitious and respectable madhouse keepers of the late eighteenth century, 'The idea of a mad-house is apt to excite . . . the strongest emotions of horror and alarm; upon a supposition not altogether ill-founded, that once a patient is doomed to take up his abode in one of those places, he will not only be exposed to very great cruelty; but it is a great chance, whether he recovers or not,

62. Lewis Southcomb, *Peace of Mind and Health of Body United*, London: Cowper, 1750, p. 57. Southcomb claimed to have successfully treated patients from Somerset, Cornwall, Devon, Dorset, Sussex, and London. Notwithstanding his reputation for treating the mad, he mostly dealt with the marginally disturbed, not those who 'have been really mad, but very frequently with such as have been madly dealt with withal before I have ever known them; and thus, some have, by Male Practice [*sic*], rendered a very curable disease, either incurable, or been the Occasion of protracting the Cure . . .'. *Ibid.*, pp. 61, 70. The most complete portrait of a clerical practitioner of this sort is Michael MacDonald's study (*Mystical Bedlam*) of the seventeenth-century Puritan divine, Richard Napier.
63. For Cowper's description of his breakdown (1763–5) and treatment by Cotton, see *Memoir of the Early Life of William Cowper, Esq. Written by Himself*, London: Edwards, 1816.
64. R. Porter, *Mind Forg'd Manacles*, p. 140.
65. *Ibid.*, p. 137.
66. W. Parry-Jones, *The Trade in Lunacy*.
67. For example, Edward Long Fox's madhouse at Cleve, and later at Brislington House, near Bristol; Laverstock House near Salisbury, run by William Finch; Fishponds Asylum, founded in mid-century by the Baptist layman, George Mason (see H. Temple Phillips, 'The History of the Old Private Lunatic Asylum at Fishponds Bristol, 1740–1859', unpublished M.Sc. thesis, Bristol University, 1973); and the Newington family's establishment at Ticehurst, Sussex (see Charlotte MacKenzie, 'A Family Asylum'). For a description of another obscure provincial example, see L.D. Smith, 'Eighteenth Century Madhouse Practice: The Prouds of Bilston', *History of Psychiatry* 3, 1992, pp. 45–52.

if he ever sees the outside of the walls.'[68] Fictional portraits of gothic madhouses run by scheming ruffians fed the unsavoury reputation of the industry at large;[69] and such complaints were echoed in a pamphlet literature which repeatedly emphasized the sinister and corrupt possibilities offered by the secrecy of the madhouse, particularly for the illicit confinement of the sane.[70]

Such complaints at length provoked a rather half-hearted Parliamentary investigation of London madhouses in 1763, which nonetheless provided evidence to substantiate many of the allegations of improper confinement.[71] However, spirited opposition from the Royal College of Physicians (several of whose fellows were now profiting handsomely from the burgeoning trade in lunacy) blocked any legislative action for more than a decade, when the 1774 Madhouses Act (14 George III *c.* 49) finally passed into law. Even then, the statute proved little more than a token gesture. Paupers were the most likely to suffer from extremes of neglect and ill-treatment in unregulated madhouses, particularly since most proprietors of the institutions in which they were confined were attempting to extract a profit from the pittance which the parish overseers allowed for their maintenance. Yet the Act expressly excluded them from its purview. Even the private patients, whom the act was ostensibly designed to protect, gained little from its provisions. While licensing was required for the first time, the licensing authority had no power to reject applications. Inspection of metropolitan madhouses was handed over to none other than the Royal College of Physicians, and the reluctant inspectors were in any

68. William Pargeter, *Observations on Maniacal Disorders*, Reading: for the author, 1792, p. 123.
69. Tobias Smollett, for instance, arranges to have his mock-heroic English Quixote, Sir Launcelot Greaves, seized and carried off to a madhouse run by the eponymous Bernard Shackle, an occasion for a warning that 'in England, the most innocent person upon earth is liable to be immured for life under the pretext of lunacy, sequestered from his wife, children, and friends, robbed of his fortune, deprived even of necessaries, and subjected to the most brutal treatment from a low-bred barbarian, who raises an ample fortune on the misery of his fellow-creatures and may, during his whole life, practise this horrid oppression, without question or control'. T. Smollett, *The Adventures of Sir Launcelot Greaves*, London: Coote, 1762.
70. See, for instance, Daniel Defoe, *Augusta Triumphans* London: Roberts edn, 1728; Anonymous, *Proposals for Redressing Some Grievances Which Greatly Affect the Whole Nation*, London: Johnson edn, 1740; Alexander Cruden, *The London Citizen Exceedingly Injured: or, A British Inquisition Displayed*, London: Cooper and Dodd edn, 1739; and Anonymous, 'A Case Humbly Offered to the Consideration of Parliament', *Gentleman's Magazine* 33, 1763, pp. 25–6.
71. For example, Turlington, the owner of one of the madhouses they investigated, 'vowed that the rule was general, to admit all persons who were brought'. His agent, King, who actually ran the house, '[u]pon being asked, if he ever refused any persons who were brought on any pretence whatsoever, provided they could pay for their board? He answered, No . . . he frankly confessed that out of the whole number of persons he had confined he had never admitted one as a lunatic during the six years he had been entrusted with the superintendence of the house'. *The History, Debates, and Proceedings of both Houses of Parliament of Great Britain from the Year 1743 to the Year 1774*, London: Debrett, 1792, pp. 125, 126.

event given no power to bring sanctions against those they found guilty of maltreatment. Consequently, the situation of the growing numbers of lunatics incarcerated in madhouses and asylums (not to mention those confined in workhouses and jails) was to provide a ready target for the efforts of early nineteenth-century philanthropists.

Notwithstanding the long-run importance of these developments, both in constituting a nursery for developing the skills of those claiming expertise in the management of the mad and in providing ammunition for a later generation of reformers, one must be careful not to exaggerate the extent to which provision for the insane – rich or poor – had assumed an institutional form even by the end of the eighteenth century. While we have no reliable figures on either the capacity of the asylums and mad-houses or the total number of lunatics in the population in this period, such places clearly provided for only a small minority of the insane.[72] Even taking into account the additional numbers confined in the local workhouses and poorhouses, it is clear that the majority were still outside institutions, being supported by some sort of household relief.[73] In this respect, they resembled the wider category of the dependent, from whom they were only beginning to be separated. For despite the passage of permissive acts in 1722 and 1782 (9 George I *c.* 7 and 22 George III *c.* 83), allowing parishes to erect workhouses for institutional care of the indigent, much of the local effort to relieve poverty continued to be on an outdoor basis. The occasional pamphleteer boldly advocated the creation of a comprehensive network of places of confinement for the defective and the unfortunate (a schematic Great Confinement of positively Foucauldian dimensions):

> There should be one General Hospital erected in each County . . . for the Reception and Maintenance of all poor Lunaticks, Ideots, Blind Persons, Maim'd Soldiers and Seamen, Cripples incapable of relieving themselves by any Manufacture or Labour, and Bedridden Persons beyond a prospect of Cure, that are or shall be Inhabitants of that County.[74]

But such visions were seen as both impractical and superfluous: potentially enormously costly, and a wholly unacceptable extension of central control and influence.

72. For similar conclusions, *cf.* R. Porter, *Mind Forg'd Manacles*, pp. 8–9, 118–9, 140–1.
73. Indirectly, of course, the continued popularity of such tracts as Edward Synge's *Sober Thoughts for the Cure of Melancholy, Especially that which Is Religious* (London: Trye, 1742) and John Wesley's *Primitive Physick* (London: Trye, 1747), with their advice on caring for lunatics, provide valuable confirmation of this, for they were primarily intended as collections of remedies for use in the home. As Roy Porter has noted, confinement of lunatics in workhouses and bridewells was seen as unnecessarily costly; moreover, 'because they distracted the institution from disciplining real law-breakers,' there were even instances of magistrates ordering the discharge of mad folk from houses of correction. *Mind Forg'd Manacles*, p. 119.
74. Anonymous, *Some Thoughts Concerning the Maintenance of the Poor in a Letter to a Member of Parliament*, London: Goodwin, 1700.

3. Madness and Market Society

Nonetheless, even the limited growth of the private trade in lunacy, and the parallel creation of a number of charity asylums, serve to demonstrate that the traditional, family-based response to insanity (and indeed to all forms of dependency) was beginning to be questioned and abandoned, a process which gathered steam as the eighteenth century drew to a close. Those who see this process, and the asylum's ultimate triumph in the nineteenth century, as a relatively direct and uncomplicated consequence of the rise of an urban-industrial society argue that the rise of segregative forms of social control represented a 'natural' response to the inability of a community- and household-based relief system to cope with the vastly greater problems created by this new form of social organization. In Mechanic's words, 'Industrialization and technological change . . . , coupled with increasing urbanization brought decreasing tolerance for bizarre and disruptive behavior and less ability to contain deviant behavior within the existing social structure.'[75] The increased geographical mobility of the population and the anonymity of existence in the urban slums were combined with the destruction of the old paternal relationships which went with a stable, hierarchically organized rural society. Furthermore, the situation of the poor and dependent classes, huddled together in the grossly overcrowded conditions which accompanied the explosive, unplanned growth of urban and industrial centres became simultaneously more visible and more desperate. In a period in which society as a whole grew richer, the rise of industry is blamed for creating for the first time an extensive proletariat, 'cut off from the ever-sustaining resources of an uncomplicated rural parish, and living at the mercy of an employment subjected to periodic intervals of slump or complete stagnation'.[76]

The suggestion is that families in these conditions were much less capable of sustaining a non-productive member, and that both the scale of the problems and the anonymity of urban existence threatened the easy and uncomplicated system of relief which had sufficed in earlier times. Though for a long time the implications of these developments were evaded, and 'the whole frame of historical and economic reference remained agrarian in an economy undergoing an industrial revolution',[77] eventually the new problems posed by poverty and dependence in an urban environment had to be faced. For the structural foundations of an effective system of parochial relief were undermined and brought close to collapse by the rise of an urban-industrial order. Despite the fact that they were no longer concerned with individuals, but with an amorphous mass, and despite their growing conviction that many of the poor were

75. David Mechanic, *Mental Health and Social Policy*, Englewood Cliffs, New Jersey: Prentice-Hall, 1969, p. 54.
76. W.K. Jordan, *Philanthropy in England*, pp. 66–7.
77. *Ibid.*, p. 67.

Table 1 The Growth of Large Urban Centres in England 1801–21.

	1801	1811	1821
Manchester	109,218	137,201	155,707
Liverpool	77,635	94,376	118,972
Birmingham	73,760	85,755	106,722
Bristol	63,645	76,433	97,779
Halifax	62,425	73,315	91,930
Leeds	54,162	62,534	83,758
Plymouth		56,000	61,112
Sheffield		53,231	62,275
Blackburn			53,330
Bradford			52,954
Oldham			52,510
Norwich			51,188

Source: Adapted from Eli Halevy, *England in 1815*, London: Benn, 1949, p. 257.

Table 2 Percentage of the Population of England and Wales Living in Cities of 20,000 and up.

1801	1811	1821	1831	1841	1851	1861	1871	1881	1891
16.94	18.11	20.82	25.05	28.90	35.00	38.21	42.00	48.00	53.58

Source: A.F. Weber, *The Growth of Cities in the Nineteenth Century*, New York: Columbia University Press, 1899, p. 47.

'undeserving', the new class of entrepreneurs could not wholly avoid making some provision for them, if only because of the revolutionary threat they posed to the social order. The asylum – and analogous institutions such as the workhouse – allegedly constituted their response to this situation.

But there are serious problems with this line of argument. While the proportion of town dwellers in England rose sharply from the late eighteenth century onwards, the process of urbanization was simply not as far advanced as this account necessarily implies when pressures developed to differentiate and institutionalize the deviant population. In the early stages of the Industrial Revolution, 'cotton was the pacemaker of industrial change, and the basis of the first regions which could not have existed but for industrialization, and which expressed a new form of society, industrial capitalism'.[78] Though technical innovations introduced into the

78. Eric Hobsbawm, *Industry and Empire*, London: Penguin, 1969, p. 56.

manufacturing process in the latter half of the eighteenth century, together
with the application of steam power, soon resulted in factory production,
the technology of cotton production remained comparatively simple; and
much of the industry remained decentralized and scattered in a variety of
small local factories, as likely located in 'industrial villages' as concentrated
in large urban centres. Even in other industries, initially 'most of the new
industrial units were small and highly localized'.[79] Consequently, although
large towns absorbed an increasing proportion of the English population,
city dwellers remained a distinct minority during the first decades of the
nineteenth century,[80] by which time powerful pressures were already
being exerted to secure the establishment of lunatic asylums (and other
segregative forms of social control) on a compulsory basis. London, it is
true, already had a population of 840,000 in 1801, and grew to contain
more than a million people by 1811 – but it remained unique. In 1801,
there were only six other cities with a population of more than 50,000; by
1811, there were eight; by 1821, there were twelve, including three which
had passed the 100,000 mark. More significantly, at the turn of the
century, 'only one third [of the English population] lived in a town of any
size, only one in six in a town over 20,000.'[81]

By themselves, these figures suggest that the notion that it was *urban*
poverty which forced the adoption of an institutional response to deviance
is by no means as self-evident as is commonly assumed.[82] And when one
looks for direct, concrete evidence of such a connection, one's faith in the
traditional wisdom is still further diminished. During the initial growth of
the private madhouse trade in the eighteenth century, the 'regions most
conspicuous for asylum building were not the industrial boom-towns.
Georgian private asylums commonly sprang up away from dense population centres, in Kent, Sussex, Wiltshire, Gloucestershire, etc; and their
catchments [*sic*] areas were quite restricted.'[83] The pattern is not altered
much, as we shall see, even in the opening decades of the nineteenth
century: in 1808 local magistrates were given discretionary power to
provide asylum accommodation for pauper lunatics. Whether any given

79. Asa Briggs, *The Making of Modern England 1783–1867*, New York: Harper and Row,
    1965, p. 18.
80. In F.M.L. Thompson's words, 'in 1830, the day when typical English men or women
    would be town dwellers, or factory workers, still lay emphatically in the future'. *The
    Rise of Respectable Society: A Social History of Victorian Britain 1830–1900*, Cambridge,
    Mass.: Harvard University Press, 1988, p. 23.
81. Harold Perkin, *The Origins of Modern English Society 1789–1880*, London: Routledge and
    Kegan Paul, 1969, p. 117. In fact, at the first census of 1801, there were only fourteen
    towns in the country with a population of more than 20,000.
82. A comparative perspective enables us to make this point still more emphatically. As
    David Rothman has shown in his *The Discovery of the Asylum* (Boston: Little Brown,
    1971), during the first half of the nineteenth century, the United States too moved
    rapidly to embrace a policy of segregative control – at a period when, as even the most
    avid proponent of the urbanization thesis must concede, the American population
    remained overwhelmingly rural.
83. R. Porter, *Mind Forg'd Manacles*, p. 162.

county adopted this solution to the problem of the dependent insane bore little or no relationship to the degree of urbanization of its population. While Lancashire and the West Riding of Yorkshire, two of the most heavily populated counties in England, were among the first to plan and open county asylums, Middlesex, the most densely populated county in the country, made no effort to do so until 1827, and then acted only under the spur of direct Parliamentary pressure. None of the counties in the West Midlands, along with the North the most industrialized and urbanized region of England, built an asylum until 1845, when they were compelled to do so.[84] At the other end of the scale, the second county to open an asylum under the 1808 Act (in 1812) was small, rural Bedfordshire. Other rural counties exhibited a similar enthusiasm for the institutional solution at a comparatively early date. Indeed, the majority of the asylums built on the basis of the permissive act were situated in rural counties: Norfolk (1814), Lincolnshire (1820), Cornwall (1820), Gloucestershire (1823), Suffolk (1829), Dorset (1832), Kent (1833).

No clear-cut connection exists, therefore, between the rise of large asylums and the growth of large cities. Instead, I suggest that the main driving force behind the rise of a segregative response to madness (and to other forms of deviance) can much more plausibly be asserted to lie in the effects of a mature capitalist market economy and the associated ever more thoroughgoing commercialization of existence. While the urban conditions produced by industrialization had a direct impact which was originally limited in geographical scope, the market system observed few such restrictions, and had increasingly subversive effects on the whole traditional rural and urban social structure. These changes in turn prompted the abandonment of long-established techniques for coping with the poor and troublesome (including troublesome members of the more affluent classes).

Some may object that these contentions rest upon a chronological confusion: that the rise of capitalism in England occurred too early to be plausibly invoked as the explanation for events occurring in the late eighteenth and the first half of the nineteenth century.[85] But such criticism is itself confused and misplaced, for I am concerned here not simply with the initial moves towards commercialized production and the rise of a

---

84. Moreover, both the West Midlands and Lancashire had been extremely thinly supplied with private madhouses before and during this period.
85. David Roberts suggested this objection to me. For a trenchant critique of this sort of exaggerated attempt to find 'commercial revolutions . . . lurking unexpectedly in mediaeval and early modern Europe', see Neil McKendrick, John Brewer, and J.H. Plumb, *The Birth of a Consumer Society*, pp. 3–6. As they scornfully note, in certain historical circles, the most modest and trivial stirrings of commercial activity have been comically and wholly inappropriately dubbed 'revolutions', and the birth of commercial capitalism pushed back into the ever more distant past. 'False pregnancies' notwithstanding, 'it requires evidence as unambiguous and changes as obvious as those which can be found in the eighteenth century to justify the vital metaphor of birth.'

market of national reach and scope, but with the massive reorganization of
an entire society along market principles – what Karl Polanyi has termed
'the running of society as an adjunct to the market'.[86] And this takes place
only in the late eighteenth and early nineteenth century.

The rise of market-oriented production in England can, of course, be
traced back at least as far as the fifteenth century. Slowly, though at an
increased pace from the early seventeenth century onwards, the market
system spread to incorporate all but the Celtic fringe, so that by 1750,
England was already in essence a single national market economy.[87] But
it was a market riddled with imperfections, one which in consequence
'exercised a weak pull on the economy'[88] and had only a limited impact on
the English social structure. As late as the 1740s, 'society and economy
remained in self-adjusting equilibrium, and there were no great pressures
towards destabilization'.[89] The pace of change then began to accelerate,
until by 'the last quarter of the century, economic activity and population
began to soar'.[90] The reasons for the persistence of a more traditional
social formation were many. Difficulties of transport and communications
hampered the market's effectiveness. Likewise, the underdevelopment of
credit mechanisms, together with the customary and institutional barriers
to the reorganization of land and labour markets along capitalist lines,[91]
meant that the rationalizing impact of capitalism, though present, only
operated within strict limits. And precisely 'because the mass of con-
sumers was poor and their effective demand restricted by low incomes,
the incentives to prompt producers to overcome these limits were still
insufficient'.[92]

The consequences of this situation are plain. The weak pull of the
market allowed the persistence of a relatively unchanging agriculture and
the survival of a social order which, reformulated in terms of eighteenth-
century philosophy, exhibited substantial continuities with the past.
Market determination of wages and prices coexisted alongside and at times
was substantially inhibited by traditional conceptions of the just wage and
the just price, as well as customary ideas about what constituted a fair
day's work. Moreover, 'wage-earners of a modern type were to be found

86. Karl Polanyi, *The Great Transformation*, Boston: Beacon, 1957.
87. E. Hobsbawm, *Industry and Empire*, pp. 27–8; Pierre Mantoux, *The Industrial Revolution
    in the Eighteenth Century*, London: Cape, 1928, p. 74.
88. L.A. Clarkson, *The Pre-Industrial Economy in England 1500–1750*, London: Batsford,
    1971, p. 22.
89. Roy Porter, *English Society in the Eighteenth Century*, London: Penguin, 1982, p. 230.
90. *Ibid.*, p. 329. Taken together, as McKendrick comments, 'these pervasive changes in
    commercial technique and consumer behaviour [were] an event of dramatic importance
    in English life . . .'. N. McKendrick, J. Brewer, and J.H. Plumb, *The Birth of a Consumer
    Society*, p. 5.
91. 'Mercantilism, with all its tendency towards commercialization, never attacked the
    safeguards which protected these two basic elements of production – labour and land –
    from becoming the objects of commerce.' Karl Polanyi, *The Great Transformation*, p. 70.
92. L.A. Clarkson, *The Pre-Industrial Economy in England*, p. 22.

only in isolated groups . . . [though] a large proportion, perhaps a majority, of workers had reached what may be considered a half-way stage between peasant and proletarian'.[93] From prince to pauper, society was held together by what Cobbett referred to as 'the chain of connection'. Social subordination rested upon reciprocal bonds of patronage, deference, and dependence, and 'permanent vertical links . . . , rather than the horizontal solidarities of class, bound society together . . . a social nexus . . . less formal and inescapable than feudal homage, more personal and comprehensive than the contractual, employment relationships of capitalist "Cash Payment" '.[94]

The changing structure of the English economy from the second half of the eighteenth century onwards undermined and then destroyed the old order. An ever more robust and abrasive commercialism established itself in every realm of social existence, scurrying around in search of opportunities for profit, and remorselessly broadening the geographical scope of the market. Profound shifts occurred in the relationships between the superordinate and the subordinate classes, and in upper-class perceptions of their responsibilities towards the less fortunate – changes which can be summarized as the transition from a master–servant to an employer–employee relationship; from a social order dominated by rank, order, and degree, to one based on class.[95] There emerged a 'general sense of betrayal of paternal responsibilities by the naked exercise of the power of property'.[96] As part of the general change from regulated to self-regulating markets, centuries-old legislation protecting workers' standard of living and conditions of work was abolished. Increasingly, 'the process of acquisition set the terms on which other social processes were allowed to operate'.[97] Capitalism broke the social bonds which had formerly held it in check, and a modern commercial consumer society was born.[98]

The impetus for these changes had a number of sources. Substantially improved transport had reduced costs and widened internal markets.[99] But more importantly, domestic population had begun to rise very rapidly indeed from the 1770s onwards (in the fifty years from 1780 it roughly

93. H. Perkin, *The Origins of Modern English Society*, p. 90.
94. *Ibid.*, p. 49. As E.P. Thompson (in *Whigs and Hunters*) and Douglas Hay (in *Albion's Fatal Tree*) have forcibly reminded us, one must not romanticize this social system. Beneath the emphasis on patronage and dependence lay a ruling class skilled and ruthless in manipulating force and terror.
95. *Cf.* Asa Briggs, 'The Language of "Class" in Early Nineteenth Century England', pp. 43–73 in A. Briggs and J. Saville (eds), *Essays in Labour History*, London: Macmillan, 1960.
96. H. Perkin, *The Origins of Modern English Society*, p. 126.
97. Asa Briggs, *The Making of Modern England*, pp. 64–5.
98. On the growth of a 'hectic economy of consumption and emulation' in these years, see the illuminating discussions in R. Porter, *English Society in the Eighteenth Century*, chapters 5 and 8; and N. McKendrick, J. Brewer, and J.H. Plumb, *The Birth of a Consumer Society*.
99. See the discussion in R. Porter, *English Society in the Eighteenth Century*, pp. 207–9.

doubled). This, coupled with the impact of the growing industrial sector of the economy, produced a large and continuing expansion of demand.[100] Nowhere was this development more marked than in the demand for food. Given an extra stimulus between 1793 and 1815 by the Napoleonic Wars, the market for foodstuffs entered upon a phase of permanent boom. (During the Wars, wheat prices, for example, reached double their prewar levels, and they remained substantially above their prewar peak even when the artificial spur of military conflict was removed.) These conditions provided rural producers with sustained pressures and incentives to rationalize agricultural production. In Asa Briggs's words, 'businesslike farming became a reasonable economic proposition'.[101] Along with the cultivation of new land, the application of systematic business calculation to farming was perhaps as important as anything in bringing about the remarkable early nineteenth-century rise in agricultural output.

Rationalization, of course, had its costs. Marginal smallholders and cottagers with some alternative sources of support beyond wage labour were squeezed out and proletarianized, in part by the Parliamentary enclosures of the late eighteenth century,[102] but also by the harsh competitive realities of an economic system dominated by industrial manufactures and an ever more thoroughly rationalized agriculture. In-servants, who had formerly lived as part of the farmer's family, were increasingly transformed into labourers, since at a time of rising prices and over-abundant labour this was cheaper. And labourers were hired for shorter and shorter terms, because that was more economically rational: the farmer did not have to pay for them when, for whatever reason, they were idle.[103] The economy as a whole came under the sway of the notion that '[the employer] owed his employees wages, and once these were paid, the men had no further claim on him'.[104]

Thus, just as surely as urbanization, the market when given its head destroyed the traditional links between rich and poor which had character-ized the old order. The 'great transformation' wrought by the advent of a thoroughly market-oriented society sharply reduced the *capacity* of the lower orders to cope with economic reverses. Wage-earners, whether they were agricultural labourers or the early representatives of an urban proletariat, shared a similar incapacity to make adequate provision for periods of economic depression. Quite apart from the centres of urban-ization and industrialization, and to a much greater degree than the geo-graphically limited scope of these processes would indicate, the burgeoning

100. The transformative effects of a rapid growth in demand are emphasized particularly strongly in N. McKendrick, J. Brewer, and J.H. Plumb, *The Birth of a Consumer Society*, chapter 1.
101. A. Briggs, *The Making of Modern England*, p. 40.
102. See the discussion in R. Porter, *English Society in the Eighteenth Century*, pp. 225–230.
103. The last two paragraphs are heavily indebted to the analysis in Eric Hobsbawm and George Rude, *Captain Swing*, London: Penguin, 1969, chapters 1 and 2.
104. P. Mantoux, *The Industrial Revolution*, p. 428.

market economy was rendering anachronistic the idealized conception of a population living amidst 'the ever-sustaining resources of an uncomplicated rural parish'.[105] To make matters worse, along with the closing off of alternatives other than wage work as a means of providing for subsistence went the tendency of the primitive capitalist economy to oscillate wildly and unpredictably between conditions of boom and slump.

All in all, among the lower classes in this period, family members unable to contribute effectively towards their own maintenance must have constituted a serious drain on family resources. In the situation which they faced, 'any interruption of the ability to work or the availability of a job spelt dire want. . . . The aged and children became a greater burden . . .',[106] as, of course, did the insane. Consequently, while a family-based system of caring for the mad may never have worked especially well, one suspects that by the turn of the century it was likely to have been functioning particularly badly.

These changes in structures, perceptions, and outlook, which marked the transition from the old paternalistic social order to a fully capitalist social system, provided a direct source of bourgeois dissatisfaction with the traditional, non-institutional response to the indigent; but they were by no means the only ones. Another derived from the dislocations of the social structure associated with the rapid rise in population and the transition to an industrial economy. Not the least of these dislocations was the sizeable late eighteenth-century expansion of the population in temporary or permanent receipt of poor relief – an expansion which took place at precisely that point in time when the growing power of the bourgeoisie and their increasing dominance of intellectual life were reducing the inclination to tolerate such a state of affairs. By 1803, 'over a million people, one in nine of the population, were said to be in receipt of poor relief, casual or permanent'.[107] Doubtless alarmed by this situation, the upper classes readily convinced themselves that laxly administered systems of household relief promoted poverty rather than relieved it, a position for which they found amply ideological justification in the writings of Malthus and others.[108] Instead, they were increasingly attracted towards an institutionally based system. Workhouses, asylums, and the like were not only expected to provide an efficient and economical solution to the problem; they enabled a close and continuing watch to be kept on who was admitted. By making living conditions in the workhouses sufficiently unattractive, all save the truly needy and 'deserving'

---

105. W.K. Jordan, *Philanthropy in England 1480–1660*, pp. 66–7.
106. Gaston Rimlinger, *Welfare Policy and Industrialization in Europe, America, and Russia*, New York: Wiley, 1971, p. 8.
107. H. Perkin, *The Origins of Modern English Society*, p. 22.
108. T.R. Malthus, *An Essay on the Principle of Population*, London: Johnson, 1798, esp. chapter V; John MacFarlan, *Inquiries Concerning the Poor*, Edinburgh: Longman and Dickson, 1782, pp. 34–6; [William Temple], *An Essay on Trade and Commerce*, London: Cunningham, 1770, p. 258.

poor could be deterred from applying for relief; and the treatment of those
so confined could always serve as an example *pour encourager les autres*. In
this way, the whole system might be made efficient and economical.[109]

Institutions seemed to promise still other advantages. A labour force
composed primarily of displaced agricultural labourers was ill-disposed to
submit to the rigours of discipline demanded by a wage labour system –
and, more especially, by the requirements of wage labour in a factory. In
Andrew Ure's words, the problem was 'to subdue the refractory tempers
of work people accustomed to irregular paroxysms of diligence . . .',[110]
and to teach them to conform to the impersonal dictates of power-driven
machinery. In devising techniques to secure these ends, there can be little
question but that 'the most available [human] material was that large
element of the people whose dependence upon charity had surrendered
them bodily into the hands of the civil power.'[111] Here, the appeal of the
institution was obvious: for it appeared to provide the opportunity for the
most intensive and thoroughgoing control over the lives of its inmates.
The quasi-military authority structure which it could institute seemed
ideally suited to be the means of establishing 'proper' work habits among
those marginal elements of the work force who were apparently most
resistant to the monotony, routine, and regularity of industrialized labour,
providing 'rigorous life conditions to discipline the labourer and purge his
character of the evil habits of "luxury" and "sloth". . . .'[112] Workhouses
and the like would thus 'perform the double service of administering
punishment for idleness and providing training in the habits of thrift and
industry'.[113] They would function, in Bentham's caustic phrase, as 'a mill
to grind rogues honest and idle men industrious . . . ,'[114] and as a stark
warning to those tempted to stray from the path of labour and virtue.

4. The Differentiation of the Mad

Thus, on the most general level, the receptivity of the English ruling class
to the notion of an institutional response to problem populations can
be traced to the underlying structural transformations of their society.
But what were the sources of the increasing tendency, not only to institutionalize the deviant, but also to depart from the traditional practice of
treating the indigent, troublesome, and morally disreputable as part of a
single amorphous mass? More specifically, given my present concerns,

109. Edgar S. Furniss, *The Position of the Laborer in a System of Nationalism*, New York:
      Kelly, 1965, p. 107; [W. Temple], *An Essay on Trade and Commerce*, pp. 151–269.
110. Andrew Ure, *The Philosophy of Manufactures*, London: Knight, 1835, p. 16.
111. E. Furniss, The *Position of the Laborer in a System of Nationalism*, p. 117.
112. *Ibid.*, p. 107; William Bailey, *A Treatise on the Better Employment and More Comfortable
      Support of the Poor in Workhouses*, London: Dodsley, 1758.
113. E. Furniss, *The Position of the Laborer in a System of Nationalism*, p. 107.
114. Bentham to Brissot, in Jeremy Bentham, *Works*, Volume X (ed. J. Bowring),
      Edinburgh: Tait, 1843, p. 226.

how and why did insanity come to be differentiated from the previously inchoate mass of deviant behaviours, so that it was seen as a distinct problem requiring specialized treatment in an institution of its own, the asylum? For it should be obvious that before the asylum could emerge as a specialized institution devoted to the problems of coping with insanity, the latter had to be distinguished as a separate variety of deviant behaviour. Insanity could not be a term narrowly applied to cases of furious mania or reserved for demented members of the upper classes. It had to be seen as a condition existing more pervasively among the lower classes of the community – a distinct species of pathology which could not be considered as just one more case of poverty and dependency.[115]

The establishment of a market economy and, more particularly, the emergence of a market in labour, provided the initial incentive to distinguish far more carefully than hitherto between different categories of deviance. If nothing else, under these conditions, stress had to be laid for the first time on the importance of distinguishing the able-bodied from the non- able-bodied poor. One of the most basic prerequisites of a capitalist system, as both Marx and Weber have emphasized, was the existence of a large mass of wage labourers who were not merely 'free' to dispose of their labour power in the open market, but who were actually forced to do so. In Marx's words, 'Capital presupposes wage labour, and wage labour presupposes capital. One is the necessary condition of the other'.[116] Indeed,

> all the peculiarities of Western capitalism have derived their significance in the last analysis only from their association with the capitalist organization of labour. Even what is generally called commercialization – the developments of negotiable securities and the rationalization of speculation, the exchanges, etc. – is connected with it. For without the rational capitalist organization of labour, all this, so far as it was possible at all, would have nothing like the same significance, above all for the social structure and all the specific problems of the modern Occident connected with it. Exact calculation – the basis of everything else – is only possible on the basis of free labour.[117]

115. Of course, I am not suggesting here that prior to this process of differentiation the population at large were naively unaware of any and all differences between the various elements making up the disreputable classes – between, say, the raving madman and the petty criminal, or the blind and the crippled. Obviously, on a very straightforward level such distinctions were apparent and could linguistically be made – and in extreme cases made some practical differences to the ways in which individuals were dealt with. The critical question, however, is when and for what reasons such perceived differences rigidified and came to be seen as *socially significant* – i.e., began routinely to provoke differential responses and to have consequential impact on the lives of the deviant. The question of the definition of insanity is discussed in chapter 7 below.
116. Karl Marx, *Capital*, Vol. 1, New York: International Publishers edn, 1967, pp. 578, 717–33.
117. Max Weber, *The Protestant Ethic and the Spirit of Capitalism*, London: Allen and Unwin, 1930, p. 22.

But to provide aid to the able-bodied threatened to undermine in a radical fashion and on many different levels the whole notion of a labour market.

Parochial provision of relief to the able-bodied interfered with labour mobility.[118] In particular, it encouraged the retention of a 'vast inert mass of redundant labour', a stagnant pool of underemployed labouring men in rural areas, where the demand for labour was subject to wide seasonal fluctuations. It distorted the operations of the labour market and, thereby, of all other markets, most especially on account of its tendency, via the vagaries of local administration, to create cost differentials between one town or region and another. Late eighteenth-century economic writers complained that relief to the able-bodied 'renders the price of labour in England very unequal, in some places so low as to afford little encouragement to industry; in others so exorbitantly high as to become ruinous to manufactures . . .' – a complaint later echoed by the Poor Law Commission.[119] Finally, by its removal of the threat of individual starvation, such relief had a pernicious effect on labour discipline and productivity, an outcome accentuated by the fact that the 'early labourer abhorred the factory, where he felt degraded and tortured. . . .'[120]

Instead, it was felt that want ought to be the stimulus to the capable, who must therefore be distinguished from the helpless. Such a distinction is deceptively simple; but in a wider perspective, this development can be seen as a crucial phase in the growing rationalization of the Western social order and the transformation of prior *extensive* structures of domination into the ever more intensive forms characteristic of the modern world. Traditional pre-capitalist conceptions viewed the domestic population as a largely unchangeable given from which an effort was made to squeeze as large a surplus as possible; the emergent modern conception of the labour pool viewed it as modifiable and manipulable human material whose yield could be steadily enlarged through improvements in use and organization, rationally designed to transform qualitatively its value as an economic resource. As Moffett has shown, during this process, 'the domestic population came increasingly to be regarded as an industrial labour force – not simply a tax reservoir as formerly – and state policies came increasingly to be oriented to forcing the entire working population into remunerative employment'.[121] The significance of the distinction between the able-bodied and non-able-bodied poor thus increases *pari passu* with the rise of the wage labour system.

118. J. MacFarlan, *Inquiries Concerning the Poor*, pp. 176ff.; Adam Smith, *The Wealth of Nations*, New York: Modern Library edn, 1937, pp. 135–40.
119. J. MacFarlan, *Inquiries Concerning the Poor*, p. 178; *Report of the Poor Law Commission of 1834*, London: Penguin, 1971, p. 43.
120. K. Polanyi, *The Great Transformation*, pp. 164–5; E.P. Thompson, *The Making of the English Working Class*, Harmondsworth: Penguin, 1963.
121. John T. Moffett, 'Bureaucracy and Social Control: A Study of the Progressive Regimentation of the Western Social Order', unpublished Ph.D. dissertation, Columbia University, 1971.

The beginnings of such a separation are evident even in the early phases of English capitalism. The great Elizabethan Poor Law, for example, classified the poor into the able but unemployed, the aged and impotent, and children; and a number of historians have been tempted to see in this and in the Statute of Artificers (1563) a primitive labour code of the period, dealing respectively with what we would call the unemployed and unemployable, and the employed. But, as Polanyi suggests, in large measure, 'the neat distinction between the employed, unemployed, and unemployable is, of course, anachronistic since it implies the existence of a modern wage system which was absent [at this time]'.[122] Until much later, the boundaries between these categories remained in practice much more fluid and ill-defined than the modern reader is apt to realize.[123] Moreover, though it is plain that the Tudors and Stuarts did not scruple to invoke harsh legal penalties in an effort to compel the poor to work, these measures were undertaken at least as much 'for the sake of political security' as for more directly economic motives.[124]

Gradually economic considerations became more and more dominant. As they did so, it became increasingly evident that 'no treatment of this matter was adequate which failed to distinguish between the able-bodied unemployed on the one hand, the aged, infirm, and children on the other.'[125] The former were to be compelled to work, initially through the direct legal compulsion inherited from an earlier period. But the upper classes came to despair of the notion that they 'may be compelled [by statute] to work according to their abilities . . .';[126] and were increasingly attracted towards an alternative method according to which, in the picturesque language of John Bellers, 'The Sluggard shall be cloathed in Raggs. He that will not work shall not eat.'[127] The superiority of this approach was put most bluntly by Joseph Townsend:

122. K. Polanyi, *The Great Transformation*, p. 86.
123. Still, Paul Slack quite correctly emphasizes that 'the dichotomy between the deserving and undeserving poor acquired much greater force in the sixteenth century. Hammered home in tracts, statutes, and proclamations, it became a commonplace concept through which contemporaries organized their view of the social order'. *Poverty and Policy in Tudor and Stuart England*, p. 23. In part, this development reflected the impact of the Reformation, which removed the need to concede the holiness of voluntary poverty; and in still larger part, it emerged out of the fear and disgust with which vagabonds came to be viewed in the sixteenth century.
124. Dorothy Marshall, *The English Poor in the Eighteenth Century*, London: Routledge, 1926, p. 17; Maurice Dobb, *Studies in the Development of Capitalism*, New York: International Publishers, 1963, pp. 233ff.
125. K. Polanyi, *The Great Transformation*, p. 94. This is not to dispute the fact that some recognition of the existence of different kinds of poverty can be traced back at least as far as the thirteenth century, but the qualitative shift in perceptions in the sixteenth century is nonetheless undeniable. *Cf.* P. Slack, *Poverty and Policy in Tudor and Stuart England*, pp. 22–3.
126. J. MacFarlan, *Inquiries Concerning the Poor*, p. 105.
127. John Bellers, *Proposals for Raising a College of Industry of All Useful Trades and Husbandry*, London: Sowle, 1696, p. 1.

Hunger will tame the fiercest animals, it will teach decency and civility, obedience and subjection to the most perverse. In general, it is only hunger which can spur and goad [the poor] on to labour; yet our laws have said they shall never hunger. The laws, it must be confessed, have likewise said, they shall be compelled to work. But then legal constraint is attended with much trouble, violence, and noise; creates ill-will, and can never be productive of good and acceptable service; whereas hunger is not only peaceable, silent, unremitting pressure, but, as the most natural motive to industry and labour, it calls forth the most violent exertions.[128]

The whiplash of hunger, that is, appeared as 'a purely economic and "objective" form of compulsion'; a suprahuman law of nature. And, as Malthus was quick to point out, 'When nature will govern and punish for us, it is a very miserable ambition to wish to snatch the rod from her hands and draw upon ourselves the odium of the executioner.'[129]

Thus the functional requirements of a market system promoted a relatively simple, if crucial, distinction between two broad classes of the indigent. Workhouses and the like were to be an important *practical* means of making this vital theoretical separation, and thereby of rendering the whole system efficient and economical. However, although workhouses were initially intended to be just that – institutions to remove the able-bodied poor from the community in order to teach them the wholesome discipline of labour – they swiftly found themselves depositories for the decaying, the decrepit, and the unemployable. And an unintended consequence of this concentration of deviants in an institutional environment was that it produced an exacerbation of the problems of handling some of them.[130] More specifically, it rendered problematic the whole question of what was to be done with those who could not or would not abide by the rules of the house – among the most important of whom were the acutely disturbed and refractory insane.

A single mad or distracted person in the community produced problems of a wholly different sort from those the same person would have produced if placed with other deviants within the walls of an institution. The order and discipline of the whole workhouse were threatened by the presence of a madman who, even by threats and punishment, could neither be persuaded nor induced to conform to the regulations. And besides, by its very nature, the workhouse was ill-suited to provide a secure safe-keeping for those who might pose a threat to life or property.

128. [Joseph Townsend], *A Dissertation on the Poor Laws by a Well Wisher of Mankind*, London: Dilly, 1786.
129. T.R. Malthus, *An Essay on the Principle of Population*, 6th edn, London: Murray, 1826, Book 2, p. 339.
130. J. MacFarlan, *Inquiries Concerning the Poor*, pp. 97ff. For some recent discussion, see Akihito Suzuki, 'Lunacy in Seventeenth and Eighteenth Century England: Analysis of Quarter Sessions Records, Part II', *History of Psychiatry* 3, 1992, pp. 29–44.

In the words of a contemporary appeal for funds to set up a second charity asylum in London, 'The law has made no particular provision for lunaticks and it must be allowed that the common parish workhouses (the inhabitants of which are mostly aged and infirm people) are very unfit places for the Reception of such ungovernable and mischievous persons, who necessarily require separate apartments.'[131] Advocates of similar institutions in the provinces also sought to capitalize on this situation, pointing out that 'when the Poorhouse shall be relieved of the insane . . . the respectable magistrates . . . will then find it easier to extirpate vice, disorder, and guilty idleness, from this great family of the lowest and most ignorant class of society'.[132] The local jail, which was frequently resorted to as a substitute place of confinement for violent maniacs, proved scarcely more satisfactory, the dislocations which the madmen's presence produced provoking widespread complaints from both prisoners and their jailers. And faced by similar problems, general hospitals began to respond by refusing to accept lunatic inmates 'on Account of the safety of other Patients'.[133]

Clearly, the adoption of an institutional response to all sorts of problem populations greatly increased the pressures to elaborate the distinctions amongst and between the deviant and dependent. By making separate institutional provision for a troublesome group like the insane, a source of potential danger and inconvenience to the community could be removed to a place where such people could no longer pose a threat to the social order. Consequently, by the late eighteenth century, many were becoming convinced of the need for specialized institutions. After all, one must surely concede that

> the case of the unhappy objects afflicted with this disorder is in a peculiar manner distressful, since besides their own sufferings, they are rendered a nuisance and a terror to others; and are not only themselves lost to society, but take up the time and attention of others. By placing a number of them in a common receptacle, they may be taken care of by a much smaller number of attendants; and at the same time they are

131. St. Luke's Hospital, *Considerations upon the Usefulness and Necessity of Establishing an Hospital as a Further Provision for Poor Lunaticks*, 1750, in manuscript, St. Luke's Woodside Hospital, London. Contractors 'farming' the poor in London were increasingly concerned about the problems created by violent and difficult cases of insanity, and began to refuse to take charge of lunatics. Richard Birch, for instance, who operated a workhouse at Spitalfields in the early 1760s, explicitly refused to accommodate such 'as are Raving and not Capable of being Controuled'; and John Flower, who ran a similar establishment in St. Giles Cripplegate, insisted in his contract dated 30 October 1771 that he would take charge of the parish poor 'Lunaticks only Excepted'. Guildhall Manuscripts 4501, 11280A/4, cited in J. Andrews, 'Bedlam Revisited', p. 497.
132. Letter to the *Liverpool Advertiser*, quoted in Michael Fears, 'Moral Treatment and British Psychiatry', paper presented at the conference of the British Sociological Association, 1975, p. 5.
133. St. Luke's Hospital, *Considerations*, p. 2.

removed from the public eye to which they are multiplied objects of alarm, and the mischiefs they are liable to do to themselves and others, are with much greater certainty prevented.[134]

Initially, with respect to the insane, this situation provided no more than an opportunity for financial speculation and pecuniary profit for those who set up private madhouses and asylums. Such, indeed, was the general character of the eighteenth-century 'trade in lunacy', which, even in the sector concerned with pauper lunatics, was a frequently lucrative business dealing with the most acutely disturbed and refractory cases – those who in the general mixed workhouses caused trouble out of all proportion to their numbers. While claims to provide cures as well as care were periodically used as a means of drumming up custom, the fundamental orientation of the system (besides profit) was towards restraint in an economical fashion of those posing a direct threat to the social order.[135] Indeed, the revelations of the nineteenth-century parliamentary inquiries into the system were to reveal that in many madhouses almost every other consideration, including the welfare of the inmates, was willingly sacrificed to the requirements of order and restraint with the least trouble to the keeper. As we shall see, however, in the long run, such a differentiation of deviance provided the essential social preconditions for the establishment of a new organized profession, claiming to possess a specific expertise in the management of insanity and oriented towards a rehabilitative ideal.

On the most general level, the English elite's receptivity to the notion that a particular occupational group possessed a scientifically based expertise in dealing with lunacy reflected the growing secular rationalization of Western society at this time, a development which, following Weber, I would argue took place under the dominant, though not the sole, impetus of the development of a capitalist market system. More specifically, it reflected the penetration of this realm of social existence by the values of science, the idea that 'there are no mysterious incalculable forces that come into play, but rather that one can, in principle, master all things by calculation'.[136] Linked to this change in perspective was a fundamental shift in the underlying paradigm of insanity, away from an emphasis on its demonological, non-human, animalistic qualities towards

134. John Aikin, *Thoughts on Hospitals*, London: Johnson, 1771, pp. 65–6.
135. W. Parry-Jones, *The Trade in Lunacy, passim*. Earlier in the century, when Bethlem made specific provision for the 'incurable', its governors rapidly moved to give priority to dangerous over harmless incurables, stipulating, on 31 October 1739, 'that for the future only such patients as . . . are outrageous and likely to do mischief to themselves or others shall be admitted into the Incurable Hospital'. Bethlem General Court Minutes, quoted in J. Andrews, 'The Lot of the "Incurably" Insane in Enlightenment England', p. 11. St. Luke's adopted a similar rule in 1763.
136. Max Weber, *From Max Weber: Essays in General Sociology*, London: Oxford University Press, 1946, p. 139.

a naturalistic perspective which viewed the madman as exhibiting a defective *human* mechanism, and which therefore saw this condition as at least potentially remediable.[137]

By the end of the eighteenth century, a growing market or trade in lunacy was emerging. Moreover, those operating in this developing market were at work in a social context in which claims to possess expertise and special competence were likely to find a receptive audience. It is thus not surprising that the development and consolidation of institutional means of coping with madness parallels that of a professionalized group of managers of the mad. For it was the existence of the institutions which permitted, or perhaps it might be more accurate to say, formed the breeding ground for, this emerging 'professionalism'. On the one hand (and particularly once the state was led to invest directly in the asylum solution), the institutions provided the incentive, in the form of a guaranteed market for the experts' services; and on the other, they provided a context within which, isolated from the community at large, the proto-profession could develop empirically based craft skills in the management of the distracted.[138] As I have already noted, one of my major concerns in what follows will be with *how* one particular group captured and organized this market, defining the problem as one they were uniquely qualified to deal with and in the process decisively shifting insanity into the medical arena. Equally important for my analysis is a further implication of the fact that they were able to do so. The emergence in the nineteenth century of what was to become the psychiatric profession lent scientific legitimacy to the process through which the various sub-categories of deviance were established and institutionalized. Or, to put it another way, this development played a critical role in transforming the vague cultural construct of madness into what now purported to be a formally coherent, scientifically distinguishable entity, which reflected and was caused by a single underlying pathology.

This was a self-reinforcing system, for the key dimensions of the emergent profession's claims to expertise came to revolve around questions of institutional management. The very essence of their approach lay in its emphasis on order, rationality, and self-control; goals which could only be reached in an institutional setting. A dialectical process was at work, whereby the separation of the insane into madhouses and asylums

---

137. In the next chapter, we shall examine in more detail the social sources and appeal of the ideology of rehabilitation; and the impact of this shift in the cultural meaning of madness (and hence in what was considered appropriate treatment for the lunatic) on the reform movement as a whole.

138. The distinction I want to emphasize here is between skills largely learned by a process of trial and error and transmitted from one generation to the next through a system of apprenticeship; and those resting upon an elaborate rational-scientific basis, allowing of a standardized, routine transmission of expertise. Ideological protestations and smokescreens notwithstanding, the former remains to this day the basis for most controllers' claims to expertise.

helped to create the conditions for the emergence of an occupational group laying claim to expertise in their care and cure, and the nature and content of the restorative ideal which the latter fostered reinforced the commitment to the institutional approach. Thereafter, the existence of both asylums and psychiatry was to testify to the 'necessity' and 'naturalness' of distinguishing the insane from other deviants.

5. The Deviant and the State

Analysing these developments from a slightly different perspective, we can see that in a number of ways the emergence of medically run asylums for the mad was predicated upon important changes in the relationship between the state and civil society, for a vital feature of this radically novel social control apparatus as it emerged and consolidated itself in the nineteenth century was the degree to which its operations became subject to central control and direction, and dependent upon state power and patronage. Until very late in its history, English society remained overwhelmingly localized in its social organization, characterized by a fragmentation of power and loyalties, and as we have already seen, the mechanisms for coping with deviance in pre-nineteenth-century England placed a corresponding reliance upon an essentially communal and family-based system of control. The assumption of direct state responsibility for these functions, which took place over the first four or five decades of the nineteenth century, thus marked a sharp departure from these traditional emphases.

While the administrative centralization and rationalization which are crucial elements of this transformation are not wholly the consequence of economic rationalization, it seems inescapable that in England, and elsewhere in Western Europe in the later and most critical phases of these processes, the advance of the capitalist economic order and the growth of the central authority of the state are twin processes intimately connected with each other.

> On the one hand, were it not for the expansion of commerce and the rise of capitalist agriculture, there would scarcely have been the economic base to finance the expanded bureaucratic state structures. But on the other hand, the state structures were themselves a major economic underpinning of the new capitalist system (not to speak of being its political guarantee).[139]

In a very literal sense, institutional control mechanisms were impracticable earlier, because of the absence both of the necessary administrative techniques and also of the surplus required to establish and maintain them.

139. Immanuel Wallerstein, *The Modern World System*, New York: Academic Press, 1974, p. 133.

The creation of more efficient administrative structures, which was both the precondition and the consequence of the growth of the state and of large-scale capitalist enterprise, possessed a dual importance. It allowed for the first time the development of a tolerably adequate administrative apparatus to mediate between the central and local authorities, and thus to extend central control down to the local level. It also provided the basis for the development of techniques for the efficient handling of large numbers of people confined for months or years on end, without which the institutional mechanisms of social control could scarcely have achieved the importance that they did.

Financially speaking, state construction and operation of institutions for the deviant and dependent was very costly. Hence the importance, as a transitional arrangement, of the state contracting with private entrepreneurs to provide jails, madhouses, and the like. By this method, the state allows the 'deviant farmer' to extort his fees and control his costs in whatever ways he can, and turns a blind eye to his methods; in return the latter relieves the state of the capital expenditure (and often many of the running costs) required by a system of segregative control. This is the structural underpinning of the free market in lunacy which formed such a note-worthy feature of eighteenth- and early nineteenth-century responses to the mad. The change to a system directly run by the state was obviously conditioned by, though by no means the automatic product of, the development of large stable tax revenues and that state's ability to borrow on a substantial scale.

In Jean Boudin's famous words, 'Financial means are the nerves of the state.' The 'nervous system' of the English state, lacking the spur of military competition, without a standing army to enforce and require efforts to extract taxes, and dominated by a gentry class fearful of the expansion of the power of the central authority, was for a long time only poorly developed when compared with the Continental Absolutisms of the period.[140] Everywhere, however, in Europe as well as in England, 'until we approach the nineteenth century ... fiscal possibilities were strictly limited by the structure and trend of the economy'.[141] In the absence of a developed market economy, the structure of economic life militated against the effective levying of taxes. Subsistence economies offer systematic obstacles to both the estimation and collection of taxes. Where there is only limited exchange, value and net earnings cannot be estimated with any degree of accuracy, and intervening in the tight cycle of production and consumption becomes very difficult. Furthermore, the fact that so much economic activity does not take a monetarized form hinders the collection of taxes – which by now are levied in money, not in kind. In these and other ways, '*tax collection and assessment are indissolubly*

140. P. Anderson, *Lineages of the Absolutist State*, chapter 5.
141. G. Ardant, 'Financial Policy and Economic Infrastructure', p. 174.

linked to an exchange economy.[142] State borrowing and the rise of the
so-called national debt are likewise intimately tied to the expansion of
the monetarized sector of the economy – to the development of capital
markets and the growth of the sophisticated credit and accounting mechanisms characteristic of capitalist economic organization.[143] In the circumstances, one can readily understand why for more than a century and
a half, the taxes in support of the poor authorized by the Elizabethan
Poor Law (1601) 'were enforced in any community only as a last resort,
for these rates were extremely unpopular and they were most difficult
to raise'.[144] And while the growing commercialization of the English
economy in the eighteenth century gradually began to break down the
technical obstacles to larger state appropriation of the social product,
political barriers did not dissolve as fast.

In the long run, the development of national and international markets
produced a diminution, if not a destruction, of the traditional influence of
local groups (especially kinship groups), which formerly played a large
role in the regulation of social life. But local opposition to centralized
intervention in an increasing range of social activities did not, of course,
simply disappear in the face of these developments. Indeed, as we shall
see, it proved remarkably tenacious, particularly in the politically sensitive area of the size and reach of 'the central coercive machinery at the
disposal of the State'.[145] Central control of the social control apparatus –
whether of the facilities for the surveillance and restraint of the poor,[146]
the apparatus for the policing of the criminal,[147] or the machinery for
certifying and managing the mad – was not won easily, and we shall
have occasion to notice the retarding impact of this factor on the lunacy
reformers' project.[148]

142. *Ibid.*, p. 166, emphasis in the original.
143. On the development of public credit and debt, see the classic study by P.G.M. Dickson,
    *The Financial Revolution in England: A Study of the Development of Public Credit, 1688–
    1756*, London: Macmillan, 1967. For a recent modification of Dickson's views,
    emphasizing the importance of the growth of the power to tax as a necessary structural
    foundation for the evolution of public indebtedness, see J. Brewer, *The Sinews of Power*,
    esp. chapter 4.
144. W.K. Jordan, *Philanthropy in England*, p. 141; W.J. Ashley, *An Introduction to English
    Economic History*, p. 360.
145. P. Anderson, *Lineages of the Absolutist State*, p. 139.
146. N.C. Edsall, *The Anti-Poor Law Movement, 1834–44*, Manchester: University of
    Manchester Press, 1971.
147. D. Hay, 'Property, Authority, and the Criminal Law', in D. Hay, P. Linebaugh, J.G.
    Rule, E.P. Thompson, and C. Winslow, *Albion's Fatal Tree: Crime and Society in
    Eighteenth Century England*, New York: Pantheon, 1975; S. Spitzer and A. Scull, 'Social
    Control in Historical Perspective: From Private to Public Responses to Crime', pp.
    281–302 in D.F. Greenberg (ed.), *Corrections and Punishment: Structure, Function, and
    Process*, Beverly Hills, California: Sage Publications, 1977.
148. The progress of lunacy reform in nineteenth-century Ireland provides a highly
    instructive contrast in this respect. In England, attempts to secure a measure of central
    authority and supervision of the asylum system, and to compel local authorities to erect
    asylums at taxpayers' expense, were hobbled by strong and entrenched forces resistant
    to anything that smacked of centralization. Legislation embodying these principles was

Nevertheless, the underlying thrust of the changes in the English social structure in this period is clear: the growth of a single national market and the rise of allegiance to the central political authority to a position of overriding importance ultimately undermined the rationale of a locally based response to deviance, based as that was on the idea of settlement and the exclusion of strangers. As local communities came to be defined and to define themselves as part of a single overarching political and economic system, it made less and less sense for one town to dispose of its problems by passing them on to the next. There was a need for some substitute mode of exclusion. All of which contributed to 'the monopolization of all "legitimate" coercive power by one universalist coercive institution . . .'.[149] and to the development of a state-sponsored system of social control.

not enacted until 1845, after some three decades of struggle; and it took almost a decade and a half longer before the last vestiges of local resistance were overcome. In Ireland, the peculiar quasi-administrative political structure English imperialism had imposed meant that conversion of a small governing elite to the virtues of the asylum solution sufficed to secure prompt passage of the necessary legislation, seemingly without much in the way of attention or debate. And, as Mark Finnane has shown (*Insanity and the Insane in Post-Famine Ireland*, London: Croom Helm, 1981), the authorities in Dublin Castle subsequently retained much greater powers over the size and operations of the system than were possessed by their counterparts in London.

149. Max Weber, *Economy and Society*, Vol. I, Totowa, New Jersey: Bedminister Press, 1968, p. 337.

CHAPTER TWO

The Social Context of Reform

Poor Ophelia
Divided from herself and her fair judgment,
Without which we are pictures, or mere beasts;
William Shakespeare, *Hamlet*

[In] either the public, or the minor and more clandestine Bethlems . . . such a mode of management is used with men, as ought not to be, although it too generally is, applied even to brutes. Derangement is not to be confused with destruction . . . [the lunatic's] unfortunate state . . . for the most part ought to be regarded not as an abolition, but as the suspension merely of the rational faculties.

John Reid, *Essays on Hypochondriasis and Other Nervous Affections*

The *senses* have therefore become directly in their practice *theoreticians*.
Karl, Marx, *Economic and Philosophic Manuscripts of 1844*

The differentiation of the insane from the wider category of the merely indigent and troublesome was made irrevocable by the events of the first half of the nineteenth century. This final phase of the process was marked by the efforts of a relatively small group of laymen to alleviate the conditions of those they saw as an oppressed segment of society. Simultaneously, however, it marked a highly significant redefinition of the moral boundaries of the community. Insanity was transformed from a vague, culturally defined phenomenon afflicting an unknown, but probably small, proportion of the population into a condition which could only be authoritatively diagnosed, certified, and dealt with by a group of legally recognized experts; and which was now seen as one of the major forms of deviance in English society. Whereas in the eighteenth century only a small fraction of those now labelled insane would have been segregated and confined apart from the rest of the community – the most violent and destructive, for instance, or those members of the propertied classes whose mental peculiarities threatened their relations with social or financial ruin – with the achievement of lunacy reform the asylum was endorsed as the sole officially approved response to the problems posed by mental illness. And, in the process, the boundaries of who was to be classified as mad, and thus was to be liable to incarceration, were themselves transformed.

Central to the reform process itself, and to the attempt to transform existing practices, was the construction of a particular vision of the past, one which portrayed the treatment of the mad in Georgian England uniformly in the darkest of hues. Nineteenth-century lunacy reformers pictured the preceding age as mired in ignorance and cruelty, conjuring up indelible images of monstrous madhouse keepers beating their patients into submission, chaining them up like wild beasts in foul holding-pens filled with shit, straw, and stench; of the callous, jeering crowd – urban sophisticates and country bumpkins alike – thronging to Bedlam in their thousands to view the splendid entertainment offered by the spectacle of the raging and raving mad. Generations of Whiggish historians, celebrating the Victorian asylum as the triumph of science over superstition, the very embodiment of an aroused moral consciousness, sang variations on the same theme, seizing on the passage from the madhouse to the mental hospital as decisive evidence of our progress towards ever greater enlightenment, and heaping opprobrium on the benighted denizens of an earlier age.

1. Augustan Views of Madness

Until very recently, modern scholarship had done little to disturb the unsavoury reputation of the pre-reform era or to alter in any fundamental fashion our view of the eighteenth century. Foucauldians followed their master in seeing the Augustan Age as the first decisive step in Reason's repression of Unreason. And even so subtle and sophisticated a historian as Michael MacDonald – whose splendid *Mystical Bedlam* used the casebooks of the astrological physician and divine Richard Napier to illuminate the mental world of the seventeenth century, and to suggest that mental alienation and distress might then have been dealt with in surprisingly sympathetic ways – joined in the chorus of condemnation of the 'violent medical treatments' which followed. 'The eighteenth century', he confidently announced, 'was a disaster for the insane'.[1]

There is unquestionably something distinctly odd about the spectacle of Victorian reformers and twentieth-century Whig historians standing arm in arm with Foucauldians and Anglo-Saxon revisionists to condemn the eighteenth century as a psychiatric dark age. Indeed, the juxtaposition is so startling that one is tempted to conclude that the mere existence of such a peculiar intellectual alliance abundantly testifies to the truth of the propositions it advances, and simultaneously provides us with compelling reassurances about the ultimate triumph of fact over ideology. I have already suggested, however, that eighteenth-century madhouses did not form a monolithic system, and that practices and patient experiences

---

1. Michael MacDonald, *Mystical Bedlam: Madness, Anxiety, and Healing in Seventeenth Century England*, Cambridge: Cambridge University Press, 1981, pp. 228, 230.

varied quite considerably among and between them. More generally, in place of the rather simplistic and formulaic views of madness in the classical age which were accepted as recently as a decade ago, a more nuanced and complex picture is now emerging.

To begin with, one must recognize that to a surprising extent, in discerning the nature of eighteenth-century responses to madness, both traditionalists and revisionists have until recently been content to rely on examples drawn from contemporary fiction and drama and the iconography of Hogarth and his epigones, supplemented by a handful of exemplary tales about the gothic horrors of the eighteenth-century madhouse (often those retailed by nineteenth-century reformers), as the sole evidentiary basis for their bill of indictment.[2] That indictment is familiar to all of us, and I shall insist that, in certain crucial respects, it should not be dismissed as unfaithful to the reality it purports to describe. Nonetheless, as a number of scholars have begun to demonstrate, when one moves beyond these sources to a more detailed and systematic examination of other available evidence about eighteenth-century responses to madness – the writings of medical and non-medical madhouse keepers, for instance, or the admittedly fugitive archival evidence about conditions in eighteenth-century asylums – a richer, more complex portrait emerges. In the process, one develops a clearer understanding of what lay behind Georgian responses to the mad.

Literary and pictorial evidence can, of course, provide us with important insights into popular *mentalités* (albeit as filtered through the sensibilities of the literate classes); and there is much here which suggests the persistence of long-standing cultural stereotypes of mad behaviour, encompassing extravagance, incoherence, incomprehensibility, menace, and ungovernable rage.[3] In Augustan literature of all sorts, the overthrow of Reason, 'the sovereign power of the soul',[4] is seen as unleashing the

2. I plead guilty to committing some version of this sin in *Museums of Madness*. For trenchant criticism of historians' failure to do the necessary spadework in the archives, see Patricia Allderidge, 'Bedlam: Fact or Fantasy?' in W.F. Bynum, Roy Porter, and Michael Shepherd (eds), *The Anatomy of Madness*, Vol. 2, London: Tavistock, 1985, pp. 17–33. (One must emphasize, however, that not all her strictures are entirely warranted, and her polemical zeal to rescue the reputation of the institution of which she is currently the archivist leads her at times to serious overstatements and distortions.) Vital for any reconsideration of eighteenth-century developments are Roy Porter, *Mind Forg'd Manacles: A History of Madness in England from the Restoration to the Regency*, London: Athlone, 1987; Michael Hay, 'Understanding Madness: Eighteenth Century Approaches to Mental Illness', unpublished Ph.D. dissertation, York University, 1979; and, especially, Jonathan Andrews, 'Bedlam Revisited: A History of Bethlem Hospital *c.* 1634–*c.* 1770', unpublished Ph.D. dissertation, London University, 1991. In what follows, I draw extensively upon this body of scholarship (with which, I should nonetheless point out, I continue to differ on some important points of interpretation). In addition, I make considerable use of one of my own earlier essays, 'The Domestication of Madness', *Medical History* 27, 1983, pp. 233–48.
3. On the emergence and consolidation of these 'popular stereotypes of insanity', see M. MacDonald, *Mystical Bedlam*, chapter 4.
4. Nicholas Robinson, *A New System of the Spleen, Vapours, and Hypochondriak Melancholy*, London: Bettesworth, Innys, and Rivington, 1729, p. 43.

appetites and the passions in their full fury: 'Fancy gets the ascendant, and Phaeton-like, drives on furiously',[5] stripping away the veneer of civilization, tossing aside all that is distinctively human,[6] and revealing the beast within.[7] Images of nakedness, irrational violence, furious raving, and incoherent bestiality mark the wreck of the intellect and the loss of the mad person's very humanity;[8] and the fate of such creatures is increasingly portrayed as being intertwined with the nefarious activities of despised and ruffianly madhouse keepers, whose rule over the wild and the ungovernable, the dangerous and the delirious, is necessarily enforced by whips and chains, discipline and depletion.

Imagery of this sort was plainly present even on the Elizabethan and Jacobean stage: in Marston's *What You Will* ('Shut the windows, darken the room, fetch whips: the fellow is mad, he raves – talks idly – lunatic') and in Shirley's *Bird in a Cage* (where the madhouse is referred to as 'a house of correction to whip us into our senses'), not to mention *Hamlet* and *King Lear*.[9] Indeed, it is precisely the commonplace character of these associations which allowed writers to employ them, not just to arouse terror and disgust, but equally for satirical and comic effect:

5. John Brydall, *Non Compos Mentis: Or, the Law Relating to Natural Fools, Mad-Folks, and Lunatick Persons*, London: Cleave, 1700, p. 53.
6. *Cf.* 'Wherever reason is, it ought to predominate and rule, and govern as supreme, and he who will not allow this to be so, is most unworthy of the endowments of this faculty, and takes part with the brute against his own nature; and ought, if his demerits did not require a far greater punishment and disgrace, to lose his natural shape and be turned and transformed into another one: that brute which he imitates, and perhaps envies; into a swine, if a glutton, into a goat, if lascivious.' Zachary Mayne, *Two Discourses Concerning Sense, and the Imagination, with an Essay on Consciousness*, London: Tonson, 1728, p. 91.
7. *Cf.* the claim that 'those that are taken with this disease seem to be as mad as wild beasts, nor do they differ much from them . . . [they possess] a prodigious Herculean strength . . . endure also the greatest hunger, cold and stripes without any sensible harm. . . . Those that are mad are as desirous to bite as mad dogs, or ravenous wolves.' William Salmon, *System Medicinale: A Complete System of Physick, Theoretical and Practical*, London: for the author, 1686, pp. 37, 56–61. For valuable discussions of images of madness in eighteenth-century literature, see Michael Deporte, *Nightmares and Hobbyhorses: Swift, Sterne, and Augustan Ideas of Madness*, San Marino, California: Huntington Library, 1974; and Max Byrd, *Visits to Bedlam*, Columbia: University of South Carolina Press, 1974. D.J. Mellett also provides some commentary on eighteenth- and nineteenth-century literary imagery in chapter 5 of *The Prerogative of Asylumdom: Social, Cultural, and Administrative Aspects of the Institutional Treatment of the Insane in Nineteenth Century Britain*, New York and London: Garland, 1982.
8. The associations were anything but accidental: 'The persistent reference to the ruined dress of lunatics, in literary stereotypes and actual descriptions of madmen, seems oddly insignificant unless this detail is understood as a symbolic repetition of essential ideas about insanity. By reducing his apparel to rags, the lunatic repudiated the hierarchical order of his society and declared himself a mental vagrant; by casting away all artificial coverings, he shed all trace of human society . . . [embracing] a kind of social suicide.' M. MacDonald, *Mystical Bedlam*, p. 131. For similar conclusions, *cf.* J. Andrews, 'Bedlam Revisited', pp. 100–2.
9. For other examples of madhouses scenes, *cf.* John Fletcher's *The Pilgrim*; Thomas Decker's *The Honest Whore*; Decker and Webster's *Northwood Ho*; and Middleton's *The Changeling*. On dramatic images of madness, see generally Edgar A. Peers, *Elizabethan Drama and Its Mad Folk*, Cambridge: Heffer, 1914; and Robert R. Reed, *Bedlam on the Jacobean Stage*, Cambridge, Mass.: Harvard University Press, 1952.

Love is merely a madness; and I tell you, deserves as well a dark house
and a whip as madmen do; and the reason why they are not so punished
and cured is, that the lunacy is so ordinary that the whippers are in love
too.[10]

If, as Sir Richard Blackmore acknowledged, the subject of madness
remained, a century later, 'a wild uncultivated region, an intellectual
Africa, that abounds with an endless variety of monsters and irregular
minds . . .',[11] it was a territory which writers in a variety of genres continued to exploit and explore. From the mock-heroic adventures of Tobias
Smollett's *Sir Launcelot Greaves*, which ends with both hero and heroine
trapped in a madhouse run by the eponymous Mr Shackle, through the
mawkish sentimentality of Henry Mackenzie's *Man of Feeling*, where a
visit to Bethlem provides an inevitable occasion for one of those floods of
tears the author repeatedly inflicted on his readers, the new world of the
novelist repeatedly relied upon and helped to reinforce the currency of
these stock images. Minor poets like Thomas Fitzgerald drew a contrast
between the 'stately Fabric' of Bethlem's walls and the disorder that
reigned within:

> Woe and Horror dwell for ever here.
> For ever from the echoing Roofs rebounds,
> A dreadful Din of heterogeneous Sounds;
> From this, from that, from ev'ry Quarter rise,
> Loud Shouts, and sullen Groans, and doleful Cries;
> Heart-soft'ning Plaints demand the pitying Tear,
> And Peals of hideous Laughter shock the Ear.[12]

And within the confines of a very different genre, Alexander Pope and
Jonathan Swift found few figures as well suited as the lunatic to serve as
the focus of their satires. While Pope warned of a world about to be
overwhelmed by dunces, in a characteristically excremental outpouring,
Swift urged the madhouse keeper to stick to his task of reining in the mad:

> Tie them keeper in a tether,
> Let them stare and stink together:
> Both are apt to be unruly,
> Lash them daily, lash them duly,
> Though 'tis hopeless to reclaim them,
> Scorpion rods perhaps may tame them.[13]

10. William Shakespeare, *As You Like It*, Act 3, Sc. 2, lines 420–6.
11. Sir Richard Blackmore, *A Treatise of the Spleen or Vapours*, London: Pemberton, 1724, p. 263.
12. Thomas Fitzgerald, 'Bedlam', in *Poems on Several Occasions*, London: Watts, 1733.
13. Jonathan Swift, *A Character, Panegyric, and Description of the Legion Club*, Dublin, 1736, reprinted in Harold Williams (ed.), *The Poems of Jonathan Swift*, 2nd edn, Oxford: The Clarendon Press, 1966, lines 831–5. Compare also the characterization of the madman in *A Tale of a Tub* (1702, pp. 112–3): 'Accost the Hole of another Kennel, first stopping

Meanwhile, on Grub Street, the Ned Wards of the world retailed ι standard literary clichés, as they entertained their audience by providing what purported to be naturalistic descriptions of the antics of the Bedlamites:

> . . . such a rattling of chains, drumming of doors, ranting, holloaing, singing, and rattling, that I could think of nothing else but Don Quevado's vision where the damned broke loose and put Hell in an uproar.[14]

2. Bedlam and the Bedlamites

It was Bedlam, indeed, which dominated most eighteenth-century portraits of lunacy, most famously and vividly of all in Hogarth's didactic representation of madness as the wages of sin, as Tom Rakewell's progress ends with his being chained and bled in the wards of Bethlem Hospital. It would be foolish, of course, to reduce the classical encounter with madness to this single setting, and yet even for contemporaries, its wards became emblematic of Unreason, and its very name synonymous with lunacy. Though it was 'the smallest, most specialized and least affluent of the great London hospitals',[15] its prominence in eighteenth-century literary and journalistic discussions of insanity was matched only by its 'immense popularity' as a source of 'public entertainment' – for, till 1770, its doors were open to virtually all comers.[16] Recent scholarship has demolished careless earlier estimates that the number of visitors thronging the galleries to view the patients approached 100,000 a year.[17] But the

---

your Nose, you will behold a surly, glaring, nasty, slovenly Mortal, raking in his own Dung, and dabbling in his Urine. The best Part of his Diet, is the Reversion of his own Ordure, which escaping into Steams, whirls perpetually about and at last reinfunds. . . .'

14. Ned Ward, *The London Spy (1698–1709)* London: The Folio Society, 1955, pp. 48–51. For scepticism about the authenticity of Ward's reports, *cf.* R. Porter, *Mind Forg'd Manacles*, pp. 37, 240.

15. J. Andrews, 'Bedlam Revisited', p. 353.

16. *Ibid.*, p. 11 Public visitation did not come to an abrupt end in 1770, but rather than Bethlem being open to all comers for a penny or tuppence a time, the hospital authorities now instituted a ticket system. Andrews suggests that 'The gradual curtailment of visiting in the 1760s cannot simply be interpreted as a reaction to the mounting disenchantment of the educated public. It was partly an internal response to an escalation of the problems posed by visitors beyond the hospital's capacity to cope.' Ironically, however, 'the situation at the hospital appears to have markedly deteriorated [after] the exclusion of public visitors in 1770. Public access to Bethlem must have constituted both a diversion from, and a constraint upon, the abuse of patients by staff, although carrying with it a whole host of other attendant ills'. *Ibid.*, pp. 93, 386.

17. See P. Allderidge, 'Bedlam: Fact or Fantasy?' in W.F. Bynum, R. Porter, and M. Shepherd (eds), *The Anatomy of Madness*, Vol. 2, pp. 17–33; J. Andrews, 'Bedlam Revisited', chapter 2, 'Visiting'. In some distinguished company, I must confess to relying upon and helping to disseminate this myth in some of my earlier work, including the first edition of this book.

Fig. 3   An Engraving of Bedlam by William Hogarth, 1735, retouched 1736, from the final episode of *The Rake's Progress* (1735), with madness represented as the wages of sin.

number who came was undoubtedly large, and a wide variety of sources testify that 'Londoners and tourists from the country flocked to Bethlem in droves, as one of the wonders of the city'.[18] For nineteenth-century reformers, as for twentieth-century historians, here was the quintessence of the classical response to madness, and the occasion for the most lurid retrospective reconstructions of the defects of the *ancien régime*: within its walls, the crazed were reduced to a spectacle, an ever varied menagerie from which an audience of both provincial bumpkins and urban sophisticates could derive almost endless amusement.

The reality, as Jonathan Andrews has recently insisted, was somewhat more complex than this generalization allows. At least some of the visitors were the patients' families and friends, who were presumably activated by sympathy and affection, and the official rationalizations of the policy on

18. J. Andrews, 'Bedlam Revisited', p. 39.

visitation emphasized more defensible motives than mere 'curiosity'[19] for allowing strangers access: Bethlem's value as a moral lesson, for instance, illustrating the product (and price) of immorality; the possibility that outsiders would act as informal overseers of the institution; and the useful-ness of visitation as an incentive or stimulus to charitable giving. Clearly, too, all of these were operative at one time or another. Not least, the fee charged to those anxious to view the inmates made a quite substantial contribution to the hospital budget, and allowed the governors to econo-mize on staff salaries – a factor which presumably explains their reluctance to abolish or restrict visits even after mid-century, when increasing numbers of the elite began to view the custom with discomfort or disdain.[20]

But even those most concerned to place public visiting in its con-temporary context concede, in the end, that Bethlem's primary attraction was as a freak show.[21] The masses reacted with 'mirth, mockery, and

19. On Bedlam patients as 'curiosities', see *The Gentleman's Magazine* 18, May 1748, p. 199. From Pepys to Boswell, seventeenth- and eighteenth-century diarists recorded visits to Bethlem, often with family, friends from out of town and children in tow, in search of 'extraordinarie' or 'remarkable' spectacles.

20. J. Andrews, 'Bedlam Revisited', chapter 2, esp. pp. 14–17, 23–38, 71–3. St. Luke's, which was founded in 1751, forbade casual visitors from the outset, and its first physician, William Battie, as part of a scarcely veiled criticism of the regime at Bethlem, urged that 'the impertinent curiosity of those, who think it pastime to converse with madmen and to play upon their passions, ought strictly to be forbidden'. William Battie, *A Treatise on Madness*, London: Whiston and White, 1758, pp. 68–9.

Differences of taste and sensibility provide a potentially invaluable mechanism for marking status boundaries, and accordingly, over the course of the eighteenth century, the emerging middle classes strove to maximize the distance between polite and popular culture. From mid-century onwards, public visits to Bethlem increasingly became the occasion for drawing invidious contrasts between elite refinement, rationality, and sensitivity, and the depraved attitudes, mindless superstition, and moral coarseness characteristic of the hoi polloi. Samuel Richardson provides an early and striking illustration. In the course of discussing a visit to Bethlem, he comments:

> I was very much at a loss to account for the behaviour of the generality of people, who were looking at these melancholy objects. Instead of the concern I think unavoidable at such a sight, a sort of mirth appeared on their countenances; and the distemper'd fancies of the miserable patients most unaccountably produced mirth and loud laughter in the unthinking auditors; and the many hideous roarings, and wild motions of others, seemed equally entertaining to them. Nay, so shamefully inhuman were some, . . . as to endeavour to provoke the patients into rage to make them sport.

(Quoted in Max Byrd, *Visits to Bedlam*, Columbia, South Carolina: University of South Carolina Press, 1974, p. 89.) Initially, as Andrews indicates, one observes a shift among the better sort away from 'searching out and describing the most entertaining and brutish of the inmates [towards a concentration] on the most moving'. Soon, however, broader objections begin to be voiced to the exhibition of the insane before the rabble. Compare, for instance, the objection raised by MacKenzie's fictional hero to a proposed visit to Bethlem: 'I think it an inhuman practice to expose the greatest misery with which our nature is afflicted to every idle visitant who can afford a trifling perquisite to the keeper; especially as it is a distress which the humane must see with the painful reflection, that it is not in their power to relieve it.' Henry MacKenzie, *The Man of Feeling*, London: Cadell, 1771, chapter 20.

21. R. Porter, *Mind Forg'd Manacles*, p. 122. As J. Andrews reluctantly concedes, 'The major enticement of Bedlamites was entertainment, pure and simple. . . . Visitors were

callous teasing' to the sight of the mad (much as they behaved at public executions, and when criminals were confined in the stocks), and their treatment of 'the patients they encountered was often vicious in the extreme'.[22] During holiday times (the peak time for visitors), the scene could verge on anarchy. As one observer reported in 1753, 'a hundred people at least [were] . . . suffered unattended to run rioting up and down the wards, making sport and diversion of the miserable inhabitants [some of whom were] provoked by the insults of this holiday mob into furies of rage; [prompting in] the spectators . . . a loud laugh of triumph at the ravings they had occasioned'.[23] Those from the upper echelons of society behaved a trifle more circumspectly, and looked down their noses at the behaviour of 'the mob'; but they, too, boasted about 'the "delight" Bethlem afforded them. [Till past mid-century,] amusing anecdotes concerning the antics witnessed during a day's visit were clearly considered thoroughly in keeping with "the gaiety and good humour" of many a polite table.'[24]

On a broader scale, one can accept, as a number of historians have recently insisted, that Georgian Bethlem ought not to be 'glibly . . . dismiss[ed] as Hell on Earth'.[25] Their less jaundiced accounts rightly stress that, seen in their contemporary context, the dirt, the vermin, the poor and monotonous diet, even the use of straw for bedding – aspects of the treatment of the inmates which drew such a negative response from later generations – did not distinguish Bedlam from the almshouses, work-houses, jails, and other institutions where the poor and disreputable were increasingly gathered together.[26] Furthermore, the Bethlem archives demonstrate that the governors periodically made efforts, feeble and ineffectual as these undoubtedly proved to be, to secure improvements in hygiene and treatment, together with some mitigation of the effects of the cold and damp conditions characteristic of Bethlem's cells and galleries; and the hospital authorities insisted, as early as 1677, that 'None of the Officers or Servants shall at any time beat or abuse any of the Lunatics in the said hospital neither shall offer any force unto them but upon absolute Necessity for the better government of the said Lunatics.'[27] Though there

essentially sightseers, for whom Bethlem was a "sight", and "a rare diversion" . . . a pleasure rather than a duty.' 'Bedlam Revisited', p. 38.

22. J. Andrews, 'Bedlam Revisited', p. 45.
23. *The World*, No. 23, 1753, p. 138, quoted in J. Andrews, 'Bedlam Revisited', p. 47. The hospital committee itself eventually conceded that 'great Riots & Disorders have been Committed in this Hospital during the Holidays'. Quoted *ibid.*, p. 92.
24. J. Andrews, 'Bedlam Revisited', p. 43.
25. R. Porter, *Mind Forg'd Manacles*, p. 125; P. Allderidge, 'Bedlam: Fact or Fantasy?'; J. Andrews, 'Bedlam Revisited'.
26. This argument is made at length in J. Andrews, 'Bedlam Revisited', esp. chapter 3.
27. Minutes of the Court of Governors of Bridewell and Bethlem, 30 March 1677, quoted in P. Allderidge, 'Bedlam: Fact or Fantasy?', p. 28. (The final qualification of this rule is surely of more significance than Allderidge allows.) For convincing documentation of the fact that 'Practice at Bethlem consistently belied the Governors' directives' see J.

can be no gainsaying the 'incontrovertible' evidence that the medical regime remained 'staunchly conservative', and 'wedded to a routine course of evacuative and antiphlogistic treatments ... applied to most patients virtually without distinction';[28] yet Bethlem's defenders have been able to show that in other respects, the treatment meted out was less uniformly harsh than has been previously represented, being at least 'partially dependent [on patients'] behaviour, their relations with staff, their status and their means of purchase'.[29] Finally, those seeking to overturn the earlier received wisdom about the hospital point to Bethlem's claim to be a curative establishment, an assertion which was periodically reinforced by the release of statistics purporting to document its role in restoring a large fraction of its inmates to sanity.[30]

In emphasizing the defects of an overly simplistic portrait of eighteenth-century practices, however, one must be careful not to swing too violently to the opposite extreme. There is much evidence, some of it provided by patients themselves,[31] which suggests that the proverbial brutality of the Bethlem attendants is a reputation justly earned. Andrews's inspection

---

Andrews, 'Bedlam Revisited', chapters 3 and 5. The hospital records are unambiguous on this point: 'One discovers the same abuses occurring again and again, in the face of repeated orders and exhortations of reform from the Governors' Courts and Committees. ... For example, "the dishonest steward", Richard Langley, was repeatedly rebuked and twice suspended, during his eight years of office, for persistent forgery of his accounts, embezzlement of hospital funds and provisions, drunkenness and obstreperousness. ...' Ibid., pp. 375–6.

28. J. Andrews, 'Bedlam Revisited', pp. 309, 300–1.
29. J. Andrews, 'Bedlam Revisited', p. 159.
30. See, for example, John Strype, A Survey of the Cities of London and Westminster, Vol. 1, London: Churchill, 1720, esp. pp. 192–7. Patricia Allderidge is particularly vocal on this point. See 'Bedlam: Fact or Fantasy?', pp. 29–32. Curiously enough, Jonathan Andrews, who is also concerned to document these claims to provide cures (see 'Bedlam Revisited', pp. 283–4), proceeds to demonstrate both that they were spurious and that this was well known at the time. From a detailed examination of parish records, he concludes that 'there seems little doubt that the great majority of parochial patients admitted to Bethlem failed to leave the hospital in a condition able to resume their ordinary lives and livelihoods'. Moreover, these failures, which contrasted starkly with the hospital's public rhetoric about being a curative establishment, were widely acknowledged. 'Not only had the vast majority of parish poor admitted to Bethlem been discharged unrecovered, or failed to sustain their remissions, but also only a minority seem to have been committed primarily for their cure. Parish records do register cure as an objective of the admission and support of patients in Bethlem, but only rarely, indicating that cure was a subordinate concern of parish officers' who worried mostly about custody and safe-keeping. Internally, too, 'the prevailing attitude ... to patients' among the staff was that they were 'stubborn objects, resisting all efforts at cure'. Ibid., pp. 309, 493.
31. Cf. Richard Stafford, Because to Many People, I have Seemed to Falsify My Word and Promise, Which I made Upon My Being Discharged Out of Bethlehem Hospital, London: for the author, c. 1692; James Carkesse, Lucida Intervalla: Containing Divers Miscellaneous Poems, Berkeley: University of California Press, 1979 (first edn, London, 1679); Alexander Cruden, The London Citizen Exceedingly Injured, Or, A British Inquisition Displayed, London: Cooper and Dodd, 1739; idem., The Adventures of Alexander the Corrector, With an Account of the Chelsea Academies, Or the Private Places of Such As Are Supposed to Be Deprived of the Exercise of Their Reason, London: for the author, 1754; Urbane Metcalf, The Interior of Bethlehem Hospital, London: for the author, 1818.

of the hospital archives has uncovered a plethora of examples of 'exploita-
tive and neglectful servants . . . misappropriation of funds, misuse of
provisions, and cruelty', and he concludes that 'Ultimately, the overwhelmingly negative assessments of contemporary visitors to the hospital
are difficult to dispute . . . there is little evidence to contradict the general
impression that it was 'terrific' discipline rather than care which epitomised
treatment of patients by staff at Bethlem.'[32] Clothing was 'coarse and
uncomfortable', the diet meagre and inadequate to maintain health, idleness and inactivity the norm, the reliance on chains and other forms of
restraint widespread and routine, the patients vulnerable to both physical
and sexual abuse and subjected to what Carkesse termed 'Mad *Physick*':
'drenching' with medicine which was at once 'uncomfortable, painful and
debilitating, producing voiding from both stomach and bowels, scarifi-
cation, sores and bruises.'[33]

3. Domesticating the Mad

Such treatment must be understood, however, as far more than simply the
product of mismanagement, material shortages, the brutality of ignorant
keepers, or (in the case of private madhouses) the desire to maximize
profits at the expense of a helpless patient population. To be sure, all of
these played some role in dictating the regimen at Bethlem, as in other
madhouses. But eighteenth-century practices were also rationalized and
justified by reference to long-standing cultural assumptions about what it
meant to be mad, and what constituted an appropriate, even an essential
response to the frantic and the frenzied.

The view of madness as a condition that required taming, as one might
domesticate and thus render predictable the behaviour of a wild beast, had
a long intellectual ancestry. Andrew Boorde, bishop of Chichester in
Henry VIII's time, had spoken of '*Mania*, . . . *Insania*, . . . or *Furor*' as 'a
madnes or woodnes like a wylde beast', and urged that by way of remedy,
one must 'use the pacient so that he do not hurt hym selfe nor no other
man, and he must be kepte in feare of one man or an other, and if nede
requyre he must be punyshed and beaten . . .'.[34] And the king's sometime
Lord Chancellor, Sir Thomas More, referred equally straightforwardly to
the need for 'betynge and correccyon' to restore the mad to their senses,
boasting of his own success in encouraging a maniac to behave himself
once the lesson had been 'beten home': 'I beyng advertysed of [his
misdeeds] . . . caused him as he came wanderyng by my dore, to be taken
by the constables and bounden to a tre in the strete before the whole

32. J. Andrews, 'Bedlam Revisited', chapter 5, esp. pp. 326, 352–5, 372–4, 398.
33. J. Andrews, 'Bedlam Revisited', p. 301.
34. Andrew Boorde, *The Breviary of Healthe: The Seconde Boke of the Brevyary of Health,
    Named the Extravagantes*, London: Powell, 1552, quoted in R.A. Hunter and I.
    MacAlpine, *Three Hundred Years of Psychiatry, 1535–1860*, London: Oxford University
    Press, 1963, pp. 14–15.

towne, and there they stryped him with roddys therfore tyl he waxed
wery and somewhat lenger' and ceased annoying the rest of the community.[35] Such beliefs and practices remained commonplace through the
seventeenth and well into the eighteenth century. Comparing lunatics to
'mad dogs, or ravenous wolves', the London practitioner William Salmon
(1644–1713) insisted that 'those who are taken with this disease seem to be
as mad as wild beasts, nor do they differ much from them. . . . [They
possess] a prodigious Herculean strength . . . endure also the greatest
hunger, cold, and stripes without any sensible harm'.[36] His more famous
contemporary, Thomas Willis, Sedleian Professor of Natural Philosophy
at Oxford, concurred: 'Madmen', he warned, 'are still strong and robust
to a prodigy, so that they can break cords and chains, break down doors
or walls, one easily overthrows many endeavouring to hold him.' More
extraordinarily yet, they 'are almost never tired . . . Madmen, what ever
they bear or suffer are not hurt; but they bear cold, heat, watching fasting,
strokes [beatings], and wounds, without any sensible hurt; to wit because
the spirits being strong and fixed, are neither daunted nor fly away.'[37]

By mid-century, Richard Mead had extended this set of immunities a
step further: the mad, it appeared, were likewise immune to the ravages of
bodily disease,[38] a claim to which John Monro took exception, as Jonathan
Andrews points out,[39] but a formulation which was to be repeated
by others almost by rote into the nineteenth century.[40] Such striking

35. Sir Thomas More, *The Apologie of Syr T. More, Knyght*, London: Rastell, 1533, folios
  197–8, quoted in R.A. Hunter and I. MacAlpine, *Three Hundred Years of Psychiatry*, p. 6.
36. William Salmon, *System Medicinale*, pp. 37, 56–61.
37. Thomas Willis, *The Practice of Physick*, London: Dring, Harper, and Leigh, 1684, p. 205.
  See also Zachary Mayne, *Two Discourses Concerning Sense, and the Imagination*, p. 91. John
  Strype, a close friend of Edward Tyson (physician to Bethlem from 1684 to 1708), drew
  upon this eminent authority to buttress the claim that the lunatic 'when raving or furious
  do not suffer much from the Weather', becoming susceptible to its ill-effects only in their
  lucid 'Intervalls'. John Stow, *A Survey of the Cities of London and Westminster Written at
  First in the Year MDXCVIII by John Stow, Corrected, Improved and Very Much Enlarged to
  the Present Time*, London: Churchill, 1720, p. 196.
38. Richard Mead, *Medical Precepts and Cautions*, London: Brindley, 1751, p. 79, also pp.
  90–1. Mead, along with many other eighteenth-century authorities, emphasized the
  general insensibility of the insane: 'all mad folks in general bear hunger, cold, and any
  other inclemency of the weather . . . all bodily inconveniences, with surprising ease'.
  'Medica Sacra', in *The Medical Works of Richard Mead*, London: Hitch and Hawes, 1762,
  p. 619. For later comments on the 'sedative power' of cold on maniacs, and their
  insensibility to its 'bad effects', *cf.* W. Pargeter, *Observations on Maniacal Disorders*,
  Reading: for the author, 1792, pp. 8, 95; Thomas Arnold, *Observations on the Nature,
  Kinds, Causes and Prevention of Insanity*, 2nd edn, Vol. 1, London: Phillips, 1806, pp. 4–5.
39. *Cf.* John Monro, *Remarks on Dr Battie's Treatise on Madness*, London: Clarke, 1758, pp.
  26–7, quoted in J. Andrews, 'Bedlam Revisited', p. 179.
40. See Thomas Arnold, *Observations on . . . Insanity*, Vol. 1, pp. 155–6 (acknowledging
  Mead as the authority on the means by which 'insanity not only preserves the patient
  from other diseases, but when it seizes him actually labouring under them, lays such
  strong claim to the whole man, that it sometimes dispossesses the body of them . . .').
  See also Joseph Mason Cox, *Practical Observations on Insanity*, London: Baldwin and
  Murray, 1806, pp. 4–5 ('Insanity, more than any other complaint, seems to take entire
  possession of the whole system, and almost secures it from other morbid attacks. Mead,

immunity to the infirmities to which human flesh is heir were purchased, though, at a heavy price, for the descent into madness marked the divestment of 'the rational Soul . . . of all its noble and distinguishing Endowments'.[41] The melancholy lunatic offered, said Nicholas Robinson, 'the most gloomy Scene of Nature, that Mankind can possibly encounter, where nothing but Horror reigns; where the noble Endowments of the reasonable Soul are often disconcerted to a surprising Degree, and this lordly creature then almost debased below the brutal Species of the animated Creation'.[42] Still more clearly was the maniac reduced in status, losing 'that Power by which we are distinguished from the brutal Class of the animated Creation; 'til at last upon a Level, or rather beneath the Condition of a mere Brute'.[43]

Thus dragged down to a state of brutish insensibility and incapacity, the lunatic occupied a wholly unenviable ontological status. Legally, as those writing on the jurisprudence of insanity acknowledged, he or she became virtually a nonentity, one whose 'Promises and Contracts' were 'void and of no force' and whose behaviour could never attain the dignity and status of human action.[44] Such a creature, 'deprived of his reason and understanding', could, said Mead, expect a miserable and humiliating career: 'to attack his fellow creatures with fury like a wild beast; to be tied down, and even beat, to prevent his doing mischief to himself or others; or, on the contrary, to be sad and dejected, to be daily terrified with vain imaginations; to fancy hobgoblins haunting him; and after a life spent in considerable anxiety, to be persuaded that his death will be the commencement of eternal punishment'.[45] Small wonder that the belief that 'There is no disease more to be dreaded than madness' became an eighteenth-century cliché, reiterated as if by rote by successive generations of commentators.[46]

I believe was the first who made the observation, and no fact in medicine is more completely established.').

41. N. Robinson, *A New System of the Spleen*, p. 241.

42. *Ibid.*, p. 243.

43. *Ibid.*, pp. 44, 50. As Andrew Snape put it, in a Spital sermon preached in behalf of 'those unhappy People, who are bereft of the dearest light, the Light of Reason':

> Distraction . . . divests the rational soul of all its noble and distinguishing Endowments, and sinks unhappy Man below the mute and senseless part of Creation: even brutal Instinct being a surer and safer guide than disturb'd Reason, and every tame Species of Animals more sociable and less hurtful than humanity thus unmann'd.

> *A Sermon Preach'd Before the Lord Mayor, the Aldermen, Sheriffs and Gouvenours of the Several Hospitals of the City of London*, London: Bowyer, 1718, p. 15. Madness, Samuel Richardson likewise concluded, brought 'the mighty reasoners of the earth, below even the insects which crawl upon it'. *The World*, 7 June 1753.

44. John Brydall, *Non Compos Mentis*.

45. R. Mead, *Medical Precepts*, pp. 74–5.

46. *Cf.* N. Robinson, *A New System of the Spleen*, p. 50; R. Mead, *Medical Precepts*, p. 74; Henry MacKenzie, *The Man of Feeling*, p. 73; T. Arnold, *Observations on . . . Insanity*, Vol. 2, p. 320; William Pargeter, *Observations on Maniacal Disorders*, pp. 122, 139 ('a state, which is even more deplorable than death itself').

Fig. 4 Charles Bell's representation of 'the madman', a portrait that purported to strip away the romanticized images prevalent among artists and to provide a faithful copy of nature. To render the madman naturalistically, Bell insisted, the artist must 'learn the character of the human countenance when devoid of expression, and reduced to the state of lower animals; and as I have already hinted, study their expression, their timidity, their watchfulness, their state of excitement, and their ferociousness'. As well as being a skilled amateur artist, Bell was one of the leading British surgeons and anatomists of the first half of the nineteenth century. His comments are graphic evidence of the persistence of old stereotypes in the highest professional circles, well past the turn of the century. From Sir Charles Bell, *Essays on the Anatomy of Expression in Painting* (London: Longman, 1806).

Willis had insisted that the madman's ferocity could only be tamed by a mixture of discipline and depletion, measures designed to put down 'the raging of the Spirits and the lifting up of the Soul'.[47] Mild methods were perhaps of some avail with 'the more remissly Mad, [who] are healed more often with flatteries, and with more gentle Physick'.[48] But in graver cases,

> To correct or allay the furies and exorbitancies of the Animal Spirits . . . requires threatenings, bonds, or strokes as well as *Physick*. For the *Madman* being placed in a House convenient for the business must be so handled both by the *Physician*, and also by the Servants that are prudent, that he may in some manner be kept in, either by warnings, chidings, or punishments inflicted upon him, to his duty, or his be-haviour, or manners. And indeed for the curing of Mad people, there is nothing more effectual or necessary than their reverence or standing in awe of such as they think their Tormentors. For by this means, the Corporeal Soul being in some measure depressed and restrained, is compelled to remit its pride and fierceness; and so afterwards by degrees grows more mild, and returns in order: wherefore, Furious Mad-men are sooner and more certainly cured by punishments and hard usage, in a strait-room, than by *Physick* or Medicines.[49]

This emphasis on 'severe government and discipline'[50] and the ac-companying reliance on fear, force, and coercion as therapeutic tactics seemed entirely appropriate to the management of 'brutes', and the equation of insanity and animality continued to be a central element of many eighteenth-century speculations on the subject,[51] with their

> almost exclusive emphasis on disturbances of the *reason*, or the higher intellectual faculties of man. Insanity was conceived as a derangement of those very faculties which were widely assumed to be universal to man; as a matter of fact, we sometimes find in the literature the presumed absence in animals of any condition analogous to insanity

47. Thomas Willis, *Two Discourses Concerning the Soul of Brutes*, translated by S. Pordage, London: Dring, Harper, and Leigh, 1683, p. 206.
48. *Ibid.*
49. *Ibid.*, emphases in the original.
50. *Ibid.*
51. Pargeter, for instance, invites us to 'figure to ourselves the situation of a fellow creature destitute of the guidance of that governing principle, reason – which chiefly distinguishes us from the inferior animals around us, and gives us a striking superiority over the beasts that perish. View man deprived of that noble endowment, and see in how melancholy a posture he appears. He retains indeed the outward appearance of the human species, but like the ruins of a once magnificent edifice, it serves only to remind us of his former dignity, and fill us with gloomy reflections for the loss of it. Within, all is confused and deranged, every look and expression testifies to internal anarchy and disorder.' *Observations on Maniacal Disorders*, pp. 2–3.

taken as proof that man's highest psychological function results from some principle totally lacking in other animals, that is, the soul.[52]

It was difficult, in consequence, not to draw the conclusion that in losing his reason, the essence of his humanity, the madman had lost his claim to be treated as a human being. And certainly, as Nicholas Robinson urged, in all such cases, a misplaced caution and timidity were at all costs to be avoided. '[I]t is Cruelty', he insisted, 'in the highest Degree, not to be bold in the Administration of Medicine. [Only] a Course of Medicines of the most violent Operation' would suffice, for in cases of madness a frontal attack was essential 'to bring down the Spirit of the Stubborn Persons [and] to reduce their artificial Strength by compulsive Methods'.[53]

To be sure, even during these years, madhouse keepers were becoming less inclined to advertise their talents as whip-masters. As Porter suggests, 'Whatever the popular stereotypes of madmen as brutes, every proprietor knew he could not cash in by harping on the severity of his treatments. . . .'[54] And even though the testimony of ex-patients casts some doubt on how far and how rapidly *practices* changed,[55] still one must accept that the greater reticence about openly acknowledging corporal punishment, which now begins to manifest itself, signals the onset of a not insignificant shift in sentiment, in certain circles at least.[56]

Some historians have gone further than this, urging us to see essential continuities between eighteenth-century practices and the utopian programmes of nineteenth-century reformers; and to recognize that the practices of the new moral treatment regime which was then established cannot be represented as a distinct break with the past. In Roy Porter's formulation, 'both in rhetoric and in reality, "moral" forms of therapy were well tried and tested long before the close of the eighteenth century.

---

52. W.F. Bynum, 'Rationales for Therapy in British Psychiatry, 1780–1835', *Medical History* 18, 1974, p. 320.

53. N. Robinson, *A New System of the Spleen*, pp. 400–1.

54. R. Porter, *Mind Forg'd Manacles*, pp. 139–40. Towards the century's close, Alexander Hunter boasted that at his York Asylum, 'the patients are treated with all the tenderness and indulgence that is compatible with a steady and effectual government; and the servants are enjoined never to use unnecessary severity'. *The Rise and Progress of the York Lunatic Asylum*, York, 1792, quoted in Anne Digby, *Madness, Morality and Medicine: A Study of the York Retreat 1796–1914*, Cambridge: Cambridge University Press, 1985, p. 12. Subsequent investigations were to reveal a regime characterized by beatings, starvation, rape, and murder, which (among much else) should serve as a reminder to some too credulous historians not to take every eighteenth-century protestation about 'tenderness and indulgence' and the absence of whipping at face value.

55. *Cf.* the complaints of beating and whipping in Alexander Cruden's *The London Citizen Exceedingly Injured*, and in his *Adventures of Alexander the Corrector* (where he complains on pp. 13, 20, and 34 of his confinement in 'the Strait-Wastecoat', bed-strapping, 'severe usage', and 'Tom o'Bedlam' treatment at Inskip's Chelsea madhouse in 1753); the earlier testimony of James Carkesse in *Lucida Intervalla*, London: [S.N.], 1679; and the gruesome accounts in Urbane Metcalf, *The Interior of Bethlehem Hospital*.

56. This is one of the primary burdens of Jonathan Andrews' discussion of these materials in 'Bedlam Revisited', especially pp. 204–18, 382–9.

It would not even be outrageous to suggest that the heyday of a *de facto* kind of moral therapy lay in the eighteenth century . . .'.[57]

But this is to misconstrue, I think, the character of the changes in the treatment of madness which we can observe emerging in the second half of the eighteenth century; to underestimate the extent to which, changes notwithstanding, methods of treatment continued to exhibit substantial continuities with the past; and to misunderstand the degree to which the versions of moral treatment which begin to emerge at the turn of the century, most famously at the York Retreat, rested on a fundamentally different approach to madness, and did indeed mark a distinct rupture or change in English responses to insanity. Certainly, from mid-century some influential voices begin to express doubts about the need to beat the mad. Richard Mead was among the first to urge that 'it is not necessary to employ stripes or other rough treatment to bring [the outrageous] into order'[58] and he promptly found an unlikely ally in John Monro, who declared the traditional belief in its salutary effects had been 'deservedly exploded . . . as unnecessary, cruel, and pernicious'.[59] More forcibly still, near century's end, William Pargeter announced 'I at once condemn this practice, as altogether erroneous, and not to be justified upon any principles or pretences whatsoever.'[60]

But there was hardly unanimity on this point. William Battie, whom Porter portrays as the author '(albeit in a rather schematic and theoretical guise) [of] the key ideas of Tukean moral therapy',[61] was one of those who continued to emphasize the utility of 'bodily pain' and 'fear' in the treatment of the insane.[62] Two decades later, as eminent a man as William Cullen, professor of the institutes of medicine at Edinburgh and the most influential medical teacher in late eighteenth-century Britain, still more bluntly insisted that it was 'necessary to employ a very constant impression of fear . . . awe and dread – emotions that should be aroused by all restraints that may occasionally be proper . . . even by stripes [whippings] and blows' – and cautioned that where physical force was necessary, stripes 'although having the appearance of severity, are much safer than strokes or blows about the head'.[63]

57. R. Porter, *Mind Forg'd Manacles*, p. 277; see also *idem.*, 'Was There a Moral Therapy in the Eighteenth Century?' *Lychnos* 1981–2, pp. 12–26.
58. R. Mead, *Medical Precepts*, p. 98.
59. J. Monro, *Remarks on Dr Battie's Treatise on Madness*, p. 38.
60. W. Pargeter, *Observations on Maniacal Disorders*, pp. 129–30.
61. R. Porter, *Mind Forg'd Manacles*, p. 276. See also the more extended discussion *ibid.*, pp. 206–9.
62. W. Battie, *A Treatise on Madness*, pp. 84–5.
63. William Cullen, *First Lines in the Practice of Physic*, 4th edn, Edinburgh: Elliot, 1784, quoted in R. Hunter and I. MacAlpine, *Three Hundred Years of Psychiatry*, p. 478. Cullen's views were especially influential since he taught some of the best-known late eighteenth-century medical men who took a serious interest in the treatment of insanity. These included Thomas Arnold, John Ferriar, William Hallaran, Joseph Mason Cox, Thomas Trotter, and Alexander Crichton, as well as the most prominent American mad-doctor of the age, Benjamin Rush of Philadelphia.

In any event, most of those who began to argue against the use of the whip in the second half of the century generally did so, not from any principled opposition to the use of force itself, but rather because they had concluded that beating was superfluous and unnecessary, and therefore to be condemned. The fundamental basis of their approach to insanity remained the traditional one of subjugating the mad, of the breaking of the will by means of external discipline and constraint, as part of an almost literal battle between reason and unreason. Whipping, however, was steadily being superseded by other, more effective means of inducing conformity.[64]

Some change might thus be warranted in the weapons one used, and certainly a greater emphasis now emerged on the charismatic authority the madhouse keeper might exercise over the furious and raving. But much of the traditional perspective on coping with madness survived intact (and to the extent that this paradigm became more closely identified with increasingly vocal medical claims to jurisdiction over the insane, this was ultimately to the medical profession's detriment). Mead's objection, for instance, was not to beating as such, but only to its being redundant, for in his view, 'all maniacal people are fearful and cowardly'.[65] In the case of those afflicted with 'sadness and fear', 'diversions' would often suffice (a judgement with which Willis would have concurred). Of course, though, even 'melancholy very frequently changes, sooner or later, into maniacal madness'. Sterner measures were then called for, but in confronting the furious, the mad-doctor would discover that 'chiding and threatening' (supplemented, to be sure, by the various unpleasant weapons in the physician's therapeutic armamentarium) were in general amply sufficient to tame their excesses and restore a measure of tranquillity.[66]

Like his observation about the exemption of the mad from the ravages of disease, Mead's doctrine about the cowardliness of the insane was to prove widely influential,[67] and came to underpin and give legitimacy

64. Compare, for instance, David MacBride's assertion that 'It has sometimes been usual to chain and beat them, but this is both cruel and absurd; since the contrivance called the Strait Waistcoat, answers every purpose of restraining the patients, without hurting them.' *A Methodical Introduction to the Theory and Practice of Physick*, London: Strahan, 1772, p. 591. Such sentiments were echoed by Erasmus Darwin in his *Zoonomia* (Vol. 1, London: Johnson, 1794, p. 352) and by Thomas Percival at the turn of the century: 'The law justified the beating of a lunatic in such a manner as the circumstances require. But it has been before remarked that a physician, who attends an asylum for insanity, is under obligation of honour as well as of humanity, to secure the unhappy sufferers, committed to his charge, all the tenderness and indulgence compatible with steady and effectual government. And the strait waistcoat, with other improvements in modern practice, now preclude the necessity of coercion by corporal punishment.' *Medical Ethics*, Manchester: Johnson and Bickerstaff, 1803, pp. 27, 68–9. The 'modern improvements in practice' which supplanted the whip will be discussed at more length below.
65. R. Mead, *Medical Precepts*, p. 98.
66. R. Mead, *Medical Precepts*, pp. 98–9.
67. See, for example, David MacBride, *A Methodical Introduction to the Theory and Practice of Physick*, p. 592; William Falconer, *A Dissertation on the Influence of the Passions upon*

to some of the most characteristic late eighteenth-century responses to madness. Four decades later, William Pargeter acknowledged that 'to superficial observers, the conduct of maniacs . . . appears extremely daring and courageous'. Direct experience had demonstrated, however, that 'in reality they are exceedingly timorous and are found to be easily terrified'.[68] To accomplish the management that both Battie[69] and Monro[70] had urged as the key to the cure of the mad, Pargeter urged that the physician should ensure that his first visit was by surprise. But he must then 'employ every moment of his time by mildness or menaces, as circumstances direct, to gain an ascendancy over them, and to obtain their favour and prepossession'.[71]

4. Wrestling with the Demons of Madness

Much stress came to be laid during the last half of the eighteenth century on the authoritative presence of the mad-doctor, whose ability to wrestle with and single-handedly subdue the demons of madness now acquired almost mythic proportions – a tactic whose utility for those laying claim to jurisdiction over the insane scarcely requires comment. The mad-doctor's skill at managing his presentation of self was pictured as being of quite central importance to the management and cure of the insane, since 'he may be obliged at one moment, according to the exigency of the case, to be placid and accommodating in his manners, and the next, angry and absolute'.[72] And this requirement sharply limited the ranks of those who

Disorders of the Body, London: Dill, 1788, p. 83; Joseph Mason Cox, Practical Observations on Insanity, 3rd edn, London: Baldwin and Underwood, 1813, p. 34.

68. W. Pargeter, Observations on Maniacal Disorders, p. 61. As we shall see, such conclusions did not serve to restrain medical men from exercising considerable ingenuity to foment that terror.

69. W. Battie, A Treatise on Madness.

70. J. Monro, Remarks on Dr Battie's Treatise on Madness.

71. W. Pargeter, Observations on Maniacal Disorders, p. 49. As I have previously pointed out, in Pargeter's case, at least, 'menacing' the patients apparently did not mean whipping them: 'I must add, that beating was a practice formerly much in use in treating the insane; and I am sorry and surprised to note, that some authors, of very late date, have countenanced such unnatural and brutish violence. But I will venture to declare, that such usage is on no occasion necessary, self-defence only excepted.' In his view, the ready availability and recourse to 'strait-waistcoats, chains, and cords' was sufficient, obviating the need for blows. Ibid., pp. 129–30, 31. Such views became increasingly orthodox among medical men specializing in the treatment of the mad. Compare, for instance, David Uwins: 'Straight waistcoats, even in private houses, prove occasionally instruments of the greatest mercy, for they effect more than several individuals could accomplish, with all the power that they could exercise; and the memory of their employment, with the fear of its repetition, will, in many cases, supersede the necessity of its repetition. . . . Strictly corporal punishments, that is, "stripes and blows", I hope are now, throughout the whole country, "obsolete things."' A Treatise on Those Disorders of the Brain and Nervous System, Which Are Usually Considered and Called Mental, London: Renshaw and Rush, 1833, pp. 148–9.

72. W. Pargeter, Observations on Maniacal Disorders, p. 50. As Joseph Mason Cox put it, 'The essence of management results from experience, address, and the natural endowments of the practitioner, and turns principally on making impressions on the senses.' Practical Observations on Insanity, 2nd edn, London: Baldwin and Murray, 1806, pp. 42–3.

could successfully specialize in the trade in lunacy, since, as Joseph Mason Cox noted,

> there are very few, whom nature has been so kind as to qualify for the practice; every man is not furnished with sufficient nerve, with the requisite features for the varied expression of countenance which may be necessary, with the degree of muscular powers, or stature, etc. [But all, at least, could recognize that] as the grand object in their moral management, is to make ourselves both feared and loved, nothing can so successfully tend to effect this as a system of kindness and mildness, address and firmness, the judicious allowance of indulgences, and the employment of irresistible force and coercion.[73]

Sometimes the coercion and control continued to be quite straight-forward. Bakewell, for example, related an instance from his own practice where 'a maniac confined in a room over my own . . . bellowed like a wild beast, and shook his chain almost constantly for several days and nights. . . . I therefore got up, took a hand whip, and gave him a few smart stripes upon the shoulder. . . . He disturbed me no more'.[74] Such techniques were generally expected to be efficacious since, as Falconer put it, 'those who attend [the insane] . . . mostly find, that although generally irrational, they retain a great consideration for personal safety, and that threats will often compel them to speak and act rationally'.[75]

Rather than whips and cudgels, however, it was chains and other forms of mechanical restraint which continued to figure most prominently in this regime of coercion, being seen as useful, even essential adjuncts to the attempt to compel right-thinking. Jonathan Andrews, for instance, has uncovered evidence in the Bethlem archives that 'sixty leg-locks and a dozen handcuffs were purchased by the Steward . . . within the space of just two years, during the 1760s', an indication that 'restraint was being very widely employed on the hospital's 260 or so patients by its skeleton nursing staff of ten or eleven'.[76] St. Luke's, which Porter would have us see as the site of experiments with new forms of moral restraint, was no

73. J.M. Cox, *Practical Observations on Insanity*, 3rd edn, 1813, p. 84.
74. Thomas Bakewell, *The Domestic Guide in Cases of Insanity*, Stafford: for the author, 1805, quoted in R. Hunter and I. MacAlpine, *Three Hundred Years of Psychiatry*, p. 705.
75. W. Falconer, *A Dissertation on the Influence of the Passions*, p. 83.
76. J. Andrews, 'Bedlam Revisited', p. 209. He acknowledges (*ibid.*, p. 210) that during the 1770s and 1780s, 'A very large proportion of patients . . . seem to have been subjected to the temporary intimidation of irons, strait-waistcoats and solitary confinement, and to have been securely restrained in their beds at night.' A minute from the Bethlem Stewards' Accounts is equally instructive in this regard. On 29 June 1791, the blacksmith was summoned to perform a series of tasks: 'To take off all the Locks Latches Catches Bolts Bars Hinges and Grates that are found bad and decayed and replace and make good with new and to provide and fix on proper Strap Irons with Chains and Staples where they may be wanted to compleat att the New Bed Steads and bed places and to take off and repair and refix the old Strap Chains &c to fix new Stay braces straps and irons as shall be directed. . . .' As we shall see, such practices continued unabated well into the nineteenth century.

Fig. 5   The interior of St. Luke's Hospital in 1809, drawn by Rowlandson and Pugin, and taken from *The Microcosm of London* (1808–10). In his notes on a visit to St. Luke's, Samuel Tuke commented: 'The superintendent . . . thinks confinement or restraint may be imposed as a punishment with some advantage, and, on the whole, thinks fear the most effectual principle by which to reduce the insane to orderly conduct. The building has entirely the appearance of a place of confinement, enclosed by high walls, and there are strong iron gates to the windows.' (Rowlandson's drawing, incidentally, greatly exaggerates the height of the ceilings. In reality, the galleries were gloomy and dark.)

less reliant than its counterpart on 'irons'. Its minute books reveal, for instance, that on a single day in October 1764, 'the following necessaries are wanted. . . . One Dozen of Chain for the kitchen. Half a Dozen for the Women Patients New Room and Same Benches around it. Chain Benches and a Table for the Men Patients Room. . . . Six pair of Handcuffs. Six large Common Stock Locks that go in Suit about the House. Ordered provided'.[77] And in planning for the charity asylum at Leicester in 1792,

77. St. Luke's Hospital House Committee Minutes, 12 October 1764, quoted in J. Andrews, 'Bedlam Revisited', p. 209. The reliance on mechanical restraint was equally striking a half century later. Samuel Tuke's manuscript notes of a visit in 1812 (reprinted in Daniel Hack Tuke, *Reform in the Treatment of the Insane: Early History of the Retreat, York; Its Objects and Influence*, London: Churchill, 1892, pp. 89–90) provide a harshly critical commentary on its practices in this and other respects. And significantly, when the authorities at St. Luke's were consulted by the Bedfordshire magistrates in that same year about the organization of their new county asylum, the first advice they provided consisted of the blacksmith's 'patterns' for making 'straight-waistcoats, handcuffs,

Thomas Arnold advised the governors that their twenty patients would require '20 strait waistcoats, as well as a great number of appropriate Straps, Locks, and other fastenings, and securities; besides Chairs of a peculiar construction for particular purposes', and urged them to set aside a special room 'to receive the various instruments of security which are not in use'.[78] As Andrews concedes, 'Restraint might be even more extreme at private madhouses... where profit-making motives were more prone to encourage the prolongation of confinement and to deprive patients of the dispensations they were apt to receive for good behaviour at a charity-funded hospital.'[79]

The routine character of the use of restraint, and the assumption that it was an inevitable, even a desirable concomitant of the confinement of the mad, is equally evident in the comments of outsiders who had occasion to view such scenes. Pierre Grosley spoke casually, and with no hint of criticism, of his observations on being conducted round Bethlem in 1770, where he saw 'a row of large cells, in each of which was a poor wretch chained down in bed.'[80] Four decades later, William Black, the medical statistician, was equally matter-of-fact about the necessity for 'the ferocious maniac' and even some 'of the Incurables' to be 'kept as wild beasts, constantly in fetters'.[81] Certainly, mad-doctors made much of their desire to improve the instruments of restraint so as to ensure 'all the tenderness and indulgence compatible with steady and effectual government'.[82] But in practice this evolved into a debate of sorts between those who preferred 'the strait waistcoat, with other improvements in modern practice', on the grounds that they 'preclude[d] the necessity of coercion by corporal punishment',[83] and those who preferred 'metallic manacles on the wrist;

leglocks, and a chain and staple for arm and leg-locks'. Letter from Thomas Dunston, the steward at St. Luke's, to the Bedfordshire Asylum Committee, 23 April 1812, bound with the Bedfordshire County Asylum Minutes, Bedfordshire County Record Office LB 1/1. Casting further doubt on Porter's claims about Battie's regime, Andrews provides detailed evidence in chapter 4 of 'Bedlam Revisited' about the 'substantial areas of continuity between' conditions at St. Luke's and at Bethlem, and 'the limited practical ramifications of the differences between the two medical regimes'.

78. Thomas Arnold, 'A Sketch of the Preparations [for] the Asylum', [1792] in the Minute Books of the Leicester Infirmary, manuscript at the Leicester City Library, quoted in I. MacAlpine and R. Hunter, *George III and the Mad-Business*, London: Allen Lane, 1969, p. 280.

79. J. Andrews, 'Bedlam Revisited', p. 217.

80. Pierre Grosley, *A Tour of London, or New Observations on England and Its Inhabitants*, translated by T. Nugent, Dublin: Ekshaw, Lynch, Williams, Montcrieffe, Walker, and Jenkin, 1772, Vol. 2, p. 9.

81. William Black, *A Dissertation on Insanity: Illustrated with Tables Extracted From Between Two and Three Thousand Cases in Bedlam*, London: Ridgway, 1810, pp. 13–14. Black noted that 'by far the great majority of Patients in Bedlam, except at temporary intervals, and exacerbations, walk peaceably about the long wards. Separate confinement in their cells, strait waistcoats, and for the ferocious maniac handcuffs and chains, soon render them tractable and obedient'.

82. Thomas Percival, *Medical Ethics*, pp. 68–9.

83. T. Percival, *Medical Ethics*, p. 69.

the skin being less liable to be injured by the friction of polished metal than by that of linen or cotton'.[84] Paul Slade Knight endorsed the latter opinion, though he cautioned that 'the clinking of the chains should be, by all means, prevented, for I have known it to impress lunatics with the most gloomy apprehension.'[85]

The ready availability and regular use of these transparent means of repressing disorder and tumult provided powerful incentives for the patients to behave themselves, and in this context, direct physical threats and punishments were not always seen as necessary. 'It is of great use in practice', said MacBride, 'to bear in mind that all mad people . . . can be awed even by the menacing look of a very expressive countenance; and when those who have charge of them once impress them with the notion of fear, they easily submit to anything that is required.'[86]

The use of 'the eye' was perhaps the most dramatic technique which the late eighteenth-century mad-doctor claimed to have at his disposal.[87] The

84. Charles Dickens and W.H. Wills, 'A Curious Dance Around a Curious Tree', (1852), reprinted in *Charles Dickens' Uncollected Writings from Household Words*, Bloomington: Indiana University Press, 1968, Vol. 2, pp. 382–3. John Haslam, the apothecary at Bethlem, was one of those opposed to the use of the strait-waistcoat, arguing that it was uncomfortable, degrading, and constricting, and placed the patient too much 'at the mercy of the keeper'. 'The more effectual and convenient mode of confining the hands is by metallic manacles; for, should the patient, as frequently occurs, be constantly endeavouring to liberate himself, the friction of the skin against a polished metallic body may be long sustained without injury; whereas excoriation shortly takes place when the surface is rubbed with linen or cotton.' During his tenure, the hospital accordingly switched back from the strait-jacket to the use of chains. See John Haslam, *Observations on Madness: With Practical Remarks on the Disease and an Account of the Morbid Appearances on Dissection*, London: Rivington, 1798, pp. 64–7. He repeated this opinion more than a decade later in his *Observations on Madness and Melancholy*, London: Callow, 1809, p. 289, and remained a vocal advocate of the merits of restraint even in the early 1840s, when such views had become distinctly unfashionable.

85. Paul Slade Knight, *Observations on the Causes, Symptoms, and Treatment of Derangement of the Mind*, London: Longman, 1827, p. 116. Knight served as the first medical superintendent of the Lancashire County Asylum, which opened its doors in 1816, and became well-known for inventing ingenious new kinds of wrist and leg-locks. His traditional views about the indispensability of these forms of coercion were fully reflected in his practice. In the words of Samuel Gaskell, who subsequently succeeded to his post,

> From the opening of this Asylum, in the year 1816, mechanical restraint appears to have been extensively employed; and at the time your officers took charge [in 1840], they found twenty-nine persons wearing either hand-cuffs, leg-locks, or strait-waistcoats, exclusive of between thirty and forty patients who were chained down in the day-time on seats so constructed as to answer all the purposes of water closets.

New patients were routinely chained up at night until they showed that they could safely be left at large. Lancashire County Asylum, *Medical Officers' Report for 1841*, p. 4. Lancashire County Record Office, Preston, QAM/5/3, pp. 18–20.

86. David MacBride, *A Methodical Introduction to the Theory and Practice of Physick*, p. 592.

87. Benjamin Rush even went so far as to claim that 'there are keys in the eye, if I may be allowed the expression', that allowed the skilled practitioner to vary 'its aspect from the highest degree of sternness, down to the mildest degree of benignity' and thus to secure minute changes in the patient's behaviour. Benjamin Rush, *Medical Inquiries and Observations Upon the Diseases of the Mind*, Philadelphia: Kimber and Richardson, 1830, pp. 173–4.

clinical literature of the period is replete with case histories testifying to its utility and efficacy. Country practitioners employed it in the management of ordinary and anonymous madmen:

> The maniac was locked in a room, raving and exceeding turbulent. I took two men with me, and learning he had no offensive weapons, I planted them at the door with directions to keep silent and out of sight, unless I should want their assistance. I then suddenly unlocked the door – rushed into the room and caught his eye in an instant. The business was then done – he became peaceable in a moment – trembled with fear, and was as governable as it was possible for a furious madman to be.[88]

And Francis Willis made highly publicized use of the technique in his treatment of the most famous late eighteenth-century lunatic of them all, George III.[89] Here was perhaps the archetypical image of late Georgian responses to the mad: the imperious keeper able to reduce the ranting and raving to docility and obedience through the moral force of his gaze.

5. The Technology of Treatment

Willis's treatment of his king illustrates how tenacious traditional notions about the proper treatment of the mad proved to be. His practice was built upon the conviction that nothing was more important that 'inculcating salutary fear'. As he was to indicate to a French visitor,

> The emotion of fear is the first and often the only one by which they can be governed. By working on it one removes their thoughts from

88. William Pargeter, *Observations on Maniacal Disorders*, pp. 50–1, also pp. 58–9. John Haslam was sceptical in the extreme of all such claims: 'It has, on some occasions, occurred to me to meet with gentlemen who have imagined themselves eminently gifted with this awful imposition of the eye, but . . . I have never been able to persuade them to practise this rare talent *tête-à-tête* with a furious lunatic.' J. Haslam, *Observations on Madness and Melancholy*, p. 276.

89. Willis's boasts about his talent for visual intimidation initially provoked incredulity and harsh criticism among politicians. The parliamentary committee which inquired into the king's treatment during his 1788 attack of 'mania', whose membership included Edmund Burke and Richard Sheridan, learned that Willis had allowed the king, while in the throes of his madness, to shave himself with a cutthroat razor. The royal physicians, considerably discomfited by being upstaged by a provincial mad-doctor, reported this alarming news with evident satisfaction, and looked forward to his interrogation before such a sceptical audience. Willis once more confounded them:

> Burke also was very severe on this point, and authoritatively and loudly demanded to know, 'If the Royal patient had become outrageous at the moment, what power the Doctor possessed of instantaneously terrifying him into obedience.' 'Place the candles between us, Mr Burke,' replied the Doctor, in an equally authoritative tone – 'and I'll give you an answer. There Sir! by the EYE! I should have looked at him *thus*, Sir – *thus!*' Burke instantaneously averted his head, and, making no reply, evidently acknowledged this *basiliskan* authority.

> *The Life and Times of F. Reynolds, Written by Himself*, Vol. 2, London: Colburn, 1826, pp. 23–4.

the phantasms occupying them and brings them back to reality, even if this entails inflicting pain and suffering. It is fear too which teaches them to judge their actions rightly and learn the consequences. By such means is their attention brought back to their surroundings.[90]

Willis's reputation for using force and fear to cow his patients was such that, when he was called in to treat George III, the queen was extremely reluctant to allow him to proceed.

It was known to her, that the first principle of Dr W's practice is to make himself formidable – to inspire awe. In these terrible maladies, those who superintend the unhappy patients must so subjugate their will, that no idea of resistance to their commands can have place in their minds. It was but too obvious, that the long and habitual exercise of high command must increase the difficulty of accomplishing this, in the present instance; – and an apprehension of peculiar rigour gave all possible aggravation to the queen's distress.[91]

But Willis refused to modify his practice,[92] insisting that

He might be permitted to act without control. He said that there was but *one method* in that complaint, by which the lowest and highest person could be treated with effect: – and that his reputation was too much concerned in the event, for him to attempt anything, if he might not be invested with unlimited powers.[93]

As Bynum has argued,[94] given the enormous stake Willis had in the king's recovery, he unquestionably acted as best he knew how to control and cure his patient. Yet, as one of the members of the court reported, once in Willis's hands, 'The unhappy patient . . . was no longer treated as a human being. His body was immediately encased in a machine which left no liberty of motion. He was sometimes chained to a stake. He was fre-

90. Anon., 'Détails sur l'établissement du Docteur Willis, pour la guérison des aliénés', *Bibliothèque Britannique, Littérature*, 1, 1796, pp. 759–73, quoted in I. MacAlpine and R. Hunter, *George III and the Mad-Business*, p. 275.
91. Anon., *Some Particulars of the Royal Indisposition of 1788 to 1789, and of Its Effects Upon Illustrious Personages and Opposite Parties Interested by It*, London: Taylor, 1804, pp. 31–3.
92. As Willis himself later put it, 'As death makes no distinction in his visits between the poor man's hut and the prince's palace, so insanity is equally impartial in her dealings with her subjects. For that reason, I made no distinction in my treatment of persons submitted to my charge. When, therefore, my gracious sovereign became violent, I felt it my duty to subject him to the same system of restraint as I should have adopted with one of his own gardeners at Kew: in plain words, I put a strait waistcoat on him. . . . The strait waistcoat was an offence to her pride which the Queen never could, and never did, overcome.' Quoted in I. MacAlpine and R. Hunter, *George III and the Mad-Business*, p. 281.
93. *Ibid*.
94. W.F. Bynum, 'Rationales for Therapy', p. 319.

quently beaten and starved, and at best he was kept in subjection by menacing and violent language.'[95]

Underlying Willis's approach, as well as the practices of many of his rivals in the rapidly expanding mad-business, was their conviction that the successful treatment of madness was dependent upon an ability to foster 'the artful association of ideas', and to invent novel ways 'of breaking false or unnatural associations, or inducing counter-associations'.[96] Sometimes, some sort of 'pious fraud' might suffice, though for such tactics to be successful, 'the actor in this drama must possess much skill, and be very perfect in his part . . .':

> It is certainly allowable [,said Cox,] to try the effect of certain decep-
> tions, contrived to make strong impressions on the senses, by means of
> unexpected, unusual, striking, or apparently supernatural agents; such
> as after waking the party from sleep, either suddenly or by a gradual
> process, by imitated thunder or soft music, according to the peculiarity
> of the case, combatting the erroneous deranged notion, either by some
> pointed sentence, or signs executed in phosphorus upon the wall of the
> bedchamber, or by some tale, assertion, or reasoning by one in the
> character of an angel, prophet, or devil.[97]

More commonly, however, the 'strong impressions on the senses' con-
tinued to depend on the excitement of fear and even the infliction of physical suffering, and new techniques were developed to induce the appropriate degree of terror.

Intellectually, these approaches rested on the growing conviction that men were the product of their circumstances and experiences, an empiricism which had found forcible expression in John Locke's *Essay Concerning Human Understanding* as much as a century earlier. Locke's portrait of the human mind as in its origins a *tabula rasa*, moulded for good or ill by the education of the senses and in consequence susceptible to error and misassociation, provided an increasingly influential theoretical account of

95. The Countess Harcourt, Lady of the Bedchamber to the Queen, quoted *ibid.* The King's equerry, Colonel Greville, reported with some distress that Willis had informed him that he '"broke in" patients' as one might '"Horses in a manege" – as his expression was.' 'His Majesty's 1st Illness in the Year 1788–9', in *The Diaries of Colonel the Hon. Robert Fulke Greville*, edited by F.M. Bladon, London: John Lane, 1930, p. 186. Remarkably, less than a century later, in the course of constructing a suitable genealogy for alienism, Andrew Wynter was to claim that Willis's treatment of George III constituted 'one of the first and most striking instances of a victory gained by non-restraint over madness' (*The Borderlands of Insanity*, 1st edn, London: Hardwicke, 1875, pp. 84–5) – an early instance of the drawbacks of an in-house history of psychiatry.
96. John Gregory, *A Comparative View of the State and Faculties of Man with Those of the Animal World*, London: Dodsley, 1765, pp. 186–8.
97. J.M. Cox, *Practical Observations on Insanity*, p. 88. Benjamin Rush endorsed this approach in his *Medical Inquiries and Observations Upon the Diseases of the Mind*, Philadelphia: Kimber and Richardson, 1812, pp. 108–12. Haslam by contrast, who was generally scornful of Cox's prescriptions, was particularly dismissive of this suggestion. See *Observations on Madness and Melancholy*, 2nd edn, London: Callow, 1809, pp. 303, 307.

what had gone wrong with the mad.[98] Simultaneously, his epistemology could be drawn upon to provide theoretical warrant for therapeutic interventions of a thoroughly practical sort.

Madness was essentially defined, indeed constituted, by the preternatural force with which certain irrational ideas dominated the mind, heedless of the ordinary corrective processes provided by experience and persuasion. Within an empiricist world-view, it seemed that mad people's loss of contact with our consensually defined reality, their spurning of common sense (in both senses of the term), must somehow reflect how deeply the chains of false impressions and associations were engraved upon their systems.[99] To be sure, there were differences in degree between mania and melancholia: 'The distinguishing character of [the latter] is an attachment of the mind to one object, concerning which the reason is defective, while in general it is perfect in what respects other subjects'; whereas mania entailed 'an irrationality on all subjects'.[100] But in both forms of the disorder, the thought processes were trapped in erroneous pathways – a language that reified and referred them to an underlying disorder of a (somewhat variously conceived) physical substratum of thought, from whose grip they must somehow be shaken loose.

The very tenacity with which maniacs adhered to their false and mistaken perceptions testified to the weight and strength with which these were impressed upon the brain, and by implication required and justified the extremity of the measures adopted to jolt the system back into sanity. Given that *the mind when waking is always active and employed*, it followed that *we have no method of banishing one set or train of ideas, but by substituting another in its place*.[101] And in view of the entrenched position occupied by the opposing ideas, one could only hope 'to eradicate the false impressions by others still more violent'.[102] 'The imagination' must 'be subdued, and kept under'; 'the passions . . . held in subjection [and] restrained.'[103] Locke's emphasis on the direct relationship between the strength of a

98. For a recent discussion of the influence of Locke's ideas on 'educated and enlightened thinking' about madness in the eighteenth century, see R. Porter, *Mind Forg'd Manacles*, pp. 188–94, 207–8.

99. In Thomas Arnold's formulation, 'the mind having once lost, in any great degree, the power of commanding, and regulating its own attention, of turning it with facility from one object to another, and of resisting the forcible, and continual recurrence, of any particular ideas, or notions, is apt at length to be so bewildered by incessantly brooding upon the same objects, as to become entirely passive, and to be carried along with the stream of that activity of the brain, and those violent vibrations, which it itself had excited, but can no longer control, or resist . . . in a word, reason will [then] be over powered, and insanity will assume her place.' *Observations on . . . Insanity*, 2nd edn, London: Phillips, 1806, Vol. 2, pp. 167–8, and p. 191 for the image of the brain getting stuck in certain grooves.

100. W. Falconer, *A Dissertation on the Influence of the Passions Upon the Disorders of the Body*, pp. 77, 82.

101. *Ibid.*, p. 4, emphasis in the original.

102. *Ibid.*, p. 82. *Cf.* also J.M. Cox, *Practical Observations on Insanity*, 3rd edn, p. 45.

103. T. Arnold, *Observations on . . . Insanity*, Vol. 2, pp. 331, 335.

particular sensation and the vividness of any given idea was thus readily coupled with the notion that the cure of madness required the supersession of defective learned patterns of thoughts, and provided a source of legitimation for the most extreme versions of therapeutic terror.

Adapting the technological inventiveness of the age to the task, some of those engaged in treating the mad proceeded to devise yet further means of coercing them back to sanity. Benjamin Rush's 'tranquillizing chair', designed to prompt a measure of good behaviour from even the most recalcitrant, found its English advocates.[104] Elaborate systems of plumbing were developed to deliver forcible streams of cold water to the head of a suitably restrained maniac.[105] More strikingly still, the suggestion by the Dutch physician, Hermann Boerhaave, that near-drowning be employed for its salutary effects gave birth to a variety of ingenious devices designed to produce this effect: hidden trapdoors in corridors designed to plunge the unsuspecting lunatic into a 'bath of surprise', and even coffins with holes drilled in their lids, into which the patient could be fastened before being lowered under water.[106] But perhaps the most famous contrivance

104. It was proposed, for instance, to the Royal physicians in 1811, as a useful means of treating the monarch, but declined. I. MacAlpine and R. Hunter, *George III and the Mad-Business*, p. 279. Rush himself boasted of his invention:

> I have contrived a chair and introduced it to our [Pennsylvania] Hospital to assist in curing madness. It binds and confines every part of the body. By keeping the trunk erect, it lessens the impetus of blood toward the brain. By preventing the muscles from acting, it reduces the force and frequency of the pulse, and the position of the head and feet favors the easy application of cold water or ice to the former and warm water to the latter. Its effects have been truly delightful to me. It acts as a sedative to the tongue and temper as well as to the blood vessels. In 24, 12, six, and in some cases in four hours, the most refractory patients have been composed. I have called it a Tranquillizer.

Rush to James Rush, 8 June 1810, reprinted in *The Letters of Benjamin Rush*, edited by L.H. Butterfield, Princeton: Princeton University Press, 1951, Vol. 2, p. 1052.

105. See Alexander Morison, *Cases of Mental Disease, With Practical Observations on the Medical Treatment*, London: Longman and Highley, 1828.

106. Just how frequently these devices were translated from the drawing board to actual use remains unclear, though the Belgian physician, Guislain, reports that Francis Willis made use of them on occasion. Guislain himself was somewhat contemptuous of these late eighteenth-century efforts to reconcile the need to obtain complete mastery over the madman while avoiding drowning him, and invented a still more elaborate version of his own:

> It consists of a little Chinese temple, the interior of which comprises a moveable iron cage, of light-weight construction, which plunges down into the water descending in rails, of its own weight, by means of pulleys and ropes. To expose the madman to the action of this device, he is led into the interior of this cage; one servant shuts the door from the outside while the other releases a brake which, by this manoeuvre, causes the patient to sink down, shut up in the cage, under the water. Having produced the desired effect, one raises the machine again. . . .

J. Guislain, *Traité sur l'aliénation mentale et sur les hospices des aliénés*, Amsterdam: Hey, 1826, pp. 43–4. He thoughtfully provided a working drawing for those wanting to construct such a device for their own madhouses.

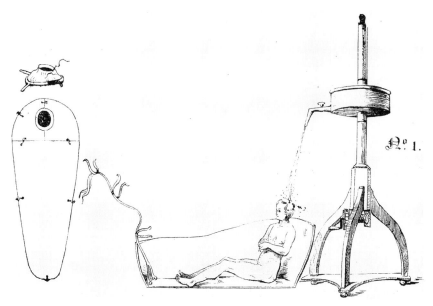

Fig. 6   Immersion in cold water was an ancient nostrum for insanity. Aquatic shock treatment, otherwise euphemistically known as 'hydrotherapy', here takes the form of the douche. The illustration is taken from Alexander Morison, *Cases of Mental Disease* (London: Longman and Highley, 1828).

of all at the time was Joseph Mason Cox's swinging device, the idea for which had been suggested by Erasmus Darwin.[107]

Cox's book describing the chair's construction and use rapidly went through three English editions,[108] as well as appearing in a French, an American, and a German edition.[109] He promoted its remarkable ability to bring both moral and physiological pressures to bear on the patient, exploiting 'the sympathy or reciprocity of action that subsists between mind and body'. In the application of his sovereign remedy, each became 'in its turn the agent, and the subject acted on, as when fear, terror, anger, and other passions, excited by the action of the swing, produce various alterations in the body, and where the revolving motion, occasioning fatigue, exhaustion, pallor, horripilatio, vertigo, etc, effect new associations and trains of thought'.[110]

107. Erasmus Darwin, *Zoonomia; or, The Laws of Organic Life*, 2 Vols, London: Johnson, 1794–6. Darwin derived the idea from classical suggestions about the value of swinging as therapy. According to Dr Vivian Nutton (personal communication), his immediate source was probably Girolamo Mercuriale, *De arte gymnastica*, Amsterdam: Frisii, 1672.
108. J.M. Cox, *Practical Observations on Insanity*: 1st edn 1804; 2nd edn 1806 (both London: Baldwin and Murray); 3rd edn 1813 (London: Baldwin and Underwood).
109. The French edition appeared in 1805, and the American and German editions in 1811.
110. J.M. Cox, *Practical Observations on Insanity*, 3rd edn, pp. 168–9.

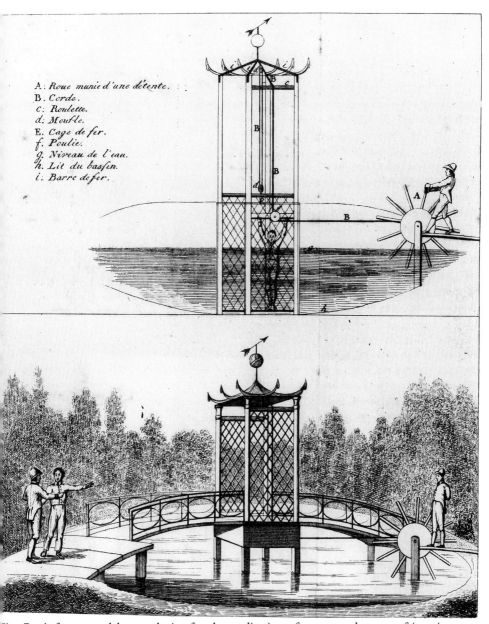

A: *Roue munie d'une détente.*
B: *Corde.*
c: *Roulette.*
d: *Moufle.*
E: *Cage de fer.*
f: *Poulie.*
g: *Niveau de l'eau.*
h: *Lit du bassin.*
i: *Barre de fer.*

Fig. 7   A far more elaborate device for the application of water to the cure of insanity was Guislain's so-called Chinese Temple. Taken from J. Guislain, *Traité sur l'aliénation mentale et sur les hospices des aliénés* (Amsterdam: Hey, 1826).

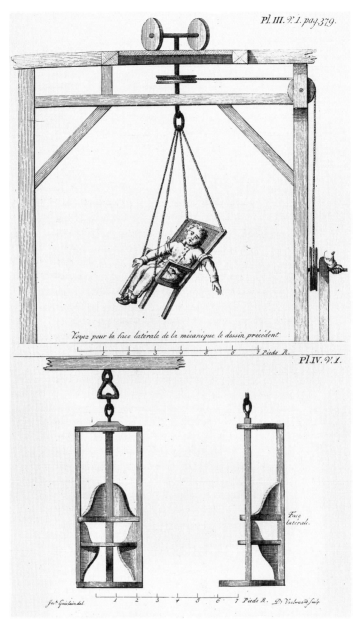

Fig. 8 A rotary machine based on Cox's swing. A number of
complicated variants on Cox's original design were developed in the
early nineteenth century. This version was briefly used at the Berlin
Charité. From J. Guislain, *Traité sur l'aliénation mentale....*
(Amsterdam: Hey, 1826).

The 'mechanical apparatus' provided the operator with the inestimable advantage of being able to regulate the whole process with extraordinary precision. One could, for example, vary its effects on the stomach so as to produce 'either temporary or continued nausea, partial or full vomiting', and if necessary could secure 'the most violent convulsions . . . the agitation and convulsion of every part of the animal frame'.[111] Even obstinate cases could not long resist its powers: if necessary, it could even be 'employed in the dark, where, from unusual noises, smells, or other powerful agents, acting forcibly on the senses, its efficacy might be amazingly increased'.[112] And by 'increasing the velocity of the swing, the motion be[ing] suddenly reversed every six or eight minutes, pausing occasionally, and stopping its circulation suddenly: the consequence is, an instant discharge of the contents of the stomach, bowels, and bladder, in quick succession'.[113]

The consequent 'very violent shock both to mind and body' was believed to exhibit a wholly salutary 'tendency to excite fear or terror'.[114] An Irish mad-doctor, William Saunders Hallaran, subsequently carried the whole process to a higher pitch of perfection, designing a seat that 'supports the cervical column better, and guards against the possibility of the head in the vertiginous state from hanging over the side [sic]'.[115] Both inventors provided elaborate case histories to document its immense usefulness as an agent of moral repression, capable of reducing the most violent and perverse to a meek obedience.[116]

6. Free Trade in Lunacy

Such therapeutic experiments and speculations were in substantial measure the by-product of the growing resort to confinement of the mad as the Georgian age drew to a close. Although by the turn of the century, the

111. *Ibid.*, pp. 143–4.
112. *Ibid.*, p. 140.
113. George Man Burrows, *Commentaries on the Causes, Forms, Symptoms, and Treatment, Moral and Medical, of Insanity*, London: Underwood, 1828, p. 601.
114. J.M. Cox, *Practical Observations on Insanity*, 3rd edn, p. 170.
115. G.M. Burrows, *Commentaries on . . . Insanity*, p. 601. *Cf.* William Saunders Hallaran, *An Enquiry into the Causes Producing the Extraordinary Addition to the Number of the Insane*, Cork, Ireland: Edwards and Savage, 1810; *idem.*, *Practical Observations on the Causes and Cure of Insanity*, Cork, Ireland: Hodges and M'Arthur, 1818. Hallaran boasted that 'since the commencement of its use, I have never been at a loss for a direct mode of establishing a supreme authority over the most turbulent and unruly'.
116. In keeping with Lockean associationism, Cox attributed his success to the swing's 'tendency decidedly to correct erroneous ideas . . . destroy the links of morbid association, and break the force and effects of vicious mental habits'. Quoted in R. Hunter and I. MacAlpine, *Three Hundred Years of Psychiatry*, p. 596. See also P.S. Knight, *Observations on the . . . Derangement of the Mind*, p. 63; George Nesse Hill, *An Essay on the Prevention and Cure of Insanity*, London: Longman, 1814, esp. pp. 291, 327 ('a very valuable addition to the common stock of general remedies of which we cannot have too extended a number').

number of lunatics locked up in specialized places remained quite modest, it was nonetheless sufficient to form the basis for the emergence of an increasingly self-conscious group of practitioners laying claim to expertise in the treatment of the mad. A network of publicly financed and state-run asylums would not assume a dominant position in the institutional management of the insane for another half century. Still, the first four decades of the new century saw a sharp expansion in the number of lunatics confined in specialized institutions.

Such expansion for the most part followed eighteenth-century pre-cedents and occurred in the private and profit-making sector of the mad-business. Between 1807 (when a House of Commons Select Committee collected and published the first nationwide figures on the number of private madhouses) and 1844 (when the Metropolitan Commissioners in Lunacy published the report which finally persuaded the legislature to compel local justices to set up publicly run asylums) the number of private licensed houses in England more than tripled. From a total of forty-five establishments in 1807, the private system had grown to encompass 139 madhouses by 1844. For the remainder of that decade, the size of this sector stayed relatively constant; thereafter, as the expansion of the public sector siphoned off almost all the pauper patients – the majority of the insane population – it declined slowly, though as many as ninety-one private houses still received patients in 1890.

In some respects, it may be misleading to speak of early nineteenth-century madhouses as a system; for, as in the eighteenth century, there continued to be an extraordinarily wide variability in the character of the houses and those who ran them. During the first half of the century, 'the greater number of provincial madhouses contained up to approximately twenty-five patients'.[117] Most of those in the London area, the so-called metropolitan houses, were also small. Of the thirty-six operating in 1816, nine were licensed to take fewer than ten patients each; and most of the remainder contained well under a hundred.[118] On the other hand, institu-tions such as Hoxton House, Haydock Lodge, or Warburton's Bethnal Green houses provided for four or five hundred in a single establishment. While places like Ticehurst and Brislington House catered almost exclu-sively to an upper-class and aristocratic clientele, the large London houses swarmed with a mixture of paupers and a smattering of the marginal middle class.

Similarly, there were wide disparities in the ratio of staff to patients, and in the kind of treatment the patients received. The magistrates charged with visiting Ticehurst reported that many patients 'spoke with pleasure of their residence at Ticehurst, and expressed unwillingness to quit it; all

117. William Parry-Jones, *The Trade in Lunacy*, London: Routledge and Kegan Paul, 1972, p. 40.
118. House of Commons, *Third Report of the Select Committee on Madhouses*, 1816, p. 75.

Fig. 9 An anonymous engraving of Brislington House, the first purpose-built asylum in England, from F.C. Fox, *History and Present State of Brislington House* (Bristol: Light and Ridler, 1836). Completed in 1806 for Edward Long Fox, it was designed for an upper-class clientele, and was located in the centre of a well-wooded estate some three miles from Bristol. In addition to the central asylum buildings, a brochure of 1836 advertises a number of houses on the estate 'inhabited by members of the nobility, who are accommodated with servants from the institution; and are allowed to pursue any style of living and expense as to carriages, horses, etc, most suitable to their former habits, and not inconsistent with their present situation'.

expressed themselves well satisfied with the arrangements made for their comfort and convenience'. Here, for fifty patients, there were as many as thirty-six attendants.[119] At Brislington House, Edward Fox was among the first to demonstrate that the insane could be managed in a more humane and less violent fashion than had hitherto been believed possible. He provided for the segregation and classification of patients according to the degree of their disorder and his management of them involved little or no restraint.[120] At the other extreme, by the standards the nineteenth-

119. Anon., *Views of Messrs. Newington's Private Asylum for the Cure of Insane Persons, Ticehurst, Sussex* n.p., *c.* 1829. A copy of this pamphlet is in the East Sussex Record Office in Lewes. The quotation is from the reprinted report of the asylum's official visitors, dated 24 November 1827.
120. House of Commons Select Committee, *Report*, 1815, p. 21; *Brislington House: An Asylum for Lunatics, Situate near Bristol, on the Road from Bath, and Lately Erected by Edward Long Fox M.D.*, Bristol: n.p., 1806. While he never received the same publicity as the Tukes, Fox was one of the pioneers of the new moral treatment. It is perhaps no coincidence that the matron at the York Retreat, Katherine Jepson (*née* Allen), had been recruited from Brislington House. For a more jaundiced view of Fox's madhouse, see John Thomas Perceval, *A Narrative of the Treatment Received by a Gentleman, During a*

century lunacy reformers were to apply (and which we largely still share), conditions in many, perhaps a majority, of the houses were appalling. Particularly early in the century, inmates suffered extremes of barbarity and neglect.

Reflecting the continuing administrative weakness of the English state bureaucratic apparatus (especially on the local level), there was an almost total absence of legal restrictions on entry into or the subsequent conduct of the mad-business.[121] At the same time, the market for the madhouse keepers' services was expanding, as the tendency to incarcerate all sorts of problem populations grew ever more marked and as the corresponding recognition that 'the Practice of confining such lunatics and other insane persons as are chargeable to their respective Parishes in Gaols, Houses of Correction, Poor Houses, and Houses of Industry, is highly dangerous and inconvenient'[122] spread ever more widely. Undoubtedly, this permissive legal climate, and the demand for places of confinement to which lunatics could be removed, encouraged speculators with no other qualifications than a little capital and an interest in quick returns to enter the mad-business. Indeed, as a contemporary observer commented, precisely because 'Few speculations can be more unpleasant than that of a private madhouse, . . . it is seldom if ever undertaken, unless with the hope of receiving large returns on the capital invested.'[123] Concerned solely with maximizing the return on their investment, the worst proprietors cast aside their scruples to become 'wholesale dealers and traffickers in this

State of Mental Derangement, 2 vols, London: Effingham Wilson, 1838, 1840. Perceval, the son of Spencer Perceval, the British Prime Minister assassinated in 1812, was committed to Brislington suffering from religious excitement and delusions, and was subsequently an inmate of Ticehurst, of which he is somewhat less critical. At Brislington House, he complained of being treated 'as if I were a piece of furniture, an image of wood, incapable of desire or will as well as judgement. . . . Men acted as though my body, and soul were fairly given up to their control, to work their mischief and folly upon. . . . I was fastened down in bed, a meagre diet was ordered for me; this and medicine forced down my throat or in the contrary direction; my will, my wishes, my repugnances, my habits, my delicacy, my inclinations, my necessities, were not consulted, I may say, thought of. I did not find the respect usually paid to a child.' Ibid., pp. 175–6, 179. To his family's great discomfiture, on his recovery and release from Ticehurst, Perceval devoted the rest of his life to 'the subject of maintaining the rights of lunatics'. Together with a number of others, including Luke Hansard, publisher of Parliament's proceedings, he formed the Alleged Lunatics' Friend Society, serving as the organization's secretary from 1846 onwards. In testimony before the Select Committee on the Care and Treatment of Lunatics, established by the House of Commons in 1859, he termed himself 'the attorney general of all Her Majesty's madmen'. On the society's activities, cf. Nicholas Hervey, 'Advocacy or Folly? The Alleged Lunatics' Friend Society, 1845–63', Medical History 30, 1986, pp. 254–75.

121. Until 1828, the only legislation purporting to regulate the care of lunatics in these institutions was an Act of 1774, providing for the licensing and inspection of metropolitan madhouses by members of the Royal College of Physicians and of provincial madhouses by local magistrates.
122. Report of the Select Committee on Criminal and Pauper Lunatics, 1807, p. 6.
123. Andrew Duncan, Observations on the Structure of Hospitals for the Treatment of Lunatics as a Branch of Medical Police, Edinburgh: Ballantyne, 1809, p. 18.

species of human misery', prepared, if necessary, to go to extreme lengths to increase their profits.[124] A doubtless unintentional product of their activity was to provide the lunacy reformers with some of their most powerful ammunition.

Primarily because of the desire to reduce the comparatively large invest-ment needed to enter the trade, at this period 'lunatic houses are mostly common dwelling houses, fitted to the purpose not originally built for it'.[125] Not only were few madhouses of the period purpose-built, but as an economy measure in those that had to be adapted to accommodate lunatics, the necessary alterations were kept to a minimum. A particularly common practice was to buy an old, abandoned country mansion, to turn the impressive-looking central structure into accommodation for the more profitable patients, and to relegate the paupers to the stables and outbuildings.[126]

The scenes of the greatest abuses were the asylums which accom-modated paupers. The profit that could be made out of a single pauper was comparatively negligible, given the pittance which the parish over-seers allowed for the support of pauper lunatics. In the absence of legal restraint, however, there were no restrictions on the number of patients that could be entrusted to a single keeper. To ensure a sufficient return on their capital, therefore, and to take advantage of these potential economies of scale, madhouses which took pauper patients were generally very large. This explains the growth in large establishments up to the middle of the nineteenth century, and their subsequent decline as the opening of county asylums drained off the pauper patients. (More licensed houses disappeared between 1850 and 1860, the decade during which most county asylums built under the 1845 Act first opened their doors, than during the next thirty years; and those that disappeared included all the largest

124. Andrew Halliday, *A General View of the Present State of Lunatics and Lunatic Asylums*, London: Underwood, 1828, p. 10.
125. *Report of the Select Committee on Madhouses*, 1815, p. 77.
126. The defects of one such establishment in Lancashire were exposed in the late 1840s. See *Report of the Commissioners in Lunacy Relative to the Haydock Lodge Lunatic Asylum*, London, 1847. Other examples of this practice include Lainston House, Winchester; Bailbrooke House, Bath; Duddleston Hall, near Birmingham; and Plympton House, Devon. In mixed asylums of this sort, paupers often fared particularly badly. Following a visit to Plympton House in 1842, for instance, the Metropolitan Commissioners in Lunacy reported that 'In one of the cells in the upper court for women, the dimensions of which were 8 feet by 4, and in which there was no table, and only two wooden seats, fastened to the wall we found three females confined. There was no glazing to the windows, and the floor of this place was perfectly wet with urine. The two dark cells which adjoin the cell used for a day room are the sleeping places for these three unfortunate beings. Two of them sleep in two cribs in one cell. The floor in the cell with two cribs was actually reeking, wet with urine and covered with straw and filth. . . . In the other cell, . . . part of the straw had been stuck to the wall . . . with excrement. . . . The whole of these cells were as damp and dark as an underground cellar and were in such a foul and disgusting state that it was scarcely possible to endure the offensive smell. We sent for a candle and a lantern to enable us to examine them.' Metropolitan Commissioners in Lunacy, *Report*, 1844, pp. 62–3.

houses.) While such large establishments were not confined to the London area – Haydock Lodge in Lancashire was licensed for 400 pauper and fifty private patients – the metropolis contained a number of the more famous (or infamous) houses. In 1815, Miles's house at Hoxton contained 486 patients, three quarters of whom were paupers; at Warburton's two houses in Bethnal Green, the White House contained 360 patients (230 paupers) and the Red House 275 patients (215 paupers). In 1844, of the metropolitan houses taking paupers, Hoxton House contained 396 patients, Peckham House 251, and Warburton's two establishments 562.

Even to our eyes, institutions containing three, four, and five hundred seem like sizeable concentrations of people. Placed in their proper historical context, however, they were simply enormous. In the early nineteenth century, few institutions, including factories, approached this size. For with any concentration of numbers, the employer had to 'submit to the constant trouble and solicitude of watching over a numerous body of workmen . . .', and were he to try to employ a workforce of two or three hundred men, not only did this mean that he could no longer directly supervise his own employees, but it even became 'exceedingly difficult to supervise his supervisors'.[127] Given the scarcity of trained managers and the poverty of management techniques of the period, most commercial enterprises perforce remained comparatively small. The size of the mad-houses is the more remarkable, then, since, unlike the factory owner, the proprietor of a madhouse faced the further problem of managing *all* aspects of the lives of an inmate population confined in his buildings for months, if not years, at a time. Moreover, this was a population com-posed of people who by definition had failed to respond to conventional efforts to manage and control their behaviour.

To make matters worse, these houses had to compete against one another for patients. And given the parsimony of parish Poor Law officials, and their lack of concern with anything save efficient custody, madhouse keepers catering to the pauper trade were forced to reduce their charges for such patients to a bare minimum. Most of these institutions were, as a result, no more than convenient receptacles for the most troublesome and socially inept. They were characteristically overcrowded, and attendants were few and far between. At Warburton's White House, for example, there were at times as few as two paid attendants for 170 male pauper lunatics. Inmates were kept alive only with the help of convalescent patients.[128]

The dearth of attendants and the unsuitability of those who were employed – together with the structural deficiencies of the buildings them-selves and the absence of effective techniques of managing and supervising

127. Cited in Sidney Pollard, *The Genesis of Modern Management*, Harmondsworth: Penguin, 1965, pp. 21–2.
128. House of Commons, *Report from the Select Committee on Pauper Lunatics in the County of Middlesex*, 1827, esp. pp. 3, 120–1, 124–6.

either patients or staff – produced an overwhelming reliance upon chains and other forms of mechanical restraint.[129] In Warburton's houses, to save trouble and expense, and to allow the attendants some free time at the weekends, patients were placed in cribs at three o'clock on a Saturday afternoon, secured with chains, and left there until Monday morning. In the worst pauper establishments, reformers scarcely exaggerated when they claimed that 'fetters and chains, moppings at the morning toilet, irregular meals, want of exercise, the infliction of abusive words, contemptuous names, blows with the fist, or with straps, or with keys, formed an almost daily part of the lives of many unprotected beings'.[130]

Conditions in the public subscription hospitals, such as Bethlem and St. Luke's, were scarcely much better. At St. Luke's in 1815, there were only sixteen keepers for 300 patients, and the galleries themselves were 'overcrowded and cheerless'. At Bethlem, there were two male keepers for fifty-two male patients, and two females for sixty-eight females. The apothecary visited the wards for about half an hour a day, and the physician scarcely at all.[131] Here, too, inmates were confined to make the attendants' work easier: 'The custom when I first went was, only to get them up three days a week – never on meat days: they lie in bed four days a week.'[132] Overcrowding and inadequate accommodation, and the constant provocation inmates offered the keepers, all too frequently then led to 'an alternation of reciprocal violence between the prisoner and the gaoler'.[133]

7. The Reformers

Conditions in the early nineteenth-century asylums consequently provided a promising arena for legislative interference. There proved to be no shortage of men interested in the subject. During this period, certain upper middle-class gentlemen began to interest themselves in projects of social reform of every description. Indeed, for a brief period (1811–17) these self-styled philanthropists were sufficiently numerous to support a periodical all their own. Lunacy reform was soon one of their favourite causes. Of equal or perhaps even greater importance for the emergence of a reform movement was the activity of several energetic local magistrates – an involvement which is scarcely surprising, for the Justice of the Peace was the primary instrument of local government at the time, and hence faced on a daily basis all the problems created by the decay of the traditional social structure. Their duties, moreover, which included

---

129. House of Commons, *Report of the Select Committee on Madhouses*, 1815, p. 46 and *passim*.
130. John Conolly, *The Treatment of the Insane Without Mechanical Restraints*, London: Smith, Elder, 1856, p. 143.
131. House of Commons, *Report of the Select Committee on Madhouses*, 1815, pp. 35–7.
132. House of Commons, *First Report of the Select Committee on Madhouses*, 1816, p. 95, evidence of the matron of Bethlem.
133. Samuel William Nicoll, *An Enquiry into the Present State of Visitation, in Asylums for the Reception of the Insane*, London: Harvey and Darton, 1828, p. 32.

inspection of the jails and workhouses, were apt to bring them into contact with the most troublesome, and on the whole most ill-treated, sections of the pauper lunatic population.

More immediately, the outcome of a particular trial in 1800 made magistrates at the turn of the century still more acutely conscious of the problems created by the violent insane. In the wake of an unsuccessful attempt on the life of George III, the would-be assassin was acquitted on the grounds of insanity. Under existing law, there was no provision for detaining someone acquitted in this fashion. Reluctant to allow Hadfield his freedom, Parliament rushed through a piece of retroactive legislation, directing that such lunatics would be detained 'in strict custody' in the County Jail or other suitable receptacle during the king's pleasure. In the first five years of its operation, thirty-seven people were detained under this act, provoking complaints that 'to confine such persons in a common Gaol, is equally destructive of the recovery of the insane and of the security and comfort of the other prisoners'.[134] More than that, some magistrates, at least, were troubled by the irrationality of acquitting some-one of a criminal charge on grounds of insanity, and then imprisoning him anyway.

Both strands of the emerging lunacy reform movement, like almost all Victorian social reforms, were heavily influenced by two compet-ing philosophical systems which were, in effect, social movements: Evangelicalism and Benthamism. The lunacy reformers' ranks included leading adherents of both factions,[135] and the final shape of lunacy legisla-tion in England clearly owes much to the Evangelicals' humanitarianism and paternalism, and to the Benthamite emphasis on expertise and effi-ciency. Evangelicalism may be thought of as a Methodism of the upper middle classes which nevertheless managed to remain firmly within the Anglican tradition. A group of proselytizing religious reformers, the Evangelicals, sought to convert a whole society to the advantages of discipline and regularity over disorder and vice. In many ways they present us with an ideal-typical example of the type of belief system which Howard Becker suggests produces the moral entrepreneur. Their mission (and how appropriate that word is) was perceived as a holy one, the

134. House of Commons, *Report of the Select Committee on Criminal and Pauper Lunatics*, 1807, p. 4.
135. Among the Evangelicals, William Wilberforce, Lord Robert Seymour, and William Smith all served on one or more of the parliamentary committees on the lunacy question, while the leading Evangelical of a later generation, Lord Ashley (later Lord Shaftesbury), was heavily involved in lunacy reform from 1827 until his death in 1885. Benthamites who took an active part in the reform process included Sir Samuel Romilly and Samuel Whitbread among MPs, and provincial magistrates like Sir George Onesiphorus Paul. Bentham himself wrote on the treatment of the insane, and even in the case of those whose commitment to lunacy reform had different sources, such as the Quaker land agent, Edward Wakefield, the influence of his ideas was strong. See the endorsement of Bentham's Panopticon scheme in Edward Wakefield's 'Plan for an Asylum for Lunatics', *The Philanthropist* 3, 1812, pp. 226–9.

conditions they chose to combat as transparently evil. They insisted that they were not merely imposing their views on others, but, in a profoundly humanitarian fashion, rescuing the lower classes from the sin and social degradation that threatened them. The Evangelical commitment to a kind of moral imperialism was perhaps most clearly exemplified by the name of one of Wilberforce's favourite associations, 'The Society for the Suppression of Vice' – which, as Sydney Smith caustically commented, was 'a society for suppressing the vices of persons whose income does not exceed 500 pounds per annum'.[136]

The moral self-righteousness implicit in their whole perspective is classically that adopted by a dominant class towards those less favourably situated in the social structure. Their simplified view of the world and their immense moral fervour provided them with both innumerable targets for reform, and the fortitude to pursue their goals in the face of ridicule from the wider society as eccentric moralizers. The religious indifference of the new industrial classes,[137] the immorality of the slave trade, widespread cruelty to children and to animals, and, of course, the treatment of the insane, were all aspects of contemporary society which they deplored, and problems which they attacked with vigour and determination. Evangelicalism was at its core a conservative movement, concerned to shore up a disintegrating social structure and a paternalistic morality against the threats posed by an undisciplined lower-class rabble, and by a purely materialistic entrepreneurial class. To achieve its ends, however, it was forced into the paradoxical position of helping to create a rash of new social rules and institutions. Ironically, too, its emphasis on discipline and order, rooted in the desire to see the old patterns of deference and dependence re-established, readily formed the basis for the entirely different morality required by the radically new industrial society.

If Evangelicalism drew its adherents from among those with a profound distaste for certain aspects of the newly emerging society, Benthamism was the creed of a class of professional administrators virtually created by that new society. Committed to the need for a 'science of government' and emphasizing the replacement of the amateur by the expert, Benthamism's natural appeal was to this growing class. Providing an intellectually powerful and wide-ranging ideology in support of their claims, it proved an important weapon in their fight against the aristocratic dilettante and the dispersal of power to the periphery. The principle of utility, a kind of primitive cost-benefit analysis, provided a 'rational' method for deciding between alternative courses of action; and since the policy thus arrived at was by definition productive of the greatest happiness of the greatest number, the remaining problem was simply to ensure

136. Quoted in Harold Perkin, *The Origins of Modern English Society 1789–1880*, London: Routledge and Kegan Paul, 1969, p. 282.
137. *Cf.* Michael Anderson, *Family Structure in Nineteenth Century Lancashire*, Cambridge: Cambridge University Press, 1971, pp. 107–8.

efficient and effective implementation of its provisions. Both at the level of policy formation and at the level of practical implementation, such an approach inevitably emphasized the desirability, even the necessity, of centralized professional administration, so that with scarcely a need for qualification, Benthamism may be termed 'the apotheosis of the professional ideal'.[138]

For adherents to a philosophy which claimed to have reduced the problem of choice between competing moral alternatives to a rationalistic, almost mechanical process of weighing the consequences of each, the Benthamites pursued their ideals in a curiously passionate way. The Evangelicals were content merely to try to moralize the individual within the existing social framework. The Utilitarians sought to moralize the social framework itself. The fusing of moral and practical considerations implicit in the decision 'to attach honour to actions solely in proportion to their tendency to increase the sum of happiness, lessen the sum of misery . . .',[139] should not be taken as requiring an abandonment of moral fervour to the dictates of expediency. Rather, it implied a shift in the means by which the good was to be sought, away from the individual and towards an emphasis on the centrality of social rules and policy. The Benthamite, with his emphasis on providing institutional mechanisms to uncover as well as to eliminate social evils, was in many ways a more effective moral entrepreneur than his equally self-righteous Evangelical contemporary. The Benthamite formula – inquiry, legislation, execution, inspection, and report – proved a fertile source of new laws and institutions throughout the nineteenth century, nowhere more so than in the area of lunacy reform.

The attraction of lunacy reform for both these groups is not difficult to understand. For the Evangelicals, the desire to ensure that those who had lost their reason should not also lose their souls inspired sometimes grotesque efforts to bring the lunatic the consolation of organized religion. Few groups besides the insane offered such a powerful appeal to the essentially paternalistic instincts of the Low Churchmen; and after the revelations of the 1815–16 House of Commons Select Committee, few could so readily claim the pity of the pious for their misery and degradation. Most important of all, unlike the sufferings of the new urban proletariat, reform of the conditions under which poor lunatics were kept provided a cause which could salve the consciences of the devout upper classes without posing a threat to existing social arrangements. For the Utilitarians, on the other hand, the conditions of the insane were a powerful argument against the haphazard, amateurish social policies of the past, and in favour of the rational, centralized approach they advocated. Their

---

138. Harold Perkin, *The Origins of Modern English Society*, p. 269.
139. *Westminster Review* February 1824, quoted in Asa Briggs, *The Age of Improvement*, London: Longmans, Green, 1959, p. 222.

distrust of local discretion and of the 'wisdom' of the Common Law was for them confirmed and justified by the patent anomalies and absurdities produced by the law as it stood; and by the revelations of appalling cruelty, filth, and neglect produced by a series of Parliamentary inquiries into the treatment of lunatics. In the face of apparently overwhelming evidence that the existing lack of a policy was responsible for gross inhumanity and yet perpetuated a threat to the social order in the form of madmen left at large in the community, the Benthamite insistence on the need for a coherent national policy, and Bentham's own emphasis on the value of disciplining the insane within a special institution,[140] had a natural attraction for those confronted with the problem of what to do with the insane. Not so coincidentally, of course, a centralized, bureaucratically run system also advanced the interests of the emerging administrative class from which so many of Bentham's supporters came.

8. The Cultural Meaning of Madness

Efforts to secure national legislation on the lunacy question came first from one of these Benthamite administrators, Sir George Onesiphorus Paul, a Gloucestershire magistrate who was also heavily involved in prison reform. Frustrated in his efforts to secure a charity asylum at Gloucester in association with the local infirmary, he bombarded the Home Office with complaints concerning the anomalies in existing laws dealing with lunatics and urged the establishment of a system of tax-supported asylums for their 'relief and comfort'. Eventually, in 1807, he secured the appointment of a Select Committee of the House of Commons charged with investigating 'the State of the Criminal and Pauper Lunatics in England and Wales'.

Despite the presence on this Committee of a number of the most active social reformers of the age – such men as Romilly, Whitbread, and Wilberforce – what seems most striking in retrospect are the narrow limits of its inquiries and recommendations. Over the next half century, much of the energy and public support the lunacy reformers mustered for their project was generated by the 'scandals' uncovered by successive legislative inquiries. But in contrast to these later reports, with their volumes of evidence and their impassioned calls for central intervention and direction, the 1807 Committee's activities seem curiously tame. Few witnesses testified before it, and having acknowledged that 'In many instances, but particularly in the Metropolis, parishes have adopted the system of boarding out their Insane Paupers in Private Madhouses', the Committee accepted without further inquiry the testimony of madhouse keepers that

140. Cf. Jeremy Bentham, *Panopticon; or, the Inspection House: Containing the Idea of a New Principle of Construction Applicable to Any Sort of Establishment, in which Persons of Any Description Are to be Kept Under Inspection*, London: Payne, 1791.

'their treatment in general appears to be extremely proper. . . .'[141] Claims that existing charity asylums were 'a great success' met with a similar credulousness, and the House of Commons was informed, with considerable confidence, but on the basis of no real evidence, that 'the Measure which appears to Your Committee most adequate to enforce the proper care and management of these unfortunate persons and the most likely to conduce to their perfect cure, is the erection of Asylums for their reception in different parts of the kingdom'.[142] However dubious the antecedents of this recommendation, it was accepted by Parliament, and in the following year a permissive act was passed, authorizing but not compelling magistrates to erect asylums in each county at public expense.

If the 1807 Committee had adopted the asylum solution with little prior investigation of its merits, it also provided the magistrates who were charged with building the asylums with few clear guidelines about what to build. Their report had simply urged that asylums be as large as possible in order to save expense, but 'not exceeding three hundred [inmates]'.[143] The 1808 Act instructed that a site be secured in 'an airy and healthy situation, with a good supply of water, and which may afford the probability of the vicinity of constant medical assistance'. But apart from this, and the provisions concerning finance, admissions, and discharges, the justices were left to their own devices.

Faced with the problems of what kind of institution to construct and how to administer it, those local magistrates who chose to build an asylum (and most Quarter Sessions did not) solved it in the most obvious fashion, by using existing asylums as models. Some appointed a superintendent and sent him to an older asylum to observe its procedures.[144] Others obtained the information they needed through correspondence with those running existing charity asylums, or accepted the help offered by madhouse keepers.[145]

141. House of Commons, *Report of the Select Committee on Criminal and Pauper Lunatics*, 1807, p. 6, evidence of Dr Willis.
142. House of Commons, *Report of the Select Committee on Criminal and Pauper Lunatics*, 1807, p. 6.
143. House of Commons, *Report of the Select Committee on Criminal and Pauper Lunatics*, 1807, p. 7.
144. Thus, the Cornwall County Asylum sent its 'Governor', James Duck, to Bethlem for this purpose, and Nottingham sent its superintendent, Dr Storey, to the York Retreat to observe its operations.
145. At Bedford, Whitbread, who was a vice president of St. Luke's, corresponded with Dunston, the head keeper there, obtaining a detailed list of the necessary furnishings, restraining apparatus, etc, as well as recommendations of suitable persons to serve as superintendent and matron. See Bedford Asylum Minute Book, 1812–22, p. 5 (in manuscript at the Bedfordshire Record Office, LB 1/1). The Warneford Asylum in Oxford corresponded with the committee setting up the Gloucester Asylum, and accepted the assistance of the Staffordshire madhouse keeper, Thomas Bakewell, and his son. See Warneford Ancient Book, 7 December 1812; memoranda dated 12 April and 6 June 1826; and Building Minutes, 6 June 1826 (all in the hospital archives). Bakewell made a similar offer to the Middlesex magistrates, but I can find no record of whether it was accepted (Greater London Record Office, MA/A/J1).

County asylums built from the late 1820s onwards were able to draw on the experience of their predecessors as an additional source of information. The magistrates' committee in charge of the Middlesex Asylum, for example, corresponded frequently with a number of other county asylums, seeking both architectural plans and information on the day-to-day administration of an asylum.[146] Eventually, too, it recruited William Ellis, the superintendent of the West Riding County Asylum, to fill the same position at Hanwell.

To some extent, the treatment the patients in these new asylums received depended on which older institution their asylum was modelled after. At Nottingham, for instance, under the influence of the Retreat, some effort was made to occupy the patients, to limit the amount of restraint that was used, and to classify the patients according to how refractory they were. With only one attendant for every twenty patients, however, it was but a pale imitation of its inspiration. Similarly, William Ellis, the superintendent of the West Riding Asylum, who was one of the earliest disciples of moral treatment, made strenuous efforts to introduce one of its central features, manual labour as a means of occupying the inmates, even over the initially fierce opposition of local residents frightened by the prospect of patients outside the walls of the asylum. On the other hand, at Bedford Asylum, one of the first actions of the magistrates' committee was to request and receive advice on the sorts of devices they could use to keep their inmates closely confined.[147]

The concern with security and the preservation of order within the institution, coupled with the magistrates' demands for economy, made this the more usual pattern, and ensured a fundamental similarity of approach.[148] Nowhere was the emphasis on custodialism more evident than in the architecture of such places. John Conolly, speaking during the brief period of therapeutic optimism that marked the 1840s, commented that the architects of this period 'appear to have had regard solely to the safe-keeping of the inmates, and the buildings resemble prisons rather than hospitals for the cure of insanity'. As another observer commented,

> Were we to draw our opinions on the treatment of insanity from the construction of the buildings designed for the reception of the patients, we should conclude that the great principle adopted in recovering the faculties of the mind was to immure the demented in gloomy and iron-

146. The asylums contacted included Cornwall, Lincoln, Bedford, Gloucester, Lancaster, Nottingham, Stafford, and the West Riding. See Visiting Justices' Minutes for the Middlesex Lunatic Asylum, Vol. 1, p. 10; Vol. 2, pp. 215–28, 236 (in manuscript at the Greater London Record Office, MA/A/J1, MA/A/J2).
147. Letter from Dunston to the Committee, dated 23 April 1812, included in the Asylum Minutes, in manuscript at the Bedfordshire County Record Office, LB 1/1.
148. See, for instance, *Lancaster Asylum Medical Officers' Report for 1841*, p. 4. For similar comments about conditions at the Lincoln Asylum, see Robert Gardiner Hill, *A Lecture on the Management of Lunatic Asylums*, London: Simpkin, Marshall, 1839.

bound fastnesses; that these were the means best adapted for restoring the wandering intellect, correcting its illusions, or quickening its torpidity: that the depraved or lost social affections were to be corrected or removed by coldness and monotony.[149]

As the experience of these early county asylums demonstrates, even those most heavily involved in lunacy reform lacked at the outset any clear idea of what sort of institution they ought to set up, how it was to be run, or why it would ameliorate the condition of the insane. Hence the new asylums' tendency to be modelled on the very places the reformers were within a few years to denounce so vehemently. A concern with protecting society from the disorder threatened by the raving; a desire to simplify life for those charged with administering local poorhouses and jails; and an equally unfocused and unsystematic feeling that the insane themselves deserved to be treated in a more 'humane' fashion: all these were shared in varying degrees by the earliest reformers. But they did not amount to a coherent alternative vision of what could, and should, be done.

This lack of a plausible alternative conception of how the insane might be managed was a severe handicap to the reformers. They remained trapped within the conventional assumptions of their society, and continued to defer to the 'expertise' of the mad-doctors. By so doing, they accepted practices which they themselves were later to condemn as needless cruelty. Widespread use of mechanical restraint, for instance, was made necessary by the structural deficiencies of existing asylums and by the inadequacies of available management techniques; but, as we have seen, it did not lack for sophisticated ideological justifications. Paul's frequent laudatory references to the York Asylum,[150] where chains and other means of restraint were extensively employed, make it clear that he, at least, accepted these doctrines; just as he accepted the contention that fear was the best method of managing maniacs.[151] Over a period of years, he repeatedly praised the asylum as 'the institution at York under the

149. John Conolly, *Treatment of the Insane*, p. 7; *Westminster Review* 43, 1845, p. 167.
150. See Sir George Onesiphorus Paul, 'Suggestions on the Subject of Criminal and Pauper Lunatics Addressed to Earl Spencer', reprinted in House of Commons, *Report of the Select Committee on Criminal and Pauper Lunatics*, 1807, pp. 14–20; *idem.*, *Minutes of Proceedings Relative to the Establishment of a General Lunatic Asylum, Near the City of Glocester*, [Gloucester], 1796; *idem.*, *Address to Subscribers to the Gloucester Lunatic Asylum*, Gloucester: for the author, 1810; *idem.*, *Observations on the Subject of Lunatic Asylums*, Gloucester: Walker, 1812, esp. pp. 28–37. Hunter himself had corresponded with Paul even earlier, giving him advice about how to organize a lunatic asylum. See *A Scheme of an Institution, and a Description of a Plan, for a General Lunatic Asylum, for the Western Counties, to Be Built in or Near the City of Glocester*, [Gloucester], 1794, p. 1.
151. 'I know it to be the opinion of medical men conversant with this malady, that although Maniacs have not the power of combining ideas, or of drawing effects from causes by deduction, yet they possess a cunning and instinctive penetration, which makes them apprehend consequences from acts, and indeed to fear them; for they are universally cowardly. It is by keeping up this apprehension on their minds, that they are so easily governed in numbers by the modern system of treating them.' G. Paul, 'Suggestions on . . . Pauper Lunatics', p. 16.

excellent management of Dr Hunter' and urged it as a model which those building public asylums should strive to emulate. Yet within less than a decade, the York Asylum came to symbolize all that the reformers sought to abolish.

As this should suggest, the perception that the traditional ways of coping with lunatics in madhouses (even such things as the use of fear, coercion, and chains to maintain a semblance of order) were inherently cruel and inhumane is by no means as simple and self-evident a judgement as both the reformers and later generations came to believe. The practices of eighteenth-century madhouse keepers seem so transparently callous and brutal that we tend to take this judgement as unproblematic, as immediately given to any and all who have occasion to view such actions. The value of Paul's case is that it demonstrates so clearly the shallowness and fallacy of such an assumption. The reformers were eager to portray their activities as motivated by a kind of disinterested moral superiority, and to picture their opponents as moral lepers, devoid of common decency and humanity. However useful such an outlook may be as support for one's own sense of self-righteousness, it remains without analytic utility. Indeed, it has been our readiness to take such claims at face value that has blinded us to a central feature of the reform process, which is that it both reflected and helped to produce a transformation in the moral boundaries of the community.

In crucial ways, I shall suggest, the constitution and consummation of the reformers' project was dependent upon (even as it helped to bring into being) a profound shift in the cultural understanding of madness. That metamorphosis proved vital in creating and sustaining the moral outrage which drove the whole process forward; and it was equally essential in giving shape and substance to the alternative approach to managing the mad for which the reformers were such effective proselytizers. Yet the very success of that series of transformations has served to distort and obscure our understanding of a prior set of approaches and responses to the lunatic which were now abandoned; and our uncritical embrace of nineteenth-century assessments of the Augustan age – assessments which were at once self-interested and uncomprehending – has simultaneously and unwittingly also helped to mask and misrepresent the true character of the Victorian reforms themselves.

Cruelty, like deviance, 'is not a quality which lies in behavior itself, but in the interaction between the person who commits the act and those who respond to it'.[152] Consequently, whether or not a set of practices is perceived as inhumane depends, in large part, on the world-view of the person who is doing the perceiving. We have seen how practices from which we now recoil in horror were once advocated by the most eminent physicians and cultured men of their day. That madmen were manacled

152. Howard Becker, *Outsiders*, Glencoe, Illinois: Free Press, 1963, p. 14.

and menaced in asylums in the eighteenth century was well known at the time. How could it be otherwise when, as we have seen, the most eminent writers on insanity openly advocated the routine employment of fear and mechanical restraint in managing the mad? Certainly, such practices were not something of which magistrates only became aware at the turn of the century. Yet it was only then that protests began to be heard that such treatment was cruel and inhumane, and that the underlying logic of these practices, the attempt to *tame* madness, was seriously misguided.[153]

To be sure, some of the treatment meted out to lunatics in private madhouses was the natural product of an unregulated free market in madness – the consequence of the unchecked cupidity of the least scrupulous, of the incentives to half-starve and neglect pauper inmates, of the temptation to rely on force as the least troublesome form of control. But there is more to it than that. Even in situations where such factors were obviously inapplicable, lunatics were treated in ways which later generations were to condemn as barbaric and counter-productive – in ways which they (and we) find virtually incomprehensible and almost by default attribute to an underdeveloped moral sensibility, if not outright inhumanity. The treatment of George III during his recurrent bouts of 'mania' makes this point most dramatically and unambiguously, and it is surely significant that Willis's treatment of him would have been unthinkable only a decade or two later.

One is inescapably led to the conclusion that a necessary condition for the emergence of the moral outrage which animated the lunacy reformers was a transformation of the cultural meaning of madness. Such a change can indeed be shown to have occurred. I have suggested that in seventeenth- and eighteenth-century practice, the madman was often treated no better than a beast; for that was precisely what, according to the prevailing paradigm of insanity, he was. In becoming crazy, the lunatic had lost the essence of his humanity, his reason. Pascal's view was typical: 'I can easily conceive of a man without hands, feet, head (for it is only experience which teaches us that the head is more necessary than the feet). But I cannot conceive of a man without thought; that would be a stone or a brute.'[154] Eminent mad-doctors of the early nineteenth century continued to adhere to this position, arguing that 'If possession of reason be the proud attribute of humanity, its diseases must be ranked among our greatest afflictions, since they sink us from our pre-eminence to a level with animal creatures.'[155]

153. Jonathan Andrews has recently reaffirmed, following a systematic review of the available evidence, that 'Few . . . had raised their voices against the liberal recourse to restraint at lunatic hospitals before the 1790s'. 'Bedlam Revisited', p. 205. I have illustrated above the persistent recourse among leading late eighteenth-century practitioners to a language of fear, force, and constraint, and their overt reliance on a technology designed to intimidate and coerce their charges into right-thinking.
154. Blaise Pascal, *Œuvres Complètes*, Paris: Gallimard, 1954, p. 1156.
155. Joseph Mason Cox, *Practical Observations on Insanity*, 3rd edition, p. ix.

It was this world view which the nineteenth-century reformers, and, indeed, society as a whole, were in the process of abandoning. Much of the reformers' revulsion on being exposed to conditions in contemporary madhouses derived from this changed perspective. For them, the lunatic was no longer an animal, stripped of all remnants of humanity. On the contrary, he remained in essence a man; a man lacking in self-restraint and order, but a man for all that. Moreover, the qualities he lacked might and must be restored to him, so that he could once more function as a sober, rational citizen.

Of course, the replacement of the traditional perspective did not come all at once. 'Unenlightened' circles clung to it long after it had been displaced as the dominant orthodoxy; by which time actions based on it were incomprehensible, and its adherents drew upon themselves the stigma of inhumanity. Paul's continuing attachment in the early years of the century to the doctrine that chains and the inculcation of fear were the best means of managing madness demonstrates that even the reformers did not succeed at a stroke in freeing themselves from the past (though this peculiarity has been overlooked by earlier historians since it conflicts with their notion of a simple humanitarianism as the well-spring of reform). Furthermore, once it is recognized that to a large extent what divided the reformers and their opponents was not the morality of one group and the immorality of the other, but rather the existence of two mutually contradictory paradigms of the essence of insanity, certain otherwise incomprehensible incidents in the history of reform begin to lose their air of paradox.

For example, one of the situations which the reformers were able to exploit to greatest advantage was their discovery of the conditions under which a Bethlem inmate, James Norris, had been kept, night and day, for somewhere between nine and fourteen years. Norris was found to be restrained by a specially constructed piece of apparatus: an iron cage encased his body from the neck down, and this in turn was attached by a short chain to an iron bar running from the floor to the ceiling of the cell. The degree of confinement was such that he could lie only on his back, and could advance no more than twelve inches from the bar to which he was attached. The keepers admitted that he had been restrained in this fashion, day and night, for at least nine years – a practice they justified by insisting on his potential for violence (Norris had attacked his keeper and fellow patients on a number of occasions), and by emphasizing that his peculiar bone structure rendered the traditional chains and handcuffs useless, since he could discard them at will.[156] The most curious aspect of all this was not that a man should be found confined in such a fashion – for

156. Remarkably, Wakefield and his party found that Norris was still able to converse rationally on a wide range of topics, though he was obviously weakened by the effects of his long confinement, and by the tuberculosis which he had contracted.

WILLIAM NORRIS:

Confined in this Manner in Bethlem Hospital.

Sketch'd from the Life May 2, 1814; & Etch'd by G. Arnald A.R.A.

Fig. 10   On their second visit to Bethlem, Wakefield's party of reformers brought with them an artist, G. Arnald, who sketched a picture of Norris in his iron cage. This picture was mass-produced in the form of cheap engravings and used to great effect by the reformers.

his treatment was merely a particularly dramatic example of the mechanical restraint which was widely and openly used at the time. Rather it lies in the response of the hospital authorities. Compelled to institute an official inquiry, the governors conceded that the facts were as the reformers had stated them, but contended that the confinement was kind and merciful rather than cruel and brutal, and expressed their undiminished confidence in the asylum's medical officers.[157]

One can place two possible interpretations on this bizarre state of affairs. Either the governors shared the callousness of their subordinates and were ingenuous enough to let this show; or their protestations were sincere, and they genuinely saw nothing wrong with treating a lunatic in such a fashion. The latter is surely the more plausible: and it is precisely what one would expect of men who still adhered to the long-established orthodox view that the lunatics were to be mastered by discipline and depletion; who lacked the alternative weapons for managing the recalcitrant which moral treatment apparently provided; and who still looked at madness in terms of the earlier paradigm[158] – of which conditions in Bethlem were almost an exact reflection.[159]

157. See *Report from the Committee of Governors of Bethlem Hospital, to the General Court Appointed to Inquire into the Case of James Norris*, reprinted as an appendix of the *Report* of the 1815 Select Committee on Madhouses. Reluctantly, the governors eventually ordered Norris's release from his restraints, only to have him inconveniently die shortly thereafter from his consumption.

158. Compare John Haslam's unblushing admission, before hostile inquisitors, that he made use of chains and other forms of mechanical restraint to render 'the most outrageous Maniac . . . an innoxious animal'. House of Commons, *Report of the Select Committee on Madhouses*, 1815, pp. 63, 67.

159. Patricia Allderidge has objected strenuously to this line of argument, contending that it unfairly maligns her hospital. She makes much of the case of James Tilly Matthews, who was confined in Bethlem for well over a decade, beginning in 1797. Matthews believed himself privy to an extraordinary plot by French revolutionaries to employ Mesmeric gangs to magnetize and take control of the British government, making use of 'airlooms' designed to transmit waves of animal magnetism. His own attempt to expose the plot had, he alleged, brought about his confinement in Bethlem, where he was assailed by airborne tortures involving 'foot-curving, lethargy-making, spark-exploding, knee-nailing, burning out, eye-screwing, sight-screwing, roof-stringing, vital-tearing, fibre-ripping' attacks on his person. Yet throughout his confinement, as Allderidge points out, he was allowed to write and draw, and even awarded a premium of 30 pounds by the hospital governors when, in 1810, he produced a set of plans for a new Bethlem Hospital. Here, she triumphantly concludes, is a decisive refutation of the image of a Bedlam wedded to the classical conception of madness. ('Bedlam: Fact or Fiction?', pp. 25–7.) I think not. Notwithstanding his remarkable delusions, Matthews was, after all, a gentle, mild-mannered, and appealing figure, precisely one of those 'more remissly Mad' people whom Thomas Willis had declared, as much as a hundred and fifty years earlier, were 'healed more often with flatteries, and with more gentle Physick'. (*Two Discourses Concerning the Soul of Brutes*, p. 206.) There was ample room within the traditional paradigm of insanity – as I have pointed out – for such variations in treatment. Moreover, the testimony of the Bethlem staff before the 1815 Select Committee on Madhouses repeatedly demonstrates their affection for him, their adoption of this odd fellow as a kind of pet or mascot; while the same testimony documents clearly enough the sharply contrasting fate of the run-of-the-mill, less privileged patients, those whom the attendants found more troublesome. (On

Such 'backward' attitudes persisted even longer in provincial settings. In 1843, for example, the Metropolitan Commissioners in Lunacy, as part of a national survey of conditions in madhouses, visited the West Auckland Licensed House a matter of hours after the local magistrates had inspected it. The former pronounced it 'utterly unfit'; the latter reported 'everything in good order'.[160] The sheer perverseness of this judgement from the reformers' perspective is the clearest evidence that their standards were not universally shared, even by the middle of the century;[161] and these different criteria of evaluation were one reason local power centres resisted efforts to set up a system of nationally supervised, publicly supported asylums.[162]

9. Moral Treatment and the York Retreat

At the outset, those who denied the legitimacy of the treatment meted out by traditional madhouse keepers, and who sought to establish a paradigm which would declare such conduct to be purposively illegitimate, faced the difficult task of overcoming the charge that their ideas were no more than the Utopian schemes of an abstract benevolence, unschooled by contact with the realities of day-to-day management of lunatics. As Samuel Tuke remarked, 'Benevolent persons in various places had long been dissatisfied with the system of management generally pursued, but

Matthews, see John Haslam's *Illustrations of Madness*, first published in 1810, and Roy Porter's introduction to the Tavistock reprint edn, London: Routledge, 1989.)

    The testimony of medical men before the 1828 Select Committee of the House of Lords provides, I think, still further support for the position I take here. Attempting to resist legislative interference in the mad-business, and to defend professional practice against oversight by outsiders, leading physicians nevertheless quite openly defended practices reformers found totally unacceptable. John Latham, President of the Royal College of Physicians (and previously one of those the College had delegated to inspect metropolitan madhouses), stoutly defended the use of coercion, quoting from the Bible in support of chaining lunatics up; and his colleague William Heberden pronounced the use of cribs and straw entirely appropriate when dealing with so-called 'dirty patients'. *Minutes of Evidence before the Select Committee of the House of Lords [on] the Bill . . . to Amend the Laws Relating to County Asylums*, 1828, pp. 65, 99.

160. Quoted in Kathleen Jones, *Lunacy, Law, and Conscience 1744–1845*, London: Routledge and Kegan Paul, 1955, p. 179.

161. Compare also, on this point, John Walton's discussion of conditions in the Lancaster County Asylum in the 1830s, which reaches similar conclusions about the gulf between the reformers' standards and what was sufficient to satisfy the expectations of the local justices. John Walton, 'The Treatment of Pauper Lunatics in Victorian England: The Case of Lancaster Asylum, 1816–1870', in A. Scull (ed.) *Madhouses, Mad-doctors, and Madmen*, Philadelphia: University of Pennsylvania Press/London: Athlone, 1981, pp. 171–2.

162. As Parry-Jones points out, another powerful motive for opposing the reformers' schemes was straightforwardly financial: county expenditures were already rising rapidly in the early nineteenth century. Demand for better communications prompted the construction or improvement of roads and bridges, and magistrates faced simultaneous pressures to provide more jails and workhouses. W. Parry-Jones, *The Trade in Lunacy*, p. 15.

benevolent theory was powerless when opposed by practical experience.'[163] Fortunately for the reformers, a number of madhouse keepers were by now groping towards methods of managing and 'treating' patients which showed that it was indeed possible to eliminate most of the 'barbarous' and 'objectionable' features of the contemporary asylum. Men like John Ferriar at the Manchester Lunatic Asylum and Edward Long Fox at his madhouse for aristocrats, Brislington House, were becoming convinced that 'the first salutary operation in the mind of a lunatic' lay in 'creating a habit of self-restraint . . .', a goal which might be reached by 'the management of hope and apprehension . . . , small favours, the show of confidence, and apparent distinction . . .', rather than by coercion.[164] In the event, though, it was the fundamentally similar notions developed by the Tuke family at the York Retreat which became nationally known and, under the guise of 'moral treatment', virtually synonymous with the very idea of reform.[165]

The proximate cause of the establishment of the Retreat in 1792 had been a purely local scandal, involving the death under mysterious circumstances of a Quaker patient at the local charity institution, the York Asylum.[166] Following the repeated urgings of William Tuke, a local tea and coffee merchant, the Quaker community was stimulated by this to construct an asylum of their own for those Friends 'deprived of the use of their reason'. Notwithstanding the apparent obscurity of its provincial, sectarian origins, the Retreat, from a quite early date in its history, attracted the attention of an occasional visitor concerned with the plight of the insane. The first tribute to its achievements came from a Swiss physician, Gaspar de la Rive, within two years of its opening, though this attracted more attention on the Continent than in England.[167] Twelve years later, the Glasgow architect, William Stark, publicized the Tukes' activities rather more successfully. Stark's pamphlet, *Remarks on the Construction of Public Hospitals for the Care of Mental Derangement*,[168] attracted considerable attention among those interested in lunacy reform. In consequence, his long eulogy on the practices at the Retreat led to a spate of inquiries and visits by the philanthropically inclined. Thus encouraged, the founder's grandson, Samuel Tuke, decided to publish an account of the institution and of the methods of treatment pursued in it. The appearance of this

163. Quoted in R. Hunter and I. MacAlpine, introduction to Samuel Tuke, *Description of the Retreat*, facsimile edition, London: Dawson, 1964, p. 5.
164. John Ferriar, *Medical Histories and Reflections*, Vol. 2, London: Cadell and Davies, 1795, pp. 111–2.
165. *Cf.* Anne Digby's definitive history, *Madness, Morality and Medicine: A Study of the York Retreat 1796–1914*, Cambridge: Cambridge University Press, 1985.
166. *Cf. ibid.*, pp. 15–8, for the death of Hannah Mills and the subsequent fundraising effort.
167. Gaspar de la Rive, *Lettre addressée aux rédacteurs de la Bibliothèque britannique sur un nouvel établissement pour la guérison des aliénés*, Geneva: for the author, 1798.
168. W. Stark, *Remarks on the Construction of Public Hospitals for the Care of Mental Derangement*, 2nd edn, Glasgow: Hedderwick, 1810.

book in 1813, and the subsequent favourable notice by Sidney Smith in the *Edinburgh Review*, brought the Retreat national attention.

One cannot readily summarize in a phrase or two what moral treatment consisted of, nor reduce it to a few standard formulae, for it was emphatically not a specific technique. Rather it was a general, pragmatic approach which recognized the lunatic's sensibility and acknowledged (albeit in a highly limited and circumscribed sense) his status as a moral subject. In Sydney Smith's words, 'It does not appear to [the operators of the Retreat] that because a man is mad on one subject, that he is to be considered in a state of complete mental degradation, or insensible to feelings of gratitude.'[169] Consequently, and contrary to previous practice, Tuke held that the madman must not be addressed 'in a childish or . . . domineering manner',[170] for this approach threatened to subvert the effort to rouse his 'moral feelings' and to use these as 'a sort of moral discipline'.[171] As one of Tuke's contemporaries put it, 'Certainly authority and order must be maintained, but these are better maintained by kindness, condescension, and indulgent attention, than by any severities whatsoever. Lunatics are not devoid of understanding, nor should they be treated as if they were; on the contrary, they should be treated as rational beings.'[172]

The emphasis on lunatics' sensitivity to many of the same inducements and emotions to which other people were prone was associated, whether as cause or consequence, with other equally profound alterations in their treatment. What was seen as perhaps the most striking, both at the time and subsequently, was the insistence on minimizing external, physical coercion – an insistence which has had much to do with the interpretation of moral treatment as unproblematically 'kind' and 'humane'.[173] William

169. [Sydney Smith], 'An Account of the Retreat', *Edinburgh Review* 23, 1814, pp. 189–198.
170. S. Tuke, *Description of the Retreat*, p. 159.
171. T. Bakewell, *The Domestic Guide in Cases of Insanity*, p. 59.
172. *Ibid.*, pp. 55–6. In her *Madness, Morality and Medicine* (p. 35), Anne Digby has suggested that 'the Retreat's lay therapists drew upon a Protestant dissenting tradition of religious healing that was non-institutional and had lasting popular appeal'. This is an intriguing notion, though she provides little more than speculation in its support. She does succeed in showing, however, that the 'moral' treatment at the Retreat originally welded together the psychological and the normative in some recognizably and distinctively Quaker ways.
173. Almost equally striking was the Retreat's architecture: self-consciously domestic, resembling, in the words of a Swiss visitor, 'une grande ferme rustique', clean, neat, and comfortable. Completely unostentatious, it avoided any appearance of a place of confinement. Tuke's determination to sustain this illusion even extended as far as disguising the iron bars on the glazed windows by encasing them within wooden sashes, and muffling the locks on the interior doors, lest the noise of keys turning in them should awaken the wrong sentiments in the minds of the inmates. William Stark was one of a number of visitors who commented on the 'air of comfort and contentment' which resulted, and the 'delicacy' with which 'the smaller feelings of the patients' were attended to. Quoted in S. Tuke, *Description of the Retreat*, p. 225. The notion of the purpose-built asylum acquires a thoroughly novel meaning in this context.

Cullen had articulated the eighteenth-century consensus when he contended that

> Restraining the anger and violence of madmen is always necessary for preventing their hurting themselves or others; but this restraint is also to be considered as a remedy. Angry passions are always rendered more violent by the indulgence of the impetuous notions they produce; and even in madmen, the feeling of restraint will sometimes prevent the efforts which their passion would otherwise occasion. Restraint, therefore, is useful and ought to be complete.[174]

Tuke's dissent from this position was sharp and unequivocal: 'Neither chains nor corporal punishment are tolerated, on any pretext, in this establishment.'[175] Less objectionable forms of restraint might be necessary to prevent bodily injury, but these ought to be a last resort, and were never to be indulged in solely for the convenience of the attendants. While Tuke did not think that restraint could entirely be done away with, he did insist on doing away with its most oppressive forms – 'gyves, chains, and manacles'[176] – and his refusal to employ it as a routine measure was a marked departure from contemporary practice. It made a profound impact on contemporary reformers, who saw his success as proof that the insane could be managed without what were now seen as harshness and cruelty.[177]

Yet this was no 'kindness for kindness' sake.[178] From its architecture to its domestic arrangements, the Retreat was designed to encourage the individual's own efforts to reassert his powers of self-control. For instead of merely resting content with controlling those who were no longer quite human, which had been the dominant concern of traditional responses to the mad, moral treatment actively sought to *transform* the lunatic, to remodel him into something approximating the bourgeois ideal of the rational individual. The problem with external coercion was that it could

---

174. William Cullen, *First Lines in the Practice of Physic*, Vol. 2, Edinburgh: Bell and Bradfute, 1808, pp. 312–3.
175. S. Tuke, *Description of the Retreat*, p. 141.
176. *Ibid.*, pp. vi, 171.
177. The novelty of the approach, and the consequent impact on those becoming acquainted with practices at the Retreat, are evident in the comments of numerous visitors. *Cf.* York Retreat Visitors' Book, 1798–1822, Borthwick Institute of Historical Research, York, D/3/1.
178. Indeed, one of the most able publicists of moral treatment was later to insist that 'There is a fallacy even in conceiving that Moral Treatment consists in being kind and humane to the insane.' W.A.F. Browne, 'The Moral Treatment of the Insane: A Lecture', *Journal of Mental Science* 10, 1864, pp. 311–2. Kindness certainly entered the picture, but 'the purely benevolent physician can never be a good practitioner'. On the contrary, it was a grave error to exhibit 'a barren sympathy' for the mad. Nothing could be more counterproductive than to 'indulge vicious propensities, [or] . . . give way to unreasonable demands . . . , [or] be active in soothing momentary pangs at the sacrifice of permanent peace'. *What Asylums Were, Are, and Ought to Be*, Edinburgh: Black, 1837, p. 179.

force outward conformity, but never the essential internalization of moral standards. The change in aim mandated a change in means.

Granted, 'it takes less trouble to fetter by means of cords, than by assiduities of sympathy or affection'.[179] But 'the natural tendency of such treatment is, to degrade the mind of the patient, and to make him indifferent to those moral feelings, which, under judicious direction and encouragement, are found capable, in no small degree, to strengthen the power of self-restraint'.[180] On purely *instrumental* grounds, then, those who rejected traditional modes of managing the mad urged that 'tenderness is better than torture, kindness more effectual than constraint. . . . Nothing has a more favourable and controlling influence over one who is disposed to or actually affected with melancholy or mania, than an exhibition of friendship or philanthropy.'[181]

Here was a thoroughgoing rejection of traditional modes of managing the mad (as well as the rationales underlying them). It was not just that the outwardly visible apparatus of physical restraint and coercion had begun to lose its legitimacy (a process that was to culminate a generation later in Gardiner Hill's and Conolly's triumphant claims to have abolished mechanical restraint entirely).[182] Rather, the very attempt to *tame* madness was increasingly seen as seriously misguided. Samuel Tuke commented that, by means of terror, lunatics

> may be made to obey their keepers with the greatest promptitude, to rise, to sit, to stand, to walk, or to run at their pleasure; though only expressed by a look. Such an obedience, and even the appearance of affection, we not infrequently see in the poor animals who are exhibited to gratify our curiosity in natural history; but, who can avoid reflecting, in observing such spectacles, that the readiness with which the savage tiger obeys his master, is the result of treatment at which humanity would shudder?[183]

Within the new orthodoxy, attempts to *compel* patients to think and act reasonably would themselves come to be stigmatized as unreasonable;[184] and formerly respectable therapeutic techniques would ultimately be viewed with a mixture of incomprehension and moral outrage.[185]

179. John Reid, *Essays on Hypochondriasis and Other Nervous Affections*, 3rd edn, London: Longman, 1823, p. 303.
180. S. Tuke, *Description of the Retreat*, pp. 159–60.
181. J. Reid, *Essays on Hypochondriasis*, pp. 303–4.
182. Robert Gardiner Hill, *A Lecture on the Management of Lunatic Asylums and the Treatment of the Insane*, London: Simpkin, Marshall, 1839; John Conolly, *The Treatment of the Insane without Mechanical Restraints*, London: Smith, Elder, 1856.
183. S. Tuke, *Description of the Retreat*, pp. 147–8.
184. *Cf.* Hanwell Lunatic Asylum, *Annual Report*, 1840, pp. 55–6, 70; T. Harrington Tuke, 'On Warm and Cold Baths in the Treatment of Insanity', *Journal of Mental Science* 5, 1858, p. 102.
185. *Cf.* Samuel Tuke's condemnation of 'those swingings, whirlings, suspensions, half-drownings and other violent expedients by which some physicians have sought to

In contrast, Tuke and his followers insisted that only by 'treating the patient as much in the manner of a rational being, as the state of mind will possibly allow', could one hope to re-educate him to discipline himself. Fortunately, and contrary to what was commonly assumed, madmen were not wholly deprived of their reason: 'Their intellectual, active, and moral powers, are usually rather perverted than obliterated; and it happens, not infrequently that one faculty only is affected.'[186] By acting as though 'patients are considered capable of rational and honourable inducement . . . ,' and making use of the vital weapon of man's *desire for esteem*, inmates could be induced to collaborate in their own recapture by the forces of reason. Walking, talking, taking tea with their superintendent, all within the confines of a carefully constructed therapeutic environment, patients were to be taught to restrain themselves. 'When properly cultivated', the desire to look well in others' eyes 'leads many to struggle to conceal and overcome their morbid propensities; and, at least, materially assists them in confining their deviations within such bounds, as do not make them obnoxious to the family'.[187] Madness could thus be reined in amid the

frighten the unhappy subject into reason, or at least into subjection'. 'Introductory Observations' to Maximilian Jacobi, *On the Construction and Management of Hospitals for the Insane*, London: Churchill, 1841, p. 54. In the face of this rapid shift in public sentiment, Cox's swinging chair enjoyed a remarkably brief half-life: by 1828, George Man Burrows was lamenting that, despite his personal conviction of the swing's therapeutic value, he dared not make use of it, fearing lest, given 'the morbid sensitivity of modern pseudo-philanthropy', any accident attending its use would leave him 'universally decried, his reputation blasted, and his family ruined'. *Commentaries on . . . Insanity*, p. 606. Twenty-five years later, such once respectable treatments had lost their last shreds of plausibility, being denounced by Charles Dickens as symptomatic of the mad-doctors' 'wildly extravagant . . . monstrously cruel monomania', the product of a bizarre insistence that 'the most violent and certain means of driving a man mad, were the only hopeful means of restoring him to reason'. C. Dickens and W.H. Wills, 'A Curious Dance Around a Curious Tree', p. 385.

186. S. Tuke, *Description of the Retreat*, pp. 133–4. There are echoes here of Locke's insistence that the mad had retained some portion of their reason: 'For [lunatics] do not appear to me to have lost the faculty of reasoning, but having joined together some ideas very wrongly, they mistake them for truths, and they err as men do that argue right from wrong principles. For, by the violence of their imaginations, having taken their fancies for realities, they make right deductions from them.' *An Essay Concerning Human Understanding*, London: Everyman, 1965, Book 1, p. 127. Locke's emphasis on misassociation and error was here employed to justify an approach based on reeducating the mad and reconditioning their minds to 'normality'. I have already stressed, however, that proponents of the older, heroic approach could with equal justice have defended their practices on Lockean grounds. The very existence of these diametrically opposed 'implications' of Locke's ideas surely points up the limitations of any purely internalist account of changing responses to madness.

187. S. Tuke, *Description of the Retreat*, p. 157. The emphasis on 'concealing' morbid propensities points up a central assumption of Tuke's therapeutics: a person's madness was not to be reasoned with or refuted. This was a useless, even a dangerous endeavour. Rather, its content was to be ignored; its existence, the patient had to be taught to suppress. *Cf.* Samuel Tuke's comment that 'No advantage has been found to arise from reasoning with them on their particular hallucinations. . . . In regard to melancholics, conversation on the subject of their despondency is found to be highly injudicious. The very opposite method is pursued. Every means is taken to seduce the mind from its favourite but unhappy musings, by bodily exercise, walks, conversation,

comforts of domesticity by the invisible yet infinitely potent fetters of the sufferer's own desire to please others, complemented by the benevolent authoritarianism of the asylum superintendent and the healthful influences of the new moral architecture.

The staff played a vital role in the re-education process: they must 'treat the patients on the fundamental principles of . . . kindness and consideration'.[188] Again, this was not because these were good in themselves, but because

> whatever tends to promote the happiness of the patient, is found to increase his desire to restrain himself, by exciting the wish not to forfeit his enjoyments; and lessening the irritation of mind which too frequently accompanies mental derangement. . . . The comfort of the patients is therefore considered of the highest importance in a curative point of view.[189]

Here, too, lay the value of work, the other major cornerstone of moral treatment, since 'of all the modes by which the patients may be induced to restrain themselves, regular employment is perhaps the most generally efficacious'.[190] Taken together, these instruments of moral treatment constituted in every respect 'a more powerful lever in acting upon the intractable'[191] than the fear and physical coercion that had previously been seen as indispensable.

By all reasonable standards, the Retreat was an outstandingly successful experiment.[192] It had demonstrated, to the reformers' satisfaction at least, that the supposedly continuous danger and frenzy to be anticipated from maniacs were the consequence of, rather than the justification for, harsh and misguided methods of management and restraint; indeed, that this reputation was in large part the self-serving creation of the madhouse keepers. It apparently showed that the asylum could provide a comfortable

reading, and other innocent recreations.' *Description of the Retreat*, pp. 151–2. Here, Tuke was in agreement with most medical opinion. Joseph Mason Cox had earlier insisted that 'Reasoning with maniacs is generally useless . . . the talking *at* will generally be found more efficacious than talking *to* a patient'. *Practical Observations on Insanity*, 1st edn, p. 45. Spurzheim was subsequently even more emphatic: 'All practitioners . . . who have conversed with insane persons, and tried to exhibit logic as a remedy for insanity, agree that such a treatment is attended with little success. . . . All argument, therefore, should be avoided. On the whole, the less notice there can be taken even of the most obstinate fancies of the insane, the less disposed they will be to retain them.' Johann Gaspar Spurzheim, *Observations on the Deranged Manifestations of the Mind, or Insanity*, London: Baldwin, Craddock, and Joy, 1817, p. 248.

188. S. Tuke, *Description of the Retreat*, p. 177.
189. *Ibid.*
190. *Ibid.*, p. 156.
191. W.A.F. Browne, *What Asylums Were, Are, and Ought to Be*, p. 156.
192. As Anne Digby points out, the remarks made by early nineteenth-century visitors provide eloquent testimony to the novelty of the approach at the Retreat; simultaneously, their comments suggest 'that at the Retreat reality reflected rhetoric and that practice did not fall too far short of its ideals'. *Madness, Morality and Medicine*, pp. 29–30.

Fig. 11   An engraving by Cooper after Cave of the original building of the York Retreat, opened in 1796, taken from D.H. Tuke, *Reform in the Treatment of the Insane: Early History of the York Retreat, York* (London: Churchill, 1892). At the front were gardens and only a small fence. The domestic architecture reminded one early visitor of 'une grande ferme rustique'. The impression of a place of confinement was further diminished by avoiding bars on the windows (instead, the frames and partitions were made of iron, painted to look like wood); and by building the wall around the exercising courts (behind the main building) at the bottom of a slope, allowing the inmates unhampered views over the surrounding countryside.

and forgiving environment, where those who could not cope with the world could find respite, and where, in a familial atmosphere, they might be spared the neglect that would otherwise have been their lot. Perhaps even more impressive than that was the fact that, despite a conservative outlook which classified as cured no one who had to be readmitted to an asylum, the statistics collected during the Retreat's first fifteen years of operation seemed to show that moral treatment could restore a large proportion of cases to sanity. Of those whose insanity was of recent origin, twenty-one out of thirty-one diagnosed as cases of mania had recovered; nineteen out of thirty cases of melancholia were restored; and four others were sufficiently improved that they no longer required confinement. Even among long-standing and apparently hopeless cases, a respectable number were discharged as recovered.[193]

193.   Ten of sixty-one classed as maniacs, and six of twenty-one melancholics. S. Tuke, *Description of the Retreat*, pp. 202–3. All the figures Tuke provided were for the period 1796–1811.

10. Sources of the Changing Conceptions of Insanity

One must grant the importance of changing conceptions of madness and its treatment as an intervening cause in the rise of the lunacy reform movement. But of course ideas and conceptions of human nature do not change in a vacuum. They arise from a concrete basis in actual human relations. Put slightly differently, the ways in which people look at the world are conditioned by their activity in it. The question which we must therefore address is what changes in the social conditions of existence lie behind the changes we have just examined.

In a society still dominated by subsistence forms of agriculture, nature rather than man is the source of activity. Just as man's role in actively remaking the world is underdeveloped and scarcely perceived – favouring theological and supernatural rather than anthropocentric accounts of the physical and social environment – so too the possibilities for transforming human beings themselves go largely unrecognized and the techniques for doing so remain strikingly primitive. In a world not humanly but divinely authored, 'to attempt reform was not only to change men, but even more awesome, to change a universe responding to and reflecting God's will' – to embark on a course akin to sacrilege.[194] And where the rationalizing impact of the marketplace is still weak, structures of domination tend to remain *extensive* rather than intensive – that is, the quality and character of the workforce are taken as given rather than plastic and amenable to improvement through appropriate management and training.

But under the rationalization forced by competition, people's active role in the process presents itself ever more insistently to their consciousness. The hazards and insecurities of most people's lives in the sixteenth and seventeenth centuries, their extreme vulnerability to physical and economic misfortune, and the general absence of well-developed economic and social institutions to mitigate the impact of events which threatened financial and social ruin, all encouraged the widespread resort to magical and religious practices and accounts of daily life.[195] But the Providence-dominated world of early modern England, the cosmos alive with spirits and witches, astrologers and the occult, the divinity and the devil, steadily gave ground in the eighteenth century, being replaced 'by the world of expanding knowledge and science, of discoverable nature and rational exploration'.[196]

---

194. Howard Solomon, *Public Welfare, Science, and Propaganda in Seventeenth Century France*, Princeton: Princeton University Press, 1972, pp. 29–30.
195. *Cf.* Keith Thomas, *Religion and the Decline of Magic*, Harmondsworth: Penguin, 1973, esp. chapter 1. Richard Napier's casebooks, analysed in Michael MacDonald's *Mystical Bedlam*, provide much evidence in support of this generalization.
196. J.H. Plumb, 'The Acceptance of Modernity', in Neil McKendrick, John Brewer, and J.H. Plumb, *The Birth of a Consumer Society: The Commercialization of Eighteenth Century England*, Bloomington, Indiana: Indiana University Press, 1982, p. 333.

The commercialization of society, the transformation and improvement of material life for large segments of the population, the massive reorientation and expansion of the economy, and the associated arrival of a world in which human invention and creation were all-pervasive phenomena – these developments necessarily altered the mental universe, not just of a privileged elite, but of increasingly sizeable portions of the population at large.[197] Feverish commercial activity was matched (and necessarily so) by an almost frenzied propensity to consume, and the logic and dynamism of the marketplace reached into every crevice and corner of English society, bringing with it the taste for innovation, for novelty, and for 'improvement'. New attitudes to the world were being inculcated, often unconsciously and certainly unintentionally, and their effects ramified in all directions.[198]

Agriculture, of course, still absorbed the energies of the bulk of the workforce. Yet so far from rural society being immune to the changes I have discussed, they 'spread through it like a contagion'.[199] Even the appearance of the countryside was dramatically transformed over the course of the eighteenth century, as the commercialization of agriculture accelerated the enclosure of the land; and as improvements in transportation and communication – the roads and canals that were at once produced by, and the precursor and precondition for, further expansion of the market – changed the face of the landscape and brought peripheral communities into contact with a wider world.[200] Most significantly of all for our present concerns, there was the importation of new flora and fauna, and the deliberate creation of new varieties of familiar forms, through selective breeding of animals, birds, fish, vegetables, and fruits – a process that accelerated markedly past mid-century. Earlier, these efforts had provoked some of the traditional concerns about the propriety of interfer-

197. In Neil McKendrick's words, 'the later eighteenth century saw such a convulsion of getting and spending, such an eruption of new prosperity, and such an explosion of new production and marketing techniques, that a greater proportion of the population than in any previous society in human history was able to enjoy the pleasures of buying consumer goods'. 'The Consumer Revolution in Eighteenth Century England', in N. McKendrick, J. Brewer, and J.H. Plumb, *The Birth of a Consumer Society*, p. 9. The following sentences draw liberally from this analysis.

198. As early as 1751, Henry Fielding was complaining that 'the introduction of trade . . . hath indeed given a new face to the whole nation, hath in great measure subverted the former state of affairs, and hath almost totally changed the manners, customs, and habits of the people, more especially of the lower sort'. *An Enquiry into the Causes of the Late Increase of Robbers*, London: Millar, 1751, quoted in N. McKendrick, *The Consumer Revolution*, p. 24.

199. Nathaniel Forster, *An Enquiry into the Causes of the Present High Price of Provisions*, London: Fletcher, 1767, p. 41. As Keith Thomas remarks, 'Agriculture, after all, was the first sector of the British economy to become thoroughly capitalized and developed in a "rational" manner. Magic was rejected by men who had faith in the potentiality of technical innovation but it must be remembered that in the sixteenth and seventeenth centuries much of this innovation was agricultural.' *Religion and the Decline of Magic*, p. 796.

200. *Cf.* J.H. Plumb, 'The Acceptance of Modernity', pp. 327–8.

ing in this way with God's creation, accentuated in this instance by the need to resort to inbreeding to fix desirable traits, seen by some as a violation of the divinely ordained prohibitions against incest. But the economic gains and the potential for creating rewarding novelties proved too great to resist: improved varieties of sheep, cattle, horses, pigs, and dogs; a cornucopia of new varieties of vegetables, flowers, and fruit. Even urban dwellers got into the act, concentrating on breeding songbirds, pigeons, and ornamental fish. Nature was revealed as anything but fixed and immutable, and the revelation of the truth of this proposition was well-nigh universal:

> in every town and in many villages, adults, and even children, were attempting to improve nature, indeed to control it. . . . The idea of experiment, of changing nature, was no longer a philosophic concept, but a widespread practical art.[201]

The development and acceptance of this new outlook were further accelerated and confirmed by the rise of manufacturing – a form of human activity in which nature is simply relegated to a source of raw materials, to be worked on and transformed via active *human* intervention. Taking things still another step further, in this sphere economic competition and the factory system were the forcing-house for a thoroughgoing transformation in the relation of man to man. For industrial capitalism demanded 'a reform of "character" on the part of every single workman, since their previous character did not fit the new industrial system.'[202] Entrepreneurs concerned to 'make such machines of men as cannot err'[203] soon discovered that physical threat and economic coercion would not suffice: people had to be taught to *internalize* the new attitudes and responses, to discipline themselves. More than that, force under capitalism became an anachronism (perhaps even an anathema) save as a last resort. For one of the central achievements of the new economic system, one of its major advantages as a system of domination, was that it brought forth 'a peculiar and mystifying . . . form of compulsion to labor for another that is purely economic and "objective" '.[204]

---

201. *Ibid.*, p. 323 and *passim*. As Plumb notes on p. 326,

> Tens of thousands of men and women, probably hundreds of thousands, were actively concerned in horticulture, eager for novelty and determined on improvement. The importance of this was the sense of modernity and novelty generated by this widespread activity, bent on changing nature. People no longer expected flowers, vegetables or trees to be static objects in the field of creation, but constantly changing, constantly improving, the change and the improvement due to the experimental activity of man.

202. S. Pollard, *The Genesis of Modern Management*, p. 297.
203. Josiah Wedgwood, quoted in Neil McKendrick, 'Josiah Wedgwood and Factory Discipline', *Historical Journal* 4, 1961, p. 46.
204. Maurice Dobb, *Studies in the Development of Capitalism*, New York: International Publishers, 1963, p. 7.

The insistence on the possibility of radical transformations of nature, including human nature; the importance of securing the internalization of norms in order to reduce a recalcitrant population to order; the conception of how this was to be done; and even the nature of the norms that were to be internalized – in all these respects, we can now see how the emerging attitude towards the insane paralleled contemporaneous shifts in the world at large, and even in the treatment of the 'normal' populace. The new attitude coincided with and formed part of what Peter Gay has dubbed 'the recovery of nerve'[205] – a growing and quite novel sense that people were the masters of their own destiny and not the helpless victims of fate. Likewise, it had obvious links with the rise of 'the materialist doctrine that people are the product of circumstance'.[206] 'Is it not evident', said James Burgh (and certainly it *was* to an ever larger circle of his contemporaries), 'that by management the human species may be moulded into any conceivable shape?'[207] The implication, boldly proclaimed by the Enlightenment *philosophes*, was that one might 'organize the empirical world in such a way that man develops an experience of and assumes a habit of that which is truly human'.[208]

This faith in the capacity for human improvement through social and environmental manipulation – summed up in Helvetius's classic dictum, 'l'éducation peut tout' – was translated in a variety of settings (factories,

205. Peter Gay, *The Enlightenment: An Interpretation*, Vol. 2, *The Science of Freedom*, New York: Knopf, 1969, p. 6.
206. B. Fine, 'Objectification and the Bourgeois Contradictions of Consciousness', *Economy and Society* 6, 1977, p. 431.
207. James Burgh, *Political Disquisitions*, Vol. 3, London: Dilly, 1775, p. 176. Social practices embed themselves in linguistic usage, of course, and the successive layers of meaning attached to particular words often reveal much about changes in the realm of the social. Seen in this light, the linguistic history of the term 'management' provides striking support for the argument developed here. Etymologically, 'management' derived from the Italian *maneggiare* and the French *management*. The word was originally used in the sense of handling or training animals, especially horses, and referred in particular to the disciplinary methods by which horses were accustomed to the bit and bridle, brought under control, and induced to submit to the rule and authority of their human masters. When the term began to be extended to human beings, it was originally employed in closely related senses. Significantly, in the early part of the eighteenth century, 'manage' retained the cluster of meanings of its original Italian and French derivation, but during the second half of the century, the standard meaning gradually began to undergo a subtle shift, and by the turn of the century the concept came to be used in the rather different sense of treating persons with indulgence or showing them consideration; or, alternatively, of using tact, care or skill to manipulate the behaviour of others. Analogously, the *manager*, once the wielder of a weapon or one who waged war, now became someone skilled in handling people and in administering a business. Linguistic developments thus reinforce my argument that the contemporaneous shift from the coercive management or taming of the insane characteristic of the regime advocated by Monro, Battie, Cullen, and Francis Willis, to the very different sense in which Tuke, Fox, Ferriar, and others employed moral management to domesticate the mad, must be seen to be rooted in a much broader set of social transformations. (I am very grateful to Charlotte MacKenzie for directing my attention to the evolution of the concept of management, and to suggesting its relevance for my larger thesis.)
208. Claude-Adrien Helvetius (1715–71), quoted in B. Fine, 'Objectifications', p. 431.

schools, prisons, asylums) into the development of a whole array of tem-
porally coincident and structurally similar techniques of social discipline.[209]
Originating among the upper and middle classes, for example, there
emerged the notion that the education and upbringing of children ought
no longer to consist in 'the suppression of evil, or the breaking of the
will'.[210] With the growth of economic opportunity and social mobility,
the old system of beating and intimidating the child to compel compliance
came to be seen as a blunt and unserviceable technique, for it ill-prepared
one's offspring for the pressures of the marketplace. The child needed to
be taught to be 'his own slave driver', and with this end in view, 'developing the child's sense of emulation and shame' was to be preferred to
'physical punishment or chastisement.'[211] John Locke, the theoretician of
these changes, provided an early elaboration of their rationale:

> Beating is the worst, and therefore the last Means to be used in the
> Correction of Children. . . . The *Rewards* and *Punishments* . . . whereby
> we should keep Children in order *are* of quite another kind. . . . *Esteem*
> and *Disgrace* are, of all others, the most powerful Incentives to the
> Mind, when it is once brought to relish them. If you can once get
> into Children a Love of Credit and an Apprehension of Shame and
> Disgrace, you have put into them the true principle.[212]

The essential continuity of approach is equally manifest in the methods
and assumptions of the early nineteenth-century prison reformers. Crime
had been seen as the product of innate and immemorial wickedness and

209. For further discussion, see Michael Ignatieff, 'Prison and Factory Discipline, 1770–
     1800: The Origins of an Idea', unpublished paper presented at the Annual Meeting of
     the American Historical Association, 1976; Michel Foucault, *Discipline and Punish: The
     Birth of the Prison*, London: Allen Lane 1977.
210. J.H. Plumb, 'The New World of Children in Eighteenth Century England', *Past and
     Present* 67, 1975, p. 69.
211. *Ibid.*, pp. 67, 69.
212. John Locke, *Educational Writings*, Cambridge: Cambridge University Press, 1968, pp.
     152–3, 183. Note the stress on esteem and disgrace, and the idea of putting them *into*
     children. Locke's educational doctrines acquired an ever greater popularity among the
     upper and middle-classes in the latter half of the eighteenth century. Plumb draws
     attention to the fact that 'by 1780 John Browne could make one of the principal virtues
     of the expensive academy for gentlemen's sons that he proposed to set up a total
     absence of corporal punishment' ('The New World of Children', p. 70). (Interestingly
     enough, one of William Tuke's early philanthropic endeavours, prior to setting up the
     York Retreat, had been the establishment of Ackworth, a school for girls.) Seen in the
     context of these slightly earlier changes, Samuel Tuke's comment (*Description of the
     Retreat*, p. 150) that 'there is much analogy between the judicious treatment of children
     and that of insane persons' takes on a new significance. In practice, the analogy was to
     extend even further. When Locke's doctrines (and their intellectual descendants) were
     modified to accommodate the children of the poor, they spawned the rigidities of the
     monitorial system: Andrew Bell's 'steam engine of the moral world', and Joseph
     Lancaster's 'new and mechanical system of education'. When the techniques of the
     small, upper-middle-class Retreat were adapted to the 'requirements' of the mass of
     pauper lunatics, moral treatment, as we shall see, was simultaneously transformed into
     a set of management techniques for a custodial holding operation.

sin. Now, however, the criminal was reassimilated to the ranks of a common humanity. As Fine puts it,

> The prisoner was to be treated as a person, *who possessed a reason in common with all other persons*, in contrast to animals and objects. However hardened the prisoner was, beneath the surface of his or her criminality an irreducible reason still remained.[213]

In consequence, as lunatics were for Tuke, felons were 'defective mechanisms' that could be 'remoulded' through their confinement in a penitentiary designed as 'a machine for the social production of guilt'.[214] And for such purposes (again the parallel with moral treatment is clear), prison reformers clearly perceived that 'gentle discipline is more efficacious than severity'.[215]

The new practices, which had their origins in the wider transformation of English society, were shared, developed further, and given a somewhat different theoretical articulation in the context of coping with the mad. In a society where self-interest was elevated to a law of human nature and where all people were subjected in a superficially equal fashion to the pressures of the marketplace, the notion that everyone shared a common humanity possessed an obvious appeal. By extension, the insane were now drawn into this community of mankind. At least among the more 'enlightened' and increasingly self-conscious adherents to an elite culture, 'the mad had become . . . not merely "creatures", but "fellow creatures" '[216] – a development whose significance was soon manifest.

As is the wider world, so too in the lunatic asylum: one could no longer be content with the old emphasis on an externally imposed and alien order, which ensured that madness was controlled, yet which could never produce self-restraint. Control must now come from within, which meant that physical violence, now dysfunctional, became abhorrent.[217] Abstract-

213. B. Fine, 'Objectification', p. 429.
214. Michael Ignatieff, *A Just Measure of Pain: The Penitentiary in the Industrial Revolution in England*, New York: Pantheon, 1978, p. 213; see also Robin Evans, ' "A Rational Plan for Softening the Mind": Prison Design, 1750–1842', unpublished Ph.D. dissertation, Essex University, 1974.
215. John Howard, *The State of the Prisons*, Warrington: Egres, 1778, p. 8.
216. J. Andrews, 'Bedlam Revisited', p. 62, quoting the *London Chronicle* of May 1761 and the *Gentleman's Magazine* 18, 1748, p. 199. Andrews correctly emphasizes that one can find anticipations of this broader shift in sentiment even in the late seventeenth century (see, for example, Thomas Tryon, *A Treatise of Dreams and Visions, to Which Is Added, a Discourse of the Causes, Nature, and Cure of Phrensie, Madness, or Distraction*, London: Sowle, 1689), and that 'the percolation of the new philosophy' was spread out over several decades. Though still far from universal, even among the educated classes, such sentiments were becoming increasingly common and influential by the last third of the eighteenth century.
217. Compare Michel Foucault's comment (*Discipline and Punish*, p. 202) on the attractions of the Panopticon to the bourgeoisie: 'It is not necessary to use force to constrain the convict to good behaviour, the madman to calm, the worker to work, the schoolboy to application, the patient to observation of the regulations . . . no more bars, no more chains, no more heavy locks.'

ing from the barely conscious activities of their fellow-capitalists, a few of
the more perspicacious employers grasped the wider implications of what
they were collectively doing: they were providing a practical demonstration of the proposition that 'Any general character, from the most ignorant
to the most enlightened, may be given to any community, even to the
world at large, by the application of proper means: which means are to a
great extent at the command and under the control of those who have
influence in the affairs of men.'[218] This realization of the power that was
latent in the ability to manipulate the environment, and of the possibility
of radically transforming the individual's 'nature', was translated in the
context of madness into a wholly new stress on the importance of cure. It
represents a major structural support of the new ethic of rehabilitation. As
the market made the individual 'responsible' for his success or failure, so
the environment in the lunatic asylum was designed to create a synthetic
link between action and consequences, such that the madman could not
escape the recognition that he alone was responsible for the punishment he
received. The insane were to be restored to reason by a system of rewards
and punishments not essentially different from those used to teach a
young child to obey the dictates of 'civilized' morality. Just as those who
formed the new industrial workforce were to be taught the 'rational' self-
interest essential for the market system to work, the lunatics, too, were to
be made over in the image of bourgeois rationality: defective human
mechanisms were to be repaired so that they could once more compete in
the marketplace.[219] And finally, just as hard work and self-discipline were
the keys to the success of the urban bourgeoisie, from whose ranks Tuke
came, so his moral treatment propounded these same qualities as the
means of reclaiming the insane.[220]

11. Private Investigations at the York Asylum and at Bethlem

The gradual emergence in the late eighteenth and early nineteenth
centuries of new responses to madness is thus scarcely fortuitous. From
the reformers' viewpoint, the importance of the York Retreat was as a
practical realization of their own half-formulated ideals. The value of the
alternative model it provided quickly became apparent.

Some months before the publication of Tuke's book, Godfrey Higgins,
a Yorkshire magistrate, had become aware of the mistreatment of a pauper
whom he had ordered to be committed to the York Asylum. At the time,

218. Robert Owen, *A New View of Society*, London: Cadell and Davies, 1813, p. 99.
219. In practice, of course, the millennial claims to possess the means of restoring and
    rehabilitating the deviant and the defective were to prove absurdly overoptimistic.
    Asylums did not become mechanisms for the mass resocialization of mad folk for
    reentry into the marketplace. Nonetheless, Utopian expectations of this sort clearly
    helped to energize the movement for reform, and to attract broader political support for
    the implementation of its proposals.
220. I owe this last point to Michael Fears.

his own efforts to secure an investigation by the institution's governors had proved unavailing.[221] Higgins now renewed his attempts to expose the abuses there. Joining forces with the Tukes, and with several of his fellow magistrates, each of whom subscribed the twenty pounds necessary to become an asylum governor, he forced an official investigation of the institution.[222] On another front, he proceeded with his own inquiry into the condition of the patients. Together, these investigations provided evidence of wrongdoing on a massive scale: maltreatment of the patients extending to rape and murder; forging of records to hide deaths among the inmates; an extraordinarily widespread use of chains and other forms of mechanical restraint; massive embezzlement of funds; and conditions of utter filth and neglect. Higgins discovered a series of cells whose entrance had been deliberately hidden from view. Conditions here were particularly bad. The cells themselves were

> in a very horrid and filthy condition . . . the walls were daubed with excrement; the airholes, of which there was one in each cell, were partly filled with it. . . . I then went upstairs . . . into a room . . . twelve feet by seven feet ten inches, in which there were thirteen women who . . . had all come out of those cells that morning. . . . I became very sick, and could not remain any longer in the room. I vomited.[223]

The reformers could not have asked for a better example of the practices they were hoping to eliminate. The value of the events at York to the cause they were seeking to promote was enhanced by the reluctance of some of the original governors, and particularly of the asylum physician, Dr Best, to concede defeat. Despite the variety and volume of evidence that the reformers produced, for almost a year Best and his supporters among the governors refused to give way. A furious press and pamphlet war took place during the whole of this time,[224] keeping the case continuously before the public, and providing a highly effective forum for the dissemination of the reformers' ideas to an ever wider audience.[225]

221. See Godfrey Higgins, *A Letter to the Right Honourable Earl Fitzwilliam Respecting the Investigation Which Has Lately Taken Place into the Abuses at the York Lunatic Asylum*, Doncaster: Sheardown, 1814, pp. 3–9.
222. For an eye-witness description of the fury with which the new governors were greeted by the existing board, see Jonathan Gray, *A History of the York Lunatic Asylum: with an Appendix, Containing the Minutes of Evidence on the Cases of Abuse Lately Inquired into by a Committee*, York: Hargrove, 1815, p. 34.
223. House of Commons, *Report of the Select Committee on Madhouses*, 1815, pp. 1, 4–5.
224. See, for example, Godfrey Higgins, *A Letter to the Right Honourable Earl Fitzwilliam*; [A New Governor], *A Vindication of Mr Higgins from the Charges of Corrector: Including a Sketch of Recent Transactions at the York Asylum*, York: Hargrove, 1814; *York Herald* 27 November, 9 December 1813; 10 January, 21 March, 4 April, 12, 19, 28 December 1814. See also Best's own letter defending himself, signed 'Evigilator', in *York Chronicle*, 25 September 1813.
225. Locally, the controversy continued even after the 1815–16 inquiry. See, for instance, Godfrey Higgins, *The Evidence Taken Before a Committee of the House of Commons Respecting the Asylum at York; With Observations and Notes*, Doncaster: Sheardown, 1816;

Inevitably, Best was ultimately forced to resign, and the asylum was reorganized under Tuke's direction.

By a curious coincidence, the publication of Samuel Tuke's *Description of the Retreat* provoked the revelation of similar abuses at Bethlem. Edward Wakefield, who was also a Quaker, had for some years been interested in providing asylums for the insane. In the *Medical and Physical Journal* for April 1814, he announced an effort to set up a 'London Asylum', to be run on the lines of the York Retreat. A committee was formed to further the project, and as part of its preparations, an investigation was undertaken of existing provisions for London's insane at Guy's Hospital, St. Luke's, and Bethlem. The conditions they discovered at the latter institution when they went round it on 2 May 1814 prompted an effort to reopen the issue of lunacy reform at the national level.

As we have seen, the name of Bethlem, or its corrupted form, 'Bedlam', had for centuries been virtually synonymous with the very idea of a separate institution for the insane. Notwithstanding occasional hints of scandal, it had been a favorite London charity. Its respectability was attested to by the eminence of its board of governors; and its physician, Thomas Monro, was himself something of a society figure.[226] Despite these upper-class trappings, however, as befitted its charity status, Bethlem contained few patients from wealthy backgrounds;[227] indeed, most of the patients were paupers. Crammed together in a decaying structure that was acknowledged to be in need of replacement,[228] these unfortunates were

Anon., *An Appendix to a Book Lately Published, Entitled, 'Incontestable Proofs, etc., etc.' (in which the Publications of Mr Higgins and Others on the York Lunatic Asylum Are Not Sparingly Criticised)*, York: Storry, 1818.

226. Monro was widely known as a promoter and connoisseur of the fine arts. A competent watercolourist himself, his protégés included J.W.M. Turner.

227. Patricia Allderidge, ironically, for one so ready to charge other historians with preferring fantasy to facts, has recently claimed that 'there were none at all actually', since Bethlem took only charity patients. 'Bedlam: Fact or Fantasy?', p. 24. This assertion is demonstrably not true. For documentation of 'the significant gradations in status, occupation and wealth, that characterised the hospital's clientele', *cf.* the detailed discussion in J. Andrews, 'Bedlam Revisited', chapter 6. As he shows, 'at least a quarter of those patients admitted to Bethlem during 1640–80 were maintained privately', and '[a]mongst incurables supported at Bethlem during 1735–1800, private patients consistently comprised between 35 and 39% of the total incurable patient population. . . . During 1733–94 at least 12 patients underwent Commissions of Lunacy while in Bethlem, demonstrating that they were possessed of rather wealthy estates' and one can identify by name a substantial number of patients of gentlemanly or even aristocratic origins. *Ibid.*, pp. 418–9.

228. By the end of the eighteenth century, the condition of the buildings at Bethlem was deteriorating badly. Sections of the asylum now became completely uninhabitable, or not secure enough to contain patients, a situation reflected in the hospital census, which declined from 266 patients in 1800 to only 119 in 1814. Many of the pauper lunatics were transferred to Warburton's private madhouses in Bethnal Green. At the very moment that Wakefield and others were exposing the conditions at Bethlem, its governors were appealing to Parliament for funds to replace the existing buildings with a new structure. (Opened in St. George's Fields in 1815, this building is now the Imperial War Museum.)

still managed along traditional lines. With only four keepers employed to supervise 120 patients, the inspecting party found that many patients continued, for weeks and months at a time, to be chained to the walls of their cells.[229] (Among these, of course, was James Norris in his iron cage.) A number of inmates were left naked, or covered with only a blanket.[230] There was no effort to classify the patients; the furious, violent, and frenetic were distributed indiscriminately among the mild and convalescent cases. And the implications of the ancient associations of madness with coercion, nudity, and bestiality were starkly exemplified for visitors convinced of the practicability of an alternative vision: of madmen sitting sipping tea and exchanging social pleasantries in an institution self-consciously designed and run like a large country house.

Here, instead, were patients treated liked animals or 'vermin':

> One of the side rooms contained about ten [female] patients, each chained by one arm to the wall; the chain allowing them merely to stand up by the bench or form fixed to the wall, or sit down on it. The nakedness of each patient was covered by a blanket gown only.... Many other unfortunate women were locked up in their cells, naked, and chained on straw.... In the men's wing, in the side room, six patients were chained close to the wall by the right arm as well as by the right leg.... Their nakedness and their mode of confinement gave this room the complete appearance of a dog kennel.[231]

In other respects, too, the inmates were largely abandoned to their fate. Extraordinarily, for an institution which could nominally call on the services of a physician and a surgeon, as well as a resident apothecary, not even the physical ills and ailments of the patients received prompt attention. Several cases were found of inmates who had lost toes or even feet from frostbite. To the efforts of the apothecary to attribute this to the greater susceptibility of the insane to 'mortified extremities', the reformers countered that not a single such incident had occurred in twenty years of the Retreat's existence. In any event, questioning of the staff brought to light the information that the 'resident' apothecary visited the asylum for only a half hour each day, and on many occasions did not bother to appear for days at a time.[232] Monro, the physician, was seen still more

229. House of Commons, *Report of the Select Committee on Madhouses*, 1815, pp. 35–6.
230. George Wallet, the Bethlem Steward, estimated that in 1815, 'about one third of the patients may be considered as dirty patients'. House of Commons, *Report of the Select Committee on Madhouses*, 1815, pp. 12, 36. Officially, these 'blanket patients', together with those maniacs prone to destroy or tear their clothing, were the only inmates who were confined without clothes.
231. [Edward Wakefield], 'Extracts from the Report of the Committee Employed to Visit Houses and Hospitals for the Confinement of Insane Persons, With Remarks, By Philanthropus', *The Medical and Physical Journal* 32, August 1814, pp. 122–8.
232. House of Commons, *Report of the Select Committee on Madhouses*, 1815, p. 37.

infrequently; evidently his time was too valuable to waste on such un-remunerative patients.[233]

Appalled by what he had found, and convinced by now of the need for a more ambitious and thoroughgoing reform than would be achieved merely by setting up a competing asylum run on the lines of the York Retreat, Wakefield contacted a group of sympathetic MP's and revisited Bethlem with them. This time he brought an artist to sketch Norris, still confined in his remarkable apparatus.[234] Armed with this first-hand experience, and with the publicity the scandals at York and Bethlem had received, these MPs pressed for a Parliamentary investigation of conditions in madhouses and charity asylums. In April 1815, a Select Committee was authorized and the inquiry began.

---

233. House of Commons, *Report of the Select Committee on Madhouses*, 1815, pp. 35–6.
234. Arnald's sketch of Norris was subsequently mass-produced, and used by the reformers as powerful propaganda in support of their proposed reforms.

CHAPTER THREE

The Chimera of the Curative Asylum

Madmen appear to have been employed to torment other madmen, in most of the places intended for their relief.
Samuel Tuke, *Description of the Retreat*

Tenderness is better than torture, kindness more effectual than constraint. . . . Nothing has a more favourable and controlling influence over one who is disposed to or actually affected with melancholy or mania, than an exhibition of friendship or philanthropy.
John Reid, *Essays on Hypochondriasis and Other Nervous Affections*

I want to stir up an intelligent and active sympathy, in behalf of the most wretched, the most oppressed, the only helpless of mankind, by proving with how much needless tyranny they are treated – and this in mockery – by men who pretend indeed their cure, but who are, in reality, their tormentors and destroyers.
John Perceval, *A Narrative of the Treatment Experienced by a Gentleman, During a State of Mental Derangement*

1. The 1815–16 Parliamentary Inquiry

The new Committee included several of those who had been members of the 1807 investigation,[1] but the inquiry which ensued was quite unlike its predecessor. Lasting almost two years and encompassing a whole series of detailed reports and minutes of evidence, the inquiry surveyed treatment in charity hospitals (Bethlem, York Asylum, St. Luke's); in the new county asylums (Nottingham, one of only three open at this time); in private madhouses (a number, ranging from Warburton's houses at Bethnal Green and Spencer's house at Fonthill Gifford at one extreme, to Brislington House and Laverstock at the other); and in workhouses. Forty-one witnesses testified before it, including fifteen members of the medical profession (ten physicians, four surgeons, and an apothecary); twelve madhouse keepers; and an assortment of magistrates, members of

---

1. These included the chairman of the Committee, George Rose (a close personal friend of George III before the latter's descent into madness and dementia); and Charles Williams-Wynn, Shaw Lefevre, and Samuel Whitbread.

the Committee itself, and various 'Gentlemen, who, from motives of benevolence, had given particular attention to inquiries connected to this subject'.[2] In addition, some of those interested in influencing the course of future legislation submitted written evidence, subsequently published in pamphlet form.[3]

The reformers were now sure of what they wanted to achieve. The focus throughout their inquiry was on the conditions endured by those insane confined in institutions, with no effort being made to gather comparable data on lunatics in the community. Yet although abuses and maltreatment of patients were found to be prevalent in virtually every type of institution they examined, both the Committee itself and those who disseminated its findings to a wider public[4] interpreted these revelations as proof of the need for more institutions (albeit under direct public control), as well as justifying (indeed making imperative) an improved system of inspection and supervision of all receptacles within which lunatics were confined. And there can be no question but that, through the impact of its portrait of the plight of the insane in existing institutions, this inquiry helped to create a climate of opinion favouring reform.

The early meetings of the Committee were largely taken up by an investigation of the recent events at the York Asylum and at Bethlem. The reformers realized that this material provided some of their most powerful ammunition against the existing system. Accordingly, they were careful to avoid all appearances of bias, offering those criticized the opportunity to rebut the testimony given against them, while making sure that the abuses and depredations earlier investigations had uncovered received a thorough airing. The reformers' case was overwhelming. At York, as we have seen, they had already succeeded in forcing the resignation of the asylum physician, Dr Best, had dismissed the staff, and had undertaken a total reorganization of the entire institution. Higgins, who had played such a prominent role in these affairs, was the Committee's first witness. He placed on record an extensive narrative of events prior to reform, including the frantic efforts of the asylum staff to conceal their wrong-doing by the destruction of records and, in all probability, by deliberately burning down a large part of the asylum building itself – a fire in which at least four patients were acknowledged to have died. His old adversary, Dr Best, was, therefore, already discredited by the time he appeared before

2. [W.H. Fitton], 'Lunatic Asylums', *Edinburgh Review* 28, 1817, p. 451.
3. For example, Thomas Bakewell, *A Letter Addressed to the Chairman of the Select Committee . . . Appointed to Enquire into the State of Madhouses*, Stafford: for the author, 1815; William Charles Ellis, *A Letter to Thomas Thompson, Esq., M.P., . . . on the Necessity of Proper Places Being Provided by the Legislature for the Reception of All Insane Persons*, Hull: Topping and Dawson, 1815; William Nisbet, *Two Letters to the Right Honourable George Rose, M.P., . . . on the State of the Madhouses*, London: Cox, 1815.
4. See esp. [W.H. Fitton], 'Lunatic Asylums', pp. 431–71; 'Insanity and Madhouses', *Quarterly Review* 15, 1816, pp. 387–417.

the Committee, and the mixture of bluster and outright denial he exhibited on the witness stand failed to rescue his reputation.[5]

The situation at Bethlem was rather different. In the aftermath of Wakefield's first visit, and his return with a party of MPs, the governors had felt compelled to institute their own inquiry into the conduct of their officers and the condition of the asylum. Incredibly, from the reformers' perspective, they had convinced themselves that the charges were without foundation, that the institution was as good as, if not better than, any in England, and that the conduct of the physician and apothecary deserved praise rather than opprobrium. Indicative of their attitude was their verdict on the case of Norris: his confinement, they solemnly averred, had been 'upon the whole, rather a merciful and a humane than a rigorous and severe imposition'.[6]

Consequently, the reformers were here concerned not merely with placing on the public record an account of past mismanagement, but also with provoking a more suitable response from the governors. Wakefield's evidence itself provided a damning indictment of the asylum's administration; but, in addition, several of the MPs had themselves witnessed the abuses he complained of on their own tour of Bethlem. When the apothecary and the physician, Haslam and Monro, appeared before the Committee, their position, following their recent vindication by their employers, was ostensibly secure. The hostile cross-examination which they now faced, however, forced both of them, first into evasion and denial, and then into self-contradiction and damaging admissions about their own conduct in office. Finally, in desperation, each man resorted to blaming the other, or the surgeon, Bryan Crowther, who had conveniently died earlier that year. In the words of a contemporary, the impression they left was of 'a physician who walked the hospital only once a month – an apothecary, who abounded in theoretical views, but was above attending to anything else – a steward, a matron, and a porter, all too important in their own eyes to attend to the wants and necessities of the patients – and a surgeon often mad himself, and almost continually drunk'.[7]

As soon as their first report was printed, the Committee ordered copies to be sent to every governor of Bethlem, a scarcely veiled suggestion that

---

5. For Higgins' evidence, see Select Committee Report, 1815, pp. 1–9; his evidence was corroborated by Bryan Cooke, a fellow magistrate and governor of the York Asylum, *ibid.*, p. 9. For Best's reply, see *ibid.*, pp. 144–7. Higgins subsequently published an annotated version of the testimony before the Committee on the events at the York Asylum, sarcastically refuting Best's defence point by point. See Godfrey Higgins, *The Evidence Taken Before a Committee of the Houses of Commons Respecting the Asylum at York, With Observations and Notes,* Doncaster: Sheardown, 1816.

6. *Report from the Committee of Governors of Bethlem Hospital [on] the Case of James Norris,* reprinted as an appendix to Select Committee, *Report,* 1815. Their bluster was rather undermined by their simultaneous order that he be released, and by Norris's own inconvenient decision to die a few weeks thereafter.

7. *Hansard's Parliamentary Debates,* Vol. 34, first series, 1816, col. 426.

the latter should reconsider their earlier action. In the face of this pressure, the governors convened a special meeting and called the physician and the apothecary before them for a second time. Each arrived with an air of injured innocence and presented the governors with a written defence of his conduct, pointing out that the charges against them were the very same ones the governors themselves had concluded were baseless only a few months previously.[8] The governors proved no less adept than their employees at contradicting themselves. Haslam was dismissed, and within six weeks, they accepted Monro's resignation.[9]

In the meantime, the Committee's inquiries had moved from a concern with conditions in the principal charity hospitals of the period[10] to a consideration of the treatment meted out to those confined in workhouses and in a number of private institutions avowedly operated for profit. Much of the testimony on these places came from a handful of reformers who appear to have made almost a full-time vocation of inspecting the conditions under which lunatics were kept. Wakefield, for example, in his travels as a land-agent, had inspected a number of provincial madhouses. A few, such as Brislington House and Laverstock House, were exceptions to the general trend, and failed to add to the catalogue of abuses the Committee was now uncovering. At Langworthy's House at Box in

---

8. John Haslam, *Observations of the Apothecary of Bethlem Hospital Upon the Evidence Taken Before the Committee of the Honourable House of Commons for Regulating Madhouses*, London: Bryer, 1816; Thomas Monro, *Observations of Dr Monro Upon the Evidence Taken Before the Committee of the Honourable House of Commons for Regulating Madhouses*, London: Bryer, 1816.

9. That this sequence of events was little more than a tactical concession is suggested by the governors' choice of a physician to succeed Thomas Monro, his son, Edward Thomas Monro.

10. The Committee secured some evidence on the lunatic ward at Guy's Hospital, and on St. Luke's. Dunston, the keeper at the latter institution, was allowed to offer uncontroverted evidence that each patient in his establishment was well fed and given a proper wooden bed, and that restraint was kept to a minimum – he claimed only five of three hundred patients were under restraint at the time of his testimony. The Committee's unusual passivity may have reflected the presence of two Governors of St. Luke's (Shaw Lefevre and Whitbread) among its own membership. Kathleen Jones (*Lunacy, Law, and Conscience, 1744–1845*, London: Routledge and Kegan Paul, 1955, pp. 96–8) has echoed the claim that St. Luke's was better than Bethlem or the York Asylum, but contemporary evidence suggests otherwise. Wakefield testified before the Committee itself that he had found the place overcrowded and cheerless, with unglazed cells, patients chained to their beds, nearly naked and clad only in rags (Select Committee, *Report*, 1815, pp. 16–7). William Tuke's notes of a visit in 1812 (reprinted in D.H. Tuke, *Chapters in the History of the Insane in the British Isles*, London: Kegan Paul and Trench, 1882, pp. 89–90) paint a similar picture: 'There are about three hundred patients, sexes about equal. . . . The superintendent has never seen much advantage in medicine and relies chiefly on management. Thinks chains a preferable mode of restraint to straps or the waistcoat in some violent cases. Thinks confinement or restraint may be imposed as a punishment with some advantage, and, on the whole, thinks fear the most effectual principle by which to reduce the insane to orderly conduct. The building has entirely the appearance of a place of confinement . . . and there are strong iron grates to the windows.' It seems clear that under other circumstances, St. Luke's would have been cited as another example of the need for reform.

Wiltshire, however, the pattern was more typical: he was refused permission to see male patients on the grounds that this was one of the days they were not allowed up. Among the women, he found two lying naked on straw pallets, and four others left entirely naked in total darkness: 'in the course of my visiting these places, I never recollect to have seen four living persons in so wretched a place.'[11] Back in London, he attempted to view Sir John Miles's madhouse in Hoxton, the largest of the metropolitan establishments. Once again, Wakefield was refused admission, the keeper conceding that to allow 'an inspection of that house would be signing its death warrant'.[12]

The most extensive evidence on the treatment of the insane confined in workhouses was provided by Henry Alexander, a banker who had developed an interest in lunacy reform. Like Wakefield, he had taken advantage of the travelling he had to do for business purposes to undertake a series of unofficial inquiries into the conditions of the insane. Some he had found in rooms 'no better than dungeons . . .'; elsewhere, the cells were 'like pigstyes'. His description of the conditions at the Tavistock Workhouse was particularly graphic. He was refused permission to see the lunatics themselves, and when he persisted, the master reluctantly showed him the quarters they were usually housed in, first warning him that he would find them unfit to enter, even though they had been washed out earlier that morning:

> I have never smelt such a stench in my life, and it was so bad, that a friend who went with me [into the first cell] said he could enter the other. After having entered one, I said I would go into the other; that if they could survive the night, I could at least inspect them. . . . The stench was so great I almost suffocated; and for hours after, if I ate anything, I still retained the same smell; I could not get rid of it; and it should be remembered that these cells had been washed out that morning, and had been opened some hours previous.[13]

---

11. House of Commons, *Report of the Select Committee on Madhouses*, 1815, p. 21.
12. *Ibid.*, p. 19.
13. *Ibid.*, p. 3. To some extent, of course, this and similar references to filth and stench reflect (and contribute to) what Corbin has termed an 'olfactory revolution', a mounting intolerance among the better sort for the dirt and foul odours which had been so much a part of organized social life in previous centuries. See Alain Corbin, *The Foul and the Fragrant: Odor and the French Social Imagination*, New York: Berg, 1986, esp., pp. 57–85 and 89–110. (Originally published as *Le miasme et la jonquille*, Paris: Aubier Montaigne, 1982.) Jonathan Andrews has similarly emphasized that 'Calls for hygiene grew more insistent, not merely out of developing theories concerning the generation of putrid distempers, but alongside a growing sensibility and insistence upon outward decorum, which began to challenge former assumptions that the squalid conditions of the poor, sick and insane were unavoidable, or even appropriate, and sought to impose cleanliness as (next to godliness) one means of subjugating the signs and symptoms that had marked these groups out so visibly as disordered.' 'Bedlam Revisited: A History of Bethlem Hospital *c.* 1634–*c.* 1770,' unpublished Ph.D. dissertation, London University, 1991, pp. 164–5.

The Committee next sought evidence on the operations of the system for inspecting metropolitan madhouses under the 1774 Act, a task which had been delegated to members of the Royal College of Physicians. Dr Richard Powell, who had acted as the secretary of the Commissioners since 1808, was their principal witness. There were thirty-four madhouses under the Commissioners' direct jurisdiction, and Powell testified that on their tours of inspection they visited 'some days, perhaps two; other days six or eight' houses within the space of a few hours. Though they suspected some houses of concealing the actual number of patients crammed into their overcrowded rooms, they made no effort to see that the legal requirement that all inmates be reported to them was observed, or to inquire into the disposition of individual cases. Given the brief duration of the average inspection, such procedures were totally impracticable. At the most recent visit to Miles's establishment at Hoxton, for example, the inspection of the whole structure and the condition of its 486 inmates had been completed within two and a half hours.[14] The lunacy reformers on the Committee were naturally aware that even had the Commissioners bothered to uncover evidence of systematic brutality and neglect, the latter lacked any legal power to intervene. But, of course, this only strengthened their resolve to replace the existing system altogether.

At the close of the inquiries in 1815, therefore, the Committee had uncovered evidence that neglect and maltreatment of lunatics was endemic in all the various types of institutions in which they were incarcerated, and its members were convinced that legislative intervention was urgent. Fearful perhaps that others might not be so readily convinced, they continued their investigations into the following session, uncovering evidence which suggested massive irregularities in two of the largest and best-known private madhouses in London, Warburton's Red and White Houses at Bethnal Green. John Rogers, the apothecary at the White House, gave evidence which suggested a state of affairs at least as sordid as that revealed at Bethlem and at the York Asylum. The houses themselves, he alleged, were infested with rats and fleas, and were so cold and damp that many patients suffered from gangrene and tuberculosis. At least one patient had had to have both feet amputated when mortification set in, and as many as a hundred patients had died in the winter of 1810–11 from typhus. Instances of gross brutality inflicted on patients by the keepers went unpunished even where they caused a patient's death. Female patients were liable to be raped. Beating and whipping were common punishments and prolonged restraint was employed as a routine means of managing patients. Incontinent patients were 'mopped down' in a none-too-gentle

14. House of Commons, 1815, p. 76. In view of Wakefield's earlier testimony, the Committee can scarcely have been reassured to learn that Powell considered Miles's house to be kept 'in very excellent order'.

fashion under a stream of cold water from a pump in the yard. Refusal to eat or to take prescribed medications was met by force: 'I have known sundry instances where the mouth had been lacerated and the teeth have been forced out. I recollect Mrs Hodges, wife of the vestry clerk at St. Andrew's Holborn, dying in this way. I do not suppose there is a keeper who has been in these houses four or five years who has not had patients die under their hand in the act of forcing.'[15]

Rogers reiterated these and other allegations in a pamphlet he had published at his own expense.[16] The detailed nature of the evidence he gave and his willingness to cite the names and dates of actual cases made him an impressive witness, and his sister, Mary Humieres (who had previously served as a housekeeper at the White House), returned from Switzerland to corroborate his accusations. Their testimony was, quite naturally, vigorously contested by Warburton and his minions. Matthew Talbot, superintendent of the White House, accused Rogers of deliberate falsification, and Warburton himself appeared before the Committee to issue a blanket denial of all the charges: 'I never knew of an instance of an injury so much as any boy has received at school from a chilblain, or not more.'[17] Unfortunately, the Committee's failure to investigate conditions at first hand left the issue of who was telling the truth unresolved, though the mere suspicion that such events might have occurred was enough for many of the reformers.[18]

By the time the 1815–16 Committee submitted its final report, there was a wealth of documentation to support the reformers' contention that what they perceived as appalling degradation and inhuman treatment were the lot of madmen in every sort of institution in which they were confined. Future investigations might (and did) add further examples of these selfsame abuses inflicted on other madmen in other asylums; but the fundamental picture was already clear, and the evidence sufficiently abundant to convince most observers of the justice of the reformers' claims about conditions in existing asylums, if not the correctness of their prescription for reform. Likewise, the reformers were already convinced that they knew what had to be done to cure the 'intolerable' evils they had

15. House of Commons, *First Report of the Select Committee on Madhouses*, 1816, pp. 7ff.
16. J.W. Rogers, *A Statement of the Cruelties, Abuses, and Frauds, Which Are Practised in Mad-Houses*, London: for the author, 2nd edn, 1816.
17. Select Committee, *First Report*, 1816, pp. 23, 38.
18. Subsequent events tended to confirm Rogers's veracity. In 1825, John Mitford published a two-part exposé of *The Crimes and Horrors of Warburton's Private Madhouses* (London: Benbow, 1825), in which he claimed that the keepers' motto was 'If a man comes in here mad we'll keep him so; if he is in his senses, we'll soon drive him out of them.' Less polemically, the proceedings of a subsequent Parliamentary inquiry in 1827 focused directly on Warburton's establishments, and provided detailed evidence in support of Rogers's allegations, some eleven years after they were first made. Rogers himself reappeared as a witness in these hearings, contending that he had been ruined by the machinations of private madhouse keepers after his previous testimony. See House of Commons, *Report of the Select Committee on Pauper Lunatics*, 1827, pp. 144–6.

exposed. There were two central elements in their plan: the provision of a system of asylums at public expense to take at least all of the pauper lunatics ought to be made compulsory, in order to eliminate the inducements to maltreatment inherent in keeping lunatics for profit;[19] and a vigorous system of inspection by outsiders with no ties to the asylum administration should be implemented, to provide a check against the tendency of all institutions to fall away from their initial ideals and against the temptations for the keepers to neglect and maltreat their helpless 'clients', the mad.[20] These two proposals remained the fundamental features of the reform plan until its eventual implementation. Yet despite the obvious propaganda value of the Committee's revelations in producing converts to the reformers' cause, it took the latter thirty years to attain their objectives.

2. The Fate of the First Reform Bills

In the aftermath of the Committee's findings, the reformers sought, in the first instance, to replace the existing moribund provisions for the inspection of madhouses with the kind of efficient national inspectorate which they considered an essential prerequisite for reform. Three times between 1816 and 1819, members of the Select Committee presented bills to introduce such a provision. Each bill proposed a permanent commission of eight, to be appointed by the Home Office, with power not merely to inspect private madhouses, but also to lay down and enforce standards for the management of these institutions and the treatment of patients. On each occasion, the Parliamentary reformers were able to make use of the massive evidence of abuse which they had uncovered, and the manifest inadequacies of the existing system of inspection, to secure majorities in the House of Commons for the bill's passage; on each occasion the measure was rejected in the Lords.

What accounts for these failures? In the first place, it is clear that the reformers made some tactical errors which hurt their cause. For example, in 1816, when the revelations of their Committee were still fresh in the public mind, the reformers made the error of including in their bill a provision for the stringent inspection of 'single lunatics'. This was a measure known to offend the aristocratic sensibilities of their Lordships, who were concerned to protect the privacy of upper class families with a

---

19. Samuel Tuke had suggested this measure in an article in *The Philanthropist* ('Essay on the State of the Insane Poor', 1, 1811, pp. 357–60), and it was vigorously advocated by W.C. Ellis in his written submission to the Committee. Its necessity was impressed on a wider public by the *Quarterly Review* (15, 1816, p. 416).

20. Again, this was a central theme in Samuel Tuke's writings (see both the *Description of the Retreat: An Institution Near York for Insane Persons of the Society of Friends*, York: Alexander, 1813, and his pamphlet, *Practical Hints on the Construction and Economy of Pauper Lunatic Asylums*, York: Alexander, 1815, reemphasized by the *Quarterly Review* 15, 1816, p. 415).

lunatic in the closet, and it undoubtedly contributed to the bill's defeat. Subsequently, this provision was so watered down in the 1817 bill as to be almost meaningless, but by then the reform movement was losing its momentum. The *Edinburgh Review* sought to rally support for the measure, urging that while 'many of the evils have already ceased to exist in some of the principal institutions for the insane . . . they were the offspring of circumstances that, without a radical change of system in the control of madhouses, cannot fail to produce again the same deplorable effects'.[21] By now, however, opponents of the bill were exerting pressure in the opposite direction.

Such opposition had a number of sources. Most obviously, it came from those whose interests in the mad-business were directly threatened by the new schemes. Madhouse proprietors complained that though the Committee's findings had 'excited a very high degree of public feeling', the testimony it had heard was not given on oath,[22] 'and, whilst it exaggerates praise in a few instances, bestows much undeserved censure in others'. The publication of such evidence was 'likely to be productive of positive injury in various ways, both to society and to individuals. Society at large must suffer if insane persons are allowed to range uncontrolled, whilst they are not regulated by reason in their conduct, and are morally irresponsible as they should therefore be, for their actions'. In consequence of the prejudice against madhouses the reformers had stirred up, 'it does indeed so suffer at present, and crimes which are referable to insanity are largely increased'.[23] In a more subtle kind of special pleading, which we will discuss at greater length in Chapter 4, the reformers' proposals were pictured as an assault on medicine's professional prerogatives, as encouraging lay interference in technical decisions about the proper treatment of the insane, and hence as productive of serious damage to the patients' best interests.[24]

One doubts, though, whether such self-interested sophistry would have carried the day but for the existence of a much more broadly based and politically powerful source of opposition to the reformers' plans. The critical strength of the resistance movement came from its links with the localist bias characteristic of English society until well into the nineteenth century. This aversion to the concentration of power at the national level was extraordinarily widespread and well-entrenched on both the structural and ideological levels. Undoubtedly, its origins lay in the gentry's success- ful resistance to Stuart attempts to impose an indigenous English form of absolutism (though such convictions concerning the threat which

21. [W.H. Fitton], 'Lunatic Asylums', p. 434.
22. George Man Burrows, *Cursory Remarks on a Bill now in the House of Peers for Regulating of Madhouses*, London: Harding, 1817, p. 1.
23. Anon., *Insanity*, London: Underwood, 1817, p. 5.
24. An earlier effort to strengthen the system for inspecting madhouses had also been stifled, in part at least, by medical opposition. See *Medical and Surgical Journal*, 1814, pp. 1–2.

centralized state power offered to the liberties and freedom of a propertied class had received more recent and dramatic confirmation in the French Revolution and its aftermath). The English upper class had secured its power by ensuring that administration remained locally based, and by convincing the common people (as well as themselves) that an increase in the authority of the state threatened to produce an engine of despotism, 'a system of tyranny . . . , the destruction of all public liberty, and the disturbance of all private happiness'.[25] The hegemony of these local landed elites, astutely legitimized through the legal system and finding practical expression in the powers of the magistrates and the innumerable autonomous local authorities, did not simply melt away at the first demands for a more rational system.[26] On the contrary, in the first decades of the nineteenth century these administrative units jealously defended their independence against the Benthamites and the rising class of professional administrators.[27]

The effort to rewrite the legal rules concerning insanity and the treatment of the insane was necessarily productive of opposition on this score, since it involved interference with the 15,000 or so local Poor Law administrations which had previously possessed untrammeled authority to dispose of the insane (along with the rest of the indigent) with virtually total freedom from central supervision and control. The reformers' proposals for a system of inspection by paid officials dependent upon the central government – officials who would have had the power to enforce centrally determined directives and standards – threatened a transformation in political relationships whose importance extended far beyond the narrow sphere of lunacy reform. In securing acceptance of this type of administrative apparatus, the central government would have obtained far greater power than it had hitherto possessed to ensure compliance with its wishes – with a corresponding setback to the power of the landowning class.

The political leverage of the rural aristocracy – locked in a losing battle with the rising manufacturing and commercial bourgeoisie – was by now clearly on the wane. As economic life – indeed, life in general – became

25. J.P. Smith (1812), quoted in E.P. Thompson, *The Making of the English Working Class*, New York: Vintage, 1963, p. 82.
26. The impact of these structural features of the English political system is vividly demonstrated in the long-running conflict over the rationalization of the English criminal law. See the discussions in Douglas Hay, Peter Linebaugh, and E.P. Thompson (eds) *Albion's Fatal Tree: Crime and Society in Eighteenth Century England*, New York: Pantheon, 1975; and in Steven Spitzer and Andrew Scull, 'Social Control in Historical Perspective: From Private to Public Responses to Crime', pp. 281–302 in D.F. Greenberg (ed.) *Corrections and Punishment*, Beverly Hills, California: Sage, 1977. Opposition to the further concentration of power at the national level was reflected in such actions as the rejection of Bentham's plans for a 'Ministry of Police' by an 1818 Parliamentary committee, and perhaps reached its apogee in the resistance to the passage and implementation of the Poor Law Amendment Act of 1834.
27. See generally, William C. Lubenow, *The Politics of Government Growth: Early Victorian Attitudes Toward State Intervention 1833–1848*, Newton Abbot: David and Charles, 1971.

increasingly oriented towards and dictated by conditions in national and international markets, so the significance of the purely local and personal dependencies to which the authority of the traditional elites was bound steadily declined in significance. Ever more aware of the advantages of impersonal forms of coercion – most especially the invisible hand of the marketplace – the bourgeoisie were in consequence ever less disposed to rely on the visible and personal authority of an earlier era. And yet, while capitalism dissolved traditional social restraints, capitalists as a class sought a previously unknown degree of stability and predictability in social relationships, for the market was extraordinarily sensitive to disorder and uncertainty. In the long run, only a greatly strengthened state apparatus could provide such guarantees, particularly on a national basis.

In the short run, however, the position of the gentry remained sufficiently entrenched to ensure that the old habits of thought and existing systems of political organization would be defended with much of their old vigour. Two additional factors stiffened resistance to the lunacy reformers' proposals. The plan to make construction of county asylums compulsory threatened local authorities with heavy capital expenditures which they were reluctant to incur, particularly since they faced simultaneous pressures to provide new jails and workhouses, and to develop a communications network adequate for the emerging industrial society. Then, too, the uneven spread of the new outlook on the insane left many sceptical of the need for change. Local magistrates continued to accept the traditional paradigm of insanity, along with its emphasis on the demonological, almost bestial character of madness. Consequently, they were frequently unable to comprehend why the reformers saw the treatment of lunatics within their jurisdictions as brutal and inhumane; why conditions they saw as unexceptionable produced shock and outrage in others. Not surprisingly, then, it was only after the manufacturing and commercial bourgeoisie had secured a substantial increase in their political power and influence through the 1832 reform of Parliament that the obstacles to central administration and direction were confronted and dealt a decisive defeat; and the issue was fought out, not over the marginal issue of lunacy reform, but over the crucially important matter of Poor Law policy – the Old Poor Law being the single most important remaining limitation on the free market in labour.

3. Renewed Parliamentary Investigation

The defeat of the 1819 bill led to a brief hiatus in the effort to secure legislative implementation of the lunacy reformers' plans. Several leading parliamentary supporters had died, while others had retired.[28] In 1827,

28. Whitbread had committed suicide in 1815, and Romilly in 1818. George Rose died of old age, also in 1818, and shortly thereafter the aging Lord Robert Seymour had given up his Parliamentary seat.

however, yet another parliamentary inquiry re-awakened interest in the issue. Between that date and 1845, when the major elements of the reform program were enacted into law, the reformers' efforts to overcome their opposition proceeded on two fronts. The first and most visible of these was the political: they made use of astute parliamentary manoeuvering and a further series of official inquiries to keep the issue before the public and eventually to wear down their opponents. As we shall see, the success of this first tactic was intimately tied to activity of a rather different sort – the development over the second quarter of the nineteenth century of an increasingly elaborate pro-institutional ideology designed to rally public support for the lunacy reformers' plans.

The revival of parliamentary interest in lunacy reform came about through the persistence of Lord Robert Seymour, a member of the 1815–16 Committee who had subsequently given up his seat in Parliament. In his remaining public capacity, as a magistrate for the county of Middlesex, he had sought for years to persuade his reluctant fellow magistrates of the need for a county asylum. Finally, in 1827, they were prevailed upon to set up a committee of magistrates to inquire into conditions in the private madhouses in the county. Armed with the evidence produced by a visit of the overseers of the poor for St. George's parish to one of Warburton's houses, Seymour also approached those interested in lunacy reform in the Commons, and pressed for a renewed inquiry into conditions in the metropolitan madhouses. Here again he was successful: on 13 June 1827, Robert Gordon, a fellow magistrate and MP for Dorset, secured the establishment of a new Select Committee charged with this task.

For the most part, the Committee confined its attention to a detailed inquiry into conditions at Warburton's White House in Bethnal Green, taking extensive testimony from magistrates and Poor Law officers who had visited it to inspect the conditions of the pauper patients, from members of the Royal College of Physicians who had inspected it under the provisions of the 1774 Madhouse Act, and also from a number of ex-patients. Almost without exception, their evidence revealed a pattern of systematic abuse, maltreatment, and neglect of the inmates. On the first day of the hearings, John Hall, a guardian and director of the poor for the parish of Marylebone, gave evidence about a visit he had made in August of the previous year. Informed that one of the lunatics from his parish was ill and was therefore being cared for in the infirmary, he had brushed aside the objections raised by the keeper, and had insisted on examining him:

we found a considerable number of very disgusting objects – a description of pauper lunatics I should conceive chiefly idiots, in a very small room, and several of them were chained to the wall. The air of the room was highly oppressive and offensive, insomuch so that I could not draw my breath. I was obliged to hold my breath while I staid to take a very short survey of the room. . . . It contained the description of patients called the wet patients; they were chiefly in petticoats . . . they appeared to be of the worst description of decided idiots; and the room was exceedingly oppressive from the excrement and smell which existed there.[29]

The evidence of other witnesses made it clear that those who had the good fortune to avoid the special care provided for the physically sick were scarcely better off. A large number of the 'patients' were kept confined in 'crib rooms', places where

> there are nothing but wooden cribs or bedsteads; cases, in fact, filled with straw and covered with a blanket, in which these unfortunate beings are placed at night; and they sleep most of them naked on the straw, covered with a blanket . . . they are mere boxes of the depth of about eighteen inches, where the person lies in; they are all fastened; some all fours, some one, some two, and some three [limbs].[30]

Fifteen of these cribs were crammed into a single room, twenty-nine feet by fifteen. Each day patients were locked into their cribs 'about three o'clock in the afternoon, and . . . did not get up until nine in the morning'.[31] To allow the keepers a day off one day a week

> on Saturday evenings, they were locked down in the same state, and kept till Monday morning, without being unchained or allowed to get up to relieve themselves in any way whatever. . . . On Monday morning, like the other mornings, when they got up, they were many of them in a very filthy state, and I have seen them, when the snow has been upon the ground, put into a tub of cold water and washed down with a mop; there was a man from Northamptonshire, who was treated in that way; I have seen that man brought up from the door of the room, and from the heat of the faeces that were lying on him, his back has been completely bare for many inches up, and he was treated in the same way, by being washed in the way I have stated.[32]

The cribs themselves were generally in a filthy state: 'I turned the straw out of some of the cribs and there were maggots at the bottom of them where sick men had laid.'[33]

No effort was made to separate patients according to the degree of their disorder, cases of all descriptions congregating in the single exercise yard

---

29. House of Commons, *Select Committee on Pauper Lunatics in Middlesex*, p. 15.
30. *Ibid.*, pp. 30–1, evidence of Richard Roberts.
31. *Ibid.*, pp. 37, 98, evidence of John Nettle, and of Thomas Jennings, Warburton's head keeper.
32. *Ibid.*, p. 32, evidence of William Soloman. This account was corroborated by several other witnesses. See *ibid.*, pp. 37, 38, 40, 128.
33. *Ibid.*, p. 37, evidence of John Nettle.

allotted inmates of each sex. The visitor would find 'some of them chained to seats, and some of them handcuffed; and there are some exceedingly noisy, and others melancholy and dull, all in the same apartments, and in a yard too small for such a number, where they have not room for exercise or for employment. . .'.[34] Patients necessarily performed most of the work in the asylum – on the men's side, for instance, there were only two paid attendants for 164 male pauper lunatics.[35] Warburton himself put in an appearance twice a week, as did Thomas Jennings, the man nominally in charge of the day-to-day administration of the establishment.[36]

As the Committee took pains to document,[37] such conditions were scarcely atypical of those metropolitan madhouses which concentrated on the pauper lunatic trade, and the reformers now made use of this ostensibly local investigation to reopen the issue of legislation to give effect to at least some of the changes they considered necessary. This time the bills were framed to avoid offending the local gentry and magistrates, and to reduce the most obvious manifestations of central control to a minimum, so as to eliminate the most important source of opposition to the earlier bills. The bill which eventually became the County Asylums Act (9 George IV *c.* 40) on the surface added very little to previous acts regulating these establishments. It did, however, create a precedent for some central government interest in the internal affairs of country asylums through the apparently trivial provisions that the magistrates were to send annual returns of admissions, discharges and deaths to the Home Office, and that the Secretary of State could, if he so chose, send a visitor to any county asylum – though such a visitor had no legal power to intervene in asylum administration. A second bill, which passed as the Madhouse Act (9 George IV *c.* 41), marked another partial success for the reformers. The 1827 inquiry had again shown that inspection on a part-time basis by the College of Physicians under the 1774 Madhouse Act was little more than a cosmetic measure with no practical force,[38] and with this new act they

34. *Ibid.*, p. 24, evidence of Garrett Dillon, a surgeon.
35. *Ibid.*, p. 34, evidence of William Soloman.
36. *Ibid.*, p. 34, evidence of William Soloman.
37. See the evidence of Garrett Dillon, Dr John Bright, Peregrine Fernandez, and Dr Alexander Franston, and the detailed evidence on the state of Casey's, Burrows's, and Holt's madhouses, House of Commons, *Report on Pauper Lunatics in the County of Middlesex*, pp. 153–8. At the latter, for instance, 'In an outhouse at the bottom of the yard, ventilated only by cracks in the wall, were enclosed three females, the door was padlocked; upon an open rail-bottomed crib herein, without straw, was chained a female by the wrists, arms, and legs, and fixed also by chains to the crib; her wrists were blistered by the handcuffs; she was covered only by a rug; the only attendant upon all the lunatics appeared to be one female servant, who stated she was helped by the patients.'
38. For discussion of the role of the College of Physicians in inspecting asylums before 1828, see Nicholas Hervey, 'A Slavish Bowing Down: the Lunacy Commission and the Psychiatric Profession 1845–60', in W. Bynum, R. Porter, and M. Shepherd (eds), *The Anatomy of Madness*, Vol. 2, London: Tavistock, 1985, pp. 99–101. Hervey documents the close personal and professional links between the physicians inspecting the madhouses and the madhouse keepers themselves, and their total failure to establish any corpus of administrative expertise.

finally secured its abolition and replacement. To achieve this, however, they were forced to engage in a temporary tactical retreat from the proposals for a full-time national 'Board of Inspection' which had been so prominent a feature of the 1816, 1817, and 1819 bills, and which remained the solution they ultimately wanted to implement.[39]

The 1828 Act did provide for the establishment of a new Commission to license and supervise lunatic asylums. Its activities were, however, to be confined to the metropolitan area. Moreover, the Commissioners were to be appointed on a purely part-time basis, with the five physician Commissioners receiving token payment, and the rest giving their services gratuitously. In this respect it represented a reversion to the amateur system of the past, an apparent abandonment of the earlier insistence on the Benthamite ideal of full-time, expert administrators; and in filling the medical positions on the Commission, the Home Secretary, Peel, deferred to Sir Henry Halford, President of the Royal College.[40] Meanwhile, in the provinces, in what was basically but a minor departure from the provisions of the 1774 Act, the duties of visitation and licensing remained in the hands of the magistrates – three justices and a medical attendant were to be appointed at the General Quarter Sessions and charged with visiting all houses licensed to receive lunatics at least three times a year. Finally, the Act's provisions for inspection applied only to private madhouses, not to county asylums, or to the charity or 'subscription' asylums.

In all these respects, the bill to regulate madhouses presented in 1828 seemed a weak measure, particularly when compared with the earlier bills the reformers had presented.[41] But it had the decisive merit of conciliating the opposition sufficiently to secure its passage (not entirely unscathed) through the Lords.[42] By allowing the magistrates to continue to perform the duties of visitors in the provinces, it avoided giving offence to the country gentry; the provision exempting the county asylums, which were run by the local magistrates, had the same effect; while the parallel exemp-

---

39. S.W. Nicoll's *An Enquiry into the Present State of Visitation, in Asylums for the Reception of the Insane* (London: Harvey and Darton, 1828), published with a view to influencing the pending legislation, had provided a forceful restatement of the earlier arguments for the establishment of a full-time national inspectorate.
40. *Cf.* Nicholas Hervey, 'A Slavish Bowing Down', p. 101.
41. The Act did embody a number of new provisions, however. The commission could, for the first time, revoke or refuse licenses; a resident medical officer was now required for asylums with more than 100 patients; changes were made in the certification process, and some minimal requirements instituted concerning returns of patients and records of their treatment; and finally, the Evangelicals in the House of Lords imposed a requirement that divine service should be performed in every licensed house each Sunday.
42. Once again, both the Royal College of Physicians and a number of prominent medical madhouse keepers campaigned vigorously against the legislation, contending that it infringed on professional prerogatives, illegitimately interfered with private contracts between physicians and patients' families, and threatened to undermine mad-doctors' therapeutic efforts. For documentation of some of the behind the scenes lobbying, see the diaries of E.T. Monro, entries for 17, 25 March, 3, 12, 29 April, 14, 16, 17 May, 1828, cited in N. Hervey, 'A Slavish Bowing Down', pp. 101, 120.

tion of the charity hospitals circumvented the possibility that the powerful lobby formed by their aristocratic boards of governors would be ranged against the bill; and the provisions for the Metropolitan Commissioners to be amateurs stilled fears that the measure would produce a further increase in the powers of the executive.

Some of the most active reformers felt that the compromises had gone too far. S.W. Nicoll, the Recorder of York, who had been a close ally of Higgins in exposing the abuses at the York Asylum, was convinced the new Commission would be unwieldy and its impact too geographically limited. Despairingly, he commented that it offered 'no new stimulus, no new motive, no new intelligence . . .'.[43] In the long run, however, the Metropolitan Commission proved to be an extremely effective pressure group on behalf of the expansion of its own activities, and for the establishment of the full-time national inspectorate which the reformers had long sought.[44] All the leading members of the Parliamentary group of lunacy reformers initially secured appointments to the Commission – eleven of the fifteen Commissioners were MPs or former MPs, and their ranks included Robert Gordon, Anthony Ashley Cooper (later Lord Shaftesbury), and Lord Granville Somerset.[45] Such a small and politically influential group was well placed to use their reports as propaganda for their own solution to the problems of insanity and to produce evidence which would convince others of the correctness of their case. Moreover, they could confidently anticipate that while they enforced the provisions of the 1828 Act relatively vigorously, and thus eliminated at least the grosser forms of abuse, a majority of the provincial magistrates would continue to ignore or laxly carry out their responsibilities. Given time, the opponents of the centralized system could be relied upon to produce evidence which would damn their cause.

Entering upon their duties in 1828, the Metropolitan Commissioners

43. S.W. Nicoll, *An Enquiry Into the Present State of Visitation*, pp. 79, 84, 88–9.
44. For somewhat contrasting and more detailed recent assessments of the Metropolitan Commission's impact, see D.J. Mellett, 'Bureaucracy and Mental Illness: The Commissioners in Lunacy 1845–90', *Medical History* 25, 1981, pp. 223–4 (inclined to be sceptical of the Commission's impact); and N. Hervey, 'A Slavish Bowing Down', pp. 101–3, and *idem.*, 'The Lunacy Commission 1845–60, with Special Reference to the Implementation of Policy in Kent and Surrey, unpublished Ph.D. dissertation, Bristol University, 1987, pp. 70–114 (suggesting it played a more substantial role). My own review of the evidence corresponds more closely with Hervey's account.
45. Not surprisingly, many of the parliamentarians were too busy to participate in the routine work of inspection. In 1832, therefore, the Lord Chancellor, Lord Brougham, introduced legislation to cut back on the number of lay commissioners, and to add, for the first time, two barristers as legal commissioners. The first occupants of these positions, Mylne and Procter, played a vital role in systematizing the Commission's work, and in maximizing its effectiveness. It was a combination of the legal and lay commissioners (and not the medical commissioners) that made the Metropolitan Commission a powerful force for further change. See the discussions in N. Hervey, 'A Slavish Bowing Down', pp. 101–3; and *idem.*, 'The Lunacy Commission 1845–60', pp. 70–1.

found buildings that were dirty and ill-ventilated; inadequate numbers of attendants, with the consequence that mechanical restraint was widely employed; and patients left to vegetate, provided with neither occupations nor amusements. Establishments which took private patients were held to suffer less from these defects, but were 'nevertheless less satisfactory than might be hoped'.[46] By 1830, however, they were (somewhat implausibly) claiming that the more obvious abuses exposed by the 1827 Select Committee were in the process of disappearing. Following an inspection of Warburton's by now notorious White House, they reported that they were 'much gratified with the general condition of the House. . . . Mr Warburton has devoted much pains to the improvement of this establishment and the result is highly creditable'.[47] And they used their subsequent reports to drive home their claims about the value of thorough inspection. In 1836, for example, they asserted that 'in several respects, the improvement [in metropolitan madhouses] still continues to be progressive: among other points may be mentioned with praise the increased attention of the superintendents to cleanliness and ventilation, to classification of patients in wards, and to providing them with occupation and amusement . . . the amelioration has been marked and uniform'.[48] They had, they concluded, 'great reason to be satisfied with the improvements which have taken place in all the asylums within their jurisdiction'.[49]

On the other hand, evidence was readily forthcoming of instances where inspection in the provinces was cursory in the extreme. By 1838, the Commissioners were complaining that in the provinces, 'the salutary provisions of the Act by which it is required that all houses . . . shall be annually licensed and periodically visited and report by the Visiting Magistrates, have been in great degree neglected or violated . . . '.[50] As Conolly had predicted, the local justices proved to be reluctant to inquire into the conduct of a madhouse proprietor who was doubtless 'a most respectable man, a neighbour, a friend perhaps, and the asylum is his fortune; to depreciate it, or to cast doubt upon a case where he has none, may be to ruin him; and the sense of duty in an honorary Visitor could hardly lead him to run such a risk'.[51]

In 1839, a Select Committee of the House of Commons, set up in response to a petition from the Herefordshire magistrates for an inquiry into conditions at the Hereford Lunatic Asylum, produced evidence of widespread administrative irregularities and ignorance of the law on the part of both local magistrates and the proprietor of the asylum, defects in

46. Metropolitan Commissioners in Lunacy, *Report for 1830*, p. 4.
47. *Ibid.*
48. Metropolitan Commissioners in Lunacy, *Report for 1836*, p. 1.
49. *Ibid.*, p. 3.
50. Metropolitan Commissioners in Lunacy, *Report for 1838*, p. 6.
51. John Conolly, *An Inquiry Concerning the Indications of Insanity. With suggestions for the better protection and care of the insane*, London: Taylor, 1830, p. 6.

inspection which were presumed to have contributed to the neglect and ill-treatment of the patients.[52] In their report for the year, the Metropolitan Commissioners drew attention to these findings, as providing independent confirmation of the deficiencies of provincial inspection. By contrast, in successive reports, they made a point of emphasizing their own growing volume of work, and hence their need for more staff and more office space.[53]

4. The Elaboration of a Pro-Institutional Ideology

The Commissioners were not alone in seeking to revise and extend the reforms of 1828. The more respectable asylum doctors, who were attempting to monopolize the mad-business and to transform it into an arena for professional practice, were consequently interested in excluding the more disreputable elements engaging in the madhouse trade. The members of this proto-profession produced large numbers of books and pamphlets which served to bolster their claims to possess a specific expertise in the treatment of the insane; but many of these writers were also concerned 'to condense, in a plain, practical, and still popular form, the results of observation in the treatment of insanity, for the specific purpose of demanding from the public an amelioration of the condition of the insane'.[54] Over the next two decades, this emerging class of professional asylum administrators, acting in concert with a number of lay reformers, developed an increasingly elaborate account of the merits and advantages of the asylum as a response to insanity. Emphasis was placed on the contrast between conditions in traditional madhouses and the possibilities of the new approach based on moral treatment – both as providing more humane care than would otherwise have been possible, and as producing cures in a large number of cases. The growing volume of literature discussing what an asylum could do and what it should be like was matched by a growing optimism about the likely results of the new system. More and more the asylum was presented as a technical, objective, scientific response to the patient's condition, an environment which provided the best possible conditions for his recovery.

In the absence of public asylums, many pauper lunatics who were 'not so violent as to be perfectly unmanageable' were frequently abandoned, and left to 'linger out their existence in a workhouse'.[55] Here, the reformers objected, 'they are under the care of persons totally and entirely ignorant of the proper treatment of lunatics . . . the rooms in which they are kept

---

52. See House of Commons, *Report from the Select Committee on Hereford Lunatic Asylum, with Minutes of Evidence*, 1839.
53. See Metropolitan Commissioners in Lunacy, *Reports for 1838, 1839, 1840*.
54. W.A.F. Browne, *What Asylums Were, Are, and Ought to Be*, Edinburgh: Black, 1837, p. 1.
55. W.C. Ellis, *Letter to Thomas Thompson*, p. 10.

are ill-adapted to the confinement of such persons, and . . . from those causes, those unfortunate persons have been constantly confined in strait waistcoats, frequently kept in bed night and day.'[56] But though the maniac was here reduced to the status of an inconvenient object, whose condition required no more than that minimal efforts be made to ensure his physical survival, yet his presence was still a burden upon the workhouse administrators, and on the lives of the sane inmates. If nothing worse, the latter were forced to tolerate the disruptions and unpleasantness brought about by the lunatics' refusal to conform to ordinary social conventions, so that under even the most brutal and unfeeling management, 'lunatics in workhouses' unavoidably remained 'an extreme annoyance to the other inhabitants of those houses'.[57]

From this perspective, 'the propriety and necessity of a separate establishment for the care of lunaticks, must be obvious' to even the meanest intelligence.[58] The mental hospital would be an asylum in a dual sense: to the workhouse, it would afford relief from the disorder always at least latent in the presence of madmen; and for the maniac himself, it would provide a sanctuary, a refuge from the world with which he could no longer cope. Here he would be cared for by those who had a greater practical experience in the management of insanity, in surroundings specifically designed to avoid the structural deficiencies which, in the workhouse, made harsh treatment of the lunatic almost inescapable.

The promise of the specialized institution lay in its ability to create a forgiving environment in which humane care on a mass basis was possible; and the probability that the efforts of those running the asylums would restore a significant number of lunatics to sanity. In the aftermath of the publicity moral treatment had received, even those who did not entirely share the reformers' optimistic faith in the virtues of the asylum found it hard to resist the notion that the grim custodial routines by which the workhouses accommodated itself to the lunatic could be transformed. And since it was assumed that the insane in workhouses were only there because they lacked either the personal resources or the sort of supportive kinship network they needed to survive outside an institution, to advocate the continued segregation of such derelicts behind the walls of a different institution was scarcely controversial. If one could overlook the powerful deterrent factor of the cost of building and maintaining asylums (as parish officials were reluctant and reformers were prone to do),[59] then on most

---

56. Select Committee, *Report*, 1815, p. 11, evidence of Edward Wakefield.
57. *Ibid.*
58. St. Luke's Asylum, *Annual Report*, 1830, p. 3.
59. For instance, even after the 1827 Parliamentary inquiry had revealed that conditions in private madhouses in Middlesex were, if anything, worse than they had been in 1815, the overwhelming majority of petitions from parishes received by the magistrates' committee charged with erecting a county asylum urged rejection of the plan (twelve against versus only one in favour). Similarly, in Sussex, even after the passage of the 1845 Act which made provision of a county asylum compulsory, the opposition

other grounds it was plausible (and probably correct) to assert that at least those lunatics who had formerly starved and rotted in workhouse cellars would be better off in asylums.

But the reformers were not content just to bring these benefits to those who had hitherto been confined in sub-standard institutions. The asylum possessed advantages which even those whose families were still willing and able to care for them should share in. And the reformers and asylum doctors were determined that they should do so.

The idea of confining the sick or helpless members of one's family in an institution was not yet a popular one, particularly among the more respectable elements of society. Even the poorest families amongst the working classes made strenuous efforts to avoid bringing the disgrace of the workhouse upon themselves. Similarly, the hospitals of the period still tended to be patronized by a clientele composed of the indigent sick and the friendless traveller far from home. The enormous mortality rates, uncompensated for by greatly increased chances of recovery (to say nothing of the lingering stigma of their charity origins), gave them the public reputation of being little better than charnel houses, vectors of disease and death to be avoided by all who had the means to do so.

As for the deranged, the evils of the *ancien régime* madhouse had been widely advertised by the reformers themselves. The picture that had emerged from successive parliamentary inquiries and from the books and pamphlets produced by those agitating for lunacy reform incorporated a mixture of sex, madness, maltreatment, and murder in a fashion calculated at once to titillate and to repel. With male and female flung together without even the pretence of classification and supervision, the public was invited to imagine the 'decorum and purity of the intercourse which ensued,' bearing in mind that 'the beings thus having uninterrupted access to each other were irrational, acting under the impulse of ungovernable passions, and unrestrained, perhaps by the sacred obligations of religion, and certainly unmindful of the conventional check of public opinion'.[60] Meanwhile, even those madwomen who retained some remnants of innate feminine purity and modesty were not safe, their bodies being at the disposal of the lascivious ruffians who served as madhouse attendants. The deplorable consequences of a system in which the mad were '[r]egarded as wild beasts, [and] all maniacs were indiscriminately treated as such'[61] extended in every direction: patients bled and drugged into insensibility; their public display, like 'the animals in a menagerie'; unregarded deaths from botched force-feeding and the brutality of uncaring attendants; the

---

at the parish level was so determined and well organized that, despite continuous pressure from the Lunacy Commissioners, no county asylum was built until 1859. (The memorials opposing asylum construction, and the correspondence with the Lunacy Commission, are in the County Record Office at Lewes.)

60. W.A.F. Browne, *What Asylums Were, Are, and Ought to Be*, p. 128.
61. *Ibid.*, p. 101.

corrupt confinement of the sane, amidst the shrieks and ravings of the mad; and the remarkable and ingenious array of 'bolts, bars, chains, muffs, collars, and strait-jackets' madhouse keepers had devised to coerce a measure of order from recalcitrant human raw materials.

In such a context, it would not be difficult to conclude that asylums were 'rather . . . places for the concentration and aggravation, than for the relief of disease';[62] and the contention that everyone becoming insane ought to be promptly removed to an institution had an obviously paradoxical air.[63] So far from embracing the idea of institutionalization, a family concerned with the welfare of a member afflicted by mental disturbance, periodically regaled with evidence which appeared to confirm their worst gothic nightmares about what transpired behind the high walls and barred windows of the madhouse, must surely conclude that 'no person who can keep such a sufferer out, ought to place him in an asylum . . . '.[64]

But if asylum superintendents and their reformist mentors were to obtain a population consisting of much more than just chronic pauper derelicts, if the asylum was to amount to more than just a convenient dumping ground for confining the most troublesome flotsam and jetsam of society, then families who could exercise some choice in the matter had somehow to be convinced that the institution should be the place of first rather than last resort. Unless this effort succeeded, asylums would surely remain starved of funds. Moreover, without a significant proportion of upper-class patients, the newly emerging psychiatric profession could look forward to no more than a dubious status as a barely legitimate branch of medicine. For close and unremitting contact with the stigmatized and powerless carries its own peculiar reward – a share of their stigma and marginality.[65]

From a variety of perspectives, then, the construction of a more benign and salubrious image of the asylum, and the insistence on the potential curability of insanity when properly treated were vital components of the reformers' efforts to reshape attitudes towards madness and the mad, and

---

62. *Ibid.*, pp. 133, 107.

63. The problem is quite openly recognized and discussed by Andrew Combe, writing to the author of a pamphlet attacking conditions in contemporary asylums: 'Your work will strengthen the prejudice against asylums as moral lazar-houses . . . [by reinforcing] the popular notion of the cruel treatment of lunatics, and the great aversion thence arising either to have the patients removed to an asylum, or even to admit that insanity really exists.' The public must rather be 'led to regard asylums as infirmaries for the cure and kind treatment of that disease. . . .' Letter dated 13 July 1840, reprinted in George Combe, *The Life and Correspondence of Andrew Combe, M.D.*, Edinburgh: Maclachlan and Stewart, 1850, pp. 376–7.

64. Anon., *On the Present State of Lunatic Asylums*, London: Drury, 1839, p. 11. *Cf.* also W.A.F. Browne, *What Asylums Were, Are, and Ought to Be*, pp. 172, 177.

65. Compare J.C. Bucknill's complaint that 'the public extends its unreasonable antipathy to the insane, to all those who are connected with insanity; even to those who wrestle with the great evil, and, to the best of their ability, hold it down . . .'. 'Presidential Address', *Journal of Mental Science* 7, 1860, p. 6.

lay at the heart of their attempts to overcome the political and economic obstacles to lunacy reform. Yet in the light of the reformers' own findings, the conclusion that institutional care was preferable to even the best and most solicitous domestic arrangements was by no means self-evident. Hence it required elaborate ideological justification. Only by emphasizing the expertise of those who ran the asylums and the positive benefits of asylum treatment could the institution's advocates make a presumptive case for extending those 'benefits' to those not compelled to use the asylum's services.

The emerging profession was not above implying that any madman, even an apparently placid and harmless case of dementia, was capable of sudden and unprovoked acts of violence, which were peculiarly liable to be directed against members of his immediate family. This element of unpredictability carried with it the clear implication that 'both for their own safety, and that of others, it is necessary that they should be placed in a state of confinement, differing, of course, in degree as the symptoms are violent'.[66] But for all its functionality, the traditional argument, based on the threat the lunatic might pose to the security of the community, was more readily used to justify custody than efforts at cure; so that asylum superintendents were reluctant to employ it as their major argument for committal. Instead, they preferred to develop an alternative thesis, stressing that the management of insanity 'is an art of itself' and that in its successful treatment, 'the requisite means and advantages can rarely, if ever, be united in the private habitations even of the opulent'.[67]

The much greater experience of asylum personnel with the shapes and forms of mental disturbance was reflected in the ease and skill with which they managed and handled their patients. By contrast, the deranged frequently suffered from the well-meaning but misconceived interventions of devoted relatives. Not surprisingly, then, 'they submit more patiently to discipline from strangers, who are experienced in their treatment, than from relatives and dependents, who are timid, unskilled, and frequently the objects of irritation.'[68] Architecturally, too, '[a] private dwelling is ill-adapted to the wants and requirements of such an unfortunate being',[69] since in addition to there being a specific expertise attached to treating the insane, there were also buildings which were particularly adapted and suited to the condition of insanity. Only a purpose-built asylum could provide the requisite conditions for 'moral and physical management . . .

---

66. W.C. Ellis, *Letter to Thomas Thompson*, p. 8. See also John Parkin, *On the Medical and Moral Treatment of Insanity*, London: Martin, [1843?]; and Robert Gardiner Hill, *A Lecture on the Management of Lunatic Asylums and the Treatment of the Insane*, London: Simpkin, Marshall, 1839, p. 6.
67. Reverend J.T. Becher, *An Address to the Public on the General Lunatic Asylum near Nottingham*, Newark: 1811, pp. iv–v.
68. [Edward Long Fox], *Brislington House: An Asylum for Lunatics*, Bristol: n.p., 1806, p. 1.
69. R.G. Hill, *Lecture on the Management of Lunatic Asylums*, p. 6.

as well as the means of preventing personal injury and inconvenience to the Patient'.[70]

Besides the fact that it lacked most of the basic necessities for the effective treatment of mental illness, the home suffered from a fatal flaw, one which made it the least suitable place of all to keep a lunatic. Quite simply, it was the environment which had nurtured the disturbance in the first place. Lunatics ought not to be treated at home, 'not only on account of the distress and confusion they there produce, but because there circumstances that excite a maniacal paroxysm frequently exist'.[71]

If any families were concerned with the welfare of their insane members, it was surely those who, rather than simply abdicating all responsibility by handing them over to strangers, were prepared to suffer the inconvenience produced by keeping such people at home. But if the asylum doctors were to be believed, such generous and self-sacrificing instincts were fraught with potentially disastrous consequences for the patient himself. After all, 'experience . . . proves that few are cured at home, but many more when removed'.[72] The overwhelming consensus of the experts in the field testified to

the improbability (I had almost said moral impossibility) of an insane person's regaining the use of his reason, except by removing him early to some Institution for that purpose. If such a result is ever to be obtained without the adoption of this plan, it is either a very rare occurrence indeed, or it has ensued from a change of residence, of scene, and of persons around, combined with a mode of treatment in some measure resembling that which can be adopted fully only in a Building constructed for the purpose.[73]

The need for reassurance that 'those we exile to madhouses are receiving treatment, not punishment'[74] seems to have emerged early in the history of the asylum, and to have been offered and accepted on the basis

70. [E.L. Fox], *Brislington House*, p. 1.
71. [E.L. Fox], *Brislington House*, p. 1. See also *The State of Lincoln Hospital in 1837: 13th Annual Report.*
72. *Westminster Review* 18, 1833, p. 134. This was a safe generalization, since nobody possessed (or was likely to possess) the information necessary to disprove it.
73. R.G. Hill, *Lecture on the Management of Lunatic Asylums*, pp. 4–5. See also Maximilian Jacobi, *On the Construction and Management of Hospitals for the Insane* (translated by John Kitching), London: Churchill, 1841, p. 7. Compare also George Man Burrows (*Commentaries on the Causes, Forms, Symptoms, and Treatment of . . . Insanity*, London: Underwood, 1828, p. 696): 'There is no general maxim in the treatment of insanity wherein medical practitioners, ancient or modern, foreign or domestic, are so unanimous, as that of separating the patient from all customary associations, his family, and his home. . . . Few of the medical profession require arguments or proof to convince them of the great utility of separation. When the friends of any insane person have a doubt, and have not confidence in the advice or probity of their physician, they should consult the works of authors who have treated of insanity, and who can have no interest in the question.'
74. Erving Goffman, *Asylums*, Garden City, New York: Doubleday, 1961, p. 369.

of very little evidence. Perhaps this should not surprise us: after all, it serves important functions for both the madhouse keepers and their true clients, the 'patient's' family. For the former, it provides the necessary material from which the self-image of expertise can be constructed. For the latter, it eases the guilt which must inevitably be attached to the prospect of confining a loved one in an institution which has never managed to obtain a very salubrious reputation. Accordingly, both groups could find comfort in the assurance that 'the treatment of insanity is now so well understood, and the requisites for forming a perfect asylum, or hospital, for the reception of insane patients so fully ascertained by experience that they admit of very little discussion'.[75]

5. The Asylum's Critics

By and large, the reformers and the asylum doctors were extremely effective in proselytizing the asylum's virtues and the need to insulate the insane from the world. From time to time, the wisdom accumulated by the experts was condensed and summarized for popular consumption in one or another of the leading reviews of the period.[76] And laymen could always be impressed by references to a veritable pantheon of names famous for their humanity and/or their skill in treating mental disorder – Cullen, Tuke, Pinel, Esquirol – all of whom were staunch advocates of the seclusion of the insane.

Occasionally, though, a few isolated figures refused to bend to the weight of professional and informed opinion, and raised their voices against the tendency to incarcerate all those labelled as mad. For Andrew Combe, the judgement that someone was insane was quite distinct from the question of whether confinement in an institution was appropriate, 'and this distinction ought never for a moment to be forgotten'.[77] Granted there were certain cases – where the home was a source of 'incessant irritation' or where 'morbid associations have . . . connected themselves inseparably with his own family and friends' – in which 'the preference ought to be given to a well-regulated asylum . . .'.[78] But '[b]ecause confinement is beneficial to the recovery of one class of patients, it has been supposed that it must be equally advantageous for the recovery of all; and

---

75. Andrew Halliday, *A Letter to the Magistrates of Middlesex on Erecting an Asylum for Pauper Lunatics*, London: Brettell, 1826, p. 13.
76. Compare 'Esquirol and the Treatment of the Insane', *Westminster Review* 18, 1833, pp. 129–38; 'Lunacy', *Westminster Review* 37, 1842, pp. 305–21; 'Lunatic Asylums', *Westminster Review* 43, 1845, pp. 162–92; [W.H. Fitton], 'Lunatic Asylums', *Edinburgh Review* 28, 1817, pp. 431–71; 'Insanity', *Quarterly Review* 24, 1821, pp. 169–94.
77. Andrew Combe, *Observations on Mental Derangement*, Edinburgh: Anderson, 1831, p. 345.
78. *Ibid.*, pp. 346–7, 349.

to pronounce a person insane, and to send him to a madhouse, have thus come to be considered as almost the same thing . . .' – a practice he dismissed as 'an utter and injurious absurdity'.[79] On the contrary, 'Many who have been hurried into premature confinement, have, by that very act, been fitted for remaining tenants for life of the cells to which heedless rashness first consigned them.'[80] In approaching the question of what to do with the insane, the first requisite was thus 'to get rid of the hitherto inseparable association between insanity and the madhouse'.[81]

Thomas Bakewell, perhaps the best-known non-medical madhouse keeper of the early nineteenth century, derived a substantial income from his small private asylum at Spring Vale. Consequently, one is tempted to dismiss his opposition to plans for a system of publicly-funded asylums as anything but disinterested. The burden of his complaint, however, echoed the concerns of less partial observers:

> Large Public Asylums for the Insane, are certainly wrong, upon system; for nothing can be more calculated to prevent recovery, from a state of Insanity, than the horrors of a large Mad House, close confinement, and a state of idleness in the company of incurable Lunatics.[82]

Others, indeed, were still more hostile to institutionalization. George Nesse Hill, author of one of the most well-known early nineteenth-century texts on the management and restoration of lunatics, insisted that 'congregating insane people together in the promiscuous way which has too long obtained is an evil of the most pernicious tendency'.[83] The separation from the sane influences which surrounded the mad in the outside world exacerbated their problems, and the unfortunate inmates of madhouses tended to feed off one another's delusions. Consequently, both 'public charities and private asylums stand opposed to all rational plans of speedy and permanent cure of insanity, and from their very nature are the most unfavourable situation in which . . . lunatics . . . can be placed'.[84] John Reid's verdict on asylums was couched in yet harsher terms: decrying 'our medical prisons . . . our *slaughter houses* for the destruction and mutilation of the human mind',[85] he alleged that they fixed the very delusions they claimed to remove. Indeed, 'Many of the depots for the captivity of intellectual invalids may be regarded only as nurseries for and manufactories of madness; magazines or reservoirs of lunacy, from which is

79. *Ibid.*, p. 346.
80. *Ibid.*, p. 348.
81. *Ibid.*, p. 343.
82. Thomas Bakewell, *A Letter . . . to . . . the Select Committee of the House of Commons*, p. 9.
83. G.N. Hill, *An Essay on the Prevention and Cure of Insanity*, London: Longman, Hurst, Rees, Orme, and Brown, 1814, p. 222.
84. *Ibid.*, p. 220.
85. John Reid, *Essays on Insanity, Hypochondriacal and Other Nervous Affections*, London: Longman, Hurst, Rees, Orme, and Brown, 1816, p. 206, emphasis in the original.

issued, from time to time, a sufficient supply for perpetuating and extending this formidable disease.'[86]

John Conolly, newly installed as Professor of the Nature and Treatment
of Diseases at the fledgling University of London,[87] pointed out that it
was seldom hard to isolate particular features of someone's behavior which
would lend credence to the idea that he was crazy. To send such a person
to an asylum was practically to ensure that the designation would stick:
'Once confined, the very confinement is admitted as the strongest of all
proofs that a man must be mad.' Hence to create more institutions would
guarantee the discovery of more madmen to fill them. Already, 'the
crowd of most of our asylums is made up of odd but harmless individuals,
not much more absurd than numbers who are at large'.[88] Moreover, even
for those who were manifestly mad, the asylum was more likely to prove
harmful than otherwise. After all, an anonymous fellow critic argued,

> what would be the consequence, if we were to take a sane person, who
> had been accustomed to enjoy society, and . . . were to lock him up in a
> small house with a keeper for his only associate, and no place for
> exercise but a miserable garden? We should certainly not look for any
> improvement to his moral and intellectual condition. Can we then
> reasonably expect that *a treatment which would be injurious to a sane mind,*
> *should tend to restore a diseased one?*[89]

The most vital deficiencies of the asylum as a curative institution were
thus inherent in its very structure. No matter that asylum directors were
'men of great intelligence and humanity'; no matter that

> they may point to the spaciousness of their grounds, to the variety
> of occupations and amusements prepared for their patients; to the
> excellence of their food and the convenience of their lodgings; and urge
> that as little restraint is employed as is compatible with their safety;

---

86. *Ibid.*, p. 205. Such statements echoed a scepticism about the merits of institutions that
can also be traced among some eighteenth-century writers (when, in general, the value of
asylum treatment was portrayed in far more circumscribed terms). Andrew Harper, for
instance, claimed that asylum care was wholly counter-productive, 'big with ignorance
and absurdity. [Confinement,] 'tis true, may answer the purpose of private interest, and
domestic convenience, but at the same time it destroys all the obligations of humanity,
robs the sufferer of every advantage, and deprives him of all the favourable
circumstances which might tend to his recovery . . . confinement never fails to aggravate
the disease. A state of coercion is a state of torture from which the mind, under any
circumstances, revolts.' Andrew Harper, *A Treatise on the Real Cause and Cure of Insanity*,
London: Stalker and Walter, 1789, pp. 59–61.
87. An appointment that lasted a scant two years, following which he (temporarily) sank
back into provincial obscurity. See my *Social Order/Mental Disorder: Anglo-American*
Psychiatry in Historical Perspective, Berkeley: University of California Press/London:
Routledge, 1989, pp. 169–85.
88. John Conolly, *An Inquiry Concerning the Indications of Insanity*, London: Taylor, 1830, pp.
4–5, 17.
89. Anon., *On the Present State of Lunatic Asylums*, p. 39, emphasis in the original.

but the fault of the association of lunatics with each other, and the infrequency of any communication between the patient and persons of sound mind mars the whole design.[90]

For those forced to remain within the walls of an asylum, 'the effect of living constantly among mad men and women is a loss of all sensibility and self-respect or care; or, not infrequently, a perverse pleasure in adding to the confusion and diversifying the eccentricity of those about them. . . . In both cases the disease grows inveterate.'[91] Such a pathological environment thus encourages the very behaviours which are then used to justify its existence: 'Paroxysms of violence alternate with fits of sullenness; both are considered further proofs of the hopelessness of the case.'[92] The peculiar routines of the asylum are quite unlike those of the outside world. Nevertheless, some inmates manage to adjust to them and it is one of the ironies of institutional existence that those who manage this transition most effectively are at the same time reducing their ability to function in the outside world. 'After many hopeless years, such patients become so accustomed to the routine of the house, as to be mere children; and are content to remain there as they commonly do, until they die.'[93] Equally pathetic were the 'numerous examples . . . in which it was evident that although the patients were not yet sufficiently recovered to be restored to their families without superintendence, a continued residence in the asylum was gradually ruining the body and the mind'.[94]

If some of these critics seemed to argue for the total abolition of lunatic asylums, others, as I have indicated, were more circumspect. Andrew Combe, while urging that many of those who could not be cared for in their own homes might nevertheless be better placed outside an asylum (in a physician's household for instance, or boarded with an attendant 'hired for the purpose'), still conceded that in certain cases, 'the preference ought to be given to a well-regulated asylum, from the superior means which such an institution affords for enforcing regularity and order, and the various other measures conducive to the safety, comfort, and recovery of the patient'.[95] John Conolly, too, urged that in certain circumstances, 'public lunatic asylums' must be regarded as 'unavoidable evils'.[96] They were, however, totally unsuitable for most of the insane: curable cases ought never to be shut up in an asylum; nor should the large class of the harmlessly demented; indeed, '[n]o patient should be confined in a Lunatic

---

90. J. Conolly, *An Inquiry Concerning the Indications of Insanity*, p. 31.
91. *Ibid.*, p. 22.
92. *Ibid.*
93. *Ibid.*, p. 21.
94. *Ibid.*, p. 20.
95. A. Combe, *Observations on Mental Derangement*, p. 349.
96. J. Conolly, *An Inquiry Concerning the Indications of Insanity*, p. 7.

Asylum, except on the particular representation of the relatives or friends, that he could not have proper care and attention out of it.'[97]

The clear implication of these arguments was that the whole effort to reform the treatment of the insane by their routine isolation in hospitals was a venture which was misconceived from the start.[98] Resting their case on a faulty and incomplete analysis of what was wrong with traditional madhouses, the reformers were committing themselves to 'solutions' which, in the nature of things, could not produce a lasting improvement in the condition of the insane.[99] Yet, despite the force and relevance of the critique, it drew no intellectually adequate response from the asylum's proponents.[100] For all the impact these words had, they might as well have never been uttered. It is not just that they had no influence on social policy, or that they were met by counterarguments which seemed plausible at the time. Rather, their fate was to be greeted by silence, to be consigned to oblivion.

Quite clearly, the critics suffered from their lack of organization and numbers, which inhibited their ability to get their opponents to take them seriously. They were, after all, attempting to overturn the conventional wisdom of the overwhelming majority of experts in the field. Those experts had a considerable intellectual investment in the asylum; over many years, they had spent considerable time and effort trying to educate the public in the necessity of building asylums. Indeed, they had already persuaded the community to make a sizeable investment of material

97. *Ibid.*, pp. 29, 30, 48, 483. I would argue that even a program of building asylums based on these minimalist assumptions would in all probability have led to the ultimate dominance of the institutional response. What Combe and Conolly failed to realize is that what a family perceives as intolerable behaviour on the part of one of its members, up with which it will not/cannot put, is itself a socially variable matter. The availability of a culturally legitimate alternative to keeping him/her in the family itself tends to reduce family tolerance (to put it another way, to expand the notion of the intolerable) to a degree which varies with how grandiose and well accepted the institution's helping claims are. For further discussion of this point, see chapter 7 below.

98. Compare Sir Robert Peel: 'There could not be a question that, unless asylums for pauper lunatics were well-conducted, they would be a curse rather than a blessing; and it would be infinitely better to have none at all, than such as would only offer temptations to send unfortunate creatures to them. There were many cases in which the patient was merely troublesome, and it was much better that such as these should be abroad, it being preferable to leave them in the custody of their relatives, than lock them up in madhouses.' Quoted in Joseph Mortimer Granville, *The Care and Cure of the Insane*, Vol. 1, London: Hardwicke and Bogue, 1877, p. 87.

99. Thomas Bakewell, himself a third generation madhouse keeper, voiced extreme scepticism at the reformers' proposal for a network of state-run asylums, suggesting that the unintended consequences of its enactment would prove worse than the defects it was supposed to remedy: 'What is the system at best but a scheme to organize by law indiscriminate coercion, from which there is no appeal, under the ostensible plea of humanity?' *A Letter . . . to . . . the Select Committee of the House of Commons*, p. 20.

100. For very qualified exceptions to this general contemporary neglect, see 'Esquirol on the Treatment of the Insane', *Westminster Review* 18, 1833, pp. 129–38; Maximilian Jacobi, *On the Construction and Management of Hospitals for the Insane*, London: Churchill, 1841.

resources in just such a program. These were not the sort of commitments which would be easily abandoned.

As I shall show later in this chapter, the proponents of institutionalization were by now so convinced of the superiority of a carefully supervised asylum system that they were prepared to overlook, or rationalize away, not merely plausible *arguments* that they were wrong, but also a mass of empirical evidence which indicated that the strategy which they had chosen would, from the outset, fall far short of the goals they had set for it. This blindness or tunnel vision derived not merely from the normal reluctance of most human beings to concede that they may be mistaken, but also from a specific trait which one must possess to be a successful reformer. It is plainly the case that awareness of the complexity of the world and the moral ambiguity of existing patterns of behavior is something which always threatens to paralyse action; so that all of us are forced to resort to some degree of cognitive simplification of the world, to take for granted the 'routine grounds of everyday action', if the world is not to overwhelm us. The reformer, though, the person who seeks to alter certain aspects of this socially constructed reality, must characteristically carry such cognitive simplification to an extreme. The ability to reduce the ambiguous to the certain, to order the world in an often grossly stereotypical fashion, is generally a necessary precondition if one is to be a successful moral crusader. If the reformer is to remain dedicated to his task in the face of the ridicule and opposition he is sure to encounter, he must possess abundant confidence in the validity of his chosen alternative; and if he is to convince others of the urgent necessity to change existing arrangements, he must provide convincing, and therefore one-sided, 'proof' of his contentions.[101]

Quite apart from the single-mindedness of the reformers, and their consequent lack of receptivity to counterarguments, certain structural factors made their solution more attractive to the governing classes than its competitor. It was all very well to suggest that the reformers' cure was worse than the disease, but what was the alternative? What were the likely implications of leaving the insane in the community?

There was no systematic evidence available to answer the latter question. Assuming that all those who would later find their way into an asylum and be labelled insane could have been readily identified while still in the community (a large assumption), an adequate assessment of how they would be treated would have been a complex and time-consuming

101. Henry Maudsley characteristically offered a harsher analysis: 'He who possesses great judgment and has his feelings completely under the control of his reason is not likely to be a great reformer in his lifetime . . . the reformer . . . is not very far removed from the monomaniac . . . [indeed,] the extreme earnestness and sincerity of a little insanity are almost essential to move a man to the unhopeful and laborious task of combating the heavy opposition of the existing state of things.' Henry Maudsley, 'Delusions', *Journal of Mental Science* 9, 1863, pp. 5–6, 8.

task. It was never attempted. The reformers, at least, were content to rely on a small number of what Goffman has called 'exemplary tales' to demonstrate their contention that leaving the insane in the community invited the grossest forms of abuse. Little or no effort was made to determine whether such stories were in fact representative. Instead, isolated reports of individual cases of maltreatment were elevated to the status of definitive proof of the barbarity of existing conditions.

It is, of course, likely that by the standards of the typical middle-class reformer, the living conditions of the pauper insane would seem appalling. On may doubt, though, whether the reasons for this lay simply in the tendency of the ignorant to maltreat the mad. Living conditions of even the sane members of the lower classes, particularly those crowded together in the new urban slums, were quite sufficient to provoke expressions of horror and disgust in those of their betters who came into contact with them. Where the sane were forced to live in squalor, disease, and misery, on the very edge of starvation, the treatment of a dependent and often troublesome group like the lunatics was unlikely to correspond with middle-class ideals.

This would remain true even if the lunatic fared no worse than other members of his or her community. Certainly, few of those concerned with the plight of the insane could contemplate with equanimity the prospect of leaving them in the sorts of conditions which commonly prevailed in the larger towns:

> It will scarcely appear credible, though it is precisely true, that persons of the lowest class do not put clean sheets on their beds three times a year; that even where no sheets are used, they never wash or scour their blankets or coverlets, nor renew them until they are no longer tenable; that curtains, if unfortunately there should be any, are never cleansed, but are suffered to continue in the same state until they fall to pieces; lastly, that from three to eight individuals of different ages often sleep in the same bed; there but one room and one bed for each family. . . .
> The room occupied is either a deep cellar, almost inaccessible to the light, and admitting of no change of air; or a garret with a low roof and small windows, the passage to which is close, kept dark, and filled not only with bad air, but with putrid excremental effluvia from a vault at the bottom of the staircase . . . the cumbrous furniture or utensils of trade with which the apartments are clogged, prevent the salutary operations of a broom . . . and favour the accumulation of a hetero-geneous filth.[102]

Millions of English men, women, and children were virtually living in shit. The immediate question seems to have been whether they weren't

---

102. R. Willan (1801), quoted in M.D. George, *London Life in the Eighteenth Century*, London: Penguin, 1965, p. 95.

drowning in it. . . . Large numbers of people lived in cellars, below the level of the street and below the water line. Thus generations of human beings, out of whose lives the wealth of England was produced, were compelled to live in wealth's symbolic counterpart. And that substance which suffused their lives was also a virtual objectification of their social condition, their place in society: that was what they were.[103]

In such a situation, those who sought to improve the lot of the pauper insane, but who were dubious about the merits of the asylum, confronted a painful dilemma. They could scarcely dispute MacGill's claim that 'the circumstances of the great body of mankind are of such a nature as to render every attempt at recovering insane persons in their own houses extremely difficult, and generally hopeless'.[104] And if they balked at the idea of keeping lunatics in such surroundings, it was hard to see how they could avoid concluding that the asylum was better than the other option available, the workhouse.

What stood in the way of ameliorating the environment of the insane still at large? To improve the conditions of existence for lunatics living in the community would have entailed the provision of relatively generous pension or welfare payments to provide for their support, implying that the living standards of families with an insane member would have been raised above those of the working class generally. Moreover, under this system, the insane alone would have been beneficiaries of something approximating a modern social welfare system, whilst their sane brethren were subjected to the rigours of a Poor Law based on the principle of less eligibility. Such an approach would clearly have been administratively unworkable, not least because of the labile nature of lunacy itself, and the consequent ever-present possibility that given sufficient incentive (or rather desperation), the poorer classes would resort to feigning insanity.

In any event, a program of this sort had absolutely no political appeal to the upper classes as a whole. Engraved deeply into bourgeois consciousness in this period was an abhorrence of all forms of outdoor relief. On the one hand, this abhorrence reflected the lessons they had learned concerning the evils of such relief from the disastrous impact of the Speenhamland system – a system which had undermined the wage labour system while pauperizing, demoralizing, and degrading 'the people it was [allegedly] designed to succour'.[105] On the other hand, the determination to avoid the payment of relief to those in the community was at once reflected and strengthened on the ideological level by the hegemony of classical liberalism. For the logical consequence of that doctrine's insistence that

103. Steven Marcus, *Engels, Manchester, and the Working Class*, New York: Vintage, 1974, pp. 184–5.
104. Stevenson MacGill, *On Lunatic Asylums*, Glasgow: for the Glasgow Asylum Committee, 1810, p. 4.
105. Karl Polanyi, *The Great Transformation*, Boston: Beacon, 1957, p. 81.

each man was to be free to pursue his fortune and at the same time was to be responsible for his own success or failure, coupled with its dogmatic certainty that interference with the dictates of the free market could only be counterproductive in the long run (a proposition that could even be proved theoretically), was to render the whole notion of social protectionism – in any form – an anathema. Moreover, by the 1830s, the English ruling classes had developed

> a sense of precariousness about society. This was expressed in the form that there was a delicate balance between institutions and their operation, and the behaviour of the labouring classes. There was a feeling that any concession to idleness might bring about a rapid and cumulative deterioration in the labourer's attitude towards work. This produced a growing sensitivity towards the Poor Law[106]

– and towards anything else that, by lessening the dependence of the labouring classes on market forces, might weaken the social fabric of Victorian society.

These obstacles presented a virtually insurmountable barrier to the adoption of any alternative scheme. Only the asylum plan offered the advantage of allowing scope for the exercise of humanitarian impulses, without requiring any fundamental changes in the structure of society and while remaining consistent with the imperatives of the New Poor Law. Bowing to the inevitable, the anti-institutional mavericks fell into line. Within a few years, we find that Conolly became a leading and zealous advocate of county asylums for pauper lunatics.[107] He had been anticipated by one of his (anonymous) fellow critics, who, for all the evils he saw in the asylum (which was 'a prison' in which 'the want of all society, the absence of all amusement and employment, both of body and mind, must tend to *increase* rather than to relieve the morbid irritation of the brain'), thought from the outset that such establishments were perfectly satisfactory for paupers: 'As . . . the county or public asylums will soon become general . . . no fear need be entertained for the future fate and condition of pauper lunatics in this country.'[108] Even its staunchest opponents now conceded the asylum's inevitability.

6. The Model Institution

Given their basic commitment to the asylum as the solution to the problem of what to do with lunatics, the reformers laboured hard to translate

106. S.G. Checkland and E.O.A. Checkland (eds) 'Introduction' to *The Poor Law Report of 1834*, London: Penguin, 1974, pp. 20–1.
107. See John Conolly, *On the Construction and Government of Lunatic Asylums*, London: Churchill, 1847, and the discussion in Andrew Scull, 'John Conolly: A Victorian Psychiatric Career', pp. 162–212 in *Social Order/Mental Disorder*, Berkeley: University of California Press/London: Routledge, 1989.
108. Anon., *On the Present State of Lunatic Asylums*, pp. 16, 41, 52. Presumably, paupers' sensibilities were insufficiently refined to notice the defects of institutional confinement.

their ideals into reality. They tried to provide detailed blueprints of how an asylum should be organized and what its principal features ought to be. Throughout, it is quite clear that the dominant influence on their minds, and the model they sought perpetually to keep before them, was the York Retreat; and the writings of Samuel Tuke remained their constant guide.

The contrast with the traditional madhouse – the shit, straw, and stench, the beatings, intimidation, and rapes – could scarcely be more marked. So far from being 'a moral lazar house'[109] wherein the deranged were hidden and hope and humanity abandoned, the asylum was to be a home, where the patient was to be known and treated as an individual, where his mind was to be constantly stimulated and encouraged to return to its natural state. Mental patients required dedicated and unremitting care, which could not be administered on a mass basis, but rather must be flexible and adapted to the needs and progress of each case. Such a regime demanded kindness and an unusual degree of forbearance on the part of the staff. If this ideal were to be successfully realized, the attendants would have to be taught to keep constantly in mind the idea 'that the patient is really under the influence of a disease, which deprives him of responsibility, and frequently leads him into expressions and conduct the most opposite to his character and natural dispositions'. For this teaching to be successful, and since the attendant was the person who had the most extensive and intimate contact with the patient, attendants should be selected for their intelligence and upright moral character.[110]

Even these precautions would probably not suffice, though. They recognized that 'the business of an attendant, requires him to counteract some of the strongest principles of our common nature'.[111] Samuel Tuke himself had pointed out that the practice of moral treatment required a degree of altruism only present in those with a true vocation. After all, 'to consider them [the insane] at the same time both as brothers, and as mere automata; to applaud all they do right; and pity, without censuring, whatever they do wrong, requires such a habit of philosophical reflection, and Christian charity, as is certainly difficult to attain.'[112] It was not considered impossible, however. The influence of the superintendent could be a powerful force for good here. In a properly run asylum, the patients must be seen daily, sometimes hourly, by the man who had charge of the institution. By paying 'minute attention' to all aspects of the day-to-day conduct of the institution, by always setting, through his own example, a high standard for subordinates to emulate in their dealings with the inmates, he could foster the kind of intimate and benevolent familial environment in which acts of violence would become rare. Indeed, as the

109. W.A.F. Browne, *What Asylums Were, Are, and Ought to Be*, p. 213.
110. S. Tuke, *Description of the Retreat*, p. 175.
111. S. Tuke, *A Letter to Thomas Eddy of New York on Pauper Lunatic Asylums*, New York: Wood, 1815, p. 27.
112. S. Tuke, *Description of the Retreat*, p. 176.

autocratic guiding spirit of the whole curative apparatus, the superior moral and intellectual character of the medical superintendent was an essential precondition for success. From their own experience, though, the reformers knew that 'education and talent are but imperfect securities against the seductions of interest and indolence,' so they tried to provide a further barrier to history repeating itself: in the last analysis, they concluded, the best, even 'the only security for the good conduct of the attendants [and medical officers] is the most frequent inspection'.[113]

The emphasis on intimacy, on patients and staff alike being members of an extended 'family', was, at the outset at least, not confined to a mere rhetorical flourish. The propagandists for the asylum vigorously promoted this idea and sought to ensure that it would be carried into effect. Hence, above all else, they emphasized the virtues of small size. Without it, 'the attempt to introduce anything approaching to domestic comfort, is altogether futile; and it becomes necessary for the attendant to rule with an iron hand, to keep in order such a formidable body of malcontents'.[114] 'It is evident,' said Ellis,

> . . . that for the patients to have all the care they require, there should never be more than can, with comfort, be attended to; from 100 to 120, are as many as ought to be in any one house; where they are beyond that the individual cases cease to excite the attention they ought; and if once that is the case, not one half the good can be expected to result.[115]

Others thought that the number might be raised to 200, or even 250; but all the major authorities agreed that it should not rise beyond this point.[116]

The concern with small size, and with recreating the family in the institution, did not end here. An institution of fewer than a hundred could dissipate all the advantages which that gave it, if it neglected to classify the patients according to the severity of their disorder, and if the wards themselves grew too large. The ideal size was not more than ten people, and Tuke warned of the consequences of breaking that rule:

> During the last year, I had frequent occasion to visit two Institutions for the insane, in which very opposite plans . . . were adopted. In one, I frequently found upwards of thirty patients in a single apartment; in the other, the number in each room rarely, if ever, exceeded ten. Here, I generally found several of the inmates engaged in some useful or amusing employment. Every class seemed to form a little family; they observed each other's eccentricities with amusement or pity; they were

113. S. Tuke, *A Letter . . . on Pauper Lunatic Asylums*, pp. 27–8.
114. *Ibid.*, p. 15.
115. William Ellis, *A Treatise on the Nature, Symptoms, Causes, and Treatment of Insanity*, London: Holdsworth, 1838, p. 17.
116. *Cf.* M. Jacobi, *On the Construction and Management of Hospitals for the Insane*, p. 23; Metropolitan Commissioners in Lunacy, *1844 Report*, p. 23.

g. 12   An engraving by Dean, after Musgrave, of Chester County Asylum, one of the
rliest county asylums, built under the permissive act of 1808 and opened in 1829, from
emingway, *Chester* (*c*.1830). Already more 'institutional' than its supposed inspiration, the
ork Retreat, its relatively modest size nonetheless contrasts sharply with the vastness of
ylums built only a decade or so later. Within a generation, such small-scale public asylums
d vanished.

interested in each other's welfare, and contracted attachments or aver-
sions. In the large society, the difference of character was very striking.
I could perceive no attachments, and very little observation of each
other. In the midst of society, everyone seemed in solitude; conversation or amusement was rarely to be observed – employment never.
Each individual appeared to be pursuing his own busy cogitations;
pacing with restless step from one end of the enclosure to another, or
lolling in slothful apathy on the benches. It was evident that society
could not exist in such a crowd.[117]

Even the architecture and the physical setting of the asylum could make
vital contributions to its success, concretely exemplifying the distance
between the reformed institution and the traditional madhouse. A modern
curative establishment should be sited where the patients could enjoy the
benefits of fresh, bracing country air, and where there was an extensive
and pleasing view of the surrounding countryside to divert the mind from
its morbid fantasies. The building itself should emphasize as little as
possible the idea of imprisonment or confinement. The insane were very
sensitive to their surroundings, and it was not extravagance to design and

117. Samuel Tuke, *A Letter on Pauper Lunatic Asylums*, pp. 14–5.

build institutions which emphasized cheerfulness by being aesthetically pleasing. Indeed, spacious and attractive accommodations could make their own contributions to the inmates' 'moral training', and to replacing 'their morbid feelings . . . [with] healthy trains of thought'.[118] To further these goals, the buildings should avoid a dull uniformity and their internal arrangements should be such as to allow a maximum of organizational flexibility. Patients, for instance, ought to be able to change rooms in the course of the day to get a change of scenery.

For essentially the same reasons, provision ought always to be made for extensive grounds to be attached to an asylum. These would allow scope for recreation and harmless diversion, the kinds of mental and physical stimulation which would counter the tendency of insanity to degenerate into outright fatuity. 'The leading principle here is to prevent idleness, to preserve every power of mind and body constantly occupied, and never to allow it to flag or to retire upon itself.'[119] And one of the best ways of putting that principle into practice was to encourage the patients to employ themselves in some useful work. Attaching a farm to every hospital would provide admirable opportunities for the kind of regular employment which greatly helped to restore men's minds.

Classification, separation, and employment – all central to the implementation of moral treatment – had a still broader significance, providing the basis for a response to those critics who objected that asylums, by 'congregating insane people together in the most promiscuous way', constituted 'an evil of the most pernicious tendency . . .'.[120] Reassurance could be offered that the tranquil and the raving, the convalescent and the incurable, were carefully separated; treatment individualized and adapted to the idiosyncrasies of the patients (an implicit and telling contrast with the indiscriminate mass-medication of the *ancien régime*); and interaction managed and controlled in carefully constructed communities of the mad. Classification also allowed asylum keepers to offer still another kind of reassurance: that no improper mingling of the social classes would be permitted. One might well imagine the 'unhappiness which would flow from bringing the ignorant and brutal into constant and compulsory contact with the enlightened and refined'.[121] Besides, 'The pauper could not appreciate, nor prize, nor derive benefit from the refinement and delicacies essential to the comfort, and instrumental in the recovery of the affluent. Most fortunately, [therefore,] this arrangement, which is called for by the usages of society, is found to correspond with those higher and less artificial distinctions which are dictated by philosophy.' Class distinctions finding support in Nature itself, the asylum superintendent could

118. W.A.F. Browne, *What Asylums Were, Are, and Ought to Be*, p. 191.
119. William Nisbet, *Two Letters to George Rose M.P. on the . . . State of the Madhouses*, London: 1815, p. 26.
120. G.N. Hill, *An Essay on Insanity*, p. 222.
121. W.A.F. Browne, *What Asylums Were, Are, and Ought to Be*, p. 201.

proceed with a clear conscience to make 'fitting preparations' with which to 'tempt the rich to have recourse to those measures from choice, which the poor have long pursued from necessity'.[122]

The advocates of the asylum, then, plainly saw that there were obstacles to the successful realization of their ideal. But they were infinitely remote from the view which saw the proposed cure as worse than the disease, or even as tending only to spread the disease. Rather they were confident that no difficulty was insurmountable, that all the problems they and others had identified could be overcome – indeed, that they already had the answers to most of them. Within the controlled confines of the institution, they announced that the paternal order Tuke and his successors had created would provide a practical demonstration that even the irrational and raving could be reduced to docility, and by moral suasion and self-sacrifice, rather than by force. With all the fervour of a new convert, John Conolly delivered a panegyric on the new asylum, the place where

> calmness will come; hope will revive; satisfaction will prevail. Some unmanageable tempers, some violent or sullen patients, there must always be; but much of the violence, much of the ill-humour, almost all the disposition to meditate mischievous or fatal revenge, or self-destruction will disappear. . . . Cleanliness and decency will be maintained or restored; and despair itself will sometimes be found to give place to cheerfulness or secure tranquility. [The asylum is the place] where humanity, if anywhere on earth, shall reign supreme.[123]

As this passage makes clear, a strong utopian strand runs through the early Victorian images of the asylum. The note of almost unbounded optimism, which its proponents so successfully communicated to their lay audience, was perhaps articulated in its purest form in Browne's vision of the asylum of the future:

> In place of multiplying individual examples of excellence, let me conclude by describing the aspect of an asylum as it ought to be. Conceive a spacious building resembling the palace of a peer, airy, and elevated, and elegant, surrounded by extensive and swelling grounds and gardens. The interior is fitted up with galleries, and workshops, and music rooms. The sun and the air are allowed to enter at every window, the view of the shrubberies and fields, and groups of labourers is unobstructed by shutters or bars; all is clean, quiet and attractive. The inmates all seem to be activated by the common impulse of enjoyment, all are busy, and delighted by being so. The house and all around appears to be a hive of industry. When you pass the lodge, it is as if you

---

122. *Ibid.*, pp. 199, 169.
123. John Conolly, *On the Construction and Government of Lunatic Asylums*, p. 143. On the convolutions of Conolly's thinking, and their connections to the vagaries of his career, see my *Social Order/Mental Disorder*, chapter 7.

had entered the precincts of some vast emporium of manufacture; labour is divided, so that it may be easy and well performed, and so apportioned, that it may suit the tastes and powers of each labourer. You meet the gardener, the common agriculturalist, the mower, the weeder, all intent on their several occupations, and loud in their merriment. The flowers are tended and trained, and watered by one, the humbler task of preparing the vegetables for table, is committed to another. Some of the inhabitants act as domestic servants, some as artisans, some rise to the rank of overseers. The bakehouse, the laundry, the kitchens, are all well supplied with indefatigable workers. In one part of the edifice are companies of straw plaiters, basket-makers, knitters, spinners, among the women; in another, weavers, tailors, saddlers, and shoemakers, among the men. For those who are ignorant of these gentle crafts, but strong and steady, there are loads to carry, water to draw, wood to cut, and for those who are both ignorant and weakly, there is oakum to tease and yarn to wind. The curious thing is, that all are anxious to be engaged, toil incessantly, and in general without any recompense other than being kept from disagreeable thought and the pains of illness. They literally work in order to please themselves, and having once experienced the possibility of doing this, and of earning peace, self-applause, and the approbation of all around, sound sleep, and it may be some small remuneration, a difficulty is found in restraining their eagerness, and moderating their exertions. There is in this community no compulsion, no chains, no whips, no corporal chastisement, simply because these are proved to be less effectual means of carrying any point than persuasion, emulation, and the desire of obtaining gratification. But there are gradations of employment. You may visit rooms where there are ladies reading, or at the harp, or piano, or flowering muslin, or engaged in some of those thousand ornamental productions in which female taste and ingenuity are displayed. You will encounter them going to church or to market, or returning from walking, riding, and driving in the country. You will see them ministering at the bedside some sick companions. Another wing contains those gentlemen who can engage in intellectual pursuits, or in the amusements and accomplishments of the station to which they belong. The billiard room will, in all probability, present an animated scene. Adjoining apartments are used as news-rooms, the politicians will be there. You will pass those who are fond of reading, drawing, music scattered throughout handsome suites of rooms, finished chastely, but beautifully and looking down upon such fair and fertile scenes as harmonize with the tranquillity which reigns within, and tend to conjure up images of beauty and serenity in the mind which are akin to happiness. But these persons have pursuits, their time is not wholly occupied in the agreeable trifling of conning a debate, or gaining so many points. One acts as an amanuensis, another is engaged in landscape painting, a third devolves to himself a course of historical reading, and submits to examination on the subject of his studies, a fourth seeks consolation from binding the books which he does not read. In short, all are so busy as to overlook, or all are so contented as to forget their misery.

'Such', Browne concluded triumphantly, 'is a faithful picture of what may be seen in many institutions, and of what might be seen in all, were asylums conducted as they ought to be'.[124]

Conjured up in these paragraphs is a quite extravagant portrait of ideal asylums as 'miniature worlds, whence all the disagreeable alloys of modern life are as much as possible excluded, and the more pleasing portions carefully cultivated'.[125] Here is a social universe that constitutes an organic, harmonious whole – a hierarchical order arrayed under its benevolent philosopher-king,[126] in which everyone knows and respects his or her place; where even the rage of madness is reigned in without whips, chains, or corporal chastisement, amidst the comforts of domesticity and the invisible yet infinitely potent fetters of the Tukean 'desire for esteem'; a community whose inhabitants 'literally work in order to please them-selves', virtually without recompense, but so readily that 'a difficulty is found in restraining their eagerness . . .'; a Potemkin village notable for its absence of conflict and strife, wherein the conventional division of occupation and inclination along gender lines 'naturally' and reassuringly reproduces itself, while the lower orders of society coexist in harmony and tranquility with their betters.

Ideologically, of course, this was a vision of extraordinary resonance and attractiveness, particularly for a ruling class surrounded by alarming signs of increasing social friction and political discontent, and forced to confront the discord, disruptions, and divisiveness that were so central a feature of the Great Transformation. Confronted by the threats of Chartism and a militant working class; surrounded by the all-but-inescapable evidence of the devastating impact of industrial capitalism on the social and physical landscape; and themselves the authors of a New

124. W.A.F. Browne, *What Asylums Were, Are, and Ought to Be*, pp. 229–31.
125. Anon., 'Review of *What Asylums Were, Are, and Ought to Be*', *Phrenological Journal* 10, 53, 1836–7, p. 697.
126. Like his fellow alienists, Browne insisted throughout his career on the centrality and necessarily untrammeled power of the asylum superintendent. The delegation of autocratic power was a vital 'element in curative discipline. He is not merely a dispenser of advice and medicine, he is a moral governor, who identifies himself with the happiness as well as the health of those around; a referee in all disputes and difficulties; a depository of all secrets and sorrows; a source of pleasure, as well as of power and direction, and who gives a tone to every proceedings'. (Crichton Royal Asylum, *11th Annual Report*, 1850, p. 39.) A decade and a half later, the royal analogy is made overt: 'The power or government by which such communities are ruled should be monarchical. The details, as well as the principles, should emanate from one central will. . . .' (W.A.F. Browne, 'The Moral Treatment of the Insane', *Journal of Mental Science* 10, 1864, p. 334.)

Fig. 13   A drawing of the twelfth-night entertainment at the Hanwell Lunatic Asylum, taken
from the *Illustrated London News*, 15 January 1848, demonstrating the happy effects of reform
and the success of Conolly's non-restraint system. The entertainments at Hanwell were still
segregated by sex – the female patients had their party on New Year's Eve. The cavernous
corridor in which the inmates are seated at dinner was one of a number which ordinarily
served as day rooms. The figures in the foreground include some of the asylum officers and
Magistrates' Committee, with their wives.

Poor Law assailed by its critics (most memorably in Dickens's *Oliver
Twist*) as the very embodiment of inhumanity and meanness of spirit, the
Victorian governing classes were here offered the opportunity to redeem
their society's progressive and humane character. Embracing the reformers'
schemes and constructing the new realm of asylumdom would allow the
replacement of violent repression, conflict, and strife by moral suasion,
docility, and willing submission to authority, even among the depraved
and unruly. The practical demonstration of the powers of 'reason and
morality' when allied to a new kind of 'moral machinery' – these constituted a potent advertisement for the merits of reformed asylums run by
practitioners initiated into the mysteries of moral treatment and medical
psychology. And, like the Invisible Hand now regulating civil society, the
new regime had the inestimable advantage of being a 'system . . . at once
beautiful and self-operating. [The] presence [of keepers] is required to
regulate the machine, but its motions are spontaneous . . .',[127] serving all

127. W.A.F. Browne, *What Asylums Were, Are, and Ought to Be*, p. 203.

but imperceptibly to secure 'the regulation and tranquillization of the unhealthy mind'.[128]

7. The Reformers Triumphant

Driven forward by such utopian reveries, and inspired with a limitless confidence in the merits of their chosen solution, the lunacy reformers now embarked upon the final and decisive phase of their campaign. Their aims remained those they had sought in 1815: the establishment on a compulsory basis of a network of public asylums for all pauper lunatics; and the creation of a full-time national inspectorate to supervise the whole system.[129] By the early 1840s, however, the chances of accomplishing these changes were greatly improved. The proponents of localism had fought the attempt to establish a similar measure of central control and direction over Poor Relief and lost. In the course of the 1830s, recalcitrant parishes had been brought around, frequently by the use of government patronage to bribe local elites. Having established the principle with reference to paupers as a whole, it was difficult to resist the conclusion that the treatment of a much smaller group like the insane ought to be subject to a similar authority, particularly since the parish was clearly too small a unit to deal with them on a specialized basis. Furthermore, the 1832 reform of Parliament had helped to weaken the power the entrenched local elites had hitherto enjoyed in the legislature, shifting the balance of political power towards the bourgeoisie – whose interests were best served by uniform national policies.

Meanwhile, as we have seen, the literate public had been provided with a surfeit of tracts arguing the superior merits of the asylum as a solution to the problems of insanity. The Metropolitan Commissioners had made use of their periodic reports to stress the improvements which could be brought about by assiduous and frequent inspection; and to contrast the marked amelioration of conditions in the metropolis with the stagnation or retrogression in the provinces, where 'the salutary provisions of the Act by which it is required that all houses . . . shall be annually licensed and periodically visited and reported by the Visiting Magistrates, have been in

128. *Ibid.*, p. 213.
129. These aims bore the clear stamp of Benthamite influence. The scheme for expert, full-time inspectors employed by the central government to provide a check on local administrators paralleled the system elaborated for the reform of the Poor Law by Chadwick and Nassau Senior in the 1832 Poor Law Inquiry, and the Poor Law Amendment Act of 1834. The insistence on the value of the institution had received the approbation of the master himself (Jeremy Bentham, *Panopticon, or the Inspection House*, London: Payne, 1791), while the Poor Law Commission had endorsed existing asylums as a model for the 'separate and appropriate management of the various sub-classes of the incompetent poor.' Similarly, the idea that the defects of existing asylums were due to the lack of efficient central oversight had its parallel in the Poor Law reformers' rationalization of the horrors of the pre-1834 general mixed workhouse as due to maladministration and the lack of central direction.

great degree neglected or violated . . .'.[130] Finally, the discovery at the Lincoln Asylum that the insane could be managed without resort to any form of mechanical restraint whatsoever, and the successful implementation of such a policy at Hanwell, the largest of all public asylums, had been promoted as a dramatic demonstration of the reformers' contention that the establishment of public asylums would eliminate the horrors of the old madhouse regime.[131] When the *Westminster Review* sought to advance the cause of reform, it simply summarized the content of a number of asylum reports, and concluded triumphantly that evidences of success 'crowd the pages of the Reports before us, and they contain not the prospective theories of an imaginary philanthropy, but the practical results of a tested system'.[132]

On other grounds, too, the desirability, even the necessity of reform had been urged upon the governing classes. Running through the burgeoning specialist literature of the early nineteenth century were pronouncements on three crucial issues: how much insanity existed in the community; what caused people to go mad; and the differential social incidence of mental alienation. Naturally enough, the more extensive the legions of the mad, the more pressing the question of lunacy reform became. The more closely insanity was bound up with the conditions of modern civilized existence, the more threatening the future prospects for society at large, and the more vital the necessity for expert and effective intervention to mitigate the problem. And the more susceptible the rich and powerful to the ravages of mental disorder, the more urgently their own self-interest commanded them to adopt the reformers' prescriptions, lest they wake some morning to find themselves incarcerated in one of those 'wild and secluded abodes of human misery' to which the mad were traditionally consigned.

The experts' conclusions on all these points were scarcely reassuring. Conceding the defects of existing statistics, their consensus was nonetheless 'that a much greater number of cases is known to exist, and to require treatment, than formerly', and that the numbers of the insane appeared to be increasing at a far more rapid rate than the population in general.[133] Nor should one be surprised to find 'the poisoned stream larger, and wider, and deeper', given 'the too palpable multiplication of the causes

---

130. *Annual Report of the Metropolitan Commissioners in Lunacy*, 1838, p. 6.
131. For discussions of the 'non-restraint' movement, see my *Social Order/Mental Disorder*, pp. 188–97; and Nancy Tomes, 'The Great Restraint Controversy: A Comparative Perspective on Anglo–American Psychiatry in the Nineteenth Century', pp. 190–225 in W.F. Bynum, R. Porter, and M. Shepherd (eds), *The Anatomy of Madness*, Vol. 3, London: Routledge, 1988.
132. *Westminster Review* 37, 1842, p. 310.
133. W.A.F. Browne, *What Asylums Were, Are, and Ought to Be*, pp. 54–5; see also Andrew Halliday, *A General View of the Present State of Lunatic Asylums in Great Britain and Ireland*, London: Underwood, 1828; Jean Etienne Dominique Esquirol, *Mental Maladies*, Philadelphia: Blanchard and Lee, 1845. For a more sceptical view, see G.M. Burrows, *Commentaries*.

which produce mania'.[134] Wherever 'the sources of moral agitation and excitement are most abundant, there', it was confidently asserted, 'will the proportion of insanity be the highest'[135] – grim news indeed for a social order characterized by wrenching social change and upheaval, and for the commercial, manufacturing, and professional elites who so relentlessly sought to exploit the resulting opportunities for social and material advancement.

The Rousseauist myth that the noble savage was somehow immune from the ravages of insanity was widely canvassed by Regency and early Victorian writers on the subject.[136] Thomas Beddoes spoke of nations 'civilized enough to be capable of insanity'[137] and Alexander Morison reported that madness appeared 'to be very small in South America, and among the Indian tribes, &c. and to be very considerable in China. It is . . . probable', he gravely concluded, 'that the increasing civilization and luxury of this country, co-operating with hereditary disposition, tends rather to increase the numbers in proportion to the population'.[138] Others were less restrained in their language: the London physician, John Reid, announced in apocalyptic tones, that 'Madness, strides like a Colossus over this island . . .'[139]; and W.A.F. Browne echoed his warning: 'as we recede, step by step, from the simple, that is, the savage, manners of our ancestors, and advance in industry and knowledge and happiness, this malignant persecutor strides onward, signalizing every era in the social progress by an increase, a new hecatomb of victims'.[140]

Here was a paradox, particularly for an audience which, as a matter of course, equated a 'higher' civilization with progress in all spheres of existence. Moreover, if the connection were to prove an inseparable and inevitable one, it was a peculiarly discomforting paradox, for it implied that one could look forward to a rapid and persistent rise in the numbers of mad folk. Fortunately, some reassurance was forthcoming. The increase occurred, not inevitably, but

---

134. W.A.F. Browne, *What Asylums Were, Are, and Ought to Be*, pp. 54–5.
135. *Ibid.*, p. 63.
136. Of course, the connections between artificiality, over-stimulation, luxury, and madness had been a staple of speculation on the causes of nervous distempers at least since the publication of George Cheyne's *The English Malady*, London: Wisk, Ewing, and Smith, 1733. For a general discussion of the persistence of this belief as a staple of nineteenth-century psychiatric theorizing, see D.J. Mellett, *The Prerogative of Asylumdom*, New York: Garland, 1982, pp. 64–9.
137. Thomas Beddoes, *Hygeia*, Bristol: Mills, 1802, Vol. 2, p. 40.
138. A. Morison, *Outlines of Lectures on Insanity*, Edinburgh: Lizars, 1825, p. 73.
139. John Reid, 'Report of Diseases', *The Monthly Magazine* 25, 1808, p. 166.
140. W.A.F. Browne, *What Asylums Were, Are, and Ought to Be*, p. 52. The conclusion was echoed by an anonymous reviewer: 'In that state of society which is now termed civilized, the sources of mental excitation and disease are almost beyond computation.' Anon., 'Review of *What Asylums Were, Are, and Ought to Be*', *Phrenological Journal* 10, #53, 1836–7, p. 691.

because the enjoyments and blessings of augmented power are abused; because the mind is roused to exertion without being disciplined, it is stimulated without being strengthened; because our selfish propensities are cultivated while our moral nature is left barren, our pleasures becoming poisonous; and because in the midst of a blaze of scientific light, and in the presence of a thousand temptations to multiply our immediate by a sacrifice of our ultimate gratifications, we remain in the darkest ignorance of our own mind. . . .[141]

If society could but be brought to listen to those who were lifting the veil of ignorance surrounding the subject (and who were simultaneously developing expertise in restoring the mad to sanity) the worst might be averted. Inaction, however, might well prove fatal.

Nor could wealth or social position provide any security against the inroads of insanity. Spurzheim's even-handed claim that 'no one is secure from [going mad]; . . . rich and poor, the laborious and sober labourer and his master who indulges in scenes of luxury are all equally liable to this affliction'[142] was soon supplanted by far more ominous warnings from no less an authority than Esquirol that madness was more usually a disease of the rich. Even the growth in the trade in lunacy itself was cited by some as evidence of the disproportionate susceptibility of the well-to-do.[143] Whilst the agricultural population, and particularly the rural poor, 'is to a great degree exempt from insanity', the bourgeoisie and the plutocrats enjoyed no such immunity from its depredations, exposed as they were 'to excitement . . . and . . . to the formation of habits of thought and action inimical to the preservation of serenity and health'.[144] The upwardly mobile were perhaps the most vulnerable of all: 'Pianos, parasols, *Edinburgh Reviews*, and Paris-going desires, are now found among a class of persons who formerly thought these things belonged to a different race; these are the true source of nervousness and mental ailments.'[145]

If the most successful in the race for consumption goods and competitive advantage were simultaneously now pictured as the most susceptible to the ravages of madness, a similar vulnerability appeared to characterize the dominant sex: not for the first time, indeed, for as Michael MacDonald has shown, in sixteenth- and seventeenth-century England, 'Madness [also] wore a masculine visage. . . . [Under the Tudors and Stuarts,] society was more concerned about men who fell insane than women . . . [and t]he stereotypical lunatic was Mad Tom, a tattered beggar, hardly

141. W.A.F. Browne, *What Asylums Were, Are, and Ought to Be*, pp. 52–3.
142. Johann Gaspar Spurzheim, *Observations on the Deranged Manifestations of the Mind, or Insanity*, London: Baldwin, Craddock, and Joy, 1817.
143. W.A.F. Browne, *What Asylums Were, Are, and Ought to Be*, p. 61.
144. *Ibid.*, pp. 56–7.
145. David Uwins, *A Treatise on Those Disorders of the Brain and Nervous System, Which Are Usually Considered and Called Mental*, London: Renshaw and Rush, 1833, p. 51.

better than a beast.'[146] But such presumptions had been overturned gradually over the course of the eighteenth century, and by the dawn of the Victorian era, alienists generally portrayed women as biologically weaker and more liable to go mad;[147] and the broader cultural images of insanity had been securely tied to the female of the species: in novels, in drama, in poetry, in painting, in popular ballads, in opera, it was disproportionately women who stood as the emblems and exemplars of irrationality.[148] And yet the newly collected statistics of insanity suggested a quite different picture. John Thurnam's findings, for instance, indicated that men outnumbered women in English asylums by about thirty per cent, and other data suggested that the discrepancy between the two had widened during the preceding quarter century, to the disadvantage of men.[149]

146. Michael MacDonald, 'Women and Madness in Tudor and Stuart England', *Social Research* 53, 2, 1986, p. 262. The predominance of men among the ranks of the mad was as apparent in practice as at the level of cultural stereotypes, notwithstanding the conventional assumption that women's 'reason was feebler than men's and less able to constrain unruly passions . . . descriptions of madness and frenzy in sixteenth- and seventeenth-century medical books always refer to the typical patient as male'. *Ibid.*, pp. 263–4, 267–8.

147. See, for instance, the discussions in John Haslam, *Observations on Insanity . . .* , p. 108; in idem, *Observations On Madness and Melancholy*, pp. 245–9; and in J.G. Spurzheim, *Observations on the Deranged Manifestations of the Mind, or Insanity*, pp. 162–3. The special causes of insanity in women were alleged to include disorders associated with menstruation, parturition, and 'preparing nutriment for the infant'. Women, too, were more exposed to disappointments in life, and were more often the victims of circumstances, while having fewer resources with which to cope with life's setbacks. Finally, in contrast to men, their feelings and emotions were generally stronger than their intellects, heightening their susceptibility to madness.

148. See, for example, the numerous portraits of 'Crazy Jane' or 'Crazy Kate'; Bertha Mason, the quintessentially gothic figure of 'the madwoman in the attic'; Sir Walter Scott's Lucy Ashton, subsequently the heroine of eight different operas, most notably Donizetti's *Lucia di Lammermoor*; and the ascension of Shakespeare's Ophelia to almost the status of a cult figure among early nineteenth-century romantics. Elaine Showalter has suggested that this association of irrationality with the female marked a cultural shift occurring over the course of the second half of the eighteenth century – that in the Augustan age by contrast, 'the cultural image of the lunatic was male'. Elaine Showalter, *The Female Malady: Women, Madness and English Culture, 1830–1980*, New York: Pantheon, 1985, p. 8.

149. *Cf.* John Thurnam, *Observations and Essays on the Statistics of Insanity*, London: Simpkin Marshall, 1845, pp. 145–55. *Cf.* the earlier findings of Richard Powell, 'Observations Upon the Comparative Prevalence of Insanity at Different Periods', *Medical Transactions* 4, 1813, pp. 131–59, that admissions to madhouses in the metropolis between 1804 and 1808 comprised 1,128 men and 1,000 women. Similarly, a Parliamentary Return for 1826 recorded 4,461 males and 3,443 females admitted to private madhouses between 1815 and 1824. Not everyone took these statistics at face value. Thomas Bakewell, who reported that the number of female patients sent to his private madhouse at Spring Vale was 'only half the number of males', was nonetheless sceptical of the claim that this corresponded to the actual incidence of the disorder. Because of the cost of confinement, 'none can be expected but the most confirmed, aggravated cases' and given that 'females may be better managed at home, therefore the expense is not incurred'. *A Letter to the Chairman of the Select Committee . . . Appointed to Inquire into the State of Madhouses*, p. 61.

To the extent that these assertions about the social geography of madness secured a measure of public credibility and acceptance, they provided
the men who formed the governing classes with still more powerful
motives to embrace the cause of lunacy reform. To be sure, once a
network of reformed asylums had been constructed, the overwhelming
bulk of the patient population would turn out to be drawn from the ranks
of the poor and the disenfranchised, and past mid-century, female pauper
lunatics soon began to outnumber their male counterparts.[150] But in
the early 1840s, the best professional opinion suggested that it was the
educated, the wealthy, the most cultured segments of the community (and
quite possibly the men, who after all were most directly exposed to the
noxious effects of heightened competition, speculation and ambition) who
had the most to fear from the spectre of madness – all of which surely
heightened the receptivity of an elite who shared these characteristics to
the claims and clamour of the lunacy reformers.

With the ground for advancing the reformers' plans so well prepared
in advance, the Metropolitan Commissioners now went beyond mere
complaints of the ineffectiveness of provincial inspection. On 17 March

150. The 1871 census, for instance, showed that while the ratio of women to men in the
population at large was 1,056 : 1,000, in asylums it was 1,182 : 1,000. Among the upper
classes, males would continue to outnumber female patients almost till the close of the
century, but there were already 1,242 female pauper lunatics for every 1,000 male
lunatics. Elaine Showalter, who cites these figures (see *The Female Malady*, pp. 52, 259),
deploys them as a central part of her argument that during the nineteenth century,
madness became 'the female malady'. I have suggested elsewhere (*Social Order/Mental
Disorder*, chapter 11) that this places more weight on these data than is really warranted.
Victorian alienists themselves remarked upon the phenomenon, but suggested (correctly
in my view) that a substantial fraction of the difference disappeared once one took
account of women's greater longevity, and their longer average stay in the asylum.
(Men were discharged more rapidly on the average, perhaps because families more
desperately needed them as breadwinners.) For discussion, see, for example, John
Conolly, *On the Construction and Government of Lunatic Asylums*, pp. 146–50; and Edgar
Sheppard, *Lectures on Madness in Its Medical, Legal, and Social Aspects*, London:
Churchill, pp. 3–5. What is intriguing and lends weight to the feminist critique of
psychiatry is surely something rather different: the fact that, notwithstanding the nearly
equal propensity of the two sexes to go mad, Victorian alienists developed theories of a
differential, gender-based etiology for mental disturbance. From neurological portraits
of females as possessed of nervous systems of greater refinement and delicacy (and
hence more susceptible to breakdown) to gynaecological theorizing about peculiarly
intimate ties between a woman's brain and her reproductive organs, medical men
constructed images of creatures whose physiological equipment was of surpassing
fragility, liable to give way at any moment under the strains of modern life or the
unavoidably perilous passage through puberty, pregnancy, parturition, lactation,
menstruation, and the menopause. In the process, the constriction of women's lives,
their legal powerlessness, and their economic marginality – the central features of
existing social relations between the sexes, thus received the sanction of science. For a
particularly egregious but by no means unrepresentative example of the genre, see
Henry Maudsley, 'Sex in Mind and Education', *The Fortnightly Review* 21, 1874, pp.
466–83. For the ominous consequences for treatment which could flow from such
assumptions, see Andrew Scull and Diane Favreau, '"A Chance to Cut is a Chance to
Cure": Sexual Surgery for Psychosis in Three Nineteenth Century Societies', in S.
Spitzer and A. Scull (eds), *Research in Law, Deviance, and Social Control*, Vol. 8,
Greenwich, Connecticut: JAI Press, 1986, pp. 3–39.

1842, Lord Granville Somerset, the chairman of the Commission, introduced a bill into the Commons to extend its powers for three years to allow it to carry out a comprehensive inspection of all asylums and madhouses in the country.[151] The inspections which followed the bill's passage in early August were extremely extensive and detailed: asylum records were checked for accuracy and conformity to the legal requirements of the various lunacy statutes; close attention was paid to the condition of the building in which the patients were housed; questions were asked about the origins of each asylum and its current sources of financial support; inquiries were made into the role of the medical attendants, and the general administration of the asylum; patients were questioned about the treatment they received; and so on. Two years later, the findings were embodied in a comprehensive report, detailing the condition of every asylum in England, with sections on the nature of insanity and its proper classification, consideration of the arguments for and against the non-restraint system, and a discussion of the admission of pauper lunatics from workhouses, concluding with detailed recommendations about the direction reform should take.

The Commission found that 'the asylums thus brought before our view exhibit instances of about every degree of merit and defect'. Institutions in several categories were found to be reasonably satisfactory, but in a number of instances there were 'Asylums and Licensed Houses which deserve almost unqualified censure.'[152] It was these extreme cases which provided the best argument for change, and which were widely cited in summaries of the Report written for popular consumption, as well as in the parliamentary debates on the legislation which the reformers introduced. The types of abused uncovered differed little from those found by parliamentary inquiries earlier in the century: At West Auckland,

> each sex had only one sitting room, with windows that did not admit of any prospect from them, and the violent and the quiet, and the dirty and the clean were shut up together. There was only one small walled yard, and when one sex was in it, the other was locked up. . . . In the small, cheerless day-room of the males, with only one (unglazed) window, five men were restrained by leg-locks . . . and two more were wearing, in addition, iron hand-cuffs and fetters from the wrist to the ankle: they were all tranquil. The reason assigned for this coercion was, that without it they would escape. . . . Chains were fastened to the floor in many places, and to many of the bedsteads. The males slept two to a bed . . . [153]

151. The legislation also added two more barristers and two more doctors to the Commission, strengthening the 'professional' element of the inspectorate.
152. *Report of the Metropolitan Commissioners in Lunacy to the Lord Chancellor*, London: Bradbury and Evans, 1844, pp. 7, 46.
153. *Ibid.*, pp. 53–4.

– something which shocked Victorian sensibilities. At a house in Derby,

> the straw in the paupers' beds was found filthy, and some of the
> bedding was in a disgusting condition from running sores, and was of
> the worst materials, and insufficient. Two cells, in which three sick
> epileptic paupers slept, were damp, unhealthy, and unfit for habitation.
> The beds of some of the private patients were in an equally bad state.[154]

Another house was described as

> deficient in every comfort and almost every convenience. The refractory
> patients were confined to strong chairs, their arms being also fastened
> to the chair. One of these – a woman – was entirely naked on both the
> days the Commissioners visited the asylum, and without doubt during
> the night. The stench was so offensive that it was almost impossible to
> remain there.[155]

A major theme of the Report was that only the creation of a powerful
national inspectorate on a permanent basis would ensure the elimination
of such abuses. Local inspection by magistrates was simply inadequate.
All the asylums the Commissioners termed 'utterly unfit' were private
asylums in the provinces receiving paupers, licensed by the local magistrates and hitherto only visited by them.[156] No house in the London area,
where the Commissioners themselves had had complete control for a
decade and a half, exhibited comparable defects. Warburton's, for instance,
which in 1828 was as bad as any of the provincial houses, was now
apparently transformed:

> We have visited few, if any, receptacles for the insane in which the
> patients were more kindly or more judiciously treated . . . the abuses
> which existed previously to the year 1828 led to the introduction of a
> system of visitation by commissioners in the metropolitan district. The
> houses at Bethnal Green, which were among the worst, now rank with
> the best receptacles for the insane.[157]

Only continued vigilant inspection could ensure such results: 'we . . . are
convinced that some of these very houses of which we now speak in terms
of commendation, would soon become scenes of great abuses were it not
for the checks interposed by constant and watchful visitation to which
they are subjected'.[158]

---

154. *Ibid.*, p. 56.
155. *Ibid.*
156. These included: West Auckland and Wrekenton in County Durham; Green Hill House
    in Derbyshire; Lainston House, Winchester and Grove Place, Nursling, Hampshire;
    Kingsdown House, Wiltshire; Plympton House, Devon; Moor Cottage, Yorkshire; and
    West Malling Place, Kent.
157. *Report of the Metropolitan Commissioners in Lunacy*, 1844, p. 44.
158. *Ibid.*, p. 35.

In emphasizing the gains inspection could produce, as they had to in order to convince others of the necessity for a national inspectorate, the Metropolitan Commissioners threatened to undermine their own case for the other major reform they sought to introduce. For if effective supervision alone could raise an institution from the ranks of the worst to among the best, why was it not sufficient by itself? Why was it necessary to introduce a measure to compel counties to make a large capital invest- ment in the erection of sufficient public asylums to accommodate every pauper patient? After all, their own description of existing county asylums had been a lukewarm endorsement at best:

> It is apparent . . . that although a few . . . are well adapted to their purpose, and a very large proportion of them are extremely well con- ducted; yet some are quite unfit for the reception of the insane, some are placed in ineligible sites, some are deficient in the necessary means of providing outdoor employment for paupers, some are ill-contrived and defective in their internal accommodations, some are cheerless and confined in their yards and airing grounds, and some are larger than seems consistent with the good management of their establishments and the proper health and care of their inmates.

But county asylums offered a decisive advantage over the private system – the judgement and conduct of those running them could not be perverted by considerations of personal profit. The defects of existing institutions of this sort were largely the product of inexperience and could readily be eliminated by more expert guidance on the part of the central authorities. Consequently, after Ashley had summarized the worst abuses the Report had uncovered for the House of Commons, he assured his listeners that 'to correct these evils there was no remedy but the multiplication of county asylums'. Experience showed that many counties were deterred from performing their manifest duty by considerations of expense, so providing adequate accommodation for pauper lunatics at public expense ought henceforth to be made compulsory.

Throughout the nineteenth century, it was an article of faith among those who dealt with lunatics that the deranged were more readily restored in the early stages of the disorder, so that delay in help could prove disastrous. Whatever its scientific merits, as ideology such a belief was of great assistance to the asylum doctors. It helped, of course, to explain the low proportion of their patients they managed to restore to sanity. More important than that, it did so in a way which demonstrated that the failure lay, not with the asylum, but with the public. If asylums did not cure, it was because the public did not send lunatics to them fast enough; since existing asylums were already flooded with chronic cases, the situation could only be remedied by building still more asylums; and given that the supply of asylum beds could never catch up with the demand, which appeared to expand in proportion with the number of available beds, the proposition would never be tested.

Here was the Commission's final and decisive argument for more public asylums:

> At the Retreat, York, at the Asylums of Lincoln and Northampton, and at the Asylum for the County of Suffolk, tables are published, exhibiting the large proportion of cures effected in cases where patients are admitted within three months of their attacks, the less proportion when admitted after three months, and the almost hopelessness of cure when persons are permitted to remain in Workhouses or elsewhere, and are not sent into proper asylums until after a lapse of a year from the period when they have been first subject to insanity.[159]

At the same time, the testimony from county asylum superintendents exhibited their virtually 'unanimous opinion that pauper lunatics are sent there at so late a period of their disease as to impede or prevent their ultimate recovery'.[160] The problem was that 'even if there did exist on the part of the guardians and overseers of the poor a full knowledge of the importance of early treatment, and the most earnest desire to avail themselves of its advantages, throughout almost the whole of England, and in the whole of Wales, there is so great a want of accommodation for the reception of the insane that they could not carry their views into effect'.[161]

The Report was completed just before the close of the 1844 session of Parliament. On 23 July, Ashley, in a long speech, outlined its major conclusions and urged legislative enactment of its central recommendations. Though action was postponed until the following year, this speech did help to draw attention to the Report's findings. Later the same year, the Tory *Quarterly Review* published a long article on the subject, endorsing all the Commission's suggestions and calling for their swift passage into law.[162] Early in 1845, its Benthamite counterpart, the *Westminster Review*, followed suit.[163] Both pieces dwelt at length on the intolerable conditions which had been found, and concluded that even on strictly economic grounds, the Commission's proposals deserved support. For 'the very great probability of cure in the early stages of insanity', provided lunatics received prompt asylum treatment, suggested that making proper provision for the insane population of the country would ultimately reduce the numbers needing support at public expense. By the time Ashley introduced legislation to give effect to the Report's recommendations, in June 1845, informed opinion had moved decisively in his favour. The two bills he proposed both received government backing and passed swiftly

159. *Ibid.*, pp. 80–1.
160. *Ibid.*, p. 80.
161. *Ibid.*, p. 82.
162. 'Report on the Treatment of Lunatics', *Quarterly Review* 74, 1844, pp. 416–47.
163. 'Lunatic Asylums', *Westminster Review* 43, 1845, pp. 162–92.

through both Houses of Parliament, becoming law on 4 and 8 August 1845.

The first, the Lunatics Act of 1845 (8 & 9 Victoria *c.* 100), established a permanent national Lunacy Commission, with power to make detailed and frequent inspections of all types of asylums – whether public, private, or charity foundations. The second Act (8 & 9 Victoria *c.* 126) made the erection of county and borough asylums to house pauper lunatics compulsory. In keeping with the recommendations of the Metropolitan Commissioners, and to ensure that the presence of large numbers of chronic patients would not interfere with the asylum doctors' ability to produce the cures they had promised, counties were authorized, though not instructed, to erect separate, less costly buildings for chronic lunatics. And to ensure that accommodation was not overcrowded or insufficient, counties which failed of their own volition to make adequate provision for their insane population could be compelled to do so.

8. *The Ideal and the Reality*

By 1845, therefore, the reformers had been successful in securing the enactment of both the key elements in their plan to remedy the condition and treatment of the insane. The insane had been sharply distinguished from other types of indigent and troublesome people and the asylum had been officially recognized as the most suitable place for them. A whole network of such institutions was now to be created at public expense, within whose walls all cases of lunacy were to be treated by members of the medical profession who had made or would make the treatment of mental disturbance their specialty. Most cases would now be cured. It was, the reformers agreed, a triumph for science and humanity.

Experience, however, was already suggesting that this optimism about the future was misplaced. As early as 1845, under the multiple and reinforcing pressures which derived from the difficulties associated with the routinization of reform, the economies imposed by cost-conscious local authorities, and the impact of an overwhelmingly lower-class clientele, there were clear signs of the collapse of the very things the reformers thought were indispensable to the success of the whole enterprise. The asylum doctors themselves contributed to this process. Bowing to political and social realities, the medical superintendents of county asylums began to compromise and water down their requirements, always consoling themselves with the thought that 'the worst asylum that can at this day by possibility be conceived, will still afford great protection' to the poor lunatic, compared to the treatment he would get elsewhere.[164]

County asylums had proved expensive to build and expensive to operate. In 1843, the average weekly cost of caring for a pauper lunatic in

---

164. J. Thurnam, *Observations and Essays on the Statistics of Insanity*, p. 104.

a public asylum was 7s. 6¾d., a sum which did not include any provision
for the capital cost of the building itself. By contrast, lunatics were maintained in the community for only 2s. 7¼d., roughly what it cost to keep a
pauper in an ordinary workhouse. Hostile Poor Law officials alleged that
'a vast sum of money has been thrown away in the erection of [asylums],'
and that running them more nearly along the lines of workhouses would
enable lunatics to 'be kept at one half or a third or a fourth of the expense
at which they are now kept'.[165]

By way of justification of their 'excessive' expenditures on paupers, the
asylum's proponents produced a number of counter-arguments. To begin
with, the inmates they had to deal with were far more difficult and
intractable as a class than the average workhouse inmate, and required
closer and more continuous supervision, all of which raised costs. Then
again, the workhouse was specifically designed to deter the able-bodied,
undeserving poor from seeking public relief, so that within its walls the
strictest regard for economy was highly functional. Not only was it unfair
to subject those who were not responsible for their own condition to such
treatment, it was also likely to be counterproductive, making permanent
what skilful attention might cure. The false economy of the Poor Law
officials overlooked the fact that it was cheaper in the long run to pay a
higher sum for a few months, and have the patients restored to sanity and
productivity, than to provide 'inexpensive' custodial care for a lifetime.

Many magistrates and parish officials remained stubbornly unconvinced,
with the result that, before the 1845 Act made their erection compulsory,
the majority of counties failed to build their own asylums. The magistrates
were reluctant to impose extra local taxes which would fall heavily on
their own class, and were strengthened in their resolve by the parish
Guardians of the poor. Where asylums *were* erected, these men sought to
keep costs to a minimum and to pare down the 'frills and luxuries'
the reformers wanted, arguing that paupers could not appreciate them
anyway. Even those who agreed that 'nothing [should] be neglected which
may tend to facilitate the recovery of the patients' were inclined to view
the more costly aspects of moral treatment with a somewhat jaundiced
eye. They insisted that 'when this accommodation is to be produced for
the poor and paid for out of Poor Rates, it is imperative that it should be
done with the strictest eye to economy'.[166]

Realizing that 'the main impediment in the way of constructing county
asylums has been . . . and at present is, the fear of the enormous expense
supposed to be necessarily attendant upon such undertakings',[167] the
reformers now discovered that some of the things they had formerly

165. *Select Committee on the Poor Law Amendment Act*, 1838, quoted in K. Jones, *Lunacy, Law,
        and Conscience, 1744–1845*, pp. 165–6.
166. *Memorial from the Parish of Brighthelmston, Sussex, Concerning the Proposed County Asylum*,
        1845, in manuscript in the East Sussex Record Office, Lewes, QAL 2/3/6.
167. Ashley, in *Hansard* 81, Third Series, 1845, column 190.

insisted on could be safely discarded. It was conceded that 'the first object that should be kept in view, after providing for the comfort and health of the patients, is economy; for, after all that can be said of the feelings of humanity towards this unfortunate class of our fellow-creatures, their sufferings are too much out of sight to create that sympathy for them'.[168] William Ellis, now superintendent at Hanwell, showed a keen awareness of the consequences of this concession for those who, like him, sought to extend the benefits of asylum treatment to all of the insane. As he revealingly put it, 'It becomes necessary to show that to render them efficient need cost very little more than to neglect them'[169] – a necessity which did not disappear because it unavoidably meant that the fundamental principles of moral treatment would have to be compromised in the process.

The Metropolitan Commissioners had found grave defects in the siting, construction, architecture, and facilities of existing county asylums. Apparently all these deficiencies could be overcome while making radical economies in the construction of future asylums, for Ashley now asserted that while the buildings at Hanwell and the Surrey Asylum had cost 160 pounds and 245 pounds a head respectively, perfectly adequate accommodation for curable cases could be built for 80 pounds. For chronic cases, the cost could be even less. The 1844 Report provides us with some notion of how this was to be achieved: 'Although we have no wish to advocate the erection of unsightly buildings, we think that no unnecessary cost should be incurred for architectural decoration; especially as these Asylums are erected for those who, when in health, are accustomed to dwell in cottages.' Ellis gives an indication of what dispensing with surplus architectural decoration would mean in practice: 'In asylums designed for paupers only, it is unnecessary to have any plaster on the walls; limewash on the bricks is all that is required.'[170] The cheerful and pleasing architecture, which in initial formulations of moral treatment played such an important role in creating and sustaining the optimistic and familial atmosphere so essential to success, was now, with the blessing of the asylum doctors, transformed into an 'unnecessary cost'. Asylum buildings became increasingly monotonous, drearily functional, prison-like.

If the reformers had collaborated, with little apparent discomfort, in this departure from their earlier ideals, they were somewhat less willing to accept some of the other changes the magistrates insisted on. One of the most important of these, symbolically and actually, was the question of asylum size. Tuke and his followers had made a powerful case for the contention that small asylums were a necessary, even if not a sufficient, condition for individualized care of patients. Several of the earliest county

168. William Ellis, *A Treatise on . . . Insanity*, p. 267.
169. *Ibid.*
170. *Ibid.*, p. 275.

asylums had conformed quite closely to these designs and to the model provided by the York Retreat. Lincoln was built for sixty patients, Nottingham for eighty, Gloucester for 120. Even those erected in highly urbanized counties were initially quite modest in size – the West Riding Asylum at Wakefield had space for 150, and that at Lancaster for 170.

The small intimate institution did not survive for long. The influx of a horde of derelict paupers brought the demise of the notion that the asylum should be a substitute household. Instead, local magistrates insisted on taking advantage of presumed economies of scale. Until well into the twentieth century, the average size of county asylums grew almost yearly. While the trend towards larger asylums became well-nigh universal after 1845, it was already well marked by then. Five of the fifteen county asylums built by 1844 contained well over the recommended maximum of 200 patients: the Kent Asylum contained 300; Surrey 360; Wakefield 420; Lancaster 611; and Hanwell as many as 975, with a nominal capacity of 1,000. The profession relaxed its standards somewhat, but not sufficiently. When the Metropolitan Commissioners censured the Middlesex magistrates, alleging that their policies were directly responsible for the 'evils and inconveniences which have been experienced at Hanwell owing to its extreme size', they were merely providing a faithful reflection of the best professional opinion. They had no effect. As Conolly put it, 'the magistrates go on adding wing to wing and story to story, contrary to the opinion of the profession and to common sense, rendering the institution most unfavourable to the treatment of patients, and their management most harassing and unsatisfactory to the medical superintendent'.[171] All the powers of persuasion the asylum doctors could muster, all their elaborate statistical proofs that it was cheaper to cure in a small asylum than to immure in a vast custodial warehouse, were in vain. The magistrates who employed them remained unconvinced, and given the choice between hypothetical cures and concrete savings, they consistently chose the latter.

'[Hanwell] was designed for three hundred patients; but, with greatly economizing the room, and making use of a part of the basement, it has been fitted to accommodate six hundred and fifteen.'[172] Whatever the consequences of this for the patients' daily existence, the magistrates were clearly delighted, for during this same period, the weekly cost of each patient's maintenance fell from 9s. a week to only 5s. 10d.[173] In similar fashion, the buildings at the Wakefield Asylum, originally intended for 150 patients, were made to accommodate 296.[174] It was not until well into

---

171. Letter from John Conolly to Sir James Clark, quoted in the *Edinburgh Review* 131, 1871, p. 221.
172. Ellis, *A Treatise on . . . Insanity*, p. 283.
173. Metropolitan Commissioners in Lunacy, *1844 Report*, pp. 86–7.
174. Samuel Tuke, 'Introductory Observations', in M. Jacobi, *On the Construction and Management of Hospitals for the Insane*, p. xxiv.

the second half of the nineteenth century that these 'monstrous asylums' became general, but the larger asylums of the 1830s and 1840s already exhibited many of the features which would later be typical of the asylum system as a whole.[175] Large numbers from the outset required the development of an orderly bureaucratic routine. Prior to the opening of Hanwell, for example, the magistrates drew up a detailed and elaborate code of rules. The duties and qualifications of each of the officers, keepers, and servants were carefully specified, and lines of authority drawn. Efforts were made to provide for every contingency: there were rules covering how dead patients were to be buried; regulations about when patients were to get up and go to bed, and when they were to eat ('Patients will breakfast at eight, dine at one, and sup at seven'); the diet tables were so detailed, they even included instructions as to how the ingredients used in the gruel given out at breakfast and supper were to be prepared.

This system of fixed rules was enforced by a discipline based on solitary confinement and deprivation of privileges, rather than whips and chains. At first, these were supplemented by the use of the shower bath as a punishment, by mild mechanical restraint, or by 'the terror . . . of the electrifying machine'. As superintendents became accustomed to managing such large numbers, however, they began to realize that they could do without mechanical restraint. They discovered in a pragmatic way what Goffman has so elegantly shown the rest of us, that in the context of a life in a total institution, manipulation of small rewards and privileges, seclusion, or the threat of removal to a 'worse' ward have such profound implications for the self that more overtly punitive strategies are seldom required.

The degree of regimentation needed to administer an institution of 600 or 1,000 inmates ensured that such asylums would be the virtual antithesis of their supposed inspiration, the York Retreat. To Tuke, moral treatment had meant the creation of a stimulating environment where routine could be sacrificed to the needs of the individual. Here the same term disguised a monotonous reality in which the needs of the patients were necessarily subordinated to those of the institution; indeed, where a patient's needs were unlikely even to find expression.

9. Controlling the Uncontrollable

All of this suggests that the county asylums were an aberrant development, a deviation from the ideals of moral treatment, as in a sense, they were. But in an ironic way they also embodied some of the core principles of the new approach. They showed, more clearly than did the Retreat, the true character of the 'reform' Tuke had unwittingly fostered.

175. The increasing size of asylum populations and the reasons for the apparent rise in the number of mad people in the course of the nineteenth century are examined at some length in chapter 7.

The central fact about moral treatment, after all, and the reason for its immediate appeal, was the way it demonstrated that the most repellent features of existing madhouses were actually unnecessary cruelties. One of Tuke's proudest claims was that 'neither chains nor corporal punishment are tolerated, on any pretext in this establishment'.[176] Instead, the patient's desire for esteem could often be exploited to induce good behaviour. Where this did not produce the desired result, 'the general comfort of the patients ought to be considered; and those who are violent require to be separated from the more tranquil, and to be prevented, by some means, from offensive conduct towards their fellow-sufferers'.[177] This could be achieved when 'the patients are arranged into classes, as much as may be, according to the degree in which they approach to rational or orderly conduct'.[178] Such a system had the crucial additional advantage of providing patients with a powerful incentive to exercise self-restraint: the insane 'quickly perceive, or if not, they are informed on the first occasion, that their treatment depends, in great measure on their conduct'.[179]

One of the questions which has puzzled historians of psychiatry (and which also puzzled some of the reformers themselves)[180] was why it took so long to realize that brutal methods of managing the mad were counter-productive, and to discover that lunatics responded better to 'humane' treatment. What was involved here was, I suggest, something more than just the development of a more refined conscience about the conditions the insane were forced to endure. So long as there existed no alternative methods of managing those who would otherwise fail to conform to the rules required for the smooth functioning of an institution, the cruelties of the madhouse keeper were, in fact, functionally necessary. In the absence of better techniques, chains and fear – though crude – were among the only mechanisms which could guarantee at least a minimum of order.

Concentration on the humanitarian aspect of moral treatment has blinded us to the fact that, from a different perspective, it was precisely such a superior way of *managing* patients. For two of what I have just shown were crucial elements in moral treatment, the ward system and the creation of an intimate tie between the patient's position in this classificatory system and his behaviour, are still the fundamental weapons which mental hospitals use to control the uncontrollable. As Goffman puts it,

> since mental patients are persons who on the outside decline to respond to efforts at social control, there is a question of how social control is

176. S. Tuke, *Description of the Retreat*, p. 141.
177. *Ibid.*
178. *Ibid.*
179. *Ibid.*, pp. 141, 157.
180. Compare Ashley's opening words in his speech on the 1845 Lunatics Bill: 'Sir, it is remarkable and very humiliating, the long and tedious process by which we have arrived at the sound practice of the treatment of the insane, which now appears to be the suggestion of common sense and ordinary humanity. . . .' *Hansard's Parliamentary Debates*, Vol. 81, 3rd series, 1845, column 194.

achieved on the inside. I believe that it is achieved largely through the 'ward system', the means of control that has slowly evolved in modern mental hospitals. The key, I feel, is a system of wards graded for the degree of allowable misbehavior and the degree of discomfort and deprivation prevalent in them. Whatever the level of the new patient's misbehavior, then, a ward can be found for him in which this conduct is routinely dealt with and to a degree allowed. In effect, by accepting the life conditions on these wards, the patient is allowed to continue his misbehavior, except that now he does not particularly bother anyone by it, since it is routinely handled, if not accepted, on the ward. When he requests some improvement in his lot he is then, in effect, made to say 'uncle', made to state verbally that he is ready to mend his ways. When he gives in verbally, he is likely to be allowed an improvement in life conditions. Should he then again misbehave in the old way, and persist in this, he is lectured and returned to his previous conditions. If instead of backsliding he states his willingness to behave even better, and retains this line for a suitable length of time, he is advanced further within the quick discharge cycle through which most first admissions are moved up and out within a year. A point is then often reached where the patient is entrusted to a kinsman, either for walks in the hospital grounds, or for town expeditions, the kinsman now being transformed into someone who has the incarcerating establishment and the law to reinforce the threat: 'Be good or else I'll send you back.' What we find here (and do not on the outside) is a very model of what psychologists might call a learning situation – all hinged on the process of an admitted giving-in.[181]

Tuke's invention of these techniques, then, made it possible for the first time to abandon the brutal and overtly harsh methods of management which had previously been inescapably connected with the concentration of large numbers of madmen together in an institutional environment. There was a quite conscious recognition among many of his followers that their central accomplishment was the creation of a new regime of 'curative discipline', and a parallel insistence that '[t]here is a fallacy even in conceiving that Moral Treatment consists in being kind and humane to the insane'.[182] Disciplining the disorderly, as they acknowledged, depended

---

181. Erving Goffman, *Asylums*, Garden City, New York: Doubleday, 1961, pp. 361–2. (London: Penguin, 1970.)
182. Crichton Royal Asylum, *11th Annual Report*, 1850, p. 39; W.A.F. Browne, 'The Moral Treatment of the Insane', pp. 311–2, and *passim*. To be sure, he insisted that 'kindness' was one element in the equation. But this must not be just 'a barren sympathy. . . . The purely benevolent physician can never be a good practitioner . . . [for one must not] indulge vicious propensities, [or] . . . give way to unreasonable demands . . . [or] be active in soothing momentary pangs at the sacrifice of permanent peace'. (*What Asylums Were, Are, and Ought to Be*, p. 179.) Compare, too, his insistence on 'the necessity for rigid, stringent, even stern discipline among the insane . . .' (Crichton Royal Asylum, *3rd Annual Report*, 1842, p. 21), and his expressed preference for dormitory sleeping

crucially upon the asylum's 'moral governor' taking advantage of the tightly controlled environment the institution provided to oversee and regulate 'the most minute workings of the great moral machine'.[183] Careful and 'discriminate use of ordinary circumstances and trifles in depressing, elevating, tranquillising, rousing, persuading, or governing the insane . . .'[184] could be employed to ensure that 'the impress of authority is never withdrawn, but is stamped on every transaction'.[185]

It was this latent strength of moral treatment as a mechanism for enforcing conformity which came to be emphasized in the vast pauper asylums. There, to the extent that moral treatment was an advance, what it did was to place a far more effective and thoroughgoing means of control in the hands of the custodians, while simultaneously, by removing the necessity of the asylum's crudest features, it made the reality of that imprisonment and control far more difficult to perceive. So that by cruel irony, it was the same central feature of moral treatment which gave it its appeal as a humanitarian reform and which allowed its transformation into a repressive instrument for controlling large numbers of people.

Increasing size inevitably made the doctors more remote, and broke the ties which were supposed to unite superintendent and patient. The daily, sometimes hourly, contact between patient and physician, which the proponents of the institution were arguing was such a valuable feature of asylum life, was already disappearing. Ellis might sometimes refer to 900 patients as his 'family', but the term was clearly a matter of rhetoric rather than reality. He was, it is true, required by the rules at Hanwell to visit each ward and each patient at least once daily, but since the rules also stipulated that he was to prepare an annual report, keep daybooks and casebooks, a record of the name, age, sex, date of admission, occupation, etc, of every patient, act as steward and treasurer of the institution and keep the accounts, as well as oversee every aspect of the operations,[186] his time for this task was naturally limited. The situation had not changed much when the Metropolitan Commissioners visited in 1844:

> The two resident Medical Officers have between them nearly 1,000 patients to attend, and are required by the rules to see every patient twice a day. Each of these officers has an average of 30 patients on the sick list, and above 50 on the extra diet list. Besides these duties, they are required to mix medicines and keep the registers and diaries. Some

accommodation for his charges, since this arrangement 'continues the discipline and inspection exercised during active pursuits into the night, and during silence and sleep. Control may thus penetrate into the very dreams of the insane'. (Crichton Royal Asylum, *10th Annual Report*, 1849, p. 38.)

183. Crichton Royal Asylum, *7th Annual Report*, 1846, p. 35.
184. Crichton Royal Asylum, *11th Annual Report*, 1850, p. 31.
185. Crichton Royal Asylum, *7th Annual Report*, 1846, p. 35.
186. Minutes of the Visiting Justices of the Hanwell Lunatic Asylum, Vol. 2, 1829–31, pp. 364–6, in manuscript at the Greater London Record Office, MA/A/J2.

attention is also required to be paid to chronic cases in which the general health and state of mind are often varying.[187]

Given the increasing remoteness of the superintendents from the patients, 'much authority . . . in large asylums is now necessarily placed in the hands of the attendants'.[188] We have seen that Tuke had emphasized how crucial their role was. Moral treatment depended for its success on the extraordinary devotion and patience of those who were called on to administer it. Especially as asylums began to fill up with incurable cases, 'success' could frequently not be measured in conventional terms. Since the incurables could provide little in exchange for the humane care they received except gratitude (and often not even that), maintaining the requisite morale and dedication among the staff was likely to be difficult, at best. Given the low rewards characteristically offered to those who do society's dirty work, aggravated by the unwillingness of any save the least successful elements of such a class-conscious society as Victorian England to tolerate the defiling close daily contact with the derelict, it proved impossible. Asylums were compelled to recruit their attendants from 'the unemployed of other professions . . . if they possess physical strength and a tolerable reputation for sobriety, it is enough; and the latter quality is frequently dispensed with. They enter upon their duties completely ignorant of what insanity is'.[189] Close supervision and carefully designed bureaucratic rules could coerce a measure of conformity from such an ill-suited lot and ensure the mechanical and perfunctory performance of custodial tasks; but they could not provide the dedicated self-sacrifice, the unflagging interest in the patient's welfare, which moral treatment required. As in other respects, moral treatment could not survive the perils of routinization.

While the reformers continued to use the increased likelihood of cure as one of the primary arguments in favour of asylum treatment, there were already signs that the asylums were filling with chronic cases for whom nothing could be done. Like most of its counterparts, Hanwell was originally planned to be for 'the reception of those only whose malady being of recent date is found to be most susceptible of cure'. In order 'not to fill the asylum with incurables, . . . all pauper Lunatics of these Parishes should be examined, and those Lunatics having the least inveterate symptoms be selected for the County Asylum'.[190] Despite every precaution, however, within three years of its opening, Ellis drew the attention of the magistrates to the 'melancholy fact of the house being filled with

187. Metropolitan Commissioners in Lunacy, *1844 Report*, p. 24.
188. *Ibid.*
189. W.A.F. Browne, *What Asylums Were, Are, and Ought to Be*, quoted in R.A. Hunter and I. MacAlpine, *Three Hundred Years of Psychiatry*, London: Oxford University Press, 1963, p. 868.
190. Middlesex Lunatic Asylum, Minutes of the Visiting Justices, Vol. 2, 1829–31, pp. 323, 412, in manuscript at the Greater London Record Office, MA/A/J2.

old and incurable cases'; something he attributed 'almost entirely to the neglect of proper remedies in the early stages of the disease'.[191] At Lancaster, too, there were complaints of 'the Asylum being crowded with chronic and almost hopeless cases'.[192] And Prichard, the superintendent of the Northampton Asylum, strove to make a virtue of necessity, arguing that

> to express a regret that these pitiable wrecks of intellectual being should find here an Asylum, that during their brief period of mere vegetative existence they should enjoy through its medium every comfort which their unfortunate situation demands, would be as foreign to the dictates of right feeling as to the benevolent views of those by whom it was founded.[193]

To convince his listeners of the advantages of the asylum, Ashley might engage in elaborate and optimistic calculations of the theoretical savings curative institutions would produce. But to do so, he had to ignore the evidence which demonstrated that existing 'county asylums have . . . become, and the evil is daily increasing, places of security rather than curative establishments'.[194] For it is one of the many ironies of the English lunacy reform movement that just as it reached its goals, and the optimism it had been so sedulously promoting reached its peak, experience was showing the fragility of the assumptions on which its whole program rested. There was much truth in the comment made by David Uwins, a London mad-doctor and writer on insanity:

> No well-regulated mind can for a moment doubt that the recent inquisitions by our statesmen and legislators on the nature of insanity and the economy of lunatic establishments have been prompted by a grandeur of design and a largeness of benevolence; the only room for doubt and distrust is in reference to the complete fulfillment of sanguine expectation. It is in the very spirit and nature of reform to be too condemnatory of what is, and too hopeful of what is to come.[195]

191. Hanwell Lunatic Asylum, *4th Annual Report*, 1835.
192. Lancaster Lunatic Asylum, *Annual Report*, 1845, p. 19.
193. Northampton General Lunatic Asylum, *Annual Report*, 1840, p. 12.
194. *Westminster Review* 43, 1845, p. 171.
195. D. Uwins, *A Treatise on those Disorders of the Brain and Nervous System, Which Are Usually Considered and Called Mental*, p. 235, footnote.

CHAPTER FOUR

From Madness to Mental Illness:
Medical Men as Moral Entrepreneurs

'When *I* use a word,' Humpty Dumpty said, in a rather scornful tone,
'it means just what I choose it to mean – neither more nor less.'

'The question is,' said Alice, 'whether you *can* make words mean so
many different things.'

'The question is,' said Humpty Dumpty, 'which is to be master –
that's all.'

Lewis Carroll, *Through the Looking Glass, and What Alice Found There*

1. *The Meanings of Madness*

The inhabitants of early modern England understandably viewed madness
as a frightening and mysterious disorder. Its most extreme manifestations – wild ravings, disturbances of the senses, deep depressions – were
profoundly disturbing and disruptive events. Representing an obvious
threat to the social order, they imposed grave social and economic costs
on the lunatics' families, while simultaneously providing a troubling
reminder of the precariousness of the rule of reason.[1]

In attempting to comprehend the depredations wrought by these protean
and bewildering forms of misfortune, Englishmen (and women) had
recourse to supernatural as well as natural accounts. Even among the
educated elite in Tudor and Stuart England, religious and magical causation
were embraced alongside naturalistic forms of explanation.[2] Divine

1. As Michael MacDonald has shown, in early modern England, such 'extravagant mental
   disorders were comparatively rare'. Still, the severity of the difficulties they created could
   not but force attention to a condition which rendered its victims 'terrifying and
   disgusting, impossible to control and oblivious to the normal rules of violence. Their
   behaviour imperiled the fundamental principles of social life: household and hierarchy'.
   Mystical Bedlam: Madness, Anxiety, and Healing in Seventeenth Century England, Cambridge:
   Cambridge University Press, 1981, pp. 147–8.
2. For example, Joseph Blagrave, *Blagrave's Astrological Practice of Physick*, London: S.G.B.G.
   for Obad. Blagrave, 1671; and for a protest against this sort of therapeutic eclecticism,
   John Cotta, *A Short Discouerie of the Vnobserved Dangers of Seuerall Sorts of Ignorant and
   Vnconsidered Practisers of Physicke in England*, London: William Jones, 1612. See generally
   Keith Thomas, *Religion and the Decline of Magic*, esp. pp. 8–14, 177–211, 275–7, 330–4,
   378–80, 536–46, 649–60. Also valuable are Michael MacDonald, 'Insanity and the

retribution, demoniacal possession, witchcraft,[3] or the misalignment of one's astrological signs was seen as being at least as plausible an explanation of distraction as was an account pitched in terms of bodily indisposition (most commonly a disequilibrium of the humours).[4] In very few circles were natural and supernatural explanations seen as mutually exclusive or contradictory, and, as in the cases of Richard Napier[5] and Robert Burton,[6] the more general pattern among those who sought to explain, to cope with, and perhaps to cure the mad was to draw eclectically on the religious, the astrological, the magical, and the psychological, alongside or in place of organically based medical interventions. Clerics, astrologers, village wizards, folk magicians, and cunning men and women were as likely as surgeons and apothecaries to be summoned to combat the malignity of mental disorder.[7]

Among the unlettered and among Protestant preachers whose 'enthusiastic' forms of Christian belief appealed primarily to the lower orders, these traditional conceptions of madness seem to have survived substantially intact through much of the eighteenth and even into the nineteenth century.[8] For Puritan divines, for sectarian Protestants like the Quakers

Realities of History in Early Modern England', *Psychological Medicine* 11, 1981, pp. 11–25; and *idem.*, 'Popular Beliefs About Mental Disorder in Early Modern England', in W. Eckhart and J. Geyer-Kordesch (eds), *Heilberufe und Kranke in 17 und 18 Jahrhundert*, Münster: Burgverlag, 1982, pp. 148–73.

3. *Cf.* John Cotta's bitter complaint about 'The general madness of this age [which] ascribeth unto witchcraft whatsoever falleth out unknown or strange unto a vulgar sense'. *A Short Discouerie of . . . Seuerall Sorts of Ignorant and Vnconsidered Practisers of Physicke*, London: William Jones, 1612, p. 59. Others were beginning to express a similar scepticism about the degree of diabolic intervention in men's lives. *Cf.* Timothie Bright, *A Treatise of Melancholie*, London: Vautrollier, 1586; Edward Jorden, *The Suffocation of the Mother*, London: Windet, 1603; and Reginald Scot, *The Discouerie of Witchcraft*, London: Clark, 1665.

4. ''Tis a common practice of some men', Burton remarked, 'to go first to a witch and then to a physician, if the one cannot [cure] then the other shall'. Robert Burton, *The Anatomy of Melancholy*, reprint edition edited by Holbrook Jackson, London: Dent, 1932, Partition 2, p. 7.

5. See M. MacDonald, *Mystical Bedlam*, esp. pp. xiii–xiv, 7–12.

6. [Robert Burton], *The Anatomy of Melancholy, What it Is. With All the Kinds, Causes, Symptomes, Prognosticks, and Severall Cures of It*, Oxford: Cripps edn, 1621, especially Partition 3. For commentary on Burton's demonology, see Roy Porter, *Mind Forg'd Manacles: A History of Madness in England from the Restoration to the Regency*, London: Athlone, 1987, pp. 62–6; and *idem.*, 'Anglicanism and Psychiatry: Robert Burton and Sir Thomas Browne', unpublished paper, Wellcome Institute for the History of Medicine.

7. M. MacDonald, *Mystical Bedlam*, chapters 1 and 5. 'Clergymen, astrologers, and magicians of all kinds treated mental disorders. Religious and magical remedies were not sharply distinguished by laymen, and traditionally the clergy had been the most respected practitioners of healing magic.' *Ibid.*, p. 176.

8. See, for example, the commentary in Lewis Southcomb, *Peace of Mind and Health of Body United*, London: Cowper, 1750, pp. 84ff.; John Wesley, *The Journals of John Wesley*, 4 volumes, edited by Ernest Rhys, London: Everyman, 1906, e.g., Vol. 1, pp. 190, 210, 363, 412, 551; Vol. 2, pp. 225, 461, 489 (Wesley fervently believed in a demonomania and advocated spiritual healing); T. Bakewell, *A Letter Addressed to the Chairman of the Select Committee . . . Appointed to Enquire into the State of Madhouses*, Stafford: for the author, 1815, p. 12. As Keith Thomas notes in the concluding pages of *Religion and the Decline of*

and the Methodists, mental turmoil was reinvested with profound spiritual significance. Anxiety and despair, the tortures provoked by the acknowledgement of guilt and sin, the perils of damnation and the promise of salvation, the literal struggle between the divine and the temptations of the Evil One for possession of an individual's soul: these were central elements of passionate forms of evangelistic Christianity which steadily gained adherents among the unlearned and the unwashed. In such circles, scriptural discussions of demons and witches served to reinforce popular belief in an almost palpable spiritual world of supernatural malevolence and satanic temptation, one of whose most visible manifestations was maladies of the mind.

Proponents of 'enthusiastic' Protestantism proffered not merely *explanations* of mental disturbance that were consonant with popular beliefs, but also alternative forms of spiritual healing and religious therapy. As Michael MacDonald has shown, through the provision of spiritual solace, rituals of exorcism, the exercise of apostolic powers, and communal healing rituals of prayer and fasting, dissenters like George Fox and John Wesley sought to console and cure the mad, often – so they reported – with success.[9] Accordingly, the secularization of mental disorder proceeded quite slowly and haltingly among the lower orders.

Paradoxically, however, MacDonald has also contended that the increasingly close identification of preternatural accounts of madness with sectarian and 'enthusiastic' forms of religious belief encouraged the English governing classes to embrace their antithesis, a secularized, somatically grounded explanation of mental disorder. The English Civil War and its aftermath had vividly demonstrated to the ruling elite the perils of Puritan zeal and religious enthusiasm, and induced in their midst a positive aversion to the pious emotionalism of the radical Protestant sects.[10]

Magic, Harmondsworth: Penguin, 1973 (pp. 797–800): 'Nineteenth-century students of popular folklore discovered everywhere that the inhabitants of rural England had not abandoned their faith in healing wells, divination, cunning folk, witchcraft, omens or ghosts.' See also J.F.C. Harrison, *The Second Coming: Popular Millenarianism, 1780–1850*, New Brunswick, New Jersey: Rutgers University Press, 1979; and James Obelkevich, *Religion and Rural Society: South Lindsey, 1825–1875*, Oxford: Clarendon Press, 1976, esp. chapter 6.

9. See especially M. MacDonald, 'Religion, Social Change, and Psychological Healing in England, 1600–1800', in W.J. Sheils (ed.), *The Church and Healing*, Oxford: Blackwell, 1982, pp. 101–25; *idem.*, 'Insanity and the Realities of History in Early Modern England', *Psychological Medicine* 11, 1981, pp. 11–25. For documentation of 'many cases of alleged diabolical possession in which Puritan ministers diagnosed the malady, entered into discourse with the devil, and triumphantly ejected it after fasting and prayer', *cf.* K. Thomas, *Religion and the Decline of Magic*, pp. 569–88.

10. For the beginnings of the revolt against enthusiasm, see Henry More, *Enthusiasmus Triumphatus, or, A Discourse of the Nature, Causes, Kinds, and Cure, of Enthusiasme*, London: Morden, 1656. For twentieth-century commentary, see George Williamson, 'The Restoration Revolt Against Enthusiasm', *Studies in Philology* 2, 1933, pp. 571–603; Thomas Steffan, 'The Social Argument Against Enthusiasm (1650–1660)', *Studies in English* 21, 1941, pp. 39–63; R.A. Knox, *Enthusiasm*, London: Oxford University Press, 1950; Susie I. Tucker, *Enthusiasm: A Study in Semantic Change*, Cambridge: Cambridge

Preferring 'rational' forms of religion, shunning zealotry and superstition, and fearing the subversive potential of claims to possess divine inspiration, the upper classes increasingly repudiated popular supernaturalism, and with it the language of religious psychology and the practice of spiritual healing. Indeed, many took their opposition a step further: so far from accepting the healing miracles of the enthusiasts, they began to equate evangelical fanaticism with 'delusion, obsession, madness'.[11] From this perspective, enthusiasm itself was 'nothing but the effect of mere madness, and arose from the stronger impulses of a warm brain'[12] – and Methodism one of the prime producers of candidates for the madhouse.[13]

MacDonald's claim that the spreading influence in upper-class circles of medical explanations of insanity was to a significant extent a reflection of underlying political and religious conflicts is an important insight, though it should not be pushed too far.[14] More broadly and, I would argue, more significantly, efforts by physicians to define madness as a uniquely and exclusively medical problem and province were aided by and dependent upon the larger social changes which for some segments of the population were bringing about the disenchantment of the universe, promoting a more secular outlook on a world increasingly seen as orderly and rational, and undercutting the earlier emphasis on a spirit-drenched cosmos.[15] And those efforts only began to take on a sustained and systematic character alongside and in intimate relationship to the movement to segregate the mad into specialized institutions.

2. Madness and Medicine

Theoretical medical disquisitions on the seriously mad, furious or moping, thus begin to become more prominent from the late seventeenth century onwards, most notably in the writings of Thomas Willis and his epigones.

University Press, 1972; George Rosen, 'Enthusiasm: "A Dark Lanthorn of the Spirit"', *Bulletin of the History of Medicine* 42, 1968, pp. 393–421.

11. Roy Porter, 'The Rage of Party: A Glorious Revolution in English Psychiatry?' *Medical History* 27, 1983, p. 40.

12. Nicholas Robinson, *A New System of the Spleen, Vapours, and Hypochondriack Melancholy*, London: Bettesworth, Innys, and Rivington, 1729, p. 250.

13. M. MacDonald, 'Insanity and the Realities of History in Early Modern England', pp. 14–5. For a late eighteenth-century reiteration of these views, *cf.* William Pargeter, *Observations on Maniacal Disorders*, Reading: for the author, 1792, esp. pp. 31ff.: 'The *doctrines* of the *Methodists* have a greater tendency than those of any other sect to produce the most deplorable effects on the human understanding. The brain is perplexed in the mazes of mystery, and the imagination overpowered by the tremendous description of future torments.'

14. Its role seems more as a catalyst helping to speed and facilitate the process than an essential precondition of it, as is suggested, not least, by similar shifts in outlook elsewhere in Europe.

15. Roy Porter has put forward a similar criticism in *Mind Forg'd Manacles*, pp. 78–9. For discussion of this crucial set of inter-connected changes in perceptions, see chapters 1 and 2.

Linked at first to a heightened interest in anatomy and especially in the glandular system common to much of late seventeenth- and early eighteenth-century medicine, these accounts uneasily combine traditional humouralism with more mechanistic accounts linking disease to the operations of the glandular and nervous systems, and to the vagaries of fluids and fibres.[16] The earliest medical treatises for the most part rested upon a remarkably restricted clinical acquaintance with the condition, perhaps indicative of distaste for any close or continuing contact with those suffering from the disorder, but they nonetheless signalled a growing intellectual and practical interest in providing a rational explanation of the origins of madness.

At first, however, these pioneering medical men were disposed to direct their primary attention elsewhere, attempting in thoroughly entrepreneurial ways to legitimize as authentic diseases new and milder (and presumably more treatable) varieties of 'nervous' disorders – the spleen, hypochondria, the vapours, hysteria – which apparently afflicted a more fashionable and desirable clientele than most of the Bedlam mad. Here was an extraordinarily attractive patient population, blessed with excessively refined sensibilities and exquisitely civilized temperaments (not to mention money),[17] the victims of 'Riot, Luxury and Excess . . . Laziness, [and their own] Ineptitude for Exercise'.[18] 'Scarce known to our Ancestors . . . these nervous Disorders' were now 'computed to make almost one *third* of the Complaints of the People of *Condition in England*'.[19]

Such *malades imaginaires* might be scoffed at by the masses, but those suffering from them proved, not surprisingly, eager to embrace the medical insistence that their pains were indeed rooted in a real disorder of the body.[20] For this reason, too, medical imperialism thus found a

16. See especially Thomas Willis, *Two Discourses Concerning the Soul of Brutes*, translated by S. Pordage, London: Dring, Harper, and Leigh, 1683; *idem.*, *The Practice of Physick*, translated by S. Pordage, London: Dring, Harper, and Leigh, 1684.
17. '[Such disorders] I think never happen or can happen to any but those of the liveliest and quickest natural parts whose Faculties are the brightest and most spiritual, and whose Genius is most keen and penetrating, and particularly where there is the most delicate Sensation and Taste, both of pleasure and pain.' George Cheyne, *The English Malady: or, A Treatise of Nervous Diseases of All Kinds*, London: Wisk, Ewing, and Smith, 1733, p. 262. 'For it is evident by common observation that Men of a splenetic Complexion . . . are usually endowed with refined and elevated parts, quick Apprehension, distinguishing Judgement, clear Reason, and great Vivacity of Imagination; and in these Perfections they are superior to the common Level of Mankind.' Sir Richard Blackmore, *A Treatise of the Spleen or Vapours*, London: Pemberton, 1724, p. 90.
18. G. Cheyne, *The English Malady*, pp. 48, 49, 52. See also Bernard Mandeville, *A Treatise of Hypochondriack and Hysterick Passions*, London, Dryden Leech, W. Taylor, 1711; Sir Richard Blackmore, *A Treatise of the Spleen or Vapours*; N. Robinson, *A New System of the Spleen*.
19. G. Cheyne, *The English Malady*, pp. i–ii, emphasis in the original.
20. 'One great Reason why these Patients are unwilling their Disease should go by its right Name is, I imagine, this, that the Spleen and Vapours are, by those that never felt their Symptoms, looked upon as an imaginary and fantastick Sickness of the Brain, filled with

receptive audience among those who moved in the highest social circles. And since the boundaries between these milder forms of nervous prostration and out-and-out madness were widely pictured as fluid and ill-defined, the one if left untreated likely to progress into the other,[21] the growing acceptance of medical accounts of nervous complaints indirectly also helped to legitimize physicians' more extended claims to jurisdiction over insanity.

Of more direct significance, most especially from the middle of the eighteenth century onwards, were the experience and writings of medical men who now enjoyed – if that is the appropriate term – a more intimate acquaintance with the raving and the melancholic. Physicians had been placed in charge of the Bethlem Hospital only from the end of the sixteenth century onwards, and for the next century and more their role in the day-to-day functioning of the institution was extremely limited, their contact with the inmates seldom extending beyond a brief visit once a week.[22] The job was certainly highly sought after, for its visibility meant that the incumbent could secure substantial financial rewards from the aristocratic patrons he was in a position to attract.[23] At least until the accession of James Monro, however, none of the Bethlem physicians attempted to specialize in the mad-doctoring trade, and none either 'investigated insanity or advanced its treatment'.[24] Richard Hale, for instance, Monro's immediate predecessor, and physician to Bethlem from 1708 to 1728, was a noted anatomist and general practitioner, skilled, as the Harveian orators put it, 'for his gifts in all branches of medicine', but his views on madness remain obscure, and his primary energies were clearly directed elsewhere.[25]

The advent of the Monro dynasty in 1728[26] substantially coincided with the development of more specialized forms of practice, with the Monro name rapidly becoming almost as closely identified with madness as

odd and irregular Ideas.' Sir Richard Blackmore, *A Treatise of the Spleen or Vapours*, pp. 98–9. I have drawn here on the useful discussion in R. Porter, *Mind Forg'd Manacles*, pp. 81–91.

21. 'It frequently happens, if great Care be not timely taken, that the Spleen and Vapours make a Transition into Madness, by which word I comprehend all the several Species of Distraction.' N. Robinson, *A New System of the Spleen*, p. 199. '[I]ndeed the Limits and Partitions that bound and discriminate the highest Hypochondriack and Hysterick Disorders, and Melancholy, Lunacy, and Phrenzy are so nice, that it is not easy to distinguish them, and set the Boundaries where one Ends, and the other Begins.' Sir Richard Blackmore, *A Treatise of the Spleen or Vapours*, p. 163.

22. In Roy Porter's words, 'Bethlem physicians saw their post . . . if not exactly as a sinecure, at least as somewhat ceremonial'. *Mind Forg'd Manacles*, p. 128.

23. *Cf.* Jonathan Andrews, 'A Respectable Mad-Doctor? Dr Richard Hale, F.R.S. (1670–1728)', *Notes and Records of the Royal Society of London* 44, 1990, pp. 179–80.

24. R. Porter, *Mind Forg'd Manacles*, p. 128.

25. J. Andrews, 'A Respectable Mad-Doctor?', pp. 172–3, 183–5. Many of Hale's predecessors, including Helkiah Crooke and Edward Tyson, shared his interest in anatomy.

26. Four Monros were to serve in succession as physician to Bethlem, over a span of more than a century: James, John, Thomas, and Edward Thomas.

Bedlam itself. But the Monros were a conservative lot who concentrated on building their own practice and fortunes, and displayed little interest or aptitude for prosletyzing in behalf of a more extended medical involvement in the treatment of insanity.[27] Given this stance, it was perforce other elements of the mad-doctoring trade who played the central role in constructing a professional literature about the treatment of madness, and who acted to advance medicine's jurisdictional claims.

Most early madhouses were private speculations run for profit. Given the difficulties others experienced in managing the insane and the lack of legal restrictions on entry into the business or upon the actual conduct of the enterprise, they were generally a very profitable investment. Initially, the traffic in this species of human misery was a trade monopolized by no single occupational group. Speculators from a wide variety of backgrounds looking for easy profits, as well as more 'respectable' groups such as the clergy, all sought to obtain a share of a lucrative market. It was at precisely this stage that the medical profession (or rather, diverse individuals laying claim to possess some sort of medical training and knowledge) first began to assert an interest in insanity. A number of doctors trying to gain a share of the lucrative new business, and possibly also to improve the treatment of the insane, began opening madhouses of their own or became involved in efforts to set up charity hospitals for the care of lunatics.

The English medical profession at this time was composed of three separate elements, physicians, surgeons, and apothecaries, each of whom catered to a different clientele. The physicians, the elite's doctors, generally possessed a medical degree, and in London at least, were members of the Royal College of Physicians: but an MD was no guarantee of more than a passing acquaintance with classical authors in the field, with no assurance of clinical experience; and membership of the College depended more on social connections than medical skill. Surgeons had only recently severed their links with the barber's trade; entry into their ranks was usually by apprenticeship and their status was distinctly lower than that of the physicians. Apothecaries catered largely to the middle and lower classes; they too were recruited by apprenticeship and lacked any real control over licensing and entry; so that those calling themselves apothecaries might vary from semi-illiterate quacks to highly competent practitioners by the standards of the time.[28]

27. Of the first three members of the dynasty, only John Monro bothered to publish on the subject, being stung into writing his *Remarks on Dr Battie's Treatise on Madness* (London: Clarke, 1758) by the latter's criticism of the Monro family's secretiveness and therapeutic conservatism. On the Monro regime, *cf.* Jonathan Andrews, 'Bedlam Revisited: A History of Bethlem Hospital *c.* 1634–*c.* 1770', unpublished Ph.D. dissertation, London University, 1991, chapter 4.
28. An excellent example of the former was provided by Finch. In his evidence before the Select Committee of 1815, he produced a certificate of insanity he had received from one such practitioner: 'Hey Broadway A Potcarey of Gillingham Certefy that Mr. James Burt

The doctors entering the mad-business were not drawn exclusively from any one of these three classes; nor, so far as one can judge, did they differ significantly from the rest of the profession in skill or respectability. While 'doctors' with little claim to the title did enter the field, so too did well-known society physicians, and those trained at some of the best medical schools of the time.[29] By no means was the mad-business a refuge of only the most disreputable elements of the medical profession. To the contrary, it was those drawn from the most educated and literate elements of the profession who were amongst the most vigorous and effective partisans of medicine's claims in this area, and who contributed most to its growing dominance of the field.

The earliest lay proprietors of madhouses had often attempted to attract clients by claiming to provide cures as well as care.[30] This idea that expert intervention could provide a means of restoring the deranged to reason naturally proved an attractive one. However, it was a much more plausible claim when asserted by the medical madhouse proprietors. To understand why this should be so, one need only recall certain basic characteristics of eighteenth-century medicine.

Unlike its modern successor, eighteenth-century medicine did not involve identifying specific disease entities and then prescribing specialized treatments directed at them.[31] Rather it possessed a number of things

Misfortin hapened by a Plow in the Hed which is the Ocasim of his Ellness and By the Rising and Falling of the Blood and I think A Blister and Bleeding and meddeson Will be A Very Great thing. But Mr. James Burt would not A Gree to be Don at Home, Hay Broadway.' House of Commons, *Report of the Select Committee on Madhouses in England, with minutes of evidence and appendices*, 1815, p. 51. The profession as a whole did not succeed in laying down uniform standards for entry until the passage of the 1858 Medical Registration Act. The Apothecaries' Act of 1815 represented an early effort to define the legal status of that segment of the medical profession. Interestingly enough, it was George Man Burrows, one of the most well-known private madhouse keepers of the early nineteenth century, and the chairman of the Association of Apothecaries and Surgeon Apothecaries, whose efforts were largely instrumental in securing its passage. See W. Parry-Jones, *The Trade in Lunacy*, London: Routledge and Kegan Paul, 1972, pp. 78, 92–3.

29. Both William Battie of St. Luke's and John Monro of Bethlem were well-known society physicians. Anthony Addington, one of George III's physicians, had formerly kept a private madhouse at Reading. Other established doctors who kept madhouses (with the university from which they received their MDs) included: Francis Willis (Oxford); Thomas Arnold (Edinburgh); James Mason Cox (Edinburgh, Paris and Leyden); Edward Long Fox (Edinburgh); William Perfect (St. Andrew's). W. Parry-Jones, *The Trade in Lunacy*, pp. 75–7.

30. See, e.g., David Irish, *Levamen Infirmi, or: Cordial Counsel to the Sick and Diseased* (London: for the author, 1700); Thomas Fallowes, *The Best Method for the Cure of Lunaticks, With Some Account of the Incomparable Oleum Cephalicum Used in the Same, Prepared and Administered by Tho. Fallowes, at his House in Lambeth-Marsh* (London: for the author, 1705). (Fallowes's MD was awarded by himself.)

31. Indeed, as Warner has shown, until well past the middle of the *nineteenth* century, disease entities were seen as fluid, not fixed, and 'disease specific treatment was in most instances professionally illegitimate'. John Harley Warner, *The Therapeutic Perspective: Medical Practice, Knowledge, and Identity in America, 1820–1885*, Cambridge, Massachusetts: Harvard University Press, 1986, p. 62. As he demonstrates, regular practitioners fiercely resisted the very idea that a particular treatment might cure a single disease, a cookbook

which in principle were regarded as useful weapons against any and all types of bodily dysfunction.[32] No English doctor went quite so far as the American, Benjamin Rush, who reduced all illnesses to one underlying pathology, and prescribed a single remedy, depletion.[33] Nevertheless, adherents of almost every one of the eighteenth-century medical 'systems' exhibited a touching faith in a number of cure-alls – such things as purges, vomits, bleedings, and various mysterious coloured powders, whose secrets were known only to their compounders.

Traditional humoural medicine, which supplied the intellectual model of disease that made sense of these therapeutic interventions, proved remarkably tenacious, not least through its ability to generate a set of shared cultural understandings of illness and its treatment. While providing solace for the sufferer, it simultaneously offered the doctor both the reassurance that he understood the disease and a set of weapons with which to intervene in the underlying physiological processes that gave rise to the observed pathology. Within this mutually reinforcing system, 'health or disease [were seen] as general states of the total organism . . . [and] the body as a system of intake and outgo – a system which had, necessarily, to remain in balance if the individual were to remain healthy'.[34] With the body portrayed as an interconnected whole, and pathology as the product of systemic imbalance, the goal of therapeutics was to restore the patient's internal equilibrium.[35] And in accomplishing this end, 'the physician's most potent weapon was his ability to "regulate the secretions" – to extract blood, to promote the perspiration, or the

approach to therapeutics which threatened to undermine their insistence on the importance of professional expertise and clinical judgement. As one American physician insisted, as late as 1859, 'No scientific physician willingly admits the existence of specifics. Such an admission is a germ of quackery.' Quoted *ibid.* On therapeutics in eighteenth-century England, see Roy Porter and Dorothy Porter, *In Sickness and in Health: The British Experience 1650–1850*, London: Fourth Estate, 1988; idem., *Patient's Progress: Doctors and Doctoring in Eighteenth Century England*, Oxford: Polity Press, 1989.

32. As Cheyne insisted, 'There can be no greater Evidence of the Truth of Principles, than their being simple and few, and readily applicable to solve all possible Appearances. Nature produces many and various Effects in different Circumstances, from one and the same Cause.' G. Cheyne, *The English Malady*, p. vii. This paradigm persisted well into the nineteenth century. *Cf.* Spurzheim's insistence that 'the art of medicine does not consist in multiplying medical formulas, but in judiciously prescribing a few select and active remedies'. *Observations on the Deranged Manifestations of the Mind, or Insanity*, London: Baldwin, Craddock, and Joy, 1817, p. 282.

33. On Rush, see Norman Dain, *Concepts of Insanity in the United States, 1786–1830*, New Brunswick, NJ: Rutgers University Press, 1964, pp. 14–24 and Richard Harrison Shyrock, *The Development of Modern Medicine*, Philadelphia: University of Pennsylvania Press, 1936, pp. 28–9.

34. Charles Rosenberg, 'The Therapeutic Revolution: Medicine, Meaning, and Social Change in Nineteenth Century America', in Morris J. Vogel and Charles E. Rosenberg (eds), *The Therapeutic Revolution; Essays in the Social History of American Medicine*, Philadelphia: University of Pennsylvania Press, 1979, p. 6.

35. *Cf.* J.H. Warner, *The Therapeutic Perspective*, p. 85; R. Porter and D. Porter, *Patient's Progress*, passim, esp. chapter 5.

urination, or defecation . . . [the] visible products of the body's otherwise inscrutable internal state'.[36]

Closely connected to the view that the body formed a wholly inter-related system was the long-standing assumption that mind and body were interdependent and 'equally capable of affecting [each] other'.[37] Medical theory and its associated remedies were therefore readily adapted to the understanding and treatment of insanity. It was but a small leap to assert that the standard Galenic therapeutics, efficacious across a wide range of diseases, would also cure lunatics.[38]

The doctors, then, had an advantage when it came to justifying their claims to cure insanity, because everybody 'knew' that they possessed powerful remedies whose use demanded special training and expertise, and whose 'efficacy' against a wide range of complaints was generally acknowledged. They exploited this advantage to good effect, arguing with renewed vigour that bleedings, vomits, purges, and the like were also efficacious in cases of insanity, which was, after all, a disease of the mind or brain. Respectable institutions must be set up under the control of physicians, for only in this way could the danger of incurability, 'either by the Disorder gaining Strength beyond the Reach of Physick, or by the patient falling into the Hands of Persons utterly unskilled in the Treatment of the Disorder, or who have found their Advantage in neglecting every Method necessary to obtain a Cure',[39] be avoided. A number of other factors entered into and added weight to the attempt to claim insanity as part of the legitimate domain of medicine. The promoters of the new St. Luke's Hospital were partly motivated by the desire to improve the medical knowledge of insanity, and their efforts to raise funds publicized the idea that medicine had something to offer the insane. The involvement of William Battie, a successful society physician later elected President of the Royal College of Physicians, first in promoting the hospital and then in serving as its first resident physician, must have helped to overcome the

36. C. Rosenberg, 'The Therapeutic Revolution', pp. 6–7. As he points out, paradoxically, it was often 'the very severity of drug action [which] assured the patient and his family that something was indeed being done.' *Ibid.*, p. 9.
37. *Ibid.*, p. 5.
38. William Perfect advocated the use of bleedings, setons, electricity, and administration of emetics, digitalis and antimony. [W. Perfect], *Select Cases in the Different Species of Insanity, Lunacy or Madness, With the Modes of Practice as Adopted in the Treatment of Each*, Rochester: Gillman, 1787, and *A Remarkable Case of Madness, with the Diet and Medicines used in the Cure*, Rochester: for the author, 1791. See also Thomas Arnold, M.D., *Observations on the Nature, Kinds, Causes, and Prevention of Insanity*, 2 Vols Leicester: Robinson and Caddell, 1782–6; William Pargeter, *Observations on Maniacal Disorders*, Reading: for the author, 1792; and J.M. Cox, *Practical Observations on Insanity: In Which Some Suggestions Are Offered Towards an Improved Mode of Treating Diseases of the Mind [. . .] to Which Are Subjoined, Remarks on Medical Jurisprudence as Connected with Diseased Intellect*, London: Baldwin and Murray, 1806.
39. St. Luke's Hospital, *Considerations upon the usefulness and necessity of establishing an Hospital as a further provision for poor Lunaticks*, manuscript dated 1750, at St. Luke's Woodside Hospital, London.

scruples of many of his colleagues, who might otherwise have hesitated to risk their reputations by entering such a positively disreputable, though highly profitable, field. As other charity asylums founded in the eighteenth century were frequently located alongside and associated with existing infirmaries, the link between insanity and medicine was strengthened in the public mind.[40] The appearance of a number of books on the medical treatment of insanity gave further support to the mad-doctors' claims, and such famous medical teachers as William Cullen began to incorporate materials on the subject into their lectures, so that some physicians could assert that they had specialized training in this area.[41] On this basis, therefore, doctors were gradually acquiring a dominant, although not a monopolistic position in the mad-business by the end of the eighteenth century. Numerically, they might still be a minority of those trafficking in madness, but their view of insanity as an illness was an increasingly influential one in upper-class circles, its attractions reinforced by the fortuitous circumstance of George III's illness, with its associated mania; for the King's disorder meant that 'the topic of insanity was widely discussed in a context which excluded the attitude of moral condemnation'.[42] On this basis, therefore, doctors were gradually acquiring a powerful, although very far from an overwhelmingly dominant position in the mad business by the end of the eighteenth century.

3. The Obstacles to a Medical Monopoly

Modern professions are not simply the *dominant* or most important providers of a particular service; instead, they effectively *monopolize* a service market, claim to do so on the basis of a unique, scientifically based expertise and training, and make use of their exclusive control of valuable markets to secure for themselves not merely monopoly profits in the monetary sense, but also significant status advantages.[43] During the nineteenth century, mad-doctors manoeuvered to secure such a position for themselves, and acceptance of their particular view of madness,

---

40. The medical approach benefitted further from the association with charity; for these institutions apparently lacked a motive for keeping sane people confined, and their benevolent status disarmed much of the public hostility then directed against the profit-seeking (most non-medical) private madhouses.

41. See William Cullen, *First Lines of the Practice of Physic*, 2 Vols, Edinburgh: Bell and Bradfute, 1808. Among his students were Arnold, Ferriar, and Hallaran, as well as Benjamin Rush.

42. Kathleen Jones, *Lunacy, Law, and Conscience 1744–1845*, London: Routledge and Kegan Paul, 1955, p. 26.

43. As Harold Perkin points out, 'scarcity may appear long before outright monopoly. [But w]hen a professional occupation has, by active persuasion of the public and the state, acquired sufficient control of the market in a particular service, it creates an artificial scarcity in the supply which has the effect of yielding a rent, in the strict Ricardian sense of a payment for the use of a scarce resource.' *The Rise of Professional Society: England Since 1880*, London: Routledge, 1989, pp. 7–8.

seeking to transform their existing foothold in the marketplace into a cognitive and practical monopoly of the field, and to acquire for those practising this line of work the status prerogatives 'owed' to professionals – most notably autonomous control by the practitioners themselves over the conditions and conduct of their work. The process was, however, by no means a simple one. Structural weaknesses of both an internal and external sort posed serious obstacles to the medical capture and reorganization of the 'trade in lunacy', and more specific conjunctural factors for a time threatened even that degree of market control which medical men had already won.

The consequence of the growth of a separate institutional provision for the mad was the creation of a guaranteed, albeit initially limited market for a new type of service, which in turn prompted the emergence of competing groups seeking to control this market. For professionalization to occur, one group had to succeed in driving out all its competitors or in subordinating all who persisted in this line of work to its authority. The ordinary operations of the marketplace were unlikely to produce such a result. For in the mad-business, the criteria of success were somewhat ambiguous, the verification of competing claims was difficult, and the very existence of a cognitive system markedly superior to any other was in doubt. So long as those in competition were forced to produce 'evidence' of their superiority, it was unlikely that a single group would succeed in securing a dominant position and in choking off the entry of potential competitors. And so long as this remained the case, the idea that anyone possessed expertise in this area remained problematic.

In the face of competing claims of apparently equal plausibility, the most rational as well as the most likely public policy was to continue to permit free entry into the trade in lunacy. Yet to allow this was to perpetuate the very conditions standing in the way of the emergence of a distinctive and relatively homogeneous occupational group possessing a plausible claim to be granted a professional monopoly. In the first place, the lack of barriers to entry into the mad-business allowed unscrupulous elements to enter the trade, and thus depressed public confidence in all its practitioners. Worse than this, the existence of a number of groups each clamouring to be recognized as *the* experts in the treatment of insanity, each purporting to produce 'evidence' in support of its claims, and each concerned to denigrate and discredit its rivals, was scarcely a situation calculated to promote public belief in the legitimacy of such pretensions on anyone's part. Lack of public confidence was likewise reflected in the low social status accorded to practitioners in the field, and this set in motion a self-fulfilling prophecy through its negative effects on the quality of those attracted to the madhouse trade. All of which meant that those dealing with lunatics had difficulty securing even a modest degree of occupational stability.

Furthermore, efforts to remedy this state of affairs faced severe obstacles of a similar sort. Since entrance into the mad-business was not contingent upon having undergone prolonged and probably costly professional training, the ability of those striving to obtain professional status for mad-doctoring to attract candidates for such training was severely curtailed – a situation made worse by their inability to provide a guaranteed connection between their type of learning and subsequent earnings. A vicious circle seemed to be at work, for lacking 'general public belief in [their] competence, in the value of [their] professed knowledge and skill',[44] mad-doctors were in a poor position to obtain the monopoly they sought. But without it, they could scarcely hope to overcome the inherent weaknesses produced by the fluid, unregulated market for the type of services which they offered.

To complicate the situation still further, there were serious internal weaknesses in the mad-doctors' position. Though use was made of therapeutic rhetoric, early medical approaches to the treatment of the insane remained in many ways firmly wedded to the past, and were legitimated more by reference to classical authority than by rational demonstration. While more overtly coercive means of controlling the lunatic (for example, whipping and the use of chains) were given a medical gloss, in practice even the standard medical techniques of the time (such as bleeding and the administration of cathartics) were primarily employed as useful ways of disciplining and restraining 'patients' who were still seen in the animalistic terms of the traditional paradigm of insanity. Temporarily, at least, this commitment rendered the mad-doctors' position a vulnerable one, when changed circumstances made these sorts of responses no longer comprehensible or acceptable.

As I have previously demonstrated, towards the end of the eighteenth century there began to occur, as part of a wider transformation in the cultural boundaries of the community, a major shift in the cultural meaning of madness, as well as an increased stress on cognitive rationality rather than traditional usage as the basis for an action's legitimacy. These developments threatened to undermine medicine's claims to jurisdiction over the insane. For the growth of a new perspective on insanity, one which viewed the lunatic as essentially human, though lacking in self-restraint and discipline, and which saw the primary task for therapy to be the development of control from within the madman's own psyche rather than concentration upon an externally imposed and alien order, led inexorably to a perception of the practices which formed the core of the medical claim to possess a special competence in the treatment of insanity as presumptively inhumane. This was a presumption which might have been overturned had there been demonstrable evidence of either the practices' therapeutic effectiveness or their practical necessity.

In fact, there was neither. And the invention by laymen of a new

---

44. Eliot Freidson, *Profession of Medicine*, New York: Dodd, Mead, 1970, p. 11, emphasis in the original.

approach, moral treatment, which controlled the insane without resort to these traditional devices, and which convincingly claimed to have demonstrated the therapeutic bankruptcy of standard medical techniques in this area, weakened and ultimately destroyed the plausibility of any such contentions. Under these circumstances, the negotiation of cognitive exclusiveness on the part of mad-doctors, whereby insanity came to be defined as a disease, and hence as a condition within the sole purview of the medical profession, was necessarily a prolonged and complicated process.

4. The Threat Posed by Moral Treatment

English ideas on the moral treatment of the insane were inextricably bound up with the experience of the York Retreat, and that experience constituted 'a rather damning attack on the medical profession's capacity to deal with mental illness'.[45] The Retreat's founder, William Tuke, was a layman with a considerable, and not entirely unmerited, distrust of the medical profession of his day.[46] His primary concern was with providing humane care for insane Quakers though he also hoped, if possible, to cure them. Sceptical as he was of medicine's value, he possessed a sufficiently open mind to investigate its claims to have specific remedies for mental illness. With his encouragement, both the first visiting physician, Dr Fowler, and his successors made a trial of all of the various medicines and techniques which members of the profession had suggested.

The results must have been a disappointment, though perhaps not a surprise. In Samuel Tuke's words, 'the experience of the Retreat [. . .] will not add much to the honour or extent of medical science. I regret [. . .] to relate the pharmaceutical means which have failed, rather than to record those which have succeeded'.[47] Fowler found that

> the sanguine expectations, which he successively formed of the benefit to be derived from various pharmaceutical remedies, were, in great measure, as successively disappointed; and, although the proportion of cures, in the early part of the Institution, was respectable, yet the medical means were so imperfectly connected with the progress of

45. William Bynum 'Rationales for Therapy in British Psychiatry, 1780–1835', *Medical History* 18, 1974, p. 323.
46. *Cf.* K. Jones, *Lunacy, Law, and Conscience 1744–1845*, pp. 58ff. and *Mental Health and Social Policy 1845–1955*, London: Routledge and Kegan Paul, 1960, p. 9. His grandfather's disapproval led Samuel Tuke to relinquish his medical studies and enter the family business instead. (*Dictionary of National Biography* [Oxford University Press].) Daniel Hack Tuke was the first of the family to qualify as a doctor. He 'only overcame the family prejudice against that profession in 1852 after refusing to enter Tuke, Son and Co., giving up a legal career in its early stages and failing lamentably to become a poet'. K. Jones, *Lunacy, Law, and Conscience, 1744–1845*, p. 60.
47. Samuel Tuke, *Description of the Retreat: An Institution Near York for Insane Persons of the Society of Friends*, York: Alexander, 1813, p. 110.

recovery, that he could not avoid suspecting them, to be rather con-comitants than causes. Further experiments and observations confirmed his suspicions, and led him to the painful conclusion (painful alike to our pride and our humanity), 'that medicine, as yet, possesses very inadequate means to relieve the most grievous of human diseases'.[48]

Fowler's death in 1801 and the swift demise of his successor meant that the Retreat had three visiting physicians within its first five years of operation. Each of the others arrived convinced of medicine's applicability and value. Both were disillusioned:

> They have had recourse to various means, suggested by either their own knowledge and ingenuity, or recommended by later writers; but their success has not been such, as to rescue this branch of their pro-fession, from the charge, unjustly exhibited by some against the art of medicine in general, of its being chiefly conjectural.[49]

Numerous trials had shown that all the various suggestions that had been made, with the exception of warm baths for melancholics, were either useless or positively harmful.

Henceforth, the visiting physician confined his attention to treating cases of bodily illness, and it was the lay people who were in charge of the day-to-day running of the institution – the Tukes and George and Katherine Jepson – who began to develop the alternative response to insanity which became known as moral treatment.[50]

As Bynum points out, 'at the Retreat, like the Bicêtre [where Pinel was independently developing his own version of moral treatment], the physician was [thus] a shadowy figure, the burden of therapeutic responsibility having fallen on the keepers and other staff whose personal contacts with the patient were so much greater than that of the physician'.[51]

48. *Ibid.*, p. 111.
49. *Ibid.*, p. 115. Pinel's experience at the Bicêtre led him to the same conclusion: 'My faith in pharmaceutical preparations was gradually lessened, and my skepticism went at length so far, as to induce me never to have recourse to them until moral remedies had completely failed.' Phillipe Pinel, *A Treatise on Insanity*, translated by D.D. Davis, Sheffield: Cadell and Davies, 1806. Here, too, moral treatment involved a rejection of the traditional medical paradigm.
50. In 1815, William Tuke reported that 'very little medicine is used at the Retreat'. House of Commons, 1815, p. 135, evidence of William Tuke.
51. W. Bynum, 'Rationales for Therapy', p. 324. Jan Goldstein has recently provided a detailed reconstruction of the circumstances surrounding Pinel's 'discovery' of moral treatment, demonstrating quite conclusively 'its non-esoteric, lay origins – which Pinel [himself] so proudly and defiantly proclaimed'. His contribution, as she painstakingly documents, was to convert a 'charlatanistic' technique developed by the lay *concierges* who had day-to-day charge of the insane 'into a respectable tenet of official medicine', a scientizing project he accomplished through philosophical (and wholly speculative) specification of the mechanisms of both cause and cure, and through the application of statistical methods to measure and confirm quantitatively the efficacy of the treatment. See Jan Goldstein, *Console and Classify: The French Psychiatric Profession in the Nineteenth Century*, Cambridge: Cambridge University Press, 1987, pp. 72–119.

By the beginning of the second decade of the nineteenth century, the staff's substitution of moral constraint and kindness for fear and physical restraint in the management of the insane, their insistence on the importance of encouraging the inmate to reexert his own powers of self-control, and their demonstration that many lunatics recovered when treated in this fashion, were being given considerable publicity – both through the efforts of a stream of visitors interested in lunacy reform, and through the writings of William Tuke's grandson, Samuel. Treated less harshly and more nearly as rational human beings, the patients at the Retreat responded by acting less like the traditional stereotype of the raving maniac. Tuke's contention that 'furious mania is almost unknown at the Retreat [. . .] and that all the patients wear clothes and are generally induced to adopt orderly habits'[52] agrees with the independent observations of visitors.[53] The refusal to use chains, the absence of physical abuse or coercion of patients, and the success in restoring them to a measure of dignity and self-respect, all contrasted sharply with the prevailing conditions in most madhouses of the period. Andrew Duncan was so impressed by his visit to the Retreat that he commented:

> The fraternity denominated Quakers have demonstrated beyond contradiction the very great advantages resulting from a mode of treatment in cases on Insanity much more mild than was before introduced into any Lunatic Asylum at home or abroad. In the management of this institution, they have set an example which claims the imitation, and deserves the thanks, of every sect and every nation.[54]

But Duncan's assessment was far from representative of his medical colleagues' views. On the contrary, the initial response of most of the medical profession to the claims of moral treatment was one of hostility. In the face of the evidence, they simply tried to reassert the value of the traditional medical approach. Hill's book on the prevention and cure of insanity, perhaps the best-known work on the subject published at this time, assured its readers that 'insanity is as generally curable as any of those violent Diseases most successfully treated by Medicine',[55] and truculently asserted that 'direct medical remedies can never be too early

---

52. S. Tuke, *Description of the Retreat*, p. 144.
53. See also Dr G. De La Rive, *Lettre adressée aux rédacteurs de la bibliothèque britannique sur un nouvel établissement pour la guérison des aliénés*, Geneva: for the author, 1798; William Stark, *Remarks on the Construction of Public Asylums for the Cure of Mental Derangement*, Glasgow: Hedderwick, 1810; and Anon., *A Short Account of the Rise, Progress, and Present State of the Lunatic Asylum at Edinburgh*, Edinburgh: Neill, 1812.
54. Dr A. Duncan, Sr., reported in *ibid.*, p. 15. Compare Tuke's own comment: 'the experience of the Retreat [. . .] has demonstrated, beyond all contradiction, the superior efficacy, both in respect of cure and security, of a mild system of treatment in all cases of mental disorder.' S. Tuke, *Description of the Retreat*, p. vi.
55. George Nesse Hill, *An Essay on the Prevention and Cure of Insanity*, London: Longman, Hurst, Rees, Orme, and Brown, 1814, p. 201.

introduced or too readily applied'.[56] William Nisbet, a leading London practitioner who wrote extensively upon a wide range of medical subjects, concurred: 'The disease of insanity in all its shades and varieties, belongs, in point of treatment, to the department of the physician alone [. . .] the medical treatment [. . .] is that part on which the whole success of the cure hangs.'[57] And when the 1815 Select Committee asked Dr John Weir, the official inspector of the conditions naval maniacs were kept under, for his opinion on the value of medical intervention, he qualified his answer only slightly: 'In recent cases, and those unconnected with organic lesions of the brain, malformation of the skull, and hereditary disposition to insanity [. . .] medical treatment is of the utmost importance.'[58] More directly still, Thomas Mayo provided what purported to be an authoritative assessment of the relative value of moral and medical therapies:

> We will suppose a patient left negatively, if we may use the expression, in respect of moral regimen. He is continued in the same comfortable state which he was in before he became insane; – he is treated, when violent, with humanity, but he is repressed by the strait waistcoat. No precaution is taken to break morbid associations – no care to furnish him with others that are agreeable – no attempt to make an impression by well-chosen appeals upon his wavering intellect. . . . Allow us the medical regimen which we have sketched, [bleeding and cupping; the use of caustic issues and setons as counter-irritants; purges and nauseants used almost daily; and a variety of sweat-producing and cooling agents] and we shall indulge fair hopes of curing the patient. But, reverse the means of cure; let the degree of medical regimen be no

56. *Ibid.*, p. 205.
57. William Nisbet, *Two Letters to the Right Honourable George Rose, M.P. on the Reports at Present before the Honourable House of Commons on the State of Madhouses*, London: Cox, 1815, pp. 7, 21.
58. House of Commons, *Report of the Select Committee on Madhouses*, 1815, p. 32. Compare, too, the comments of Sir William Lawrence, who, among his other activities, served as surgeon to Bethlem from 1815 until 1867:

> They who consider the mental operations as acts of an immaterial being, and thus disconnect the sound state of the mind from organization, act very consistently in disjoining insanity also from the corporeal structure, and in representing it as a disease, not of the brain, but of the mind. Thus we come to disease of an immaterial being, for which, suitably enough, moral treatment has been recommended. I firmly believe, on the contrary, that the various forms of insanity, that all the affections comprehended under the general term of mental derangement are only evidences of cerebral affections [. . .] symptoms of diseased brain [. . . .] Sometimes, indeed, the mental phenomena are disturbed, without any visible deviation from the healthy structure of the brain [. . .] we find the brain, like other parts, subject to what is called functional disorder; but, although we cannot actually demonstrate the fact, we have no more doubt that the material cause of the symptoms or external signs of disease is in this organ, than we do that impaired biliary secretion has its source in the liver, or faulty digestion in the stomach [. . . .]

> William Lawrence, *Lectures on Physiology, Zoology, and the Natural History of Man*, London: Callow, 1819, p. 114.

more than analogous to the moral in the first case which we have supposed, – we shall no longer answer for the event. . . .[59]

Medicine, in other words, was quite essential, and moral treatment wholly incidental, to any attempt to cure.

Nor should this reaction come as a surprise. After all, moral treatment challenged medicine's traditional paradigm of what was suitable as a method of treating illness of any sort. Furthermore, its wholesale rejection of standard medical techniques naturally ran counter to the profession's deep intellectual and emotional investment in the value of its own theory and practice. As William Bynum has noted, 'if physicians *qua* physician could do nothing for the lunatic except treat his bodily afflictions, then the medical man had no special claim to a unique place in the treatment of mental illness. Their income, prestige, and medical theories were all threatened'.[60]

As a consequence of this initial reluctance to abandon outmoded conceptions and treatments of insanity, the medical profession's continuing status as the most prominent group involved in coping with the insane became, for a time, distinctly problematic. For those outside the profession, of course, lacked its prior commitments, and so were readier converts to the value of the new approach – the more so since the evidence of even the medical witnesses before the 1815–16 Select Committee provided substantial support for William Tuke's contention that 'in cases of mental derangement . . . very little can be done [by way of medical treatment]'.[61] It should come as no surprise, therefore, that those laymen who, for a number of years, had been agitating for lunacy reform on humanitarian grounds, but who had previously lacked a viable alternative model to existing asylums, eagerly seized on moral treatment. Since it was these lay people, primarily magistrates and upper-middle-class philanthropists, who were the prime movers in the effort to reorganize the treatment of insanity through changes in the law, their conversion was a highly significant one.

The evidence given by Best and Monro, physicians at York and Bethlem respectively, had proved to be particularly damaging to medicine's reputation and standing. The Monro family had been physicians to Bethlem for almost a century, and prior to this Thomas Monro himself had been thought of as one of the foremost experts of the medical treatment of insanity. As with Best, though, the credibility of his testimony was coloured by the Committee's knowledge of conditions in his asylum, and

59. Thomas Mayo, *Remarks on Insanity; Founded on the Practice of John Mayo, M.D.*, London: Underwood, 1817, pp. 19, 26, 71–2.
60. W.F. Bynum, 'Rationales for Therapy', p. 325.
61. House of Commons, *Report of the Select Committee on Madhouses*, 1815, p. 135, evidence of William Tuke.

he was treated as a hostile witness. Under close questioning by the Committee, the extent of his medical treatment was now revealed to the public:

> In the months of May, June, July, August and September, we generally administer medicines; we do not in the winter season, because the house is so excessively cold that it is not thought proper [. . . .] We apply generally bleeding, purging, and vomit; those are the general remedies we apply [. . . .] All the patients who require bleeding are generally bled on a particular day, and they are purged on a particular day.[62]

Later in his testimony, Monro gave a few more details: all the patients under his care, except those manifestly too weak to survive such a heroic regime,

> are ordered to be bled about the latter end of May, or the beginning of May, according to the weather; and after they have been bled they take vomits once a week for a certain number of weeks, after that we purge the patients. . . .[63]

Thereafter, of course, patients were kept chained to their beds at least four days out of every seven.

A committee convinced of the value of moral treatment's emphasis on treating every lunatic as an individual was in principle unlikely to approve of such indiscriminate mass medication. Under the even more hostile questioning he now faced, Monro was forced to make a still more damaging admission. 'Do you think,' he was asked, 'it is within the scope of medical knowledge to discover any other efficacious means of treating Insane persons?' 'With respect to the means used, I really do not depend a vast deal upon medicine; I do not think medicine is the sheet anchor; it is more by management that those patients are cured than by medicine [. . .] *the disease is not cured by medicine, in my opinion. If I am obliged to make that public I must do so.*'[64] The only question which remained was why Monro continued to employ therapies he conceded were useless. He himself had

---

62. *Ibid.*, p. 93, evidence of Thomas Monro.
63. *Ibid.*, p. 95.
64. *Ibid.*, p. 99, my emphasis. Compare Ellis's comment, 'Of the abuses that have existed, the cause of a great proportion of them may be traced to the mystery with which many of those who have had the management of the insane have constantly endeavoured to envelop it. . . .' William Charles Ellis, *A Letter to Thomas Thompson, Esq. M.P., containing Considerations on the Necessity of Proper Places being provided by the Legislature for the Reception of all Insane Persons and on Some of the Abuses which have been found to exist in Madhouses, with a Plan to remedy them*, Hull: Topping and Dawson, 1815. Expertise always flourishes where its techniques are somewhat mysterious; the expert, wherever possible, '*minimizes the role of persuasive evidence in his interaction with his clientele*'. E. Freidson, *Professional Dominance*, New York: Atherton, 1970, p. 110, emphasis in the original. Being forced to justify his actions to laymen almost always weakens the professional's authority (*cf. ibid.*, ch. 4, *passim*). Nowhere is this more clearly the case than when a challenge to produce rational grounds for one's procedures cannot be met.

already provided an answer to that: 'That has been the practice invariably for years, long before my time; it was handed down to me by my father, and *I do not know any better practice*.'[65]

St. Luke's Hospital, London's other charity asylum, had not come in for the severe criticism directed at Bethlem. Nevertheless, when its physician, Dr Sutherland, was called to give evidence his answers were extremely circumspect, and he sought to be as non-controversial as possible. While he felt that medicines for the stomach might be of some indirect benefit, he conceded that 'moral treatment is of course more especially important in the treatment of mental disorder'.[66] Similarly, when Dr John Harness, a Commissioner of the Transport Board, was asked 'what was his opinion as to the utility of medical treatment of Insanity,' he replied: 'Although much may be effected by medical treatment, I have before stated that I am not sanguine in the expectation of a permanent advantage from it.'[67]

Doctors at this time played another important role vis-à-vis the insane. Five Commissioners selected from the members of the Royal College of Physicians were charged with annually inspecting metropolitan madhouses under the 1774 Act. Even conceding the defects of the Act, as the reformers did, their record was hardly one to inspire confidence in a system of medical policing of asylums, or in physicians' willingness to judge the work of their colleagues. According to Dr Richard Powell, the Secretary to the Royal College, and himself a Commissioner, the visits took no more than six days a year to perform. Often, as many as six or eight madhouses were visited in a day. No attempt was made to check

65. House of Commons, *Select Committee on Madhouses*, 1815, p. 95 – a nice example of medicine's bias towards active intervention. *Cf.* Thomas Scheff, *Being Mentally Ill: A Sociological Theory*, Chicago: Aldine, 1966, chapter 4, 'Diseases in Medicine'; and Freidson, *Profession of Medicine*, chapter 12, 'Professional Construction of Concepts of Illness'. In his testimony, Monro if anything understated the therapeutic conservatism of his predecessors. Despite a systematic bias in favour of presenting conditions at Bethlem in the best possible light, and a consistent tendency to read ambiguous archival evidence with a generous eye, Jonathan Andrews was recently forced to concede that a thorough review of the available documents demonstrates that

> the array of medicaments and methods of treatment deployed on the hospital's population remained essentially unchanged [from the mid-seventeenth through the early nineteenth century]. . . . I would not seek to dispute the standard and incontrovertible assessment that Bethlem remained wedded to a routine course of evacuative and antiphlogistic treatments, which without doubt were not only ineffective, but were occasionally, positively harmful, to the patients who experienced them. Just how routine doses were is suggested by the lack of any mention in the Governors' Minutes of the precise nature of the medicines administered at the hospital. . . . Doses were so uniform for the insane, and the insane themselves looked upon as so innately averse to, and ignorant of, what was good for them, that medical men frequently did not even bother to examine them first. ('Bedlam Revisited: A History of Bethlem Hospital *c.* 1634–*c.* 1770', unpublished Ph.D. dissertation, London University, 1991, pp. 288, 300, 301.)

66. House of Commons, *Report of the Select Committee on Madhouses*, 1815, p. 136.
67. *Ibid.*, p. 159.

to see whether the numbers resident corresponded to those the Commissioners had received notification of. The justification for medical visitation was primarily that no one else was competent to assess the medical treatment administered. Yet Powell conceded that, apart from cursory inquiries as to the condition of the patients, no effort was made to discover what medical treatment the patients received, let alone to find out how effective it was. Such inquiries were doubtless seen as an unjustified interference in another gentleman's professional practice, a studied reticence which also reflected 'the close personal and professional links [the inspecting physicians] maintained with asylum proprietors'.[68]

The most respectable medical figure to appear before the Committee was Sir Henry Halford, who was already 'indisputably at the head of London practice'. A favourite of George III's, he was later physician to George IV, and Victoria, and from 1820 to his death in 1844, President of the Royal College of Physicians.[69] As the official spokesman for the most prestigious branch of the medical profession, and an influential figure in elite circles, he obviously presented his evidence with a view to making a strong case for the value of the medical approach and in an effort to rectify the damage done by Best's and Monro's testimony. In practice, his evidence was too rambling and confused for that. Having begun by asserting that medical intervention was valuable, at least in the early stages of the disorder, he subsequently conceded that 'our knowledge of insanity has not kept pace with our knowledge of other distempers', a situation he blamed on 'the habit we find established, of transferring patients under this malady, as soon as it has declared itself, to the care of persons who too frequently limit their attention to the mere personal security of their patients, without attempting to assist them by the resources of medicine'. 'The profession,' he acknowledged, had 'much to learn on the subject of mental derangement.' By the end of his testimony, he had given the impression that medicine lacked reliable knowledge in this area, and could offer little by way of effective therapy. In mitigation, he urged that 'we want facts in the history of the disease,' coupled with the vague hope that 'if they are carefully recorded, under the observation of enlightened physicians, no doubt, they will sooner or later be collected in sufficient number, to admit of safe and useful inductions.'[70] As a performance, this

---

68. Nicholas Hervey, 'The Lunacy Commission 1845–60, with Special Reference to the Implementation of Policy in Kent and Surrey', unpublished Ph.D. dissertation, Bristol University, 1987, p. 61. Members of the College serving as inspectors often engaged in joint consultations with certain mad-doctors, and regularly referred patients to them. Beyond the financial ties this situation created, they enjoyed friendly personal ties with 'the top echelon of madhouse keepers, [whose] clientele . . . mostly consisted of the aristocracy or gentry'. Hervey suggests that the exclusivity of these mad-doctors' practices (and the limited size of the stigmatizing pauper lunatic sector early in the century) may have made these alienists more acceptable in the highest medical circles than their counterparts later became. Ibid., pp. 61–3.
69. Dictionary of National Biography, s.v. Halford, (Sir) Henry.
70. House of Commons, First Report of the Select Committee on Madhouses, 1816, pp. 13–4.

was scarcely calculated to convince the somewhat sceptical audience which he faced. He had provided neither evidence nor plausible argument to refute the contention of those who favoured moral treatment that 'against mere insanity, unaccompanied by bodily derangement, [medicine] appear[s] to be almost powerless.'[71] Nor had he succeeded in erasing the unfavourable impression created by earlier medical testimony.[72]

If Monro did not know of any better weapons to use against insanity than the traditional anti-phlogistic system, the laymen who were acquainted at first hand with the results of moral treatment obviously thought that *they* did. Both their testimony before official inquiries and the pamphlets they were busily writing now took on a tone of considerable hostility to medicine's claims to jurisdiction in this area. When Edward Wakefield was asked: 'In consequence of the observations you have made on the state and management of the Lunatic Establishments, and the manner of inspecting them, are you of the opinion that medical persons exclusively ought to be Inspectors and Controllers of Madhouses?' his response was:

> I think they are the most unfit of any class of persons. In the first place, from every enquiry I have made, I am satisfied that medicine has little or no effect on the disease, and the only reason for their selection is the confidence which is placed in their being able to apply a remedy to the malady. They are all persons interested more or less. It is extremely difficult in examining either the public Institutions or private houses, not to have strong impression upon your mind, that medical men derive a profit in some shape or form from those different establishments [. . . .] The rendering therefore, [of] any interested class of persons the Inspectors and Controllers, I hold to be mischievous in the greatest possible degree.[73]

Higgins, the Yorkshire magistrate who had done much to uncover the scandals at the York Asylum, had witnessed at first hand over many

71. [Sydney Smith], 'An Account of the York Retreat', *Edinburgh Review* 23, 1814, p. 196.
72. Taken as a whole, medical testimony on the treatment of insanity before this and subsequent committees of inquiry was a highly damaging mixture of contradictions, inconsistencies, and evasions. 'This one lauded one plan of treatment, that another; emetics were to do everything, according to the opinion of some, purgatives were supported by others, as almost the only medicinals upon which any reliance could be placed. This party talked of reducing, that of exciting; cold bathing was almost the catholicon of some physicians, others were avowedly partial to warm bathing – but the remarkable circumstance was, that many respectable men expressed their opinion, that very little could be done by any medicinal measures, while others asserted insanity to be the most curable of all the maladies to which man is subject.' David Uwins, *A Treatise on Those Disorders of the Brain and Nervous System, Which Are Usually Considered and Called Mental*, London: Renshaw and Rush, 1833, p. 189.
73. House of Commons, *op. cit.*, p. 24. Wakefield was to modify this judgement the following year, after a visit to William Finch's establishment at Laverstock House, near Salisbury (see *First Report of the Select Committee on Madhouses*, 1816, p. 36), but it was his earlier view that was reflected in the bills introduced into Parliament over the next few years.

months the practices of one of the most famous medical 'specialists' in the field. His comments were, if anything, still more hostile. He pointed out that in the aftermath of Dr Best's departure from the York Asylum, and the establishment of an efficient system of lay visitation there, the number of deaths of patients fell from twenty a year to only four. Furthermore, thirty patients were almost at once found fit for discharge. In his caustic fashion he demanded to know 'who after this will doubt the efficacy of my medicine – visitors and committees? I will warrant it superior even to Dr Hunter's famous secret – *insane powders* – either green or grey – or his patent Brazil salts into the bargain'.[74] Higgins was clearly angered by the efforts on the part of the medical profession to explain away what he perceived as cruelty as legitimate medical techniques for 'treating' insanity, or to attribute to the progress of the condition itself what he saw as the consequences of neglect. In contemptuous tones, he commented:

> Amongst much medical nonsense, published by physicians interested to conceal their neglect, and the abuses of their establishments, it has been said, that persons afflicted with insanity are more liable than others to mortification of their extremities. Nothing of the kind was ever experienced at the institution of the Quakers. If the members of the royal and learned College of Physicians were chained, or shut up naked, on straw saturated with urine and excrement, with a scanty allowance of food, exposed to the indecency of a northern climate, in cells having windows unglazed, I have no doubt that they would soon exhibit as strong a tendency to mortified extremities, as any of their patients.[75]

William Ellis, though himself medically qualified,[76] by now possessed firsthand acquaintance with Tuke's work at the Retreat, and had absorbed much of the latter's scepticism about the activities of his fellow professionals. His *Letter to Thomas Thompson, M.P.* (a member of the Select Committee) contained a number of critical remarks directed at them. In particular, he alleged that

> the management of the insane has been in too few hands; and many of those who have been engaged in it, finding it a very lucrative concern, have wished to involve it in great mystery, and, in order to prevent institutions for their cure from becoming more general, were desirous that it should be thought that there was some secret in the way of

---

74. Godfrey Higgins, *The Evidence Taken Before a Committee of the House of Commons Respecting the Asylum at York; with Observations and Notes, and a Letter to the Committee,* Doncaster: Sheardown, 1816, p. 48. Dr Hunter was, until his death (when he was succeeded by his protégé, Dr Best), the physician to the York Asylum. In addition to his lucrative trade at the Asylum, which included extensive embezzlement of its funds, he energetically promoted his 'powders' as a certain, if expensive, home-remedy for insanity for those who could not afford his full-time ministrations.
75. G. Higgins, *The Evidence Taken Before a Committee of the House of Commons Respecting the Asylum at York,* p. 48, footnote.
76. MD St. Andrew's, MRCS.

medicine for the cure, not easily to be found out. Some medical men have gone so far as even to condescend to the greatest quackery in the treatment of insanity.[77]

To the contrary, Ellis contended there were no medical specifics for the successful treatment of insanity, and acceptance of the idea that care of the insane was best left to experts, medical or otherwise, was the surest guarantee of abuse. In his own proposals for reform, therefore, he advocated constant lay supervision of all asylums by local magistrates.[78]

5. The Weaknesses of Moral Treatment as a Professional Ideology

The propagation of the notion that 'very little dependence is to be placed on medicine alone for the cure of insanity'[79] posed a clear threat to the professional dominance of this field.[80] Given that those most convinced of the truth of this proposition were also the prime movers in trying to obtain lunacy reform, the doctors interested in insanity were unable any longer to ignore or depreciate moral treatment. They had to find some way to accommodate it.

Challenges over jurisdictional boundaries are, as Andrew Abbott has recently emphasized, a perpetual feature of professional life. Indeed, such disputes constitute 'the real, the determining history of the professions . . .',[81] with the outcomes both reflecting and affecting any particular group's intellectual and organizational standing, and thus their social status and market situation. To control knowledge and its application, to define, in fact, what shall count as knowledge and constitute efficacious and appropriate techniques of intervention is the very essence of what distinguishes the successful profession.

At first sight, moral treatment seemed to be an unpromising basis for any profession trying to assert special competence in the treatment of the insane. In Freidson's words, 'one of the things that marks off professions from occupations is the professions' claims to schooling in knowledge of

---

77. Ellis, *A Letter to Thomas Thompson, Esq., M.P.*, p. 7.
78. *Ibid.*, p. 35. Still he thought asylums should on a day-to-day basis be administered by a doctor, a position restated more emphatically in his later work.
79. [Sydney Smith], 'An Account of the York Retreat', p. 196.
80. Compare, for instance, Spurzheim's comments, following a review of the therapeutics employed at Bethlem:

    If insane patients are only consigned to such a routine of practice, to painful coercion, to starving, indiscriminate abstraction of light, to bleeding and purging, *ad libitum*, there is no doubt that neither physicians nor the public can gain confidence in medicine with respect to insanity. I fully agree that, if we continue such proceeding in insanity, our profession ought to be interdicted by those who have the will and the power to improve the public good.

    Observations on the Deranged Manifestations of Mind, or Insanity, pp. 273–4.
81. Andrew Abbott, *The System of Professions: An Essay on the Division of Expert Labor*, Chicago: University of Chicago Press, 1988, p. 2.

an especially esoteric, scientific, or abstract character that is markedly superior to the mere experience of suffering from the illness or having attempted pragmatically to heal a procession of sufferers from the illness.'[82] Moral treatment had begun by rejecting existing 'scientific' responses as worse than useless; and the remedies proposed in their place – warm baths and kindness – hardly provided much of a foundation for claims to possess the kinds of expertise and special skills which ordinarily form the basis for the grant of professional autonomy.

In practice, however, this feature of moral treatment proved an advantage to those bent on reasserting medicine's jurisdiction in this area. The very difficulty of erecting professional claims on such a flimsy basis largely precluded the emergence of an organized group of competitors – lay therapists. Abstraction is essential to survival in the rough and tumble of jurisdictional competition, for 'only a knowledge system governed by abstractions can redefine its problems and tasks, defend them from interlopers, and seize new problems. . . .'[83] Certainly, cognitive and practical dominion over a particular territory can be loosened or lost when a group claiming jurisdiction lacks effective treatments for the conditions it claims as its own – precisely the threat that confronted medical mad-doctors once the emergence of moral treatment had publicly and successfully called into question the efficacy of traditional anti-phlogistic therapeutics in the treatment of the mad. But jurisdictional claims not rooted in claims to possess abstract knowledge are at least equally vulnerable: likely to be dismissed by a broader audience as mere 'craft knowledge'; and to be viewed as too commonsensical, too transparently obvious to constitute the sorts of special skills that make up *professional* work.[84]

Yet Tuke had explicitly *not* sought to create or train a group of experts in moral treatment and had systematically avoided abstract theorizing about the approach he had introduced. To the contrary, he and his followers were deeply suspicious of any plan to hand the treatment of lunatics over to any group of 'experts'. Those who had developed moral treatment claimed that the new approach was little more than an application of common sense and humanity; and these were scarcely qualities monopolized by professionals. Indeed, the grant of a measure of autonomy which accompanied the acceptance of someone as an expert threatened to remove the surest guarantee of humane treatment of the insane, searching inquiry and oversight by outsiders.

Interestingly enough, the earliest recruits to moral treatment were primarily those who were interested in the cause of lunacy reform, but who were unlikely, given their social status, to undertake themselves the task of administering an asylum – magistrates and upper-class philanthropists.

82. Freidson, *Professional Dominance*, p. 106.
83. A. Abbott, *The System of Professions*, p. 9.
84. *Cf.* the discussion in A. Abbott, *The System of Professions*, pp. 102–4.

The major exception to this generalization, William Ellis (who from 1814 on ran the Refuge, a private madhouse at Hull), was a doctor rather than just an expert on moral treatment. In the absence of any rival helping group, medicine set about assimilating moral treatment within its own sphere of competence.

Even while specifically denying medical claims to expertise in the area of insanity, the promoters of moral treatment had continued to employ a vocabulary laden with terms borrowed from medicine – 'patient', 'mental illness', 'moral treatment', and so on. This failure to develop an alternative jargon itself made the reassertion of medical control somewhat easier, inasmuch as one of the most important connotations of the label 'illness', and its associated array of concepts, is the idea that the syndrome to which it is applied is essentially a medical one. Given the critical role of language in shaping the social construction of reality, to employ terms which imply that something is a medical problem, and yet to deny that doctors are those most competent to deal with it, seems perverse.

The lack of an alternative to the model of insanity in terms of a coherent, well-articulated theory had this further consequence: that the denial of the applicability of medicinal remedies implied a view of insanity as essentially irremediable ('incurable') or as remediable ('curable') only by accident or through the operation of spontaneous tendencies towards recovery. Tuke himself seems to have adhered to the latter view. Thus, in his efforts to secure the establishment of asylums for the insane poor, he urged that 'though we can do but little by the aid of medicine towards the cure of insanity, it is surely not the less our duty to use every means in our power to alleviate the complaint, or at least place the poor sufferer in a situation where nature may take her own course, and not be obstructed in the relief which she herself would probably bring to him'.[85] And his discussion of the Retreat's success in restoring patients to sanity concludes: 'As we have not discovered any anti-maniacal specific, and profess to do little more than assist Nature, in the performance of her own cure, the term *recovered*, is adopted in preference to that of *cured*.'[86] Such modesty may well have been warranted; yet it was scarcely as appealing as the claim that one could actively influence the outcome in the desired direction. Practically speaking, it left moral treatment vulnerable to assimilation by a medical profession less scrupulously modest in its claims.

All this meant that the challenge moral treatment posed to the medical dominance of insanity was not as clear-cut as it might have been. Further-more, the medical profession possessed certain initial advantages as it sought to reassert its jurisdiction, advantages which could, however, have proved purely ephemeral. After all, there were, as yet, no legal barriers to the development of an organized rival group of therapists, and language

85. Samuel Tuke, 'Essay on the State of the Insane Poor', *The Philanthropist* 1, 1811, p. 357.
86. S. Tuke, *Description of the Retreat*, pp. 216–7.

is not immutable. The interested segments of the medical profession now moved to secure what they rightly perceived to be their imperilled position.[87]

The potential consequences of taking Tuke seriously were most clearly articulated by Browne half a century later:

> If therapeutical agents are cast aside or degraded from their legitimate rank, it will become the duty of the physician to give place to the divine or moralist, whose chosen mission it is to minister to the mind diseased; and of the heads of establishments like this [lunatic asylum] to depute their authority to the well-educated man of the world, who could, I feel assured, conduct an asylum fiscally, and as an intellectual boarding-house, a great deal better than any of us.[88]

Earlier he had complained that

> a want of power or inclination to discriminate between the inutility of medicine from its being inapplicable, and from its being injudiciously applied, had led to the adoption of the absurd opinion that the insane ought not to be committed to the charge of medical men. A manager of a large and excellent institution, entertaining this view, has declared the exhibition of medicine in insanity was useless, and that disease was to be cured by moral treatment only.[89]

The pernicious doctrine that traditional medical remedies were useless had spread dangerously far, even among those who continued to insist that doctors were the most qualified to treat lunatics. 'We must confess', said Spurzheim, 'that hitherto medical art has acquired very little merit in the cure of insanity; nature alone does almost everything.'[90] When the *Quarterly Review*'s correspondent argued for medical control, he simultaneously made the dangerous concession that

> the powers of medicine, merely upon mental hallucination are exceedingly circumscribed and feeble [. . .] we want principles on which to form any satisfactory indications of treatment [. . . .] Almost the whole [. . .] of what may be called the strict medical treatment of madness must be regarded, at present, at least, as empirical, and the most extensive experience proves that very little is to be done.[91]

---

87. In tones verging on panic, Thomas Mayo, one of the most well-connected mad-doctors, spoke of jurisdiction over the insane as being 'almost . . . wrestled by the philosopher out of the hands of the physician'. T. Mayo, *Remarks on Insanity*, London: Underwood, 1817, p. v.

88. William Alexander Francis Browne, *The Moral Treatment of the Insane: A Lecture*, London: Adlard, 1864, p. 5.

89. W.A.F. Browne, *What Asylums Were, Are, and Ought to Be*, Edinburgh: Black, 1837, p. 178.

90. J.G. Spurzheim, *Observations on the Deranged Manifestations of the Mind, or Insanity*, p. 197.

91. [David Uwins], 'Insanity and Madhouses', *Quarterly Review* 15, 1816, p. 402.

Casting about for justifications for his insistence on medicine's entitlement to preeminence, he found remarkably few. The administration of warm baths now became something which could only be done under careful professional supervision. After all, the use of such a powerful technique had to be guided by an expert assessment of the condition of the individual patient. Cathartics were somehow rescued from the oblivion into which other medical remedies had been cast, once more with the caution that 'the practice of purging' was by no means 'of so simple and straight-forward a nature as might be at first sight conceived'.[92] Conscious that these contentions might seem less than compelling, he resorted to the argument from experience: 'Were it only an account of the frequent opportunities which more strictly medical practitioners have of witnessing aberrations of the intellect, from different sources, these would appear to be the fittest persons for the treatment of lunacy.'[93]

6. Medical Resistance to Reform

The necessity for a more strenuous and convincing defense of professional prerogatives was clear, and was rendered the more urgent as the lunacy reformers sought to give legislative effect to their schemes. As we have seen in the previous chapter, in the aftermath of the findings of the 1815–16 Select Committee, the reformers in the Commons made a sustained effort to devise a system of strict outside supervision and control of madhouse keepers, to ensure against the repetition of previous abuses. In 1816 and 1817, bills were introduced to set up a Board of Inspection of madhouses for each county, to be chosen annually from among the county magistrates. The proposal was revived in 1819, with the addition of a permanent Board of Inspection for the whole country, which was to visit all houses 'at different and uncertain times'.

All three of these bills would have empowered the boards of laymen to inquire into the treatment and management of patients, to direct discontinuance of practices they considered cruel or unnecessarily harsh, and to order the discharge of any patient they considered restored to sanity.[94] If one follows Freidson in considering autonomy, the right to deny legitimacy to outside criticism of work and its performance, as the core characteristic of any profession, such proposals to introduce lay control and evaluation

92. *Ibid.*, pp. 402–3.
93. *Ibid.*, p. 403. Ellis, in the same bind, justified medical control of asylums as necessary to ensure that the physical ailments of the insane were properly treated: 'Insane patients being liable to every complaint that others are subject to, together with those brought on by the body's sympathising with the mind, it seems now generally admitted that it is necessary to have a medical man to administer such establishments.' W. Ellis, *A Letter to Thomas Thompson, Esq., M.P.*, p. 11.
94. For detailed discussion of these bills' provisions, see N. Hervey, 'The Lunacy Commission 1845–60', pp. 64–7. On other grounds, Hervey dismisses these legislative proposals as 'totally impractical'.

of expert performance must clearly be seen as of enormous strategic importance; and as likely to provoke intense opposition from those threatened by such control. Opposition of this sort was indeed forthcoming from doctors in the mad-business.

Burrows, in particular, was scathing in his criticisms of these bills. Somewhat disingenuously, he commented:

> The provision of this [1817] Bill induces me to conclude that I certainly misinterpreted the import of many of the queries of the Members of the Committee of Inquiry; for I was led to think that a conviction had arisen out of the investigation, that all houses for the reception of insane persons ought to be under the superintendence of men of character and ability, and particularly of medical men.[95]

Assuming that this was so (a large assumption, of course), it was simply absurd to allow the judgement of rank amateurs to override the mature judgement of a competent expert. If the legislature was convinced of the necessity of appointing Commissioners to inspect madhouses, these ought, as in the past, to be medical men. One faced a situation in which 'the most experienced will acknowledge the liability of being deceived, even where frequent opportunities of judging of the sanity of the mind have occurred. How then can those who are not only casual but unprofessional visitors pretend to decide on any particular case, or prescribe any alteration, or condemn any mode of treatment?'[96] It made no sense to ask a layman to pass judgement on the curative treatment of a patient, 'for if any difference of opinion were to arise upon a question relative to the management or release of a patient, it were surely most proper that the medical opinion should prevail.'[97] Furthermore, allowing 'country gentlemen' to visit asylums, unaccompanied by medical men, in order to check for possible abuses, threatened the welfare of the patients in the most serious possible degree. The commotion their visits would cause, and the interference their ignorance might lead them to indulge in, would set at naught the asylum doctor's most skillful efforts to cure his patients. Consequently, the reformers could proceed with their plans only at 'the hazard of great injury to the patients'.[98]

95. George Man Burrows, *Cursory Remarks on a Bill now in the House of Peers for Regulating of Madhouses, [. . .] With Observations on the Defects of the Present System*, London: Harding, 1817, p. 51. This pamphlet was dedicated: 'To the Royal College of Physicians in London, the Constitutional Guardians of the Public Health, and the only Public Body which, by reason of its learning and experience, is truly competent to arrange and to carry into execution an Efficient Plan for the Amelioration of the Condition of the Insane.'

96. *Ibid.*, p. 23.

97. *Ibid.*, p. 24.

98. *Ibid.*, p. 25. There is an obvious parallel here with the modern psychiatrist's emphasis that the patient can 'be greatly damaged if unskilled action is taken in [. . .] crucial, precarious therapeutic matters, necessitating the strict control of non-medically qualified mental hospital staff lest they engage in amateur psychotherapy'. Erving Goffman,

In the Commons, the lunacy reformers remained unmoved by these arguments, and managed to secure the passage of each of the bills they introduced. The House of Lords, however, proved more receptive, and in each instance exercised its veto powers. Their Lordships' opposition was undoubtedly motivated by more than just the desire to protect the prerogatives of the medical profession. A strong faction there was opposed to any effort to extend the scope of central government authority. Aristocratic families with a lunatic in the closet were determined to avoid publicity, and hence the provisions in the 1816 and 1817 bills for a central register of 'single lunatics' provoked further opposition.[99] Furthermore, the High Tories in the Upper House were disposed to reject on principle

Asylums: Essays on the Social Situation of Mental Patients and Other Inmates, New York: Doubleday, 1961, pp. 377–8. As Freidson has shown for the medical profession as a whole, 'where dangerous consequences can follow upon improper work [. . .] the *claim* of emergency and of possible dangerous consequences is a potent protective device'. Freidson, *Profession of Medicine*, p. 45. Compare, in this connection, Burrows's stated objections to the 1817 Bill:

> It may be asserted [. . .] that if the insane be visited in the indiscriminate and judicial manner which this Bill invites and empowers, that neither medical nor moral remedies will be of the least avail [. . . .] Who can say but some meddling inconsiderate justice [. . .] might from ignorance [. . .] interfere; and by doing so blast all prospect of future happiness even of scores of his miserable fellow creatures [. . . .] The humane and skilful superintendent is, perhaps, on the point of seeing the fruition of all his cares and anxieties; and is anticipating the restoration of the faculties of his charge, and the well-earned remuneration for his troubles and cares; the relatives and friends of the patient, from the depths of despondency [. . .] are raised to the utmost pinnacle of hope and expectation; when lo! comes a fatal visitation – the patient must not be denied – he must be examined as to the state of his mind – the fatal chord is touched on which depends harmony of his mental with his corporeal frame; a tremendous explosion follows, and in one moment, the toil of months is destroyed: the wavering reason is lost, and sometimes forever!

G.M. Burrows, *Cursory Remarks*, pp. 25, 27, 29–30.
If further evidence is needed that the purpose of this protest was the protection of professional prerogatives, Burrows' own version of the type of reform acceptable to the profession provides it:

> The fundamental principles of all reformation or improvement in the management of madhouses or in the medical treatment of insane persons, therefore, consist: 1. In the fitness of the qualifications of those who are permitted to take charge of them; 2. In having regular members of the faculty as superintendents; 3. In leaving superintendents uncontrolled in their management; 4. In protecting *Superintendents* against the malicious allegations of patients or outsiders; 5. In employing competent (i.e. Medical) Visitors. (*Ibid.*, p. 79.)

An opponent summarized his position as follows:

> Dr Burrows contends that Parliament has no right to interfere with the internal management of private lunatic asylums, and that the visits of medical men on the part of patients or their friends, is an intrusion, and no more warranted than the surveillance of the same persons in private practice.

[Anonymous], *On the Present State of Lunatic Asylums: with suggestions for their improvement*, London: Drury, 1839, p. 14.
99. Similar concerns had played a part in restricting the scope of the 1763 House of Commons inquiry and emasculating the 1774 Madhouse Act.

all types of 'liberal' reform – their principal spokesman, Lord Eldon, the Lord Chancellor, once referred to 'philanthropists' as 'men pretending to humanity but brimful of intolerance, and swollen with malignity, which they all are'.[100]

At the very least, however, the protests of the medical profession provided the Lords with a convenient ideological cloak for their opposition, and while votes may actually have been swayed by other considerations, they were justified on these neutral, technical grounds. The Marquis of Lansdowne, who introduced the 1819 bill into the Lords, clearly foresaw the direction the debate would take, and sought to reassure his audience that, while some systems of visitation and control by outsiders 'might retard the cure of persons so affected', the insane would only benefit from the specific provisions of this bill.[101] Speaking against the bill, Eldon brushed this aside, and reiterated the standard professional line: 'It was of the utmost importance, with a view to the proper care of these unhappy individuals, and with a view to their recovery that they should be under the superintendance [sic] of men who had made this branch of medicine their peculiar study, and that the superintendence of physicians should not be interfered with.' Yet this was precisely what the bill before them sought to do, and in consequence, 'he conscientiously believed its regulations would tend to aggravate the malady with which the unfortunate persons were afflicted, or to retard their cure'. One of the most objectionable features of the bill from his (and the medical profession's) perspective was that it

> gave a number of penalties, half of which were to go to the informer, and it was evident that the informer would be found amongst the attendants and servants in receptacles for lunatics, who would thus be made the judges of the conduct of the physicians, and it would be impossible for the latter, under such circumstances, to resort to many of these means which their experience had taught them were most effectual for the cure of their unhappy patients.[102]

Eldon had the authority of the best medical opinion behind him, when he asserted that 'there could not be a more false humanity than an over-humanity with regard to persons afflicted with insanity', and in the division which followed, the bill was rejected 35 to 14.[103]

---

100. Brenda Parry-Jones, 'A Calendar of the Eldon-Richards Correspondence c. 1809–1822', *Journal of the Merioneth Historical and Record Society*, 1965, pp. 39–50, cited in W.L. Parry-Jones, *The Trade in Lunacy*, pp. 16–7.
101. Hansard's *Parliamentary Debates*, Vol. 40, first series, 1819, Column 1345.
102. *Ibid.*
103. *Ibid.* K. Jones, *Lunacy, Law and Conscience*, pp. 109–11, condemns this action as 'illiberal', but entirely neglects the role of the medical lobbying in ensuring the defeat of these early efforts at 'reform', presumably because it would be at odds with her naive Whiggish perspective, which sees the doctors as the purveyors of scientific enlightenment. As we have seen in the previous chapter, elite mad-doctors were at least equally active in attempting to block reform legislation in 1828.

7. The Defence of Medical Hegemony

Temporarily, at least, the mad-doctors had successfully resisted efforts to restrict their professional autonomy, for with the rejection of the 1819 bill, the reform moment lost its momentum. Their victory was a fragile and uncertain one, however, so long as it rested on a marriage of convenience with political forces whose power was on the wane, and as long as they remained vulnerable to charges from enthusiasts for moral treatment that their expertise had no scientific or practical foundation. If they were to overcome their vulnerability, they had to develop a more sophisticated justification of their privileged position.

As part of this process, from about 1815 onwards, a veritable spate of books and articles purporting to be medical treatises on the treatment of insanity began to appear.[104] Similarly, the claim that instruction in its

104. Among those which I have consulted are: Matthew Allen, *Cases of Insanity, with Medical, Moral and Philosophical Observations upon them* (London: Swire, 1831) and *Essay on the Classification of the Insane* (London: Taylor, 1837); Samuel Glover Bakewell, *An Essay on Insanity* (Edinburgh: Neill, 1833); Nathaniel Bingham, *Observations on the Religious Delusions of Insane Persons [. . .] with which are combined a copious practical description [. . .] of mental disease, and of its appropriate medical and moral treatment* (London: Hatchard, 1841); George Man Burrows, *An Inquiry into Certain Errors Relative to Insanity* (London: Underwood, 1820) and *Commentaries on the Causes, Forms, Symptoms, and Treatment, Moral and Medical, of Insanity* (London: Underwood, 1828); Andrew Combe, *Observations on Mental Derangement: Being an Application of the Principles of Phrenology to the Elucidation of the Causes, Symptoms, Nature, and Treatment of Insanity* (Edinburgh: Anderson, 1831); John Conolly, *An Inquiry Concerning the Indications of Insanity, with suggestions for the better protection and care of the insane* (London: Taylor, 1830), facsimile edition by Hunter and MacAlpine (London: Dawsons, 1964); W.C. Ellis, *A Treatise on the Nature, Symptoms, Causes, and Treatment of Insanity, with practical observations on Lunatic asylums, and a description of the Pauper Lunatic Asylum for the County of Middlesex at Hanwell, with a detailed account of its management* (London: Holdsworth, 1838); R. Fletcher, *Sketches from the Casebook to Illustrate the Influence of the Mind on the Body, with the treatment of some of the more important brain and nervous disturbances* (London: Longman, 1833); Thomas Forster, *Observations on the Phenomena of Insanity* (London: Underwood, 1817); William Saunders Hallaran, *Practical Observations on the Causes and Cure of Insanity* (Cork: Edwards and Savage, 1818); John Haslam, *Medical Jurisprudence as it Relates to Insanity, According to the Law of England* (London: Hunter, 1817); Thomas Mayo, *An Essay on the Relation of the Theory of Morals to Insanity* (London: Fellowes, 1834); John Mayo and T. Mayo, *Remarks on Insanity* (London: Underwood, 1817); J.G. Millingen, *Aphorisms on the Treatment and Management of the Insane, with considerations on public and private lunatic asylums, pointing out the errors in the present system* (London: Churchill, 1840); (Sir) Alexander Morison, *Outlines of Lectures on the Nature, Causes, and Treatment of Insanity*, edited by Thomas C. Morison (London: Longman, Green, Brown and Longman, 1st edn, 1825, 4th edn, 1848); William B. Neville, *On Insanity; its nature, causes, and cure* (London: Longman, Rees, Orme, Brown, Green and Longman, 1836); John Parkin, *On the Medical and Moral Treatment of Insanity, including a notice on the establishment for the treatment of nervous and mental maladies: Manor Cottage, King's Road, Chelsea, established in 1780* (London: Martin, 1843 [?]); James Cowles Prichard, *A Treatise on Insanity and Other Disorders Affecting the Mind* (London: Sherwood, Gilbert and Piper, 1835) and *On the Different Forms of Insanity in Relation to Jurisprudence* (London: Bailliere, 1842); John Reid, *Essays on Insanity, Hypochondriacal and other Nervous Affections* (London: Longman, Hurst, Rees, Orme, and Brown, 1816); Edward J. Seymour, *Observations on the Medical Treatment of Insanity* (London: Longman, Rees Orme, Brown, and Co., 1832); J.G. Spurzheim, *Observations on the Deranged*

treatment formed a part of the normal curriculum of medical training, which had been made by earlier generations of mad-doctors, was reinforced when Dr (later Sir) Alexander Morison, a well-known society physician, began a course of lectures on the topic. These he repeated annually from 1823 to the late 1840s, while the published version simultaneously went through a number of editions. All this activity was probably stimulated at least in part by the increased attention all members of the educated elite were giving to insanity, in the wake of two major parliamentary inquiries into the subject within the short space of eight years, and in consequence of the revelations of the second of these about conditions in madhouses. But more importantly than that, it represented an effort to reassert the validity of the medical model of mental disturbance, and to ensure a maximum of professional autonomy in the treatment of lunatics.

Dr Francis Willis, grandson of the Lincolnshire divine who had treated George III's madness, explicitly wrote his treatise to emphasize the medical nature of insanity, an endeavour rendered 'the more necessary, because derangement has been considered by some to be merely and exclusively a mental disease, curable without the aid of medicine, by what are termed moral remedies; such as travelling and various kinds of amusements'.[105] The language used by Thomas Mayo was even more revealing. His announced purpose in publishing his *Remarks on Insanity* was 'to vindicate the rights of [our] profession over Insanity, and to elucidate its medical treatment',[106] two tasks which were obviously closely connected. For the mere existence of a large body of what purported to be technical literature passing on the fruits of scientific knowledge about the management of the insane gave impressive-seeming substance to the claim of expertise, regardless of its practical usefulness or merits. Complicated nosographies like that developed by Prichard bewildered and impressed the average layman; given such an array of diagnostic categories, recognition of the precise form of mental disease an individual lunatic was labouring under clearly became a matter for expert determination.

When medical ideas about insanity had to be presented to a lay audience, the availability of a large body of specialized 'knowledge' was valuable in a different way. For it enabled writers who wanted to advance medicine's cause to circumvent the ordinary requirement that they produce evidence in support of their contentions. Non-technical discussion of the medical treatment of insanity could be justified on the grounds of the general

Manifestations of the Mind, or Insanity; John Thurnam, *Observations and Essays on the Statistics of Insanity: Including an Inquiry into the Causes Influencing the Results of Treatment in Establishments for the Insane: To Which are Added Statistics for the Retreat near York* (London: Simpkin Marshall, 1845); David Uwins, *A Treatise on those Disorders of the Brain and Nervous System, Which Are Usually Considered and Called Mental* (London: Renshaw and Rush, 1833); Francis Willis, *A Treatise on Mental Derangement* (London: Longman, Hurst, Rees, Orme and Brown, 1823, second edition, 1843).
105. F. Willis, *A Treatise on Mental Derangement*, p. 2.
106. T. Mayo, *Remarks on Insanity*.

importance of making the public aware of the potential contribution medicine could make, but any pressures to move beyond vague generalities could now be resisted as being 'more properly the province of journals exclusively devoted to technical science'.[107] To enter upon such 'purely professional' topics would 'only be interesting to a comparatively small number of our readers',[108] and would simply be above the heads of the majority of lay readers, since they lacked the requisite training.[109]

Morison's lectures were the most visible sign that members of the medical profession were in fact receiving training. It scarcely mattered that Morison himself had no practical experience that would have given him justification for claiming expertise in this area; or that his lectures were an unoriginal mélange of ideas uncritically assembled from existing works in the field.[110] Instruction in 'a curriculum that includes some special theoretical content (whether scientifically proven or not) may represent a declaration that there is a body of special knowledge and skill necessary for the occupation',[111] which is not otherwise obtainable. Here, the availability of special education, regardless of its specific content or scientific validity, bolstered the medical profession's claims to expertise and esoteric knowledge.

The effort to press these claims proceeded on other fronts as well. The more respectable part of the medical profession used its prestige and ready access to elite circles to promote its cause.[112] As part of this process, medical men running asylums made strenuous and eventually successful efforts to persuade their lay audience that they possessed a more common and/or intense commitment to a service orientation than did their non-medically qualified competitors. At a time when madhouses were acquiring considerable disrepute, Nisbet took pains to emphasize that 'out of thirty-

107. [David Uwins], 'Inquiries Relative to Insanity', *Quarterly Review* 24, 1820–21, p. 169.
108. *Ibid.*
109. In the discussion of specific techniques, this point was emphasized over and over again: 'It would be altogether inconsistent with our *plan* to enter into the detail of such cases [. . .] (*ibid.*, p. 403); 'We have not the leisure to enter into any detail respecting the mode of employing this remedial process, and shall therefore merely observe that its use requires always to be regulated by the circumstances and constitutional condition of the patient' (*ibid.*, p. 402) – which, it goes without saying, were matters only a doctor was competent to evaluate.
110. Morison undertook these lectures primarily as an exercise in self-promotion, and with the hope that the publicity would expand his practice among the upper classes. In these respects he was successful, even though his course attracted a total of only 150 students between 1823 and 1845. *Cf.* R.A. Hunter and I. MacAlpine, *Three Hundred Years of Psychiatry*, London: Oxford University Press, 1963, pp. 305–9; Daniel Hack Tuke, *The Moral Management of the Insane*, London: Churchill, 1854, p. 78.
111. Freidson, *Professional Dominance*, pp. 134–5.
112. For examples of discreet lobbying during the drafting of lunacy legislation, see the diary of E.T. Monro, entries for 17, 25 March, 3, 12, 29 April, 15, 16, 17 May 1828 (describing approaches to such influential figures as the Lord Chancellor, Lord Lyndhurst, the Home Secretary, Robert Peel, Lord Malmesbury, the Bishop of Llandaff, and Robert Gordon). Monro's diaries for 1808–33 are in private hands in Sevenoaks, Kent. I am grateful to Nicholas Hervey for this reference.

three licenses for the metropolis, only three are in the hands of medical men. The chief part is in the hands of persons unacquainted with medicine, who take up this branch of medicine as a beneficial pursuit, and whose object is to make the most of it'.[113] Similarly, Conolly urged the importance 'of making medical men as familiar with disorders of the mind as with other disorders; and thus of rescuing lunatics from those whose interest it is to represent such maladies as more obscure, and more difficult to manage than they are'.[114] Burrows's writings[115] and his evidence before the 1828 Select Committee of the House of Lords likewise both reflected and promoted 'the widespread view that lay proprietors were more likely to be corrupt and avaricious than their medically trained colleagues'.[116] So that when the *Quarterly Review* informed its readers that 'the superintendent of a mad-house ought to be a man of character and responsibility', it recommended in the same breath that 'he should always be chosen from the medical profession'.[117]

The articles which appeared in the leading periodicals of the time either were themselves written by a physician[118] or presented an account of insanity sympathetic to the medical viewpoint.[119] The profession did not neglect the opportunity to present itself in a favourable light. Those, for instance, who relied on the *Edinburgh Review*'s summary for an account of the findings of the 1815–16 Inquiry learned that 'it is the decided opinion of *all* the most judicious and experienced witnesses examined before the Committee, that the proper employment of medicine, though neglected most deplorably in several public asylums, and in almost all the private establishments, has the best effect in cases of insanity'.[120] Similarly, Burrows informed his readers that 'from a perusal of the replies to the Questions put by the Committee, it is evident that insanity is greatly under the control of medicine – a fact that strictly accords with my own observations'.[121]

The profession was able to use its representation in Parliament, and its position as one of the three ancient learned professions, to ensure that its views received due consideration. When there was a renewed inquiry into

113. William Nisbet, *Two Letters to the Right Honourable George Rose, M.P. on the Reports at Present before the Honourable House of Commons on the State of Madhouses*, London: Cox, 1815, pp. 8–9.
114. Conolly, *An Inquiry Concerning the Indications of Insanity*, p. 7.
115. See especially Burrows, *An Inquiry into Certain Errors Relative to Insanity*.
116. W. Parry-Jones, *The Trade in Lunacy*, p. 82.
117. [D. Uwins], 'Inquiries Relative to Insanity', p. 190.
118. For example, [W.H. Fitton], 'Lunatic Asylums', *Edinburgh Review* 28, 1817, pp. 431–71; [David Uwins], 'Insanity and Madhouses'; *idem.*, 'Inquiries Relative to Insanity', pp. 169–94, both in the *Quarterly Review*.
119. [Anonymous], 'Esquirol on the Treatment of the Insane', *Westminster Review* 18, 1833, pp. 129–38. (Though the author remains unknown, internal evidence suggests that this essay, too, may have been written by a medical man.)
120. [W.H. Fitton], 'Lunatic Asylums', pp. 454–5.
121. G.M. Burrows, *Cursory Remarks*, p. 97.

conditions in private madhouses, it could call on the services of eminently
respectable society physicians like Sir Anthony Carlisle and Dr John
Bright to lend their authority to the contention that this was a medical
problem. Medical certification of insanity (for private patients only) had
been required by the 1774 Madhouse Act as an additional security against
improper confinement of the sane, and the doctors now sought to clarify
and extend their authority in this area, so as to develop an officially
approved monopoly of the right to define [mental] health and illness.[122]
Further efforts were made to get medicine's special competence vis-à-vis
the insane recognized and written into the growing volume of lunacy
legislation. When a statute based on the findings of the 1827 Select Committee was pending in the House of Lords, for instance, a special committee sat to hear the views of the medical profession on the proposed
changes. The testimony of men like E.L. Fox, W. Finch and E.T. Monro
is indicative of considerable resentment of supervision and inspection
by magistrates, particularly when efforts were made by these laymen
to meddle with decisions which were properly the prerogative of the
professional, such as when a patient was ready for discharge.[123] While
legislation was under consideration, the Royal College of Physicians
appointed a Committee of its own to (as Parry-Jones delicately puts it)
'enquire into the expediency of the provisions of the 1828 Bill'.[124] And at
the same time, a rash of pamphlets written by members of the medical
profession appeared urging that further inspection was 'a useless inquisition
into private concerns, destructive of all that privacy that is truly desirable
for the patient', and that the proposal itself 'betrays a want of confidence
in their [mad-doctors'] moral and medical character'.[125]

Some outside regulation and inspection of asylums was made inevitable
by the continuing revelation in their absence of abuses and maltreatment
of patients. Hence, the doctors sought to turn this into a system of
professional self-regulation by obtaining a dominant role for medical
practitioners. Under the 1828 Act, in the provinces only the medical
visitor, and not the magistrates who accompanied him, received payment,
while among the newly created Metropolitan Commissioners in Lunacy,
five out of fifteen were physicians. This representation was not achieved
and maintained without a struggle. In 1842, for instance, Ashley expressed

122. Freidson, *Profession of Medicine*, p. 5. Compare Dr John Bright's complaints about the
    ease of certification and the vagueness of the qualifications demanded of the certifiers.
    He could attract support for his recommendation that two physicians', surgeons' or
    apothecaries' signatures be required because of the widespread concern lest some people
    were incarcerated in madhouses by corrupt relatives seeking control of their property.
    See House of Commons, *Report of the Select Committee on Pauper Lunatics and on Lunatic
    Asylums*, 1827, p. 154, evidence of Dr John Bright.
123. See House of Lords, *Minutes of Evidence taken before the Select Committee of the House of
    Lords on the Bills Relating to Lunatics and Lunatic Asylums*, 1828.
124. W. Parry-Jones, *The Trade in Lunacy*, p. 19.
125. All cited in Hunter and MacAlpine, *Three Hundred Years of Psychiatry*, p. 791.

considerable scepticism about any requirement that commissioners, to inspect asylums, should be medically qualified, arguing that 'although so far as health was concerned the opinion of a medical man was of the greatest importance, yet it having been once established that the insanity of a patient did not arise from the state of his bodily health, a man of common sense could give as good an opinion as any medical man he knew [respecting his treatment and the question of his sanity]'.[126] Thomas Wakley, MP, the editor of the leading medical periodical, the *Lancet*, and the major spokesman for the emerging group of general practitioners, defended his profession's prerogatives, terming insanity 'a grievous disease', and stigmatizing any proposal to have lunatic asylums inspected by lawyers alone as 'an insult to the medical profession'.[127] Such a proposal now formed a part of the Licensed Lunatics Asylums Bill, introduced to expand temporarily the jurisdiction of the Metropolitan Commissioners to allow them to inspect asylums throughout the country, to prepare for a further national reform. When the bill came up again, Wakley renewed his attack:

> He objected to the clause appointing barristers to the office of commissioners of lunatic asylums. What could be more absurd than to select members of the legal profession to sit in judgement on cases of mental derangement? Was not insanity invariably associated with bodily disease? The investigations in which the commissioners would be involved would be purely of a medical character, and therefore barristers, if they were appointed, would be incompetent to perform the duties which would devolve upon them.[128]

'On the contrary', observed Lord Granville Somerset, 'the commissioners were solely concerned with whether [the lunatic] was treated properly and with kindness', and this could as well be discovered by a lawyer as a doctor.[129] Both sides had their adherents in the debate which followed, and eventually some sentiment emerged for a compromise, whereby the commissioners would operate in pairs, one with legal and one with medical training. This was the solution eventually adopted, so that the number of Metropolitan Commissioners was expanded to include seven doctors – in addition to Bright, Southey and Hume, and Thomas Turner, Thomas Waterfield, Francis Bisset Hawkins, and James Cowles Prichard.[130]

---

126. Hansard's *Parliamentary Debates*, Vol. 61, third series, 1842, column 806. Actually, this was far from being the last occasion on which he cast public doubt on the medical profession's capacities in the diagnosis and treatment of insanity. See, for example, Parliamentary Papers, 1859, 1st session, p. 23; and *Journal of the House of Lords*, March 22, 1862.
127. Hansard's *Parliamentary Debates*, Vol. 61, 3rd series, column 804.
128. *Ibid.*, column 886.
129. *Ibid.*, column 887.
130. This arrangement was continued when the national Lunacy Commission was set up. It permitted a useful professional division of labour. While the lawyers checked that the

Since the 1844 Commission Report formed the basis of the 1845 reforms, this expanded medical representation was of considerable importance. When the Report discussed the nature of insanity and its medical and moral treatment, the lay members of the Commission deferred to the specialized knowledge of their medical colleagues, and thus these sections of the Report faithfully reflected the orthodox medical viewpoint. In turn, this official acknowledgement of medicine's legitimate interest in insanity (and, at least nominally, Ashley was now one of the converted) helped to shape the legislation and its subsequent implementation.

8. Persuasion at the Local Level

Simultaneously, the profession was active on the local level, where the magistrates who were engaged in setting up the new system of public asylums were an obvious target for their efforts. In some counties the magistrates were already convinced that insanity was a medical province, and hence needed no prompting to place their asylum in the hands of the local doctor. At Nottingham, for instance, Becher, who was the man most responsible for getting the asylum built, was convinced that the management of insanity 'is an art of itself',[131] a disease having its basis in organic lesions of the body which only doctors were competent to treat.[132] In consequence, an apothecary was placed in charge of the day-to-day management of the asylum, subject to the control of a visiting physician 'who shall be entrusted with the medical treatment of the patients'.[133] The magistrates at Hanwell and Wakefield followed a similar plan, except that here ultimate authority rested in 'the hands of the Resident Physician'.[134]

Elsewhere, however, asylum committees chose to place the daily control of the institution in the hands of a lay superintendent, or even tried to run it themselves. The Staffordshire magistrates chose a layman as their chief resident officer. At the Cornwall Asylum at Bodmin, after the first appointment of a surgeon, James Duck, as superintendent proved unsatisfactory, he was replaced by a lay 'Governor and Contractor'.[135]

The magistrates at Bedford initially also chose this latter plan. Among

legal niceties had been observed with respect to admission and discharge documents, record-keeping, and so forth, the doctors attended more strictly 'medical' matters such as diet and clothing.

131. Rev. John Thomas Becher, *An Address to the Public on the Nature, Design, and Constitution of the General Lunatic Asylum Near Nottingham*, Newark, Nottinghamshire: Ridge, 1811, p. iv.

132. *Ibid.*, pp. xi–xii.

133. Nottingham Lunatic Asylum: *The Articles of Union entered into and agreed upon between the Justices of the Peace for the County of Nottingham; the Justices of the Peace for [. . .] the town of Nottingham; and the subscribers to a voluntary institution; for the purpose of providing a General Lunatic Asylum*, Newark: Ridge, 1811, pp. 17–9.

134. *Middlesex Lunatic Asylum: Visiting Justices' Minutes*, Vol. 2, 1830. In manuscript at the GLC Record Office, London, MA/A/J2.

135. K. Jones, *Lunacy, Law and Conscience*, pp. 118–20.

the candidates they considered to head their asylum were a former assistant keeper at St. Luke's, and a house painter, who had some experience looking after a lunatic he had come across in the course of his business.[136] They had previously decided that, since the medical care needed by the lunatics was slight, and they 'will not [. . .] require the same species of unremitting attention during the whole of the four and twenty hours as Patients in Hospitals do', therefore 'Mr Leach, our House Surgeon at the Infirmary who so ably discharges his duties there might from the Contiguity of the Establishments' be induced to attend to the occasional medical needs of the Asylum patients.[137] At a subsequent meeting held on 27 April 1812, the house painter, William Pether, and his wife were appointed 'the Governor and Matron of the Lunatic Asylum with a Salary of Sixty Guineas per Annum'.[138]

Within less than a year, local physicians were seeking their first foothold in the new institution. A letter was received from a Dr G.O. Yeats offering 'to undertake the office of the Medical Superintendent and Physician of this Institution gratuitously'.[139] He justified the need for such assistance by pointing out that there were 'a considerable number of lunatics whose diseases will require medical aid'. Naturally enough, the offer was accepted.[140] A few more months went by before Yeats tried to convince the magistrates that medicine could be used not merely to cure the patients' physical ailments, but also to help restore them to sanity. In a second long letter to the managing committee, he argued that

> however anxious the legislature has been strictly to confine the inmates of the house and to guard against the possibility of there being restored to the world unfit members of society, yet equal anxiety is expressed that every possible care should be taken by medical means for such restoration [. . . .] It is very desirable then, in order to render the Asylum, not only a place for incarceration, but one where every facility may be given for the amelioration of the condition and for the cure of the maladies of its unfortunate inmates,

that the medical officer be given broader powers over the treatment of the patient.[141]

The process by which the physician invoked the privileges of his office to subordinate the lay superintendent to medical control, and eventually to squeeze him out altogether, had now begun. Three days later Pether

---

136. Bedfordshire County Asylum: *Minute Book*, Vol. 1, 1812, p. 7, in manuscript at the Bedfordshire County Record Office, LB 1/1.
137. *Ibid.*, pp. 4–5.
138. *Ibid.*, p. 9.
139. *Ibid.*, 2 January 1813, p. 39.
140. *Ibid.*, p. 41.
141. Letter from Dr G.O. Yeats to the Committee of Magistrates on the Asylum dated 21 April 1813, in Bedfordshire County Record Office, Miscellaneous Papers relating to the Foundation of the County Lunatic Asylum, LBP 1.

received his new instructions: 'It was ordered that the Governor in all matters relating to the Health and Distribution of the Patients with a view to their Convalescence or their Medical Treatment, do obey implicitly the instructions of the Physician.'[142] In February of the following year, Yeats was obliged to submit his resignation as non-resident Medical Superintendent, as he was moving to London; but his colleague, Dr Thackeray, offered to assume the position, once more gratuitously.[143]

During Thackeray's term in office, he and various other doctors made efforts to educate the magistrates to the fact that insanity was a disease just like any other disease physicians were called on to treat, and that there ought therefore to be provision for a full-time resident medical officer to run the Asylum. In 1815, he complained in a letter to the magistrates of

> the insufficiency of the present Medical Means to fulfill the benevolent designs of the Institution. Their asylum affords a solitary example in which a large and important medical establishment is conducted without the assistance of a Resident director in the character of House apothecary. The defect in its constitution by totally precluding the employment of all remedies requiring attention to their effects and by preventing the observation and accumulation of Facts for the advancement of the Science of medicine greatly limits its service as a Medical Institution.[144]

Such a state of affairs was rendered the more deplorable because proper classification of the various varieties of mental disease revealed that each major sub-type was almost certainly the consequence of an underlying physical pathology – mania reflected a disorder of the brain, melancholia of the abdominal viscera, and nervousness, a disturbed state of the nervous system.

Thackeray felt that 'if there be any foundation for this classification of mental disease, great encouragement I think is held out in it for placing a Lunatic Asylum on the footing of a Medical Institution'.[145] The magistrates clearly did not. Dr Maclean, who had replaced Leech as House Surgeon at the Infirmary, continued to hold that post, and to perform the duties of Secretary and Head Apothecary at the Infirmary, so that his attendance on the Asylum patients was a distinctly part-time affair; and Thackeray still contributed his services on a voluntary, unpaid, visiting basis. On Maclean's resignation from his various posts in June 1823,[146] the governors ordered that his successor should perform these same duties, and in September a Mr Harris accepted the appointment.

142. Bedfordshire County Asylum: *Minute Book*, 24 April 1813, p. 46, LB 1/1.
143. *Ibid.*, 5 February and 5 March 1814.
144. Thackeray to the Magistrates' Committee, 7 August 1815, in Bedfordshire County Asylum Miscellaneous Papers, LBP 1.
145. *Ibid.*
146. Bedfordshire County Asylum Visitors' Book A, 2 June 1823, LB 1/8.

Further efforts were now made to dislodge the layman, Pether, and to replace him with a resident medical officer. The large proportion of chronic derelicts among the asylum population here posed a problem for those advocating a greater role for medicine, since it was not clear what benefits, if any, the increased expenditure for a full-time medical officer would bring. Thackeray conceded the difficulty, but sought to persuade the magistrates that it was a temporary state of affairs, the consequence of the failure to employ medical treatment while such cases were still curable, a mistake they should take care to avoid in the future.

> The present state of the house in which there are but few subjects under medical treatment may perhaps have led to the idea that little occasion exists for the establishment of such a department. Were this state a *permanent* condition of the house the conclusion would be just; but it should be regarded [as] wholly an *accidental* one, depending on the Infancy of the Institution. The asylum is at present filled chiefly with patients whose disorders from their *long* standing, discourage every hope of benefit from medical exertion. In the progress, however, of time *recent* cases of derangement will be continually presenting themselves, when much encouragement will be offered for the active interference of Art.[147]

For a while, the magistrates still proved recalcitrant. Thackeray and Harris submitted further memoranda in support of their position, and obtained testimonials reinforcing their contentions from other physicians who happened to visit the asylum. Finally, the magistrates bowed to the weight of professional opinion:

> Dr Thackeray and Mr Harris having separately called the attention of the magistrates to the expediency of providing regular resident medical aid to the Institution and the Magistrates having noticed a similar suggestion entered in the visitors' journal by the Medical Superintendent of the Bicêtre of Paris and another foreigner and Dr Thompson of the twenty-fifth of July last, and having taken the same into their consideration, resolved to recommend the subject to the next court of Quarter Sessions.[148]

Pether's position swiftly became untenable, as he lost almost all his remaining authority. Finally, in 1828 he resigned his position as General Manager, and was succeeded by Harris.[149] Paramount authority over all aspects of asylum administration now rested in medical hands.

---

147. Memorandum from Dr Thackeray, MD, in Bedfordshire County Asylum Miscellaneous Papers, LBP 1, emphasis in the original.
148. Bedfordshire County Asylum Visitors' Book, 5 February 1827, LB 1/8.
149. *Ibid.*, 6 October 1828.

9. Madness as Mental Illness

The activities, both local and national, which we have just been discussing, all made use of, and owed much of their success to, the arguments which were developed in the medical literature of the period. For it was the contentions advanced here which convinced almost all the educated classes that insanity was indeed a disease and that its treatment ought therefore to be entrusted to doctors. Consequently, I now want to devote some time to a consideration of just what such arguments were.

Moral treatment lacked a well-developed ideological rationale for why it should work. Tuke had explicitly eschewed any desire to develop a theoretical account of the nature of mental disturbance, and had refused to elaborate moral treatment into a rigid 'scientific' therapy.[150] In the past, 'the want of facts relative to this subject, and our disposition to hasty generalization, have led to many conclusions equally unfriendly to the progress of knowledge, and the comfort of patients'.[151] He therefore resisted efforts to achieve a premature systematization of knowledge, and encouraged a pragmatic approach: 'I have happily little occasion for theory, since my province is to relate, not only what ought to be done, but also what, in most instances, is actually performed.'[152] He even refused to choose between a psychological and somatic etiology of insanity, arguing that 'whatever theory we maintain in regard to the remote causes of insanity, we must consider moral treatment of very high importance'.[153] If its origins lay in the mind, 'applications made immediately to it are the most natural, and the most likely to be attended with success'; if in the body, 'we shall still readily admit, from the reciprocal action of the two parts of our system upon each other, that the greatest attention is necessary to whatever is calculated to affect the mind'.[154]

Undoubtedly, though, the nature of the therapy he advanced, and the manner in which advocates of moral treatment persistently and explicitly denied the value of a medical approach, could, at the very least, be more readily reconciled with a mental rather than a somatic etiology of insanity. Francis Willis was not alone in accusing those favouring moral treatment of propagating the doctrine that 'mental derangement must arise from

---

150. For instance, he was 'far from imagining that this Asylum is a perfect model for others, either in regards to construction or management. If several improvements have been successfully introduced, it is probable that many others remain unattempted'. S. Tuke, *Description of the Retreat*, p. xxii.
151. *Ibid.*, p. viii.
152. *Ibid.*, p. 138. This refusal to reduce moral treatment to a set of formulae, and the insistence that it rested in a common-sense approach to the problem of insanity, aimed at eliminating artificial obstacles to recovery, made for a refreshing lack of dogmatism. At the same time, they were a crucial factor in weakening its ability to resist takeover and transformation by those espousing a less modest ideal; for by denying that schooled human knowledge and intervention were needed to cope with insanity, they at least delayed the rise of an occupational group claiming training in the new therapy.
153. *Ibid.*, p. 131.
154. *Ibid.*, pp. 131–2.

causes, and be cured by remedies, that solely and exclusively operate on the mind'.[155] Physicians stigmatized this as an 'absurd opinion'[156] but were obviously afraid of the threat it posed to their position.[157]

The single most effective response to an attack along these lines would have been to demonstrate that insanity was in fact caused by biophysical variables. A somatic interpretation of insanity would place it beyond dispute within medicine's recognized sphere of competence, and make plausible the assertion that it responded to medicine's conventional remedies for disease. The trouble was that the doctors could not show the existence of the necessary physical lesions, and this inconvenient fact was already in the public domain.[158]

Unable to produce a consensus about the existence of visual[159] or other

155. F. Willis, *A Treatise on Mental Derangement*, p. 4. This was an idea which he thought 'cannot [. . .] for a moment be rationally entertained'. (*Ibid.*) I shall show why in a moment. William Saunders Hallaran was quite unusual among his medical colleagues in accepting the logic of this position and adopting it anyway. He explicitly distinguished 'two species of insanity', those attributable to physical causes and those which he held were due to strictly mental causes, and argued for 'opposite modes of treatment': medical treatment in the former cases, and moral treatment in the latter. See W.S. Hallaran, *An Enquiry into the Causes Producing the Extraordinary Addition to the Number of Insane, Together with Extended Observations on the Cure of Insanity*, Cork: Edwards and Savage, 1810; *idem.*, *Practical Observations on the Causes and Cure of Insanity*.
156. W.A.F. Browne, *What Asylums Were, Are, and Ought to Be*, p. 178.
157. Thomas Bakewell, for instance, perhaps the best-known non-medical madhouse keeper of the early nineteenth century, acknowledged that when it came to the dispensing of medicines for bodily disorders, 'I have the greatest cause for humility. But in the moral treatment, merely as an experienced Keeper, I ask for no other opinions.' *A Letter to the Chairman of the Select Committee . . . [on] Madhouses*, p. 53.
158. As Andrew Halliday lamented,

> the anatomists sought in vain for some visible derangement of structure, or a diseased state of the parts in many cases where it was perfectly ascertainable that death had ensued from insanity . . . hence the common opinion seemed to be confirmed, that it was an incomprehensible and consequently an incurable malady of mind. Taking this view of the disease, it is not at all wonderful that it was considered as beyond the reach of medical science.

Andrew Halliday, *A General View of the Present State of Lunatics and Lunatic Asylums*, London: Underwood, 1828, p. 2; see also Joseph Mason Cox, *Practical Observations on Insanity*, 2nd edn, pp. x–xi. Others were even more specific: 'In three fourths of the cases of insanity, where they have been subjected to, dissection after death, the knife of the anatomist has not been able, with the most scrutinizing care, to trace any organic change to which the cause of the disease could be traced' (W. Nisbet, *Two Letters . . . on the Reports . . . on the State of Madhouses*, pp. 21–2). For still more pessimistic conclusions (from the medical viewpoint), see J. Haslam, *Medical Jurisprudence*; House of Commons, *Report of the Select Committee on Pauper Lunatics*, 1827, evidence of Sir Anthony Carlisle. Those medical men who, in the teeth of this testimony, continued to insist that their theoretical commitment to somaticism had an unimpeachable empirical basis, and that death made the physical basis of the disease transparent, had their credibility seriously undermined by the general inability, even in their own midst, to reach agreement about 'just what was visible'. *Cf.* R. Smith, *Trial by Medicine: Insanity and Responsibility in Victorian Trials*, Edinburgh: Edinburgh University Press, 1981, p. 44.
159. Even where there *were* some visible abnormalities of the brain, difficulties remained: 'In the first place, the alterations themselves are exceedingly wanting in correspondence with what one should, *a priori*, conceive; and in the next, it is not always easy to say

inter-subjectively verifiable evidence which supported their personal and professional predilection for a somatic interpretation,[160] a handful of mavericks resolved the difficulty by the simple expedient of defining the mind as a function of the brain and wholly dependent on it. In this view (an uncompromising physicalism which had obvious similarities to the

how far appearances, after death, have been the cause of disease, or consequence of disease, or consequence of death itself.' David Uwins, *A Treatise on Those Disorders of the Brain and Nervous System, Which Are Usually Considered and Called Mental*, pp. 83–4.

160. That insanity was a somatic disease was asserted with complete confidence and virtual unanimity in the medical literature of the time: 'Madness has always been connected with disease of the brain and its membranes' (J. Haslam, *Medical Jurisprudence*, p. 238); 'Insanity, always originates in a corporeal cause: derangement of the intellectual faculties is but the effect' (G.M. Burrows, *Cursory Remarks*, p. 102); 'Insanity it must be contended for, is as much within the province of medical acumen, as any other disorder incidental to animal life [. . . .] Insanity, it will be shewn, is, in every instance, associated with organic lesion' (J. Hallaran, *Practical Observations on the Causes and Cure of Insanity*, 2nd edn, p. 2); 'Instead of delirium, derangement and insanity, being nearly mental disorders, each of them must be, in fact, and in its origin, a bodily one' (F. Willis, *Mental Derangement*, p. 5, 2nd edn, p. 3); 'I believe that insanity is as much a bodily disease as a fever or a bunyon on any finger [. . . .] It is a disease of the brain just as much as dyspepsia [is] of the stomach' (House of Commons, *Report of the Select Committee on Pauper Lunatics*, 1827, evidence of Dr Edward Wright, superintendent of Bethlem); 'The remote causes of insanity may be [. . .] undefined and countless; but the proximate cause, or in fact the disease itself, will always be found to arise from the diseased state of the structure of the brain' ([Sir] Andrew Halliday, *A General View of the Present State of Lunatics and Lunatic Asylums in Great Britain and Ireland, and in some other Kingdoms*, London: Underwood, 1828, p. 5); 'Madness is sometimes immediately excited by mental circumstances but even when that is the case, the disorder is bodily' (D. Uwins, *A Treatise on . . . Disorders of the Brain and Nervous System*, p. 229); 'Insanity may be defined as "disordered" function of the brain generally' (W.B. Neville, *On Insanity*, p. 18); '[Insanity is] strictly a bodily disease having its origins in organic lesions of the brain' (W.A.F. Browne, *What Asylums Were, Are, and Ought to Be*, pp. 4–7); 'Insanity has been considered in all cases, to be a disease of the brain' (W.C. Ellis, *A Treatise on . . . Insanity*, p. 146 and *cf.* chapter 2, pp. 22–40); 'Now it was well known, that insanity never existed without some organic affection of the human body – that the mind itself never became deranged or disordered in its functions but from some derangement in the structure of the human frame [. . . .] In general, there was an inflammatory attack going on, requiring to be treated and subdued and when subdued the derangement disappeared' (Thomas Wakley in Hansard's *Parliamentary Debates*, Vol. 66, third series, 1844, column 1278). See also T. Mayo (*Remarks on Insanity*), who emphasizes 'the physical phenomena' of insanity; J.C. Prichard, *A Treatise on Insanity*, pp. 234–49; A. Morison, *Outlines of Lectures on . . . Insanity*, 4th edn, pp. 422–3. A few doctors located the cause somewhere other than the brain: 'I would say, that where a hurt or disease or disorder exists in the brain, there is at least an equal number where it exists in the stomach [. . .]' (House of Commons, *Report of the Select Committee on Pauper Lunatics*, 1827, p. 52, evidence of Sir Anthony Carlisle); J.C. Prichard (*A Treatise on Insanity*, p. 249) and J.G. Spurzheim (*Observations on the Deranged Manifestations of the Mind*, p. 300) concurred; But for Burnett, 'both reason and science favour the idea that insanity is not and ought not in the first instance, and often to the very last, to be regarded as a disease of the brain, but as a disease floating in the blood, having no fixed or local character' (C.M. Burnett, MD, *Insanity Tested by Science, and Shown to Be a Disease Rarely Connected With Organic Lesion of the Brain, and on That Account Far More Susceptible of Cure Than Has Hitherto Been Supposed*, London: Highley, 1848, p. 5); Andrew Halliday informed the public of the importance of the 'discovery' that insanity had a somatic basis: the earlier, mistaken notion that insanity was a disease of the mind could not but lead to a deep therapeutic pessimism, since neither doctors nor anyone

views of La Mettrie and Cabanis),[161] the distinction between mind and brain was illusory and mental events were thus mere epiphenomena. 'Mind' being purely a function of the brain, mental functions must be identical with the physiological processes which were allegedly their invariable concomitant. Accordingly (and self-evidently), there could be no such thing as mind disease. Rather, 'all the affections comprehended under the general term of mental derangement, are only evidences of cerebral affections; – disordered manifestations of those organs, whose healthy action produces the phenomena called mental; – in short, symptoms of the diseased brain'.[162]

Perhaps the most aggressive proponent of this stance was William Lawrence, Crowther's successor as surgeon to Bethlem. 'The effects of medical treatment', he truculently asserted,

> completely corroborate these views. Indeed they, who talk of and believe in diseases of the mind, are too wise to put their trust in mental remedies. Arguments, syllogisms, discourses, sermons, have never yet restored any patient; the moral pharmacopoeia is quite inefficient, and no real benefit can be conferred without vigorous medical treatment, which is as efficacious in these affections, as in the diseases of any other organs.[163]

An unabashed materialist, Lawrence did not shrink from the implications of his own position, denouncing dismissively the 'hypothesis or fiction of a subtle invisible matter, animating the visible textures of animal bodies' as merely an illustration 'of that propensity of the human mind [sic], which has led men at all times to account for those phenomena, of which the causes are not obvious, by the mysterious aid of higher and imaginary beings . . . and . . . the immediate operation of the divinity'.[164] Three years later, he reiterated that 'physiologically speaking . . . the mind,

else could act on this immaterial substance. However, 'truth has taken the place of fiction and madness is found to proceed in all cases from some real tangible bodily ailment. It can now be treated according to the known rules of practice – made amenable to the ordinary discipline of the apothecary's shop – and is often more easily removed than less important diseases that have made a temporary logement in the human frame' (A. Halliday, *A General View of the Present State of Lunatics*, p. 444).

161. *Cf.* Julian La Mettrie, *L'Homme machine*, Princeton: Princeton University Press, 1960 (original edn 1748); and Pierre Cabanis, *Rapports du physique et du moral de l'homme*, in *Œuvres complètes* (ed. P.J.G. Thurot), Paris: Bossange Frères, 1823–5 (original edn 1802), where the claim is advanced that the brain secretes thought just as the liver secretes bile.

162. William Lawrence, *Lectures on Physiology, Zoology, and the Natural History of Man, Delivered at the Royal College of Surgeons*, London: Callow, 1819, p. 112. The reference to Cabanis is made manifest in the next sentence: 'These symptoms have the same relation to the brain, as vomiting, indigestion, heartburn, to the stomach; cough, asthma, to the lungs; or any other deranged functions to their corresponding organs.'

163. *Ibid.*, p. 114.

164. William Lawrence, *An Introduction to Comparative Anatomy and Physiology*, London: Callow, 1816, quoted in R.A. Hunter and I. MacAlpine, *Three Hundred Years of Psychiatry*, p. 748.

the grand prerogative of the brain' was simply a function of that organ. The symptoms of insanity thus possessed 'the same relation to the brain, as vomiting, indigestion, heartburn to the stomach; cough, asthma to the lungs; or any other deranged functions to their corresponding organs'.[165]

The reaction to these remarks suggests why most alienists eschewed the materialist strategy. Lawrence immediately came under strong attack as an atheist and a menace to the social order. Even his former teacher and fellow surgeon at St. Bartholomew's, John Abernathy, sharply criticized him for 'propagating opinions detrimental to society, and of . . . loosening those [moral and religious] restraints, on which the welfare of mankind depends.'[166] Accused of atheism and of denying the divine immortality of the soul, Lawrence saw 'public indignation . . . threaten his position at Bethlem, as well as at Bridewell's, and St. Bartholomew's'[167] – a potentially fatal blow to his professional prospects. He survived this threat of professional ruin by the skin of his teeth, and only by taking the extraordinary step of withdrawing his book from sale, and resigning as lecturer to the Royal College of Surgeons.[168]

Lawrence was nonetheless not the only medical man to embrace this straightforward means of unambiguously tying insanity to disorders of the body. While still a student at Edinburgh, W.A.F. Browne impoliticly advanced similar views. At the 27 March 1827 meeting of the Plinian Society at the University (to which he had just proposed the admission of the young Charles Darwin as a member), Browne rose to deliver a paper on the nature of organisms and mind. 'Mind', he announced, 'as far as one individual's sense and consciousness are concerned, is material.' Uproar followed, and in the aftermath it was decided, not just to strike Browne's paper from the record, but to go back to the minutes of the previous meeting to expunge the announcement that he *intended* to read such a paper.[169] Browne learned his lesson, and was to take great care in his later work not to raise the bugaboo of materialism.

Small wonder that so few of Lawrence and Browne's colleagues chose to adopt such an exposed position – one that was in any event politically so inexpedient if one sought to defend professional prerogatives.[170] As a

165. W. Lawrence, *Lectures on Physiology, Zoology, and the Natural History of Man.*
166. Quoted in R.A. Hunter and I. MacAlpine, *Three Hundred Years of Psychiatry*, p. 748.
167. William Bynum, 'Rationales for Therapy', pp. 48–9.
168. *Cf.* June Goodfield-Toulmin, 'Some Aspects of English Physiology, 1780–1840', *Journal of the History of Biology* 2, 1969, pp. 283–320.
169. See the account in Howard E. Gruber and Paul H. Barrett, *Darwin on Man . . . Together with Darwin's Early and Unpublished Notebooks*, New York: Dutton, 1974, pp. 39–41, 479.
170. For discussion of a similar tactical choice by phrenologists, who could ill-afford to confirm their opponents' charges of materialism and irreligion, see D. De Giustino, *The*

proto-profession with only the most tenuous claims to legitimacy and scientific status, alienism could scarcely afford to adopt a controversial stance on an issue which provoked fiercely negative reactions from established elites.[171] Consequently, whether because their own theological convictions barred such materialism, or from motives of prudence, few mad-doctors can have felt encouraged to justify their predilection for a somatic account of insanity in straightforwardly materialist terms. Nonetheless, their most fundamental assumptions about pathological processes, powerfully reinforced by their professional interest in unambiguously tying insanity to disorders of the body, impelled them to find some alternative means of demonstrating this linkage.

Over the next decade and more, it therefore comes as no surprise to discover that most medical men who wrote on the subject came to embrace an ingenious metaphysical argument which, presented as if it were the findings of empirical investigation, appeared to provide a definitive resolution to the difficulty. They began by postulating a Cartesian dualism between mind and body. The mind, which was an immortal, immaterial substance, identical with the Christian doctrine of the soul,[172] was forced to operate in this world through the medium of a material instrument, namely the brain. This was an apparently innocuous distinction, but once it had been conceded, the doctors had no trouble 'proving' their case. For to argue that the mind was subject to disease, debility, or even, in the case of outright idiotism, death, was to contradict the very

---

Conquest of Mind: Phrenology and Victorian Social Thought, London: Croom Helm, 1975, pp. 114–5.

171. Some indication of the likely outcome of adopting an openly materialist stance may be deduced from the reception given by the ecclesiastical establishment to evolutionary theory, which similarly implied 'the union . . . between man's spiritual nature and his body, particularly his nervous system'. One should remember, for instance, that Robert Chambers, rightly fearing the potential effect on his publishing business, took enormous pains to disguise his authorship of *The Vestiges of the Natural History of Creation*, which appeared anonymously in 1844 to the accompaniment of ferocious criticism from Adam Sedgwick and other establishment figures. And Darwin himself, having worked out the essentials of his theory in the early 1840s, delayed publishing his ideas for almost two decades, perhaps not unmindful of Browne's treatment, and certainly well aware of how Georges Buffon had been forced into a public retraction of his account of the geological history of the earth, when scientific geology collided with the myth of creation presented in the book of Genesis. (The delay, of course, did not save Darwin from merciless attacks, even from Sedgwick, one of his scientific mentors. See the discussion in H.E. Gruber and P.H. Barrett, *Darwin on Man*, especially chapter 2, 'The Threat of Persecution', and pp. 85–9; and in Robert M. Young, *Mind, Brain, and Adaptation in the Nineteenth Century*, Oxford: Clarendon Press, 1970, p. 20 and *passim.*

172. As W.F. Bynum points out, the French even use the same word, *l'âme*, for the two concepts. ('Rationales for Therapy', p. 320.) The conflation of mind and soul has an ancient lineage, and can be traced even in the physical model of mind offered in David Hartley, *Observations on Man, His Frame, His Duties, and His Expectations*, London: Leake and Frederick, 1749.

foundation of Christianity, the belief in an immortal soul.[173] On the other hand, adoption of a somatic viewpoint provided a wholly satisfactory resolution to the dilemma: 'From the admission of this principle, derangement is no longer considered a disease of the understanding, but of the centre of the nervous system, upon the unimpaired condition of which the exercise of the understanding depends. The brain is at fault and not the mind.'[174] The brain, as a material organ, was liable to irritation and inflammation, and it was this which produced insanity.[175] 'But let this oppression [of the brain] be relieved, this irritation be removed, and the mind rises in its native strength, clear and calm, uninjured, immutable, immortal. In all cases where disorder of the mind is detectable, from the faintest peculiarity to the widest deviation from health, it must and can only be traced directly or indirectly to the brain.'[176] Commitment to a

173. In Andrew Halliday's words,

> we may suppose that many very able men, led away by what appeared to be the general opinion of mankind [that insanity was a disease of mind], would shrink from the investigation of a subject that seemed to lead to a doubt of the immateriality of mind; a truth so evident to their own feelings and so expressly established by divine revelation. If they admitted that the mind could become diseased, it would follow, as a matter of course, that the mind might die. They therefore refrained from meeting a question which involved such dangerous consequences.

A. Halliday, *A General View of the Present State of Lunatics and Lunatic Asylums*, p. 4. As Spurzheim expressed the medical consensus, 'I have no idea of any disease, or of any derangement of an immaterial being itself, such as the mind or soul is. The soul cannot fall sick, any more than it can die.' J.G. Spurzheim, *Observations on the Deranged Manifestations of the Mind, or Insanity*, p. 101.

174. W.A.F. Browne, *What Asylums Were, Are, and Ought to Be*, p. 4.

175. Morison, *Outlines of Lectures on . . . Insanity*, pp. 35–7. The immortal and immaterial on this side of the grave was utterly and intimately dependent on the material and therefore corrupt sensory apparatus of the body:

> so dependent is the immaterial soul upon the material organs, both for what it receives and what it transmits, that a slight disorder in the circulation of the blood through different portions of the nervous substance, can disturb all sensation, all emotion, all relation with the external and living world.

John Conolly, *An Inquiry Concerning the Indications of Insanity*, p. 62.

176. Browne, *What Asylums Were, Are, and Ought to Be*, p. 4. For the elaborations of this entire somatic ideology which most clearly reveal the ultimately theological grounds on which the explanation was offered (and accepted), see A. Morison, *Outlines of Lectures on . . . Insanity*, pp. 34–44, and Halliday, *A General View of the Present State of Lunatics*, pp. 5–8. Halliday even went so far as to suggest that the threat to religious belief had held back the scientific investigation of madness, *ibid.*, pp. 2–3. Revealing in a rather different sense was Burrows's contention that 'no impression, perhaps, has been more detrimental than the scholastic dogma, that the mind, being independent of the body, can simulate all its functions and actions; can sicken, be administered to, recover, and relapse; and that consequently all but moral remedies must be secondary, if not nearly useless, every other being incompatible with an immaterial essence like mind' (G.M. Burrows, *An Inquiry into Certain Errors Relative to Insanity*, pp. 6–7). One is led to ask, detrimental to what? And it is difficult to avoid the conclusion, detrimental to the claim that insanity is a medical problem, one that only doctors are qualified to handle.

radical psycho-physical dualism thus provided the strongest of guarantees that scientific advance would do nothing to undermine revealed religion – rendered it, indeed, logically inconceivable that it should do so[177] – while simultaneously providing the necessary social warrant for medicine's jurisdictional claims.[178]

The failure to *observe* physical lesions of the brain in most cases of insanity could now be explained in either of two ways, neither of which threatened the somatic interpretation. On the one hand, it might be that existing instruments and techniques were simply too crude to detect the very subtle changes involved.[179] On the other hand, it could be that insanity in its early stages was correlated only with functional changes in the brain, which only at a later stage, when the patient became chronic, passed over into structural ones.[180]

With delightful if unconscious irony, medical men thus made use of theological dogma to dispose of what they dismissively referred to as 'metaphysical views of insanity'.[181] Psychogenetic theories of mental disorder were exposed as subtly and seductively threatening to call into

177. Hence the alacrity with which theologians seized upon and endorsed this account of madness. *Cf.* William Newnham:

> A great error has arisen, and has been perpetuated even to the present day, in considering cerebral disorder as *mental*; requiring, and indeed admitting, *only* of moral remedies . . . ; whereas the brain is the mere *organ* of mind, not the mind itself; and its disorder of function arises from its ceasing to be a proper medium for the manifestation of the varied action and passion of the presiding spirit.

'Essay on Superstition', *Christian Observer* 29, 1829, p. 265, quoted in W.F. Bynum, 'Rationales for Therapy', p. 49.

178. *Cf.* Herbert Mayo, *Anatomical and Physiological Commentaries*, Vol. 1, London: Underwood, 1822, esp. pp. 7–8, and the discussion in Charlotte MacKenzie, 'A Family Asylum: A History of the Private Madhouse at Ticehurst in Sussex, 1792–1917', unpublished Ph.D. thesis, University of London, 1987, chapter 2.

179. 'If no organic affections are said to have been discovered in some few instances, we should not reason negatively from dissections, perhaps cursorily and ignorantly made, and with instruments ill adapted to detect minute, and apparently trivial deviations from the general structure.' Joseph Mason Cox, *Practical Observations on Insanity*, 3rd edn, London: Baldwin and Underwood, 1813, p. 40. *Cf.* also A. Morison, *Outlines of Lectures on . . . Insanity*, p. 411. Morison produced a subtle and ingenious argument to show that the changes in the brain must be slight in the early stages of the disease. It was a common observation that recent cases of insanity recovered in greater numbers than those of long standing. This must mean that the changes in the structure of their brains had not proceeded very far, for serious structural changes would naturally be irreversible, and hence impossible to cure. *Ibid.*, p. 422.

180. W.B. Neville, *On Insanity*, p. 60. The proof of *this* position was that 'cases of any standing that terminate fatally are, we may venture to say, *never* investigated by the skillful pathological anatomist without obvious traces of structural disease being discovered', pp. 60–1, emphasis in the original.

181. T. Mayo, *Remarks on Insanity*, p. 83. The dismissal of any save somatic accounts of madness as metaphysical continued to be a prominent theme in psychiatric discourse in the second half of the nineteenth century, and is particularly apparent in the work of Henry Maudsley.

question the central truths of revealed religion – the immortality and immateriality of the soul, and the existence of a divinely ordained 'free will' – and spiritual assumptions were simultaneously transformed into a thoroughly secure foundation for a fundamentally materialist case. Such an account was sure to possess an enormous intuitive appeal to an audience of convinced Christians, and suffered scarcely at all from its extra-empirical character. And by 'proving' that insanity was a somatic complaint, it decisively reinforced medical claims to be granted sole authority over madness and the institutions within which it was treated.

The obvious achievements of moral treatment could not be simply overlooked – they were too well established in the public mind for that. However, moral therapy could be (and was) absorbed into the realm of ordinary medical techniques. Moral treatment now became just one weapon among many (even if a particularly valuable one), which the skillful physician used in his battle against mental illness. Texts like Prichard's included a chapter on moral treatment as a matter of course,[182] while those who rejected the conventional medical methods were accused of unnecessarily reducing their chances of curing their patients. In support of this position, certain mad-doctors claimed to have cured a higher percentage of their patients than had the Retreat[183] and attributed this to their willingness to use both moral *and* medical means.[184] Others claimed to provide proof of the efficacy of medical means in certain cases, proof which took the form of citing instances of insanity known to the author where the patients had recovered at some time after the administration of traditional medical remedies.[185]

---

182. *Cf.* J.C. Prichard, *A Treatise on Insanity*.

183. Burrows claimed he had cured 'on recent cases, 91 in 100; and on old cases, 35 in 100' (G.M. Burrows, *An Inquiry into Certain Errors Relative to Insanity*, p. 48).

184. Burrows commented that 'insanity was formerly in that asylum [The Retreat] scarcely considered to be a remediable complaint; and consequently, medical aid was resorted to only when patients were affected with other disorders' (G.M. Burrows, *Commentaries on the Causes [. . .] of Insanity*, p. 558). For himself: 'Having the fullest conviction of the great efficacy of medicine in the majority of cases of insanity, I have ever viewed with regret the little confidence professed by the benevolent conductors of the Retreat in its powers; and have always considered that the exercise of a more energetic remedial plan of treatment was the only thing required to render the system they pursue perfect' (G.M. Burrows, *An Inquiry into Certain Errors Relative to Insanity*, p. 31).

185. Prichard, having defended medical treatment as 'the use of remedies which act upon the body and are designed to remove the disorder of cerebral or other functions, known or believed to be the cause of derangement in the mind', cited a string of such cures following the use of bleeding, purges, vomits, opium, digitalis, etc. (J.C. Prichard, *A Treatise on Insanity*, pp. 250–6). Thurnam conceded that 'perhaps we cannot produce any facts which actually prove that pharmaceutic treatment, considered separately, has in any particular institution influenced the results on any large scale; yet we cannot doubt that the proportion of recoveries is greater, and in particular, that the mean mortality will be less in a hospital for the insane, in which attention is paid to a discriminating and judicious medical treatment' (J. Thurnam, *Observations and Essays on the Statistics of Insanity*, pp. 100–1). After all, if insanity was a medical problem, no

There remained the philosophically tricky question of just how mind and body were connected – a topic on which much medical discourse remained 'strikingly incoherent'.[186] Vague reassurances that 'the connection of the faculties of the mind with the brain, or, to speak more accurately, their dependence on this organ, is a point . . . certainly demonstrated by the labours of modern physiologists and pathologists',[187] were not matched to any persuasive interpretation of just how these two things were linked. Nor, in many accounts, was there any clear explanation of how it was that a purely psychological therapy like moral treatment (which the doctors were in the process of claiming as their own) could affect a physical disorder. Certainly, the idea that mind and body were mutually interdependent had long been taken for granted by doctors and the laity alike, forming one of the core assumptions on which traditional accounts of health, illness, and therapeutics implicitly rested.[188] Moreover, perhaps fortunately in the circumstances, the proponents of moral treatment had not developed a clearly articulated theoretical account of how or why their treatment worked. Some medical men opted, therefore, simply to ignore the potential difficulty, and to argue for the adoption of moral treatment on purely pragmatic grounds. Others played the theological card once more ('Here our researches must stop, and we must declare, that "Wonderful are the works of the Lord, and his ways are past finding out".');[189] or else tried to dismiss the problem of psycho–physical interaction as insoluble ('In what manner this connection between mind and matter is effected, is not here inquired into. The link will, perhaps, ever escape human research . . .');[190] or simply irrelevant ('to discuss the validity of this or that hypothesis would be plunging into an inextricable labyrinth . . .').[191]

other conclusion made sense. The same resort to *petitio principii* was apparent in his account of the results of his own treatment of cases at the York Retreat: given a belief that insanity was a physical disease, 'I cannot but attach great importance to the use of physical means in the treatment of mental disorders, for if insanity really depends on some morbid conditions of the bodily frame, it follows, as at least highly probable, that everything tending to the restoration or maintenance of bodily health must be of primary importance in its treatment' (*ibid.*, p. 28).

186. R. Smith, *Trial by Medicine*, p. 43.
187. W.B. Neville, *On Insanity*, p. 18.
188. The best discussion of this cultural belief system, albeit based upon trans-Atlantic materials, is Charles Rosenberg's essay, 'The Therapeutic Revolution'. In traditional accounts of disease, 'Just as man's body interacted continuously with his environment, so too did his mind with his body, his morals with his health'. For the persistence of these holistic assumptions well into the nineteenth century, *cf. idem., The Care of Strangers: The Rise of America's Hospital System*, New York: Basic Books, 1987, p. 218.
189. W. Pargeter, *Observations on Maniacal Disorders*, p. 15.
190. W.A.F. Browne, *What Asylums Were, Are, and Ought to Be*, p. 4. Alienists towards the close of the century were still more dismissive: 'What is mind, and how can we explain it? Our answer is, and must ever be, we don't know. And we can never know.' T.B. Hyslop, *Mental Physiology* London: Churchill, 1895, p. 8.
191. G.M. Burrows, *An Inquiry into Certain Errors Relative to Insanity*, p. 7.

Many alienists, however, embraced what initially appeared to be a more intellectually satisfying way of reconciling their predilection for a somatic account of madness with the pressures to adopt psychological forms of treatment – the phrenological system of Gall and Spurzheim.[192] As Roger Cooter has pointed out,[193] the adoption of phrenological doctrine by those engaged in treating insanity is properly seen as overdetermined. Socially, phrenological ideas were of the utmost significance in early nineteenth-century Britain, being linked closely to campaigns for 'penal reform, . . . the provision of scientific education for the working classes, the education of women, the modification of capital punishment laws, and the re-thinking of British colonial policy' as well as 'more enlightened treatment of the insane'.[194] Beyond its symbolic and practical association with reform, however, phrenology was enormously attractive *intellectually*. Gall's and Spurzheim's researches into the anatomical structure of the brain were anything but the work of charlatans, and to many, they appeared to have taken a decisive step towards resolving the enigma of mind – an advance the younger Combe insisted was of direct and immediate *practical* significance. After all, 'If Phrenology is any thing, it is an exposition of the brain, which implicates the integrity of the mental functions'.[195] And from the insights it provided into the structure and functioning of the brain, 'Phrenology gives us a power of acting, and of adapting external circumstances to the exigencies of the case, with a

---

192. John Conolly, Sir William Charles Ellis, Disney Alexander, Richard Poole, David Uwins, William Alexander Francis Browne, and Forbes Winslow, to name but a few of the more prominent, professed themselves converts to phrenology during the 1820s and 1830s. Conolly, Browne, and Poole were particularly active proponents of the doctrine. Spurzheim's *Observations on the Deranged Manifestations of Mind*; Andrew Combe's *Observations on Mental Derangement: Being an Application of the Principles of Phrenology to the Elucidation of the Causes, Symptoms, Nature, and Treatment of Insanity*; and Forbes Winslow's *Principles of Phrenology as Applied to the Elucidation and Cure of Insanity* (London: Highley, 1832) purported to provide direct applications of the doctrine to the treatment of the insane.

193. Roger Cooter, 'Phrenology and British Alienists, ca. 1825–1845', *Medical History* 20, 1976, pp. 1–21, 135–51, reprinted in A. Scull, (ed.), *Madhouses, Mad-doctors, and Madmen: The Social History of Psychiatry in the Victorian Era*, Philadelphia: University of Pennsylvania Press/London: Athlone, 1981, pp. 58–104. See also R. Cooter, *The Cultural Meaning of Popular Science: Phrenology and the Organization of Consent in Nineteenth Century Britain*, Cambridge: Cambridge University Press, 1984; David A. De Giustino, *The Conquest of Mind*; and R.M. Young, *Mind, Brain, and Adaptation*.

194. Steven Shapin, 'Phrenological Knowledge and the Social Structure of Nineteenth Century Edinburgh', *Annals of Science* 32, 1975, pp. 219–43. Compare the claim of George Combe, the great popularizer of Gall's and Spurzheim's ideas, that 'phrenology . . . is peculiarly fitted to throw a powerful light [on] Education, Genius, the Philosophy of Criticism, Criminal Legislation, and Insanity'. [George Combe], *Essays on Phrenology*, Edinburgh: Bell and Bradfute, 1819, pp. 304–6.

195. Andrew Combe to an unknown correspondent, quoted in George Combe, *The Life and Correspondence of Andrew Combe, MD*, Edinburgh: Maclachlan and Stewart, 1850, p. 189.

precision, confidence, and consistency, which it is impossible to obtain in any other way.'[196]

Most valuably of all, phrenology provided a clear physiological account of the operations of the brain, one which permitted a parsimonious explanation of both normal and abnormal mental functioning, and which provided a coherent rationale for the application of *both* medical and moral treatment in cases of insanity. As such, it was enormously attractive to those who sought to assimilate moral treatment into the medical armamentarium, providing 'a language for talking about mental faculties and brain activity simultaneously [and in the process serving] as a linguistic and conceptual bridge in the transition to physicalist views'.[197] As Cooter points out, phrenology's 'neat mechanical view of the brain divided into organs that functioned somewhat analogous with muscles provided a ready and accessible means for comprehending the basis on which the psychological treatment might logically be supposed to operate . . . [:] the disturbed organs were to be suppressed by calling the other mental organs into greater action'.[198]

However useful such accounts of insanity initially proved to be, though, the value of phrenology to those bent on reasserting medicine's claims to jurisdiction over insanity was essentially transitory. By the late 1830s, Gall's system was beginning to lose credibility among serious intellectuals, and shortly thereafter was 'effectively rejected as a scientific system'.[199] Increasingly the province of itinerant head-readers and mountebanks, at whose hands it was being transformed into 'a form of entertainment',[200] phrenology was simply becoming far too dangerous a doctrine to be openly embraced by a profession as marginal as alienism.[201] While its

196. A. Combe, *Observations on Mental Derangement*, p. 353. In particular, 'it gives the physician immense command over such patients when by the examination of the head he can, as generally happens, discover the natural dispositions so accurately as to know what are the probable points of attack in the mental constitution'. *Ibid.*, p. 354. And on a more abstract level, like psychoanalysis a century later, phrenology offered the distinct advantage of appearing to have 'made understandable order out of chaos'. (*Cf.* Nathan Hale, *Freud and the Americans*, New York: Oxford University Press, 1971, p. 48.)

197. R. Smith, *Trial by Medicine*, p. 44. Even craniology, the aspect of phrenology that many found most doubtful from the outset, and which ultimately caused the whole body of doctrine to be ridiculed as a pseudo-science of 'lumps and bumps', was initially attractive to many alienists, offering the (spurious) promise of providing them with an external guide to the nature of the internal pathology they sought to treat.

198. R. Cooter, 'Phrenology and British Alienists', pp. 77–8. As Spurzheim himself summarized the matter, 'Inactivity weakens the functions of the brain, proper exercise strengthens them. . . . It is an essential point, that all faculties which are deranged should be kept inactive, and others exercised.' *Observations on the Deranged Manifestations of the Mind, or Insanity*, pp. 147, 253.

199. Steven Shapin, 'The Politics of Observation: Cerebral Anatomy and Social Interests in the Edinburgh Phrenology Disputes', in R. Wallis (ed.), *On the Margins of Science*, Keele, Staffordshire: Sociological Review Monograph, 27, 1978, p. 142.

200. D. De Giustino, *The Conquest of Mind*, p. 100.

201. Even W.A.F. Browne, perhaps the most active of all alienists in the phrenological cause, found it advisable to suppress all mention of it in the substance of his discussion

erstwhile supporters may have felt that its doctrines were of potentially great utility in anchoring the treatment of madness in medicine,[202] the reputation of the science nonetheless declined further still, until it was little more than 'the object of popular ridicule'.[203]

Before subsiding to the status of a pseudoscience, though, phrenology had indeed lent crucial support to alienists' claims to monopolize the dispensing of medical *and* moral treatment. Instead of arguing (implausibly) for the primacy of traditional therapeutics, it allowed the more perspicacious among them to propose a truce on terms that overwhelmingly favoured the medical cause. Extremists on both sides might argue for the unique value of a moral or a medical approach. But all reasonable men could see that a judicious *combination* of these two therapies was likely to be more valuable than either taken by itself.[204] 'To those acquainted with

in *What Asylums Were, Are, and Ought to Be.* His apostasy drew a sharp rebuke from Andrew Combe:

> I am not aware whether you intend to introduce Phrenology openly as your guide in the investigation and treatment of insanity. In the first sheet there is no allusion to it, and it therefore seems *possible* that you do not mean to notice it. If you really do not, I would strongly advise a contrary course, as due both to the cause of truth and to yourself. . . . It is true, present popularity is gained; but my conviction is, that truth is retarded in the long run.

Andrew Combe to Browne, 28 January 1837, reprinted in George Combe, *The Life and Correspondence of Andrew Combe*, pp. 281–2. In the contest between 'truth' and political expediency, truth continued to lose, however. Despite Browne's private conviction that 'whatever success may have attended my efforts to ameliorate the condition of those confided to my charge . . . I am inclined to attribute to [phrenology]', he continued in public 'to avoid . . . the phraseology of the science'. Browne to A. Combe, 28 January 1845, reprinted as an appendix to A. Combe, *Phrenology: Its Nature and Uses*, Edinburgh: Maclachlan, Stewart, 1846, p. 30; W.A.F. Browne, *What Asylums Were, Are, and Ought to Be*, p. viii.

202. On the persistent attractions of the doctrine among alienists, long past the time it had lost all scientific credibility, *cf.* R. Cooter, 'Phrenology and British Alienists', p. 73.

203. L.S. Jacyna, 'Somatic Theories of Mind and the Interests of Medicine in Britain, 1850–1879', *Medical History* 26, 1982, p. 248.

204. Looking back on the time when the threat to medical control was greatest, Browne commented: 'Benevolence and sympathy suggested and developed, and in my opinion, unfortunately enhanced the employment of moral means, either to the exclusion or to the undue disparagement of physical means, of cure and alleviation. I confess to have aided at one time in this revolution; *which cannot be regarded in any better light than as treason to the principles of our profession*' (Browne, *The Moral Treatment of the Insane: A Lecture*, p. 5, my emphasis). Most doctors who were converts to moral treatment continued to give their primary loyalty to medicine, and so emphasized that medical skill still had a role (e.g., Browne and Ellis). Gardiner Hill did not, and his case provides us with an interesting indication of a profession's response to a heretic from within its own ranks who challenges its competence. Hill had every right to be recognized as one of the outstanding figures of nineteenth-century psychiatry. It was his efforts at Lincoln which showed the feasibility of the total abolition of mechanical restraint. His practical demonstration convinced Conolly, and the latter adopted it at Hanwell, from which it spread to become the reigning orthodoxy in all British asylums. Conolly achieved a high place in the psychiatric historians' pantheon of heroes, and widespread honour in his own time. Hill, within two years of his first success, was forced to resign from his position at Lincoln, assailed over a period of years in the *Lancet* as a charlatan, saw his achievement attributed to Charlesworth, his nominal

the workings of the malady and its peculiar characteristics', said Neville, 'it will be easy to perceive the errors and partial views of such as profess to apply a medicinal agent only, as a specific, or those who advocate a course of moral treatment only for a cure. There is no doubt that a cooperation of medicinal and moral means is requisite to effect a thorough cure.'[205] Now while from one perspective this represented a concession, particularly when compared with earlier emphases on the exclusive value of medicine, the concession was a harmless one. For it left the physician, as the only person who could legitimately dispense the medical side of the treatment, firmly in control.[206] Thus, Neville thought that moral and medical treat-

superior at Lincoln, and remained a perpetually marginal figure in his chosen profession. His response was to write a series of books vindicating his claim and attempting to gain public recognition of his accomplishment, books that, given his isolation, took on an increasingly paranoid tone: Robert Gardiner Hill, *A Lecture on the Management of Lunatic Asylums, and the Treatment of the Insane* (London: Simpkin Marshall, 1839); *A Concise History of the Entire Abolition of Mechanical Restraint in the treatment of the Insane* (London: Longman, Brown, Green, and Longman, 1857); *Lunacy: Its Past and Present* (London: Longman, Green, Reader and Dyer, 1870). The enmity of the medical profession and the venom of the attacks in the leading medical periodical of the time seem puzzling at first sight. But we must remember that, in Browne's words, Hill was a 'traitor' to his profession: from the outset he had insisted that 'in the treatment of the insane, medicine is of little avail, except (of course) when they are suffering from other diseases, to which lunatics as well as sane persons are liable. *Moral treatment with a view to induce habits of self-control, is all and everything*. [In consequence] the use of the lancet, leeches, cupping, glasses, blisters, drastic purgatives, and the practice of shaving the head are totally proscribed in this Asylum [. . .]' (*A Lecture on the Management of Lunatic Asylums*, p. 45, emphasis in the original). When, in the teeth of the interests of the profession, he persisted in this opinion (it was reiterated word for word in *A Concise History of the Entire Abolition of Mechanical Restraint*, p. 72), he was rewarded with ostracism and abuse. For further discussion of Conolly and Hill, see chapter 7 of my *Social Order/Mental Disorder: Anglo-American Psychiatry in Historical Perspective*, Berkeley: University of California Press/London: Routledge, 1989.

205. W.B. Neville, *On Insanity*, p. 14. Compare also N. Bingham, *Observations on . . . Religious Delusions*, esp. pp. 62–3; and David Uwins, *A Treatise on . . . Disorders of the Brain*, p. 81: 'he who rests upon drugs and draughts alone for the cure of [mental] disorder, whether he be a minute homiopathist [*sic*], a sweeping Brunonian, a Boerhaavean humouralist, or a determined empiric, with find himself miserably out in his calculations of efficacy.'

   The shift from an emphasis on the physical etiology and physical treatment of insanity to a stress on the need to combine conventional medical remedies with a 'moral regimen' can be seen very clearly by comparing Thomas Mayo's 1817 text, *Remarks on Insanity* (which sought 'to push into notice the comparatively neglected tribe of physical phenomena [of insanity], to play down the importance of moral treatment, and to emphasize the crucial importance of 'the medical regimen'), with his later treatise on the *Elements of the Pathology of the Human Mind*, London: Murray, 1838 (which exhibits a far stronger emphasis on the 'mental pathology' of insanity and the 'very valuable influence [that] may be obtained over the insane mind' by the judicious employment of the techniques of moral therapy and 'a system of mental discipline'). Having previously denigrated moral remedies, he now contended that physicians needed instruction in 'the mental treatment of a mental disease' because 'this view of the subject . . . is always liable to be neglected in favour of physical treatment founded upon physical views'.

206. The somatic basis of madness also made it plain which class of remedies was the more important: 'indispensable as moral means are, "they are preposterous", as is well observed by Dr Ramsay, "as the sole, or even as the chief remedy of madness, where the cause is of a physical or corporeal nature, as it very frequently is; or, as it always is,

ment could only be carried out 'under the guidance of persons of sound professional education, and mature experience of the disease',[207] while Ellis commented: 'From what has been said on the treatment of the insane in Lunatic Asylums, it will be obvious, that, according to my notions, no-one, except a medical man, and a benevolent one, ought to be entrusted with the management of them.'[208]

And indeed, that was exactly what did happen. By the 1830s almost all the public mental hospitals had a resident medical director. Moreover, the magistrates' committees, which in several instances had been heavily involved in the day-to-day administration of asylums, increasingly left everything to the experts. The Metropolitan Commissioners, not entirely approvingly, commented in 1844 that the pattern at Bedford was being generally emulated, with 'almost the entire control of the County Asylum being delegated to the Medical and General Superintendent'.[209] Similarly, in the private sector, the more reputable private institutions acquired either a medical proprietor or a full-time resident medical superintendent.[210] Symptomatic of medicine's gains in this respect was the appointment of a resident physician to run the York Retreat, where moral treatment had originated, and which, for the first forty-two years of its existence, had had a succession of lay superintendents.[211]

Finally, as the last step in this process, the asylum doctor solved the problem of restricting access to his clientele, and transforming his dominance of the treatment of mental illness into a virtual monopoly, in a typically professional manner, by arranging 'to have himself designated as the expert in such a way as to exclude all other claimants, his designation being official and bureaucratic insofar as it is formally established by

according to the opinion of many learned and able physicians"... . In such cases a reliance on moral regimen were as absurd as a course of logic for the delirium of typhus fever.' Andrew Combe, *Observations on Mental Derangement*, p. 333.

207. W.B. Neville, *On Insanity*, p. 14.

208. W.C. Ellis, *A Treatise on ... Insanity*, p. 314. Compare also W.A.F. Browne, *What Asylums Were, Are, and Ought to Be*, p. 178: 'But to whom, rather than the well-educated physician, is such a sacred and momentous trust to be consigned?'

209. Metropolitan Commissioners in Lunacy, *Report*, 1844, pp. 25–6. The Commissioners were concerned lest the superintendent's power was becoming unduly autocratic: 'We consider that the appointment and dismissal of servants is a trust of great importance, which is vested in the Visiting Justices for the purpose of checking any undue power or influence being used by the superintendent over the servants of the Asylum' (*ibid.*, p. 26). But by the time of their *7th Annual Report*, in 1853, however, the national Commissioners had concluded that such a concentration of power *was* desirable, and that lay interference in all aspects of asylum affairs ought to be kept to a minimum.

210. For example, by 1831, forty-four out of sixty-eight provincial licensed houses were described as having a proprietor with medical or surgical qualifications (Parry-Jones, *The Trade in Lunacy*, p. 78). Among families in the mad-business, many whose fathers had been laymen now obtained medical qualifications. These included the Coxes, the Bakewells, the Finches and the Warburtons.

211. The appointment was of Dr Thurnam, later the first superintendent of the Wiltshire County Asylum at Devizes, and took place in 1838 (J. Thurnam, *Observations and Essays on the Statistics of Insanity*, p. 15).

law'.[212] The Madhouse Act of 1828 introduced the first legal requirements with respect to medical attendance: each asylum had to make arrangements for a doctor to visit the patients at least once a week, and for him to sign a Weekly Register. Where an asylum contained more than a hundred patients, it had to employ a medical superintendent. These requirements were stiffened by the 1845 Lunatics Act, which required, among other things, that all asylums keep a Medical Visitation Book, and a record of the medical treatment of each patient in a Medical Case Book. And from 1846 on, the Lunacy Commissioners, who included a large contingent from the medical profession, manifested a steadily growing hostility to non-medically run asylums. With the help of elite sponsorship, the asylum doctors were now able to drive competing lay people out of the same line of work, and to subordinate those who stayed in the field to their authority. And their position controlling the only legitimate institutions for coping with the mentally ill gave them powerful leverage to discourage any future efforts to enter the field.[213]

212. E. Freidson, *Professional Dominance*, p. 161.
213. Two final points: first, notice that the lay people the asylum doctors had to convert to the recognition of medical expertise, and the elite who sponsored them, weren't at all the same as those they had to persuade/coerce/treat. The upper class shared their universe of discourse; their 'clients' did not. A crucial sociological question arising out of this situation concerns the means by which the experts on insanity maintained their professional authority in the context of the asylum. (See chapter 5) Secondly, what this account has emphasized, and what Freidson has suggested is true for the professions in general, is that when this emerging profession sought to establish its dominance and authority, 'the process determining the outcome was essentially political and social rather than technical in character, a process in which power and persuasive rhetoric were of greater importance than the objective character of the knowledge, training, and work' (Freidson, *Profession of Medicine*, p. 79). For a more elaborate discussion of the processes by which modern professions seek to establishing and maintain jurisdictional claims, *cf.* A. Abbott, *The System of Professions*.

CHAPTER FIVE

Mad-doctors and Magistrates: Psychiatry's Struggle for Professional Autonomy

Half the harm that is done in this world
Is due to people who want to feel important.
They don't mean to do harm – but the harm does not interest them
Because they are involved in the endless struggle
To think well of themselves.

T.S. Eliot, *The Cocktail Party*

1. Problems for the New Profession

By 1845 the medical profession had secured powerful support for the proposition that insanity was a disease, and thus was naturally something which doctors alone were qualified to treat. Medicine's claims had received statutory endorsement in legal requirements which gave it a protected, quasi-monopolistic position in the field, largely through its control of the only legitimate institutions for the insane. For the rest of the century, the asylum doctors were primarily preoccupied with consolidating their position, being particularly concerned to develop and secure a large measure of professional autonomy.

One of the first moves towards the establishment of a distinct identity for this new group of 'experts' was the creation of their own professional organization, the Association of Medical Officers of Asylums and Hospitals for the Insane. Founded in 1841 at the initiative of Samuel Hitch, super-intendent of the Gloucester County Asylum, the Association drew its membership from the medical staff of both public and private asylums. This created problems, since there existed a 'distinct line of demarcation between the medical officers of public asylums and the proprietors of private asylums'[1] – an internal division which reflected their very different

---

1. *Journal of Mental Science* 6, 1860, p. 22. The division reflected wide differences in the social status of most of the patients treated by the two sets of practitioners, and the inevitable divergences of interest and outlook between salaried public employees and private, fee-dependent entrepreneurs.

status and interests.[2] The split hampered moves to unify the profession[3] and, for much of the nineteenth century, diminished the organization's effectiveness.[4]

Temporarily, at least, the Association was further weakened as a weapon in the professionalization process by its failure to publish its own journal – no one being willing to assume the position of editor[5] – for this meant that contacts among the membership were effectively limited to those provided by a single conference once a year.[6] When the first English periodical wholly devoted to the treatment of insanity as a medical specialty appeared, in 1848, it was published completely independently of the Association. Owned and edited by Dr Forbes Winslow, the proprietor of two Metropolitan Licensed Houses, the *Journal of Psychological Medicine and Mental Pathology* not surprisingly exhibited an editorial bias in favour of private asylums. But it was the public sector which was expanding most rapidly by now, and the county asylum superintendents were obtaining a dominant position in the Association. In 1853, the society commenced publication of its own periodical, the *Asylum Journal*, under the editorship of John Charles Bucknill of the Devon County Asylum, providing a vital 'means of vivifying and extending and uniting' a scattered membership, and forming the 'centre of our vitality'.[7]

'Any profession bases its claim for its position on the possession of a skill so esoteric or complex that non-members of the profession cannot perform the work safely or satisfactorily and cannot even evaluate the

2. For early examples of the tensions and antagonism between the two segments of the profession that lurked only just below the surface, see W.A.F. Browne, *What Asylums Were, Are, and Ought to Be*, Edinburgh: Black, 1837, pp. 174–5 (casting aspersions on the proprietors of private madhouses); and Forbes Benignus Winslow, 'Editorial', *Journal of Psychological Medicine and Mental Pathology* 5, 1852, pp. 399–401 (returning the favour).
3. *Cf. Asylum Journal* 9, 15 November 1854, pp. 130–2.
4. As president of the Association, Bucknill urged his colleagues to recognize that 'the welfare of the whole body of medical men practising in lunacy is immediately and indissolubly the same'. ('Presidential Address', *Journal of Mental Science* 7, 1860, p. 22.) But the profession, quite rightly, proved incapable of sustaining this sort of collective delusion. The interests and outlook of the salaried employees of a network of Poor Law institutions were quite sharply divergent from those of the entrepreneurial branch of the profession which catered to the well-to-do and the rich via a loosely articulated group of private asylums; and the divisions within the profession were only further compounded once men like Maudsley, Savage, and Bucknill himself succeeded in carving out consulting practices almost wholly outside the asylum system itself. The disingenuous quality of Bucknill's remark is made transparent by his own later suggestions that private asylums ought to be abolished. See J.C. Bucknill, *The Care of the Insane and their Legal Control*, London: Macmillan, 1880, p. 128 and *idem.*, 'The Abolition of Proprietary Madhouses', *Nineteenth Century* 17, 1885, pp. 263–79; and the response by Hayes Newington of Ticehurst, 'The Abolition of Private Asylums', *Journal of Mental Science* 31, 1885, pp. 138–47.
5. *Asylum Journal* 1, 5 November 1853, p. 3.
6. On the halting and uncertain status of the organization in its early years, *cf. Asylum Journal* 9, 15 November 1854, p. 132, and the comments of John Charles Bucknill in his 'Presidential Address', *Journal of Mental Science* 7, 1860, pp. 4–5.
7. *Ibid.*, (Bucknill) p. 5.

work properly.'[8] Herein lay much of the significance of the appearance of two specialized technical journals on the medical treatment of insanity. For their existence, when coupled with the large number of monographs on the subject which had been published over the previous twenty or thirty years, made it difficult for outsiders to avoid concluding that considerable expertise had already been developed in handling and treating the insane, and that existing knowledge was in the process of being further refined and extended. Both journals lost no opportunity of emphasizing that 'Insanity is purely a disease of the brain. The physician is now the responsible guardian of the lunatic and must ever remain so',[9] a theme which was also prominent in the medical texts which continued to appear on the subject.[10]

In the early part of the century, entry into the ranks of asylum superintendents was largely an unstructured process. Even among the medical men entering the field, few could claim to have had any formal training in the care and cure of the insane; though some had presumably attended lectures on the subject given by Cullen or Morison, while others had relatives already in the business, and thus had some practical experience by way of preparation.[11] As most county asylums opened after a considerable expansion of the private madhouse system had already taken place, a number recruited their first superintendent from those who had had prior experience in the private sector.[12] Others simply installed a local doctor who professed an interest in the job.[13]

In later years, the recruitment pattern changed somewhat, and the means of entry into the profession became more stable and formalized. This was particularly marked in the case of the county asylums, where the distinctive system generally employed contributed to the development of an increasingly isolated specialty. As these asylums grew in size, first one, then a number of assistant physicians were employed by each to ease the burden falling on the medical superintendent. The assistants became,

8. E. Freidson, *Profession of Medicine*, New York: Dodd, Mead, 1970, p. 45.
9. *Journal of Mental Science* 2 October 1858.
10. For an example of a continuing anxiety that, without a strenuous defense of its professional prerogatives, medicine might lose its jurisdiction over insanity, see the comments of Thomas Wakley in *The Lancet*, 13 January 1849.
11. For example, Samuel Glover Bakewell, son of the best-known non-medical madhouse keeper of the early nineteenth century, Thomas Bakewell; Francis Willis, Jr, grandson of the Lincoln divine who had treated George III's madness; and the Newingtons, descendants of the surgeon who had founded the Ticehurst private madhouse in Sussex.
12. For example, William Ellis came from the Hull Refuge to the Wakefield County Asylum; John Thurnam from the York Retreat to the Wiltshire County Asylum; William Charles Hood from Fiddlington Licensed House to the Colney Hatch County Asylum; and John Millar from Bethnal Green Licensed House to the Buckinghamshire County Asylum. However, the traffic flowed in both directions: to mention only some of the more prominent examples, William Ellis, John Conolly, and T.O. Prichard all opened private asylums after a period as superintendent of a county asylum.
13. For example, Harris at Bedford, Storey at Nottingham, Duck in Cornwall, and Prichard at Northampton.

in effect, apprentices, superintendents in training, and it was from this pool of experienced men that most senior positions were filled. In some of the largest asylums, a hierarchical structure emerged in the ranks of the assistants, each step up the ladder bringing increased administrative responsibility and less direct contact with patients.[14] Long years spent in humdrum routine work wore away whatever initiative and independence may once have been present, and ensured the complacent and unimaginative conservativism of those who finally succeeded to a superintendency.[15]

Bucknill and Tuke's claim that by mid-century 'a knowledge of the nature and treatment of Insanity is now expected of every well-educated man' was certainly an exaggeration. Granville was nearer the mark when he asserted that, among most general practitioners of the period, 'The lack of acquaintance with lunacy is extraordinary. The great body of medical men appear to know scarcely more of arrangements and method of treatment adopted in asylums than the general public.'[16] Nevertheless, at least some of those interested in a career as an asylum doctor managed to obtain limited instruction in asylum methods as part of their normal medical training – most commonly through attendance at a course of 'clinical lectures' given annually at St. Luke's Hospital in London. Only a handful of medical students bothered to attend. But for all that, the existence of the course allowed at least some of those applying for positions at asylums to claim that they had received some formal training in the specialty; and

14. As the expansion of the system slowed, so the opportunities for advancement came more rarely. With modest incomes and only slender hopes for promotion, the assistant physician 'sees the best years of his life slipping away from him without any advancement of his interests or improvement in his prospects'. Charles Mercier, *Lunatic Asylums: Their Organization and Management*, London: Griffin, 1894, p. 246. Most of those who could afford to do so left for alternative careers, and those left behind complained that they were undervalued and underappreciated. *Cf.* Dr Dodds, Dr Strahan, and Dr Greenlees, 'Assistant Medical Officers in Asylums: Their Status in the Speciality', *Journal of Mental Science* 36, 1890, pp. 43–50. (Having ruefully compared their situation with that of 'dutiful relatives, most patiently await[ing] the falling in of their estate', the assistants here voice a mounting dissatisfaction over their conditions and prospects. The contrast of 'the fat salaries of the Superintendents with the lean ones of the assistants' had perhaps been bearable 'when the Assistant Medical Officers were few and superintendencies ripened in four or five years, but [their elders' counsel to be patient] loses all its sweet reasonableness when we have to wait ten, twelve, or more years for the golden fruit, and even run the risk of its being plucked by some outsider from over the wall just as we thought it about to drop'.)

15. For some useful discussion of these developments, see Richard Russell, 'The Lunacy Profession and its Staff in the Second Half of the Nineteenth Century, with Special Reference to the West Riding Lunatic Asylum', in W.F. Bynum, R. Porter, and M. Shepherd (eds), *The Anatomy of Madness*, Vol. 3, London: Routledge, 1988, pp. 297–315.

16. J.C. Bucknill and D.H. Tuke, *A Manual of Psychological Medicine*, Philadelphia: Blanchard & Lee, 1858, p. ix; J.M. Granville, *The Care and Cure of the Insane*, Vol. 1, London: Hardwicke & Bogue, 1877, p. 328. Compare also the testimony of Crichton Browne, Harrington Tuke, Balfour, and Bucknill himself before the House of Commons, *Report of the Select Committee on the Operation of the Lunacy Law*, pp. 78, 93, 117, 151–2, all complaining of the ordinary medical man's ignorance about insanity.

the asylum authorities themselves promoted this as one of the important 'benefits conferred upon the community by the hospital. . . .'[17]

The notion that insanity was caused by organic lesions of the brain remained a vital prop for the asylum doctors' contention that it was fundamentally and incontestably a medical problem.[18] Medical jurisdiction and medical prerogatives could only be securely established on this foundation: 'Unless insanity is *a disease*, a disease of the brain affecting the mind, I do not see what we have to do with it more than other people: but if it is a disease, I maintain that we are bound to know more about it than other people.'[19] For this reason, in the words of the leading psychiatric textbook of the age,

> Whatever definition of insanity is adopted by the student, it is all important that he should regard disease as an essential condition; in other words, that insanity is a condition in which the intellectual faculties, or the moral sentiments, or the animal propensities, any one or all of them, have their free action destroyed by disease, whether congenital or acquired. He will not go far wrong if he regards insanity as a disease of the brain.[20]

'It is *certain*', the profession and public were informed, 'that all we know of mental disease is as a symptom, an *expression*, of morbid changes in our bodies. . . .'[21] The psychological symptoms of insanity, though they constituted the visible manifestations of the disorder and the features which provoked social intervention, were, from the medical perspective, purely epiphenomenal,[22] mere surface reflections of the under-

17. St. Luke's Hospital, *Annual Report*, 1886, p. 19.
18. This is not to say that alienists allowed no place for psychological and social factors in the etiology of mental disorder. That they mattered was a commonplace among mad-doctors. But these non-material factors acted only *indirectly*, by producing modifications in the patient's physical constitution. David Yellowlees, 'Presidential Address', *Journal of Mental Science* 36, 1890, p. 475. It was at this point, when the body was implicated, that insanity took hold.
19. David Skae, 'On the Legal Relations of Insanity', *Edinburgh Medical Journal* 12, 1867, p. 813.
20. John Charles Bucknill and Daniel Hack Tuke, *A Manual of Psychological Medicine*, 2nd edn, London: Churchill, 1862, p. 88.
21. W.A.F. Browne, 'The Moral Treatment of the Insane: A Lecture', *Journal of Mental Science* 10, 1864, p. 311, emphasis in the original. Hence 'the absurdity of a pure metaphysician being entrusted with the study of the mind diseased'. *Idem.*, 'On Medico-Psychology', *Journal of Mental Science* 12, 1866, p. 311. The reiterated emphasis is precisely proportional to the flimsiness of the evidentiary basis on which these assertions rested.
22. For further discussion of this point, and an elaboration of its important implications for the late Victorian understanding of and therapy for insanity, see Michael Clark, 'The Rejection of Psychological Approaches to Mental Disorder in Late Nineteenth-Century British Psychiatry', in A. Scull (ed.), *Madhouses, Mad-doctors, and Madmen: The Social History of Psychiatry in the Victorian Era*, Philadelphia: University of Pennsylvania Press/ London: Athlone, 1981, pp. 271–312.

lying morbid state of the brain and nervous system: mental disorders are 'neither more nor less than nervous diseases in which mental symptoms predominate . . .';[23] and 'psychical symptoms are to medical men only signs of what is wrong in a material system'.[24] For this reason,

> It is not our business, it is not in our power, to explain *psychologically* the origins and nature of any of [the] depraved instincts [manifested in typical cases of insanity] . . . it is sufficient to establish their existence as facts of observation, and to set forth the pathological conditions under which they are produced: they are the facts of pathology, which should be observed and classified like other phenomena of disease. The explanation, when it comes, will come not from the mental, but from the physical side – from the study of the *neurosis* [the brain and nervous system], not from the analysis of the psychosis.[25]

The insistence on the material basis of madness was in no sense novel, of course, but it was given a new plausibility by tying it to recent advances in neurophysiology. During the 1830s and 1840s, largely circumstantial and inferential accounts of the nervous system had been increasingly replaced, as a result of the researches of men like Marshall Hall, Thomas Laycock, and Johannes Müller,[26] by more elaborate conceptions of reflex physiology grounded in experimental evidence. Borrowing and modifying

23. Henry Maudsley, *Body and Mind* London: Macmillan, 1870, p. 41. In cases of mental derangement, 'a part of the man as material as his liver is unhinged, and . . . , like his liver, it is the seat of some morbid action, and just as much a subject for medical treatment'. John Arlidge, 'Review of *An Examination of the Practice of Bloodletting* by Pliny Earle', *Journal of Mental Science* 2, 1856, p. 168.
24. John Hughlings Jackson, *Selected Writings*, Vol. 1, London: Hodder and Stoughton, 1931, p. 452. Even with respect to causation, the role of non-somatic factors was increasingly deprecated. Browne, for instance, claimed that 'the influence of moral causes in inducing derangement is not doubted; but these act by and through the physical changes or conditions of which the moral phenomena are the consequences and symptoms'. Crichton Royal Asylum, *16th Annual Report*, 1855, p. 10. Others were prepared to grant a marginally more significant role to psychological factors, but in the last analysis were every bit as insistent on the primacy of the physical: 'insanity often begins in mental conditions which at first may be perfectly sane and normal, but by undue continuance or undue intensity they establish grooves of thought so deep as to create a disturbance or perversion of normal brain activity, which in times becomes truly morbid.' David Yellowlees, 'Presidential Address', p. 475. Though experience indicated that 'nervous structure may be as much injured by a means as impalpable as a thought, as it would be by a blow', the crucial fact remained that 'No one goes mad until his brain is injured. . . .' Henry Monro, 'On the Nomenclature of the Various Forms of Insanity', *Journal of Mental Science* 2, 1856, p. 295.
25. Henry Maudsley, *Responsibility in Mental Disease*, 2nd edn, London: Kegan Paul, 1874, p. 154, emphasis in the original.
26. See, for instance, Marshall Hall, *Memoirs on the Nervous System*, London: Sherwood, Gilbert, and Piper, 1837; Thomas Laycock, *A Treatise on the Nervous Diseases of Women*, London: Longman, Orme, Brown, Green and Longmans, 1840; *idem.*, 'Reflex, Automatic, and Unconscious Cerebration: A History and Criticism', *Journal of Mental Science* 21, 1876, pp. 477–98, and 22, 1876, pp. 1–17; Johannes Müller, *Elements of Physiology*, 2 vols, London: Taylor and Walton, 1839–42.

the concept of reflex action, alienists in the 1850s and 1860s increasingly portrayed insanity as the result of the breakdown of the inhibitory power of higher levels of the nervous system, a failure which produced 'regression to lower, more automatic modes of mental action'.[27] Even in the early nineteenth century, alienists had pointed to defective heredity as an important etiological factor, predisposing the vulnerable to madness;[28] but hereditarian explanations of the origins of defective inhibitory control now acquired a new force and significance, particularly from the 1860s onwards, when they were reformulated in the language of degeneration.[29]

Over time, the metaphors that linked the organic with the symptomatic manifestations of madness were periodically reworked to keep psychiatric language in plausible correspondence with the reigning models of the somatic machine which characterized the medical mainstream. As an emphasis on cellular pathology gained ground in medicine at large, so alienists emphasized that the brain cells were 'the agents of all that is called mind'.[30] During the 1850s and 1860s, the brain was increasingly pictured as 'secreting' thought, in an essentially glandular fashion, and its inflammation, brought about by hypothetical disorders of the vascular system, was seen as an especially likely cause of insanity.[31] Underlying

27. M. Clark, 'The Rejection of Psychological Approaches to Mental Disorder', p. 275. On the uses of reflex theory and neurophysiology more generally to construct accounts of insanity, see the discussions in L.S. Jacyna, 'Somatic Theories of Mind and the Interests of Medicine in Britain, 1850–79', *Medical History* 26, 1982, pp. 233–58; and Roger Smith, *Trial by Medicine: Insanity and Responsibility in Victorian Trials*, Edinburgh: Edinburgh University Press, 1981, *passim*, esp., pp. 45–8.

28. See, for example, George Man Burrows, *Commentaries on the Causes . . . of Insanity* London: Underwood, 1828, pp. 101–2; Thomas Laycock, *A Treatise on the Nervous Diseases of Women*, pp. 137–9; Andrew Combe, *Observations on Mental Derangement*, Edinburgh: Anderson, 1831, p. 91.

29. Degenerationist ideas were first given cogent form in Benedict Augustin Morel, *Traité des dégénérescences*, Paris: Masson, 1857. On the spread and the sources of the appeal of the theory of morbid heredity and degeneration in France, see Ian Dowbiggin, 'Degeneration and Hereditarianism in French Mental Medicine 1840–90', in W.F. Bynum, R. Porter, and M. Shepherd (eds), *The Anatomy of Madness*, Vol. 1, London: Tavistock, 1985, pp. 188–232; I. Dowbiggin, 'French Psychiatry, Hereditarianism, and Professional Legitimacy 1840–1900', *Research in Law, Deviance, and Social Control* 7, 1985, pp. 135–65; Robert A. Nye, *Crime, Madness, and Politics in Modern France*, Princeton: Princeton University Press, 1984, pp. 121–4; and Robert Castel, *The Regulation of Madness*, Berkeley: University of California Press, 1988, pp. 227–33. Morel's ideas were immediately transmitted to and taken up by British alienists, notably through an anonymous review article, 'On the Degeneration of the Human Race', which appeared in the *Journal of Psychological Medicine* 10, 1857, pp. 159–208. For the subsequent theoretical elaboration of degenerationist ideas in England, see Michael Clark, ' "The Data of Alienism": Evolutionary Neurology, Physiological Psychology, and the Reconstruction of British Psychiatric Theory, *c.* 1850–*c.* 1900,' unpublished D.Phil. dissertation, Oxford University, 1982, pp. 158–72; and Janet Oppenheim, *'Shattered Nerves': Doctors, Patients, and Depression in Victorian England*, New York: Oxford University Press, 1991, chapter 8. I discuss the significance of the rise of degenerationist accounts of insanity for English psychiatry in chapter 6.

30. J.C. Bucknill and D.H. Tuke, *A Manual of Psychological Medicine*, 2nd edn, p. 385.

31. *Cf.* the discussion in L.S. Jacyna, 'Somatic Theories of Mind', pp. 241–2.

these changes was a shift from an earlier dualistic model of mind and brain to the new doctrine of a strict psycho-physical parallelism, of which the neurologist John Hughlings Jackson was the most notable exponent.[32]

The stress on the material and the claim to be developing a 'mental physiology'[33] or a 'physiological psychology'[34] corresponded to the increased emphasis within mainstream Victorian medicine, and in science more generally, on 'scientific naturalism'.[35] Simultaneously, it represented an attempt by alienists to assimilate their theorizing to the received ideas about what constituted scientific explanation, and to appropriate for themselves some of the growing cultural authority of science. But such assimilation took place primarily at the level of rhetoric, and, even here, 'medical aetiology was strikingly incoherent in its language of mind and body'.[36] In reality, the links between physicalist theorizing and alienists' practice were tenuous in the extreme, with their pathological theories bearing little discernible relationship to the therapeutic techniques they employed.[37] More importantly, as Jacyna has demonstrated, these artfully constructed verbal connections masked a huge gap between scientific pretensions and reality. The use of reflex theory was crude and casual. What masqueraded as inferences from the latest developments in neurology were in fact simply the restatement of 'old doctrines in a novel idiom'. And beneath 'the thin veneer of modernity', and for all the references to reflex theory, microscopic analysis, cell theory, and the intimate structure of the nervous system, even their theorizing exhibited 'a substantial continuity with earlier physicalist aetiologies of madness'.[38]

Among Victorian alienists, the somatic basis of insanity was a proposition not intelligibly subject to doubt, for to question it was to challenge

32. In Jackson's words, 'Sensori-motor processes are the physical side of, or, as I prefer to say, form the anatomical substrata of, mental states. It is with these substrata only that we, in our character as physicians, are directly concerned.' *Selected Writings*, Vol. 1, London: Staples, 1958, p. 49.
33. Sir Henry Holland *Chapters on Mental Physiology*, 2nd edn, London: Longmans, 1858.
34. Robert Dunn *An Essay on Physiological Psychology*, London: Churchill, 1858.
35. *Cf.* M. Clark, 'The Rejection of Psychological Approaches to Mental Disorder', pp. 277–8; on physiological psychology and the growth of scientific naturalism, see, in addition to the secondary literature cited above, Roger Smith, 'Physiological Psychology and the Philosophy of Nature in Mid-Nineteenth-Century Britain', unpublished Ph.D. dissertation, Cambridge University, 1970; L.S. Jacyna, 'Scientific Naturalism in Victorian Britain: An Essay in the Social History of Ideas', unpublished Ph.D. dissertation, Edinburgh University, 1980; and M. Clark, 'The Data of Alienism.'
36. R. Smith, *Trial by Medicine*, p. 43.
37. *Ibid.*, pp. 59–60; L.S. Jacyna, 'Somatic Theories of Mind', pp. 245–6. As Smith points out, Bucknill and Tuke's *A Manual of Psychological Medicine* has wholly separate sections on the diagnosis and the pathology of insanity, the one cast in psychological, the other in physical language. Practice and theory are entirely separate, and physicalism is simply irrelevant to the former.
38. L.S. Jacyna, 'Somatic Theories of Mind', pp. 241, 244, 248, 258. Thus complaints like Wakley's, that Morison's 'physiological account of the brain and nerves [is]...an unnecessary chapter, since it is but the rudest sketch of what is known' (*The Lancet* 9 February 1849, 2, p. 141), were simply beside the point.

their claims to objectivity and to scientific status, the very basis of their privileged and authoritative role in the diagnosis and disposition of the lunatic.[39] The contrary view that insanity was 'a spiritual malady – a functional disease . . . an affection of the immaterial essence . . . a disorder of the soul and not simply the result of the derangement of the material instrument of the mind interfering with the healthy action of its manifestations . . . naturally led to the conclusion – false in theory and destructive in practice – that for the alleviation and cure of this spiritual malady, spiritual remedies were the most important and essential'.[40] Such contentions were 'at variance with all a priori and a posteriori reasoning', and would suggest 'the clergyman rather than the physician as the logical person to treat insanity'. They gave 'force and longevity to the idea that the administration of physical agents is of little or no avail in the treatment of the disorders of the mind'.[41] Yet on the contrary, the best medical knowledge indicated that 'a system of cerebral pathology' must be built upon 'the physiological principle . . . that mental health is dependent upon the due nutrition, stimulation and repose of the brain; that is, upon the conditions of exhaustion and reparation of its nerve substance being maintained in a healthy and regular state; and that mental disease results from the interruption or disturbance of these conditions'.[42] Those who refused to acknowledge insanity's somatic basis threatened 'to reverse medical progress, and to stop all the large advance in mental science made of late years'[43] – all in the quixotic pursuit of 'a phantom of the mind – a pathological enigma, having no actual existence apart from the actual imagination which gave it birth'.[44]

The difficulty which all this strong language was designed to gloss over was that no evidence could in fact be produced to show that insanity had a somatic origin. Bucknill and Tuke conceded as much: 'A rational pathology must ever be founded upon the basis of physiology. . . . In all the organs of the body, except the brain, great advances have been made in the knowledge of their physiological laws. . . . But it is quite otherwise with the noble organ which lords it over the rest of the body.'[45] Here, the most

39. As Forbes Winslow put it, 'No mind can properly be considered to be "unsound" or "insane" which is not subject to actual disease, the "insanity" or "unsoundness" being invariably the products – the effects – the consequences, of some deviation from the healthy condition of the brain, its vessels, or investments, disordering the mental manifestations.' *Lettisomian Lectures on Insanity*, London: Churchill, 1854, p. 144.
40. *Ibid.*, p. 50.
41. *Ibid.*, pp. 50–1.
42. J.C. Bucknill and D.H. Tuke, *A Manual of Psychological Medicine*, p. 342, emphasis in the original.
43. Thomas Laycock, 'The Antagonism of Law and Medicine in Insanity, and its Consequences', *Journal of Mental Science* 8, 1863, p. 597.
44. F. Winslow, *Lettisomian Lectures on Insanity*, p. 51.
45. J.C. Bucknill and D.H. Tuke, *A Manual of Psychological Medicine*, p. 341. The difficulty, as Andrew Wynter ruefully acknowledged, was acute. It was not just that, 'in the vast majority of the brains of the insane, when examined after death, [pathologists could detect] no appreciable sign of change – nay, the brain has suffered very severe injuries,

diligent investigation could produce no positive evidence in support of the somatic hypothesis.[46] Nevertheless, this did not prevent confident assertions being made that 'Insanity never exists without a physical cause . . . whence it seems to follow that physical agents ought to be resorted to in the first instance, as the means of restoring the healthy and natural state.'[47] The public was assured that 'Daily experience confirms the opinion that Insanity is a disease, and as such, that it is essential that appropriate remedies should be prescribed for each case, and this is the reason why the duties of dispensing medicines have become more onerous' for asylum superintendents.[48]

As this suggests, a corollary of the consistent efforts to emphasize that insanity was produced by a physical pathology was the widespread predilection or bias among asylum doctors in favour of physical treatment or 'remedies'. To an important extent, that is, psychiatry derived not just its mandate, but also its therapeutics from its metaphysical embrace of the body. Henry Maudsley articulated the logic of this position with characteristic bluntness: 'That which . . . has its foundation in a definite physical cause must have its cure in the production of a definite physical change.'[49] The alternative could be speedily (and of course scornfully) dismissed:

and yet been followed by no symptoms of mental disturbance'. He hastened to emphasize, however, that these findings simply showed that 'The changes that take place physically are of too delicate a nature for our science to reach in its present condition.' The public must nonetheless be brought to realize that 'The more the fact of the physical nature of insanity is acknowledged, the more it is recognized as an ailment, which can be reached by physical agents, the greater will be the chance of its successful treatment.' *The Borderlands of Insanity*, 1st edn, London: Hardwicke, 1875, pp. 14–5.

46. The situation was little better as the century drew to a close. In the words of David Ferrier, Professor of Neuropathology at Kings College Hospital, one of the four founding editors of *Brain*, and among the most distinguished Victorian students of the physiology of the brain: 'Much has been written on the symptomology and classification of the various forms of insanity; but I think we really know nothing whatever with regard to the physical conditions underlying those manifestations. Until we are able to correlate mental disorders with their physical substrata, and this we are very far from being able to do, we cannot be said to possess any real knowledge on the subject.' So far from the materialist hypothesis being securely established, he was reduced to urging 'the most minute examination of every region and tissue of the brain, with a view to discover, if possible, the organic foundations of the morbid manifestations characteristic of insanity in its various forms'. Quoted in H.C. Burdett, *Hospitals and Asylums of the World*, Vol. 2, London: Churchill, 1891, pp. 186, 230. Compare also Henry Maudsley's admission that 'The morbid anatomy of insanity would take little room were speculation rigidly excluded and it limited to what is actually seen and known. Nor does that which is seen, it must be confessed, throw much light on the symptoms. . . . The intimate chemical and molecular changes which are presumably the conditions of mental disorder go on in a domain of nature the subtleties of which far exceed the subtleties of observation.' Quoted in Aubrey Lewis, 'Henry Maudsley: His Work and Influence', *Journal of Mental Science* 97, 1951, reprinted in his *The State of Psychiatry: Essays and Addresses*, London: Routledge and Kegan Paul, 1967, p. 42.

47. Commissioners in Lunacy, *2nd Annual Report*, 1847, p. 229. This passage forms part of a summary of contemporary medical opinion which was derived from a questionnaire the Commissioners had sent to all asylum superintendents.

48. St. Luke's Asylum, *Annual Report*, 1854, p. 9.

49. Henry Maudsley, *The Physiology and Pathology of Mind*, London: Macmillan, 1867, p. 83.

No culture of the mind, however careful, no effort of will, however strong, will avail to prevent irregular and convulsive action when a certain degree of instability of nervous element has, from one cause or another, been produced in the spinal cells. It would be equally absurd to preach control to the spasms of chorea, or restraint to the convulsions of epilepsy, as to preach moderation to the east wind, or gentleness to the hurricane.[50]

This should not be taken to imply, though, that there was agreement as to the particular treatment to be adopted in any given case, or even as to the value of any one agent in countering mental disturbance, for there was not.

Both the emphasis on the value of conventional medical treatment and the disagreement as to which particular procedures were in fact effective were evident when the Commissioners in Lunacy sought to obtain a representative sampling of professional opinion on the treatment of insanity for their 1847 Report. There was, it is true, nearly unanimous condemnation of the use of massive general blood-letting in cases of mania; but while some condemned local bleeding with leeches as harmful or useless, many others testified to its great value.[51] Emetics and purgatives were endorsed by practically everyone, though with sharp disagreements as to when they should be employed, and wide variations in the degree of enthusiasm displayed. The use of opium had formerly been held to be injurious: 'This is now looked upon as prejudice by many of the most experienced physicians' – though not by others – and it was used to calm excited patients.[52] The profession was similarly unable to reach a consensus over the treatment of melancholia. 'Most of the medical officers who had given us an account of their practices in this form of mental disorder, seem to agree in directing their attention to the state of the alimentary canal, and the organs subservient to the digestive functions, and to be of the opinion that in cases of Melancholia the primary cause is to be sought in some derangement there seated.'[53] Again, however, there were others who dissented, and who alleged that the problem lay with 'the vascular system of the brain'.[54] General paralysis and epilepsy were widely regarded as incurable, but where efforts were made to treat cases, recourse was had to 'the usual physical remedies'. The following is typical: 'Dr Tyerman had tried shaving the head, blisters to the nape or vertex, occasional local depletion, once arteriotomy, calomel followed by purga-

---

50. *Ibid.*, p. 83. Compare also W.A.F. Browne: 'We know it as a physiological truth that we cannot reach the mind even when employing purely *psychical* means, when bringing mind to act on mind, except through material organs.' 'Moral Treatment', p. 311.
51. Commissioners in Lunacy, *2nd Annual Report*, 1847, pp. 180–6.
52. *Ibid.*, p. 189.
53. *Ibid.*, p. 204.
54. *Ibid.*

tives, hot and cold shower baths during severe paroxysms, tonics' – none with particularly happy results.[55]

Indeed, it was on the question of results that the asylum doctors' claims as to the efficacy of medicine proved most difficult to sustain. The enthusiasm of many physicians for the type of remedies they employed against other forms of disease cannot be doubted. At St. Luke's, for instance, the superintendent boasted that 'The average number of curable cases . . . has been during the last year 87; the number of prescriptions dispensed has been 6,846 during the year – a proof that our faith in medicine as a most efficient means of treatment has not been shaken.'[56] But the demonstrated inability of a policy of active medical intervention to produce recoveries amounting to more than a fraction of each year's admissions soon forced a more sober assessment of the value of existing somatic treatments. Little more than ten years after the establishment of county asylums on a compulsory basis, the publication of what was to be the standard medical text on insanity contained the admission that 'In the chronic stages of insanity active remedies are rarely admissible, except to obviate some intercurrent condition, which produces too much disturbance and danger to be permitted to run a natural course and wear itself out. In recent insanity, with symptoms of physical disturbance of little violence and urgency, active medicinal treatment may oftentimes be dispensed with.'[57] So that in what amounted to the overwhelming majority of cases admitted to asylums, it was conceded that 'any active medicinal interference is more likely to do harm than good'.[58]

For most asylum doctors, the acknowledged failure of this generation of medical treatments to sustain the hopes the profession had originally entertained produced, not an abandonment of their conviction as to medicine's value in curing insanity, but rather a search for new somatic remedies which would give more plausible substance to the claim. The problem, it was concluded, must lie in the administration of the wrong remedies or of the right remedies in the wrong way, and not in the nature of the undertaking itself. In an almost haphazard fashion, a veritable plethora of drugs and medical techniques was enlisted in the battle against insanity. 'Hypodermic injections of morphia, the administration of the bromides, chloral hydrate, hyoscine, physostigma, cannabis indica, amyl nitrate, conium, digitalis, ergot, pilocarpine, the application of electricity, the use of the turkish bath and the wet pack, and other remedies too

55. *Ibid.*, p. 213. On the persistent inability of the profession to agree on the relative merits of particular remedies, see D.H. Tuke, *Chapters in the History of the Insane in the British Isles*, London: Kegan Paul & Trench, 1882, pp. 485–7.
56. St. Luke's Hospital, *Annual Report*, 1853, p. 11.
57. J.C. Bucknill and D.H. Tuke *A Manual of Psychological Medicine*, Philadelphia: Blanchard and Lee, 1858, p. 481.
58. *Ibid.*, p. 482.

numerous to mention, have had their strenuous advocates during late years.'[59]

'Perhaps the fundamental reason for physical treatments, whatever their later rationale, [was that] without them doctors would have had no lever with which to operate on diseases of the mind. . . .'[60] Given the gap between their claims and their capacities, 'doctors could not afford not to try anything that was ever reported to have achieved results'.[61] Yet although the advocates of conventional medical treatment neglected nothing in their contemporary medical armamentarium, they discovered nothing which worked. Quite clearly, 'If the success of the treatment of insanity bore any considerable proportion to the number of remedies which have been brought forward, it would be my easy and agreeable duty to record the triumphs of medicine in the distressing malady which they are employed to combat. But this, unhappily, is not the case . . . each remedy . . . failing to fulfil all the hopes raised on its first trial.'[62] The medical remedies first suggested had proved almost wholly ineffective, and unfortunately, 'there are no new remedies or modes of relief which can be recommended with confidence'.[63] As a practical matter, therefore, asylum superintendents were forced to fall back on their one remaining claim to expertise, their knowledge of moral treatment (which by now meant little more than the efficient management of large numbers of inmates).

2. Managers of the Mad

All this left the asylum doctors in a distinctly vulnerable position. Their legal monopoly over the treatment of madness had been justified by contending that insanity was a disorder of the body, an assertion for which alienists remained unable to produce empirical and inter-subjectively verifiable evidence that could satisfy themselves – let alone an audience of disinterested outsiders. Although they had successfully appropriated moral treatment, it was difficult to disguise its failure in their hands to produce the cures they had promised. Periodically, too, their diagnostic acumen was impeached by embarrassing and well-publicized intra-professional squabbles over the mental status of particular individuals. Granted, as the only people with experience in dealing with large masses of crazy people in an institutional environment, they had developed certain empirically derived skills in managing asylums. Still, even in the

59. D.H. Tuke, *Chapters in the History of the Insane*, p. 485.
60. Richard Hunter and Ida MacAlpine, *Three Hundred Years of Psychiatry*, London: Oxford University Press, 1963, p. 743.
61. *Ibid.*
62. D.H. Tuke *Chapters in the History of the Insane*, p. 485.
63. J.M. Granville, *The Care and Cure of the Insane*, Vol. 2, London: Hardwicke and Bogue, 1877, p. 112.

closing decades of the nineteenth century, large claims to expertize and insight continued to rest on remarkably slender foundations.

It remains an open question, however, how far the asylum doctors' inability to translate their claimed expertize into tangible results undermined either their authority over the asylum or their capacity to sustain a viable degree of professional autonomy. By the Acts of 1828 and 1845, the medical profession had acquired a virtually exclusive right to direct the treatment of the insane, and thereafter, its concern became one of maintaining, rather than obtaining, a monopolistic position. The profession's control of asylums, the only legitimate institutions for the treatment of insanity, effectively shut out all potential competitors, for the latter would have had to oppose unsubstantiated claims to demonstrated performance. Furthermore, the asylum doctors' institutional base gave them a powerful leverage for getting the community to utilize their services (thereby indirectly supporting their professional authority), quite apart from whether those doing so were convinced of their competence. For while employment of the asylum by the relatives of 'crazy' people or by local Poor Law authorities did not necessarily reflect acceptance of the superintendent's claims or his esoteric definition of what was 'really' wrong with the troublesome people they sent him, their ready use of his services unavoidably added to the aura of legitimacy surrounding his activities. So long as his services were in such demand, it was difficult to avoid concluding that he was performing a useful and valuable task for the community.

If the attractions of a convenient institution in which to dump the troublesome and undesirable sufficed to ensure at least the passive acquiescence of the asylum doctors' true clients, the families and parish officials, in their continued existence, their nominal clients, the asylum's inmates, had little choice but to cooperate in sustaining their definition of the situation. Freidson has argued that, for the profession of medicine as a whole, 'a significant monopoly could not occur until a secure and practical technology of work was developed'. In essence this was because doctors could not force clients to come to them, they had to attract them. It was as well, therefore, that because of the peculiar structural characteristics of their practice, psychiatrists formed an exception to this generalization. Once they had secured control over asylums, they no longer had to attract clients – the institution did that for them. And once patients were obtained, they formed literally a captive audience held in a context which gave immense power to their captors. Consequently, psychiatry was able, like the scholarly professions, to 'survive solely by gaining the interest and patronage of a special, powerful sponsor without having to gain general lay confidence'.[64]

It was fortunate, as well, that the psychiatric profession's inability to produce significant numbers of cures was of only slight concern to their

64. E. Freidson, *Profession of Medicine*, pp. 21–2.

sponsors. For there had emerged a widespread consensus among local and national elites on the value of a custodial operation, so that the impact of occasional grumbling about the asylum doctors' performance was muted, and the sort of sustained criticism which might have undermined their position simply failed to materialize. Bucknill urged his colleagues to recognize the debt they owed the Lunacy Commissioners on this score: whatever differences of opinion might exist on other matters, 'on the large and broad principle of action, which may be expressed as the supremacy of the medical man in the treatment of the insane', they had consistently lined up on the correct side. 'Individually and collectively, we owe the Commissioners a debt of gratitude on this score [, otherwise] we might still have seen county asylums under the management of lay governors, the former masters of union [work]houses or men promoted from the ranks of attendants.'[65] Perhaps this overstated the case to flatter the Commission, since the ability (or inability) to produce cures by no means exhausted the asylum doctors' usefulness. They were, after all, no worse than anyone else as administrators, and their medical skills were useful in ministering to the numerous physical ailments of the decrepit specimens the asylums were continuously receiving. And by sustaining the illusion that asylums were medical institutions, they placed a humanitarian and scientific gloss on the community's behaviour, legitimizing the removal of difficult and troublesome people whose confinement would have been awkward to justify on other grounds.

However, if there was little reason for the authorities to revoke the monopoly they had originally granted to the asylum doctors, there were also slender grounds for granting them the kind of autonomy which ordinarily goes with professional status. The best medical opinion conceded that 'Ordinary medicines, which are the principal remedies for disease of the body, are only exceptional and accidental agents in the treatment of disease of the mind.'[66] And the low cure rates characteristic of the asylum system as a whole rendered implausible the claim that psychiatrists possessed even non-pharmaceutical remedies with any real efficacy.

In this situation,

> magistrates, like other mortals, have had their convictions strengthened, that medical superintendents, considered in their professional capacity, are rather ornamental than essential members of an asylum staff; very well in their way in cases of casual sickness or injury, useful to legalize the exit of the inmates from the world, and not bad scape-goats in misadventures and unpleasant investigations into the management, and

65. J.C. Bucknill, 'Presidential Address', p. 20.
66. J.M. Granville, *The Care and Cure of the Insane*, Vol. 1, p. 76.

in general not worse administrators . . . than would be members of most other occupations and professions.[67]

The magistrates on asylum committees were in sufficiently close and frequent contact with the routine practices in these institutions that they could scarcely avoid the perception that 'the medical superintendent of most English asylums is simply an overseer or onlooker, and his place might be filled by a layman of moderate intelligence, did not the law require medical qualifications, and did not accidents and emergencies arise in such establishments for which medical skill is called in requisition.'[68] From quite an early period in the history of the county asylums, there were complaints from the superintendents of their employers' 'forgetfulness that insanity is a disease, and their consequent want of due appreciation of medical science in its treatment'.[69]

Legally speaking, the superintendents of county and borough asylums were merely the salaried employees of individual asylum committees, each of which consisted of a group of magistrates chosen for the task at the local General Quarter Sessions. These laymen could, if they so chose, issue detailed directives as to the conduct of the institution, and could, if necessary, enforce their views by using their power to dismiss a superintendent without further appeal at any time. A few extraordinarily energetic committees actually exercised their enormous discretionary powers, and were heavily involved in the routine governance of 'their' asylums. Most, however, did not go to these lengths, satisfying themselves with laying down general guidelines as to the conduct of the institution. Having control over the key area of finance, they were content to leave the more mundane matters in the hands of their presumably capable subordinate, subject always to his rendering an annual account of his discharge of that trust, and to their own periodic tours of inspection.

Where the conduct of their underlings did not satisfy them, committees did not hesitate to invoke their authority to dismiss them, even over the objections of professional colleagues and of the Commissioners in Lunacy. Not surprisingly, the Association of Medical Officers of Asylums and Hospitals for the Insane proved acutely sensitive about this power of arbitrary dismissal. One case it fought particularly hard was John Millar's dismissal as head of the Buckinghamshire County Asylum in 1856.

Millar was widely regarded as a competent superintendent and possessed a high professional reputation. Even the magistrates who discharged him conceded that in previous years, 'Mr Millar possessed the general confidence of successive committees',[70] and the records for this period show

67. J.T. Arlidge, *On the State of Lunacy and the Legal Provision for the Insane*, London: Churchill, 1859, p. 104.
68. Sir James Clark, *Memoir of John Conolly*, London: Murray, 1869, p. 233.
69. *Asylum Journal* 1, 15 November 1853, p. 6.
70. Buckinghamshire County Asylum, *Annual Report*, 1857, p. 3.

that his skill had frequently been commended both by his employers and by the Commissioners in Lunacy. However, following the emigration of his chief supporter, Mr Carrington, who had served as chairman of the magistrates' committee, he abruptly lost the support of the remaining magistrates, and was dismissed, ostensibly on the grounds of vague charges of maladministration.[71]

Millar refused to concede defeat. He published a pamphlet on his own behalf, and obtained the intervention of the Association of which he was a member. John Hitchman, superintendent of the Derbyshire County Asylum and the Association's president, began by sending a letter in his official capacity inquiring into the Committee's reasons for its decision. The response was a curt note indicating that 'the Committee do not recognize the authority of any such constituted Association to submit to them the questions your letter . . . contained'. In an effort to bring further pressure to bear, the Association drew up a letter and secured the signatures of eighty-six doctors, including the major figures in contemporary English psychiatry – men like Daniel Hack Tuke, John Charles Bucknill, and John Conolly.[72] This was then extensively circulated to all the leading people in the county, the signatories complaining that 'This dismissal has been the occasion of alarm and profound discouragement to the medical men who have charge of fifteen thousand of the insane poor of this kingdom', and deploring the likely effects on the quality of men attracted to the field were this 'ignominious dismissal' upheld.

The Commissioners in Lunacy added their regrets 'that the Institution is about to lose the services of Mr Millar to whom the present creditable state of the patients is, in our opinion, mainly due'.[73] But the Committee simply stood its ground, and lacking any sanctions with which to force a change of mind, the Association and Millar himself were forced to concede defeat. In this, as in other similar cases,[74] the asylum doctors were simply unable to establish themselves as *the prime source of the criteria that qualify a man to work in an acceptable fashion*.[75] Thus, in an important sense, psychiatry, at least in the public sphere, still lacked one of the crucial appurtenances of a profession. It remained an isolated specialty, with only superficial ties with the rest of the medical enterprise. And while the asylum doctors' class origins and medical training prevented such

---

71. For a discussion of the events surrounding Millar's dismissal, see John Crammer, *Asylum History: Buckinghamshire County Pauper Lunatic Asylum – St. John's*, London: Gaskell, 1990, pp. 47–53. I shall suggest in chapter 6 that a major factor in his departure was probably pressure from cost-conscious Poor Law officials.

72. All this correspondence is reproduced in the Buckinghamshire County Asylum, *Annual Report*, 1857.

73. *Ibid.*, p. 34.

74. For protests against the dismissal of the medical officer of the Norfolk County Asylum, see *Asylum Journal* 7, 15 August 1854, pp. 99–102. For the discharging of Dr Millson, the first superintendent of the Northampton County Asylum, see chapter 6.

75. E. Freidson, *Profession of Medicine*, p. 10, emphasis in the original.

developments being carried to an extreme, both their salaries and their prestige remained conspicuously low.[76]

The superintendents' working conditions contributed to this isolation. Almost all of them were lodged either in special quarters in the main asylum buildings, or, more typically, in a house built for them in the grounds; and their manifold duties ensured that they ventured beyond the asylum walls scarcely more frequently than their patients. This physical and social segregation was encouraged by (one might almost say enforced by) their employers, who adhered to the recommendation made by the Lunacy Commissioners that the asylum doctor should 'be precluded from private Practice, and should devote his whole time and Energies to the Duties of his Office'.[77] Indeed, his administrative burdens were so heavy as to make the asylum almost a self-contained world, wherein

> the medical officer is especially prompted – if he wish to stand well with the Committee – to develop the moral management and domestic economy to the utmost; to exhibit well-kept wards, well-clothed and well-fed patients, well-filled workrooms, and a well-stocked and worked farm; and, above all, a good balance from the patients' earnings, as a set-off to the cost of their maintenance.[78]

The superintendent's employment was relatively secure, and his personal authority within his own artificial world largely unquestioned, but in other respects, his lot was scarcely an enviable one. Bucknill complained of having 'to spend our lives in a morbid mental atmosphere . . . a perpetual "Walpurgis Night" of lurid delusion' – a prospect he found 'so trying and so depressing that if it were continuous it would be unbearable'.[79] Two years later, it was, and, as we shall see, he abandoned asylum practice for greener professional pastures. Others were not so

76. See, for example, the almost wholly negative commentary in John Conolly, 'On the Prospects of Physicians Engaged in Practice in Cases of Insanity', *Journal of Mental Science* 7, 1861, pp. 180–94. Compare, too, Bucknill's complaint that 'the public extends its unreasonable antipathy to the insane, to all those who are connected with insanity; even to those who wrestle with the great evil, and, to the best of their ability, hold it down. . . .' 'Presidential Address', p. 6. In 1854, an editorial in the *Medical Circular* 4, 12 April 1854, p. 255, had complained bitterly about magistrates' failure to accord due deference to the profession, blaming continued abuses and low cure rates in asylums on the disposition to place laymen in control and to make medical men their subordinates. The salaries awarded alienists 'do not deserve the name of remuneration: they are both an injustice and a scandal'. (At Norfolk, for instance, Dr Foote was paid a mere 65 pounds per annum, and at Bedford, Dr Harris received only 150 pounds.) 'The first step towards improving the condition of the insane', the editor insisted, 'is to improve the condition of the medical superintendents, upon whose freedom of action and satisfaction with their offices, the recovery of the sick mainly depends'. 'Editorial', *Medical Circular* 4, 12 April 1854, p. 255.

77. Commissioners in Lunacy, *7th Annual Report*, 1852, quoted in R. Hunter and I. MacAlpine, *Three Hundred Years of Psychiatry*, p. 1010.

78. J.T. Arlidge, 'Review of *An Examination of the Practice of Bloodletting in Mental Disorders*, by Pliny Earle', *Journal of Mental Science* 2, 1856, p. 168.

79. J.C. Bucknill, 'Presidential Address', p. 7.

fortunate, talented, or well-connected, and, like their junior assistants, found themselves with little option but to continue to wrestle 'with the most repulsive features of man's weakness, an atmosphere of moral miasma, an almost hopeless struggle, day by day, to retrieve or reset the broken fragments of reason . . .'[80] – even at the expense of their own mental stability.[81] Small wonder that John Conolly, by this time the doyen of English alienism, concluded ruefully that '[a] young medical man, who has received a complete medical and surgical education, must either be very sadly situated, or very advantageously, who can make up his mind to devote himself to the study and treatment of Insanity'.[82] Imprisoned within the walls of their own institutions, albeit on better terms than the inmates whose lives they supervised, asylum doctors had ample time at their disposal to reflect on a bleak and dismal situation:

> Our calling is in its nature a depressing and trying one. . . . The constant tension, the continual feeling of responsibility under which we ourselves work, are wearing on all, exquisitely so on some. The routine nature and the seeming triviality of much of our labour . . . weary us. The peculiar combination of worry and monotony which characterize asylum life often torture us. . . .[83]

The relevant group with which to compare the status of psychiatrists remained the medical profession as a whole, though judging by their responses, the latter seem to have found the mad-doctors a somewhat embarrassing excrescence. Almost twenty years after the establishment of their professional association, and despite numerous efforts to rectify the situation, psychiatrists had to concede that

> the study of mental disorders is studiously excluded from the medical curriculum, alienist physicians, as they are therefore well called, work in a department of science the first principles of which are not recognized by their medical brethren, and seem often to speak a language not understood by those around them . . . so few of even our most accom-

80. J.M. Hawkes, *On the General Management of Public Lunatic Asylums in England and Wales*, London: Churchill, 1871, p. 32.
81. Bucknill, for instance, commented on 'The number of mental physicians who have suffered more or less from the seeming contagion of mental disease' ('Presidential Address', p. 7); and Hawkes expressed little doubt that this derived from 'the peculiar monotony' of asylum life – an atmosphere that must surely 'have an injurious effect on the mental characteristics of those who for a prolonged period are continuously exposed to its influence' and 'in the course of time, affect even the brightest and strongest minds'. *On the General Management of Public Lunatic Asylums*, pp. 32–3. An interesting line of argument for those who elsewhere made so much of the curative influences of asylum treatment!
82. J. Conolly, 'On the Prospects of Physicians Engaged in Practice In Cases of Insanity', p. 185. To make matters worse for the unfortunate alienist, 'In the very beginning, and to the very end, the law merely treats him as one of the dangerous classes, exercising a suspected trade, and solely intent on gain.'
83. Conolly Norman, 'Presidential Address', *Journal of Mental Science* 40, 1894, p. 492.

plished professors [of medicine] have any knowledge of the various types of mental derangement. . . .[84]

And according to Hunter and MacAlpine, the 'segregation of psychiatry from medicine if anything became more pronounced as time went on'.[85]

Recognition that 'We seem to be very Levites among our medical brethren. We cannot look to them for support, for they do not understand us . . .'[86] brought calls for the formation of a united front among asylum doctors.[87] But the results of any such activity were meagre. Subsequent presidents of the Medico-Psychological Association acknowledged despairingly that the specialty appeared to be becoming 'wholly divorced from the progress of medical science'[88] and that, having made little progress in understanding the condition they purported to treat, they had at best only 'partially succeeded in bringing their specialty within the pale of medical science'.[89]

3. Extra-Institutional Practice

By and large, asylum superintendents seem to have accepted this somewhat ambiguous professional status, and to have worked uncomplainingly within the limits of the authority granted them by their employers. It was otherwise with a handful of the leading figures in the field. Such men confronted the harsh reality that

> There are but few rewards and distinctions within the reach of our specialty. In connecting ourselves with lunacy we are almost compelled to share the seclusion of our patients. Certainly we have to renounce our chances of many posts of professional distinction.[90]

Earlier in the century, even John Conolly, made famous by his labours in introducing non-restraint at Hanwell, had been unable to translate his celebrity into anything approximating a stable extra-institutional career. Electing to resign from his post as superintendent when the Middlesex magistrates proposed to place a lay administrator in charge of administering the asylum, rather than submit to what clearly constituted a severe blow to his own authority and status, Conolly found himself cut off from the one stable source mid-century alienists possessed of obtaining a professional livelihood. Despite the reams of publicity and public honours his

84. T. Harrington Tuke, cited in R.A. Hunter and I. MacAlpine, *Three Hundred Years of Psychiatry*, p. 1053.
85. R.A. Hunter and I. MacAlpine, *Three Hundred Years of Psychiatry*, p. 1053.
86. W.H.O. Sankey, 'Presidential Address', *Journal of Mental Science* 14, 1868, pp. 297–304.
87. T.L. Rogers, 'Presidential Address', *Journal of Mental Science* 20, 1874, pp. 327–51.
88. W.T. Gairdner, 'Presidential Address', *Journal of Mental Science* 28, 1882, pp. 321–32.
89. Herbert Hayes Newington, 'Presidential Address', *Journal of Mental Science* 35, 1889, pp. 293–315.
90. W.H.O. Sankey, 'Presidential Address', pp. 297–304.

efforts at Hanwell had brought him,[91] he nonetheless faced a struggle to avoid penury, and was forced to swallow his pride and seek financial reward where he could find it. Drawing some income from being called in as a consultant in difficult cases,[92] and from 'expert' testimony in criminal trials,[93] he was forced to supplement this by taking a handful of well-paying lady lunatics into his newly leased property, Lawn House.[94] And even this barely sufficed: on his death, Conolly's estate was valued at less than £3,000.

To be sure, Conolly's pecuniary embarrassments were to some degree a product of his lifelong fecklessness and incompetence where his finances were concerned,[95] and he never possessed the personal qualities he would have needed to succeed in single-handedly defining a new form of specialist practice.[96] Still, others experienced similar difficulties, and it was only from the 1860s onwards that members of the psychiatric elite successfully began to carve out alternative career paths outside the walls of the asylum.[97] Men like John Charles Bucknill and Charles Lockhart Robertson, superintendents of the Devon and Sussex County Asylums and the first two editors of the *Journal of Mental Science*, were clearly not

91. See, for example, *The Times* 18 November 1849, p. 6, col. E; 10 December 1840, p. 6, col. E; 30 December 1840, p. 3, col. B; 8 December 1841, p. 3, col. A; 14 December 1841, p. 3, col. D; 5 January 1842, col. F; 8 March 1842, p. 13, col. E; *Hansard's Parliamentary Debates*, 3rd series, 76, July 23, 1844, cols 1275–1281; *Illustrated London News* 21 May 1843. The *Morning Chronicle* (5 October 1843) dubbed him 'one of the most distinguished men of the age'. Honours included election as a Fellow of the Royal College of Physicians in 1844; award of an honorary D.C.L. by Oxford University; and being feted at the 1850 meeting of the Provincial Medical and Surgical Association.

92. These included, for example, the celebrated lunacy inquisitions of W.F. Windham, Sir Henry Meux, and Mrs Catherine Cummings, and the well-publicized scandal surrounding the confinement of Lady Rosina Bulwer Lytton, wife of the prominent novelist and politician.

93. For example, those of Robert Tate, Edward Oxford, and Luigi Buranelli. On this aspect of Victorian psychiatric practice, see Roger Smith, *Trial by Medicine*.

94. This was a particularly difficult step for Conolly to take, since for years he had been one of the major critics of the private madhouse trade, and he did not escape criticism for his hypocrisy, both from the novelist Charles Reade (who savagely burlesqued Conolly as the bumbling 'Dr Wycherly' in his best-selling *Hard Cash*); and from such eminent colleagues as Bucknill (see *The Care of the Insane and their Legal Control*, pp. 60, 128).

95. *Cf.* the comments by his son-in-law, Henry Maudsley, in 'Memoir of the Late John Conolly', *Journal of Mental Science* 12, 1866, pp. 151–74.

96. See the extended discussion of these issues in Andrew Scull, *Social Order/Mental Disorder: Anglo-American Psychiatry in Historical Perspective*, Berkeley: University of California Press/London: Routledge, 1989, chapter 7.

97. Vital as these developments proved to be in the long term, they have attracted surprisingly little scholarly attention to date. For some preliminary observations on the subject, see A. Digby, *Madness, Morality and Medicine: A Study of the York Retreat 1796–1914*, Cambridge: Cambridge University Press, 1985, pp. 119–20; L.J. Ray, 'Models of Madness in Victorian Asylum Practice', *European Journal of Sociology* 22, 1981, pp. 258–60; E. Showalter, *The Female Malady: Women, Madness and English Culture, 1830–1980*, New York: Pantheon, 1985, chapters 4 and 5; and Trevor Turner, 'Henry Maudsley', *passim*. Also useful are Janet Oppenheim, '*Shattered Nerves*'; and Edward Shorter, *From Paralysis to Fatigue: A History of Psychosomatic Illness in the Modern Era*, New York: Free Press, 1992.

satisfied with the marginal professional status and the physical and social isolation that were inescapably the price demanded for the measure of security their jobs provided. Making matters worse, their professional autonomy was compromised by the obvious lack of application of the medical model in the huge custodial institutions of the period, and by their vulnerability to the whims of the visiting committee of magistrates. Conolly, who knew whereof he spoke, objected that such incompetent laymen

> discourage and, as far as they can, repudiate the aid of the medical officers, and disregard their advice, restricting their duties and their influence with an apparent want of discrimination between the requirements of the insane and those of mere paupers, or of prisoners in jails. . . . One result of this kind of government of lunatic asylums will, I fear, be that the best educated men of our profession will be found less and less willing to devote themselves to duties which . . . are not appreciated.[98]

Briefly, it appeared that at least one exception to the rule might establish itself: James Crichton-Browne, who was perhaps the most energetic and effective of the younger generation of asylum superintendents, worked prodigiously to break the stultifying mould within which he found himself. The son of the eminent Scottish alienist, W.A.F. Browne, he had grown up in the elite institution after which he was named, and he arrived at the West Riding Asylum in 1866 determined to reinvigorate its programme of moral treatment, but also to refute the 'often repeated accusation that the medical officers of these establishments are so absorbed in general or fiscal management, in farming or in devising ill-judged amusements for their charges, that they have no time and energy left to devote to professional research'.[99] On both fronts, during the decade he remained at the asylum, he enjoyed notable success. The administration of the institution was transformed: classes were offered in reading, writing, and arithmetic; patient employment was extended, and a large fraction of the workforce were employed to build a Turkish bath and hydrotherapy wing; problems with drains and the water supply solved; and an array of amusements and recreations – plays, magic lantern shows, conjuring exhibitions, gymnastics – was introduced, reaching a high point with a performance of Gilbert and Sullivan's *Pygmalion and Galatea*, with W.S. Gilbert himself playing the part of Leucippus. On a wholly different front, Crichton-Browne attracted a remarkable medical staff, many of whom were later to become major figures in British neurology – David Ferrier,

98. John Conolly, 'Presidential Address', *Journal of Mental Science* 5, 1858, pp. 74–5.
99. James Crichton-Browne, 'Preface', *West Riding Lunatic Asylum Medical Reports*, 1, London: Churchill, 1871, quoted in John Todd and Lawrence Ashworth, 'The West Riding Asylum and James Crichton-Browne, 1818–76', in G.E. Berrios and H. Freeman (eds), *150 Years of British Psychiatry 1841–1991*, London: Gaskell, 1991, p. 392.

John Hughlings Jackson, and Clifford Allbutt, among others – who exploited the laboratory and other facilities at the asylum to produce a stream of basic research which appeared in the *West Riding Lunatic Asylum Medical Reports*, published annually between 1871 and 1876.[100]

Crichton-Browne's activities and enterprise stood out all the more starkly in contrast with the apathy and demoralized routine which had by now settled over most of the rest of Victorian asylumdom. But his commitment to asylum medicine did not last. Desirous of performing on a larger stage, in 1875 he accepted an appointment as Lord Chancellor's Visitor in Lunacy, the same position Bucknill and Robertson had used as a springboard to extra-institutional careers.[101] The *West Riding Lunatic Asylum Medical Reports* ceased publication with its next issue, and the asylum slid gradually back into the torpor that characterized the rest of the system.[102] Revealing what was perhaps one of the sources of his own disenchantment, Crichton-Browne subsequently warned that the 'presence of Poor Law Guardians on Visiting Committees will render lunatic asylum service more distasteful than it is now to cultivated medical men, so that the tone and status of those engaged in this service will undergo gradual deterioration'.[103]

Bucknill, Robertson, and Crichton-Browne were able to use their position as Chancery Visitors to gain access to a lucrative private clientele and to build highly rewarding office-based consulting practices. Other aspirants to elite status in the profession by-passed the county asylum system altogether. Some, like Maudsley, Mercier, and Savage, had some limited experience at the head of a well-known charity asylum.[104] A few, like George Fielding Blandford, emulated Conolly, and derived a portion

100. For details, see J. Todd and L. Ashworth, 'The West Riding Asylum and James Crichton-Browne'; Henry R. Viets, 'West Riding, 1871–76', *Bulletin of the History of Medicine* 6, 1938, pp. 477–87; C.A. Gatehouse, 'The West Riding Lunatic Asylum: The History of a Medical Research Laboratory', unpublished M.Sc. thesis, University of Manchester, 1981. Ferrier's work, in particular, which involved electrical experiments on the brains of small animals, had only the most indirect connections with the nominal work of the asylum.

101. Chancery lunatics, who were generally patients with substantial property, underwent a separate and expensive certification process (the so-called lunacy inquisition, held before a Master in Lunacy and a jury) and came directly under the jurisdiction of the Lord Chancellor. On Crichton-Browne's later career, see Janet Oppenheim, '*Shattered Nerves*', esp. chapter 2.

102. *Cf.* Richard Russell, 'The Lunacy Profession and its Staff in the Second Half of the Nineteenth Century, with Special Reference to the West Riding Lunatic Asylum', in W.F. Bynum, R. Porter, and M. Shepherd (eds), *The Anatomy of Madness*, Vol. 3, pp. 297–315.

103. James Crichton-Browne, 'Presidential Address', *Journal of Mental Science* 24, 1878, p. 351.

104. Maudsley spent three years as superintendent of the Manchester Royal Lunatic Asylum (1858–61); Mercier was superintendent of the Bethel Hospital, Norwich before moving to London to lecture on nervous diseases at the Westminster and Charing Cross Hospitals; and Savage spent ten years as superintendent at Bethlem (1879–89) before establishing a thriving consulting practice. For some rather superficial discussion of Savage's career and ideas, see Stephen Trombley, *All That Summer She Was Mad: Virginia Woolf and Her Doctors*, London: Junction Books, 1981, pp. 107–58.

of their income from ownership of a small private asylum.[105] And a handful of others, including Andrew Wynter and Mortimer Granville, avoided acquiring the stigma of an association with institutional practice altogether. Alongside the hospital affiliations that from the eighteenth century onwards had been the stock-in-trade of any ambitious physician,[106] a large fraction of these men made use of highly visible positions as editors of major medical journals to advance their careers and build their reputations,[107] attracting an affluent clientele and often achieving considerable financial success. (Maudsley, for instance, left an estate of over £100,000 at his death.) To lavish consultation fees from cases they recommended for asylum treatment,[108] they increasingly added income from a whole new class of 'nervous' patients, the denizens of the shadowy regions Mortimer Granville labelled 'Mazeland, Dazeland, and Driftland', those who inhabited a perilous territory others dubbed the 'borderlands of insanity'.[109]

Such 'incipient lunatics', the carriers of 'latent brain disease', included a whole array of neurotics, hysterics, anorexics, and sufferers from the newly fashionable 'neurasthenia', or weakness of the nerves.[110] Dis-

---

105. Blandford combined a lectureship on Psychological Medicine at St. George's Hospital with ownership of Munster House Asylum, Fulham, between 1865 and 1902.
106. On the emerging importance of hospital affiliations in medical careers in the preceding century, see William F. Bynum, 'Physicians, Hospitals, and Career Structures in Eighteenth Century London', in W.F. Bynum and R. Porter (eds), *William Hunter and the Eighteenth Century Medical World*, Cambridge: Cambridge University Press, 1985, pp. 105–28; for their still greater significance in the nineteenth century, see M.J. Peterson, *The Medical Profession in Mid-Victorian England*, Berkeley: University of California Press, 1978.
107. Bucknill (1853–62), Robertson (1862–70), Maudsley (1862–78), and Savage (1878–94) all served terms as editors of the *Journal of Mental Science*. Bucknill and Crichton-Browne were, together with Hughlings Jackson and Ferrier, the founding editors of *Brain*. Andrew Wynter, besides being a frequent contributor to both the *Edinburgh Review* and the *Quarterly Review* on psychiatric matters, was also the founding editor of the *British Medical Journal*. Turner notes Maudsley's foresight in being among the first to realize that 'the very role of editor was in itself a new means for advancing scientific careers'. Trevor Turner, 'Henry Maudsley: Psychiatrist, Philosopher, and Entrepreneur', in W.F. Bynum, R. Porter, and M. Shepherd (eds), *The Anatomy of Madness*, Vol. 3, p. 160.
108. Maudsley and Savage, for instance, sent a substantial number of patients to the English aristocracy's favourite asylum, Ticehurst (Savage alone certified 25 of the patients admitted between 1885 and 1915, amounting to almost 8 per cent of the admissions in that period); and they continued to consult from time to time on their treatment.
109. Andrew Wynter, *The Borderlands of Insanity*, 2nd edn, London: Renshaw, 1877. (Granville contributed five chapters to this edition.)
110. Neurasthenia was a diagnosis invented by the American neurologist, George M. Beard, and quickly adopted by others. On its uses in the United States, see Charles Rosenberg, 'The Place of George M. Beard in Nineteenth-Century Psychiatry', *Bulletin of the History of Medicine* 36, 1962, pp. 245–59; and Barbara Sicherman, 'The Uses of a Diagnosis: Doctors, Patients, and Neurasthenia', *Journal of the History of Medicine and the Allied Sciences* 32, 1977, pp. 33–54. For its rapid influence in England, see, for example, Thomas Stretch Dowse, *On Brain and Nerve Exhaustion: 'Neurasthenia', Its Nature and Curative Treatment*, London: Baillière, Tindall, and Cox, 1880; W.S. Playfair, 'Some Observations Concerning What Is Called Neurasthenia', *British Medical Journal* 6

proportionately female,[111] and desperate to avoid the stigma and hopelessness associated with certification and confinement in an asylum, they provided a promising basis for an office-based practice,[112] and one that the leading alienists saw as naturally falling within their jurisdiction. Here were whole new realms of patients 'who pass about the world with a clean bill of health'[113] but who, left untreated, were destined to add to the population of the hopeless mad – either themselves becoming frankly insane, or (perhaps worse still) breeding[114] and passing on the 'hereditary taint' to future generations.[115]

November 1886, p. 854; and Thomas Dixon Savill, *Clinical Lectures on Neurasthenia*, 3rd edn, London: Glaisher, 1906 (first edn 1899). As George Savage subsequently acknowledged, the invention of the diagnosis 'has been a great comfort both to doctors, and to the friends of patients. Not unnaturally, these friends dread the term insanity, and rejoice to hear that the patient is only suffering from neurasthenia'. 'A Lecture on Neurasthenia and Mental Disorders', *Medical Magazine* 20, 1911, p. 620.

111. *Cf.* Elaine Showalter, *The Female Malady*, especially chapters 4, 5, and 6; and, for an alternative review of the evidence, linked to a sharply contrasting assessment of the linkages between gender and mental disorder, Janet Oppenheim, '*Shattered Nerves*', chapter 6. Oppenheim provides a forcible criticism of the contention 'now almost unquestioned among feminist scholars that middle-class Victorian women subconsciously turned to illness to vent their rage against limited, unsatisfying lives, devoid of personal significance and imposed on them by a male-dominated society'. Her related insistence that 'An unrelenting emphasis on the gendered nature of experience is not always a help in solving historical puzzles' strikes me as a useful corrective to the fashionable polemic that is implicit in the title of Showalter's book. Like the medical profession at large, Victorian alienists mobilised their scientific and cultural authority in support of a constricted and in many respects misogynist portrait of the female of the species. (For a survey of this phenomenon based on American texts, *cf.* Carroll Smith-Rosenberg and Charles Rosenberg, 'The Female Animal: Medical and Biological Views of Woman and Her Role in Nineteenth Century America', *Journal of American History* 60, 1973, pp. 332–6.) And throughout the nineteenth century (as in our own time) our culture's stereotypical images of madness and professional explanations and treatments for mental disorder were saturated with overt and subliminal sexual references and assumptions. But to recognize that gender mattered with respect to madness in a variety of ways, both gross and subtle, does not require us to embrace the extreme position which would reduce insanity to a 'female malady'. Victorian statistics reveal a broadly equal representation of men and women among those officially identified as the most severe cases of mental disorder, and the experiences of male and female lunatics populating the empire of asylumdom have more points of similarity than of difference.

112. *Cf.* Thomas Dowse's acknowledgement that neurotic women constituted 'a class of invalids who really do a great deal to support the doctors'. *Lectures on Massage and Electricity in the Treatment of Disease*, London: Hamilton, Adams, 1889, p. 128.

113. Andrew Wynter, *The Borderlands of Insanity*, 1875, pp. 45–6.

114. Fortunately, the physical signs of physiological decay were written particularly plainly on the bodies of women, and given the hopelessness of curative efforts and the vital significance of healthy offspring for the future of the race, prospective husbands were urged to inspect the merchandise carefully, searching for 'physical signs . . . which betray degeneracy of stock . . . any malformations of the head, face, mouth, teeth and ears. Outward defects and deformities are the visible signs of inward and invisible faults which will have their influence in breeding'. Henry Maudsley, *The Pathology of Mind: A Study of Its Distempers, Deformities, and Disorders*, London: Macmillan, 1895, p. 536.

115. In seeking to stave off a looming epidemic of madness, late Victorian psychiatrists saw women as being at particular risk, through the potentially disastrous consequences of their growing extra-domestic entanglements. The selfish women who in growing

Those alienists who sought to build an extra-institutional practice found themselves facing considerable competition for control of this financially rewarding, if therapeutically frustrating population. English neurology, itself emerging as a self-conscious and organized speciality in the 1870s and 1880s, was from its earliest years structurally orientated, and offered less of a direct challenge to psychiatry than its American counterpart.[116] Nonetheless, even though neurologists 'took little interest in such cases', they were publicly recognized as 'nerve-doctors', and found that 'functional "nervous" disorders always formed a very large [and financially indispensable] part of [their] practice'.[117] Less half-heartedly, a number of Harley Street physicians[118] and some general practitioners, as well as members of the increasingly aggressive specialty of gynaecology and obstetrics, attempted to contest this territory, and with some success.[119] The latter, in particular, possessed some obvious competitive advantages – they enjoyed privileged access to female patients, they lacked the alienists' stigmatizing ties to the world of the asylum, and they could offer diagnoses

numbers sought to pursue education and professional careers instead of focusing on their primary role of preserving the vigour of the English race, overtaxed their innate capacities and would inflict a terrible price on successive generations. '[It] would be an ill thing', as Maudsley put it, 'if it should so happen, that we got the advantages of a quantity of female intellectual work at the price of a puny, enfeebled, and sickly race'. In a similar vein, Clouston warned of the prospect that 'all the [female] brain energy would be used up in cramming a knowledge of the sciences, and there would be none left at all for . . . reproductive purposes'. See Henry Maudsley, 'Sex in Mind and Education', *Fortnightly Review* new series, 15, 1874, pp. 466–83; T.S. Clouston, *Female Education from a Medical Point of View*, Edinburgh: Macniven and Wallace, 1882. Such views became a staple of the Victorian mental hygiene literature, and were echoed by a number of women writers: see, for example, Eliza Lynn Linton, 'The Higher Education of Women', *Fortnightly Review*, new series, 40, 1886, pp. 498–510; Mary Scharlieb, *Womanhood and Race Regeneration*, New York: Moffat, Yard, 1912; and Arabella Kenealy, *Feminism and Sex-Extinction*, London: Fisher Unwin, 1920. For a sharply contrasting view, see Elizabeth Garrett Anderson, 'Sex in Mind and Education: A Reply', *Fortnightly Review*, new series, 15, 1874, pp. 582–94. For recent discussions of this aspect of Victorian mental 'science', *cf*. Janet Oppenheim, '*Shattered Nerves*', chapter 8; and Elaine Showalter, *The Female Malady*, chapter 5.

116. See W.F. Bynum, 'The Nervous Patient in Eighteenth- and Nineteenth-Century Britain: the Psychiatric Origins of British Neurology', in W.F. Bynum, R. Porter, and M. Shepherd (eds), *The Anatomy of Madness*, Vol. 1, pp. 89–102. On the American situation, see Bonnie Blustein, '"A Hollow Square of Psychological Science": American Psychiatry and Neurology in Conflict', in A. Scull (ed.), *Madhouses, Maddoctors, and Madmen*, pp. 241–70.

117. Harold Merskey, 'Shell Shock', in G.E. Berrios and H. Freeman, *150 Years of British Psychiatry 1841–1991*, p. 262.

118. See, for example, the casebooks of Frederick Parkes Weber, preserved in the Contemporary Medical Archives Centre of the Wellcome Institute for the History of Medicine in London. Parkes Weber's practice with 'nervous patients' is discussed in Edward Shorter, *From Paralysis to Fatigue*, pp. 60–62, 204–5, 273–7.

119. W.S. Playfair, Professor of obstetric medicine at King's College, London, was, for instance, primarily responsible for introducing the American neurologist Weir Mitchell's rest cure to England in the 1880s. See W.S. Playfair, *The Systematic Treatment of Nerve Prostration and Hysteria*, London: Smith, Elder, 1883.

that were reassuringly 'medical' and remote from the taint of madness.[120] Still, they often overreached themselves, advocating novel therapies which raised doubts about their own professionalism, and on more than one occasion they were therefore forced to moderate their claims.[121] Ultimately, too, all the alienists' competitors were constrained by the fact that a diagnosis of insanity legally required confinement in an asylum, so that the attempt by any other group of doctors to claim expertise in the treatment of mental disorders could never be pushed very far, lest it incurred the wrath of the Lunacy Commissioners.[122]

By its very nature, the practice of medicine in private consulting rooms tends to remain hidden from the historian's gaze.[123] With nervous and mental disorders, of course, our difficulties are compounded, since 'the essence of keeping such a clientele would have been absolute discretion and the guaranteed disposal of any damning documents or notes'.[124] Still, there is no reason to doubt the testimony of Clifford Allbutt, that 'the stir in neurotic problems' meant that 'daily we see neurotics, neurasthenics,

120. Charlotte MacKenzie discusses the jurisdictional conflict with gynecology, and the desperate attempts of some patients 'to try to find a localized physical cause for their disorders, and to avoid certification', in her dissertation, 'A Family Asylum: A History of the Private Madhouse at Ticehurst in Sussex, 1792–1917,' unpublished Ph.D. thesis, University of London, 1987, esp. pp. 272–4.

121. Two such episodes stand out with particular clarity: in the 1860s, a leading London gynaecologist, Isaac Baker Brown, attempted to establish the clitoridectomy as a surgical remedy for hysteria and insanity; and in the 1870s and 1880s, led by Lawson Tait, English gynaecologists briefly flirted with the use of 'normal ovariotomies' for the same purpose. (The operation was dubbed a 'normal' ovariotomy because it involved the removal of an apparently healthy set of ovaries.) Despite the willingness, even eagerness, of some patients to undergo these mutilating surgical interventions, they were highly controversial, and the medical elite on both occasions closed ranks, and acted to suppress techniques which came to be regarded as a species of quackery. For a detailed discussion of these events, and an analysis of the reasons they provoked such strongly negative reactions among the leaders of the profession, see Andrew Scull and Diane Favreau, ' "A Chance to Cut is a Chance to Cure": Sexual Surgery for Psychosis in Three Nineteenth Century Societies', in Steven Spitzer and Andrew Scull (eds), *Research in Law, Deviance, and Social Control*, Vol. 8, pp. 3–39.

122. This was, indeed, one of many sources of Isaac Baker Brown's difficulties. Threatened with prosecution by the Lunacy Commissioners for claiming to treat and cure lunatics in his proprietary hospital, his fumbling attempts to contradict his own prior public statements to this effect cost him crucial support among his peers, and helped to bring about his professional demise. See *British Medical Journal* 26 January 1867, p. 94; 2 February 1867, p. 119; 9 February 1867, p. 144; 6 April 1867, p. 400. The alienists' legally enforceable monopoly of the treatment of the gravest cases of mental disorder enabled them, more nearly than any of their potential competitors, to create a realm of practice resting upon a foundation Warner has rightly argued that all physicians seek, 'a stable source of therapeutic authority'. Cf. John Harley Warner, 'The Edinburgh Bloodletting Controversy', *Medical History* 24, 1980, pp. 241–58.

123. For a discussion of this problem, cf. John Harley Warner, *The Therapeutic Perspective: Medical Practice, Knowledge, and Identity in America, 1820–1885*, Cambridge, Massachusetts: Harvard University Press, 1986, pp. 83ff.

124. T. Turner, 'Henry Maudsley', pp. 175–6. Turner plausibly suggests that this requirement for successful practice explains the dearth of biographical material which survives on Maudsley himself.

hysterics, and the like' – with the result that 'every large city [is] filled with nerve-specialists and their chambers with patients'.[125] And amongst the more prominent of these specialists were undoubtedly that small group of alienists who had successfully broken away from the gloomy and isolated world of the asylum in which the bulk of their erstwhile colleagues remained so hopelessly immured.

4. The Defence of Mental Medicine

Ironically, as we shall see, it was from the ranks of men like these, at the very summit of the specialty, and including several presidents of the Medico-Psychological Association,[126] that the most vigorous critics of the asylums' complacent custodialism were recruited. At the same time, however, it was the professional elite who sought, almost desperately, to assert that all aspects of the treatment of insanity were a medical province, and that asylum doctors should therefore be immune from interference by unqualified laymen. The profession was warned that 'the notion that medicine is inoperative in mental disorder had produced much mischief'[127] and was urged to guard against 'the exclusion or . . . the undue disparagement of physical means of cure and alleviation',[128] lest there be a return to the 'past when the skill and experience of the physician was thought to be less important than the watchful care of the matron or steward'.[129] It was the asylum superintendent's task to emphasize that 'the just medium has been passed, and the insane are suffering by the present extreme views'[130] which depreciated the value of medicine. On the contrary, the importance of conventional medical treatment must be repeatedly stressed.[131]

125. Thomas Clifford Allbutt, 'Nervous Diseases and Modern Life', *Contemporary Review* 67, 1895, p. 217.

126. Maudsley, Bucknill, Robertson, Blandford, and Crichton-Browne.

127. J.T. Arlidge, 'Review of *An Examination of the Practice of Bloodletting in Mental Disorders* by Pliny Earle', *Asylum Journal of Mental Science* 2, 1856, p. 168.

128. W.A.F. Browne, *The Moral Treatment of the Insane: A Lecture*, London: Adlard, 1864, p. 5. Recognizing how tenuous the foundations of alienism's privileged status still remained, he warned that

> If therapeutic agents are cast aside or degraded from their legitimate rank, it will become the duty of the physician to give place to the divine or moralist, whose chosen mission it is to minister to the mind diseased; and of the heads of [asylums] to depute their authority to the well-educated man of the world, who could, I feel assured, conduct an asylum fiscally, and as an intellectual boarding house, a great deal better than any of us.

129. W.C. Hood, *The Statistics of Insanity* London: Batten, 1862, p. 104 – an obvious reference to the York Retreat.

130. J.T. Arlidge, 'Review of *An Examination of the Practice of Bloodletting in Mental Disorders,*' p. 167. In language all-too-revelatory of the political issues at stake, W.A.F. Browne used the occasion of his Presidential Address to the newly renamed Medico-Psychological Association to denounce '[h]e who refuses the aid of medicine [as being] as much a heretic to the true faith as he who doubts the efficacy of moral agents.' 'On Medico-Psychology', p. 312.

131. Since there were plainly no effective medical therapies for the treatment of the insane, it

The difficulty here lay in the fact that it did little good to advocate a greater emphasis on medical techniques as a means of raising psychiatry's prestige, or to attribute the low status of asylum doctors to 'the laudation by physicians of the so-called moral means of treatment, and the oblivion into which medical aid has been allowed to fall',[132] when the medical remedies which could prove their worth in practice simply did not exist. An alternative tack therefore became popular with those intent on raising the profession's prestige and resisting outside, 'lay' interference. If the proportion of patients cured failed to rise in the years following the rapid expansion of the asylum system, so that claims that the medical (i.e. pharmaceutical) treatment of insanity had greatly improved were likely to be received with scepticism, there remained one aspect of the condition of lunatics where no one doubted that there had been progress. As Daniel Hack Tuke put it, 'so far as this includes moral treatment and management, it has advanced in all civilized countries in a manner calculated, all will admit, to cause the liveliest feelings of satisfaction'.[133] In consequence, those who were convinced that 'There is no more dangerous delusion in the range of lunacy than this notion that the care and treatment of the insane is not wholly medical',[134] now sought to claim that moral treatment itself (or as some preferred to call it, 'medico-moral treatment')[135] was something only physicians were qualified to dispense.

Beginning with the simple assumption that 'the moral system of treatment can only be properly carried out under the constant superintendence and by the continuous assistance of a physician',[136] the profession eventually developed a more elaborate set of arguments for the position that moral treatment by itself provided sufficient justification for ensuring that it is 'the medical authority that controls everything in an asylum for mental disease',[137] entirely free of all outside interference. As Granville put it,

> It would be just as reasonable, or unreasonable, for the lay officials of an ordinary hospital to prescribe the drugs or instruments with which physicians and surgeons treat physical disease, as for lay authority to be combined with the medical in an asylum for the insane ... for the

is not at all clear how the authorities' scepticism about the value of medical treatment could have been harming the insane, though it is obvious why their doctors should find it detrimental. As Arlidge pointed out, 'It has induced magistrates to hold medical men in little estimation as physicians of asylums, and to view them merely as useful and superior stewards in directing the general management and moral treatment, and as safeguards of casualties and of accidental disease.' *Ibid.*, p. 168.

132. John Arlidge, *On the State of Lunacy and the Legal Provision for the Insane*, London: Churchill, 1859, p. 104.

133. Daniel Hack Tuke, *Chapters in the History of the Insane in the British Isles*, p. 484.

134. J.M. Granville, *The Care and Cure of the Insane*, Vol. 2, p. 149. It is obvious who was endangered by such beliefs.

135. For example, William Ley, in Littlemore County Asylum, *Annual Report*, 1855, p. 9.

136. *Asylum Journal*, 'Editorial', 1, 3, 1854, p. 33.

137. J.M. Granville, *The Care and Cure of the Insane*, Vol. 1, p. 150.

simple and obvious reasons, that disease of the mind is amenable only
to the influence of moral remedies, and the discipline, the control, the
daily routine and management of the insane are the 'drugs' with which
the physician of the mind must work the cure of his cases.[138]

As this implies, all aspects of asylum administration were now alleged to
form part of the system of moral treatment, a system whose components
were so closely linked one to another that unschooled intervention at any
point threatened the whole edifice.

From the very outset, the design of the physical structure of any asylum
required continuous consultation with, and deference to, the accumulated
expertise of this branch of the medical profession. After all, 'An asylum is
a special apparatus for the cure of lunacy, and ought to be constructed
under the direction of the physician by whom it is to be employed, or by
an expert in the uses to which it will be subsequently applied.'[139] And
once the asylum was in operation, magistrates' committees must somehow be taught to resist the temptation to meddle in questions which were
beyond their competence to decide. As to where that boundary might
lie, if the more uninhibited protagonists of medical control were to
be believed, almost everything was beyond any layman's competence.
Granville, for instance, reported that the Middlesex magistrates had ordered
their superintendents to make changes in the asylum's diet, so as to lessen
its monotony. But while their actions were clearly well-intentioned,
and the consequences in this particular instance were harmless (or even
beneficial), 'It is impossible to admit that a lay committee has any ground
or qualification for the task of forming a judgement on a point of this
nature.'[140] Apparently only a physician was qualified to recognize and
'treat' monotony. The trouble was that 'This, unfortunately, is what
visiting committees do not perceive',[141] and persisted in not perceiving.
Questions of diet, decoration, and amusement were ones in which many
laymen continued to feel they were as qualified as any professional (as, of
course, the originators of moral treatment had contended they were); and
consequently, for all the well-wrought arguments of men like Granville,
asylum committees continued to interfere in the administration of their
asylums whenever it suited them to do so.

138. *Ibid.*, pp. 77, 150. The moral and the medical were still more firmly cemented together
    in Bucknill and Tuke's *A Manual of Psychological Medicine*, (p. 509). Though they veiled
    in obscurity the precise mechanism by which the mysterious alchemy was
    accomplished, Bucknill and Tuke insisted that by combining 'moral power and
    discipline . . . a firm will, the faculty of self-control, a sympathising distress at moral
    pain, [and] a strong desire to remove it', alienists were able to mobilize a 'fascinating
    biologising power. . . .' And it was this biological power 'which enable men to
    domineer for good purposes over the minds of others'. (The choice of the term
    'domineer' is, of course, highly revealing in another way.)
139. J.M. Granville, *The Care and Cure of the Insane*, Vol. 1, p. 15.
140. *Ibid.*, p. 111.
141. *Ibid.*, p. 15.

5. Medical Authority in the Asylum

So far, I have been largely concerned with the external aspects of the psychiatric profession's efforts to consolidate its position – that is, with the threats to the asylum doctors' status and dominance originating outside the institution. Although decisions in these areas clearly had implications, often serious ones, for the superintendents' conduct of the asylums themselves, there also existed a set of problems which bore more directly on the issue of the physician's authority within the institution.

John Arlidge, who for a time had served as resident medical officer at St. Luke's, complained that asylums had grown so large that 'asylum superintendents . . . are driven to a system of routine and general discipline, as the only one whereby the huge machine in their charge can work, and look upon recoveries as casual or undesigned coincidences'.[142] What he overlooked was the potent protective function such a situation provided for the psychiatric profession. For one of the crucial problems for any occupation whose results blatantly fail to measure up to its claims is to insulate its members from the consequences of this failure – partly, of course, those which may flow from the discontent of its clients; but also, and perhaps of equal importance, the loss of morale and belief in themselves among its own members.

The asylum doctors' inability to do anything for the overwhelming majority of their patients meant that interaction with inmates threatened daily denial of their effectiveness. In this situation, being asked to undertake impossibly heavy case-loads in a patently over-large institution provided the profession with a convenient scapegoat on which to blame many of its troubles. As one would expect in the circumstances, there were complaints that because the physician had 'his mile or so of wards and offices to perambulate daily', and four or five hundred inmates to consider, he could not possibly be expected to employ the full resources of his healing art; and stories were told before official inquiries to illustrate just how unreasonable it was, in consequence, to expect cures, given the trying conditions doctors were forced to work under.[143] But there was no sustained effort on the part of the asylum doctors to reduce their task to manageable proportions, or to secure adequate staffing of asylums. On the contrary, they resisted suggestions which would have relieved

---

142. J.T. Arlidge, *On the State of Lunacy*, p. 103.
143. Some asylum committees actually required their medical officers to see each patient each day. Insight into how this apparently Herculean task was accomplished was elicited in 1859: 'Q. According to your regulations [at Hanwell], you expect them to see every patient? A. Yes; once at least every day. Q. Take the case of the 600 female patients, if each of them were seen for only a minute [by the one doctor], it would take ten hours a day? A. But there are many who might be seen in less than half a minute; you walk through the wards, you know them all [*sic!*], and it is not a medical examination which takes place of every patient on every side.' House of Commons, *Report of the Select Committee on the Care and Treatment of Lunatics*, 1859, p. 238.

them of the burden of caring for chronic patients;[144] and instead of welcoming efforts by outsiders to rid them of their administrative functions, so as to allow them to devote their full energies to the cure of patients, they fiercely resisted all such proposals, and insisted on burying themselves ever deeper in administrative concerns. Asylums were so large, and so crowded with physically decrepit specimens, that the superintendent's assistant physicians, who were forced to have some daily contact with the patients, could safely spend all that time in providing routine medical care for ordinary physical ailments; thereby, of course, affording confirmation that they were engaged in supplying a medical service to the inmates.

Even the assistants, however, found ways to minimize the amount of time they were forced to spend in the unpleasant and disturbing company of (live) patients. Particularly popular, if the figures given in the annual reports of the Commissioners in Lunacy are to be believed, was research on dead bodies, which, even though it might be repetitive and lead nowhere, at least bore a passing resemblance to more conventional medical practices.[145] More importantly, perhaps, the autopsy was potentially 'the key to integrating alienism and scientific medicine... [since] only with death could the physical basis of disease be made visible'.[146] In the meantime, the dirty work of dealing with the patients on a day-to-day, hour-by-hour basis was left to a staff of attendants, themselves recruited from the dregs of society, men and women who, in return for long hours spent in close, defiling contact with the insane, received suitably low status and financial rewards. Thus insulated from the reality of asylum existence, the superintendent was able to remain a remote, if

144. See chapter 6.
145. The practice grew in popularity in the course of the century. In 1870, for example, 1,336 autopsies were conducted, corresponding to 42 per cent of all asylum deaths that year. By 1890, the number had risen to 4,336, or 76.6 per cent of asylum deaths for the year. *Cf.* Commissioners in Lunacy, *25th Annual Report*, 1871, p. 39; and *45th Annual Report*, 1891, p. 40.
146. Roger Smith, *Trial by Medicine*, p. 44. Alienists were not in the least shy about announcing the success of their investigations. James Davey, for instance, proclaimed that the brains of only eight of one hundred insane persons were without visible structural defects in the grey matter, medullary substance, ventricles, or membranes. (*Cf.* J.G. Davey, *On the Nature, and Proximate Causes of Insanity*, London: Churchill, 1853, p. 58.) However, as Roger Smith comments on such claims in general, 'it was by no means clear just what was visible. Reports of brain alteration were made regularly, but the criteria for assessing alterations were not compatible with each other nor with a healthy norm'. *Ibid.* The purported evidence was thus simply the product of preexisting theoretical commitments. For an acknowledgement of the profession's total inability 'to correlate mental disorders with their [hypothesized] physical substrata...' see the comments of David Ferrier, reprinted in H.C. Burdett, *Hospitals and Asylums of the World*, Vol. 2, London: Churchill, 1891, p. 186. As Henry Maudsley commented, 'However one might wish it to be otherwise, and however sure that it will one day be otherwise, it is still the fact that mental disorder may exist during life without the least morbid change being visible in the brain after death.' *The Pathology of Mind*, 1895 edn, p. 519.

benevolent despot, his position above the crowd and freedom from too close and frequent contact with the patients protecting him from the contamination, not just of his social position, but, indirectly, of his authority as well.[147]

Perhaps a more serious threat to the asylum doctor's authority than his potential loss of confidence in his own skills, or of the deference shown him by his patients, was one which is generic to all types of professional authority, but which was here experienced in a peculiarly acute form. As Freidson has pointed out, 'the authority of expertise is in fact problematic, requiring in its pure functional form the time-consuming and not always successful effort of persuading others that its "orders" are appropriate',[148] rather than relying, as does bureaucratic authority, on the application of rewards and penalties to obtain compliance. Obviously, the task of persuasion is made easier to the extent that a given group of experts can provide plausible evidence that its approach brings substantially superior results to those which would have ensued in the absence of the application of their special skills, and/or the more nearly the experts and those for whom their service is intended share a common universe of discourse. Both of these factors, however, served only to exacerbate the problems psychiatry faced in maintaining its professional authority. In the first place, the asylum doctors' basic claim to possess expertise in the treatment of insanity was a fragile one, and not one in support of which they could readily produce convincing evidence in the form of large numbers of cures. Secondly, it is probable that there existed here an even more profound disjunction than usual between professional and lay worldviews. Neither the uneducated classes recruited as attendants in asylums, nor the social derelicts who formed the bulk of the asylums' population, were likely to share to any significant degree the profession's perspective on insanity. That perspective, after all, was a relatively novel one; and it was one to which the asylum doctors had been concerned to convert the elite, not the masses.

Even in those instances where the special skill possessed is demonstrably powerful and effective, 'professions have attempted to solve the problem of persuasion by obtaining institutional powers and prerogatives that at the very least set limits on the freedom of their prospective clients and that

147. The pernicious effects of too familiar and intimate association with one's inferiors upon the deference accorded those of higher status (which was so deeply rooted a feature of Victorian society) were duly noted by Granville (*The Care and Cure of the Insane*, Vol. 1, p. 99), who warned, 'The circumstance of a superintendent's wife acting as matron involves a sacrifice of social position injurious, if not fatal, to success. It is above all things indispensable that medical superintendents of asylums should be educated gentlemen; and if that is to be the case, their wives cannot be matrons. Indeed, it is inconceivable that a man of position and culture would allow his family to have any connection with an asylum.' So much for his emphasis that the insane were 'sick people'!

148. E. Freidson, *Professional Dominance*, New York: Atherton, 1970, p. 131.

on occasion even coerce their clients into compliance. The expertise of the professional is institutionalized into something similar to bureaucratic office'.[149] Consequently, where claims to the authority of expertise are themselves weak and tenuous, one can certainly expect that the quest to supplement this with the authority of office will acquire extraordinary urgency and importance.

In the context of the asylum, securing the authority of office meant restricting the position of asylum superintendent to medical men, and investing that position with power over all aspects of asylum administration, including personnel questions as well as matters more strictly related to the treatment of patients. In the earliest asylums, the medical profession accumulated such powers almost fortuitously. The asylums were small, and the local magistrates were but little inclined to pay two salaries where one would do. Accordingly, once the justices had been convinced that lunatics required almost constant medical assistance, the doctor employed for this purpose was generally expected in addition to take charge of the day-to-day administration of the asylum.

However, the rapid expansion of the number of lunatics and the associated rise in the average size of public asylums posed something of a threat to this cosy arrangement. For in asylums containing several hundred inmates, 'when to the medical and moral treatment of the patients are added the multifarious duties comprised under the terms "general management and superintendence" . . . it will be readily conceded that . . . those labours are far too onerous to be adequately performed by a single individual'.[150] A logical solution to the problem, which could be expected to occur to some asylum committees at least, was to hire a full-time lay administrator to assume the routine duties of running the institution, thus allowing the asylum doctor to devote his full time and energy to the task for which his professional training had presumably prepared him, the cure of patients.

The superintendents, though, evinced no desire whatsoever to adopt this policy or to rid themselves of their mounting burden of administrative duties. On the contrary, they insisted on assuming them. Where, as at Hanwell, asylum committees attempted to institute such a separation of powers, the physicians in residence, backed by the profession as a whole, did their best to render such schemes unworkable.[151] More generally, recognizing that the question of lay versus medical administrators 'is one in which the profession as a body has a direct concern, and in which every

149. *Ibid.*
150. Commissioners in Lunacy, *Report on Bethlem Hospital*, 1852, p. 15.
151. On the two occasions (1838–9 and 1843–4) on which the Hanwell Committee sought to install a lay administrator, the superintendent then in office promptly resigned. In both instances, his successors as resident medical officers fought fiercely with their lay competitor. Within weeks, the degree of administrative chaos and internal disorder was such as to force the magistrates to dispense with the layman and reinstitute uniform medical control. For details, see A. Scull, *Social Order/Mental Disorder*, pp. 197–200.

practitioner of "psychological medicine" must feel his status immediately involved', psychiatry's publicists sought by all means at their disposal to convince the public that 'the interests of science and the obligation of true economy alike require that public asylums should be "hospitals" under medical management . . .'.[152] These efforts were crowned with success. Asylum committees everywhere, even those which had flirted with the idea of lay administrators, conceded what the doctors wanted. Rather than dividing his authority with a lay administrator, the medical superintendent was to be given the assistance of one or more assistant physicians to perform the necessary medical chores, while he concentrated almost his entire energies on administration. Henceforth, the further an asylum doctor's career progressed, and the more experience he gained, the less his contact with the insane. But at least psychiatry had buttressed its weak claims to the authority of expertise with the more reliable authority of a near-autocratic office.

152. J.M. Granville, *The Care and Cure of the Insane*, Vol. 1, p. 150, emphasis in the original. To threaten medical control over asylums was, so it was alleged, to opt for a relapse into barbarism: 'Is it possible that any medical man who valued his reputation – I say nothing of his peace of mind – would consent to subordination to a lay manager or even to be parallel to him? It is a wonder someone does not suggest a return to fetters and strait-jackets.' Richard Greene, 'The Care and Cure of the Insane', *Universal Review* July 1889, pp. 506–7.

CHAPTER SIX

'Museums for the Collection of Insanity'[1]

Some Persons of a desponding Spirit are in great concern about that vast Number of poor People, who are Aged, Diseased, or Maimed; and I have been desired to employ my Thoughts what Course may be taken, to ease the Nation of so grievous an Incumbrance. But I am not in the least Pain upon that Matter; because it is very well known, that they are every Day dying, and rotting, by Cold and Famine, and Filth and Vermine, as fast as can reasonably be expected.

Jonathan Swift, *A Modest Proposal for Preventing the Children of Poor People in Ireland, from being a Burden to their Parents or Country*

It is a feature of many systems of thought, and not only of primitive ones, that they possess a self-confirming character. Once their initial premises are accepted, no subsequent discovery will shake the believer's faith, for he can explain it away in terms of the existing system. Neither will his convictions be weakened by the failure of some accepted ritual to accomplish its desired end, for this too can be accounted for. Such systems of belief possess a resilience which makes them virtually immune to external argument.

Keith Thomas, *Religion and the Decline of Magic*

1. The Growth of the County Asylum System

According to the 1845 Lunatic Asylums Act, every county and borough in England and Wales had a statutory obligation to provide, within three years, adequate asylum accommodation at public expense for its pauper lunatic population. Most made efforts to comply with the law: by the end of 1847, thirty-six of the fifty-two counties had built asylums of their own, some of the less densely populated rural counties, with fewer known lunatics, opting to combine with one another to open joint institutions. Nevertheless, the reluctance in many quarters to incur the large capital expenditures necessarily required by such a programme did not simply disappear once the reformers had won the battle on the Parliamentary level, and they were forced to concede that 'considerable opposition has

---

1. Francis Scott in the *Fortnightly Review*, 1879.

arisen in several counties to any proposals for erecting a county asylum'.[2]

Unwilling to provoke a full-scale conflict with local authorities by invoking the powers the Act gave them to compel compliance, lest by doing so they stirred up the widespread if temporarily dormant fear of central direction, the Commissioners in Lunacy and their allies sought instead to use their powers of persuasion to bring errant magistrates into line. John Conolly, whose successful introduction of the non-restraint system into the huge establishment at Hanwell had done much to give substance to the claim that asylum treatment of the insane represented a humanitarian advance over the rigours of the jail and the workhouse, now became one of the most able publicists on behalf of the creation of county asylums. In a series of essays first appearing in the *Lancet* in 1846, republished as the monograph, *On the Construction and Government of Lunatic Asylums*, in the following year, he restated the reformers' standard objections to providing for the insane in private madhouses or in wards attached to workhouses, contending that only a purpose-built, publicly supported asylum would suffice. In similar fashion, the Commissioners in Lunacy used their annual reports as a handy medium for propaganda on behalf of the merits of county asylums. The prospect of cure provided an attractive basis on which to advocate the creation of costly new institutions, and both in their regular reports, and in the supplemental report they issued in 1847 on the proper moral and medical treatment of insanity, they urged the certainty of a high proportion of cures, provided only that the counties shouldered their responsibilities and furnished sufficient asylums wherein recent cases of insanity could receive prompt treatment. Asylum superintendents sought to employ their own reports to further this same spirit of optimism and to insist on the potential benefits of early intervention.

To avoid the danger that all this work might remain just an exercise in preaching to the converted, the Commissioners engaged in lengthy correspondence with the magistrates of areas reluctant to implement the Act's provisions. While these further efforts to convince the recalcitrant of the error of their ways were not always immediately successful,[3] they did

2. John Conolly, *On the Construction and Government of Lunatic Asylums and Hospitals for the Insane*, London: Churchill, 1847, p. 2. In Sussex, for instance, there was clearly a highly organized campaign against building a county asylum, the magistrates receiving many identically worded memorials on the subject from individual parishes. See East Sussex Record Office, Lewes, QAL/2/6. In Buckinghamshire, within a few months of the passage of the legislation, ten parishes had petitioned the Quarter Sessions not to comply with the 1845 Act; and in January 1849, six hundred ratepayers, led by Benjamin Disraeli, renewed their opposition, complaining that they had already been taxed for a new jail and judges' lodgings, and were now being asked to underwrite another expensive capital project, costing some 30,000 pounds. See John Crammer, *Asylum History: Buckinghamshire County Pauper Lunatic Asylum – St. John's*, London: Gaskell, 1990, pp. 29–30, 38–9.
3. Parish authorities in Sussex, for instance, were still boarding more than a hundred patients at Warburton's London madhouse in 1849. An outbreak of typhus, which prompted correspondence from the Lunacy Commissioners and then from the Secretary of State

provide a continuous discreet pressure which eventually wore down the opposition of all but the most determined adversaries. Counties like Cambridge and Sussex, and boroughs like London and Norwich, fought a prolonged rearguard action, but eventually most capitulated without the Commissioners being forced to resort to compulsion. As more and more counties made provision for their pauper lunatics at public expense, so licensed houses catering to paupers began to close,[4] increasing the pressure on the remaining local authorities to follow suit. By 1854, the number of counties which had made public provision for their insane had risen to forty-one, and by the end of the decade, the task of obtaining at least an initial commitment to the care of the pauper insane on the part of each county and borough was substantially complete. The legal commitment to the asylum had now been strengthened by a considerable financial investment in this solution.

2. The Accumulation of Chronic Cases

In one highly significant respect, the extensive programme of asylum construction had departed from the provisions of the 1845 Act. The Metropolitan Commissioners' tour of inspection had convinced them that

> the disease of Lunacy . . . is essentially different in its character from other maladies. In a certain proportion of cases, the patient neither recovers nor dies, but remains an incurable lunatic, requiring little medical skill in respect to his mental disease and frequently living many years. A patient in this state requires a place of refuge, but his disease being beyond the reach of medical skill it is quite evident that he should be removed from Asylums instituted for the cure of insanity in order to make room for others whose cases have not yet become hopeless. If some plan of this sort be not adopted the Asylums admitting paupers will necessarily continue full of incurable patients . . . and the skill and labour of the physician will thus be wasted upon improper objects.[5]

Accordingly, their Report recommended, and the Act embodied, a provision permitting the erection of separate receptacles for the chronic at the discretion of any county authority.[6] Once the legislation was enacted,

himself, made no impression on the local magistrates, who continued to exhibit a stubborn opposition to building a county asylum. Ten more years passed before their opposition was worn down. The correspondence is preserved at the East Sussex Record Office, Lewes (QAL 2/3/6).

4. For example, three large licensed houses – Kingsland House near Shrewsbury, Haydock Lodge near Warrington, and Laverstock House near Salisbury – closed their pauper departments in 1852.

5. *Report of the Metropolitan Commissioners in Lunacy*, 1844, p. 92.

6. This provision can be traced to the personal views of James Cowles Prichard, who had served as one of the Metropolitan Commission's medical members. *Cf.* the discussion in Nicholas Hervey, 'The Lunacy Commission 1845–60, with Special Reference to the Implementation of Policy in Kent and Surrey', unpublished Ph.D. dissertation, Bristol

however, no constituency pressed for its implementation, and no county chose to do so.

The asylum doctors conceded, even insisted, that 'the pauper lunatic is not merely to be secured; he is, if possible, to be restored to reason'.[7] But for a number of reasons, they resisted the notion that this goal could best be realized by providing separately for the acute and the chronic. The publicly stated grounds for this opposition were that any such system, while superficially attractive, would necessarily be productive of a repetition of the very abuses the reform of the lunacy laws had been designed to avoid.[8] In particular, it would be difficult, if not impossible, to recruit suitable staff, and to maintain the requisite morale and dedication in institutions which were avowedly custodial. Furthermore, in all save cases of confirmed idiocy, there always remained a possibility, however remote, of cure, so that it would be both cruel and unwise to consign even apparently hopeless cases to places where efforts directed towards their restoration would cease. The Lunacy Commissioners simply adopted the opinion of the profession as their own, and therefore did not press local authorities to provide for such a segregation. And the magistrates themselves, who were reluctant to incur the expense of erecting and providing for the management of two separate institutions, opted instead for the immediate capital savings of a single asylum for curable and incurable alike.

Underlying the asylum superintendents' no doubt genuine concern lest institutions for the incurable should degenerate into the snake-pits from which asylums were meant to rescue the insane, one suspects that they were also seeking to inhibit the construction of a set of organizations which might potentially compete with their own for the limited funds available. Almshouses for the chronic were particularly dangerous, since they would not only be a cheaper alternative, but according to existing plans, would also achieve part of their savings by dispensing with the expense of a full-time medical staff. In view of their subsequent inability to cure most of those labelled insane, it was fortunate for the asylum doctors' own future that they resisted any such proposals – for had they been left to cope with only those they themselves considered curable, control over almost all lunatics would quickly have passed out of their hands.[9] Instead, the continued retention of chronic cases in ordinary

University, 1987, pp. 31–2. As Hervey notes, from the outset Prichard's views on this matter differed from those of many other alienists.

7. John Conolly, *On the Construction and Government of Lunatic Asylums*, p. 58.
8. *Ibid.*, pp. 4–5.
9. Thus, a quarter-century after county asylums were made compulsory, a well-placed critic acknowledged that 'It is this class of patients, beyond human help, that now choke up the public asylums throughout the land, converting them from houses of cure into mere prisons.' Indeed, according to the asylum superintendents' own estimates, 'out of the total number of 24,748 pauper-patients in county and borough asylums, and in registered hospitals, in the year 1867, no less than 22,257 were past all medical cure. . . .' Andrew Wynter, *The Borderlands of Insanity*, 1st edn, London: Hardwicke, 1875, p. 127.

asylums in time allowed them to make a graceful retreat from the difficult and risky task of curing significant numbers of lunatics. Having chosen to deal with cases that were acknowledged to be, by and large, beyond hope, the asylum doctors gradually manoeuvred to redefine success in terms of comfort, cleanliness, and freedom from the more obvious forms of physical maltreatment, rather than the elusive and often unattainable goal of cure.

Not that patients, once admitted, were necessarily confined to the asylum for life: to the contrary, a substantial fraction of those who entered an asylum in any twelve-month period could expect to be discharged within the year.[10] Laurence Ray's study, for instance, which examines several cohorts of patients admitted to the Surrey County Asylum at Brookwood and to the Lancaster County Asylum, suggests that just over a third of them were released in under a year, and a handful more over the ensuing twelve months.[11] John Crammer reports similar outcomes at the Buckinghamshire County Asylum.[12] To these, one must add a further fraction, somewhere between 6 and 17 per cent of the total, which was transferred to other asylums, forming 'part of a "circulating" chronic population'.[13]

At the margin, therefore, among those newly admitted to an asylum, the turnover was reasonably rapid, particularly when one adds in the 10 to 18 per cent of the insane who died within a year of admission.[14] Each year, however, a very substantial proportion of the admissions remained behind to swell the population of long-stay, chronic patients, and as the size of county asylums grew remorselessly, annual admissions formed a smaller and smaller fraction of the whole. Paradoxically, this state of affairs meant that while the median length of stay for a new asylum inmate was generally between a year and a year and a half, an overwhelming

10. Charlotte MacKenzie points out that this reasonably fluid interchange between the asylum and the outside world reflected the fact that temporary removal of a difficult patient to an institution was often sufficient to ease family tensions, so that the insane person might subsequently be returned to the family even when not improved. 'A Family Asylum: A History of the Private Madhouse at Ticehurst in Sussex, 1792–1917', unpublished Ph.D. thesis, University of London, 1987, p. 320.
11. Laurence Ray, 'Models of Madness in Victorian Asylum Practice', *European Journal of Sociology* 22, 1981, pp. 229–64. After the first two years of residence in an asylum, however, the chances of discharge fell to almost nil.
12. J. Crammer, *Asylum History: Buckinghamshire County Pauper Lunatic Asylum – St. John's*, pp. 119–22.
13. L. Ray, 'Models of Madness', p. 233.
14. Adding together those who died; those discharged as 'recovered'; patients handed back to their families or returned to the workhouse as 'relieved' or 'unimproved'; and those transferred to other institutions, Ray calculates that 47 per cent and 53 per cent respectively of the 'admissions batches' he sampled in the 1870s and the 1890s were 'resolved' (i.e. no longer resident in the asylum) after twelve months, figures that rose to 62 per cent and 66 per cent at the end of two years. For both groups, 16 per cent of the patients died within a year of admission, and removals to other asylums accounted for 17.5 per cent of the cases resolved in the 1870s batch, and 6.3 per cent of the 1890s batch. L. Ray, 'Models of Madness', pp. 233, 261–2.

and growing proportion of the asylum population quickly came to be composed of chronic, long-stay patients. And it was this spectre of chronicity, this horde of the hopeless, which was to haunt the popular imagination, to constitute the public identity of the asylums,[15] and to dominate Victorian psychiatric theorizing and practice.

When we estimate their successes in relation to the annual influx of new cases, asylum superintendents could lay claim to cure between one fifth and just over a third of those they treated. Even these results were a far cry from the 60, 70, or 80 per cent of cures which the more optimistic in their midst had confidently promised to deliver. But what interested rate-payers was what proportion of the asylum population as a whole could be restored to sanity (that is, to independence); and when cures were calculated on the total number under treatment, the discrepancy between promise and performance was yet more glaring. Pressed to provide estimates of how many of those confined in their asylums could be expected to be restored to sanity, alienists responded by issuing ever gloomier pronouncements, each of which subsequently turned out to correspond with a still bleaker set of outcomes.[16]

As Table 3 shows, even in 1844, before the influx of the mass of pauper inmates generated by the expansion of the county asylum system, the estimated number of curable cases in most types of asylum was really quite low. With the exception of Bethlem and St. Luke's, both institutions which rigorously selected their inmate population to exclude those who lacked a high potential for recovery, no class of asylums estimated that as many as a third of its patients would ultimately recover; in most cases, fewer than a fifth were expected to do so. At this stage, the discrepancy between these rather low figures and the optimistic projections some of those running the institutions were simultaneously employing in an effort to secure the erection of more institutions at public expense was attributed to the public's reluctance or inability to secure prompt asylum treatment

15. As one well-informed observer put it, 'the idea which the public now have of an asylum is, that it is a place where madmen are consigned until they die'. H.C. Burdett, *Hospitals and Asylums of the World*, Vol. 2, London: Churchill, 1891, p. viii.

16. Gerald Grob (in 'Marxian Analysis and Mental Illness', *History of Psychiatry* 1, 1990, p. 229) has taken strong exception to these assertions. He claims that 'Before 1880 the proportion of chronic patients (Scull's description notwithstanding) was relatively low. Most patients were admitted and discharged within four to six months, and only a small minority remained for as much as a year or longer.' To put it bluntly, Grob's criticisms here are wildly off the mark, and are refuted both by a very substantial body of nineteenth-century materials (including the Lunacy Commissioners' statistics and the writings of the asylum superintendents themselves), and by the recent re-analyses of Ray, Walton, and Crammer. Even confining ourselves to admissions, not even a majority (far less 'most') patients were discharged within a year (unless Grob wishes to count the dead among the asylum's successes in this regard); and as a proportion of the whole, chronic patients rapidly constituted 'most' of those officially identified as insane. Significantly, in advancing this line of criticism, Grob relies upon *American* data to criticize my generalizations about *English* mental hospitals – a very odd tactic for one who elsewhere makes a fetish of the particularities and peculiarities of person and place.

Table 3   Asylum Superintendents' Estimates of the Number and Percentage of Curable Patients in Asylums in England and Wales in 1844.

Type of Asylum	Private			Pauper		
	Total Patients	Number Curable	Per Cent Curable	Total Patients	Number Curable	Per Cent Curable
Provincial Licensed Houses	1,426	412	28.9	1,920	637	33.2
Metropolitan Licensed Houses	973	153	15.7	854	111	13.0
County Asylums	245	61	24.9	4,244	651	15.3
Charity Hospitals	536	127	23.7	343	59	17.2
Military/Naval	168	18	10.7	–	–	–
Bethlem	265	181	68.3	90	no estimate	
St. Luke's	177	93	52.5	31	16	51.6

Source: Metropolitan Commissioners in Lunacy, 1844 Report, pp. 185, 187.

for their insane relatives. Cure rates for recent cases were asserted to be much higher; and the combination of a wider availability of asylum treatment, greater public confidence in the treatment accorded the insane, and the educational campaign of the medical superintendents themselves, stressing the advantages of early treatment, was expected to effect a substantial improvement in the asylum's overall performance as a curative institution.

The predicted rise in the proportion of cures quite simply failed to occur.[17] At the Littlemore Asylum, for instance (the joint asylum for the counties of Oxfordshire and Berkshire), 17.1 per cent of the total number resident were discharged as recovered in 1847, the first full year of its operation. In his next annual report, however, William Ley, the superintendent, was obliged to caution his readers that such a favourable outcome was due to a combination of fortuitous circumstances, and hence was unlikely to be repeated: 'The Recoveries in 1847 were unusually numerous, arising from the class of Patients admitted, and from the greater quiet maintained in the Asylum – The average rate of Discharge by recovery in 1848 has been ten per cent upon the whole number of patients.' The chaplain's report suggests how quickly optimism about curability had evaporated, in this asylum at least:

17. Statistically, of course, this was inevitable, given the steadily declining ratio of admissions to total numbers resident. Yet this numerical 'confirmation' that insanity was a chronic and incurable disorder contributed powerfully to an official discourse of hopelessness, and the pronouncements of the Lunacy Commissioners, the assessments of informed laymen, and the medical literature on madness all bear witness to its pervasive impact.

It is a melancholy reflection to think, that out of the number of those who attended the Services, how few, in all probability, will ever again have their reasoning faculties restored; but I still trust that their constant attendance at the Sunday Services and daily Prayers, will be productive of an eternal benefit to them, so that my ministry among these my afflicted fellow-creatures may not be altogether in vain.[18]

The Littlemore Asylum was, if anything, more successful as a curative institution than the majority of the county asylums. At all events, Ley discharged more of his patients as recovered than did most of his counterparts, something he did not neglect to draw to the attention of the local magistrates.[19] From the outset, superintendents of county asylums complained that they were being swamped by hopeless cases. In the first year of the Derby County Asylum's operation, Hitchman, the director, commented: 'The majority of the Patients admitted here have not only been in a chronic state of insanity, but also in a feeble state of bodily health.'[20] The tendency of the asylum to become the resting-place for the broken-down and physically decrepit grew still more marked in subsequent years.

The diary of John Millar, the first superintendent of the Bucks Asylum at Stone, indicates that a similar pattern held there too. On 24 March 1857, for instance, less than three years after the asylum first opened its doors, Millar estimated that while nine males and eleven females might possibly be restored to reason, the condition of the remainder – sixty-six males and 100 females – was quite hopeless.[21] His dismissal later that year brought no essential change in this respect. Humphry, his successor, conceded in his first report that 'there is reasonable hope of recovery in only 13 of the 213 persons [then resident] in the asylum'.[22] Since only a fraction of the inmates were sent back to the community recovered (or even 'improved') each year, and since the elimination of others by death had slowed as the eradication of the grosser instances of physical neglect reduced mortality

---

18. Littlemore Asylum, *Annual Report*, 1848, pp. 4, 8.
19. In his 1850 report, for instance, he published a table comparing the percentage of cures at his own institution in the previous twelve months (12.8 per cent) with those of the other seventeen county asylums then in operation (8.9 per cent), complied from their annual reports. See Littlemore County Asylum, *Annual Report*, 1850, pp. 5–8. At the Lancaster County Asylum, the claimed cure rate, calculated on the total number of patients treated, was as high as 23.5 per cent in 1837, but had already fallen to 13.4 per cent by 1841. Six years later, it had declined again, to 7.1 per cent; and by 1860, it was only 4.6 per cent. From 1850 onwards, the death rate almost always exceeded the cure rate, a pattern which was, as we shall see, the general rule. (Statistics from Lancashire Record Office, QAM 5/19 Table IV, quoted in J. Walton, 'Casting Out and Bringing Back in Victorian England', pp. 141–2.)
20. Derby County Asylum, *1st Annual Report*, 1852, p. 29.
21. Superintendent's Diary, 24 March 1857, in manuscript at St. John's Hospital, Stone, Buckinghamshire.
22. Derby County Asylum, *Annual Report*, 1852, p. 29; Bucks County Asylum, *5th Annual Report*, 1858, p. 9.

rates, over time the asylums became clogged with masses of incurables, and the proportion cured calculated on the total number under treatment tended to fall even further.

The superintendents continued to blame the asylum's apparently poor performance in what they had initially claimed to be their most vital task on their inability to secure enough cases of incipient insanity, before time had confirmed the disease and while their largely unspecified, but undoubtedly powerful, techniques were maximally effective. The large numbers of existing chronic cases were also at least partially to blame for the problem: 'It is greatly to be regretted that owing to the want of room, the difficulty of obtaining Admission to Asylums, and the mistaken kindness and reluctance on the part of relatives and friends in many Cases, the early removal of Patients to Asylums should be so long delayed... thereby diminishing their chances of recovery.'[23] Yet no matter how many new asylums the magistrates were persuaded to build, and no matter how hard the asylum doctors promoted the idea that early treatment was in the long run the most economical response to insanity, a sufficient number of curable cases apparently never materialized.

In 1875, the superintendent at the Littlemore was still lamenting, in familiar fashion, that 'This Asylum is becoming full of old and incurable cases who fill our Infirmaries with Patients wanting little else than the comfort and nursing required by all aged and infirm Persons. The percentage of Recoveries is gradually becoming less, and only 13 [patients now in the asylum] are deemed curable.'[24] With rates routinely calculated on the basis of the total number 'under treatment', the proportion of reported cures was now abysmally low: in 1872, 'The percentage of Recoveries in the year was a little less than six...';[25] the following year 'a little less than seven...';[26] and in 1874, 'a little over seven....'.[27] In neighbouring Buckinghamshire, 'Of the 421 lunatics resident [in 1870], only eighteen can be considered curable, and probably several of these may not realize the hopes of recovery now entertained.'[28] Six years later, the Lunacy Commissioners inspecting the asylum were informed 'by Dr Humphry that of the 416 inmates of the wards, he considers not more than six to be curable'.[29] So it went.

When the Lunacy Commissioners published tables estimating the likely proportion of inmates who would recover at some time in the future, comparable to that published in 1844, every single type of institution

23. Hanwell County Asylum, *Annual Report*, 1871, p. 33.
24. Littlemore County Asylum, *Annual Report*, 1875, pp. 8–9.
25. *Ibid.*, 1872, p. 19.
26. *Ibid.*, 1873, p. 10.
27. *Ibid.*, 1874, p. 10.
28. Buckinghamshire County Asylum, *17th Annual Report*, 1870, p. 3.
29. *Ibid.*, *23rd Annual Report*, 1876, p. 7. The litany continued: see, for example, *28th Annual Report*, 1881, p. 9; *31st Annual Report*, 1884, p. 15.

Table 4   Estimated Number of Curable Patients in Asylums in England and Wales in 1860 and 1870.

	1860			1870		
	Total Patients	Number Curable	Per Cent Curable	Total Patients	Number Curable	Per Cent Curable
Provincial Licensed Houses	2,356	361	15.4	2,204	285	12.9
Metropolitan Licensed Houses	1,944	253	13.0	2,700	283	10.5
County and Borough Asylums	17,432	1,952	11.2	27,890	2,149	7.7
Registered Hospitals	1,985	320	16.1	2,369	436	18.4

Sources: 14th Annual Report of the Commissioners in Lunacy, 1860, p. 117; 24th Annual Report, 1870, p. 97.

Table 5   Cure and Mortality Rates in County and Borough Asylums 1870–90.

	Number cured of total number resident – per cent	Number died of total number resident – per cent
1870	8.54	8.48
1880	8.31	7.40
1890	7.68	8.20

Sources: 25th Annual Report of the Commissioners in Lunacy, 1871, pp. 112–15; 35th Annual Report, 1881, pp. 148–51; 45th Annual Report, 1891, pp. 96–9.

exhibited a decline from earlier levels. The county asylum superintendents' prophecies – self-fulfilling or otherwise – that less than one in ten of their patients would recover were apparently accurate. Between 1870 and 1890, the proportion they claimed to cure continued to fall steadily, until ultimately more of their charges left the asylum in coffins each year than were restored to society in the possession of their senses.[30]

30. This was true even though the turnover among the small proportion of the asylum population who constituted new admissions remained relatively high. At Lancaster Asylum, for instance, 'After 1850 the figure [for cures] never again reached 10 per cent, and the death rate was almost always higher than the cures. [In cures and mortality rates,] Lancaster was not exceptional . . . and if [it] is at all representative, most of the

3. Mammoth Asylums

The collapse of the asylum's pretensions to provide cure was matched by the decay and disappearance of all the crucial features of moral treatment – those elements which were supposed to distinguish the asylum from the prison. The departure from early ideals was perhaps most visible in the architecture of these institutions. The buildings themselves offered mute testimony to the fact that the asylum was now 'a mere refuge or house of detention for a mass of hopeless and incurable cases'.[31] Whereas it had been an article of faith with the reformers that 'the main object to be borne in mind, in the construction of lunatic asylums, is to combine cheerfulness with security, and to avoid everything which might give the impression that he is in prison',[32] within little more than a decade there were complaints that county asylums were 'built externally on the model of a palace, and internally on that of a workhouse.'[33]

The Lunacy Commissioners viewed this development more complacently than most outside observers, though a note of criticism crept into many of their reports. Of Colney Hatch, the second asylum for the County of Middlesex, they commented: 'Several of the wards of both divisions in the old block, are very dark and gloomy towards the centre . . . the wards generally, still have a very comfortless look. . . . Everywhere there is a deficiency of comfortable and ordinary domestic furniture.'[34] Generally, however, they were satisfied with small improvements, such as flowered wallpaper, a few cheap framed prints on the walls, and an enlargement of tiny and heavily barred windows.

Other critics were less charitably disposed. Mortimer Granville, who investigated conditions in the metropolitan asylums on behalf of the *Lancet* during the mid-1870s, commented that

> the Middlesex County asylum at Colney Hatch is a colossal mistake. . . . It combines and illustrates more faults in construction and errors of arrangement than it might have been supposed possible in a single effort of bewildered or misdirected ingenuity . . . the wards are long, narrow, gloomy, and comfortless, the staircases cramped and cold, the corridors oppressive, the atmosphere of the place dingy, the halls huge and cheerless. The airing courts, although in some instances carefully planted, are uninviting and prison-like.[35]

successes were alcoholics who had dried out, exhausted, half-starved overworked women who recovered after a few weeks of limited exertion and reasonable diet, and cases of post-natal depression.' John Walton, 'Casting Out and Bringing Back in Victorian England: Pauper Lunatics, 1840–70', in W.F. Bynum, R. Porter, and M. Shepherd (eds), *The Anatomy of Madness*, Vol. 2, London: Tavistock, 1985, p. 142.

31. Joseph Mortimer Granville, *The Care and Cure of the Insane*, Vol. 1, London: Hardwicke and Bogue, 1877, p. 8.
32. 'Lunatic Asylums', *Westminster Review* 43, 1845, p. 168.
33. 'Lunatic Asylums', *Quarterly Review* 101, 1857, p. 383.
34. Commissioners in Lunacy, *16th Annual Report*, 1862, p. 139.
35. J.M. Granville, *The Care and Cure of the Insane*, Vol. 1, pp. 145, 154.

At the City of London Asylum at Dartford, the staircases were 'cramped and draughty', the lavatories 'very defective', and the structure as a whole, while given to 'outward show', was pervaded by a 'spirit of parsimony' with respect to the internal arrangements.[36] Hanwell, too, was a classic example of the asylum architecture of the period, typified by 'long, cold corridors, huge wards, and a general aspect of cheerlessness'. From without,

> it is a vast and straggling building, in which the characteristics of a prison, a self-advertising charitable institution, and some ambitious piece of Poor Law architecture struggle for prominence. The gates are kept by an official who is attired in a garb as nearly as possible like that of a gaoler. All the male attendants are made to display the same forbidding uniform.[37]

Small wonder, then, that for all the protests that such ideas were unfounded, 'many among the higher, and nearly all among the lower classes, still look upon the County Asylum as the Bluebeard's cupboard of the neighbourhood'.[38]

Gigantic asylums such as these were already common within a decade of the passage of the 1845 Act. Colney Hatch, which opened in 1851, was from the outset designed for more than 1,000 patients. Its wards and passages amounted in the aggregate to more than six miles. The exterior was 'almost palatial' in character:

> Its facade, of nearly a third of a mile, is broken at intervals by Italian campaniles and cupolas, and the whole aspect of the exterior leads the visitor to expect an interior of commensurate pretensions. He no sooner crosses the threshold, however, than the scene changes. As he passes along the corridor, which runs from end to end of the building, he is oppressed with the gloom; the little light admitted by the loop-holed windows is absorbed by the inky asphalt paving, and coupled with the low vaulting of the ceiling, gives a stifling feeling and a sense of detention as in a prison. The staircases scarcely equal those of a workhouse; plaster there is none, and a coat of paint, or whitewash, does not even conceal the rugged surface of the brickwork. In the wards, a similar state of affairs exists: airy and spacious, they are without a doubt, but of human interest they possess nothing.[39]

With the exception of the external harmony of its architectural style, in which respect it was somewhat atypical, Colney Hatch might have served as the archetype of the county asylums of the latter decades of the nine-

---

36. *Ibid.*, p. 75.
37. *Ibid.*
38. 'Lunatic Asylums', *Quarterly Review* 101 p. 353.
39. *Ibid.*, p. 364.

Fig. 14   Colney Hatch Asylum from an engraving by Laing, opened in 1851 in the year of the Great Exhibition, and touted as the most modern in Europe. Within a decade it had been expanded to accommodate more than 2,000 patients. With rooms on both sides of the six miles of corridors in its interior, there were serious problems securing sufficient ventilation and light. In the words of Richard Hunter, who served as a consultant to the renamed Friern Barnet Hospital in the mid-twentieth century, 'the wards were tunnel-like and dark at the centre, ill-heated, sparsely furnished, and unpainted, with lavatories opening directly into the gallery, and deficient wash and bath facilities'. To make matters worse, the Middlesex magistrates instructed their architect to save money by skimping on the foundations, and within a decade, the walls were separating from the roof, rain leaked in, and the whole edifice was threatened with collapse.

teenth century. Propelled by the overriding desire to economize, local magistrates almost universally adopted the practice of tacking on wing after wing, story upon story, building next to building, in a haphazard and fortuitous fashion, as they strove to keep pace with the demand for accommodation for more and more lunatics. For all the Lunacy Commissioners' attempts to impose order on the chaos, as asylums grew steadily larger in the course of the century, and yet remained stubbornly overcrowded and overrun by hopeless and decrepit cases, it became impossible to aspire to providing more than minimal custodial care. Asylums began to seem 'more like towns than houses'; they became institutions which 'partake rather of the nature of industrial than of medical establishments'.[40]

40. House of Commons, *Report of the Select Committee on the Care and Treatment of Lunatics*, 1859, p. 90, evidence of Lord Shaftesbury; J.T. Arlidge, *On the State of Lunacy and the Legal Provision for the Insane*, London: Churchill, 1859, p. 123. Both these impressions were strengthened by asylum architects' endeavours to make the running of the asylum as self-contained as possible. For example, Griffith, who provided the plans for several late nineteenth-century asylums, designed the new asylum for Northamptonshire at Berrywood to include a gasworks, a farm, a chapel for the patients and staff, a mortuary, and so forth. Hidden behind an extensive screen of trees on a hill some miles outside Northampton, its symmetrical red-brick walls were equipped to provide for almost all

Increasing size was the one aspect of the drift towards custodialism that the Lunacy Commissioners strove hardest to resist. Throughout the 1850s, for example, they conducted an acrimonious correspondence with the Middlesex magistrates over plans to expand Hanwell and Colney Hatch, both of which already contained well in excess of 1,000 inmates. Here, as elsewhere, their inability to compel compliance with their directives proved decisive. All new asylums, or plans to extend existing institutions, needed their prior approval, but this failed to provide them with adequate leverage to force the justices to adopt their views. Local authorities balked at the proposal that they should respond to the growing demand for asylum accommodation by providing for a proliferation of small, costly institutions. Whenever the Commissioners rejected their plans to extend already large institutions, asylum committees simply made minor modifications to the existing designs and re-submitted them. The Commissioners' complaints that 'the more extended the asylums are, the more abridged become their means of cure',[41] that 'it is manifest that anything like individual treatment must be limited to a very small proportion of cases, and we fear that with the mass of the Patients the Superintendents must necessarily depend upon the good conduct and trustworthiness of the attendants',[42] were met by a stony indifference.

Given their conviction that any asylum, no matter how far it strayed from the initial conception of what an asylum should be, was better than no asylum at all, the Lunacy Commissioners then faced three not very palatable alternatives. They could continue to reject the proposals, in which case the lunatics for whom there was no room in existing asylums would be deprived of the benefits of asylum treatment, and would likely languish under not very salubrious conditions in the local workhouses. They could appeal to the Home Secretary, who possessed ultimate authority in these matters, except that, on questions of size, he usually sided with the magistrates.[43] (The central government was no more inclined than its

the wants of its six or seven hundred inhabitants, if not from the cradle, then at least from admission to the grave.

41. Commissioners in Lunacy, *11th Annual Report*, 1857, p. 11.
42. Commissioners in Lunacy, *13th Annual Report*, 1859, p. 23.
43. Nicholas Hervey has objected to my analysis on this point, correctly noting that, in disputes about other matters, the Home Office often sided with the Lunacy Commissioners. But the question of size was, as the Commissioners themselves acknowledged, crucial to the future of asylumdom, and here, in the last analysis, successive Home Secretaries withheld their support, being reluctant to court the charge of central interference in local decision making. 'At the end of the day', as Hervey himself concedes, the Home Secretary 'was not prepared to order [local magistrates] to build new asylums, although empowered to do so'. See N. Hervey, 'The Lunacy Commission 1845–60', pp. 285–7. For Shaftesbury's acknowledgement that the Commission could do little but acquiesce where magistrates insisted on increasing the size of asylums already in existence, see his testimony in House of Commons, *Report of the Select Committee on the Care and Treatment of Lunatics*, 1859, p. 235. On the Commission's persistent, and consistently ineffectual, attempts to keep down the size of Hanwell and Colney Hatch Asylums, see their correspondence with the Middlesex magistrates, reprinted *ibid.*, Appendix 6, pp. 306–15 and Appendix 7, pp. 315–24.

Table 6 Average Size of County and Borough Asylums in England and Wales in the Nineteenth Century.

Date	Number of Asylums	Average Number of Patients
1 Jan. 1827	9	116.0
1 Jan. 1850	24	297.5
1 Jan. 1860	41	386.7
1 Jan. 1870	51	548.6
1 Jan. 1880	61	657.2
1 Jan. 1890	66	802.1

Source: Annual Reports of the Commissioners in Lunacy, except 1827 figures, which are from K. Jones, *Lunacy, Law, and Conscience*, London: Routledge and Kegan Paul, 1955, p. 116.

local representatives to sanction 'excessive' expenditures on a segment of the disreputable poor.)[44] Or they could bow to the inevitable, concede that further opposition was 'impracticable', and approve the plans themselves. Perceiving the futility of resistance, their objections grew less and less frequent, though periodically they plaintively noted that 'each succeeding year . . . confirms us in the opinions we have so often expressed as to the many evils resulting from the congregation of very large numbers of the insane under one roof and one management'.[45] Each succeeding year also brought a further increase in the average size of the patient population of county and borough asylums.

Most superintendents voiced only muted protest at this remorseless trend, and the process of adjusting professional ideology to practical realities was soon under way. Addressing his professional brethren in 1860, the newly elected President of the Asylum Officers' Association, Joseph Lalor, conceded that his views on asylum size were 'at variance with those upheld [till then] by the highest authorities on this subject'.[46] But, as his audience well knew, the number of lunatics to be provided for was simply 'enormous', and the authorities, for 'reasons of economy', had repeatedly demonstrated their preference for large asylums. Their actions ran counter to the conventional wisdom of an earlier generation of alienists, who had been convinced that 'the influence of the moral governor . . .

44. See, for example, the report on the projected expansion of the Kent County Asylum, in Commissioners in Lunacy, *21st Annual Report*, 1867, p. 4.
45. Commissioners in Lunacy, *18th Annual Report*, 1864, p. 2; see also *11th Annual Report*, 1857, p. 14.
46. Joseph Lalor, 'Observations on the Size and Construction of Lunatic Asylums', *Journal of Mental Science* 7, 1860, pp. 104–5.

should be brought to bear on each case individually'.[47] But, fortunately for all concerned, this ought now to be seen to be an 'exploded principle' since more recent experience had shown that 'large are preferable to small asylums, no less on scientific principles, and from benevolent considerations, than from motives of economy'.[48] So far 'from producing . . . general turbulence and confusion, . . . the association of large masses of insane people . . . is found to be highly conducive to good order and quietude'.[49] 'Above all', he noted, 'the influence of the example of the large mass of the quiet and orderly, on their more disorderly fellow inmates will be more powerful and more available instruments of good in large than in small asylums.'[50]

If the Panglossian claim that the large asylum represented 'a happy combination of science, benevolence, and economy'[51] was a novelty in 1860,[52] by the close of the century it had hardened into orthodoxy among the asylum officers. English county asylums were proclaimed to be 'marvels of order and regularity' resembling 'a well-constructed piece of mechanism, which, once set in motion, needs but a certain amount of regular attention to keep it working smoothly and successfully'.[53] In sustaining their operations, as Lalor had recognized, old, long-stay patients were vital 'to give the newcomers the necessary example of industry, order, and obedience'.[54] Indeed, it was 'the quiet, chronic patients who give stability to the asylum microcosm . . . the phalanx of failures, whose well-considered routine constitutes the *force majeure* of an ordinary asylum, into whose orderly ways the newcomer of ill-regulated brain drops by sheer force of superior numbers'.[55] Effective treatment, it was insistently proclaimed, was dependent on 'the steadying effect of discipline, certainly curative in its tendency, which can only be properly carried out when the chronic insane lend the magnetism of their numbers to it'.[56] And, as

47. *Ibid.*, pp. 105–106.
48. *Ibid.* Note what this implies about the goals of asylum treatment.
49. *Ibid.*, p. 108.
50. *Ibid.*, p. 106.
51. *Ibid.*
52. For an example of the persistence of the older view, see S.W.D. Williams, 'Our Over-Crowded Lunatic Asylums', *Journal of Mental Science* 17, 1871, pp. 515–18. (Williams was superintendent of the Sussex County Asylum.)
53. H.C. Burdett, *Hospitals and Asylums of the World*, Vol. 1, London: Churchill, 1891, pp. 189–90.
54. David Yellowlees, 'Presidential Address', *Journal of Mental Science* 36, 1890, p. 488.
55. Dr Urquhart, superintendent of Perth Asylum, quoted in H.C. Burdett, *Hospitals and Asylums of the World*, Vol. 2, p. 255.
56. Richard Greene, 'Hospitals for the Insane and Clinical Instruction in Asylums', paper presented to the Hospitals Association, 1890, reprinted in H.C. Burdett, *Hospitals and Asylums of the World*, Vol. 2, p. 251. Greene's paper was provoked by a proposal launched by Robert Brudenell Carter in 1889 to establish a hospital for the treatment of acute insanity, wholly independent of the existing asylum system and employing the resources of somatic medicine (as distinct from what he clearly regarded as a therapeutically and scientifically bankrupt psychiatry). Carter's proposal (the basis for a document he wrote, *Report of the Committee of the London County Council on a Hospital for*

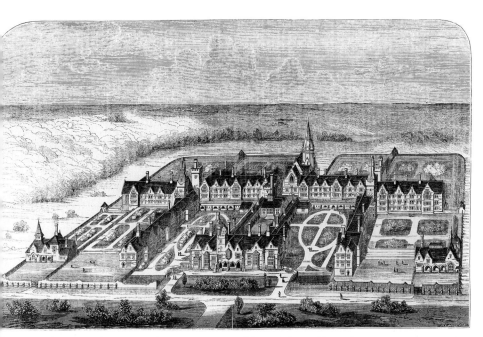

Fig. 15   The Essex County Asylum at Brentwood from *The Builder*, 16 May 1857. A typically symmetrical design, with the administrative block at the front, and the accommodation and airing courts for each sex behind and to each side.

Fielding Blandford hastened to add, 'it was for this reason that large asylums were so very much better than small ones, and why so many persons would not recover in a small institution who would in one of several hundred inmates, where perfect order and discipline obtained'.[57]

the Insane, 30 January 1890, reprinted *ibid.*, pp. 159–247) prompted some initial interest from the newly established London County Council, much to the alarm of most English alienists. Greene's counterblast was drawn up after extensive consultation with his colleagues, and explicitly represented 'the views of the chief English Lunatic Authorities and Superintendents'. Appearing in Burdett's volume with some additional commentary by other leading alienists, it demonstrates how firmly most of the profession had now committed itself to the task of administering and justifying the barracks-asylum. In 1890, David Yellowlees devoted his Presidential Address to the Medico-Psychological Association to a further assault on Carter's ideas, which he denounced as a 'wholesale slander' (though, somewhat embarrassingly, by the time he came to deliver his speech, the LCC had shelved the proposal, making his address largely redundant). See *Journal of Mental Science* 36, 1890, pp. 473–89; and the discussion by other alienists *ibid.*, pp. 583–7; as well as earlier editorials on the same subject *ibid.*, pp. 79, 232–6. The basic idea was to be revived, of course, under rather different auspices, as the Maudsley Hospital.

57. G. Fielding Blandford, quoted in H.C. Burdett, *Hospitals and Asylums of the World*, Vol. 2, p. 261.

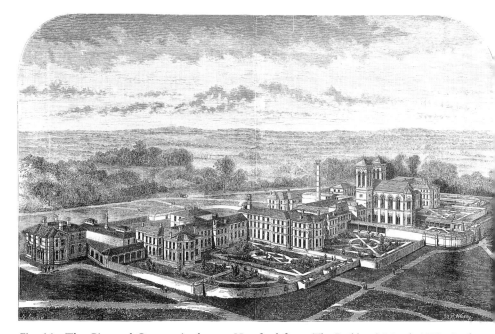

Fig. 16   The City and County Asylum at Hereford from *The Builder*, 2 March 1872. Asylum architects endeavoured to make the running of each institution as self-contained as possible. Their designs commonly made provision for such things as a gasworks, a farm, a chapel for the patients (note its prominence in this and in the preceding example), a mortuary, a graveyard, a laundry, housing for the staff on the grounds. Asylums were thus equipped to provide for almost all the wants of their inhabitants, from admission to the grave.

4. The Custodial Institution

Within these mammoth institutions, the reality of the patient's existence departed further and further from the conditions in the outside world, for his return to which the asylum was still ostensibly preparing him. As Browne put it, '[i]n the vast asylums now extant . . . all transactions, moral as well as economic, must be done wholesale'.[58] John Arlidge voiced a similar assessment:

> They have grown into lunatic colonies of eight or nine hundred, or even a thousand or more inhabitants, comfortably lodged and clothed, fed by a not illiberal commissariat, watched and waited on by well-paid attendants, disciplined and drilled to a well-ordered routine.[59]

And the key to comprehending asylum existence was obviously routine. Critics insisted that such organized monotony was

58. W.A.F. Browne, *The Moral Treatment of the Insane: A Lecture*, London, Adlard, 1864, p. 18.
59. J.T. Arlidge, *On the State of Lunacy and the Legal Provision For the Insane*, p. 102.

very well suited to a workhouse, but totally unfitted to an asylum for mental cure. Individuality is entirely overlooked; indeed the whole asylum life is the opposite of the ordinary mode of living of the working classes. When the visitor strolls along the galleries filled with listless patients, the utter absence of any object to afford amusement or occupation strikes him most painfully. It is remarked with infinite approval now and then by the Commissioners that the walls have been enlivened with some cheap paper, that a few prints have been hung in the galleries, that a fernery has been established – matters all very well in their way, but utterly inadequate to take the place of the moving sights of the outside world.[60]

Superintendents of the larger asylums conceded that 'it is totally impossible to do more than know [the inmates] by name'.[61]

'Individual interest in patients is all but dead.' How could it be otherwise? For 'their number renders the inmates mere automatons, acted on in this or that fashion according to the rules governing the great machine'.[62] Even the patients' diversions and recreations were organized and bureaucratized, shaped to fit the asylum's timetable and routine. In the words of the superintendent at the Northampton General Asylum: 'Amusement has now become so much an established and recognized part of the treatment of the insane, that it is requisite that it should be conducted in a regular and systematic manner.'[63] What this meant in practice is suggested by a description of one of the patients' dances now becoming a feature of asylum life:

On the occasion of our visit there were about 200 patients present. . . . In a raised orchestra, five musicians, three of whom were lunatics, soon struck up a merry polka, and immediately the room was alive with dancers. . . . Had the men been differently dressed, it would have been impossible to have guessed that we were in the midst of a company of lunatics, the mere sweepings of the parish workhouses; but the prison uniform of sad coloured grey appeared like a jarring note amidst the general harmony of the scene. . . . At nine precisely, although in the midst of a dance, a shrill note is blown, and the entire assembly, like so many Cinderellas, breaks up at once and the company hurry off to their dormitories.[64]

60. [Andrew Wynter], 'Non-Restraint in the Treatment of the Insane', *Edinburgh Review* 131, 1870, p. 223.
61. House of Commons, *Select Committee on the Operation of the Lunacy Law*, 1877, p. 389, evidence of Francis Scott.
62. J.T. Arlidge, *On the State of Lunacy*, p. 107.
63. Northampton General Lunatic Asylum, *Annual Report*, 1861, p. 10.
64. 'Lunatic Asylums', *Quarterly Review* 101, pp. 375–6. Such dances were an exception to the general insistence upon a strict separation of the sexes. Carefully stage-managed affairs, they constituted a weekly demonstration of the powers of moral management over the sexual passions. Apparently the segregation of the sexes was meant to extend

Fig. 17 Reproduction of a lithograph by Katherine Drake (*c.* 1847) of a lunatics' ball at the Somerset County Asylum, with the superintendent, Robert Boyd, in the foreground. The 'ballroom' is a converted kitchen. Here was a demonstration that even the forces of sexuality had been tamed and brought under control: madness was domesticated, and more effectively than the eighteenth century could ever have imagined.

The mechanical metaphor recurs again and again in contemporary descriptions of the asylum. Granville insisted that 'you want rather to encourage self-control then to convert a patient into a machine or a part of a machine'. But his own investigations of asylums showed that

> the classification generally made is for the purpose of shelving cases; that is to say, practically it has that effect. . . . in consequence of the treatment not being personal, but simply a treatment in classes, there is a tendency to make whole classes sink down into a sort of chronic state. . . . I think they come under a sort of routine discipline which ends in their passing into a state of dementia.[65]

even to the corpses: one of the principal defects noted by the Lunacy Commissioners at the Cambridge Asylum was 'the present dead-house, which serves for both sexes (an arrangement, we think, objectionable)' (Commissioners in Lunacy, *25th Annual Report*, 1871, p. 131).

65. House of Commons, *Select Committee on the Operations of the Lunacy Law*, 1877, pp. 396–7, evidence of J.M. Granville.

The asylum was 'a mere house of perpetual detention'[66] – 'simply a larger prison [with its] inmates sitting listlessly and depressed in the lengthened corridors . . . mocked [by surroundings] of which they took no heed'.[67] Unusually ambitious superintendents, like James Crichton-Browne, might insist that 'We cannot be content with a system which would imply providing convenient storage of heaps of social debris.'[68] But the system stubbornly resisted change, leaving internal critics no choice save to sink back into apathy, or to find some other line of work.[69]

Most institutions possessed a ward or two for show, where the better-behaved patients and those whose stay in the asylum was likely to be comparatively brief were kept in an environment less immediately depressing. But the contrast with the rest of the asylum only emphasized the more cruelly the bleak existence provided for the overwhelming majority of patients who were left to languish in the back-wards.[70] On one visit to Hanwell, for instance, the Lunacy Commissioners praised one day-room on the women's side as 'lofty, cheerful, and well furnished'; but it transpired that only about fifty of the 886 female patients 'are ever brought from their wards into this very cheerful sitting room'. When attention was transferred to the conditions under which the bulk of the asylum's population were forced to exist, the picture changed drastically:

> There is generally to be observed, in passing through the wards and ordinary day rooms, a marked deficiency in the means afforded for encouraging cheerfulness or intelligence among the Patients, by relieving the lifelessness of their lives from day to day. Some recreation is doubtless supplied to the better class of Patients . . . but these . . . belong to extraordinary occasions and to one class, and do not obviate that daily want among all classes.[71]

Similarly, following an inspection of the Prestwich Asylum in Lancashire: the newer wards were described as 'extremely good' with

66. *Ibid.*, p. 388, evidence of Francis Scott.
67. W. Napier Reed, reporting to the visiting committee of the Leicestershire and Rutland County Asylum on a visit to another, recently opened county asylum, quoted in W. Parry-Jones, *The Trade in Lunacy*, London: Routledge and Kegan Paul, 1972, p. 259.
68. James Crichton-Browne in *Annual Report of the West Riding Lunatic Asylum*, 1873, quoted in John Todd and Lawrence Ashworth, 'The West Riding Asylum and James Crichton-Browne, 1818–76', in G.E. Berrios and H. Freeman (eds), *150 Years of British Psychiatry 1841–1991*, London: Gaskell, 1991, p. 408.
69. Crichton-Browne himself chose the latter option, leaving Wakefield in 1875 to take up a position as Lord Chancellor's Visitor in Lunacy.
70. John Walton's detailed study of conditions in the Lancaster Asylum provides further confirmation of this pattern of 'a double standard of care, with chronic patients being allowed increasingly to vegetate'. See John Walton, 'The Treatment of Pauper Lunatics in Victorian England: The Case of Lancaster Asylum, 1816–1870', pp. 166–97 in Andrew Scull (ed.), *Madhouses, Mad-doctors, and Madmen: The Social History of Psychiatry in the Victorian Era*, Philadelphia: University of Pennsylvania Press/London: Athlone, 1981.
71. Commissioners in Lunacy, *16th Annual Report*, 1862, pp. 143–4.

respect to accommodation and the provision of amusements; 'of the older wards we have to speak much less favourably. Unfortunately, a very large number of the patients in them belong to what is called the worst class; the most noisy or violent and the most feeble or helpless.' While their separation was productive of order in the new section, it was undoubtedly detrimental to their own care.[72] At Rainhill, also in Lancashire, the 'refractory' received the same treatment:

> The Day-Rooms of these wards, without exception, are small and over-filled; there are very few comforts in them, and we saw no adequate provision for the amusement of the Patients who do not employ themselves, which form more than four or five sixths of the whole number.[73]

Conditions were equally awful at Colney Hatch. In 1862, the Commissioners commented on 'the utter absence of any means for engaging the attention of the Patients, interesting them in any occupations or amusements or affording them a sufficient variety of exercise outdoors'. In consequence, inspections of the patients found that 'besides a large number crouching on the floors, many were in or upon their beds, some for very trivial causes, and some, as if they had merely sought relief there from the noise and monotony of the galleries'.[74] The atmosphere was no better a decade later:

> The imbeciles, the demented, and those of epileptic, noisy, or violent sort, too largely or loosely classified here as more or less 'refractory', continue to be as they have always been. There is little in the objects around them, either of cheerfulness or comfort, to give them any sense but of their own miserable infirmities; and there is no check or diversion interposed, by means of any kind of employment, to the indulgence of their dirty or degraded habits. What alone is done with a staff of attendants sufficient in number . . . is to keep these particular wards as orderly as may be, and protect their inmates from violence to each other.[75]

From the outset, the advocates of moral treatment had laid much stress on the therapeutic benefits of providing employment for asylum inmates, a suggestion which met with a ready response from those charged with providing receptacles for the pauper insane. An inquiry into the number of patients employed and the type of tasks they performed was accordingly diligently made by the Lunacy Commissioners on each of their visits to an asylum, and the answers carefully written up in their subsequent reports.

72. *Ibid.*, *18th Annual Report*, 1867, p. 151.
73. *Ibid.*, p. 149.
74. House of Commons, *Select Committee on the Operation of the Lunacy Law*, 1877, pp. 396–7, 388; Commissioners in Lunacy, *16th Annual Report*, 1862, p. 138.
75. Commissioners in Lunacy, *25th Annual Report*, 1871, p. 179.

Two things clearly emerge from this mass of material. In the first place, the employment provided was hardly that envisaged by the early reformers. Instead of having as its primary goal the benefits which would accrue to the patients, the jobs provided were those that enabled the institution to run more smoothly and more cheaply – doing the laundry, repairing clothes and uniforms, acting as farm labourers on the asylum farm, or performing various menial tasks around the institution. Secondly, even given a generous definition of what constituted employment, a sizeable proportion of the inmates were not given any task, however trivial.[76] Many patients were simply left to rot.

5. The Maintenance of Order

For those who had to run these enormous receptacles for the insane, the question of most obvious concern was how such collections of crazy people – who had been placed in an institution because of their failure to conform to the ordinary rules and conventions of society – could be brought to sustain some semblance of order. The abandonment of the traditional weapons for achieving this, chains and the whip, was constantly invoked as the symbol of the humanity with which the patients were now treated when compared with past enormities, and as a shield against the perception that asylums had, on the reformers' own terms, proved a disastrous failure. On the face of things, this made the asylum administrators' task much more difficult, but in practice it was scarcely a major handicap. As is so often the case in the area of social control, the behavior which restraint had been designed to regulate turned out to be exacerbated, if not produced, by the very measures taken to control it. Its abolition showed that restraint

> was in fact creative of many of the outrages and disorders to repress which its application was commonly deemed indispensable . . . the wards of lunatic asylums no longer exhibit the harrowing description of their former state. Mania, not exasperated by severity, and melancholia, not deepened by the want of all ordinary consolations, lose the exaggerated character in which they were formerly beheld.[77]

With the employment of a larger number of attendants and the continuing availability of solitary confinement or 'seclusion' for the most stubbornly uncooperative inmates, the more extravagant prophecies of doom uttered by those attached to the old methods of management proved largely unfounded.

A subtle irony lay behind the whole subject of the control of asylum inmates' behaviour. For the creation of such a network of expensive

76. See, for example, Commissioners in Lunacy, *21st Annual Report*, 1867, pp. 152, 165; *22nd Annual Report*, 1868, p. 179.
77. Conolly, cited in J.M. Granville, *The Care and Cure of the Insane*, Vol. 1, p. 111.

specialized institutions in the first place had drawn its legitimacy from the constantly reiterated contention that lunatics were sick and/or not responsible for their own actions. Yet, if these vast asylums were to operate at all, patients had to be made to conform to the rules of the institutions, and this could only be done by utilizing the ordinary system of rewards and punishments to elicit the desired behaviour. But the resort to positive and negative sanctions was a tacit concession that it made some sort of sense to hold the lunatic responsible for his actions, and that by doing so his behaviour could be manipulated. In practice, then, the definition of actions as symptoms could not be maintained if the institution was to continue to function, and could scarcely be discarded if asylum doctors were to continue to maintain the fiction that their work was essentially medical in character.[78]

The need to disguise this awkward reality largely explains the linguistic contortions to which asylum superintendents resorted when speaking of the techniques they used to control their patients, and, in particular, their disingenuous insistence that disciplinary measures were, in fact, 'medical treatment'. In the same breath, John Millar could concede that 'the shower bath is used as a corrective discipline. The matron uses the shower bath for swearing, bad language and filthy habits' and then assert: 'The whole question [of its use] I consider to be entirely within the province of the Superintendent, as much as any other medical treatment he may think necessary to employ.'[79] The use of drugs to tranquillize patients undoubtedly increased in the course of the nineteenth century:

> Since the abolition of mechanical restraint in asylums there is no doubt that the use of medicines intended to produce sleep has very largely increased; not perhaps those that would send patients off into a state of positive somnolency, but to quiet them down; such, for example, as chloral, bromide of potassium, and remedies of that class.[80]

78. As Erving Goffman puts it in *Asylums: Essays on the Social Situation of Mental Patients and Other Inmates* (Garden City, New York: Doubleday, 1961, pp. 350–66; London: Penguin, 1970), 'the interesting point here is that psychiatric staff are in a position neither to forgo the fiction of neutrality nor to sustain it'. I have obviously drawn heavily here on his analysis.

79. Bucks County Asylum, Superintendent's Diary, 18 August 1856, in manuscript at St. John's Hospital, Stone, Bucks. On the use of shower baths as punishment, compare the discussion in Nicholas Hervey, 'The Lunacy Commission 1845–60', Vol. 1, p. 204, which draws on Alexander Morison's papers to document their being given at Hanwell, the Mecca of non-restraint, 'for impertinence to Conolly, breaking windows, hitting other inmates and nurses, and throwing food. Several patients were extremely violent when being placed in the shower, and one, Elizabeth Williams, required seven nurses to hold her down. She was tied up with a sheet over her head, and kept in the bath for over half an hour.'

80. House of Commons, *Select Committee on the Operation of the Lunacy Law*, 1877, p. 397, evidence of J.M. Granville. The drugs used often produced profound iatrogenic illnesses. During his years as superintendent of Bethlem, Sir George Savage noted that 'chloral may produce physical ill health, hypochondriasis and insanity. . . . It may produce sleep in some cases with advantage, but more commonly disadvantageously. It may be used as

Again, the rationale was explicitly therapeutic, and Granville was angry at what he saw as a perversion of medical techniques:

> The use of narcotics in the fashion I am condemning is only a modification of the old practice of giving patients antimony under the pretence of reducing the fever heat and fury of mania, or of employing a strong shower-bath, the douche, or the cold pack with the same ostensible purpose. The pretence of curative treatment was a sophistry. The real object was to secure quiet wards, and the modern version of the same policy is a free use of sedatives.[81]

The tranquillity the Lunacy Commissioners sought had other sources as well. One of the less obvious ways of ensuring that obstreperous patients did not remain that way for long was the practice of keeping all inmates on a diet barely above starvation level:

> The dietary in the asylums, certainly around London, is much below the normal standard, according to the received quantities. I have calculated the dietaries at different asylums, or got them calculated, and I find that they are below the average determined by Dr Lyon Playfair's inductive experiments for even moderate exercise; they are barely above the requirements for quiet. An excited person in an asylum would be wasting more tissue than would be replaced by such a diet.[82]

restraint rather than treatment in violent cases.' 'Uses and Abuses of Chloral Hydrate', *Journal of Mental Science* 25, 1879, p. 8. With hyoscyamine, the physical effects could be, if anything, still more dramatic: even a dose as small as a twenty-sixth of a grain could produce physical collapse and mental depression, confusion, and hallucinations of sight and touch, coupled with a feeling of 'dread, so that the patients would struggle violently rather than have a second dose' – all of which, Savage commented, created a 'moral effect lasting much longer [than the physical incapacity]'. 'Hyoscyamine and its Uses', *Journal of Mental Science* 25, 1879, pp. 178–9.

81. J.M. Granville, *The Care and Cure of the Insane*, Vol. 1, p. 59. For documentation of the extensive use of chloral and the bromides in the 1870s and 1880s even in the bastion of moral treatment, the York Retreat, see A. Digby, *Madness, Morality and Medicine: A Study of the York Retreat 1796–1914*, Cambridge: Cambridge University Press, 1985, pp. 129–30. My own examination of the casebooks of Harrington Tuke's private asylum, Manor House, Chiswick, and of Ticehurst Asylum uncovered a similarly routine reliance on drugs, particularly narcotics and soporifics. Ironically, perhaps because of the associated expense, evidence from the casebooks of county asylums points to a more sparing use of pharmaceutical restraints in the huge pauper asylums. For the London asylums, for instance, 'The total amount dispensed suggests that drugs were employed to "flatten" individual outbursts of disturbed behaviour, rather than to effect prolonged states of tranquillization. The more routine tranquillizers employed were so-called strong dresses; garments in heavy canvass which restricted movement.' D. Cochrane, ' "Humane, Economical, and Medically Wise": The LCC as Administrators of Victorian Lunacy Policy', in W.F. Bynum, R. Porter and M. Shepherd (eds), *The Anatomy of Madness*, Vol. 3, London: Routledge, 1988, p. 262.

82. House of Commons, *Select Committee on the Operation of the Lunacy Law*, 1877, p. 307. Such a policy had an additional advantage: it saved on the cost of maintenance. An even more extreme example of this policy was to be carried out at the Buckinghamshire County Asylum in the early twentieth century. By 1916, even the official dietary tables suggest that a male patient's daily food allowance provided only 40 grams of protein and 750 calories (which may be compared with what is now estimated to be a minimum

Order was also maintained by depriving recalcitrant inmates of 'privileges' which helped make the intolerable bearable. Crichton-Browne, for instance, conceded that 'there is a penal code in every pauper asylum in this country, but it is of a very mild description. The punishment consists generally in the deprivation of a man's tobacco, or in his enforced absence from the amusements provided; the balls, concerts, and entertainments'.[83] Less mentionable in official circles was the use of physical violence by attendants to compel the inmates' obedience. Yet the fact that almost every year, despite the difficulty of obtaining evidence sufficient for a conviction, the Commissioners' reports contain details of prosecutions brought against attendants for breaking patients' ribs, or even bringing about their deaths, indicates that such practices continued, albeit less frequently and openly than before.[84]

All of which meant that the order and superficial calm which the

requirement for a sedentary man of 60 grams of protein and 2,100 calories). Female patients received even less. With a deliberate policy of semi-starvation carried to this extreme, the result was a very sharp increase in asylum mortality rates. (The worst year was 1918, when a third of the asylum population died in the space of twelve months. This outcome was sufficiently extreme to shame the authorities into reversing themselves, and following a sharp increase in expenditures on food, the death rate was cut in half the following year.) See John Crammer, *Asylum History: Buckinghamshire County Pauper Lunatic Asylum*, pp. 76–7, 113, 126–7.

83. House of Commons, *Select Committee on the Operation of the Lunacy Law*, 1877, p. 72. The following revealing exchange occurred a little later in J. Crichton-Browne's testimony: Q. 'They have so much sense of responsibility, in fact, that they are influenced by the knowledge that they well be deprived of those luxuries if they violate the rules of the asylum?' A. 'Most certainly; and it is the practice in almost every county asylum in England to act on that principle, and to assume a knowledge of right and wrong in the majority of inmates.' As Goffman has so skillfully shown in his *Asylums*, those who live outside a total institution ordinarily do not appreciate the terrible significance having to do without trivial things possesses for those confined in such a bleak environment.

84. For detailed evidence on this point, see the discussion in J. Walton, 'The Treatment of Pauper Lunatics in Victorian England', pp. 186–8. In 1870, for example, the Lunacy Commissioners reported that 122 attendants had been dismissed from asylums during the preceding year, 46 for being violent or rough towards patients. This included a prosecution discussed by Walton, in which two attendants from Lancaster Asylum were sentenced to seven years' penal servitude for manslaughter. See Commissioners in Lunacy, *24th Annual Report*, 1870, p. 80. For other examples, see Richard Russell, 'The Lunacy Profession and its Staff in the Second Half of the Nineteenth Century, with Special Reference to the West Riding Lunatic Asylum,' in W.F. Bynum, R. Porter and M. Shepherd (eds), *The Anatomy of Madness*, Vol. 3, pp. 309–10; and Nicholas Hervey, 'A Slavish Bowing Down', pp. 111–12 (Kent County Asylum). Decrying the 'ludicrously inadequate' supervision that characterized the system, Andrew Wynter reflected on the consequences. Rather than the physicians, 'it is the attendant who is the real master of the patient: hour by hour he is at his mercy. The many small cruelties he perpetrates, sometimes from temper; the many neglects he is guilty of, often in consequence of fatigue, are seldom known and are but rarely recorded. It is only when some dreadful cruelty happens that the world is made cognisant through an inquest, that restraint has not altogether vanished with the destruction of bonds. [Then] we hear, as we have too often of late, that a poor demented creature has had his ribs crushed in by the knees of his attendant whilst kneeling on him, or trampling on his chest in that position.' *The Borderlands of Insanity*, 1st edn, pp. 115, 117–18.

Lunacy Commissioners and asylum authorities came to value so highly were actually attainable goals, the more so since

> The effect of long continued discipline is to remove all salient parts of the character, all obtrusive and irregular propensities and peculiarities . . . [with the result that] the majority [of asylum inmates], enfeebled by monotony, by the absence of strong impulses and new impressions, tamed, and stilled, and frozen, by the very means to which they may owe life, and some remains of reason, exhibit a stolidity and torpor which are obviously superadded to their original malady.[85]

6. Asylums for the Upper Classes

While county asylums contained the overwhelming majority of those incarcerated for insanity, their admissions were restricted by law to pauper lunatics, i.e. those maintained in whole or in part at public expense by parishes or Poor Law unions. Fee-paying upper and upper-middle-class patients patronized an entirely separate network of institutions, consisting of a mixture of the old charity or 'registered' hospitals and the profit-making private licensed houses. And, as one might expect, there were some sharp differences between these establishments and those catering to paupers, differences which were naturally most marked in the asylums servicing the aristocracy.[86]

From the outset, private patients were accommodated in small asylums. For example, the Lunacy Commissioners' first report showed that the average size of the ninety-six provincial licensed houses taking private patients, eliminating one atypically large institution, was almost exactly thirty-six patients; most took fewer than a hundred, and several as few as two. Moreover, unlike county asylums, the size of the institutions taking private patients scarcely grew in the course of the nineteenth century. In 1879, only thirteen of the thirty-three metropolitan licensed houses and twelve of sixty provincial licensed housed contained thirty patients or more. On 1 January 1890, the average patient population of a metropolitan licensed house was seventy-six patients, and of a provincial licensed house only thirty-two.[87] Consequently, private patients were spared the

85. Crichton Royal Asylum, *9th Annual Report*, 1848, p. 35.
86. One thing that should constantly be borne in mind is that the differences between the various kinds of institutions catering to private patients were almost as great as those between private and pauper asylums. One crude index of this is the range of fees charged to inmates. In 1879, these broke down as follows: 'In 32 of the houses, receiving about 1,300 patients, the average payment is under 100 pounds per annum. In 22, receiving about 750, the average payment is from 100 pounds to 150 pounds per annum. . . . In 18 the average payments range from 150 pounds to 200 pounds. In 13, from 200 pounds to 280 pounds. In four from 280 pounds to 330 pounds, and in one house [Ticehurst] they reach 470 pounds, including the cost of carriages and other expensive luxuries' (Commissioners in Lunacy, *33rd Annual Report*, 1879, p. 113).
87. Commissioners in Lunacy, *45th Annual Report*, 1891, pp. 108–9. By comparison, the average size of a county asylum had now reached 802 patients.

more grossly institutional features characteristic of the public asylums. Indeed, an uncertain but unquestionably sizeable number avoided asylums altogether. Female patients, especially, were often kept at home,[88] while many well-to-do lunatics were funnelled into a shadowy network of unlicensed and often illegal establishments specializing in single patients,[89] or even sent abroad beyond the reach of the prying eyes of the Lunacy Commissioners,[90] primarily to spare the family the stigma and disgrace associated with certification and confinement in an asylum.[91]

Reluctant as they might be, however, many wealthy families ultimately found they had no option but to commit their relations to asylums. Once admitted, private patients could generally expect much more assiduous medical attention, and, given the much lower doctor/patient ratio typical of these establishments, the average patient was likely to have at least some contact with a physician in the course of the week. The proportion of attendants was usually much greater than the ratio of 1:10 or 1:12 which was the standard in the better county asylums. In their second annual report, for instance, the Lunacy Commissioners noted that 'In some of the Private Establishments receiving Patients of a high class (such as Dr Fox's Asylum at Brislington, Dr Willis's at Shillingthorpe,[92] and Mr Newington's at Ticehurst) the number of Attendants and Servants averages about one for every two patients.'[93]

With the establishment of a regular system of inspection and the removal of pauper patients, the grosser forms of abuse and maltreatment

88. *Cf.* C. MacKenzie, 'A Family Asylum: A History of the Private Madhouse at Ticehurst in Sussex, 1792–1917', unpublished Ph.D. thesis, University of London, 1987, p. 185.
89. For details on many of these single lodgings, and a tracing of their linkages to well-known alienists with an aristocratic and upper-middle class clientele (the product of an extraordinary piece of historical detective work), see Nicholas Hervey, 'The Lunacy Commission 1845–60', Vol. 1, pp. 234–7, 242–62, and Vol. 2, p. 131; and idem, '"A Slavish Bowing Down": the Lunacy Commission and the Psychiatric Profession 1845–60', in W. Bynum, R. Porter and M. Shepherd (eds) *The Anatomy of Madness*, Vol. 2, pp. 115–18. As Hervey notes, with their confinement 'shrouded in secrecy, and protected by the powerful cloak of family sensibility', these patients were largely bereft of the protections provided by inspection, and were often the victims of appalling conditions and treatment. Their families seem to have accepted these drawbacks as the price of privacy and of avoiding social disgrace. The number of patients in single care began to be shown in the Lunacy Commissioners' reports beginning in 1865, and (though one should be cautious because these are only the cases known to the authorities) women consistently formed the majority by a substantial margin. See *Reports*, 1865, p. 29; 1875, p. 51; 1885, p. 111.
90. Ironically enough, when Shaftesbury's own son Maurice became mentally disturbed with epilepsy, he was shipped abroad and confined in private lodgings in Lausanne, Switzerland, notwithstanding Shaftesbury's vociferous and lifelong public opposition to this practice.
91. *Cf.* the discussion and evidence presented in Charlotte MacKenzie, 'A Family Asylum', pp. 279–95.
92. Shillingthorpe advertised itself as being 'conducted in the style of a country gentleman's residence'. Advertisement in the *London and Provincial Medical Directory*, 1847, reprinted in W. Parry-Jones, *The Trade in Lunacy*, p. 106.
93. Commissioners in Lunacy, *2nd Annual Report*, 1847, p. 56.

of patients seem by and large to have disappeared from these asylums.[94] In return for their much larger payments, most private patients were kept in much greater comfort than their pauper counterparts. Of no county asylum could it be said, as it was of the metropolitan licensed houses, that 'the accommodation provided for the patients of the private class in no way differs from what is usually found in an ordinary [sc. upper-class] dwelling house.'[95] While chronic pauper cases were herded about in a dull, witless mass, their upper-class equivalents usually received relatively unregimented domestic care. At Ashbrooke Hall, for example, a Mrs Hitch received 'six quiet and harmless female patients. . . . Each patient has an attendant and is visited by a medical man at least once a month – these ladies go to church, and their amusement is provided for, by out-door occupation, and music and other means of amusement is provided indoors. . . . The patients live in Mrs. Hitch's family.'[96] At Kenton House, a similar institution near Exeter, 'two ladies receive excellent accommodation of a quiet domestic kind, and much personal care and attention from the lady having charge of them'.[97]

A number of these receptacles for the upper classes more closely resembled an asylum, though. The Crichton Royal Asylum in Dumfries was a particular favourite of many well-to-do English families. It was a richly endowed institution, and one of its major attractions was its geographical location just over the border in Scotland, a situation that ensured an additional measure of privacy, since this placed it beyond the surveillance of the English Lunacy Commissioners. Moreover, its super-intendent from 1837 to 1857, William Alexander Francis Browne, had been one of the earliest and most eloquent spokesmen on behalf of the new system of reformed asylums, and his widely circulated book, *What Asylums Were, Are, and Ought to Be,* had done much to promote the image of the asylum as the place of first rather than last resort, preferable to even

---

94. There were occasional exceptions. In 1856, for example, the Commissioners reported that at Sandfield House in Staffordshire, 'The beds and bedding are for the most part in the worst state, the beds and mattresses being thin, and many of them being full of knots. The blankets, some of which are in fragments, are thin, and quite insufficient for this cold season. Much of bedding is soiled. Some of the floors are wet, saturated with urine. In one room, containing four beds, we found a patient just dead, his body exhibiting sores, and deep and extensive sloughs. . . . The clothing of the patients is in several instances ragged and bad, and is generally very defective in cleanliness and neatness. The day rooms occupied by the patients are very small; they have benches only for seats; they are very gloomy and uncomfortable, and the bedrooms are equally so.' Commissioners in Lunacy, *10th Annual Report,* 1856, p. 23.
95. Commissioners in Lunacy, *22nd Annual Report,* 1868, p. 8.
96. Ashbrooke Hall Licensed House, *Visitors and Patients Book,* 31 August 1886 and 1 March 1887, in manuscript, East Sussex Record Office, Lewes, QAL/1/5/E5.
97. Commissioners in Lunacy, *26th Annual Report,* 1872, p. 32. Apparently the Commissioners' comment that 'There is a class of cases for which nothing is so suitable or beneficial as a small, well-conducted house of this nature, pleasantly situated, and where quiet domestic comforts are obtainable' (*ibid.,* p. 36) did not apply to pauper lunatics.

the best and most solicitous of domestic arrangements. Recognizing the
need to 'tempt the rich to have recourse to those measures from choice
which the poor have long pursued from necessity',[98] he had devoted much
of his institution's not inconsiderable resources to the provision of 'the
refinement and delicacies essential to the comfort, and instrumental in the
recovery of the affluent'[99] and was rewarded with a continuing influx of
such patients from south of the border.[100]

Browne devoted enormous energy and ingenuity to the moral discipline
and treatment of his charges.[101] A wide range of activities was made
available in an effort to restore the patients to sanity (and, as he later
confessed, as ways of 'combating monotony, the giant evil of even well-
regulated seclusion').[102] Within the asylum walls, 'concerts, public read-
ings, evening parties, dances, games at bowls, billiards, summer ice,
cards, chess, backgammon, have afforded means of diversifying the dull
routine of discipline; although, perhaps, the exhibition of the magic
lantern yielded the most unalloyed pleasure, and to the greatest number'.
And despite much initial trepidation and complaints from the townsfolk,
patients were escorted outside the asylum walls to participate 'in every
public amusement which combined present gratification with prospective
benefit, and in which they could mingle without excitement or injury to
themselves, or offence or disturbance to others': races, regattas, art and
natural history exhibits, fishing, walks, concerts, the circus, outings to
the theatre.[103] Subsequently, the array of activities designed to create
'a healthy tone and an invigorating moral climate' was extended in yet
more elaborate ways: gymnastics, hymn writing, instrumental music
and singing, drawing and painting, language lessons in Greek, Arabic,
Hebrew, French and Latin, the keeping of pets, the publication of a
monthly literary magazine, the putting on of plays, with patients as both
performers and audience.[104] 'Every hour', Browne boasted, 'has its
appropriate object and occupation; and [as a result, patients] become more
the creatures of a system, and less the sport of their own distempered
inclinations.'[105]

Within the tightly controlled asylum environment, Browne, as its

98. W.A.F. Browne, *What Asylums Were, Are, and Ought to Be*, Edinburgh: Black, 1837, p.
    169.
99. *Ibid.*, p. 199.
100. In his last report as superintendent, for instance, he records receiving 100 applications
    for admission from the affluent classes, 'the majority from England'. There was room
    for only 26. See Crichton Royal Asylum, *18th Annual Report*, 1857, p. 6.
101. The paragraphs that follow draw upon the more extended discussion of Browne's
    career and the regime at the Crichton Royal in Andrew Scull, *The Asylum as Utopia:
    W.A.F. Browne and the Mid-Nineteenth Century Consolidation of Psychiatry*, London:
    Routledge, 1990.
102. Crichton Royal Asylum, *13th Annual Report*, 1852, p. 36.
103. *Idem.*, *3rd Annual Report*, 1842, pp. 15–6.
104. *Idem.*, *12th Annual Report*, 1851, pp. 22–8.
105. *Idem.*, *3rd Annual Report*, 1842, p. 22.

'moral governor', sought to ensure that 'the impress of authority is never withdrawn, but is stamped on every transaction'[106] and to make 'discriminate use of ordinary circumstances and trifles in depressing, elevating, tranquillising, rousing, persuading, or governing the insane. . . .'[107] But all his ingenuity and skill, even when coupled with an aggressive willingness to experiment with any and all medical means of treatment that suggested themselves, were of little avail in remoralizing the mad and restoring them to sanity. Where he had previously encouraged his potential clients to view the asylum as a reliable mechanism for manufacturing sane citizens from mad raw materials, he now cautioned them that

> All men entrusted with the care of the insane must be conscious of how infinitely inferior the actual benefit conferred is to the standard originally formed of the efficacy of medicine, or of the powers of the calm and healthy over the agitated and perverted mind . . . how intractable nervous disease is found to be and how indelible its ravages are even when reason appears to be restored.[108]

As in pauper institutions, efforts were now made to redefine the criteria of 'success'. Every bit as important as the cures one promoted were 'the development of sources of calm and contentment, where restoration cannot be effected [one must look to] . . . the general amount of mental health and happiness secured to all residing in the Institution, and especially to those whose calamities must render them permanent inhabitants . . . [and seek to create] a new and artificial modification of society adapted to the altered dispositions and circumstances of the insane. . . .'[109] But for all Browne's attempts to reassure his audience (and himself) that 'the progress is in the right direction',[110] reality on a daily basis remained recalcitrant and bleak. A note of quiet desperation about 'the intrinsic repulsiveness of the records of sorrow and suffering'[111] which he must constantly encounter now entered his reports, and he conceded that

> There are no more painful convictions in the mind of those engaged in the care and cure of the insane than that so little can be done to restore health, to re-establish order and tranquillity, than that, after the best application of the most sagacious and ingenious measures, the results are so barren and incommensurate, that in defiance of sympathy and solicitude, misery and violence, and vindictiveness should predominate. . . .'[112]

106. *Idem.*, *7th Annual Report*, 1846, p. 35.
107. *Idem.*, *11th Annual Report*, 1850, p. 31.
108. *Idem.*, *9th Annual Report*, 1848, p. 5.
109. *Idem.*, *12th Annual Report*, 1851, p. 5.
110. *Idem.*, *13th Annual Report*, 1852, p. 40.
111. *Idem.*, *15th Annual Report*, 1854, p. 5.
112. *Idem.*, *13th Annual Report*, 1852, p. 40. Five years later, in his final report, the romanticized commentary on the amusements and attractions of asylum life was

Even in this generously endowed and imaginatively run establishment, moral treatment was deteriorating into a repressive form of moral management (a process that accelerated once Browne left in 1857 to become one of the first Lunacy Commissioners for Scotland).

Very similar patterns can be observed at other upper-class establishments. The York Retreat, for instance, had originally been a purely Quaker establishment, but in 1820 it took its first non-Quaker patient. Gradually, those running it gave way to the temptation to add a more affluent clientele from beyond the ranks of the Society of Friends, consoling themselves with the thought that this allowed them to subsidize poorer Quaker patients. (By the mid 1870s, more than sixty per cent of the admissions had no Quaker affiliation.) As Anne Digby has demonstrated, however, while this influx of richer patients led the Retreat to provide much more luxurious accommodations, so that, during the latter decades of the nineteenth century, its 'pampered patients lived in a cozy cluttered cocoon of material abundance . . .',[113] it was also associated with the trivialization of moral treatment 'into a means of amusing or occupying patients, with no very defined therapeutic value'.[114] Though 'individuality was not crushed into helpless anonymity'[115] (as in the county asylums), still, by the last third of the century, control and discipline were the paramount goals of the institution, and 'patients were no longer subjects to be treated but objects to be managed'.[116]

entirely set aside, to be replaced by a startlingly frank description of his patients' dismal progress:

> It has been customary to draw a veil over the degradation of nature, which is so often a symptom of insanity. But it is right that the real difficulties of the management of large bodies of the insane should be disclosed; it is salutary that the involuntary debasement, the animalism, the horrors, which so many voluntary acts tend to, should be laid bare. No representation of blind frenzy, or of vindictive ferocity, so perfectly realizes, so apparently justifies, the ancient theory of metempsychosis, or the belief in demoniacal possession, as the manic glorying in obscenity and filth; devouring garbage or ordure, surpassing those brutalities which may to the savage be a heritage and a superstition. . . . These practices are not engrafted upon disease by vulgar customs, by vicious or neglected training, or by original elements of character. They are encountered in victims from the refined and polished portions of society, of the purest life, the most exquisite sensibility. Females of birth drink their urine. . . . Outlines of high artistic pretensions have been painted in excrement; poetry has been written in blood, or more revolting media. . . . Patients are met with . . . who daub and drench the walls as hideously as their disturbed fancy suggests; who wash or plaster their bodies, fill every crevice in the room, their ears, noses, hair, with ordure; who conceal these precious pigments in their mattresses, gloves, shoes, and will wage battle to defend their property.

Crichton Royal Asylum, *18th Annual Report*, 1857, pp. 24–6.
113. Anne Digby, *Madness, Morality, and Medicine*, Cambridge: Cambridge University Press, 1985, p. 40.
114. *Ibid.*, p. 115.
115. *Ibid.*, p. 199.
116. *Ibid.*, p. 56. Digby notes that 'Symptomatic of this change was the fact that from the 1850s patients' case-notes referred much more frequently to "discipline" and "control".' *Ibid.*, p. 76. Ironically enough, the 'management' of the inmates was furthered by the

g. 18   View of a portion of the grounds at Ticehurst Asylum from a brochure published in
30, showing the hermitage and bowling green. Even at this early date, the asylum provided
extraordinary range of amenities for its aristocratic clientele.

Curiously, despite its fame, the Retreat settled down to become
essentially a regional, even a local institution, with most of its affluent,
non-Quaker patients coming from Yorkshire and the immediately
surrounding counties.[117] By contrast, Ticehurst, a profit-making establishment on the borders of Sussex and Kent, achieved much more prominence
among the asylums catering to the rich, and was able to attract a clientele
from all over the country.[118] By all accounts ranking as among the best,

substitution of 'an increasingly authoritarian medical regime' for the earlier lay-run
programme, with bromides and chloral hydrate being extensively used (in the words of
one patient) to 'quench the poor sufferers into quietness'. *Ibid.*, pp. 129–30. Case notes
likewise reveal an increasing 'lack of sympathy' for the patients, alongside the shift
'from mechanical to chemical means of restraining violence and subduing excitement';
and they repeatedly demonstrate the 'continuing concern of Retreat therapists to
convert their patients into industrious, well-behaved conformists. . . .' *Ibid.*, p. 261.

117. *Ibid.*, pp. 178, 186.
118. In fact, patients even came to the Sussex countryside from abroad. The Honourable
James A.E., for instance, first secretary to the British Legation in Greece, was sent back
'direct and in haste from Athens' on 2 March 1868, his insanity allegedly caused by local
climate. (Four years later, on 31 December 1872, he was dead of tertiary syphilis.) A
still more extraordinary case was the Egyptian Prince Ahmed S. ed D., brought to
Ticehurst on 20 December 1899 from Cairo after shooting and killing his sister's
husband, Fouad Pasha, the previous year. (This was an extremely lucrative patient even
by Ticehurst standards. The Newingtons constructed a small palace in their grounds to
accommodate the Eastern potentate, for whose care they received more than 2,000

and certainly as the most expensive private asylum in England, Ticehurst rose from modest beginnings to become a favourite with the English aristocracy during the 1820s and 1830s.

Founded in the late eighteenth century, it remained in the hands of the Newington family throughout the nineteenth century. In the early 1800s it already possessed grounds of approximately fifty acres, afterwards increased to 300 acres; and by 1830 it was equipped with an aviary, bowling green, pagoda and summer house, music room, reading room, and so forth.[119] Throughout the century, its patient population fluctuated between sixty and eighty, evenly divided between the sexes. An extraordinarily large staff attended to the wants of the inmates: 'The Medical Superintendents, three in number, are assisted by seven lady superintendents and companions, four gentlemen acting as companions.'[120] The latter, 'living as they do, constantly with the patients, must materially influence for the good the demeanour and general conduct of the attendants, and the comfort to the patient to have one of his own position as his companion in his room and during his walks must be very great'.[121] In 1879 there were in all over 150 attendants of one sort or another – 'twenty-seven male attendants, thirty nurses, forty-three indoor domestics, thirty-eight outdoor, including coachmen and gardeners,' as well as fifteen carriages and twenty-six horses.[122] Almost every visit by the Commissioners produced a comment on the 'great comfort [which] as usual prevailed in every part of the Establishment . . . the fact that this is a private asylum is, as far as possible, veiled by the comfort and elegancies of the House and furniture'.[123] Not surprisingly, 'the general feeling is undoubtedly content with the domestic arrangements . . . indeed it would be difficult to add to the comforts which the Patients have in this Establishment, absolute liberty excepted'.[124] Lest the asylum's 300 acres of grounds provided

pounds per annum in the early 1900s. George Savage was one of several eminent physicians brought in to consult on the case, and share in the financial windfall. It is perhaps of interest to add that this particular case had a very unusual ending. After many years of confinement at Ticehurst, the Prince escaped and fled across Europe disguised as a woman, ultimately joining his mother in Turkey.) See Ticehurst Asylum Casebooks 15–17, 38, 39, and Patients Bill Book, 1901–1908, in manuscript, Contemporary Medical Archives, Wellcome Institute for the History of Medicine, London.

119. See the engravings in the brochure published by the Newingtons in 1830: *Views of Messrs. Newington's Private Asylum for the Care of Insane Persons.* A copy is preserved in the East Sussex Record Office, Lewes (QAL 1/1/1).

120. Commissioners in Lunacy, *33rd Annual Report*, 1879.

121. Ticehurst Licensed House and Asylum, *Visitors' Book*, 30 May 1877, in manuscript, East Sussex Record Office, Lewes (QAL 1/5/1).

122. Commissioners in Lunacy, *33rd Annual Report*, 1879.

123. Ticehurst *Visitors' Book*, 23 March 1874; 10 June 1880, in manuscript, East Sussex Record Office, Lewes (QAL 1/5/1, 2). At least one patient, Lucy Bing T., took the resemblance to a country house at face value: 'Does not appear to recognize the ladies about her are insane, looks upon this building as an hotel.' Ticehurst Asylum Casebook 32, 1888, in manuscript, Contemporary Medical Archives, Wellcome Institute for the History of Medicine, London.

124. Ticehurst *Visitors' Book*, 10 June 1880.

insufficient diversions, two houses were rented by the sea, at St. Leonard's, to which patients could repair for a change of air and scenery.

At the asylum itself, every effort was made to occupy and amuse the patients. Lectures were given on popular subjects. There were fortnightly concerts in the summer, 'as many as thirty-six patients taking part in them'.[125] Many patients dined regularly with their physicians. 'An excellent theatre with scenery' was constructed for the use of the patients.[126] Some patients were 'taken to festivities in the neighbourhood, cricket matches, archery, fêtes, flower shows, and others have been taken out for picnics'.[127] Horses, donkeys, and carriages were available for riding, and a pack of hounds for hunting. (Aristocrats could not be deprived of their favourite diversion simply because they were crazy.) In short, while moral treatment may have disappeared without trace in the public asylums, it was applied with a vengeance at some of the private ones. In the words of the Commissioners, 'the recreation grounds are large and well adapted to restore health to diseased minds . . . and we can speak in high terms of . . . the efforts made to promote the recovery and welfare of those placed here for treatment'.[128]

The results, to say the least, were disappointing.[129] In report after report, the Commissioners were compelled to acknowledge that 'we spoke to all, but did not obtain many relevant replies';[130] 'all are apparently in good health but no one shows any sign of mental improvement';[131] and

125. *Ibid.*, 9 October 1871; 5 December 1870.
126. *Ibid.*, 8 December 1877.
127. *Ibid.*, 27 July 1878.
128. *Ibid.*, 7 December 1877.
129. Moreover, as elsewhere, the accumulating disappointments and the loss of therapeutic optimism were matched by a decline in the quality of the treatment afforded to chronic cases in the last third of the nineteenth century, a decline which the lavish deployment of material comforts could mask but not reverse. *Cf.* C. MacKenzie, 'A Family Asylum', chapter 4 and Conclusion.
130. Ticehurst Asylum, *Visitors' Book*, 12 April 1892, in manuscript, East Sussex Record Office, Lewes (QAL 1/5/2).
131. *Ibid.*, 23 May 1888.
132. For example, of Lord Charles H., son of the 8th Marquis of T. (confined in Ticehurst from 14 July 1866 onwards, together with his brother Lord Frederick H.), the Newingtons themselves reported: 'Leads a mechanical and vegetative life, sitting the whole day long in his easy chair in a dreamy, listless semi-torpid state, avoiding all intercourse or occupation of mind or body. Desires to eat his meals alone, and, in fact, to live within himself. . . . Intellect in a dull confused state and without concentration or comparison. Feelings languid and passive.' He was aroused to anger only when any of his fellow inmates failed to offer him the proper degree of deference. Ticehurst Asylum Case Book 12, 21 July 1866, 30 September 1868, 31 March 1869. Jonathan Neale B., a 66-year-old gentleman admitted a few months earlier than the H.'s, was likewise reported to lead 'an indolent vegetative life. . . . Is extremely demented, being utterly incapable of carrying on a conversation; most frequently when questioned, answers yes or no indifferently, rarely giving utterance to more than one word, and that so indistinctly that it more resembles a moan, than an articulate sound . . . exhibits scarcely a ray of intelligence. . . . He hangs around in the passages and wanders carelessly in grounds.' Three years later, the Newingtons reported 'Continues the same in all respects – His behaviour at the dinner table became so dirty and disagreeable to other

Table 7   Percentage of Cures of Private Patients in
Asylums in England and Wales, 1870–90 Calculated
on the Whole Number Resident, 1 January–31
December.

Type of Institution	1870	1880	1890
Metropolitan Licensed Houses	7.57%	6.25%	5.75%
Provincial Licensed Houses	11.15%	7.43%	6.41%
Registered Hospitals	12.11%	9.05%	11.25%

Sources: Commissioners in Lunacy, 25th, 35th, and
45th Annual Reports, 1871, 1881, 1891.

so on.[132] Patients were provided with a high standard of physical care,[133] and 'could continue to enjoy many of the benefits of their privileged position despite their illness . . .',[134] while their families were assured of privacy and confidentiality, and that male and female patients would remain strictly segregated. But as a rule, Ticehurst performed less well with respect to cures than many county asylums: to take just the years 1870, 1880, and 1890, in each twelve-month period, the numbers discharged cured as a percentage of the total numbers resident were respectively 3.75 per cent, 5.68 per cent, and 4.13 per cent.[135] It was not alone in

gentlemen that he now dines in his own room, he has occasional drives which he enjoys very much.' *Ibid.*, Case Books 12–16, 22 February, 31 December 1866, 25 June 1869. Not all patients, by any means, were this demented and withdrawn. Others took fuller advantage of the range of amenities provided to help ease the monotony of their days.

133. This is particularly evident in the case notes on the substantial number of male patients who suffered from progressive paralysis caused by tertiary syphilis. See, for example, the case of Adolphus B., a 52-year-old retired hop merchant admitted on 12 December 1867. Careful nursing care extended his life for almost five years, to 1 June 1873, despite increasing signs of debility and physical decay. The similarly afflicted Honourable James A.E. lasted from 2 March 1868 to 31 December 1872. From as early as October 1870, his speech was 'so much impaired that it is impossible to understand him' and he was 'incontinent of urine', but he continued to go out for drives twice a week with his wife in 'a donkey carriage' until a month and a half before his death. See Ticehurst Casebooks 14–18, in manuscript, Contemporary Medical Archives, Wellcome Institute for the History of Medicine, London.

134. C. MacKenzie, 'A Family Asylum', p. 319.

135. Charlotte MacKenzie points out that if outcomes are calculated on admissions, rather than the number of patients resident, the results look a little less bleak: between 1845 and 1885, 27 per cent of first admissions were discharged 'recovered', and a further 23 per cent as 'relieved'. Once again, however, these statistics differ little, if at all, from the figures Laurence Ray reports for the county asylums he studied. (Moreover, those discharged as 'relieved' were generally, so far as one can judge from the case notes, but little better than when they had entered the establishment.) A more telling measure of the basic mission of the asylum is provided by another statistic she quotes: of those in Ticehurst at any one time, between 60 and 80 per cent could expect to die there, and

this respect, as Table 7 shows. In general, the proportion of cures achieved by all this effort was no better than what was accomplished in the pauper bins.[136] Apparently, the rich could buy opulent accommodation, greater attention and more eminent psychiatrists for their crazy relatives, but not more cures. For all the lavish expenditure of funds, private asylums remained, in Bucknill's words, 'institutions for private imprisonment'.[137]

7. Warehousing the Patients

Though several of the Lunacy Commissioners had been in the forefront of the effort to secure reform, and had then been at pains to emphasize the asylum's virtues as a curative institution, they adjusted their levels of expectation without visible discomfort to reflect the custodial reality which from the outset characterized almost all types of asylums. Indeed, the pressures emanating from the Commissioners' office generally served rather to reinforce than to mitigate the custodialism of the system. The optimism surrounding the achievement of reform persisted, at least in attenuated form, through the remainder of the 1840s and perhaps even into the early 1850s, and the Commissioners' reports in those years did pay some attention to the issue of cure. In 1847, they went so far as to issue a supplementary report largely devoted to a survey of existing techniques and methods of curing mental disorder as practised in English asylums of the period, hoping thereby to raise the general proportion of cures and to stimulate further advances in the field. But as the actual results achieved in the new asylums started to belie the easy optimism about curability which characterized these early years, they began to concentrate their attention on more mundane administrative matters. To judge by the space and emphasis allotted each topic, by the mid-1850s the question of curing asylum inmates ranked considerably below the urgent issue of the composition of the inmates' soup. Henceforth, the asylum's role in providing treatment and cures was emphasized only when defending asylums against proposals to retain lunatics in workhouses, or when

only between 2 and 11 per cent could expect to be discharged as recovered. It comes as no surprise, therefore, that between 1845 and 1895, the median length of stay of those resident in Ticehurst fluctuated between 22 and 30 years. See C. MacKenzie, 'A Family Asylum', pp. 185–6, 202, 315–17; and *idem.*, 'Social Factors in the Admission, Discharge, and Continuing Stay of Patients at Ticehurst Asylum, 1845–1917', in W.F. Bynum, R. Porter, and M. Shepherd (eds), *The Anatomy of Madness*, Vol. 2, pp. 148–51.

136. For documentation of 'a steady decline in the proportion of patients [recovering at the York Retreat] from the late eighteenth to the late nineteenth century', see A. Digby, *Madness, Morality, and Medicine*, pp. 231–3. Under the first superintendent, George Jepson, some 45 per cent of those admitted were discharged as recovered. Under Bedford Pierce, superintendent from 1892 to 1910, reported recoveries amounted to under 26 per cent of admissions.

137. John Charles Bucknill, *The Care of the Insane and their Legal Control*, London: Macmillan, 1880, p. 128.

magistrates failed to build enough asylum accommodation to keep up with the demand.

Over the many years it took to achieve their goals, lunacy reformers had developed a faith in the virtues of the institution which was not easily destroyed. But it was not just a human reluctance to admit their own mistake which led the Commissioners to collaborate in and encourage the adoption of an efficient custodialism as the primary goal of the asylum system. In the first place, the bourgeois emphasis on the virtues of self-discipline and regularity which was so prominent a feature of the ideology of moral treatment was not always carefully distinguished, even in the minds of its principal advocates, from a celebration of order and obedience for their own sakes[138] – and such a perversion of the original intent was particularly likely to occur and to be overlooked once asylums began to deal with an essentially lower-class population. In a sense, the potential for its transformation into an instrument of repression was always latent in moral treatment. Equally important, the campaign for lunacy reform had derived much of its energy and had attracted much of its support from those who sought to protect helpless paupers from the abominable conditions and cruelties to which they had been subjected in private madhouses. From such a perspective, it is at least understandable that the abolition of chains and the elimination of the grosser excesses of the earlier institutions could be viewed as the fulfillment of the promise of reform, impeding the perception of their replacement's perhaps equally unattractive features.

The Commissioners' standard of comparison was explicitly not the goals the reformers had set for themselves, but rather the previous conditions in the worst private madhouses. They pointed to examples like Warburton's houses at Bethnal Green, where prior to an efficient system of inspection,

> mechanical restraint was carried out to such an extent that there were seventy out of about four hundred patients almost invariably in irons . . . there was no bath, no library, not even a book or a newspaper; little or no employment; no means of amusement; a small and inefficient staff of attendants (there being only one to about fifty patients) . . . the rooms were defective in cleanliness, warmth and general comfort . . . parts of the asylum were damp and offensive from want of drainage . . .

and so on.[139] Given such a starting-point, it was difficult not to find evidence of improvement, even in institutions which remained clearly custodial.

---

138. See, on this point, the discussion in Fiona Godlee, 'Aspects of Non-Conformity: Quakers and the Lunatic Fringe', in W.F. Bynum, R. Porter, and M. Shepherd (eds), *The Anatomy of Madness*, Vol. 2, pp. 73–85, esp. pp. 75–6.
139. Commissioners in Lunacy, *2nd Annual Report*, 1847, p. 85.

As the rising cure-rate which the Commissioners had originally hoped for failed to materialize, they adopted still more conservative criteria on which to base their judgement as to an asylum's effectiveness. The reader of the four- and five-hundred-page reports the Commission produced year after year soon encounters certain words and phrases which then recur with monotonous regularity, indicating the Commissioners' pleasure or displeasure with what they found, while revealing at the same time the implicit values which lay behind their actions. Good asylums were those where the bedding was 'clean and sufficient'; the treatment 'humane and judicious'; the patients 'orderly, quiet, free from excitement and satisfactorily clothed'; the institution 'clean and tidy'; mortality rates low and attendance at chapel high; and where there was a general air of efficiency. On the other hand, institutions which deviated in any of these respects, those whose physical structure was defective or whose water supply was insufficient, could expect to be censured.

The performance of medical superintendents was not assessed in terms of how successful they were in treating or curing patients, or how diligently they were pursuing research into the causes or treatment of mental disorder. Such matters were scarcely mentioned, which was probably just as well, since the available evidence suggests that according to these criteria, asylum doctors were almost all failures. Instead, they were praised for the efficient performance of mundane administrative tasks, for their 'kindliness' and their efforts to provide for the comfort of their charges; and reprimanded if they failed to keep up to date with the mountain of legal paperwork – casebooks, admission records, discharge records, books recording instances of restraint and seclusion, and so on – required by the lunacy statutes. Any deviations from routine, even those which had a therapeutic intent, were likely to draw a stern reproof from the Commissioners, since they almost inevitably involved some increased risk, however slight, that the patients would abscond or succeed in doing away with themselves. Despite the fact that there were only six full-time Commissioners to supervise the treatment of as many as sixty or seventy thousand lunatics, all suicides and sudden, unexpected deaths were the subject of minute inquiry and concern. Often this involved a special visit from the Commissioners themselves, a quasi-legal proceeding, with evidence given on oath and an attempt to develop a careful reconstruction of the events surrounding the patient's demise – which was followed by a long and detailed report of the findings, and a censure of the asylum officers if it was shown to have been within their power to have prevented the death.[140]

The intent was the humane one of preventing a repetition of the abuses

140. For an example of this process at work, see the report of the inquiry into the death of one Joseph Owen at Hanwell, in Commissioners in Lunacy, *25th Annual Report*, 1871, pp. 249–57.

to which lunatics had been exposed prior to 1845. But the consequence was to stifle initiative and innovation on the part of the asylum doctors, and to foster a dull, protective environment where merely keeping the patient alive became an end in itself.[141] The reader of the Commissioners' reports cannot avoid concluding that their model institution was one where there was the greatest attention to economy, the fewest accidents, suicides, and escapes, and the lowest annual mortality rates. Ruthlessly, albeit perhaps unintentionally, the guardians of reform themselves thus played a central and 'instrumental role . . . in turning county asylums into cocoons of dullness'.[142]

Not surprisingly in the circumstances, asylum superintendents were content to turn necessity into a virtue. When the county asylums built in accordance with the 1845 Act first opened, the superintendents had emphasized that 'the recovery or improvement of the inmates is to be the primary consideration, and . . . [is] the purpose [for which] the Asylum was specially intended'.[143] The custodial care of long-term patients was to be only a secondary, residual function. As the prospect of curing significant numbers came to seem more and more remote, however, the commissioners' attitudes and preferences enabled the doctors to make a relatively smooth transition to a situation where these priorities were almost precisely reversed. The asylum's ability to keep crazy people out of harm's way, and to provide them with more humane care than they would otherwise receive, increasingly became the justification for its continued existence. 'In fact', the public were informed,

a County Asylum which receives pauper patients, chronic cases of ordinary Insanity from other Counties, as well as Idiot children from its own and other districts can never hope to show a very high percentage of recoveries. But the asylum is carrying out the objects of its creation – namely the cure of curable cases and the care of all cases of the Insane who are incurable,[144]

even if the ratio of incurable to curable cases had turned out to be much larger than had been originally anticipated.

141. Extraordinary precautions were taken, of course, to prevent patient suicides, but perhaps the best example of the policy of preserving the patients' lives at all costs was the elaborate nursing care accorded to the moribund. At Colney Hatch, for instance, 36 of the 75 patients who died in 1859 'had been bedridden, paralysed and helpless for months. Just feeding them was a major undertaking'. As the Annual Report for 1860 recorded,

All these cases required, before their termination, the more or less lengthened use of the water bed; and great attention was paid to the diet; beef-tea, arrowroot, jellies, wine and fruit being added to, or substituted for the ordinary diet, when, owing to paralysis of the muscles of the tongue and throat, the power of deglutition was greatly impaired, and asphyxia by suffocation from lodging of food in the pharynx was to be dreaded.

(Quoted in Richard Hunter and Ida MacAlpine, *Psychiatry for the Poor. 1851 Colney Hatch Asylum: Friern Hospital 1973*, London: Dawsons, 1974, p. 89.)

Aware of the overwhelmingly lower-class composition of the awkward, inconvenient, and troublesome people the asylums had now collected within their walls, and conscious of the lack of alternative structures and mechanisms for coping with such a potentially disruptive lot, most of those who counted in Victorian England found it easy to reconcile themselves to the collapse of earlier pretensions to cure. With scarcely a murmur of protest, both national and local elites were converted to the merits of a holding operation which kept these undesirables, the very refuse of society, out of sight, and preferably out of mind.[145] On the national level, the Select Committees of 1859–60 and 1877, both of which inquired into the treatment of the insane, exhibited little or no concern with the issue of the cure of (or rather the asylums' failure to cure) lower-class patients. The 1859–60 Committee displayed some anxiety about the condition of those pauper lunatics still confined in workhouses, but otherwise merely sought to establish that serious instances of physical abuse of the insane, such as those uncovered by parliamentary inquiries earlier in the century, had indeed disappeared. Both this Committee and the one appointed in 1877 obviously retained an unshakable faith in the fundamental applicability of the asylum solution, and their major shared concern was simply to prevent the accidental or conspired-at incarceration of sane (upper- and upper-middle-class) individuals.

The very terms of reference of the 1877 Committee, which was 'to inquire into the operations of the Lunacy Law, so far as regards the Security offered by it against violations of Personal Liberty',[146] reveal Parliament's lack of concern over the asylum's custodial status. The fact that the sole focus of concern was on fellow members of the middle and upper classes was indicated particularly clearly in the Committee's questions about whether it might be advisable to require certification by a Justice of the Peace before patients were admitted to an asylum. When the suggestion was put to Henry Maudsley, it was instantly dismissed: 'I think

142. N. Hervey, 'A Slavish Bowing Down: The Lunacy Commission and the Psychiatric Profession', p. 109.
143. Buckinghamshire County Asylum, *1st Annual Report*, 1854, p. 22.
144. Northampton County Asylum, *Annual Report*, 1888, p. 12. In similar vein, the authorities at Colney Hatch reminded the public that theirs was 'an Asylum designed for the crazy sweepings of the largest and most deprived city in the world' and sought 'to warn the community from instituting invidious comparisons and supposing that the good which we do should be measured by the number of our "Recoveries."' Colney Hatch Asylum, *12th Annual Report*, 1863, p. 114.
145. The English upper classes exhibited a similar fortitude when the passage of time revealed the bankruptcy of the claim that running workhouses on the principle of less eligibility would greatly reduce, if not eradicate, the problem of the disreputable poor. At the very least, the workhouses allowed the authorities to keep track of such potentially dangerous elements, and if harsh conditions could not deter the pauper, they at least kept the cost of his maintenance low. Consequently, the 'better sort', unlike the lower classes (who might experience its rigours at first hand), could contemplate the perpetuation of the original design with a measure of equanimity.
146. House of Commons, *Select Committee on the Operation of the Lunacy Law*, 1877, p. iii.

it would be either a monotonous routine with him, a mere form, and of no benefit therefore; or he would find the position intolerable, if he really attempted to go seriously into every case.'[147] In the next breath, he indicated that a Justice's signature was *already* required in pauper cases, which, of course, made up the overwhelming bulk of asylum admissions. The inescapable implication, that certification in such cases was simply a matter of routine, was left unacknowledged, since it was an issue that the Committee, despite their ostensible concern with 'liberty', simply did not want to pursue. Only a Committee fundamentally unconcerned about the issue of cure could have concluded, after several highly respected alienists had testified that County Asylums were merely glorified medical prisons, that the defects that their inquiry had uncovered were of a 'comparatively trifling nature . . . [and] amounted to little more than differences of opinion among medical men'.[148] Likewise, the central government's decision in 1874 to grant each parish a subsidy of four shillings a head for every pauper lunatic confined in an asylum (an action which was announced long after it was apparent that asylums were little more than convenient dumping grounds for the decrepit) represented a tacit – if very practical – endorsement of the value of custodialism.

The comments of Poor Law officials, who were shown over asylums when they came to inspect their local lunatics, indicate that they too were ready to compliment the asylum administrators on the excellence of their custodial care, and were seldom inclined to question the value of the enterprise just because cure proved out of reach. Following one such visit, the officials from the Devizes Union noted complacently that 'Most of the Lunatics belonging to this union seem to be very hopeless cases (many of them never having possessed any mind cannot of course become sane) and the Medical Superintendent who very courteously went through the Establishment with me stated that he thought that there were only about two cases which would be likely to recover.' Subsequent visits gave little hope of change: 'There does not appear to be much probability of the ultimate recovery of the patients. . . . The Medical Superintendent could only give hope of being discharged to three patients.' The inspectors from Highworth and Swindon Union were taken over the asylum, 'which we found in excellent order, the whole of the wards and corridors and day rooms being made as bright and cheerful and particularly clean and attractive for the unfortunate inmates as possible'. The forty-six inmates from their Union unfortunately showed no sign of mental improvement: 'What is still more sad is the report of the Medical Superintendent that out of this large number, not more than two men and three women can reasonably be expected to be ultimately discharged from restraint.'[149] Such therapeutic

147. *Ibid.*, p. 181.
148. House of Commons, *Report of the Select Committee on the Operation of the Lunacy Law*, 1878, pp. iii–iv.
149. Wiltshire County Asylum Visitors' Book, 1876–87, pp. 42, 103, 185–6, in manuscript at Roundway Mental Hospital, Devizes.

nihilism being accepted as a fact of life, local officials typically concentrated, as here, on emphasizing the amenities and physical comfort of the institution.

On a wider canvass, the community beyond the asylum walls evinced no enthusiasm for the prospect of lunatics at large. Bucknill, whose efforts to mitigate the isolation of his patients at the Devon County Asylum had provoked widespread public outrage and opposition,[150] bitterly concluded that

> The feeling and conduct of the British public towards the insane reminds one of nothing so much as that of the enlightened citizens of the free States of America. Noble and just sentiments towards the negro race are in every one's mouth, but personal antipathy is in every man's heart.[151]

Though 'the idea which the public now have of an asylum is, that it is a place where madmen are consigned until they die . . .',[152] the prospect appeared to disturb them not one whit, for it safely removed from their midst 'the branded bondsmen of disease', and spared them the polluting presence of these products 'of morbid passions, of ignorant and wicked habits, of the physical accidents and the tainted descent which cause their disease'.[153]

The relatives of the mad plainly possessed more ambivalent attitudes towards the asylum. As Charlotte Mackenzie has noted, 'There is ample evidence from Victorian letters, diaries and autobiographies that upper and middle class families feared asylums as much as they feared hospitals, and had low expectations of the kind of care their relatives might receive there.'[154] And while, for obvious reasons, we lack directly comparable evidence about the attitudes of the poor, both the comments of alienists in the admissions registers, and the fact that the stigma of confinement in county asylums was compounded by an association with the Poor Law, leave little doubt that a similar outlook prevailed here as well. Yet once

150. See 'Annual Reports of County Lunatic Asylums for 1856', *Journal of Mental Science* 3, 1857, pp. 477–8. For other examples of community outrage at the idea of lunatics in their midst, cf. Peter McCandless, ' "Build! Build!" The Controversy over the Care for the Chronically Insane in England, 1855–1870,' *Bulletin of the History of Medicine* 53, 1979, pp. 571–2.
151. John Charles Bucknill, 'President's Address', *Journal of Mental Science* 7, 1860, p. 6.
152. H.C. Burdett, *Hospitals and Asylums of the World*, Vol. 2, p. viii. Compare the earlier complaint from Thomas Laycock, in his Presidential Address to the Medico-Psychological Association, that the public 'look upon asylums as places of detention and on the Medical Superintendents as little better than jailers'. 'The Objects and Organization of the Medico-Psychological Association', *Journal of Mental Science* 15, 1869, p. 332.
153. J.C. Bucknill, 'President's Address', p. 6. As Maudsley put it, in the eyes of the public at large, 'lunacy [w]as something so horrible and dangerous that its victims must be pushed like the leper of old, beyond the gates of the city'. H. Maudsley, *The Physiology and Pathology of Mind*, London: Macmillan, 1867, pp. 494–5.
154. Charlotte MacKenzie, 'A Family Asylum', p. 278.

family tolerance had reached the breaking-point, ties of blood may well have tended to accentuate rather than diminish the desire for seclusion, as families sought to hide what was unquestionably a source of profound shame and potential disgrace from public view and knowledge. Some outside observers found 'the desire to withdraw [insanity] from the observation of the world . . . both natural and commendable . . .'[155] while others complained about 'the efforts of relatives and friends to conceal what they consider a stigma on the family'.[156] But both recognized how powerfully such motivations reinforced the commitment to the asylum.[157]

8. Pressures to Economize

The emerging consensus among almost all the interested parties on the value of a custodial operation was bolstered by the Lunacy Commissioners' staunch adherence to the notion that institutionalization remained the only acceptable solution to the problems of insanity. While this alliance could not entirely stifle complaints about the asylum doctors' performance[158] and suggestions that the asylum system had failed and ought to be disbanded,[159] it could and did operate to blunt the force and effectiveness of these attacks. But this relative immunity was bought at a price: the availability of funds for a custodial operation aimed at warehousing a predominantly lower-class population was never likely to be great. Consequently, asylums were perpetually starved of money, not to the extent that they had to close – for that would release their inmates back into the community, and community tolerance for the presence of the defective and decrepit in its midst was by now quite low – but always to a degree that precluded the provision of more than a minimum of care.

Local authorities were perpetually reluctant to spend 'extravagant' sums

155. 'Report from the Select Committee on Lunatics, July 1860', *Journal of Mental Science* 7, 1860, p. 146.
156. S.A.K. Strahan, 'The Propagation of Insanity and Allied Neuroses', *Journal of Mental Science* 36, 1890, p. 330.
157. Nancy Tomes has made a relevant related point, based upon a study of the correspondence of American families coping with the emotions aroused by consigning a relative to an asylum: 'Hospitalization justified the removal of a disruptive individual while at the same time promising medical treatment and a possible cure. Hospital treatment thus addressed the powerful sense of guilt and helplessness expressed by so many families when dealing with an insane relative.' Nancy Tomes, 'The Persuasive Institution: Thomas Story Kirkbride and the Art of Asylum Keeping, 1841–83', unpublished Ph.D. dissertation, University of Pennsylvania, 1978, p. 13.
158. Compare *The Scotsman*, 1 September 1871: 'build as we may, in every succeeding year we find the same demand for further accommodation . . . a work which shows as little promise of coming to an end as that of filling a bottomless pitcher. . . . Instead of finding that the great outlay which has been incurred in erecting asylums has led to the decrease of insanity, we find, on the contrary, an enormous and continuous development.'
159. For a discussion of this critique of the asylum, see Andrew Scull, *Decarceration: Community Treatment and the Deviant: A Radical View*, 2nd edn, Oxford: Polity Press, 1984, chapters 6 and 7.

of money on paupers. Consequently, although this became a more intense and pervasive concern in later years, magistrates on many asylum committees sought from the outset to keep costs to a bare minimum. As they became more experienced at running such large institutions, and perhaps less concerned to provide expensive accommodation once cures failed to materialize, they often realized considerable savings. To take just one example, in 1848, two years after the Littlemore Asylum opened its doors, the weekly charge to each parish for each patient was 11 shillings a week. By 1851, the magistrates had succeeded in reducing it to 8 shillings a week; and despite rising prices for provisions and being compelled to pay higher wages to the asylum staff, two years later they had effected a further reduction to only 7s. 6d.

A few asylum committees, convinced of the doctors' ability to make good their claims to cure, were prepared to permit larger expenditures in the expectation that the recoveries which would result would justify the apparently greater costs incurred. Such a policy was not popular with the local Poor Law officials, as the experience of the Buckinghamshire Asylum indicates. From its opening, the magistrates exhibited a marked defensiveness about costs. In their very first report, which was distributed to all the parish Poor Law officers, they sought to persuade their audience that:

> in this as in many other instances a liberal policy is identical with a true economy, as a means of saving the local rates, and the duty of humanity to arrest the incipient disease before it has time to assume a chronic and hopeless character, coincides with the pecuniary interests of the ratepayers.

They felt compelled to treat the subject at some length, because

> an erroneous impression seems to have prevailed in some quarters that the accommodation to be afforded in a Lunatic Asylum was no more than that required in a Union Workhouse, and that the Building might be erected for much the same cost, the essential difference between the two Institutions and the capacity, habits, and necessities of the inmates being greatly overlooked.[160]

---

160. Buckinghamshire County Asylum, *Annual Report*, 1854, pp. 5, 10. As John Walton has pointed out, when it came to funding levels, county asylums usually enjoyed a great advantage over workhouses because of the structural arrangements surrounding their financing. Whereas workhouses were controlled by boards of guardians elected by local ratepayers, and thus 'tightly controlled by parsimonious farmers, shopkeepers, and tradesmen', asylums were run by 'justices of the peace who were nominated by the central government (subject to the consensual approval of the leading county gentry) and were thus less vulnerable to pressure from those who paid for their policies'. J. Walton, 'Casting Out and Bringing Back', p. 133. Less vulnerable, but as this and subsequent examples will show, scarcely immune.

Evidently the committee's efforts failed to carry conviction. Two years later, the asylum superintendent took up the same task. Millar's defence of the asylum was typically spirited:

> Odium is cast upon those having [the insane's] immediate care because an expenditure is incurred greater than is to be found to be sufficient in the Unions for Sane persons, the disease, habits, and propensities of the Insane being quite overlooked. Why those suffering from a disorder the most terrible to which the human race is liable, which the world regards with fear and horror, which affixes a stigma on the sufferer for life, and against whose recovery a premium is even offered, should be branded with the vagrant and the mendicant, thus exposed to a degradation and economy which even the convicted criminals – those pests and outcasts of society – are spared, appears to me to be an evil which requires amendment. Parochial authorities never complain that convicts cost about ten shillings a week.[161]

This was stirring stuff, though scarcely calculated to make Millar many friends. From the outset, he had been firmly committed to a curative regime, and had sought to minimize the barriers between the asylum and the community by allowing patients frequent opportunities to visit the nearby town of Aylesbury. In essence, he had staked his future on being able to produce a sufficient proportion of cures, and initially, at least, had won the support of the magistrates. But he simply could not stem the influx of chronic and hopeless cases. The following year, after more than three years of uniformly favourable, even enthusiastic, reports on his conduct of the asylum by both the magistrates and the Lunacy Commissioners, he was abruptly dismissed, ostensibly for permitting administrative irregularities on the part of the asylum staff. Unable to produce the results to justify their liberal approach, the magistrates appear to have capitulated to local pressures for economy. Under Millar's successor, Humphry, the asylum became just another custodial institution,[162] and later in the century the Buckinghamshire magistrates were to prove as adept as their counterparts elsewhere at being cheeseparing.[163]

161. Buckinghamshire County Asylum, *Annual Report*, 1856, p. 14.
162. It was surely not accidental that from a field of 57 candidates, including several with previous asylum experience, the magistrates chose someone who had previously served as a workhouse doctor. Most of Millar's staff now resigned or were sacked, and the matron, too, was soon replaced by a recruit from a Surrey workhouse. Humphry was to remain as superintendent from 1856 to 1908, finally retiring when past eighty years of age.
163. The complacent acceptance of a custodial role is evident even in the tone of the annual reports, which lose the interest and optimism of the earlier years and become just another dull bureaucratic routine – a development, incidentally, which is common to all asylum reports in the course of the century. For cost-cutting, see, for example, the Commissioners' comments recorded Buckinghamshire County Asylum, *Visitors' Book*, 13 June 1892 (manuscript at St. John's Hospital, Stone, Bucks.): 'We are sorry to find that the dietary has been changed for the worse by the substitution of bacon for fresh

The link between an asylum's popularity in the local community and its cost to local taxpayers was further demonstrated by events at Northampton in the 1870s and 1880s. The Northamptonshire magistrates had for many years avoided incurring the heavy expenses the erection of a county asylum necessarily entailed. The legal requirements of the 1845 Act had been circumvented by a unique arrangement whereby the local charity hospital (the Northampton General Lunatic Asylum, which had opened in 1839) took all the county pauper patients on a contractual basis. During the 1860s, however, the pressures on the physical capacity of this asylum became acute, and it became apparent that further buildings would be required to house the rising numbers of pauper lunatics. The county's contract with the asylum trustees was now about to expire anyway, and the Commissioners in Lunacy took the opportunity to press for the erection of a conventional county asylum at a separate site, refusing to countenance the renewal of the existing contract. Local resistance to the idea was fierce, but for once the Commissioners obtained the backing of the Secretary of State, and the local authorities were reluctantly forced to concede defeat. Grudgingly, they embarked on an asylum building programme. Here too, the statutory requirement that the Commissioners approve all the plans and specifications checked any inclination they might have had to economize on construction costs; and they were compelled to build, not just an asylum, but a costly asylum.

When the asylum finally opened its doors, its unpopularity with the local people was made patently clear in letters and editorials in the local newspaper, the *Northampton Herald*. The general sentiment was that 'the long suffering ratepayers have not much to be proud of except it is a most hideous building'.[164] The Lunacy Commissioners visited and pronounced themselves highly satisfied with the condition of the asylum, which only served to inflame local ire further:

> Of course the Commissioners in Lunacy were much gratified by their visit. They have not to pay. . . . But now comes almost the worst part of the story. You sir and I and other victims, would expect to obtain something for their money, a building that the county would be proud of. . . . And what have we obtained? – a monstrously ugly structure whose chief architectural feature is a 'tall chimney'.[165]

meat on one day . . . and the reduction of the nutritious character of the soup . . . the weekly maintenance being reduced from nine shillings and four pence to eight shillings and twopence – the staff of attendants consisting of thirteen men and nineteen women for day duty, too few for the requirements of the [461] patients.' On some days, 'dinner' now consisted of rhubarb tart and water or watery soup and bread. Proud of the fact that they had reduced weekly maintenance costs at the asylum to a shilling less than the national average, the new County Council repeatedly boasted of their 'success'. Protests from the Lunacy Commissioners about the effects on patients were wholly unavailing. See the discussion in J. Crammer, *Asylum History: Buckinghamshire County Pauper Lunatic Asylum*, pp. 109–13.

164. *The Northampton Herald*, 10 March 1878.
165. *Ibid.*, 25 May 1878.

The opposition continued, and extended even to allegations that behind the high walls and the trees which shielded the asylum from the public gaze, patients were being brutally maltreated. But the prime target was always the alleged extravagance with which the asylum was administered. The superintendent, Dr Millson, had rashly insisted that since the asylum was supposed to be a hospital, patients were entitled to more than the spartan existence of a workhouse environment. The *Herald* began to suggest that the magistrates' committee running the asylum 'were dissatisfied with the lavish expenditure of public money evident in everything, even to the cups and saucers, which were far better in quality than necessary'.[166] In April 1878, under fire from all directions, Millson submitted his resignation.

In less than a year, his successor effected a remarkable reversal of public attitudes. On 4 January 1879, the *Herald* informed its readers that 'the county Lunatic Asylum now, as far as its management is concerned, seems to have entered upon a satisfactory course'. In subsequent issues, obvious delight was expressed at the condition of the hospital. A passage in the asylum report for the year indicates how such a spectacular transformation had been achieved. The surplus accommodation in the new buildings had been filled with lunatics from other counties and boroughs whose asylums were already full:

> there are now in the Asylum 128 out-county and private patients, irrespective of those chargeable to the boroughs of Northampton and Peterborough. The trouble which these cases entail on the staff is very considerable; but the profits accruing from them are also considerable, and should the Asylum need any further additions or alterations, the Northampton ratepayer will not again be called upon for the money.[167]

It was this fact, that the asylum was now running at a profit, which was emphasized over and over again in press comments,[168] and in the institution's own annual reports.[169] In 1880, 'the cost of patients' maintenance was reduced from three years ago . . . although this was effected despite an increase in the dietary and the clothing supplies'.[170] The following year, 'another reduction in maintenance was reported . . . bringing the charge at this hospital to an amount lower than the general average of similar institutions'.[171] The overcrowding, which was by now quite severe,[172]

---

166. *Ibid.*, 16 February 1878.
167. Northampton County Lunatic Asylum, *Annual Report*, 1878, p. 16.
168. See, for example, *The Northampton Herald*, 17 January 1880.
169. See the *Annual Reports* for 1880, 1881, 1882, 1886, 1887.
170. *Ibid.*, 1880, p. 14.
171. *Ibid.*, 1881, p. 8.
172. In 1881, for instance, the Lunacy Commissioners commented that in some of the male wards, '[the numbers of] patients vary from sixty to seventy while there are beds for but twenty seven'. *Ibid.*, 1881, pp. 18–19. Already a lavatory on the men's side and a sewing room on the women's had been converted to dormitory space.

undoubtedly helped in this respect. By 1886, the average cost per patient per week had fallen from the original founding rate of 10s. 6d. to 8s. And while the continual influx of patients eventually forced some minor alterations to the original structure, to raise the capacity from less than 500 initially to 700 in September 1883 and 850 by 1889, the profits from out-county patients were sufficient to pay for the needed 'improvements'. 'Thus the necessity for having recourse to the County Rates has been avoided',[173] and the asylum was able to maintain its new-found popularity.

Seriously overcrowded living conditions were clearly not unique to the Northampton County Asylum. Almost every year, the Lunacy Commissioners reported that such conditions were widespread.[174] Other institutions, too, saw it as a way of avoiding increased capital expenditure. And since it allowed fixed costs, such as the superintendent's salary and repairs to buildings, to be spread more thinly over a larger number of cases, it helped to reduce or stabilize maintenance costs for each patient. Caterham and Leavesden were explicitly custodial institutions opened for the metropolitan area's chronic lunatics. Patients were gathered together there in huge, barn-like dormitories, and were such hopeless cases that almost none were expected to (or did) leave them, except in coffins. (In an average year, fewer than one per cent were discharged cured.) In 1885, the weekly cost of each inmate dumped at these asylums was, respectively, 7s. 11d. and 7s. $3\frac{1}{2}$d. It is indicative of the success of the policy of saving money through excessive overcrowding of facilities and the practice of a cheeseparing economy, that at county asylums claiming to provide therapeutic treatment, costs were not very different – for example, at the Lancashire County Asylum at Whittingham, the charge was 8s. 8d.; at the Northampton County Asylum, 8s.; and at both the Worcester County Asylum and the Wiltshire County Asylum, 7s. $10\frac{3}{4}$d.[175]

9. The Critics of Asylumdom

While most asylum superintendents, as we have seen, readily reconciled themselves to the task of managing custodial warehouses, their complacency was not universally shared. Victorian asylumdom by the 1860s and 1870s began to attract its share of articulate and outspoken detractors: men who were unwilling to accept the retreat from earlier ideals; who raised the question of whether the whole prescription for reform rested on

173. *Ibid.*, 1887, p. 8.
174. In 1876, for instance, a typical year, 23 of the 49 county asylums· were officially described as overcrowded, while most others were clearly up against the upper limits of their accommodation. See Commissioners in Lunacy, *30th Annual Report*, 1876, Appendix C.
175. A few years later, Sir James Crichton-Browne complained of an 'unfortunate tendency' amongst those running county asylums 'to enter upon a competition in reducing the rates of maintenance. In one asylum they have got it down to 6s. a week'. Quoted in H.C. Burdett, *Hospitals and Asylums of the World*, Vol. 2, p. 238.

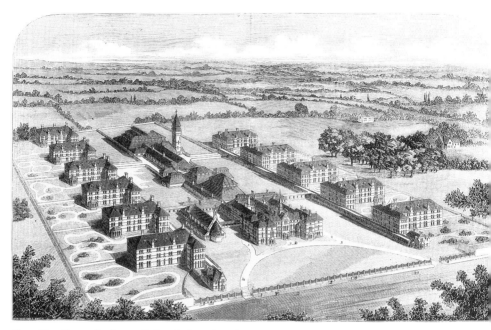

Fig. 19 General view of the design for the Metropolitan asylums for chronic lunatics at Caterham and Leavesden, from *The Builder*, 25 July 1868. Here, the drive for economy reached its apotheosis in plainly-built utilitarian brick structures, devoid of all 'superfluous' ornamentation. These barracks–asylums were designed in the 'pavilion' style, which allowed the replication of uniform blocks in two parallel rows, each housing between 150 and 200 patients, one row for the male patients and the other for females. Between the buildings assigned to each sex was a third row of buildings, containing the administration, accommodation for the superintendent and staff, and that critical part of every well-wrought Victorian asylum, the chapel, in which the inmates could be brought the consolations of organized religion. The same design was subsequently reused for a third time in 1877, in the construction of the third Middlesex County Asylum at Banstead.

Fig. 20 (right) Floor plans of a general block and an infirmary block at the Metropolitan asylums for chronic lunatics from *The Builder*, 25 July 1868. These institutions were designed to cram as many patients as possible into the available space. The dormitories also served as day rooms. Each was partitioned only once, into two groups of forty beds, with scarcely room for passage between them; and subsequently, they were to be 'adapted' to cram in still more patients. The inmates' entire existence, with the exception of meals taken in the dining hall and occasional excursions to the exercise yard, was spent contemplating these four walls.

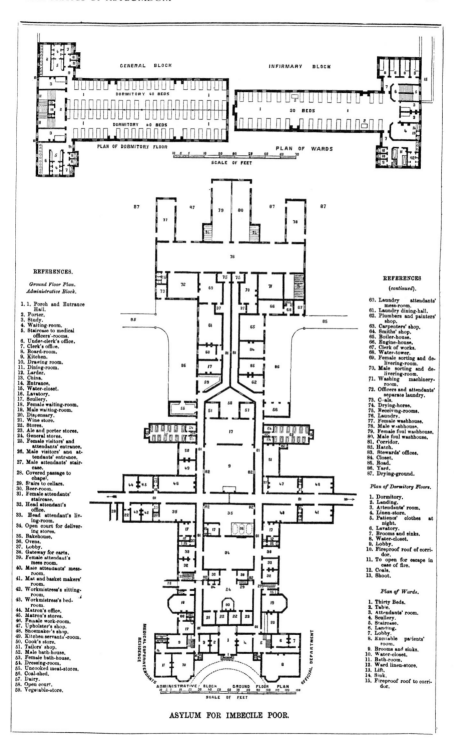

REFERENCES.

Ground Floor Plan.
Administrative Block.

1, 1. Porch and Entrance Hall.
2. Porter.
3. Study.
4. Waiting-room.
5. Staircase to medical officers'-rooms.
6. Under-clerk's office.
7. Clerk's office.
8. Board-room.
9. Kitchen.
10. Drawing room.
11. Dining-room.
12. Larder.
13. China.
14. Entrance.
15. Water-closet.
16. Lavatory.
17. Scullery.
18. Female waiting-room.
19. Male waiting-room.
20. Dispensary.
21. Wine store.
22. Stores.
23. Ale and porter stores.
24. General stores.
25. Female visitors' and attendants' entrance.
26. Male visitors' and attendants' entrance.
27. Male attendants' staircase.
28. Covered passage to chapel.
29. Stairs to cellars.
30. Beer-room.
31. Female attendants' staircase.
32. Head attendant's office.
33. Head attendant's living-room.
34. Open court for delivering stores.
35. Bakehouse.
36. Ovens.
37. Lobby.
38. Gateway for carts.
39. Female attendant's mess room.
40. Male attendants' mess-room.
41. Mat and basket makers' room.
42. Workmistress's sitting-room.
43. Workmistress's bedroom.
44. Matron's office.
45. Matron's stores.
46. Female work-room.
47. Upholster's shop.
48. Shoemaker's shop.
49. Kitchen servants'-room.
50. Cook's office.
51. Tailors' shop.
52. Male bath-house.
53. Female bath-house.
54. Dressing-room.
55. Uncooked meat-stores.
56. Coal-shed.
57. Dairy.
58. Open court.
59. Vegetable-store.

REFERENCES
(continued).

60. Laundry attendants' mess-room.
61. Laundry dining-hall.
62. Plumbers and painters' shop.
63. Carpenters' shop.
64. Smiths' shop.
65. Boiler-house.
66. Engine-house.
67. Clerk of works.
68. Water-tower.
69. Female sorting and delivering-room.
70. Male sorting and delivering-room.
71. Washing machinery-room.
72. Officers and attendants' separate laundry.
73. Coals.
74. Drying-horse.
75. Receiving-rooms.
76. Laundry.
77. Female washhouse.
78. Male washhouse.
79. Female foul washhouse.
80. Male foul washhouse.
81. Corridor.
82. Hatch.
83. Stewards' offices.
84. Closet.
85. Road.
86. Yard.
87. Drying-ground.

Plan of Dormitory Floors.

1. Dormitory.
2. Landing.
3. Attendants' room.
4. Linen-store.
5. Patients' clothes at night.
6. Lavatory.
7. Brooms and sinks.
8. Water-closet.
9. Lobby.
10. Fireproof roof of corridor.
11. To open for escape in case of fire.
12. Coals.
13. Shoot.

Plan of Wards.

1. Thirty Beds.
2. Table.
3. Attendants' room.
4. Scullery.
5. Staircase.
6. Landing.
7. Lobby.
8. Excitable patients' room.
9. Brooms and sinks.
10. Water-closet.
11. Bath-room.
12. Ward linen-store.
13. Lift.
14. Sink.
15. Fireproof roof to corridor.

ASYLUM FOR IMBECILE POOR.

misguided premises; and who suggested that if the existence of asylums could not be justified on the grounds that they were curative institutions, then for many patients it could scarcely be justified at all. Nor were all those who objected to existing policies marginal figures, or disgruntled ex-patients insisting that the (psychiatric) emperor had no clothes. On the contrary, the critics included some eminently respectable figures: two Chancery Visitors in Lunacy (John Charles Bucknill and Lockhart Robertson),[176] both of whom had served as county asylum superintendents, and ranked among the most prominent of English alienists; Henry Maudsley,[177] intellectually the dominant alienist of his generation, and someone who possessed a European-wide reputation; Joseph Mortimer Granville, who was commissioned to conduct a wide-ranging inspection of asylums in the London area for the *Lancet* in the mid-1870s; John Arlidge, a student of John Conolly's, formerly superintendent of St. Luke's and a prolific writer on psychiatric matters; Andrew Wynter, founding editor of the *British Medical Journal*; and Sir James Clark, Conolly's memorialist and close friend, and physician in ordinary to Queen Victoria from the time of her accession to the throne.[178]

Increasingly, these people came to view the asylum system as seriously,

176. Bucknill, formerly superintendent of the Devon County Asylum, was the first editor of the *Journal of Mental Science*, and author (with Hack Tuke) of *A Manual of Psychological Medicine*, for many years the standard psychiatric text on both sides of the Atlantic. He served as President of the Association of Medical Officers of Asylums in 1860, was elected a Fellow of the Royal Society in 1866, and was subsequently (in 1878) one of the co-founders and editors of *Brain*. Robertson had previously been superintendent of the Sussex County Asylum, and co-edited the *Journal of Mental Science* from 1862 to 1870.

177. Maudsley was joint editor of the *Journal of Mental Science* between 1862 and 1878. Son-in-law of the patron saint of Victorian alienism, John Conolly, his asylum experience was limited to brief stints as an assistant medical officer at county asylums in Essex and the West Riding, and three years as superintendent of the charity asylum in Manchester. Intellectually arrogant and aloof, he carved out a highly successful career as a consultant to the rich and titled on psychiatric matters, while his writings established him as the most widely-read and respected medical psychologist of his age. The best treatment of his career and influence is Trevor Turner, 'Henry Maudsley: Psychiatrist, Philosopher, and Entrepreneur', in W.F. Bynum, R. Porter, and M. Shepherd (eds), *The Anatomy of Madness*, Vol. 3, pp. 151–89; see also Elaine Showalter, *The Female Malady: Women, Madness and English Culture, 1830–1980*, New York: Pantheon, 1980, chapter 4; Henry Rollin, 'Whatever Happened to Henry Maudsley?' in G.E. Berrios and H. Freeman (eds), *150 Years of British Psychiatry 1841–1991*, pp. 351–8; and, for a more positive view, Aubrey Lewis, 'Henry Maudsley: His Work and Influence', *Journal of Mental Science* 97, 1951, pp. 259–77. A moderately useful survey of his published writings can be found in Michael Collie, *Henry Maudsley: Victorian Psychiatrist – A Bibliographic Study*, Winchester: St. Paul's Bibliographies, 1988.

178. As it is perhaps needless to remark, all these critics stood outside the ranks of asylumdom, either having used it as a stepping-stone to more lucrative and higher status careers, or having avoided the stigma of asylum work altogether. The stature of men like Maudsley and Bucknill was only harmed by the embarrassing limitations and failures of the rank and file alienists at whose head they nominally stood. From a sociological standpoint, therefore, it should come as no surprise that such elite figures sought to distance themselves from the beliefs and practices of their erstwhile colleagues.

perhaps fatally flawed.[179] The earliest proponents of moral treatment in an asylum setting had insisted that 'the grand object to be kept in view when providing for the accommodation of the insane, is to assimilate their condition and the circumstances surrounding them as closely as possible to those of ordinary life . . .'. The unprejudiced observer must concede that conditions in the contemporary mausoleums of the mad constituted 'about as wide a departure from those conditions as can well be conceived'.[180] Nor did this reflect any want of good intentions: as Granville put it, 'I think the management of asylums generally is now certainly as honest, and, I believe, as earnest and intelligent as possible. The faults in the present system are rather incidental to the system itself than to the manner in which it is worked.'[181]

Asylums were supposedly places where people went to be cured of mental disease. The superintendents' own figures showed, not just that they were abysmal failures in this regard, but that the situation was deteriorating:

> In 1857 the number of lunatics deemed curable in the county asylums of England and Wales amounted to 1,890 out of 15,194 patients, or to 12.47 per cent. . . . Those 'deemed curable' in 1874 and 1875, throughout England and Wales, were $7\frac{1}{2}$ per cent; those 'deemed curable' in the County of Surrey, were $4\frac{1}{2}$ per cent. I do not know of anything more disheartening than that . . . you do not cure as many as you did before you made these great mausoleums during the last twenty years [so that] you are certainly on the wrong scent now if you seek to multiply them for curative purposes or for economy . . . you have gone on in this way for twenty-five years, and you have got worse instead of better, and you have increased the number of lunatics and you have decreased the cures.[182]

Alienists had always insisted that leaving a patient at home diminished his chances of cure. Risking the charge of heresy, Bucknill denied it:

> The author's fullest and latest experience has convinced him that the curative influences of asylums have been vastly overrated, and those of

179. Maudsley ultimately gave practical expression to this disillusion by donating 30,000 pounds to the London County Council in 1907, to endow the hospital for psychiatric research and short-term treatment of curable patients which bears his name.
180. John Arlidge, *On the State of Lunacy and the Legal Provision for the Insane*, p. 201.
181. House of Commons, *Select Committee on the Operation of the Lunacy Law*, 1877, p. 397, evidence of Mortimer Granville.
182. *Ibid.*, pp. 386, 391–2, evidence of Francis Scott. Scott was a Surrey magistrate who had been heavily involved in the erection and management of the new county asylum at Brookwood, which already contained more than a thousand inmates. He was convinced that asylum doctors were entitled to some share of the blame for reform's failures: 'medical gentlemen tell you that they can treat up to 1,000 or 1,500 but they used not to say so. Three or four hundred was large enough for them to manage in a curative establishment; they cease to be curative; we do not cure; ours are large places of detention.' *Ibid.*, p. 386.

isolated treatment in domestic care have been greatly undervalued. . . .
It has long been the accepted doctrine [among alienists] that insanity can
only be treated curatively in asylums. . . . A wider knowledge of
insanity . . . would have taught them that a very considerable number
of cases of actual insanity run a short course and recover in domestic life
with no great amount of treatment, and that perhaps not of a very
scientific kind.[183]

It was not just curable cases who should be spared the asylum: among
the chronically crazy,

> large numbers are needlessly detained. Of the ninety percent of chronic
> cases, at least thirty, by the admission of the medical superintendents,
> and probably nearer forty to less official views, are both harmless and
> quiet, capable of giving some little help in the world . . . immediately
> the physician has ascertained that they are past care they should be
> drafted out into private houses and keeping.[184]

Lockhart Robertson thought at least a third of the chronic patients would
benefit from such a program. Formerly a staunch advocate of asylum
treatment, he had been convinced otherwise by his experience as a
Chancery Visitor: 'I could never have believed that patients who were
such confirmed lunatics could be treated in private families, the way
Chancery lunatics are, if I had not personally watched these cases.'[185]

The critics were convinced that the public and Parliament must somehow be educated out of the 'stereotyped prejudice that a lunatic is a lunatic
and an asylum is the best place for him'.[186] Such 'brick and mortar
humanity' rested on what experience and due reflection had exposed as a
fallacy: 'To drive weak and perverted minds into a crowd, and there keep
them as a class apart, is clearly against the teachings of common sense, and
is opposed to scientific observation; and to keep them there unnecessarily
is a crime.'[187] In a more rational view, 'future progress in the improvement of the treatment of the insane', Maudsley boldly proclaimed, 'lies in
the direction of lessening the sequestration and increasing the liberty of
them'.[188]

183. J.C. Bucknill, *The Care of the Insane*, 1880, p. 114 – a perilous admission for an alienist
to make.
184. [Andrew Wynter], 'Non-Restraint in the Treatment of the Insane', *Edinburgh Review*
131, 1870, pp. 225, 229.
185. House of Commons, *Select Committee on the Operation of the Lunacy Law*, 1877, pp.
53–5.
186. J.C. Bucknill, *The Care of the Insane*, p. x. Bucknill, of course, had assiduously fostered
and promoted this very notion at an earlier stage of his career.
187. [Andrew Wynter], 'Non-Restraint in the Treatment of the Insane', pp. 418, 436–8;
British Medical Journal 1859, p. 152.
188. Quoted in Sir James Clark, *A Memoir of John Conolly, M.D., D.C.L.*, London: Murray,
1869, pp. 98–9. 'It is a question', he was subsequently to suggest, '. . . whether the
present practice of crowding the insane of all sorts into large asylums, where the
interests of life are extinguished, and where anything like individual treatment is

But Maudsley's 1871 presidential address to the Medico-Psychological Association, roundly criticizing the failures of Victorian asylumdom,[189] won few admirers amongst his erstwhile colleagues in day-to-day charge of the system. He was chided for the 'very serious mistake' of encouraging 'a notion that there is something horrible about an asylum' and instructed that 'our object should be rather to encourage people to believe that an asylum is a home with nothing that a patient or his friend need dread'.[190] And Thomas Clouston, who but a year earlier had proposed him in fulsome terms for the presidency,[191] denounced the address for its 'utter and entire scepticism'.[192] Maudsley's complaints, like those of his fellow critics, were without discernible practical effect. Even modest attempts to modify existing policies – the replacement of monolithic asylums by a 'cottage system', the founding of a Mental After-Care Association in 1879 – were scorned by orthodox alienists as 'utopian and absurd',[193] and exercised only the most trivial influence on official practices.[194]

Institutions whose humane and charitable design had been persistently stressed over the years were not readily susceptible to charges that they damaged and dehumanized their patients. Moreover, the kinds of spectacular, obvious abuse and maltreatment of patients which earlier reformers had been able to utilize to rouse a largely indifferent public to a concern with the treatment of the insane had by and large disappeared. Complaints about the dullness and destructiveness of routine simply did not possess the same impact as allegations about the chaining, flogging,

---

well-nigh impracticable, is so much superior to the old system in effecting recoveries as some persons [such as his erstwhile professional colleagues] imagine'. Henry Maudsley, 'On the Alleged Increase of Insanity', *Journal of Mental Science* 23, 1877, p. 54. Contrast his earlier views, when superintendent of the Manchester Royal Lunatic Asylum: 'repeated experience has shown it to be really a rash folly, if not a positive cruelty, to send [patients] forth into the trials of life, when they are utterly unable to encounter them'. Manchester Royal Lunatic Asylum, *Annual Report*, 1860.

189. Henry Maudsley, 'Insanity and Its Treatment', *Journal of Mental Science* 17, 1871, pp. 311–34.

190. Dr Wood, 'Commentary on the Presidential Address', *Journal of Mental Science* 17, 1871, p. 459.

191. See *Journal of Mental Science* 16, 1870, pp. 454–6.

192. *Journal of Mental Science* 17, 1871, p. 456. For a more extended and waspish commentary on Maudsley's speech, by the superintendent of the Male Department at Colney Hatch, see Edgar Sheppard, 'On Some of the Modern Teachings on Insanity', *Journal of Mental Science* 17, 1871, pp. 499–514. Within a few years, Maudsley's cynicism and 'hypercriticality', and his overt contempt for most of the profession brought about his resignation as editor of the *Journal of Mental Science* and a virtually complete withdrawal from the business of the Association. See the excellent discussion in Trevor Turner, 'Henry Maudsley: Psychiatrist, Philosopher, and Entrepreneur', in W.F. Bynum, R. Porter, and M. Shepherd (eds), *The Anatomy of Madness*, Vol. 3, pp. 151–89.

193. Harrington Tuke, comment on 'Dr Mundy on the Cottage Asylum System', *Journal of Mental Science* 8, 1862, p. 333.

194. *Cf.* the discussion in William Ll. Parry-Jones, 'The Model of the Geel Lunatic Colony and Its Influence on the Nineteenth Century Asylum System in Britain', pp. 201–17 in A. Scull (ed.), *Madhouses, Mad-doctors, and Madmen*; and Peter McCandless, '"Build! Build!" . . . ,' pp. 553–74.

rape, and murder of inmates. Then again, as the critics ruefully acknowledged, the sheer scale of investment in the asylum solution over the
preceding half century created a kind of institutional inertia. In Andrew
Wynter's words, 'The amount of capital sunk in the costly palaces of the
insane is becoming a growing impediment. So much money sunk creates a
conservativism in their builders, the county magistrates, which resists
change.'[195]

A further obstacle to any modification of existing policy (Maudsley
wrongly thought it was the only serious one) 'lies in public ignorance, the
unreasonable fear, and the selfish avoidance of insanity'.[196] Those critical
of the asylum were inclined to deride these fears – Robertson assured a
Parliamentary inquiry that 'I consider the persons who are dangerous to
the public are very few, and the danger very often is the first warning we
have. The large mass of patients in asylums are not very dangerous to the
public'[197] – but they were real enough. As Wynter acknowledged, there
could be 'No doubt [that] in the eyes of the public these establishments
are the necessary places of detention of troops of violent madness, too
dangerous to be allowed outside the walls.'[198] Closer acquaintance with
the inside of an asylum would, he assured his readers, soon dispel these
fears:

> the visitor to an asylum enters the wards with the expectation of
> meeting violent maniacs. . . . He has not taken many steps, however,
> before the illusion begins to vanish; he may even ask, 'Where are the
> mad people?' as he sees nothing but groups of patients seated around
> the fire or lolling about in a dreary sort of way, perfectly quiet, and
> only curious about the curiosity of the stranger. This is the class of
> people that form at least 90 per cent of the inhabitants of our asylums,
> chronic and incurable cases that no treatment will ever improve. . . .[199]

But the point was that most people were never likely to see inside an
asylum. By removing the insane from the community and sequestering

195. [Andrew Wynter], 'Non-Restraint', p. 231. Wynter was convinced that, nonetheless,
     change was inevitable: 'As we see wing after wing spreading, and story after story
     ascending, in every asylum throughout the country, we are reminded of the overgrown
     monastic system, which entangled so many interests and seemed so powerful that it
     could defy all change, but for that very reason toppled and fell by its own weight, never
     to be renewed. Asylum life may not come to so sudden an end, but the longer its
     present unnatural and oppressive system is maintained, the greater will be the
     revolution when at last it arrives.' *The Borderlands of Insanity*, 1st edn, pp. 162–3. His
     anticipated 'revolution', of course, failed to materialize until the second half of the
     twentieth century, and, like most revolutions, has only doubtfully increased the sum of
     human happiness.
196. Quoted in House of Commons, *Select Committee on the Operation of the Lunacy Law*,
     1877, p. 55, evidence of Lockhart Robertson.
197. *Ibid.* The Committee, like the public at large, was frankly incredulous of such claims,
     citing in rebuttal an exemplary tale of a woman lunatic, released against the advice of an
     asylum superintendent, who proceeded to murder her child.
198. [A. Wynter], 'Non-Restraint', p. 224.
199. *Ibid.*

them behind the walls of an institution, the possibility of ordinary people misperceiving and exaggerating the most common features of mental disturbance had been greatly exacerbated. The cases of lunacy most likely to draw public attention were those of violent mania – mild and moping cases scarcely merited attention. And after all, why else were lunatics locked up in the first place, unless it was because it was not safe to leave them at large?

In any event, the best professional opinion could always be cited in support of the contention that the insane were dangerous. As cure rates fell, and justifying asylum treatment on this basis came to seem less and less convincing, asylum doctors had been quick to reemphasize the traditional notion that they were protecting the public and guaranteeing social order. Exemplary tales circulated to 'prove' that the most apparently harmless lunatics were liable to commit totally unpredictable and often unprovoked acts of senseless violence. 'Unfortunately', the public was informed, 'it is in just those cases in which the signs of insanity seem slight to an ordinary observer that the greatest danger exists. The homicidal lunatic often shows scarcely a sign of the disease, and the suicide may show nothing at all beyond a slight amount of depression.'[200] To emphasize the threat, when the *Quarterly Review*'s correspondent visited Hanwell and Colney Hatch, he was assured that 'the utmost precaution will not always ensure safety; for patients considered quite harmless will now and then commit the most horrible acts'. His hosts provided him with two examples with which he proceeded vividly to impress this conclusion on his readers:

A black man, a butcher, who had been many years in an American asylum, and had never shown any violence, one night secreted a knife, and induced another patient to enter his cell. When his companion had laid down, he cut his throat, divided him into joints, and arranged the pieces around his cell as he had been accustomed to arrange his meat in his shop. He then offered his horrible wares to his fellow-lunatics, carrying such parts as they desired to those who were chained. The keeper, hearing the uproar, examined the cells, and found one man missing; upon inquiring of the black butcher if he had seen him, he calmly replied, 'he had sold the last joint!' Even those who have apparently harmless delusions will sometimes, if thwarted, commit unlooked-for atrocities. Not many years since an inquisition was heard before Mr Commissioner Winslow upon a young gentleman who would travel considerable distances to see a windmill, and sit watching it for days. His friends, to put an end to his absurd propensity, removed him to a place where there were no mills. The youth, to counteract the design, murdered a child in a wood, mangling his limbs

200. Richard Greene, 'The Care and Cure of the Insane', *Universal Review* July 1889, p. 498.

in a terrible manner, in the hope that he should be transferred, as a punishment, to a situation where a mill could be seen.[201]

10. Degeneration and Decay

But there was a yet more powerful argument for sequestering lunatics than the threat of this sort of random violence. As asylums silted up with the chronically crazy, 'the waifs and strays, the weak and wayward of our race',[202] so Victorian psychiatry moved steadily towards a grim determinism, a view of madness as the irreversible product of a process of mental degeneration and decay.[203] In the process, the asylum was accorded a wholly new significance in the battle to contain social pathology and defend the social order.

The madman, as Maudsley put it, 'is the necessary organic consequent of certain organic antecedents: and it is impossible he should escape the tyranny of his organization'.[204] Insanity constituted nothing less than a form of phylogenetic regression – which accounted, of course, for its social location ('There is most madness where there are the fewest ideas, the simplest feelings, and the coarsest desires and ways');[205] and for the lunatic's loss of civilized standards of behaviour and regression to the status of a brute:

> Whence came the savage snarl, the destructive disposition, the obscene language, the wild howl, the offensive habits displayed by some of the insane? Why should a human being deprived of his reason ever become so brutal in character as some do, unless he has the brute nature within him?[206]

Employing ever harsher language which combined a physiological account with 'the look and tone of moral condemnation',[207] psychiatric discourse now exhibited a barely disguised contempt for the mad, those 'tainted persons'[208] whom it sequestered on society's behalf. Patently, they were a defective and inferior lot:

> Insanity does not occur in people who are of sound mental constitution. It does not, like smallpox and malaria, attack indifferently the weak and the strong. It occurs chiefly in those whose mental constitution is

---

201. 'Lunatic Asylums', *Quarterly Review* 74, 1857, pp. 369–70. For a British example, see *The Scotsman*, October 6, 1865, reprinted in *Journal of Mental Science* 11, 1866, p. 614.
202. W.A.F. Browne, quoted in *Journal of Mental Science* 4, 1857, p. 201.
203. For an early statement of this position, see Henry Maudsley, 'Considerations with Regard to Hereditary Influence', *Journal of Mental Science* 8, 1863, pp. 482–513.
204. Henry Maudsley, *The Pathology of Mind*, London: Macmillan, 1879, p. 88.
205. Henry Maudsley, *The Pathology of Mind* (1895 edn), p. 30.
206. Henry Maudsley, *Body and Mind*, London: Macmillan, 1870, p. 53.
207. Trevor Turner, 'Henry Maudsley: Psychiatrist, Philosopher, and Entrepreneur', p. 179.
208. S.A.K. Strahan, 'The Propagation of Insanity and Other Neuroses', p. 337.

originally defective, and whose defect is manifested in a lack of the power of self-control and of forgoing immediate indulgence.[209]

The lunatic were, said Daniel Hack Tuke, the most unembarrassed apologist for Victorian asylumdom, 'an infirm type of humanity . . . [and] on admission "No good" is plainly inscribed on their foreheads'.[210]

The profession's rigid and pessimistic somaticism, while it appeared to leave but little scope for expert intervention,[211] had the compensating advantage of explaining away psychiatry's dismal therapeutic performance: 'the unhopeful prospect has been due, not to want of recourse to early treatment [or to the deficiencies of psychiatric therapeutics], but, so to speak, to inherent unfavourableness determined from the very outset of the mental symptoms'.[212] More than that, it transformed those 'failures' into a blessing in disguise, a demonstration that Nature herself embraced Hegel's 'cunning of reason'. One must recognize the bitter truth that

> The subversion of reason involves not only present incompetency, but a prospective susceptibility of disease, a proclivity to relapse. . . . The mind does not pass out of the ordeal unchanged. . . . Recovery . . . may

209. Charles Mercier, *A Textbook of Insanity*, 2nd edn, London: Allen and Unwin, 1914, p. 17.
210. Daniel Hack Tuke, *Insanity in Ancient and Modern Life, with Chapters on its Prevention*, London: Macmillan, 1878, p. 152.
211. Daniel Hack Tuke, William's great-grandson, mournfully announced that psychiatry was already 'very near the limit of curability'. Quoted in H.C. Burdett, *Hospitals and Asylums of the World*, Vol. 2, p. 250. (The mad, as another observer commented, came from defective stock, and 'in cases representing so deplorable an ancestry as this, medicine will do little in altering the condition of the individual, which may be considered virtually unmodifiable'. Anon., On the Degeneration of the Human Race', *Journal of Psychological Medicine* 10, 1857, p. 187.) Burdett himself tried to put the best face on this state of affairs, consoling his audience with the thought that 'there is always much to be done to alleviate and smooth the march to the grave'. *Hospitals and Asylums of World*, Vol. 1, p. 198.
212. Dr Major, superintendent of the Wakefield County Asylum quoted in R. Greene, 'Hospitals for the Insane and Clinical Instruction in Asylums', 1890, p. 250. Compare Morel's own explanation of how he had first come to realize that insanity was the product of degeneration:

> In proportion as I advanced in the career which I had adopted as a speciality, I was not long in perceiving that the curability of mental affections became a problem more and more difficult of solution. [I decided that] the every increasing proportion of incurable cases [must have] their reason in the intimate nature of the evil to be combatted. . . . Never since the origin of medical institutions had such strenuous efforts been made for the interests of the insane. How was it, then, that, in reference to cures, these efforts were so disappointing? . . . I saw only one mode of accounting for the fact, which was, to consider, in the generality of cases, mental alienation as the final result of a series of moral, physical, and intellectual causes, which, by determining in man successive transformations, connect him with the morbid varieties of the race, which we have called degenerations.

> Quoted in Anon., 'On the Degeneration of the Human Race', pp. 186–7. Charles Rosenberg makes a similar argument to the one I make here in his examination of the influence of hereditarian thought in nineteenth-century American medicine, 'The Bitter Fruit: Heredity, Disease, and Social Thought in Nineteenth Century America', *Perspectives in American History* 8, 1974, pp. 189–235.

be little more than the exercise of great cunning, or self-control, in concealing the signs of error and extravagance.[213]

But if 'normality' is a mere facsimile of the genuine article, if, as Robert Castel puts it, 'a cure risks being only "apparent", [then] the only good insane are those in the asylum'.[214] In the words of the superintendent of the Norfolk County Asylum, 'It is not probable that we can ever diminish the insane by any increase in recoveries; indeed, *the converse is more probable.*'[215] The matter was of some delicacy, since, of course, 'it is the duty of every physician to exhaust all the sources at his command to cure or relieve disease. . . .'[216] But perhaps one should not, after all, try so very hard, or lament very long one's therapeutic limitations. For, in truth,

> No human power can eradicate from insanity its terrible hereditary nature, and every so-called 'cure' in one generation will be liable to increase the tale of lunacy in the next . . . [when all is said and done] it is evident that the higher the percentage of recoveries in the present, the greater will be the proportion of insanity in the future.[217]

The very defects in willpower and self-control which most character-ized these 'tainted persons' encouraged them to 'attend upon the calls of their instincts and passions as does the unreasoning beast';[218] and, in

213. W.A.F. Browne in Crichton Royal Asylum, *18th Annual Report*, 1857, pp. 12–13.
214. Robert Castel, *The Regulation of Madness*, Berkeley: University of California Press, 1988, p. 153.
215. David G. Thompson, 'Letter to the Editor', *Journal of Mental Science* 36, 1890, p. 157, emphasis in the original. Compare Henry Maudsley's characteristically pessimistic assessment of his specialty's contribution to society:

> A physician who had spent his life in ministering to diseased minds might be excused if, asking at the end of it whether he had spent his life well, he accused the fortune of an evil hour which threw him on that track of work. He could not well help feeling something of bitterness in the certitude that one-half of the diseased he had dealt with never could get well, and something of misgiving in the reflection whether he had done real service to his kind by restoring the other half to do reproductive work.

The Pathology of Mind (1895 edn), p. 563.
216. R. Greene, 'The Care and Cure of the Insane', p. 503.
217. *Ibid.*; see also R. Greene, 'Hospitals for the Insane', p. 256. Such ideas found a ready audience among the Victorian bourgeoisie. Compare, for instance, the comments of the first General in the Salvation Army: once it has been 'recognised that he has become lunatic, morally demented, incapable of self-government, . . . upon him therefore must be passed the sentence of permanent seclusion from a world in which he is not fit to be at large. . . . It is a crime against the race to allow those who are so inveterately depraved the freedom to wander abroad, infect their fellows, prey upon Society and to multiply their kind'. General W. Booth, *Darkest England and the Way Out*, London: Salvation Army, 1890, pp. 204–5.
218. S.A.K. Strahan, 'The Propagation of Insanity', p. 337. Compare T.E.K. Stansfield, superintendent of the Bexley Asylum, 'There is a floating mass of degeneracy in the population which is constantly augmented by the victims of social vice and its satellites, syphilis and drink, and from this mass we derive the bulk of our asylum population. . . . Marriage with members of insane stock is comparatively rare amongst the upper and middle classes, seldom among the intelligent working class, but with the

consequence, 'every year thousands of children are born with pedigrees that would condemn puppies to the horsepond'.[219] Left to herself, Nature would set things right, since each of the several varieties of insanity 'is but a stage in the descent towards sterile idiocy'.[220] But misguided attempts to cure the mad and restore them to society 'prevent, so far as is possible, the operation of those laws which weed out and exterminate the diseased and otherwise unfit in every grade of natural life';[221] the insane are 'not only permitted, but are aided by every device known to science to propagate their kind . . .';[222] they are 'turned loose to act as parents to the next generation . . . centres of infection deliberately laid down, and yet we marvel that nervous disease increases'.[223]

The conclusion was obvious: 'Science, until it discovers a way of correcting bad stock . . . must say: "Do not propagate it." '[224] Given the mad's unbridled propensity to breed, 'only coercion will keep them in the right path' – something which (it was thought) should raise no

degenerates, insanity does not appear to be considered a bar to matrimony.' Quoted in David Cochrane, ' "Humane, Economical, and Medically Wise": The LCC as Administrators of Victorian Lunacy Policy', in W.F. Bynum, R. Porter, and M. Shepherd (eds), *The Anatomy of Madness*, Vol. 3, pp. 265–6.

219. S.A.K. Strahan, 'The Propagation of Insanity', p. 334. Maudsley had earlier focused attention on the presence of 'remarkable animal traits and instincts' in the insane, and compared the brains of idiots with those of chimpanzees and other apes. See Henry Maudsley, *Body and Mind*, pp. 43–7.

220. Henry Maudsley, *The Physiology and Pathology of Mind*, p. 247. In Savage and Goodall's formulation, 'the transmission of insanity leads gradually to the abasement and ultimate extinction of the race'. George Henry Savage and Edwin Goodall, *Insanity and its Allied Neuroses*, 4th edn, London: Cassell, 1907, p. 44.

221. S.A.K. Strahan, 'The Propagation of Insanity', p. 331.

222. *Ibid.*, p. 332.

223. *Ibid.*, p. 334. Hayes Newington, the superintendent at Ticehurst, presided over the meeting at which Strahan presented this paper, and in the discussion that followed, he expressed doubts that the situation was as bleak as Strahan claimed. Benjamin Ward Richardson immediately rallied to Strahan's defense, and the other alienists who then chimed in were also largely supportive. See *Journal of Mental Science* 36, 1890, pp. 457–62. Significantly, as Charlotte MacKenzie has demonstrated, 'the Newingtons were reluctant to assign "heredity" as a cause to their upper class and aristocratic patients' and did so rarely even where they were well aware of a family history of insanity. See 'A Family Asylum', pp. 258–9. In all probability, the same motives lay behind his (rather mild) objections to Strahan's paper, and dissent from what was by now the orthodox psychiatric viewpoint.

224. Thomas Clouston, *Clinical Lectures on Mental Disease*, London: Churchill, 1887, p. 633. See also Lionel A. Weatherly, 'Can We Instill Rational Ideas Regarding Insanity into the Public Mind?' *British Medical Journal* 16 September 1899, p. 710. Maudsley had voiced similar sentiments in 1871: 'It is certain that if we were interested in breeding a variety of animals, we should not think of continuing to breed from a stock which was wanting in those qualities that were the highest characteristics of the species. . . . Is it then right to sanction propagation of his kind by an individual who is wanting in that which is the highest attribute of man – a sound and stable mental constitution?' But he had hesitated at the last: 'I cannot think science yet has the right to forbid marriage to those in whom some tendency to insanity exists.' H. Maudsley, 'Insanity and its Treatment', pp. 314, 318. By the 1890s, the urgent need to avoid 'the contamination of the race' (Strahan, 'The Propagation of Insanity', p. 331) led many of his erstwhile colleagues to cast aside such lingering scruples.

ethical qualms since 'these wretched creatures far down in the scale of degeneration . . . have no more right to claim freedom of action as to procreation than has the leper to mingle with the populace'.[225] In principle, a policy of this sort – which would guarantee 'a wonderful reduction in the number of . . . insane as compared with the present'[226] – could be implemented in more than one way. One might 'adopt the old Scotch custom of castration and spaying, Mr Lawson Tait[227] would willingly spay the females for a limited sum, and we could work the males ourselves.'[228] Or one could avoid 'results . . . deplorable and saddening beyond conception [sic]' by ensuring 'in the cases of chronically insane persons, their detention for life, as good not only for themselves, but for society. . . .'[229]

In practice, few took the first option seriously, at least in Britain,[230] and for a further half century and more, the authorities continued to rely on an expanding system of mass segregation as the 'solution' to the problems posed by the mad. London, as befitted the capital and the largest asylums authority in England and Wales, took the lead in setting an example for the rest of society. When local government was reorganized by the 1888 Local Government Act, the new London County Council inherited an extensive asylum network which included the establishments at Hanwell, Colney Hatch, Banstead and Cane Hill. (The warehouses for the chronic at Caterham and Leavesden, now augmented by three further establishments of a similar sort at Darenth, Sutton, and Tooting Bec, continued to

225. S.A.K. Strahan, 'The Propagation of Insanity', pp. 337–8. In the face of sentiments like these, Weatherly's complaint that 'this disease . . . is not looked upon by the general public at all in the same light as other diseases; . . . it is considered to be something to be ashamed of, something to be kept a profound secret as long as possible' has a distinctly disingenuous ring to it. See L.A. Weatherly, 'Can We Install Rational Ideas Regarding Insanity into the Public Mind?', pp. 709–10.
226. R. Greene, 'The Care and Cure of the Insane', p. 508.
227. On Lawson Tait's gynaecological treatments for nervous disorders, cf. Andrew Scull and Diane Favreau, ' "A Chance to Cut is a Chance to Cure": Sexual Surgery for Psychosis in Three Nineteenth Century Societies,' in S. Spitzer and A. Scull (eds), Research in Law, Deviance, and Social Control, Vol. 8, Greenwich, Connecticut: JAI Press, 1986, pp. 3–39.
228. Strahan, 'The Propagation of Insanity', p. 462.
229. Charles Lockhart Robertson, 'Commentary on R. Greene, "Hospitals for the Insane" ', reprinted in H.C. Burdett, Hospitals and Asylums of the World, Vol. 2, pp. 263–4. Robertson had chaired the meeting of alienists gathered to discuss Greene's paper, and he was summarizing and closing the proceedings. Obviously, he now repented his earlier endorsement of non-asylum treatment for the insane, and drawing attention to 'how doubtful many of the so-called cures were, [he] strongly condemned the liberation of many passed as cured'. Even earlier, by the late 1870s, Maudsley had begun to speak of the need for 'sequestration' or 'violent extrusion' of 'morbid varieties or degenerates of the human kind'. H. Maudsley, The Pathology of Mind, 1879, p. 115.
230. For the rather different outcome in the United States, cf. Gerald Grob, Mental Illness and American Society, 1875–1940, Princeton: Princeton University Press, 1983, p. 173: 'Between 1907 and 1940, a total of 18,552 mentally ill persons in state hospitals were surgically sterilized.'

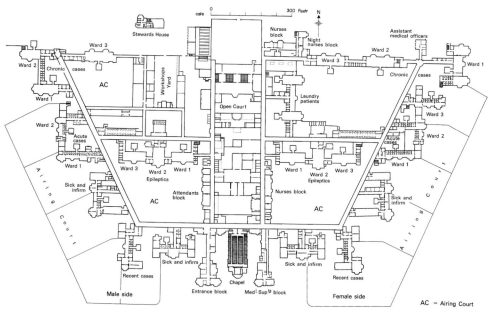

Fig. 21 Ground floor plan of the Claybury County Asylum at Woodford, Essex, begun in 1887, adapted from *The Builder*, 23 November 1889. In this vast colony for 2,000 patients, attended by several hundred staff, physical space was systematically employed to classify the inmate population and to reinforce moral boundaries. The degenerate refuse of the community was here confined in buildings which provided an important symbolic reminder of the awful consequences of non-conformity, shut away in a 'bald and monotonous architecture, which has scarcely recognized more than physical necessities'.[231]

be administered separately.) Yet another vast asylum was already under construction at Claybury in Essex, but its completion in 1894 completely failed to relieve the pressure on existing facilities, as did the opening of yet another 2,000 bed asylum at Bexley in 1898. In desperation, and with the active support of the Commissioners in Lunacy, the LCC now bought a thousand acre site near Epsom, on which it proceeded to build no fewer than five separate barracks-like asylums, practically doubling the available accommodation in the space of a mere twenty years.[232]

231. P.J. Bancroft, 'The Bearing of Hospital Adjustments Upon the Efficiency of Remedial and Meliorating Treatments in Mental Diseases', Appendix to H.C. Burdett, *Hospitals and Asylums of the World*, Vol. 2, p. 271.

232. Asylums for the county of London contained 15,293 inmates in 1891, and 25,924 in 1909. Ever more extensive efforts were made to cut costs as this massive building programme proceeded, 'including on site brick manufacture and the use of glazed brick to line the corridors and staircases to save both on plaster and subsequent painting and cleaning bills . . . centralizing the supplies of water, gas and electricity, . . . [fencing off]

Fig. 22   General view of the Claybury County Asylum from *The Builder*, 23 November 1889.
Designed for patients from the East End of London, these buildings included a recreation hall
capable of seating 1200 and a chapel able to accomodate 850 patients at a time. The construction required the manufacture of some 22 million bricks and cost a reported £337,945. Begun by
the Middlesex magistrates, the asylum was subsequently bequeathed to the new London
County Council, who promptly proclaimed that it was 'much too ornamental and sumptuous'!

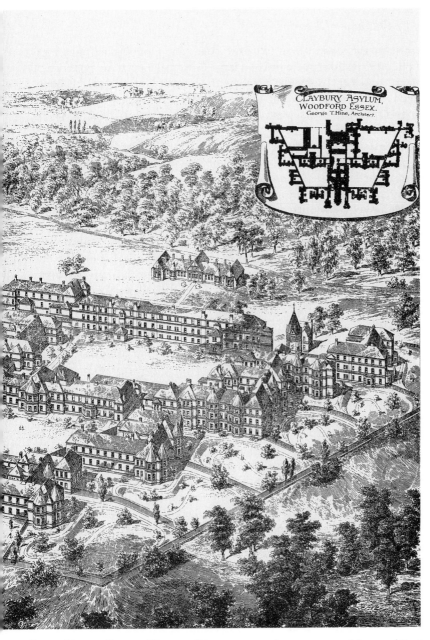

Its architect, George Thomas Hine, was to become consulting architect to the Lunacy Commissioners from 1897 onwards, and, despite the initial complaints from the LCC, was responsible for four major London asylums, new county asylums for Hertfordshire, Lincolnshire, Surrey, East Sussex, and Worcestershire, and additions and alterations to many others. (The London asylums at Bexley, Horton, and Long Grove, and the new East Sussex Asylum at Hellingly all were recycled and barely modified versions of the Claybury design.)

11. The Outcome of Reform

The worst predictions of men like Hill, Reid, and Conolly had thus been borne out, and asylums were now so large as to make even the pretence of treatment a mockery. Indeed, 'even the fresh cases which come in, being associated with such large numbers, drift into a state of dementia'.[233] The lunatic was then left 'worse than dead, with darkened soul dwelling in the living grave of his own body'.[234]

In the metropolis as in the rest of the country, the asylum's early association with social reform gave a humanitarian gloss to these huge, cheap, more or less overtly custodial dumps where the refuse of humanity was now collected together and left to endure 'the downward spiral of crumbling personal identity, mental decrepitude, and the inevitability of burial as a forgotten, pauper lunatic'.[235] At the same time, the medical control of asylums, and the propaganda about treatment rather than punishment, served to provide a thin veneer of legitimation for the custodial warehousing of these, the most difficult and problematic elements of the disreputable poor. Official policy functioned to 'herd lunatics together in special institutions where they can be more easily visited and accounted for by the authorities',[236] and the practical advantages of collecting together these dead souls in cemeteries for the still-breathing sufficed to ensure the continued expansion of existing asylums and the construction of many new ones.

Working-class opposition to the elimination of parish relief, and their hatred of the new workhouse 'Bastilles', had brought only a limited modification of the rigours of the new Poor Law, and not its abandonment. The poor thus had little alternative but to make use of the asylum as a way of ridding themselves of what, in the circumstances of nineteenth-century working-class existence, was undoubtedly an intolerable burden, the caring for their sick, aged, or otherwise incapacitated relatives. From the bourgeoisie's perspective, the existence of asylums to 'treat' the mentally ill at public expense could be invoked as a practical demonstration of their own philanthropic concern with the less fortunate. But far from asylums having been 'altruistic institutions . . . detached from the

a strip of land in the elevated and well-drained north-east corner of the estate . . . to serve as an unconsecrated burial ground for pauper patients', and building a separate rail line to serve the whole monstrous collection of asylums. See D. Cochrane, ' "Humane, Economical, and Medically Wise": The LCC as Administrators of Victorian Lunacy Policy', pp. 257–8 and passim.

233. House of Commons, *Select Committee on the Operation of the Lunacy Law*, 1877, p. 386, evidence of Francis Scott.
234. [John Charles Bucknill], '14th Report of the Commissioners in Lunacy', *Journal of Mental Science* 7, 1860, p. 117.
235. *Ibid.*, p. 263.
236. J.C. Bucknill, *The Care of the Insane and their Legal Control*, p. 122.

social structures that perpetuate poverty',[237] one must recognize that they were important elements in sustaining those structures: important because of their symbolic value, and as a reminder of the awful consequences of non-conformity.

The distressing truth, then, which confronted those who looked back on the work of the reformers in the early part of the century was 'how closely the complaints and aims of the reformers, in the days when there were few county or borough asylums, resemble our own. It is in respect to the very evils these . . . institutions were designed to remedy that they are themselves conspicuously defective'.[238] Arlidge's bitter comment on the outcome of reform succinctly summed up the consequences of its central achievement, the creation of vast receptacles for the confinement of those without hope:

> In a colossal refuge for the insane, a patient may be said to lose his individuality and to become a member of a machine so put together, as to move with precise regularity and invariable routine; a triumph of skill adapted to show how such unpromising materials as crazy men and women may be drilled into order and guided by rule, but not an apparatus calculated to restore their pristine condition and their independent self-governing existence. In all cases admitting of recovery, or of material amelioration, a gigantic asylum is a gigantic evil, and figuratively speaking, a manufactory of chronic insanity.[239]

237. Herbert Gans, preface to Colin Greer, *The Great School Legend*, New York: Basic Books, 1971.
238. J.M. Granville, *The Care and Cure of the Insane*, Vol. 1, p. 86.
239. J.T. Arlidge, *On the State of Lunacy*, p. 102. Compare W.A.F. Browne's similar conclusions about 'the moral evils of a vast assemblage of incurable cases in one building':

> The community becomes unwieldy; the cares are beyond the capacity of the medical officers; personal intimacy is impossible; recent cases are lost, and overlooked in the mass; and patients are treated in groups and classes. An unhealthy moral atmosphere is created; a mental epidemic arises, where delusion, and debility, and extravagance are propagated from individual to individual, and the intellect is dwarfed and enfeebled by monotony, routine, and subjection.

Crichton Royal Asylum, *18th Annual Report*, 1857, p. 8.

CHAPTER SEVEN

The Social Production of Insanity

'But I don't want to go among mad people,' Alice remarked.
'Oh, you can't help that,' said the Cat: 'we're all mad here. I'm mad. You're mad.'
'How do you know I'm mad?' said Alice.
'You must be,' said the Cat, 'or you wouldn't have come here.'
Lewis Carroll, *Alice's Adventures in Wonderland*

HAMLET: 'Ay marry, why was he sent into England?'
CLOWN: 'Why because he was mad. He shall recover his wits there; or if he do not, it is no great matter there.'
HAMLET: 'Why?'
CLOWN: ''Twill not be seen in him; there the men are as mad as he.'
William Shakespeare, *Hamlet*

The reformers had launched their proposals backed by the claim and sustained by the conviction that proper asylum treatment would cure a significant proportion of the insane, and so reduce the incidence of insanity. The public had been assured that providing county asylums 'will, no doubt, require a considerable sum in the first instance, but hereafter the parishes will be relieved from a very heavy and increasing burden'.[1] It would be something of an understatement to suggest that these expectations proved delusory. Indeed, it remains perhaps the most paradoxical feature of the entire reform process that the adoption of a policy avowedly aimed at rehabilitation and the rise of a profession claiming expertise in this regard should have been accompanied by a startling and continuing rise in the proportion of the population officially recognized as insane.[2]

1. Sir A. Halliday, *A General View of the Present State of Lunatics and Lunatic Asylums in Great Britain and Ireland*, London: Underwood, 1928, p. 24.
2. Edward Hare has recently argued that the increase was a real one, reflecting a rise in the most serious form of mental disorder, more specifically, 'a slow epidemic of schizophrenia'. In his eyes, the increased prevalence of this disorder, which he speculates has a viral origin, provides 'a medical explanation of the asylum era'. One cannot but admire the boldness and ingenuity of an account which purports to reduce surface complexities to the simplicity of a single underlying somatic cause, even as one is left a trifle breathless by the speculative leaps of faith involved. As the remainder of this chapter will demonstrate, however, my own preference is for a more complex, less reductionist

1. Rising Numbers of Madmen

Figures presented in the Report of the 1807 Select Committee, the first of the numerous nineteenth-century Parliamentary investigations into the lunacy question, gave 2,248 as the official tally of all persons identified as insane in England and Wales at the beginning of that year, on which basis the incidence of insanity was roughly 2.26 cases in every 10,000 of the general population – scarcely a rate calculated to produce anxiety that this was a common condition.[3] As efforts at 'reform' focused further attention on the plight of the insane, however, so their estimated proportion in the total population began to rise.[4] 'In 1810', before the first county asylum built under the 1808 Act opened its doors, 'the existing number of the insane in this kingdom was estimated by Dr Powell at one in 7,300; in 1820 by Dr Burrows, at one in 2,000; and in 1829 by Sir Andrew Halliday, at 16,500 or one in 769.'[5] The Metropolitan Commissioners' 1844 Report provided official confirmation that such a rapid rise, at least in the number of cases known to the authorities, had indeed taken place. The number of insane now amounted to over 20,000 and the incidence had risen to 12.66 cases per 10,000, almost six times that reported in 1807. This increase now became another of the reformers' arguments for new legislation to deal with the insane. For insanity was now a serious social problem, and 'pauper Lunatics have unfortunately become so numerous throughout the whole kingdom, that the proper construction and cost of asylums for their use has ceased to be a subject which affects a few counties only, and has become a matter of national interest and importance'.[6]

The achievement of reform – the construction of asylums and the employment of doctors to effect the cure of the insane – did not bring about a halt or even a diminution in the rapid upward spiral of cases of lunacy. Between 1844 and 1860, while the population as a whole grew by

account, one that leaves but a minute place for the microbes, but which nonetheless in my view makes more compelling sense of the available evidence. Hare's original case was made in his Maudsley Lecture, 'Was Insanity on the Increase?' *British Journal of Psychiatry* 142, 1983, pp. 439–55. For an earlier critique, large portions of which are incorporated here, see Andrew Scull, 'Was Insanity Increasing? A Response to Edward Hare', *British Journal of Psychiatry* 144, 1984, pp. 432–6.

3. House of Commons, *Report of the Select Committee on Criminal and Pauper Lunatics*, 1807, p. 5. Robert Castel cites comparably low contemporary estimates of the number of lunatics in early nineteenth-century France and notes that the officially identified insane population were 'very few in comparison with [other indigent and morally suspect sub-populations]'. See *The Regulation of Madness*, Berkeley: University of California Press, 1988, p. 14.

4. I want to defer for the moment any discussion of the adequacy or accuracy of these and subsequent data on the numbers of lunatics. For the present, I am solely concerned to demonstrate the extent of the increase in the number of people officially identified as insane, and to illustrate its effect on the prevailing conceptions of just how serious a problem insanity was.

5. John Thurnam, *Observations and Essays on the Statistics of Insanity*, London: Simpkin Marshall, 1845, p. 170, footnote.

6. Metropolitan Commissioners in Lunacy, *Report*, 1844, p. 30.

just over twenty per cent, the number of lunatics all but doubled; and the growth in the number of the insane continued to far outstrip the rate of increase of the general population for the rest of the century. By 1890, there were 86,067 officially certified cases of mental illness in England and Wales, which meant that in the forty-five years immediately following the establishment of a compulsory system of public asylums for the early treatment and cure of lunatics, while the total population had risen by a mere 78 per cent, the number of lunatics had more than quadrupled. To put it another way, in 1844 the rate of certified cases of mental illness in the population as a whole was 12.66 per 10,000; by 1890, the figure was 29.6 per 10,000.

In the years immediately following the opening of the county asylum system, those who ran the asylums tended to dismiss the apparent rise in numbers as a temporary phenomenon. Their claim was that before asylum treatment had been made widely available, there had been a submerged reservoir of crazy people, hidden from public view, and hence not recorded in official statistics. Asylum committees were convinced that they had adequate 'reasons to believe that, since the asylum had been opened, and the advantages it affords to lunatics have become known and recognized throughout the county, many poor insane persons, long previously neglected at home', were brought into the institution. Families now realized that the inhumanity of the madhouse was a thing of the past, and had become aware of the benefits which scientific treatment in an asylum could confer, so that those with a lunatic in the closet or attic brought forth cases 'never before known to the parish officers'.[7]

Obviously, such a state of affairs could not be expected to continue for ever. The community ought sooner or later to run out of this accumulated surplus. But unfortunately for the asylum authorities, it began to appear as though the rise in the number of lunatics *would* continue indefinitely. Consequently, this explanation, at least when standing alone, quickly came to seem inadequate. The Lunacy Commissioners might argue that a

---

7. Report of the Visiting Justices of the Wandsworth County Asylum, Surrey, 1850, cited in J.M. Granville, *The Care and Cure of the Insane*, Vol. 1, London: Hardwicke & Bogue, 1877, p. 224. Edward Jarvis had advanced a similar explanation of the apparent increase in insanity in the United States. The opening of asylums built in accordance with the reformers' plans,

> the spread of their reports, the extension of the knowledge of their character, power, and usefulness, by the means of the patients that they protect and cure, have created, and continue to create, more and more interest in the subject of insanity, and more confidence in its curability. Consequently, more and more persons and families, who, or such as who, formerly kept their insane friends and relations at home, or allowed them to stroll abroad about the street or country, now believe, that they can be restored, or improved, or, at least made more comfortable in these public institutions, and, therefore, they send their patients to these asylums, and thus swell the lists of their inmates.

Edward Jarvis, 'On the Supposed Increase of Insanity', *American Journal of Insanity* 8, 1852, p. 344.

Table 8 Total Population, Total Number Officially Identified as Insane, and Rate of Insanity per 10,000 People in England and Wales in the Nineteenth Century.

1 Jan.	Population	Number officially identified as insane*	Rate per 10,000	Source of data on number insane
1807	9,960,000	2,248	2.26	House of Commons 1807
1819	11,106,000	6,000	5.40	Burrows 1820
1828	13,106,000	8,000	6.10	Halliday 1828
1829	13,370,000	16,500	12.34	Halliday 1829
1836	14,900,000	13,667	9.18	Parliamentary Return 1836
1844	16,480,000	20,893	12.66	Metropolitan Commissioners in Lunacy
1850			NOT AVAILABLE	
1855	18,786,914	30,993**	16.49	Commissioners in Lunacy Annual Reports
1860	19,902,713	38,058	19.12	
1865	21,145,151	45,950	21.73	
1870	22,501,316	54,713	24.31	
1875	23,944,459	63,793	26.64	
1880	25,480,161	71,191	27.94	
1885	27,499,041	79,704	28.98	
1890	29,407,649	86,067	29.26	

* Includes lunatics confined in asylums, but also those in workhouses, at large in the community, etc.

** The Commissioners found 20,493 lunatics in asylums of all types in 1855; lacking a complete enumeration of all lunatics not so confined, they estimated that these amounted to some 10,500 persons. (Commissioners in Lunacy Annual Report 1855, Vol. 9, p. 39.)

by-product of their inspection of workhouses, and their other activities, was the uncovering of previously unnoticed cases of insanity, but even they conceded that this was no longer sufficient to account for the persistent sharp increase in the total number of the insane.

Naturally enough, such a rapid accumulation did not occur without arousing public unease and concern at the course of events. Most people drew the obvious conclusion that the changes in official statistics reflected a real increase in the incidence of the disorder, and the Lunacy Commissioners commented that 'the opinion generally entertained was that the community are more subject than formerly to attacks of insanity'.[8] Public fear of the legions of crazy men and women that society was

8. Commissioners in Lunacy, 15th Annual Report, 1861, p. 84.

apparently spawning at times verged on panic. Bucknill, for rhetorical effect, complained of 'the customs and laws which the sane majority has sanctioned for what is called the care and treatment, but to speak more truly for the custody and control, of that which is still fortunately the insane minority of the people';[9] but such hyperbole was lost on a general public which was convinced that such statements were almost literally true. Not three years previously, an editorial in *The Times* had commented that 'if lunacy continues to increase as at present, the insane will be in the majority, and, freeing themselves, will put the sane in asylums'.[10]

It was partly to allay these anxieties that the Commissioners had sought to explain (or rather to explain away) the reasons for the multiplication of cases of lunacy. On other grounds, though, they could scarcely have avoided examining the question. The progressive increase in insanity was obvious to those with even the most casual acquaintance with the subject. It can hardly be a source of wonder that those officially charged with overseeing the asylum system on a full-time basis should have chosen to investigate the reasons for such a development.

We must remember that those engaged in this enterprise were trying to account for a paradoxical state of affairs. The 'scientific' discovery of mental illness, and the adoption of a more 'rational' approach based upon this discovery which aimed at treating and curing the lunatic rather than neglecting him or incarcerating him in a jail or workhouse, were advances which might have been expected to coincide with a decline in the prevalence of insanity. Instead they were associated with an explosive growth in the number of the insane. When the Lunacy Commissioners sought to reconcile this seemingly contradictory state of affairs, they did so as men who had been among the prime movers in the reform process, and who were convinced of the superiority and value of the medical approach to insanity. Naturally, therefore, they were disposed to look for answers which laid the blame on something other than reform, and which accounted for the apparent failure of the asylum in practice.

2. *Official Explanations of the Increase*

In 1844, more than 80 per cent of those diagnosed as insane were classified as paupers. Subsequently, the increase in the number of lunatics came overwhelmingly from their ranks. Between 1844 and 1860 the number of pauper lunatics rose by 96.4 per cent, while that of private lunatics grew only 24.4 per cent. Understandably, the Commissioners concentrated their attention on explaining the reasons for the increase among the former. Seeking 'to take into account every circumstance bearing directly or indirectly on the condition of the insane poor, which might have the

9. J. Bucknill, *The Care of the Insane and their Legal Control*, London: Macmillan, 1880, pp. 1–2.
10. *The Times*, 5 April 1877.

apparent effect of increasing their number . . .',[11] the Commissioners first checked the most obvious point. Perhaps there had been a rise in the number of paupers, accounting for all or part of the increase in insanity among this class? On the contrary, 'we have positive information that pauperism has decreased . . .'.[12] The Poor Law Board had recently produced figures which showed that 'the decrease in the average number of paupers of all classes in receipt of relief at one time in 1859, as compared with 1849, is 20.5 per cent, and as regards able-bodied paupers, the decrease in 1859, as compared with 1849, is 40.7 per cent'.[13] The other suggestion which most readily presented itself was, at least as far as the Commissioners were concerned, equally easily disposed of. The rise could not reflect an increased incidence of insanity among the lower classes, since 'we have been unable to discover any material changes in the social conditions of the labouring population rendering them more prone to mental disease'.[14] If there were no increase in the proportion of paupers in the general population which could account for the increasing number of pauper lunatics, and if those paupers who remained were no more susceptible to insanity than their predecessors had been, one conclusion seemed inescapable: the figures which showed that such an upward trend existed must somehow be faulty. Accordingly, the Commissioners sought to reassure the public that the rise was more apparent than real.

In the first place, they contended, the methods of gathering statistics on insanity had previously been slipshod and inadequate. Local authorities had often failed to keep accurate accounts in the first place, and had compounded the error by submitting careless reports to the central government. The more thorough and uniform system of reporting they themselves had introduced had had the effect of adding large numbers to the official national statistics, even though such cases had existed all along. Much of the apparent rise could thus be attributed to 'the large number of cases previously unreported, and only recently brought under observation'.[15] Other factors were also at work. The alleged failure of the Poor Law authorities to send their cases of lunacy to asylums at a sufficiently early stage in the disease meant that asylums were filled to overflowing with the most inveterate and hopeless cases. The Commissioners conceded that it was impossible to determine with precision the effect of institutionalization on the lifespan of the insane, as the necessary figures on mortality rates prior to the rise of the asylum system were lacking:

> But we are warranted in assuming that when destitute and diseased persons are placed under care in Establishments well-conducted, well-

---

11. Commissioners in Lunacy, *15th Annual Report*, 1861, p. 77.
12. *Ibid.*
13. *12th Report of the Poor Law Board*, quoted *ibid.*, p. 77, footnote.
14. Commissioners in Lunacy, *15th Annual Report*, 1861, p. 77.
15. *Ibid.*, p. 78; see also House of Commons, *Report of the Select Committee on the Operation of the Lunacy Law*, 1877, p. 6, evidence of Lord Shaftesbury.

regulated, and specially adapted for their protection and treatment, and in which they receive succour, abundant food, and careful medical supervision, the result will be the prolongation of lives which would otherwise have been of short duration.[16]

Partial confirmation of this hypothesis was provided by figures on mortality rates in asylums, which showed a sharp diminution since the early 1840s, when they ran as high as 18 per cent and more per annum in some Metropolitan Licensed Houses; a decrease which coincided with the introduction of the new system of inspection and the general improvement of asylum conditions. The greater life expectancy associated with asylum care accentuated the existing tendencies towards the long-term accumulation of chronic cases; and their increased longevity had the apparent effect of augmenting the incidence of insanity in the community.[17]

More cases of insanity had existed in the community in the past than anyone had realized because they had often been mistaken for something else. Recent 'scientific' advances now enabled such cases to be recognized for what they 'really' were, and, for the first time, to be looked after and treated properly. 'There can be very little doubt', the Commissioners in Lunacy informed Parliament, 'that the system of observation and inquiry adopted of late years, however imperfect it still may be, had led to the detection and classification as Insane, of many persons formerly looked upon as ordinary Paupers.'[18]

These, then, were the most common official explanations of why the statistics of insanity showed a persistent rising trend. By and large, they all suggested that the apparent increase was primarily a statistical artifact and did not reflect the true state of affairs. In addition, however, there was one other theory which enjoyed periodical bursts of popularity among some of the asylum doctors, and the public also. Advocates of this position conceded that there had indeed been some real increase in the prevalence of insanity, an increase they attributed to the stresses attendant upon life in a higher 'mechanical civilization'. This view was first articulated by Powell, and subsequently received support from Halliday, both of whom adduced the rise over time in the number of people identified as insane as the principal evidence for such a position. Browne, too, was convinced that 'the occupations, amusements, follies, and above all the vices of the present race are infinitely more favourable for the development of the disease than at any previous period'.[19]

16. Commissioners in Lunacy, *15th Annual Report*, 1861, p. 79.
17. Thus the accumulation of lunatics in the system was adduced as evidence of the benefits the asylum conferred on the insane, and hence of the success of reform.
18. Commissioners in Lunacy, *15th Annual Report*, 1861, p. 78. As I shall argue at more length below, this remark, and similar ones about recognizing previously 'misclassified' cases of insanity, unconsciously suggest what was actually going on, an expansion of the boundaries of the mad.
19. Richard Powell, *Observations on the Comparative Prevalence of Insanity at Different Periods*, London: Woodfall, 1813; Sir Andrew Halliday, *A Letter to Lord Robert Seymour: with a*

Later in the century, Bucknill and Tuke exhibited a greater scepticism about the quality of the statistical data in favour of this generalization. Nevertheless, they then succeeded in reaching an identical conclusion, though by a somewhat more circuitous route. Direct measures of the comparative prevalence of insanity at different periods being somewhat unreliable, the issue could only be resolved by observing 'whether the most frequent causes of insanity are to be found in greater force in civilized societies'. Evidently realizing that an audience of orthodox adherents of a Victorian evolutionism which as a matter of course equated a 'higher' civilization with progress in almost all spheres would find the conclusion that a more civilized existence was also more productive of mental defectives an unpalatable one, they sought to soften the blow. They too, 'regarding the question in an abstract and theoretical point of view . . . should certainly be disposed to expect that the development of civilization. . . . would conduce to the mental health of any people subjected to its influence'. But from a different perspective, one was forced to recognize the possible drawbacks of the pace and fluidity of modern life, at least when taken to extremes. So that 'practically, we submit, that, in consequence of the abuse of the very blessings attendant on the progress of civilization, and of the temptation which civilization offers to overtax the faculties; and, lastly, in consequence of the greatly increased degree in which the emotions are developed, the result is, that an advanced civilization tends to increase the number of the insane'.[20]

Actually, neither Bucknill and Tuke, nor their predecessors who had argued for the same conclusion, had proved in any scientifically acceptable sense that a connection existed between civilization and insanity. Their case seems plausible only because of what they claimed were the causes of insanity; but no scientific evidence was (or has yet been) produced to demonstrate that 'artificiality', 'excitement', 'stress', and the like are instrumental in bringing about insanity. Moreover, since 'civilization' consisted of precisely those things which were supposed to cause insanity, the alleged proof turns out to have been a mere tautology. While this is not to say, of course, that the original hypothesis is necessarily false, only that it remains unproven, it does leave open the possibility that the statistical rise in insanity has quite different sources.

For a somewhat different set of reasons, the suggestion that an improved system of reporting cases of insanity was a major factor lying behind the rise in the apparent incidence of the 'disease' is similarly unsatisfactory. It does possess a certain surface plausibility, deriving from the fact that from 1844 onwards, the statistics of insanity were indeed more carefully

Report on the Number of Lunatics and Idiots in England and Wales, London: Underwood, 1829, p. v; W.A.F. Browne, *What Asylums Were, Are, and Ought to Be*, Edinburgh: Black, 1837, pp. 51–5.

20. J.C. Bucknill and D.H. Tuke, *A Manual of Psychological Medicine*, Philadelphia: Blanchard & Lee, 1858, pp. 48, 58.

collected than they had hitherto been. When the 1807 Select Committee presented the figures it had obtained, it felt bound to caution the Report's readers that 'these are so evidently deficient in several instances that a very large addition must be made in any computation of the whole number'.[21] And while subsequent numbers given by Burrows and Halliday were based on official returns, both considered it necessary to 'correct' those figures by adding an estimate of cases omitted from the returns for one reason or another; so that prior to the 1844 Report of the Metropolitan Commissioners in Lunacy, no entirely satisfactory accounting existed. On the other hand, it strains credulity to believe that the early nineteenth-century observers underestimated the incidence of what they called insanity as badly as the figures make it seem. While the 1807 Select Committee thought in terms of a 'large' addition to existing figures, the tone of their report nowhere suggests that they considered the real rate to be five or six times the existing estimate (as it would have needed to be to account for the size of the discrepancy between these and later statistics).

The Committee's recommendation that sixteen District Asylums, 'calculated to contain as large a number as possible, not exceeding three hundred', should be erected to provide for all the country's insane population indicates that they thought the likely underestimate was of the order of one or two thousand, or roughly fifty to a hundred per cent;[22] for the total capacity of such a system would have been only 4,800. Two pieces of evidence suggest that such a conclusion was not wildly unreasonable. In 1807, Dr Andrew Halliday conducted a parish by parish survey of the counties of Norfolk and Suffolk to provide a check on the official returns, and found a total of 112 and 114 lunatics respectively, as compared with the reported figures of 42 and 103 – an increase of approximately 56 per cent.[23] Using Halliday's data, the rate of insanity per 10,000 people in each county (based on populations in 1811 of 291,982 and 239,153 respectively) was 3.83 and 4.77, compared with a national rate, calculated from the Committee's figures, of 2.26.

Evidence from Bedfordshire provides further confirmation of the fact that, even when careful inquiries were instituted in the early nineteenth century to discover the number of insane persons in a county, the rate of incidence of insanity, while greater than that given in the 1807 Report, was not spectacularly so. When the local county asylum opened in 1812, there was found to be a shortage of lunatics with which to fill it, only twelve candidates for admission being received. Threatening letters to parish overseers, warning that heavy fines would be levied were they found to be concealing cases to avoid incurring the expense of asylum treatment, and a subsequent tour of the county by Samuel Whitbread,

21. House of Commons, *Select Committee on Criminal and Pauper Lunatics*, 1807, p. 5.
22. *Ibid.*, pp. 7, 27.
23. House of Commons, *Report of the Select Committee on Criminal and Pauper Lunatics*, 1807, pp. 7, 27, and Appendices 2 and 3, letters from Andrew Halliday.

Table 9 Total Population, Total Admissions into All Asylums in the Year, and Admissions Expressed as a Rate per 10,000 of the Total Population of England and Wales, 1855–90.

	Population estimated for middle of year	Total admissions excluding transfers	Rate of admissions per 10,000
1855	18,786,914	7,366*	3.92*
1860	19,902,713	9,512*	4.77*
1865	20,990,946	10,424*	4.96*
1870	22,501,316	10,219	4.54
1875	23,944,459	12,442	5.19
1880	25,480,161	13,240	5.19
1885	27,499,041	13,354	4.85
1890	29,407,649	16,197	5.51

Source: Annual Reports of the Commissioners in Lunacy.
*For these years, the Commissioners' figures on admissions include patients transferred from one asylum to another. Accordingly, the ratio of admissions to population is overstated by an unknown, but sizeable amount. In 1870, for example, transfers amounted to 10.7 per cent of total admissions, and in 1880, to 11.7 per cent. Assuming (conservatively) that transfers in the period 1855–65 were approximately 10 per cent of admissions, the rate of admissions per 10,000 people would reduce to 3.53 in 1855, 4.30 in 1860, and 4.47 in 1865.

explicitly undertaken to drum up more inmates to fill the new institution, failed to produce more than twelve additional cases. The census of the previous year had estimated a population of 70,203 for the county. This would suggest a rate of insanity of approximately 3.59 per 10,000 people, once more only slightly greater than the 2.26 which the 1807 figures gave for the country as a whole.[24]

By the time Burrows and Halliday made their estimates of the prevalence of insanity, the number of asylums and madhouses had already increased considerably, as, if they were to be believed, had the number of lunatics. Once again it seems unlikely that their estimates were as bad as the Lunacy Commissioners later implied. Both were men with a long and extensive acquaintance with questions related to insanity. Both prepared their estimates with considerable care, and were aware of and corrected for the most serious discrepancies in the official returns. And given their mutual concern with rousing public attention to the seriousness of the problem of insanity, one would expect them, if anything, to have erred on the side of generosity when estimating the numbers requiring treatment.

There is yet a further objection to the hypothesis that a more accurate enumeration was a major factor. The system of collecting data on all

24. Bedfordshire County Asylum Minutes, 15 July, 3 October 1812, in manuscript at the Bedfordshire County Record Office, LB 1/1.

aspects of insanity which was established on a permanent basis in 1846 remained substantially unchanged during the rest of the century. Yet the increase in the recorded cases of lunacy slowed little, if at all, in the latter part of the nineteenth century. It might take a few years, perhaps even a decade, for the full effects of the new arrangements to show themselves, but in the absence of further major changes in the way that data were gathered, assertions that increases in the rate of insanity reflected a more exact count come to seem progressively more implausible.

The Commissioners' contention that much of the rise in the lunatic population merely reflected the accumulation of chronic cases in asylums has a somewhat more solid foundation in fact. Since at best about a third of each year's admissions recovered the use of their wits (and less than fifteen or twenty per cent of those admitted were released – as 'relieved' or 'not improved' – without doing so); and since the annual mortality rate, while fluctuating, usually amounted to about a third of annual admissions, a fairly substantial proportion of each year's intake remained behind to swell the total number of insane people in the population.[25] Even so, taken alone, this factor obviously did not account for the rising number of lunatics. For one thing, as the Commissioners themselves realized, the growth in numbers was simply too rapid for that. Secondly, as the admission rates per 10,000 of the general population indicate, although there were some fluctuations from year to year, the secular trend which underlay these was clearly in an upward direction. Finally, if the accumulation of chronic cases was the sole, or even the single, major factor in the rise in the rate of insanity, we would expect the increase to have been approximately the same in the case of both private and pauper patients; for the cure rates in most private asylums were even lower than in their public counterparts, and mortality rates were roughly comparable. Yet in practice, the number of private patients rose 101.4 per cent between 1844 and 1890, while the number of pauper patients increased more than three and a half times as fast, by some 363.7 per cent.[26]

3. An Alternative Explanation

All of the 'explanations' given at the time for the growth in numbers of the insane share two fundamental assumptions: (1) that there is some finite universe of 'crazy people' out there in the world; and (2) that identifying who is and who is not to be defined as mad is an activity governed by some objective, uniform, and unchanging standard. Neither assumption will withstand critical examination.

25. See the previous discussion of 'cure rates' and mortality in chapter 6.
26. The other 'explanations' we have considered so far are subject to analogous objections, since they too fail to indicate why patient numbers should rise so much more rapidly among the paupers than among the private patients.

Definitions of insanity and discussion of how the condition is to be recognized abound in early nineteenth-century literature on madness. The problem is that while the definitions are full of medical terms and phrases, and are frequently long and cumbersome, they make no progress at all towards the actual identification of cases. Indeed, their uselessness for all practical purposes (save as support for the contention that identifying such a complex entity is an expert's task) is so great that many of these very same writers cheerfully concede, elsewhere in their treatises, that their formal distinctions are of no help whatsoever when it comes to the question of deciding someone's sanity.[27]

The arbitrariness of the whole business is suggested by the need most writers felt to coin a definition of their own. The verbal gymnastics are entertaining, even if the results are somewhat meagre. A man is sane only 'when . . . the manifestations of his mind, his sentiments, passions, and general conduct, continue either to improve or to keep in accordance with the exhibitions of his previous powers and habits';[28] so that 'strictly speaking, every individual who exhibits an involuntary alteration in his mental manifestation denoting the most trifling disorder is not at that moment in a state of perfect sanity or health, that is, he is insane'.[29] Alternatively, the insane person is 'one whose intellect has been perverted'.[30] His insanity is 'a consequence of loss of nervous tone . . . all insane phenomena may be ascribed to the two well-known consequences of loss of nervous tone (acting coincidently), – namely excess of nervous energy or irritable accumulation, and paralysis or loss of nervous tone'.[31] At the same time,

27. Significantly, my examination of the casebooks at a wide variety of asylums, pauper and private, reveals that diagnostic labels bore no relationship whatsoever to the treatment a patient received. The British psychiatrist Trevor Turner, following intensive research on the casebooks of the Ticehurst Asylum, concludes that 'the symptoms and behaviour noted in the casebooks are often left to stand for themselves instead of forming a diagnosis. . . . Few attempts were made at classification, psychological speculation or aetiological concern.' (T. Turner, 'Rich and Mad in Victorian England', *Psychological Medicine* 19, 1989, p. 43.) Where diagnostic labels were not even conferred, they obviously could have no effect on treatment, and Ann Digby's detailed examination of patient records at the York Retreat reveals that here, too, 'a systematic nosology fell into disuse. . . . During much of the second half of the nineteenth century, medical labelling of patients seems to have been honoured more in the breach than in the observance'. (A. Digby, *Madness, Morality and Medicine: A Study of the York Retreat 1796–1914*, Cambridge: Cambridge University Press, 1985, p. 137.) It is scarcely surprising, in the circumstances, that the iconoclastic Henry Maudsley rejected the very attempt to differentiate insanity, emphasizing 'how close are the fundamental relations of nervous diseases, and how artificial the divisions between them'. Each of the traditional subcategories – mania, melancholia, moral insanity, dementia – was, he insisted, 'but a stage in the descent towards sterile idiocy'. H. Maudsley, *The Physiology and Pathology of Mind*, London: Macmillan, 1868, pp. 246, 247.
28. W.C. Ellis, *A Treatise on the Nature, Symptoms, Causes, and Treatment of Insanity*, London: Holdsworth, 1838, p. 16.
29. *Ibid.*, pp. 30–31.
30. Thomas Mayo, *Medical Testimony and Evidence in Cases of Lunacy*, London: Parker, 1854, p. 4.
31. Henry Monro, *Remarks on Insanity: Its Nature and Treatment, and Articles on the Reform of Private Lunatic Asylums*, London: Churchill, 1850, p. vi.

medical science shows us that 'Insanity . . . is inordinate or irregular, or impaired action of the mind, of the instincts, sentiments, intellectual or perceptive powers, depending upon and produced by an organic change in the brain.'[32] We should understand that 'a precise definition of madness cannot be attempted as its degrees and intensity depend upon the extent to which the mental faculties have been perverted from their normal condition';[33] but the impossible may yet be attempted, and it turns out that 'every morbid state that influences our reflective, observant and imaginative faculties, disables an individual from conducting the processes of reasoning, or the sound and healthy exercise of his mental attributes, constitutes insanity'.[34] It might seem the counsel of despair to seek 'much help from definitions given by different medical authorities, for not only were some of them, as Dr Good has truly observed, "so narrow as to set at liberty half the patients at Bethlem or the Bicêtre and others so loose and capacious as to give a strait waistcoat to half the world", but . . . when medical men were required to explain what meaning they attached to the word Insanity, they generally satisfied themselves by giving such as had been repeated by one author after another, apparently without examination'.[35] But none of this should dissuade one from exhibiting one's own skill at concocting new forms of words: 'Insanity . . . is *the impairment of any one or more of the faculties of the mind, accompanied with, or inducing, a defect in the comparing faculty.*'[36]

On top of the basic pathology were then piled a myriad of subtypes and varieties: idiocy, fatuity, monomania, mania, and melancholia all assumed a veritable plethora of disguises. With definitions such as these, it can scarcely be a source of wonder that lesser luminaries who tried to rely on the pontifications of the most eminent men in the field were soon obliged to abandon the attempt in despair. Monro's complaints were typical:

> All who have charge of asylums must well know how very different the clear and distinct classification of books is from that medley of symptoms which is presented by real cases. . . . to be nice in dividing instinctive insanity from moral insanity, is a subtlety more easily accomplished in books than in practice, and more useful in a legal than a medical point of view. Again, to divide one sort of dementia from another – to go to the length Mr Esquirol has, and distinguish imbecility by four stages . . . is curious rather than useful.[37]

32. W.A.F. Browne, *What Asylums Were, Are, and Ought to Be*, p. 6.
33. J.G. Millingen, *Aphorisms on the Treatment and Management of the Insane*, London: Churchill, 1840, p. 3.
34. *Ibid.*, p. 1.
35. John Conolly, *An Inquiry Concerning the Indications of Insanity*, London: Taylor, 1830, pp. 292–3.
36. *Ibid.*, p. 300, emphasis in the original.
37. Henry Monro, *Remarks on Insanity*, pp. 1–2. Still earlier, David Uwins had insisted that 'in measure, more than in kind, do nervous derangements differ' and had urged his

As for himself, he preferred the simpler, but more serviceable distinction between acute, chronic, and imbecilic insanity. 'I have tried in vain to classify cases to any practical purpose on any more rigid plan than I have mentioned above. It is useless to paint pictures with more vivid colours than nature presents, and worse than useless if practical men (or rather, I would say, men obliged to practise) receive these pictures as true representations.'[38]

Events seem to have borne out Haslam's gloomy conclusion that to discover 'an infallible definition of madness ... will I believe be found impossible'.[39] After three decades of fruitless efforts to prove him wrong by an array of medical experts on the subject, the judgement remained the same. Unfortunately, 'the attempts of medical writers to define insanity, have not been more successful than those of legal authorities to define what constitutes unsoundness of mind. It is, perhaps, not possible to propose a definition which shall be both positively and negatively correct; that is, which shall include all who are insane and exclude all who are not.'[40] The consequences of trying were evident: 'Medical men have been subjected to much ridicule in our courts of law for the great variety, and sometimes total dissimilarity, of opinions entertained by them with reference to a correct definition of insanity. The great fault consists

colleagues to recognize that 'nosological distinctions and nomenclatural designations are often worse than useless ... not only arbitrary and conventional, but positively fallacious and absurd'. *A Treatise on Those Disorders of the Brain and Nervous System, Which Are Usually Considered and Called Mental*, London: Renshaw and Rush, 1833, pp. 5, 227. For similarly sceptical comments about nosological distinctions, see also J.G. Spurzheim, *Observations on the Deranged Manifestations of the Mind, or Insanity*, London: Baldwin, Craddock, and Joy, 1817, pp. 90–91. Henry Maudsley was characteristically scathing at century's end:

I have purposely avoided mention of the numerous and elaborate classifications which, in almost distracting succession, have been formally proposed as exhaustive and tacitly condemned as useless. ... I have shunned the use of the many learned names – of Greek, Latin, and Graeco-Latin derivation – which have been invented in appalling numbers to denote simple things, and sometimes, it may be feared, with the effect of confounding apprehension of them. ... The effect of such a procedure can hardly fail to be to make artificial distinctions where divisions exist not in nature, and thus to set up barriers to true observation and inference.

The Pathology of Mind: A Study of Its Distempers, Deformities, and Disorders, London: Macmillan, 1895, p. vi.

38. H. Monro, *Remarks on Insanity*, p. 3. Compare the remarkably similar conclusions of Bedford Pierce, superintendent of the York Retreat, a half century and more later: 'It is not possible as yet to make a scientific classification of mental disorders. Were it not for this humiliating reflection, the conflict of opinions would be amusing. ... An essential point in a statistical enquiry is that the things counted under one head shall be of like nature and shall be distinct from other things placed under other heads. But when we consider the forms of mental disorder this essential point is not attained.' York Retreat, *Annual Report*, 1904, quoted in A. Digby, *Madness, Morality and Medicine*, p. 137.

39. John Haslam, *Observations on Madness and Melancholy*, 2nd edn, London: Callow, 1809, p. 5.

40. J.M. Pagan, *The Medical Jurisprudence of Insanity*, London: Ball, Arnold, and Company, 1840, p. 25.

in attempting to define with precision what does not admit of being defined.'[41]

This might perhaps have amounted to no more than a mere verbal dispute over definitions, of no practical importance, had there existed fundamental agreement on the criteria for distinguishing the mad from the sane. But this was far from the case. Indeed, the best authorities were convinced that no such rules could be drawn up. '[Medical men] have sought for and imagined a strong and definable boundary between sanity and insanity, which has ... been imaginary and arbitrarily placed.'[42] These efforts notwithstanding, 'no palpable distinction exists, no line of demarcation can be traced between the sane and the insane. It must be confessed, that the line is either ideal or purely geometrical'.[43] General agreement was easily secured in extreme cases of violent mania or complete dementia, but with these exceptions, 'the task of declaring this to be reason and that insanity is exceedingly embarrassing, and, to a great degree, arbitrary. People have puzzled themselves to discover this line, a terra incognita, in fact, which does not exist.'[44] Yet if the decision as to what was or was not to count as madness was essentially 'arbitrary', the assumption that the universe of crazy people was in any sense strictly delimited was clearly not substantiated.[45]

41. William B. Neville, *On Insanity: Its Nature, Causes and Cure*, London: Longman, Rees, Orme, Brown, Green and Longman, 1836, p. 7. The two legal settings in which alienists were most publicly called upon to testify as to the presence or absence of insanity were lunacy inquisitions (the formal and expensive proceedings at which the sanity of members of the propertied classes was sometimes adjudicated, determining whether they became 'Chancery lunatics'); and criminal trials at which the insanity plea was entered. Though both were relatively rare events, they attracted attention out of all proportion to their frequency. Given alienists' aspirations to professional status, the question of their role in determining the boundary between insanity and responsibility was naturally a highly charged and symbolically crucial one. Yet their performance in these arenas turned out to be endlessly and fiercely controversial. Not least, their pretensions to possess privileged access to a realm of knowledge that secured for their judgements a unique and unchallengeable truth status was repeatedly impeached by their own inability to agree on a diagnosis. The embarrassment of having eminent men testify that the same individual was both unambiguously mad and unquestionably sane was one the profession felt deeply, but could never adequately resolve. Nor could their incantations of scientific truth and appeals to physicalist causation entirely hide the striking similarities between medico-psychological descriptions of someone's actions and commonsense, everyday descriptions of that same conduct. For a sophisticated examination of the resulting conflict, confusion, and disarray, *cf.* Roger Smith, *Trial by Medicine: Insanity and Responsibility in Victorian Trials*, Edinburgh: Edinburgh University Press, 1981.
42. J. Conolly, *An Inquiry Concerning the Indications of Insanity*, pp. 295–6.
43. W.A.F. Browne, *What Asylums Were, Are, and Ought to Be*, p. 8.
44. *Ibid.*
45. One consequence of this state of affairs was a persistent disquiet among the public at large, characterized by periodic spasms of anxiety lest the amorphous boundary between madness and sanity were to be exploited so as to equate any deviation from conventional moral and social standards with insanity. Recurrently, alienists found themselves the object of quite sharp adversarial assaults on their procedures and practices, their claims to expert status and authority questioned or even mocked. *Cf.* Andrew Scull, 'The Theory and Practice of Civil Commitment', *Michigan Law Review* 82, 1984, pp. 793–809; and Peter McCandless, 'Liberty and Lunacy: The Victorians and Wrongful Confinement', in

Lacking any other basis, the defenders of medicine's claim to possess a special skill in diagnosing cases of insanity were forced to appeal to clinical experience to legitimize and certify the authenticity of the individual practitioner's decisions. At first sight, it might be somewhat disconcerting to learn that 'the practitioner's own mind must be the criterion, by which he infers the insanity of any other person'.[46] In practice, though (they claimed), this was not as risky a procedure as it might seem. In the first place, 'it may be assumed that sound mind and insanity stand in the same predicament, and are opposed to each other in the same manner, as right to wrong, and as truth to lie. In a general view no mistake can arise, and where particular instances create embarrassment, those most conversant with such persons will be best able to determine [their sanity]'.[47] Secondly, 'it must be borne in mind, that a great unanimity may exist among experienced observers as to the presence of certain mental states, characterized by certain generally accepted names, which states, at the same time, it would be very difficult to describe in any form of words, insomuch that the undefined name, in the use of which all experienced men are agreed respecting these states, will convey to all a more clear and distinct impression than any attempt at definition or even description.'[48] Finally, the public were assured, 'although . . . contrariety of sentiment has prevailed concerning the precise meaning of the word madness, mental practitioners have been sufficiently reconciled as to the thing itself: so that when they have seen an insane person, they have readily coincided that the patient was mad'.[49] But apart from these vague assurances, no evidence was produced to demonstrate the reliability or the validity (whatever that might mean in this context) of the decisions taken by individual medical men. The stress was entirely upon firsthand experience or 'judgement'. Yet 'such emphasis', as Freidson has noted, 'is directly contrary to the emphasis of science on shared knowledge, collected and tested on the basis of methods meant to overcome the deficiencies of individual experience. And its efficacy and reliability are suspect'.[50]

The implications of this situation were profound. Beyond the initial hard core of easily recognizable behavioural and/or mental disturbance, the boundary between the normal and the pathological was left extraordinarily vague and indeterminate. In consequence, insanity was such an amorphous, all-embracing concept, that the range of behaviour it could be stretched to encompass was almost infinite. The asylum doctors themselves were but little inclined to resolve this ambiguity in favour of a

A. Scull (ed.), *Madhouses, Mad-doctors, and Madmen*, Philadelphia: University of Pennsylvania Press/London: Athlone, 1981, pp. 339–62.
46. J. Haslam, *Observations on Madness*, p. 37.
47. *Ibid.*, p. 38.
48. T. Mayo, *Medical Testimony and Evidence in Cases of Lunacy*, p. 14.
49. J. Haslam, *Observations on Madness*, p. 2.
50. E. Freidson, *Profession of Medicine*, New York: Dodd, Mead, 1970, p. 347.

narrow construction of their own sphere of competence. On humanitarian grounds, since they had convinced themselves that asylums were benevolent and therapeutic institutions, and believed that laymen were incompetent to cope with and liable to maltreat the mad, they were impelled to seek out still more cases, rather than to reject any who were proffered. There were other incentives providing support for the adoption of such an orientation. Most notably, there was an obvious link between how serious a problem insanity was perceived to be, and the importance and prestige bestowed upon those thought to be experts in its treatment. Naturally, by increasing the population which fell within their purview, the profession also became entitled to obtain increased resources to support their activities.

Taken together, these considerations impelled the profession to 'solve' these boundary problems by incorporation rather than by exclusion.[51] In practice, they did not all go as far as Haslam, who succeeded in establishing a finite universe of crazy people by the simple expedient of defining everyone as mad.[52] Such an approach was liable to provoke ridicule, and so prove counterproductive. In any event, apparently more sober and restrictive definitions possessed more than sufficient latitude.[53] Perhaps without even being conscious in many cases that this was what they were engaged in doing, the profession began to create whole new realms of madness, all the while leaving their original verbal definitions intact.

It is this shift in the way the term was applied, rather than improvements in record-keeping or the alleged influence of civilization on the incidence of insanity, that I believe was the second major factor behind the rapid rise during the nineteenth century in the number of people identified as insane.[54] Yet although it should be clear by now that the asylum

51. For an analysis of professional strategies in the struggle for jurisdiction, cf. Andrew Abbott, *The System of Professions: An Essay on the Division of Expert Labor*, Chicago: University of Chicago Press, 1988.
52. Compare his 'expert' testimony at the trial of a Miss Bagster in 1832: He avowed, 'I never saw any human being who was of sound mind.' On being pressed as to whether he meant this literally, he responded acidly, 'I presume the Deity is of sound mind, and he alone.' Quoted in W.A.F. Browne, *What Asylums Were, Are, and Ought to Be*, p. 7.
53. For a discussion of contemporary scepticism about alienists' diagnostic acumen, cf. Peter McCandless, 'Insanity and Society: A Study of the English Lunacy Reform Movement 1815–70', unpublished Ph.D. dissertation, University of Wisconsin, 1974. One of the most public, prominent (and embarrassing) sceptics about the legitimacy of medicine's claims to possess any special expertise whatsoever in the diagnosis of insanity was the Earl of Shaftesbury, for forty years the Chairman of the Lunacy Commissioners:

> For my own part, I do not hesitate to say from very long experience, putting aside all its complications with bodily disorder, the mere judgement of the fact whether a man is in a state of unsound mind, and incapable of managing his affairs, and going about the world, requires no professional knowledge: my firm belief is, that a sensible layman . . . can give not only as good an opinion, but a better opinion than all the medical men put together.

Testimony before the House of Commons, *Report of the Select Committee on the Care and Treatment of Lunatics*, 1859, p. 23.
54. For comparative evidence suggesting similar trends in France, Canada, and the United States, cf. R. Castel, *The Regulation of Madness*, chapter 4; I. Dowbiggin, 'The

doctors were quite content, indeed positively eager, to take on the duties of coping with an ever larger population of mad people, one must beware of the tendency to conclude that the mere existence of even a considerable degree of professional imperialism provides a sufficient explanation of the ever wider practical application of the term insanity. If the profession was eager, the public had also to be willing. For it is doubtful whether many groups of experts possess a secure enough position to impose an outlook too widely divergent from that of the general public; and certainly a group whose claims to special expertise and competence were as fragile as those of the asylum doctors could not have succeeded in doing so.

One important consequence, however, did flow from the asylum doctors' outlook. Since the profession had, in effect, evinced a willingness to deal with almost any and all people whose behaviour the community found intolerable, it was the lay conception of what was and was not behaviour which could be borne which fixed the boundary between the sane and the insane.[55] The initiative required to launch the process of casting out the undesirable from the community and into asylum necessarily rested mostly in non-medical hands – whether this meant the lunatic's own family, or those in authority (employers, police, magistrates, and workhouse masters, as well as the occasional workhouse doctor).[56] So

Professional, Sociopolitical, and Cultural Dimensions of Psychiatric Theory in France 1840–1900', unpublished Ph.D. dissertation, University of Rochester, 1987, esp. pp. 386ff.; S.E.D. Shortt, *Victorian Lunacy: Richard M. Bucke and the Practice of Late Nineteenth-Century Psychiatry*, Cambridge: Cambridge University Press, 1986, esp. pp. 51–2; Richard W. Fox, *So Far Disordered in Mind: Insanity in California*, Berkeley: University of California Press, 1978, *passim*.

55. *Cf.* Nancy Tomes' insistence on 'the fundamental fact that, as is still the case, commitment involved a social, primarily familial, judgment on sanity. Relatives, not doctors or public authorities, usually made the first determination that an individual was insane. Their decision to commit did not follow from some objective measure of the patient's condition, but rather from an assessment of the family's financial and emotional resources to deal with the individual's mental disability'. N. Tomes, 'The Anglo-American Asylum in Historical Perspective', in J. Giggs and C. Smith (eds), *Location and Stigma*, London: Unwin Hyman, 1988, p. 14. Based on a study of admissions to Colney Hatch, Hunter and MacAlpine reach very similar conclusions: 'The decision to send a patient to the asylum was made on social as much as on medical grounds . . . asylum doctors . . . had no control over admissions, never saw patients before they came in, and could only advise when a patient was well enough to be discharged'. R.A. Hunter and I. MacAlpine, *Psychiatry for the Poor. 1851 Colney Hatch Asylum: Friern Hospital 1973. A Medical and Social History*, London: Dawsons, 1974, pp. 16–7. See also the discussion in John Walton, 'Lunacy in the Industrial Revolution: A Study of Asylum Admissions in Lancashire, 1848–50', *Journal of Social History* 13, 1979, pp. 4–5, which concludes: 'it seems clear that social perceptions and considerations, coupled with administrative convenience and the quest for economy, must have played the predominant part in determining whether individuals should be regarded as lunatics and committed to asylums in early Victorian England . . . the pattern of admissions to asylums . . . was largely independent of any objective analysis of well-defined disease entities by competent practitioners.'

56. For a pauper to be committed as a lunatic, a deposition had to be sworn before two magistrates that he or she was insane. But, as John Walton has noted, 'we cannot reconstruct the circumstances leading up to the involvement of the officials in any regular or systematic way. We do not know what social processes lay behind the initiation of the

that it is to this extra-professional world that one must look for the sources of a more expansive view of madness.

4. The Multiplication of Madness

Very early on in the history of the asylum, it became apparent that its primary value to the community was as a handy place to which to consign the disturbing, the vaguely menacing, the unwanted, and the useless – those potentially and actually troublesome people who posed threats to the social order and to the business of daily living which were not readily subject to control by the legal system.[57] Quite obviously, there is no absolute standard by means of which people are placed or not placed in one of these categories. On the contrary, the whole notion of intolerable behaviour, of which these are merely particular examples, is clearly a culturally and situationally variable one. The importance of the asylum lies in the fact that it makes available a culturally legitimate alternative, for both the community as a whole and the separate families which make it up, to keeping the intolerable individual in the family. The very existence of the institution not only provides a means of dispensing with all sorts of disorderly, disturbing, and disruptive individuals; it also, by offering another means of coping, affects the degree to which people are prepared

administrative procedures'. His own detailed examination of patient records from the Lancaster Asylum demonstrates that 'Some asylum admissions clearly did originate with people in authority, anxious to dispose of the difficult and dissolute . . . [but also suggests that] the roots of most asylum committals clearly lay in domestic troubles, as families at the end of their tether sought succour even though it meant the Poor Law and the asylum.' Unfortunately, however, as he acknowledges, attempts to move beyond these generalizations, and to track and quantify precisely how and why it was that people ended up institutionalized as mad, raise enormously difficult conceptual and interpretative issues, and the surviving evidence bearing on these questions is 'abundant but ultimately frustrating'. John Walton, 'Casting Out and Bringing Back in Victorian England: Pauper Lunatics, 1840–70', in W.F. Bynum, R. Porter, and M. Shepherd (eds), *The Anatomy of Madness*, Vol. 2, London: Tavistock, 1985, pp. 137–9, 143.

57. Ideologically, the crux of the difficulty posed by the mad was that the social definition of their condition rendered the very notion of holding them personally responsible for their behaviour highly problematic. By implication, the disturbance and disruption they caused could not be readily and appropriately dealt with by ordinary legal sanctions, since the logic and legitimacy of legal intervention rested upon the attribution of intentionality to the person who offended. Intentionality and responsibility in the ordinary senses of those terms were, of course, precisely what the lunatic were deemed to lack (though at the margin, decisions about when to absolve someone of responsibility could themselves provoke great controversy). Robert Castel has rightly stressed how psychiatric discourse allowed for the displacement and disguise of '[t]he contradiction existing between the need for the sequestration of the insane and the respect for judicial rules that should accompany any measure that deprives a person of liberty. . . . The notion of "therapeutic isolation" was the magic agent in the act of alchemy. . . . It was without any doubt a measure as imperative, rigorous and sure as the harshest police custodial action. Yet through it the place of detention became the best therapeutic environment and, reciprocally, the "special institution" ensured an isolation as effective as that of the best prisons.' R. Castel, *The Regulation of Madness*, pp. 165–7.

to put up with those who persistently create havoc, discord, and disarray, as well as with those whose extreme helplessness and dependency creates extraordinary burdens for others. Thus I would argue that the asylum inevitably operated to reduce family and community tolerance (or, to put it the other way round, to expand the notion of the intolerable), to a degree which varied with how grandiose and well accepted the helping claims of those who ran it were. In so doing, it simultaneously induced a wider conception of the nature of insanity.

The historical evidence does not allow a direct test of this hypothesis, but there are a number of indirect ways of deciding whether or not it is correct. Among the most important of these are the following: (1) If who is defined as mad is primarily dependent upon community and family tolerance of such things as dependency, domestic violence or the threat of violence, and inability or refusal to abide by ordinary social conventions, then the poor, who have fewer resources for coping with deviant, dependent and abusive relatives, and who are less able to resist pressures from others to incarcerate such intractable individuals, should contribute the bulk of the increase in asylum admissions. Moreover, where, among the working classes themselves, differences can be discerned in access to familial and financial resources, these should be inversely related to the likelihood of being labelled a lunatic. (2) If the availability of institutions is in fact productive of decreased tolerance, then expansion of the asylum system should always produce increased numbers of crazy people. As a correlative of this, one would expect estimates of the prevalence of insanity to reflect the degree of institutional provision for the insane; so that at the beginning of the nineteenth century, when such provision was slight or non-existent in most areas, contemporary estimates should seem almost ludicrously low by comparison with later ones, arrived at once the asylum system is firmly established. Whenever asylums are built, there should be a persistent tendency to underestimate the demand for accommodation; no matter how careful a survey is made of the local requirements, it should always turn out to be wrong. More strikingly, additional facilities built to meet the apparent excess demand ought swiftly themselves to be filled to capacity, and the original cycle should then be repeated all over again for so long as more money is available for more buildings. And if changes in social policy reduce the cost differential between the asylum and other forms of provision, the incidence of 'lunacy' should increase as troublesome people are redefined as mad. (3) If the asylum's main function is to serve as a dumping ground for the bizarre and the broken down, the awkward and the withdrawn, and the socially incompetent though often harmless, then it should in fact be filled with such. Moreover, since these are the sort of people whom nobody is very keen to see return to the community, there ought, particularly as the passage of time accentuates these characteristics of the patient population, to be comparatively little pressure placed on psychiatrists to fulfil their early claims to cure, even though they prove, if anything, less successful than in the past in this respect.[58]

At first sight, the official statistics on insanity kept by the Lunacy Commissioners fail to provide any straightforward way of deciding whether the yearly increase in the number of the insane came disproportionately from the poorer segments of the community. The records of admissions of new cases are aggregated into a single undifferentiated total. But the annual figures of the total number of lunatics were broken down into two component parts – private and pauper lunatics. And since the performance of private and pauper asylums with respect to cures and mortality rates was so essentially similar, these complicating factors can be set on one side. Any differences in the speed with which patients accumulate in the two sectors can thus be expected to reflect accurately an underlying difference between them as regards the appearance of fresh cases of insanity.

How accurately, though, did the distinction between pauper and private patients correspond to a lunatic's social class? And how reliably was the distinction made in practice? A lunatic was termed a pauper lunatic if the money for his maintenance came in whole or in part from public funds. This was a simple distinction to make, and since the Lunacy Commissioners insisted that records be accurate on this point, misclassification must certainly have been exceedingly rare. The label 'pauper', of course, carried with it an additional stigma which almost every family which could possible do so sought to avoid.[59] Had they been inclined to place their pockets ahead of their pride, they would doubtless have found the equally parsimonious local authorities a formidable barrier to overcome. So that, as the term itself would suggest, pauper lunatics were quite definitely recruited from only the poorer segments of the community.

It would be wrong to conclude, however, that they were drawn simply from the ranks of the official pauper class. On the contrary, many must have come from the 'respectable' working classes, for, 'except among the opulent classes, any protracted attack of insanity, from the heavy expenses which its treatment entails, and the fatal interruption it causes to everything like active industry, seldom fails to reduce its immediate victims, and generally also their families with them, to poverty, and ultimately to pauperism'.[60] But quite plainly, the division between the pauper and the

58. The evidence for this last proposition has already been presented in chapter 4, so I shall not repeat it here.
59. See, for example, the discussion in Michael Anderson, *Family Structure in Nineteenth Century Lancashire*, Cambridge: Cambridge University Press, 1971, pp. 137–9.
60. Commissioners in Lunacy, *9th Annual Report*, 1855, p. 35. Even very wealthy families, who were not reduced to financial ruin, could find the costs of long-term institutional care taxing. Hence, we find private patients starting out at the most opulent and expensive private asylums, and subsequently being transferred to less expensive establishments, or to one of the registered hospitals or charity asylums as they fail to improve and as the financial strain mounts. See, for example, the case of Arthur Richard

private lunatic reflected accurately the basic class division of Victorian society.

If we begin by looking at the data on lunatics in asylums for the decade 1849–59, the first in which the county asylum system became fully operational, a simple pattern emerges; one which, with minor variations, remains essentially unaltered until at least the end of the century, and quite possible beyond. On 1 January 1849 the total number of patients in all types of asylums was 14,560; by 1 January 1859 it had risen to 22,853. Almost all the increase had taken place in the county and borough asylums, which now accommodated 15,845 inmates compared with only 6,494 ten years earlier. By comparison, the numbers in private licensed houses had actually declined by 1,915. These figures reflected the fact that although there had been a spectacular rise in the number of pauper lunatics confined in asylums, the number of private patients institutionalized had remained virtually static. While the number of pauper patients had grown from 10,801 to 18,022, an increase of 7,221, the figures for private patients showed an increase of only 1,072, from 3,759 to 4,831. Moreover, even this slight rise was largely a statistical artifact, since the 1859 total included a number of elements – the patients at Bethlem, military and criminal lunatics – which had not been counted in arriving at the 1849 total; so that the Commissioners were doubtful whether there had been 'any increase in the number of Registered Private Patients during the period of ten years ending 1st January 1859'.[61]

To some extent, the availability of the institution decreased the tolerance of all sections of society. In the words of Joseph John Henley, General Inspector of the Local Government Board,

> I . . . think there is a disposition among all classes now not to bear with the troubles that may arise in their own houses. If a person is troublesome from senile dementia, dirty in his habits, they will not bear with it now. Persons are more easily removed to an asylum than they were a few years ago.[62]

But it was among the poor that this change was most marked:

> . . . persons in humble life soon become wearied of the presence of their insane relatives and regardless of their age desire relief. Persons above this class more readily tolerate infirmity and can command the time and attention. The occasion may never occur in the one case, which is

W., admitted to Manor House, Chiswick, on 15 November 1884, and transferred to Bethlem just over two months later; Major Arthur Robert P., admitted on 9 April 1888 and transferred 'for pecuniary reasons' to St. Andrew's Hospital, Northampton on 26 February 1889. Manor House Male Casebook, 1884–1891, in manuscript, Wellcome Institute for the History of Medicine, London.

61. Commissioners in Lunacy, *15th Annual Report*, 1861, pp. 75–6.
62. House of Commons, *Report of the Select Committee on the Operation of the Lunacy Law*, 1877, p. 166.

urgent in the other. Hence an Asylum to the poor and needy is the only refuge. To the man of many friends it is the last resort.[63]

Huxley, superintendent of the Kent County Asylum, reached essentially the same conclusion:

> Poverty, truly, is the great evil; it has no friends able to help. Persons in middle society do not put away their aged relatives because of their infirmities, and I think it was not always the custom for worn-out paupers to be sent to the asylum. . . . It is one more of the ways in which, at this day, the apparent increase of insanity is sustained. It is not a real increase, since the aged have ever been subject to this sort of unsoundness.[64]

The detailed casebooks kept at elite private asylums provide convincing evidence about the considerable lengths to which the well-to-do went to avoid (or at least defer) placing their relatives in an asylum. Miss Letitia Elizabeth W., for instance, a forty-six-year-old single 'gentlewoman' admitted to Ticehurst on 17 July 1857, was sent only after the family had coped for an extraordinarily extended period with her peculiarities. Periodically, 'for two or three weeks at a time', she would withdraw into her room and cut off contact with the household, exhibiting 'great irritability if interfered with. She would afterwards of her own accord return to the family circle and resume her place and active duties as if no break had occurred'. After ten years, the attacks grew 'more prolonged and more serious' and she began to evidence 'nervous excitement [and] a disposition to be violent if even slightly opposed', at other times refusing to eat and seeming depressed. The family tolerated these eccentricities for several months, before at length 'by Dr Conolly's advice' sending her to an 'Establishment' run by a Mrs Idea in St. John's Wood. Returning home after exhibiting some signs of improvement, she relapsed and retreated to her room 'for weeks together, . . . [when] any endeavour to force society upon her seemed invariably to produce the worst results'. After a year and a half of enduring this behaviour, her family once more sent her off to Mrs Idea's establishment, and when that failed to produce any improvement, she was transferred to board with 'a clergyman's family in the country'. Only when it became apparent, after two even more trying months, that she required 'more control than could be exercised over her in a private household' was she at length, after a dozen and more years of effort to avoid the stigma of certification, finally packed off to an asylum.[65]

63. Northampton General Lunatic Asylum, *Annual Report*, 1858, p. 11
64. Quoted in J.T. Arlidge, *On the State of Lunacy and the Legal Provision for the Insane*, London, Churchill, 1859, p. 95.
65. At Ticehurst, she was scarcely more manageable, being frequently 'excited and restless . . . very talkative and annoying to those about her . . . throwing herself down when walking, endeavouring to meet men and looking at them in a wanton manner'.

Miss Hannah Julia K., a forty-year-old 'gentlewoman' admitted on 28 January 1861 with 'an imbecile expression of countenance', was reported to be 'very quiet and silent' on her arrival at Ticehurst. Appearances were deceiving. For the previous six and a half years, her family had coped with her 'at home, being visited occasionally by a medical man', somehow dealing with someone prone to sudden outbursts of 'violence and excitement' and periods of 'unconnected chattering' with 'imaginary voices', to say nothing of 'destructiveness, pyromania, and indecency' – a tendency to 'break, tear or burn anything she can lay her hands upon, also tear her clothes off, and rush naked about the room, or stand at the window'. It remains unclear what specific incident provoked her relatives into finally capitulating and sending her to Ticehurst, though the great difficulty the Newingtons subsequently experienced in managing her, even in an asylum, makes clear how much some rich families were willing and able to put up with before resorting to institutionalization. Within days of her arrival, repeated episodes of violence, hurling furniture around her rooms, throwing hot coals from the fireplace, stripping naked and attempting to run out in the hallways, coupled with biting, scratching, and hitting her attendants led Charles Newington to complain that 'Miss K's case has been falsely reported to us – her friends said she was generally quiet and tractable altho' occasionally violent – the reverse is the truth'. Within a few days more, the asylum authorities were provoked into placing her under physical restraint. This, too, proved unavailing, and exactly a month after her admission, they 'requested Miss K's friends to remove her'. Though suitable alternative accommodation proved difficult to arrange, on 17 March she was finally sent under close guard to 'Dr Monro's', with the admonition that 'a more dangerous and violent person can scarce be met with'.[66]

Trouble can come in many forms, of course. Mrs Anne F., another 'gentlewoman', imposed a rather different set of trials on her wealthy husband. From 1844 onwards, after a fall during a pregnancy, she had gradually withdrawn into the role of an invalid, finally taking to her bed on a full-time basis some time in 1854 or 1855. Having a morbid dread of falling out of the 'very large' bed to which she had retired, she piled 'tables, sofas, chairs, etc' around it. Nor was this her only eccentricity:

She has laid in bed for the last three years and not allowed herself to be properly washed or attended to – body and bed linen not changed for

After less than six months of this, and following complaints from her fellow patients, the Newingtons requested that her sister remove her to some alternative accommodation. Ticehurst Casebook 4, 17 February, 23 March, 7, 25 April, 6 June 1857, in manuscript, Contemporary Medical Archives, Wellcome Institute for the History of Medicine, London.

66. Ticehurst Casebook 6, 28, 29 January, 2, 5, 16, 28 February, 8, 17 March 1861, in manuscript, Contemporary Medical Archives, Wellcome Institute for the History of Medicine, London.

months – hands and arms begrimed with dried faeces – shutters and windows tightly closed – curtains drawn around her bed – a large fire in hot weather, none in cold – covered with dirty shawls and old flannel petticoats . . . sleeps the greater part of the day and keeps awake at night, takes her food, which she eats more like an animal than a human being at all hours night and day – generally chews her animal food and spits it out

and so on. All the while, 'she has been either visited by or been under the care of the most eminent medical men in England'[67] without ever being officially labelled as insane.[68]

Not surprisingly, men who were active in business or the professions tended to be institutionalized more rapidly than their womenfolk. Where their peculiarities reduced or eliminated their earning capacity, or where their conduct threatened to dissipate the family's resources, confinement took on an obvious additional urgency. In other cases, their greater capacity for physical violence[69] – whether brought on by drink or other factors – must have exacerbated the problems of handling them by extra-institutional means.[70] Even in cases like these, however, the rich used their resources to avoid asylum treatment for as long as possible, sometimes succeeding completely.[71]

67. Ticehurst Asylum Casebook 5, 2 July 1858. Three days after Mrs F.'s admission, one of the attendants who had fetched her from her home in Blackheath still complained of sickness brought on by the experience of entering her room, 'the atmosphere of it was so foul and the stench so great'. The variety of eminent medical men dancing attendance on her sick bed had not done much for Mrs F.'s physical health. On admission, 'her person was filthily dirty and her face and hands and other parts of her body were covered with boils. Her complexion was very yellow having just recovered from an attack of jaundice . . . vascular system weak, liver torpid, and its functions greatly deranged – bowels very obstinate, tongue white and much coated at the back, skin flabby and unhealthy.'

68. As these facts suggest, and as the Newingtons' observations were subsequently to confirm, 'Mrs F. appears to have the power of inducing her husband to fall in with her wishes in everything'. *Ibid.*, 28 August 1858. Her certification as lunatic was signed by John Conolly, the doyen of English alienists.

69. On the role of violence to people or property, and threats or attempts at suicide in prompting certification as insane and admission into Ticehurst, *cf.* the discussion in Charlotte MacKenzie, 'A Family Asylum: A History of the Private Madhouse at Ticehurst in Sussex, 1792–1917,' unpublished Ph.D. thesis, University of London, 1987, pp. 287–8.

70. In addition, a far higher fraction of the male patients were suffering from tertiary syphilis, which often produced dramatic psychiatric and neurological symptomatology, but also great and progressive physical debility, necessitating the sort of attentive and full-time nursing care which the elite private asylums were particularly well placed to provide. Of fifty cases recorded in the Manor House, Chiswick, Male Casebook for 1884–91, 11 were diagnosed as definite cases of General Paresis, and a further 6 possibly suffered from the same disorder. Even allowing for diagnostic imprecision prior to the introduction of the Wassermann test, these are striking figures. By contrast, GPI cases were extremely rare, verging on non-existent, among the female population. See Manor House Male Casebook, 1884–1891; and Female Casebook, 1884–1893, in manuscript at the Wellcome Institute for the History of Medicine, London.

71. Samuel Greg, a reformist mill-owner whose history is summarized by Charlotte

Albert S., for example, a thirty-three-year-old admitted to Manor House Chiswick on 20 January 1885, had begun a business career in Manchester, but forsook this when the firm he had joined changed hands. Returning home to his parents, he soon abandoned thoughts of returning to the world of employment, looked after his aged father until his death, 'was busy with home management, then . . . took to the garden alone and then gave this up and read a good deal. Next this was greatly given up and he seemed to get weaker and weaker in mind'. By 1882, he was expressing delusions that his parents had attempted to poison him and that he was being 'mesmerized'. Shipped off to India to see one of his brothers, he returned in some respects still more disturbed than before, convinced, for example, that he could 'change his form at will and ha[d] travelled all over the world in different shapes'. But he was 'dull and listless' and his behaviour was 'sober and not given to any excess'. His family therefore continued to provide for him at home for two more years, before his older brother, presumably tiring of the burdens this imposed, finally elected to have him committed as insane. Even then Walter S. took the precaution of writing to the proprietors to ask them to conceal Manor House's real character from his mother, since she objected to sending her son to an asylum.[72]

Charles V. de V.B., an old Etonian who later became Duke of A., had a still more variegated career prior to fetching up at Ticehurst. Sent off to Australia and New Zealand in the early nineties while suffering from vaguely defined ill-health, he was subsequently commissioned into the army (though he was already claiming that his father and stepmother were bent on killing him, and a 'brain specialist' brought in to treat him had pronounced him mentally unsound). Unable to manage his affairs, he ran up massive debts over the next three years. Once more his family stepped

MacKenzie, is a case in point. As she notes, he suffered a nervous breakdown in 1846, when the workforce at his mill in Cheshire opposed the introduction of new stretching machinery. Following this, he remained a total recluse for nine years, before essaying hydropathic treatment at Malvern and on the Continent. Failing to secure any relief, 'he came at length to feel that he must sit down under his burden and live with it as best he could to the end'. 'Social Factors in the Admission, Discharge, and Continuing Stay of Patients at Ticehurst Asylum, 1845–1917', in W.F. Bynum, R. Porter, and M. Shepherd (eds), *The Anatomy of Madness*, Vol. 2, p. 154, quoting Samuel Greg, *A Layman's Legacy*, London: Macmillan, 1877. With considerable understatement, MacKenzie notes that 'Such resignation could require tolerance and fortitude from family and friends.'
72. Manor House Male Casebook, 1884–91, 20 January 1885. Walter M.S. to C. Molesworth Tuke, January 22, 1885. (His mother, Walter reported, 'was horribly shocked when mention of certificates was made'.) Almost two years later, on 28 September 1886, Albert S. was 'Transferred to private care and discharged, relieved' (in fact, no better in any discernible respect). This may be an appropriate point to note that the term 'relieved' covered a multitude of conditions. Any improvement in bodily health, in habits, or in mental state, however minor, was used to justify such a judgement, one all parties had an interest in reaching, since it provided reassurance to both physician and family that the expense of confinement had produced some tangible benefits, albeit not the hoped for cure. Consequently, only the most extraordinarily difficult and recalcitrant patients were discharged as 'unimproved'.

in, paying off his obligations on condition that he remove himself to India (where, extraordinarily, they had arranged for him to serve as aide-de-camp to Lord Elgin). A year later, he was back, like a bad penny, threatening to create a scandal by suing his father for causing him to go bald. His eccentricities now multiplied rapidly: he became wholly inactive, ate four or five portions at every meal, and spent most of his time asleep. Still, his family's great wealth allowed them to cope with his presence in the household, till on his father's death, his succession to the family title and estate forced their hand, leading to his confinement under certificates at Ticehurst in January of 1899.[73]

These cases make clear some of the ways in which wealth and social standing allowed families to circumvent or postpone the disgrace of incarcerating one of their nearest and dearest in the asylum.[74] If such extreme forms of deviance could be successfully managed in domestic settings for years at a time, then certainly the less taxing problems associated with the natural failings of old age, or with, for instance, the side-effects of overindulgence in alcohol, were unlikely to precipitate institutionalization among the better sort. Hayes Newington, the proprietor of Ticehurst Asylum, mournfully acknowledged the reluctance of his potential clientele to make use of his services:

> Many of the upper classes can and do retain the services of independent specialists and get well without leaving home, or are sent away to medical men's houses. We, therefore, can say that . . . what we . . . get are not infrequently the residue of unsuccessful treatment elsewhere . . . in the case of the wealthy it is well known that an asylum is generally the last thing thought of.[75]

---

73. Ticehurst House Casebook 39, 1897–1903. The Duke remained at Ticehurst until his death in 1934.

74. I do not propose these cases, of course, as statistically 'representative' (whatever that might mean in this context). Case notes, though an increasingly fashionable window into the world of the insane (and certainly a rich resource for historians to explore), raise difficult problems of interpretation. They record the patients' world and behaviours largely through the eyes of those supervising their incarceration, and to this element of selectivity there are superadded the usual problems of the differential survival of materials of this sort, and the vast differences in what was originally recorded and preserved (the elaborate and detailed records of elite private establishments like Ticehurst and Manor House, Chiswick, as contrasted with the scanty and utilitarian records of the public barracks-asylums). There are always questions, therefore, about how far one can generalize from a particular example or handful of examples. (For discussion of a number of other similar cases among those eventually admitted to Ticehurst, and of this general approach among the well-to-do, see Charlotte MacKenzie, 'A Family Asylum', chapter 3.) Nonetheless, for my present purposes, I believe that even the small sample reported here serves to document the essential point at issue: these elaborate strategies for coping with some fraction of the distracted clearly helped to shape the universe of those officially identified as deranged, and strategies of this sort were simply unavailable to the lower classes. The consequences for the asylum censuses are plain.

75. H.F. Hayes Newington, 'The Abolition of Private Asylums', *Journal of Mental Science* 31, 1885, p. 143, quoted in Charlotte MacKenzie, 'Social Factors in the Admission, Discharge, and Continuing Stay of Patients at Ticehurst Asylum, 1845–1917', p. 166.

Upper- and upper-middle-class families possessed financial wherewithal to cope with the unproductive; the ability to employ large numbers of servants to manage their troublesome relatives; the capacity, if need be, to send them off to a quiet and secluded part of the country, or even abroad; and strong motivation to avoid the scandal and stigma that were still the inevitable consequence of having a relative officially certified as mad.

Strikingly, the impact of social factors, substantially operating in the opposite direction, is equally apparent when one confines one's attention to the lower orders – though comparable kinds of individual information about the social and familial situation of paupers remain elusive and generally unobtainable. The one detailed study we presently possess of the demographic profile of admissions to a county asylum reveals the existence of important systematic variations in the likelihood of being labelled insane even among different segments of the working classes. John Walton's examination of the social profile of admissions to the Lancaster Asylum between 1848 and 1850[76] documents a sharp and significant over-representation of pauper lunatics drawn from the county's two largest cities, Liverpool and Manchester, and a significant *under*-representation of those living in smaller towns and textile villages (where admission rates were lower even than those from more rural areas of the county). As he carefully demonstrates, these differences cannot be plausibly attributed to regional variations in administrative policies. Instead, they appear to reflect a differential ability to cope, with 'families in the textile district [being] better able, and more willing, to shelter and look after such people than were families elsewhere in Lancashire'.[77] The relatively small size of textile towns and villages, the tendency for migration into them to take place over relatively short distances, and the somewhat higher incomes of those employed in the cotton industry meant that 'existing informal links based on family and neighbouring relationships could be readily adapted to the urban setting'.[78] In the larger conurbations, by contrast, in-migration had occurred over much longer distances, kinship ties were thoroughly disrupted, employment was on average more poorly paid and insecure, and the sheer scale of urban living militated against the maintenance of close communal ties. As my larger hypothesis would suggest, it is these differences at the social structural level which largely 'explain the peculiar pattern of asylum admissions in mid-nineteenth-century Lancashire' – the lower lunacy rate of the regions with alternatives to the asylum, and the equally marked propensity of large cities to be 'generous providers of lunatics for the new custodial institutions'.[79]

76. John Walton, 'Lunacy in the Industrial Revolution'.
77. *Ibid.*, p. 14.
78. *Ibid.*, p. 13.
79. *Ibid.*, pp. 17–18. His emphasis on the crucial significance of social factors is particularly convincing since, by linking admissions data to the 1851 census, he is able to demonstrate that independent of whether one lived in a large city or a textile village, a direct relationship existed between long-distance migration and the chances of becoming an inmate of an asylum.

Table 10   Number of Private and Pauper Lunatics, that Number Expressed as a Rate per 10,000 of the General Population, and Pauper Lunatics as a Percentage of the Total Number of Lunatics.

	Private		Pauper		Total number of lunatics	Pauper lunatics as a percentage of the total number of lunatics
	Number	Rate/ 10,000	Number	Rate/ 10,000		
1844	4,072	2.47	16,821	10.21	20,893	80.5
1860	5,065	2.54	32,993	16.58	38,058	86.7
1865	5,790	2.74	40,160	18.99	45,950	87.4
1870	6,280	2.79	48,433	22.94	54,713	88.5
1875	7,340	3.09	56,403	23.55	63,743	88.5
1880	7,620	2.99	63,571	24.94	71,191	89.3
1885	7,751	2.82	71,215	25.89	78,966	90.2
1890	8,095	2.75	77,257	26.27	85,352	90.5

Sources: 1844 Report of the Metropolitan Commissioners in Lunacy, and Annual Reports of the Commissioners in Lunacy.

If kinship structures among the lower orders to varying degrees proved incapable of coping with burdensome forms of deviance and dependence, and consequently caused poor families to jettison the most troublesome into the arms of the asylum, there is considerable evidence that workhouse authorities, too, sought to use the asylums to 'relieve their wards of many old people who are suffering from nothing else than the natural failing of old age', as well as to rid themselves of troublesome people in general.[80] 'A very large amount of additional accommodation having been thrown open . . . the Parochial Authorities have availed themselves of it, and removed to Asylums numbers of paupers who would otherwise have remained in Workhouses or cottages.'[81] The asylum doctors played

80. House of Commons, *Report of the Select Committee on the Operation of the Lunacy Law*, 1877, p. 152, evidence of Dr Balfour, medical inspector of the London Workhouses. Henry Maudsley blamed these practices in substantial measure on the financial incentives to utilize asylums provided by the 1862 Act to Amend the Law Relating to Lunatics, 'which rendered lunatics chargeable upon the common fund of the union of parishes' instead of the individual parish. The consequence of this legislation, as he saw it, was that 'Parish and workhouse officers willingly saw lunacy in forms of imbecility and illness in which they would never have dreamt at one time of doing so; and their one idea, once they had made the discovery, was to get rid of the responsibility attaching to the care and treatment of the patient, by sending him to the asylum.' Henry Maudsley, 'On the Alleged Increase of Insanity', *Journal of Mental Science* 23, 1877, pp. 45–54.
81. Commissioners in Lunacy, *15th Annual Report*, 1861, p. 15. For instance, from the earliest years in Buckinghamshire, 'The magistrates began sending in the partially paralysed, the deaf and blind, the physically incapacitated and unemployed, the old and the young without family to care for them, provided they showed some behavioural disturbance as well.' J. Crammer, *Asylum History: Buckinghamshire County Pauper Lunatic Asylum – St. John's*, London: Gaskell, 1990, p. 116.

their part by employing a double standard of insanity: 'Orders for the admission of Paupers into the County Asylum are given more freely than would be thought right as regards the imputation of Lunacy, towards persons equally debilitated in body and mind who have the means of providing for their own care.'[82] Table 10 provides a graphic illustration of the effects of these class-linked differentials in community tolerance and in the availability of resources for coping with difficult people. The number of private patients rises only gradually and modestly; the number of pauper lunatics all but quadruples, and the increase remains large even when the effects of population growth are taken into account.

5. The Expanding Empire of Asylumdom and the Growth of Lunacy

The general relationship between the construction of asylums and the increase in insanity again suggests that on the whole it was the existence and expansion of the asylum system which created the increased demand for its own services, rather than the other way round. In the first place, it is simply remarkable how small the insane population was estimated to be when the first significant growth of the asylum system began in the late eighteenth century. When the York Asylum was first proposed, for example, in 1772, those planning the new institution prudently decided that they needed some estimate of the potential demand for its services. Accordingly, they conducted a careful inquiry 'as to the number of lunatics in the Three Ridings [of Yorkshire]'. When the survey was complete, the number of cases uncovered 'was found so alarming that it was determined to erect a building capable of receiving fifty-four patients...'.[83] One doubts whether a finding that, in a population probably well in excess of half a million, asylum provision was needed for fifty-four patients would have been viewed with 'alarm' a century later. Rather the response would likely have been to inquire into the reasons why this community had had the good fortune to escape the plague of insanity.

Twenty years later, William Tuke secured the establishment of the Retreat in the same city to provide for the care of all insane English Quakers. When the Retreat was proposed, insanity was thought to be a very rare condition among so sober and level-headed a group as the Quakers. Haslam, in his *Observations on Madness*, had claimed that their judicious religious beliefs and personal habits made them 'nearly exempt' from its ravages. Consequently, 'the projectors of the Retreat were thought, by some of their own friends, to be making too large a provision for its wants, in proposing a building for thirty patients'.[84] Indeed, many

82. Littlemore County Asylum, *Superintendent's Report*, 1855.
83. [J. Blackwell], 'Report on the Treatment of Lunatics', *Quarterly Review* 74, 1844, p. 420.
84. Cited in Samuel Tuke, 'Introductory Observations' to *On the Construction and Management of Hospitals for the Insane* by M. Jacobi, London: Churchill, 1841, p. liv. In

Quakers originally opposed the whole project, on the grounds that there were insufficient numbers of Quaker lunatics to justify it, and that to fill any institution, inmates would have to be admitted who were not members of the Society of Friends. In practice, however, the supply of patients proved more than adequate. The average number of Quaker inmates each year between 1796 and 1820 was 49; between 1820 and 1840 it rose to 71. Apparently the Quakers were as liable to insanity as everybody else.

If the opening of the York Retreat had produced more Quaker lunatics than anyone had hitherto realized existed, an analogous pattern was observed when many of the county asylums built under the 1808 Act began to receive patients. At Nottingham, for instance, where the first county asylum in the country was opened in 1811, the parish authorities had reported a total of thirty-five cases of insanity in the 1806 return to Parliament. To err on the side of caution, the magistrates built the asylum to accommodate 76–80 patients, and were mortified when this was almost immediately found to be totally inadequate. Initially, not every community found the alternative offered by the new institutions equally seductive. Perhaps because their economic 'backwardness' brought with it a certain insulation from the corrosive effects of capitalism on the strength of family ties,[85] the inhabitants of some regions proved less eager to

---

Jonathan Swift's Ireland insanity was also perceived to be a rare condition. When Swift died, he left a legacy in his will to establish a lunatic asylum in Dublin, on the model of Bethlem, for 140 patients. Fearing that so many lunatics might not be found, he added a provision that surplus beds could be used for other purposes.

85. Michael Anderson, while demonstrating the continuing and tenacious importance of kinship relations even for the urban-industrial working class (largely because of the virtual absence of any alternative and more formal sources of support), nonetheless documents an unambiguous erosion of the strength of those ties, particularly in the emerging urban conurbations: 'The high commitment to family relationships which was so typical of the rural areas, was not generally to be found in the towns', where all sorts of structural factors conspired to weaken these linkages. (In rural areas, for instance, 'the father had complete control over the only really viable source of income', while in the towns, urban wages allowed the young 'to free themselves from total economic dependence on the nuclear family.') In medium-sized towns (though not in the largest), 'kin seem to have [still] been a major source of assistance', but this primarily applied to 'those in not too much need'. Anderson argues that the general attitude even towards kin became highly instrumental and calculative, and the narrow and straightened circumstances of working-class existence simply precluded more extensive help: where 'even short or comparatively minor crises caused severe destitution, . . . extreme privation . . . would have resulted if kin had tried to care for those in [more permanent] need. . . .' See Michael Anderson, *Family Structure in Nineteenth Century Lancashire*, esp. pp. 18, 21, 31–2, 62, 66–7, 91, 97, 136–61. John Walton ('Lunacy in the Industrial Revolution') modifies this picture in some important respects, questioning the strength of the evidence for Anderson's claim that families behaved in a primarily calculative fashion, and providing a more nuanced analysis of the linkages between urbanization, industrialization, and the responsiveness of kinship networks to destitution and dependence. Granting the cogency of much of what Walton has to say, however, it should not be pushed too far. The fundamental strains and pressures on working-class families remained powerful and unrelenting, and operated in the basic directions Anderson analyzes. For further discussion of the uncertainties and destitution that were

consign their troublesome relatives to the asylum. In many Welsh counties, where subsistence farming remained the dominant form of economic activity, such attitudes persisted well into the second half of the nineteenth century.[86] Away from the Celtic fringe, counties like Bedford succumbed much more quickly. Long before the 1845 Asylums Act, the initial shortage of inmates for the local asylum had been replaced by such a superfluity of applicants that the local magistrates had been forced to enlarge the original structure considerably. When the Metropolitan Commissioners conducted the first nationwide survey of the adequacy of existing provisions for lunatics, they drew attention to how general a phenomenon this was:

> it must be observed as a remarkable circumstance with respect to counties having pauper Lunatic Asylums, that it has been found necessary to enlarge almost every asylum of that sort that has hitherto been erected. The Asylums for the counties of Bedford, Cornwall, Gloucester, Kent, Lancaster, Leicester, Middlesex and Nottingham, and for the West Riding of York have all been enlarged, and some of them several times.[87]

When the 1845 Act made county asylums compulsory everywhere, this pattern simply spread through the rest of the country. County asylums had been expected to reduce the lunatic population by providing early treatment and hence cure; but everywhere,

> notwithstanding very considerable pains have been taken, on the proposition to build a new asylum, to ascertain the probable number of claimants, and a wide margin over and above that estimate has been allowed in fixing on the extent of accommodation provided, yet no

an endemic feature of nineteenth-century working-class life, cf. J.D. Foster, 'Capitalism and Class Consciousness in Earlier Nineteenth Century Oldham', unpublished Ph.D. dissertation, Cambridge University, 1967.

86. As late as 1872, for example, approximately 60 per cent of the known lunatics in Cardiganshire, Carmarthenshire, and Pembrokeshire still resided at home with relatives and others. In Anglesey the proportion was as high as 72 per cent. By contrast, in the more economically advanced and increasingly industrial county of Glamorgan, it had declined to less than 27 per cent; while in largely urbanized English counties like Lancashire (5 per cent), Surrey (5 per cent), or Middlesex (4 per cent), the practice had largely died out. Following complaints from the board of the joint asylum for the three rural Welsh counties about the effects of domestic care, two Lunacy Commissioners arrived on the scene in 1875. Armed with a Welsh-speaking interpreter, they launched a case-by-case survey of the treatment of the non-institutionalized lunatics, 'scattered about in very remote and inaccessible situations'. Despite vigorous efforts to uncover episodes of abuse, they concluded that the lunatics were for the most part treated in a kindly fashion by their families, and that their relatives were vehemently opposed to institutionalization. The only serious problem they reported was that the Poor Law allowances given to aid with the lunatics' maintenance were too small, and they recommended that these be increased. See Commissioners in Lunacy, *30th Annual Report*, 1876, pp. 74–6, 346–9.

87. Metropolitan Commissioners in Lunacy, *Report*, 1844, p. 84.

sooner has the institution got into operation, than its doors have been besieged by unheard of applicants for admission, and within one third or one half of the estimated time, its wards have been filled and an extension rendered imperative.[88]

By the mid-1850s, most county institutions had been open for only five or six years. Yet in their 1856 Report, the Lunacy Commissioners were lamenting 'the crowded state of nearly all the County Asylums, and the urgent necessity of making further immediate provision for the care and treatment of the Insane Poor. . . . in nearly every County the accommodation provided in Asylums is, at present, or shortly will be, inadequate'. Building more asylums and expanding the existing ones failed to resolve the underlying problem. By 1867, there were forty-nine county and borough asylums, taking a total of 24,748 patients, compared with the sixteen receiving 4,336 in 1844. 'Notwithstanding this large increase of provision for Pauper Lunatics, the pressure for further accommodation in many districts is most urgent, particularly in Middlesex, Lancashire, and Yorkshire, the most urban counties, with the largest asylums and the greatest provision for their insane.'[89] At the Littlemore Asylum, which after 1850 took patients from both Oxfordshire and Berkshire, 'it was believed, from a Parliamentary return, that the number of Pauper Lunatics (inclusive of idiots) maintained by the parishes of the whole Union, did not exceed 480 . . .', and increased accommodation was provided for the Berkshire patients on this basis. When this swiftly proved inadequate, the asylum authorities adopted the standard conclusion 'that this Return was but imperfect'.[90] To cite one more example, the Surrey Asylum at Wandsworth was opened in 1841 with provision for 350 patients. By 1843 it was overcrowded and had to be enlarged; three years later, further enlargement was necessary, and provision was now made for 875 patients. This brought only a brief respite, for by 1853 accommodation was again insufficient. The magistrates now balked at further capital expenditures, and by cramming additional patients into the existing structure, it was made to suffice. Finally, in 1862, with Wandsworth taking 1,083 patients (more than three times the original estimate of what was required), construction of a second asylum at Brookwood was begun.[91] That, too, was designed to take more than 1,000 patients.

The general pattern of an initial estimate of demand, which then proves wildly wide of the mark, leading to the construction of additional facilities designed to more than meet the apparent deficit, which themselves prove grossly inadequate, leading to a repetition of the whole cycle, is perhaps exhibited most clearly in the case of the Middlesex asylums, which

88. J.T. Arlidge, *On the State of Lunacy*, p. 7.
89. Commissioners in Lunacy, *21st Annual Report*, 1867, pp. 67–8.
90. Littlemore County Asylum, *Annual Report*, 1863, pp. 13–4.
91. J.M. Granville, *The Care and Cure of the Insane*, Vol. 1, London: Hardwicke and Bogue, 1877, pp. 225–34.

provided for most of London's lunatics. Provision for pauper lunatics in public asylums in Middlesex began with the erection of Hanwell Asylum, completed in 1831. The original intention had been to build an asylum for 300 inmates, but following the figures revealed by the Parliamentary Return of 28 April 1830, it was decided to make provision for 500. At the time, this seemed not unreasonable, for although the return had shown a total of 824 lunatics and idiots, 480 of these were reported to be harmless, and 228 of these were not in any kind of confinement. In 1834, however, Ellis, the superintendent, reported that 'no fresh patients can be received, except on vacancies occurring from the cures or deaths of some of the present inmates; and the applications for admission are so numerous, that, with the utmost success that can be hoped for in cures, many months must now elapse after an application has been made before a patient can be received'. A year later, 'it was reported to contain a hundred patients more than it had been built for; after another two years, it had to be enlarged for 300 more . . .'.[92] At the end of the decade, it had space for 1,000 patients, and applications were still piling up.

Following an 1844 return to the Quarter Sessions which showed that there were 722 more lunatics in the county than there was space for in Hanwell, the magistrates decided that more accommodation would have to be provided. Their initial plan simply to add on to the existing structure meeting with objections from the Lunacy Commissioners, they proceeded to build a second separate asylum for over 1,200 patients, a generous margin over those known to exist.[93] 'Colney Hatch was opened in 1851; within a period of less than five years, it became necessary to appeal to the ratepayers for further accommodation . . .'.[94] The Hanwell Annual Report for 1855 concluded gloomily that 'it is probable . . . notwithstanding the additional accommodation lately made . . . that there must be at this moment 500 unprovided for'. The magistrates resisted pressures from the Lunacy Commissioners to provide yet another asylum, commenting that 'a third Asylum is a vast and expensive evil', especially since the patients were almost entirely 'the most hopeless and the most objectionable'.[95] Instead, they simply adapted Hanwell and Colney Hatch to take in the neighbourhood of 2,000 patients each.

Inevitably, history repeated itself once again. By the late 1860s, the shortage of beds was so acute that surplus patients were sent outside the county, wherever room could be found for them, some as far away as Yorkshire.[96] The opening, over the next few years, of the two huge

92. Ellis quoted in R. Hunter and I. MacAlpine, 'Introduction' to John Conolly, *On the Construction and Government of Lunatic Asylums*, facsimile edition, London: Dawsons, 1968, p. 16; Commissioners in Lunacy, *11th Annual Report*, 1857, p. 12.
93. J.M. Granville, *The Care and Cure of the Insane*, Vol. 1, pp. 161–3.
94. Commissioners in Lunacy, *11th Annual Report*, 1857, p. 12.
95. Hanwell County Asylum, *Annual Report*, 1855, p. 9.
96. 'The mass transfer of groups of disabled chronic in-patients for months or even years was a common practice' through the nineteenth and well into the twentieth century.

custodial warehouses at Caterham and Leavesden for the most chronic cases from the metropolitan area provided considerable relief, for each took over 2,000 cases. Again, however, this proved merely temporary. In 1877, a third regular asylum had to be opened at Banstead, only for the increase to swell beyond even its capacity. By 1880, the asylum for insane children at Darenth had to be converted to take adults as well, the over-flow from Caterham and Leavesden. And even after this addition, the superintendent at Hanwell once more reported that 'the demand for beds continues largely in excess of the Asylum accommodation . . .'.[97]

Looked at in a broader comparative framework, the mental hospital census for the London area provides dramatic evidence of the permeable and unstable nature of the boundary between sanity and madness, and of the susceptibility of rates of incarceration in asylums to social influences. The Metropolitan Poor Act of 1867, which licensed the construction of barracks-asylums for the chronically mad, was a more general piece of legislation creating a central administrative and financial framework within which London could modify its approach to the non-able-bodied poor. In funding new institutions from a London-wide Common Poor Fund, the Act fuelled an 'immense and disproportionate growth in Poor Law expenditure in the capital which flattened the cost differentials between lunatic asylums and other forms of poor relief'.[98] With the Common Poor Fund contributing to the cost of maintaining pauper lunatics in county asylums (augmented, from 1875 onwards, by a weekly capitation grant of four shillings per asylum inmate from the central government), and with

---

'[T]hose selected for transfer tended to be the idiots, the quiet demented, the speechless – those most disabled and presumed to be least sentient.' J.M. Crammer, *Asylum History*, p. 56.

97. Hanwell County Asylum, *Annual Report*, 1882, p. 5. One other interesting piece of information supporting the idea that the availability of the asylum creates its own supply of lunatics is provided in the Commissioners in Lunacy, *15th Annual Report*, 1861, pp. 79–80. Maidstone and Canterbury, two boroughs in Kent, then possessed equal populations. While Maidstone had made provision for its lunatics to be admitted to the Kent County Asylum, however, Canterbury had not: 'the returns now show double the number of Insane Paupers in the provided over the unprovided borough.' This is in no sense an idiosyncratic finding. A decade earlier, the American alienist Edward Jarvis had undertaken a detailed statistical examination of data on the resident population of almost every asylum in the United States, and had conclusively established the existence of an inverse relationship between distance from a mental hospital and liability to be incarcerated as insane. As he demonstrated, the nearer a family lived to an asylum, the more likely it was to discover that one of its members was a lunatic in need of confinement. The incidence of 'insanity' was in consequence as much as four times as great in areas immediately adjacent to asylums as in more distant communities. See Edward Jarvis, 'The Influence of Distance from and Proximity to an Insane Hospital, on Its Use by Any People', *Boston Medical and Surgical Journal* 42, 17 April 1850, pp. 209–22; *idem.*, 'The Influence of Distance and Nearness to an Insane Hospital on Its Use by the People', *American Journal of Insanity* 7, 1851, pp. 281–5.

98. David Cochrane, '"Humane, Economical, and Medically Wise": The LCC as Administrators of Victorian Lunacy Policy', in W.F. Bynum, R. Porter, and M. Shepherd (eds), *The Anatomy of Madness*, Vol. 3, London: Routledge, 1988, p. 251. The two following paragraphs are heavily indebted to Cochrane's analysis.

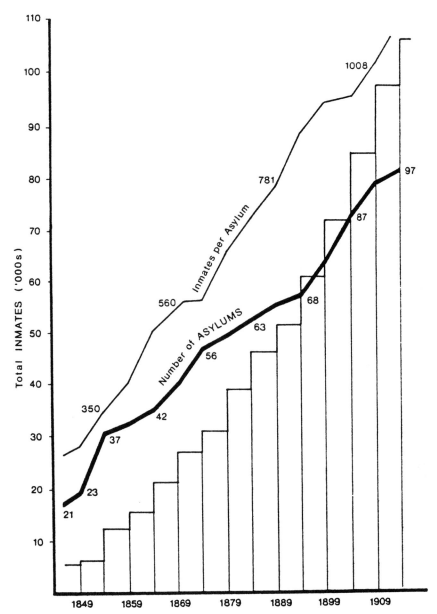

Fig. 23 The Triumph of Asylumdom. This diagram, adapted from the *68th Annual Report* of the Commissioners in Lunacy, 1914, and taken from Jeremy Taylor, *Hospital and Asylum Architecture in England 1840–1914* (London: Mansell, 1991), graphically illustrates the growth of the asylum sector from the mid-nineteenth century to the eve of the First World War: the continuous rise in the number of inmates in county and borough asylums; the steady increase in the number of institutions; and the even more rapid escalation of the average size of pauper asylums.

workhouses being maintained wholly by parish rates, London Poor Law unions found they could transfer inmates to the asylum system at virtually no additional cost.[99] Indeed, '[b]y the turn of the century, a local metropolitan union could save 60 per cent of its monetary obligation to maintain paupers if they were transferred to a county . . . asylum.'[100] By contrast, in the rest of the country, while the cost differential between asylum and workhouse was narrowed somewhat after the introduction of the central capitation grant, it remained substantial.

The effects of these financial incentives were dramatic: by 1890, a far larger fraction of London's pauper lunatics were confined in asylums, rather than being left with relatives or kept in workhouses.[101] More significantly still, the number of cases of insanity per 1,000 of the city's population already exceeded that for the rest of the country by some 23 per cent. Over the next two decades, the differential widened drastically. To give some idea of the magnitude of the increase in the officially identified cases of insanity, in 1891 there were 15,853 pauper lunatics in London, and by 1909 there were 26,293; and while the lunacy rate per 1,000 of the general population had risen relatively slowly in the rest of England and Wales, from 2.87 in 1890 to 3.31 in 1910, in London the rate grew from 3.7 to almost 6 cases per 1,000 over the same period – an explosive increase which forced the newly constituted London County Council to embark on a programme of asylum building 'almost desperate in its scale and momentum'.[102]

6. Warehouses of the Unwanted

I have suggested that asylums were largely receptacles for the confinement of the impossible, the inconvenient, and the inept. The comments of the asylum superintendents and the Lunacy Commissioners on the character of asylum inmates provide abundant support for this view. From the moment most asylums opened, they functioned as museums for the collection of the unwanted. John Millar, the superintendent at the Buckinghamshire Asylum, commented on the nature of his earliest admissions in his diary. Of eleven males brought in on 1 February 1853, for instance, 'Four . . . are incurable, two of them being advanced in years and

---

99. Maudsley saw the four shilling subsidy as by itself likely to contribute substantially to a further expansion of the numbers officially diagnosed as mad: 'we may expect this premium on lunacy will diminish materially, and, perhaps, gradually render extinct, the race of sane paupers in England.' H. Maudsley, 'On the Alleged Increase of Insanity', p. 51.

100. D. Cochrane, '"Humane, Economical, and Medically Wise": the LCC as Administrators of Victorian Lunacy Policy', p. 252.

101. David Cochrane (ibid., p. 250) cites data which give the proportion of pauper lunatics in county asylums as 78 per cent in 1889, as compared with 96 per cent in London. By 1909, the proportions had risen to 85 per cent and 98 per cent respectively.

102. Ibid., pp. 248–50, 255; see also the discussion in chapter 6.

two are paralytic. There is also a hopeless epileptic'.[103] Those over sixty consistently constituted more than a fifth of the annual admissions in Buckinghamshire between 1861 and 1881, and, after a brief dip in 1891, the proportion of the elderly and senile rose to a quarter of all admissions by the turn of the century.[104] Suffolk Asylum in 1852 included ten people 'nearly seventy years of age, nine over seventy, three over eighty; sixteen in a state of bodily exhaustion; nine either idiots from birth, or imbeciles for a very long period; one child with well-known disease of the heart, and a woman, a cripple, scrofulous, blind and deaf'. The Worcester Asylum received many patients between sixty and eighty years old, 'while others were the subjects of organic disease of the brain, lungs and heart, or suffered from long-continued mental disease, or from the superannuation of old age'. At Kent, 'the age of eleven persons admitted in 1853 averaged 64, twelve were from 72 to 75. In many of these the malady was simply decay of the mind, or was due to apoplectic seizures, and attended by palsy'. John Bucknill of the Devonshire County Asylum found that

> Patients have been admitted suffering from heart disease, aneurism, and cancer, with scarcely a greater amount of melancholy than might be expected to take place in many sane persons at the near and certain prospect of death. Some have been received in the last stages of con- sumption, with that amount only of cerebral excitement so common in this disorder; others have been received in the delirium or stupor of typhus; while in several cases the mental condition was totally unknown after admission, and must have been unknown before, since an advanced condition of bodily disease prevented speech, and the expression of intelligence or emotion, either normal or morbid.[105]

Frequent reference to the large proportion of cases of senile decay among asylum admissions continued to be made in later years, and by the

103. Buckinghamshire County Asylum, *Superintendent's Diary*, 1 February 1853. (In manuscript at St. John's Hospital, Stone.)
104. J.M. Crammer, *Asylum History*, pp. 119–20. By contrast, John Walton finds that those over 60 formed only 10 per cent of admissions to the Lancaster County Asylum in 1871. See J. Walton, 'The Treatment of Pauper Lunatics in Victorian England: The Case of Lancaster Asylum, 1816–1870,' in Andrew Scull (ed.) *Madhouses, Mad-doctors, and Madmen*, p. 189.
105. All quotations taken from county asylum annual reports, quoted in J. Arlidge, *On the State of Lunacy*, pp. 92–6. A careful review of admissions to Colney Hatch during the nineteenth century reached very similar conclusions:

> Patients rendered socially unacceptable or intolerable by disease were certified as 'lunatic' irrespective of what made them ill. They included the subnormal, even the deaf and dumb and blind for whom there was no other provision . . . [and victims of] the kind of diseases then prevalent and little understood and certainly untreatable – vitamin deficiencies, metabolic disorders like diabetes, intoxications of various kinds including lead poisoning, encephalitic syndromes, intracranial tumours, infections like syphilis and tuberculosis, and brain, heart and kidney disease complicating streptococcal infection, birth trauma, etc.

> R.A. Hunter and I. MacAlpine, *Psychiatry for the Poor*, p. 16.

fourth quarter of the nineteenth century some asylum superintendents had begun to object to the burden that this group was to care for, and to suggest that asylum treatment was inappropriate for this class[106] – not that this dissuaded either the Poor Law officers[107] or the families of such people from continuing to send them. Quite apart from the inconvenient and decrepit old people who formed perhaps a fifth or a quarter of asylum admissions, there was no shortage of other individuals whom the community was glad to get rid of. Asylums became a dumping ground for a heterogeneous mass of physical and mental wrecks[108] – chronic alcoholics afflicted with delirium tremens or, with permanently pickled brains, reduced to a state of dementia; epileptics; tertiary syphilitics; consumptives in the throes of terminal delirium; cases of organic brain damage; diabetics; victims of lead or other forms of heavy metal poisoning; the malnourished; the simple-minded;[109] women exhausted and depressed by the perpetual round of pregnancy and childbirth; and those poor worn-out souls who had simply given up the struggle for existence.[110]

106. For example, 'In several instances the patients have been so old and feeble that they have had to be carried direct from the vehicle that brought them to bed, and there they remain until they die. . . . All the treatment the majority of them require is simply kind nursing and sustaining diet; and this ought to be secured as well in the workhouse as in the Asylum, and thus avoid the risk of removal.' (Hanwell County Asylum, *Annual Report*, 1875, p. 23.) 'Very old and palsied people continue to be sent and very few, almost none, are in even moderate bodily health. . . . I fail to see any reason for not retaining many . . . in workhouses. Doubtless their minds are somewhat enfeebled by the causes above named, but they cannot be considered as truly imbecile or insane. *If they are so, every person who lives beyond his sixtieth or seventieth year, or who may have an attack of paralysis is liable to be so classed.*' (Caterham Lunatic Asylum, *Annual Report*, 1873, pp. 4–5, emphasis in the original.)
107. As Clifford Allbutt put it in testimony to an inquiry set up by the new London County Council, 'Worn-out old dements, imbeciles, and aged people are shovelled in upon asylums from the workhouses [along with] . . . the lunatic wreckage more properly so-called.' Quoted in H.C. Burdett, *Hospitals and Asylums of the World*, Vol. 2, London: Churchill, 1891, p. 195.
108. As one well placed contemporary observer put it, 'The standard of what constitutes lunacy suitable for asylum treatment has changed and immensely widened. All who have experience are agreed on this point. Far more mild cases, far more congenital imbeciles, far more eccentrically-behaved monomaniacs and contorted harmless specimens of humanity, and . . . very many more senile dotards and hemiplegic wrecks are now sent to asylums than formerly.' 'Review of The Care and Cure of the Insane by J. Mortimer Granville', Journal of Mental Science 23, 1877, pp. 895–6. (This anonymous review was almost certainly written by either Maudsley or Clouston.)
109. Janet Saunders has provided some evidence that 'asylum superintendents were not keen to detain people who were merely weak-minded, and continued to discharge them throughout a period of increasing fears about social degeneracy'. J. Saunders, 'Quarantining the Weak-Minded: Psychiatric Definitions of Degeneracy and the Late-Victorian Asylum', in W.F. Bynum, R. Porter, and M. Shepherd (eds), *The Anatomy of Madness*, Vol. 3, p. 291. The reasons for these attitudes and practices remain unclear.
110. John Walton is quite right to stress the extraordinary burden many of these people represented, and the 'squalid and humiliating conditions' which many of them endured outside the asylum. See his 'Casting Out and Bringing Back in Victorian England: Pauper Lunatics, 1840–70', esp. pp. 136, 140–1. The heterogeneity of the inmates' troubles (or 'presenting symptoms'), and the fact that, in the absence of the asylum, families would have had little alternative but to tolerate and cope with these people

This, for Bucknill, was the great difference 'between the inmates of the old madhouses and the modern asylum – The former containing only obvious and dangerous cases of lunacy, the latter containing great numbers of quiet and harmless patients whose insanity is often difficult to determine'.[111] More specifically, among the

> inmates who filled the new madhouses which existed before the alleviating action of the lunacy laws . . . outrageous madness was the rule, and the detention of patients after they had become tranquil and harmless was against the rule. Nowadays, our numerous asylums swarm with a motley crowd of persons of weak minds or low spirits; with tranquil and reasonable persons said to have suicidal tendencies if they are not always under supervision; with paralytics and epileptics, and with persons in various stages of mental decay; no doubt all of them, with very rare exceptions, persons of unsound mind, but not madmen or lunatics, or even insane persons, as our fathers understood these terms.[112]

It is surely not the least of the many ironies with which lunacy reform abounds that its very success in making available the 'humanitarian' and 'scientific' alternative of asylum treatment tended to encourage families to abandon the struggle to cope with the troublesome – a temptation many fell prey to:

> The very imposing appearance of these establishments acts as an advertisement to draw patients towards them. If we make a convenient lumber room, we all know how speedily it becomes filled up with lumber. The county asylum is the mental lumber room of the surrounding district; friends are only too willing, in their poverty, to place away

nonetheless remain crucially important aspects of the growth of 'lunacy' in the nineteenth century.

111. J.C. Bucknill, *The Care of the Insane and their Legal Control*, p. xxvii. Compare also Granville's comment that 'It is impossible not to recognize the presence of a considerable number of "patients" in these asylums who are not lunatic. They may be weak, dirty, troublesome, but they are certainly no[t] . . . affected with mental disease.' Indirectly, his contention that 'Speaking generally the causation of insanity everywhere, special organic disease apart, is an affair of three W's – worry, want and wickedness. Its cure is a matter of three M's – method, meat and morality' (J.M. Granville, *The Care and Cure of the Insane*, Vol. 1, pp. 264, 48) reveals more about the sort of people being sent to asylums than about the causes of 'mental illness'; more about the persistence of the middle-class prejudice in favour of order and discipline than the existence of any scientifically grounded therapy for its cure.

112. J. Bucknill, *The Care of the Insane and their Legal Control*, p. 3. As Maudsley and Robertson commented, looking at the character of those admitted to county asylums, 'we are almost driven to the conclusion that our system tends to include among our so-called pauper lunatics many persons who ought either to have been never included or who have ceased to properly belong to that category'. Editorial, 'On the Increase of Pauper Lunacy', *Journal of Mental Science* 17, 1871, p. 464.

the human encumbrance of the family in a palatial building at county expense.[113]

In consequence,

> the law providing that madmen, dangerous to themselves and others, shall be secluded in madhouses for absolutely needful care and protection, has been extended in its application to large classes of persons who would never have been considered lunatics when this legislation was entered upon. Since 1845, medical science has discovered whole realms of lunacy, and the nicer touch of a finikin civilization has shrunk away from the contact of imperfect fellow-creatures, and thus the manifold receptacles of lunacy are filled to overflow with a population more nearly resembling that which is still at large.[114]

113. [Andrew Wynter], 'Non-Restraint in the Treatment of the Insane', *Edinburgh Review* 131, 1870, p. 221. Three decades later, another critic employed a slightly different analogy to describe the same phenomenon: 'There are now asylums of all kinds . . . possessing . . . a sort of fascination like spiders' webs for flies.' Anonymous, *Lunatick Asylums*, London, 1898, pp. 2–3.

114. J. Bucknill, *The Care of the Insane and their Legal Control*, p. 4. Compare the very similar observations of Sir James Coxe:

> There must be taken into consideration all the different influences which in modern society lead to persons being reckoned as lunatics, and removed as such from home. Chief among these are the facilities afforded by the poor-law for the gratuitous disposal of indigent patients in asylums; and next to these the opportunities which the asylums afford of getting quit of persons who from temper, disease, vice, intemperance, or old age, have become troublesome or expensive inmates at home. *Under such influences the definition of lunacy has expanded, and many a one is accordingly now treated as a lunatic who formerly would not have been regarded as coming within the meaning of the term.*

'Presidential Address', *Journal of Mental Science* 18, 1872, pp. 311–33, emphasis added, quoted in Edward Renvoize, 'The Association of Medical Officers of Asylums and Hospitals for the Insane, the Medico-Psychological Association, and their Presidents', in G.E. Berrios and H. Freeman (eds), *150 Years of British Psychiatry 1841–1991*, London: Gaskell, 1991, p. 61.

CHAPTER EIGHT

The Legacy of Reform

> In any society the dominant groups are the ones with the most to hide about the way society works. Very often therefore truthful analyses are bound to have a critical ring, to seem like exposés rather than objective statements, as the term is conventionally used [to denote mild-mannered statements in favour of the status quo]. . . . For all students of human society, sympathy with the victims of historical processes and scepticism about the victors' claims provide essential safeguards against being taken in by the dominant mythology. A scholar who tries to be objective needs these feelings as part of his ordinary working equipment.
>
> Barrington Moore, *The Social Origins of Dictatorship and Democracy*

If being locked up had been a not uncommon fate for some of the frenzied long before the age of the asylum, nonetheless the routine consignment of the deranged, the depressed, and the distracted to confinement in a network of specialized and purpose-built institutions is essentially a nineteenth-century phenomenon. Likewise, it is only from the Victorian era forwards that one can speak without anachronism of psychiatry as an historical actor. It was on the basis of their control over the novel and rapidly expanding realm of asylumdom that alienists constituted themselves as a newly self-conscious profession, making use of their medical identity to attribute a particular status and meaning to the objects of their attention. Moreover, it is psychiatrists' absolute supremacy over the asylum and its techniques of isolation, and the monopoly this gave them over the legitimate treatment of madness, which have subsequently formed the foundation from which the profession has sought to expand its jurisdictional reach, multiplying the range of behaviours and the classes of deviants subject to its intervention and often dubiously therapeutic ministrations. I have been concerned here to analyse and account for the crystallization of this new ensemble of social practices and meanings: their striking and ultimately somewhat sinister embodiment in new physical forms that constitute such a notable example of the 'moral architecture' of the nineteenth century;[1] the reciprocal constitution of new forms of expertise

---

1. The best discussion and analysis of this novel arrangement and utilization of space in a systematic attempt to remoralize the dangerous and defective is to be found in Robin

and knowledge alongside and in intimate relationships with this new institutional apparatus; the development of new theoretical codes and technologies of intervention; the redrawing of the boundaries between the normal and the pathological; and the shutting away of the mad in what was pronounced to be a therapeutic isolation. Taken together, these mark the emergence for the first time of a relatively stable psychiatric complex, and the irruption of new modes and mechanisms of intervention and treatment, care and confinement, dominance and control.

1. Competing Accounts of Lunacy Reform

Whatever lunacy reform ultimately achieved for its ostensible clients, it certainly has had its uses for the retrospective (and contemporary) vindication of the humanity of the English bourgeoisie. Perhaps few present-day observers can quite summon up the note of positive enthusiasm and complacent self-congratulation with which the Victorian middle classes regarded their museums of the mad. Even the least informed of us feels a certain scepticism and discomfort when confronted with the claim that 'the county asylum is the most blessed manifestation of true civilization the world can present'.[2] Yet still the reformers' claims for the purity and humanitarianism of their own motives (supplemented by the labours of generations of historians who saw in the evolving treatment of the mentally distracted a source of support for their own Whiggish predilections) have served to inculcate in most people the notion that the rise of the mental hospital represents progress towards enlightenment and a practical expression of concern and assistance for one's suffering fellow man.

   Perceptions of this sort are not easily overturned or modified. After all, not only do they correspond to what the most powerful protagonists in these events wished to believe about themselves and embody what they wanted us to accept about their actions, but such beliefs also perpetuate a set of myths with enduring contemporary value. Moreover, their optimistic assumptions are embedded in the very language we use – words like 'reform,' 'psychiatrist,' 'mental hospital,' and so on – and it is a sociological truism, but true nonetheless, that the concepts which we use to delimit and discuss any particular segment of reality inevitably colour our perceptions of that reality. In the circumstances, there has been an understandable tendency to discount facts which fail to fit a 'progressive' interpretation as atypical and exceptional, and to attribute them to the inevitable imperfection of all human institutions.

Evans, *The Fabrication of Virtue: English Prison Architecture 1750–1842*, Cambridge: Cambridge University Press, 1982. Foucault, of course, develops much of his analysis of modern penality and of the structures of social control with reference to the most famous architectural contrivance of this sort, Jeremy Bentham's Panopticon. See M. Foucault, *Discipline and Punish: The Birth of the Prison*, London: Allen Lane 1977.
2. Cited in Andrew Wynter, *The Borderlands of Insanity*, 2nd edn, London: Renshaw, 1877, p. 112.

In the simplified version of history preferred by modern psychiatry and its apologists – an account which remained unchallenged until the mid-1960s[3] – the Dark Ages of the mad persisted right up to the birth of alienism and of the asylum in the early nineteenth century, the period when science and humanity at last united to produce a revolution in the treatment of the mentally ill. Certain episodes here acquired an almost totemic force and significance: Tuke calmly sipping tea with his charges; the picture of Pinel literally and metaphorically striking off the chains from the lunatics in the Bicetre and (in the midst of the bloodiest excesses of the French Revolution) inaugurating the first rational and humane approach to the treatment of the mentally disordered;[4] and the companion portrait of John Conolly completing this triumph of science and humanity by creating an asylum regime that totally dispensed with even the remnants of the ancient reliance on 'mechanical restraint' – whips and chains, manacles and muffs, stripes and straitjackets.[5] The outcome of these selfless interventions was the creation of a new set of purpose-built institutions, presided over by an increasingly self-conscious community of scientists and healers, and devoted to the provision of humane care and cures for their patients.

It would be difficult to image a more thoroughgoing assault on these orthodox triumphalist pieties than that launched by Michel Foucault almost three decades ago now.[6] But the Foucauldian critique was only one of a number of strands contributing to the development of a very different assessment of the history of psychiatry. Equally salient in the formulation of a more sceptical perspective were ideas drawn from the American sociology of deviance, and, more particularly, from those known as 'societal reaction theorists', who had made agencies of social control one of the focal points of their research. For central to this work was an ironical claim: that control structures, far from being a basically benign

3. See, for example, Kathleen Jones, *Lunacy, Law, and Conscience 1744–1845*, London: Routledge and Kegan Paul, 1955; idem., *Mental Health and Social Policy 1845–1955*, London: Routledge and Kegan Paul, 1960; David Roberts, *Victorian Origins of the British Welfare State*, New Haven: Yale University Press, 1960.
4. In this case, there are quite literally two pictures of Pinel in action, painted some half century and more after the event they purport to record: 'Pinel at the Bicêtre', painted by Charles Muller in 1849; and 'Pinel Removes the Chains of the Insane Women at the Salpêtrière', painted in 1878 by Robert-Fleury. But the episode, as Dora Weiner and Jan Goldstein have documented at length, is wholly fictitious, the pictorial 'records' completely spurious artifacts, and Pinel's presumed role as the author of moral treatment a major distortion of the historical record. As perhaps befits an Ur-myth, the claimed factual foundation dissolves under empirical scrutiny. See Dora Weiner, 'The Origins of Psychiatry: Pinel or the Zeitgeist?' in O. Baur and O. Glandien (eds), *Zusammenhang: Festschrift für Marielene Putscher*, Vol. 2, Köln: Wienand, 1984, pp. 617–31; Jan Goldstein, *Console and Classify: The French Psychiatric Profession in the Nineteenth Century*, Cambridge: Cambridge University Press, 1987, pp. 72–119.
5. For a reexamination of Conolly, the patron saint of English psychiatry, see my *Social Order/Mental Disorder: Anglo-American Psychiatry in Historical Perspective*, Berkeley: University of California Press/London: Routledge, 1989, chapter 7.
6. Cf. M. Foucault, *Madness and Civilization*, New York: Pantheon, 1965.

and defensive response to individual pathology, themselves acted to shape, create, and sustain deviance; that 'the very effort to prevent, intervene, arrest and "cure" persons of their alleged pathologies may . . . precipitate or seriously aggravate the tendency society wishes to guard against.'[7] Then, too, the attractions of the facile equation of history with progress had long since lost their lustre in most historical circles, and during the 1960s, such disenchantment somewhat belatedly began to influence discussions of lunacy reform – a development fostered in part by the growing disillusion in intellectual and policy-making circles with the value of institutional approaches to the management of the mad. Revisionists who reexamined nineteenth-century responses to the insane in the light of these notions drew a portrait which amounted to a virtual mirror image of the old Whiggish picture. Where one saw flaws and imperfections in a fundamentally sound approach, the other saw institutions with but few redeeming features – not a scientific or therapeutic response to illness, but a penal, custodial repression of threats to the social order. In place of an earlier portrait of the freeing of the insane from their fetters of iron and the shackles of superstition, the revisionist discourse spoke of the imposition of an ever more thoroughgoing 'moral uniformity and social denunciation',[8] a species of progress in which '[l]iberation from the racking of the body merely meant new tortures for the mind . . . , the imposition of more subtly terrifying "mind forg'd manacles" of guilt and self-control'.[9]

Such polemical assaults have had their uses in dissipating some of the fog of righteousness which has enveloped and nearly smothered past efforts to come to terms with the treatment of the insane in the nineteenth century; but they have scarcely provided a satisfactory alternative analysis of the phenomenon. Like the sociological tradition upon which they draw, the work of men like Szasz and Rothman portrays those consigned to asylums as caught up on some largely arbitrary scapegoating process, and views the lunatic as the 'put-upon victim, with the social control agencies the villain of the piece'.[10] But this is grossly to oversimplify and distort what happened. It romanticizes those incarcerated as crazy, and plays down the degree to which their behaviour was (and is) genuinely problematic. Even worse, by way of response to the central question of why an institutional approach to madness emerged in the first place, these

---

7. David Matza, *Becoming Deviant*, Englewood Cliffs, New Jersey: Prentice-Hall, 1969, p. 80.
8. M. Foucault, *Madness and Civilization*, p. 259.
9. W.F. Bynum, R. Porter, and M. Shepherd, 'Introduction' to *The Anatomy of Madness*, Vol. 1. London: Tavistock, 1985, p. 2.
10. J. Lorber, 'Deviance as Performance: The Case of Illness', *Social Problems* 14, 1967, p. 309. See Thomas Szasz, *The Manufacture of Madness*, New York: Dell, 1970/London: Routledge and Kegan Paul, 1971; Robert Perrucci, *Circle of Madness*, Englewood Cliffs, New Jersey: Prentice-Hall, 1974; David Rothman, *The Discovery of the Asylum*, Boston: Little Brown, 1971.

writers can offer little more than either crude conspiracy theory; or an account pitched in terms of a nebulous cultural angst – arising one knows not whence – about the stability of the social order.[11]

More generally, I have argued here that both the traditional Whig histories and the revisionist accounts of the 1960s and 1970s are too crude and one-sided. In its origins, at least, nineteenth-century lunacy reform was Janus-faced: simultaneously embodying (at the outset) 'a humanitarian concern for the protection, against visible abuses, of people who were coming to be seen as curable sufferers whose condition was not their fault';[12] while (to some degree unwittingly) fostering a concealed yet ever more systematic regulation of lunatics' lives. The new realm of asylumdom depended crucially upon the new technology of moral treatment developed independently by men like Tuke and Pinel; and embedded within moral treatment were structural tensions between repression and rehabilitation, between the imposition of moral discipline and the development of self-government and self-control. Only over time were these tensions systematically resolved in favour of an oppressive system of moral management, enforced conformity, and disciplined subordination.

The revisionists are quite correct to suggest that to see only the benevolent face of moral treatment – its break with the crude coercion of the past – is to ignore the latent power of its techniques as a mechanism for enforcing moral conformity. The pervasive authority of the alienist, and his ability to link classification with a system of rewards and punishments, constituted an extraordinarily powerful new form of 'moral machinery',[13] a superior mode of *managing* patients. As I have suggested in previous chapters, the use of space in the form of the ward system to constitute and make salient moral boundaries, and the creation of an intimate tie between the patient's position in this classificatory system and his behaviour, enabled alienists to use every aspect of the environment as 'a more powerful lever in acting upon the intractable'.[14] It was, of course, precisely the hidden strengths of moral treatment as a mechanism for the management and regulation of conduct and the production of docile bodies which made possible the abandonment of the brutal and harsh methods which had previously been inextricably connected with the concentration of large numbers of lunatics in an institutional environment. And in placing far more effective and thoroughgoing means of control in the hands of the custodians while simultaneously removing the necessity for the asylum's

11. Szasz's work inclines towards the conspiratorial view; Rothman's to cultural idealism. For more extensive criticism of the latter's approach, see Andrew Scull, 'Madness and Segregative Control: The Rise of the Insane Asylum', *Social Problems* 24, 1977, pp. 337–51.

12. J.K. Walton, 'Casting Out and Bringing Back in Victorian England: Pauper Lunatics, 1840–70', in W.F. Bynum, R. Porter, and M. Shepherd (eds), *The Anatomy of Madness*, Vol. 2, London: Tavistock, 1985, pp. 132–33.

13. The term comes from W.A.F. Browne, *What Asylums Were, Are, and Ought to Be*.

14. W.A.F. Brown, *What Asylums Were, Are, and Ought to Be*, p. 156.

crudest features, the reality of that imprisonment and control became far more difficult to perceive. In crucial respects, it was the possession of this technology of domination that made it possible, in a very practical sense, for alienists to manage and clothe with a veil of legitimacy their expanding empire, the nineteenth- and twentieth-century museums for the collection and confinement of the mad.

Yet to stress only the repressive side of moral treatment leaves one with no adequate explanation of the moral energy and commitment which sustained and underpinned the drawn out campaign for lunacy reform. The abandonment of external coercion, the emphasis that the insane were susceptible to many of the same emotions and inducements as the rest of us, the belief that the qualities that the lunatic lacked could and should be recreated or reawakened: taken together, these marked an authentic shift in moral consciousness whose dimensions and cultural resonance are clear. At the same time, these appealing dimensions of the new approach are equally indispensable to understanding the strong utopian strain that ran through early nineteenth-century discussions of the asylum[15] and the reformers' new-found conviction about the redemptive powers of the institution.

The very weaknesses and excesses of revisionist explanations have prompted the revival, albeit in a more sophisticated and seductive modern guise, of the traditional meliorist interpretation. Historians of this school concede that, looked at without rose-tinted spectacles, Victorian lunatic asylums present in many ways a dismal and depressing picture. But if the results can scarcely be applauded, or must be damned with faint praise, the benevolent intentions remain. Apparently, the history of lunacy reform records the efforts of a largely well-intentioned group of men (and the occasional woman), whose endeavours mysteriously always produced accidental and unintended unpleasant consequences. However unattractive, the institutions they founded were not 'inherently evil'. On the contrary, 'mental hospitals were not fundamentally dissimilar from most human institutions, the achievements of which usually fall far short of the hopes and aspirations of the individuals who founded and led them'.[16]

But this simply will not do either. For the view of reform as the product of the 'accidental', malevolent distortions of a Manichean world represents a denial of or a failure to come to terms with the multiple ways in which structural factors constrain, prompt, and channel human activities in particular directions. On a deeper level, consequences which appear unintended and 'accidental' considered from the viewpoint of the individual actor remain susceptible to investigation and explanation. As I have tried to demonstrate here, the genesis and subsequent development of

15. *Cf.* Andrew Scull, *The Asylum as Utopia: W.A.F. Browne and the Mid-Nineteenth Century Consolidation of Psychiatry*, London: Routledge, 1990.
16. Gerald Grob, *Mental Institutions in America: Social Policy to 1875*, New York: Free Press, 1973, p. 342.

specialized segregative techniques for the handling of the mad was neither fortuitous, nor the product of the mere piling up of a series of incremental, ad hoc decisions which were bereft of any underlying dynamic or logic. Instead, the trajectory taken by lunacy reform in nineteenth-century England must be seen as the product of historically specific and closely interrelated changes in that society's political, economic, and social structure; and of the associated shifts in the intellectual and cultural horizons of the English bourgeoisie.[17]

2. 'Experts' and the Control of Deviance

The cumulative impact of the entire process has proved extraordinarily long-lasting. We have examined the social processes by which 'madness' became unambiguously and definitively 'mental illness'. Quite clearly, people's responses to bizarre and otherwise inexplicable behaviour continue to be mediated by and through that socially constructed meaning, just as the medical monopoly over the treatment of the mad, first established in the mid-nineteenth century, remains substantially secure. Indeed, in many respects, medicine is even more firmly entrenched in this field than at the close of the nineteenth century – though, notwithstanding extravagant claims for the effectiveness of anti-psychotic medication,[18] not because of any dramatic improvements in its therapeutic performance.

Indeed, on their own terms, with respect to their ability to 'cure' their subjects, the experts on the control of deviance in modern societies have been spectacularly unsuccessful – which raises the question of why they are still accorded the status of experts. Looking at the case of psychiatry, with which I have here been concerned, it is clear that in practice psychiatrists in the nineteenth century did little more than act as caretakers of custodial dumping institutions. Nor did it require much sophistication or inquiry to uncover the fact. It was too blatantly obvious to be overlooked – or so it might seem. Yet despite this, the medical superintendents of asylums continued to claim and to be recognized as experts in the treatment of 'mental illness'. Only a few cranks, and some of the asylum inmates,[19] seem to have voiced the opinion that the emperor had no clothes.

Such a persistent, almost wilful blindness must derive from something

---

17. For an analysis of how these changes prompted equally major transformations in the English crime control apparatus in this period, see Steven Spitzer and Andrew T. Scull, 'Social Control in Historical Perspective: From Private to Public Responses to Crime', in D.F. Greenberg (ed.), *Corrections and Punishment: Structure, Function, and Process*, Beverly Hills, California: Sage Publications, 1977, pp. 281–302.
18. *Cf.* Andrew Scull, *Decarceration: Community Treatment and the Deviant – A Radical View*, Englewood Cliffs, New Jersey: Prentice-Hall, 1977, chapter 5.
19. A constant complaint made by inmates of English lunatic asylums to the Lunacy Commissioners, throughout the nineteenth century, was that they did not belong in asylums, and that nothing was being done to cure them anyway.

more than the sacred and hence unquestioned quality with which modern societies have endowed science and certified expertise. It is true, of course, that such unexamined deference is habitually exhibited in its most acute form in the realm of medicine. Indeed, the doctor–patient relationship is so structured as to demand routinely that the client abdicate his own reasoning capacity.[20] In its place is fostered a naive child-like faith that the physician is operating in the patients's best interests; and that when he does so, he is guided by an esoteric training and knowledge giving him insights which are beyond the powers of ordinary mortals to grasp or understand. But when all is said and done, modern medicine, much of the time at least, has results, if not God, on its side. British psychiatry at the end of the nineteenth century (and most of the 'experts' currently engaged in the control of deviance) clearly did (do) not.

And yet, if asylums, and the activities of those running them, did not transform their inmates into upright citizens, they did at least get rid of troublesome people for the rest of us. By not inquiring too deeply into what went on behind asylum walls, by not pressing too hard to find out what superintendents actually did with their patients, and by not being too sceptical of the officially constructed reality, people were (are) rewarded with a comforting reassurance about the essentially benign character of their society and the way it dealt (deals) with its deviants and misfits. Granting a few individuals the status and perquisites ordinarily thought to be reserved for those with genuine expertise and esoteric knowledge was a small price to pay for the satisfaction of knowing that crazy people were getting the best treatment science could provide, and for the comfortable feelings which could be aroused by contemplating the contrast between the present 'humane' and 'civilized' approach to the 'mentally ill' with the barbarism of the past.

At the close of the nineteenth century, however, the professional status of asylum doctors remained distinctly questionable. Conspicuously mired in the status of salaried employees, and forced to confront and cope with a clientele consisting almost exclusively of the least attractive members of the lower orders of society, they shared with similarly situated groups like workhouse doctors and public health officers at best a tenuous hold on social respectability and but a paltry measure of the autonomy usually granted to those engaged in professional work. Since then, however, practitioners of psychological medicine have, with somewhat more success, laid claim to these standard accoutrements of professional status.

Paradoxically, I suggest that psychiatry's retention of its institutional base in the asylum was of considerable importance in accounting for the long-term improvement in its fortunes. The asylum assured the profession its cognitive monopoly and guaranteed a (captive) market for its services, even though the central mission of institutional psychiatry came to be

20. *Cf.* E. Freidson, *Professional Dominance*, New York: Atheton, 1970, pp. 119–21.

defined as one of quarantining the incurable rather than restoring the temporarily distracted to sanity. Portraying madness as the inevitable and irreversible product of mental degeneration and decay, the outward expression of a morbid constitutional defect, psychiatrists in the late Victorian age could present themselves as providing a social function of inestimable value, the 'sequestration', even the 'violent extrusion' of 'morbid varieties of degenerates of the human kind'.[21]

But if madness was almost wholly resistant to treatment once fully established, this did 'not lead to pessimism and even less to abandoning the will to intervene'. To the contrary, fin-de-siècle psychiatry sought rather 'to shift the point at which this intervention was applied'[22] to an earlier period in the process, to promote prevention, programs of mental hygiene,[23] the treatment of the mildly disordered and still potentially salvageable.[24] Psychiatry now cast about for a place in those arenas where madness might emerge if not forestalled by expert intervention: the family, the school, the factory, the army – all were sites where it offered its services and advice, claiming to have at its disposal the means to secure, as Morel put it, the 'moralization of the masses' through a 'preservative prophylaxis'.[25]

Its hereditarian emphasis brought late nineteenth- and early twentieth-century psychiatry into close relationship with eugenic ideas, and not the least of the 'services' it offered to clients beyond the confines of asylumdom was the provision of advice about who was, and was not, fit to marry. This effort to impose restraints on the profligate breeding of the unfit, and thus, within a generation, to trim the increase in the ranks of the mad, was as successful at stemming the rising tide of insanity as the commands of King Canute on an earlier occasion. The emerging mental hygiene movement sought, with an equal lack of therapeutic success, to forestall mental illness, or to catch it in its incipient stages. But from another perspective, alienists' propaganda about the prevention of mental illness, the promo-

21. Henry Maudsley, *The Pathology of Mind*, London: Macmillan, 1879, p. 115.

22. Robert Castel, *The Regulation of Madness: The Origins of Incarceration in France*, Berkeley: University of California Press, 1988, p. 232.

23. For some discussion of Sir James Crichton-Browne's activities in this arena, see Janet Oppenheim, *'Shattered Nerves': Doctors, Patients, and Depression in Victorian England*, New York: Oxford University Press, 1991, esp. pp. 75–8 and chapter 8. For early advice on mental hygiene, see, for example, Thomas S. Clouston, 'Puberty and Adolescence Medico-Psychologically Considered', *Edinburgh Medical Journal* 26, 1880, pp. 5–17; idem., *The Hygiene of Mind*, London: Methuen, 1906.

24. Bonnie Blustein, 'New York Neurologists and the Specialization of American Medicine', *Bulletin of the History of Medicine* 53, 1979, pp. 170–83; Charles Rosenberg, 'The Place of George M. Beard in Nineteenth Century Psychiatry', *Bulletin of the History of Medicine* 36, 1962, pp. 245–59; Elaine Showalter, *The Female Malady: Women, Madness, and English Culture, 1830–1980*, New York: Pantheon, 1985, pp. 121–64; Jan Goldstein, *Console and Classify: The French Psychiatric Profession in the Nineteenth Century*, Chicago: University of Chicago Press, 1987, pp. 322–77.

25. B.A. Morel, *Traité des dégénérescences physiques, intellectuelles, et morales de l'espèce humaine*, Paris: Masson, 1857, p. 687.

tion of mental health, and the value of treating cases of incipient mental disorder both reflected and reinforced a new receptivity on the profession's part to the still-functioning, though symptom-bearing patient who could form the basis of an office-based practice. Such a development was vital if the profession was to transform the image of mental medicine as over-whelmingly concerned with the institutional custody of a chronically incapacitated and generally economically deprived clientele.

Psychiatry in the twentieth century has thus been operating in the context of a rapid proliferation of the sites and targets of intervention. Outpatient clinics and office-based practices had begun to develop in the last decades of Victoria's reign, as the profession defined and refined new syndromes requiring its services. Whole realms of 'functional' nervous disorders were 'discovered' and efforts made to invest them with a respectable status as genuine disease entities. With characteristic symp-toms as varied as 'sick headache, noises in the ear, atonic voice, deficient mental control, bad dreams, insomnia, nervous dyspepsia, heaviness of loin and limb, flushing and fidgetiness, palpitations, vague pains and flying neuralgia, spinal irritation, uterine irritability, impotence, hopelessness, and such morbid fears as claustrophobia and dread of contamination',[26] the newly defined neuroses promised psychiatrists a large and varied clientele.

The invention of the neuroses was soon followed by a widening series of interventions in the psychiatric management of domestic life. Tradition-ally a profession structurally hamstrung by the extraordinary weakness of its claims to possess special knowledge and capacities, and thus compelled to hold on tightly to the reassuring social power that derived from its autocratic control over asylumdom, psychiatry in the second and third decades of the twentieth century now began to venture forth, and to attempt to capture an ever wider sphere for its ministrations and interven-tions.[27] The psychiatric casualties of war,[28] the management of infancy

26. Barbara Sicherman, 'The Uses of a Diagnosis: Doctors, Patients, and Neurasthenia', *Journal of the History of Medicine and Allied Sciences* 32, 1977, pp. 33–54. For some preliminary discussion of these developments, see Edward Shorter, *From Paralysis to Fatigue: A History of Psychosomatic Illness in the Modern Era*, New York: Free Press, 1992, chapters 9 and 10.

27. See, for example, J. Carswell, 'Some Sociological Considerations Bearing Upon the Occurrence, Prevention, and Treatment of Mental Disorders', *Journal of Mental Science* 70, 1924, pp. 347–62; G.M. Robertson, 'The Prevention of Insanity: A Preliminary Survey of the Problem', *Journal of Mental Science* 72, 1926, pp. 454–91.

28. *Cf.* L.R. Yealland, *Hysterical Disorders of Warfare*, London: Macmillan, 1918; F.W. Mott, *War Neuroses and Shell Shock*, London: Hodder and Stoughton, 1919; C.S. Myers, *Shell-Shock in France 1914–1918*, Cambridge: Cambridge University Press, 1940; Martin Stone, 'Shellshock and the Psychologists', in W.F. Bynum, R. Porter, and M. Shepherd (eds), *The Anatomy of Madness*, Vol. 2, pp. 242–71; Harold Merksey, 'Shell-shock', in G.E. Berrios and H. Freeman (eds), *150 Years of British Psychiatry 1841–1991*, London: Gaskell, 1991, pp. 245–67; Elaine Showalter, *The Female Malady*, chapter 7.

and childhood (and particularly of delinquent childhood),[29] alcoholism and other forms of intemperance and excess, marital disharmony and divorce, the alienation of the industrial workforce,[30] the translation of these and other moral problems and disturbances not readily susceptible to legal sanctions and intervention into technical, medicalized conditions provided psychiatry with what was potentially a greatly expanded territory within which to practice.[31] A widening array of forms of deviance came to be systematized within an orderly framework, and in reducing them to a medical paradigm, an attempt was made to reconstitute them as conditions 'completely emptied of moral significance'.[32]

The advent of psychoanalysis, at first merely one among several competing forms of psychotherapeutics with which the profession experimented,[33] played a not insignificant role in these developments, though its influence in Britain was clearly more limited than it turned out to be in North America.[34] Quite obviously, the Freudian system possessed some extraordinary virtues as a professional ideology. It had the great merit of being non-testable, and hence non-refutable; and, like Marxism, it lent itself to simplification for the simple and sophistication for the sophisticated. Requiring prolonged and costly training, it developed in its devotees a presumptive expertise which readily justified the rejection of

29. Cf. Thomas Smith Clouston, The Neuroses of Development: Being the Morison Lectures for 1890, Edinburgh: Oliver and Boyd, 1891; Leonard G. Guthrie, Functional Nervous Disorders in Childhood, London: Oxford University Press, 1907; H.V. Dicks, 50 Years of the Tavistock Clinic, London: Routledge and Kegan Paul, 1970; J.G. Howells and M.L. Osborn, 'The History of Child Psychiatry in Britain', Acta Paedopsychiatrica 46, 1980, pp. 193–202; and, for very different assessments, Peter Miller and Nikolas Rose, 'The Tavistock Programme: The Government of Subjectivity and Social Life', Sociology 22, 1988, pp. 171–92; and Nikolas Rose, The Psychological Complex: Psychology, Politics, and Society in England, 1869–1939, London: Routledge and Kegan Paul, 1985, pp. 197–209.

30. Martin Stone, 'The Military and Industrial Roots of Clinical Psychology in Britain, 1900–1945', unpublished Ph.D. dissertation, London School of Economics and Political Science, 1985.

31. For general discussions of these developments, see Nicholas Kittrie, The Right to be Different: Deviance and Enforced Therapy, Baltimore: Johns Hopkins University Press, 1972; Peter Miller, 'The Territory of the Psychiatrist', Ideology and Consciousness 7, 1980, pp. 63–106; F. Castel, R. Castel, and A. Lovell, La Société psychiatrique avancée, Paris: Editions Grasset, 1979, translated as The Psychiatric Society, New York: Columbia University Press, 1982; and David Armstrong, 'Madness and Coping', Sociology of Health and Illness 2, 1980, pp. 293–316.

32. David Ingleby, 'Mental Health and Social Order', in S. Cohen and A. Scull (eds), Social Control and the State: Historical and Comparative Essays, Oxford: Martin Robertson, 1983, p. 162. For an early discussion of the growing role of medicine in the enforcement of moral norms, cf. I.K. Zola, 'Medicine as an Institution of Social Control', The Sociological Review 20, 1972, pp. 487–504.

33. See Andrew Scull, 'The Social History of Psychiatry in the Victorian Era', in A. Scull (ed.), Madhouses, Mad-doctors, and Madmen: The Social History of Psychiatry in the Victorian Era, Philadelphia: University of Pennsylvania Press/London: Athlone, 1981, pp. 21–3; R.D. Hinshelwood, 'Psychodynamic Psychiatry Before World War I', in G.E. Berrios and H. Freeman (eds), 150 Years of British Psychiatry 1841–1991, pp. 198–200.

34. For a preliminary survey, see Malcolm Pines, 'The Development of the Psychodynamic Movement', in G.E. Berrios and H. Freeman (eds), 150 Years of British Psychiatry 1841–1991, pp. 206–31.

outside, non-professional interference – a dogma which even provided an 'explanation' of why such 'irrational' resistance to its method should arise in the first place, thus discrediting its critics while protecting itself from the dangerous task of actually having to supply substantive answers to the objections they might raise. It provided, as early American converts proclaimed, an elaborate technology of treatment, 'certain definite methods of procedure of a rational sort',[35] which could underpin and give substance to an outpatient practice, a psychotherapeutics which its practitioners solemnly compared to 'a surgical operation of the most delicate sort'.[36] And perhaps most attractive of all, Freud's system 'made sense' of a whole range of phenomena previously left outside the realm of systematic observation, and in the process created 'understandable order out of chaos'.[37]

While obviously impractical in an asylum context (save, perhaps, as ideological window-dressing), psychoanalysis offered much greater potential when applied to the development of the new realm of office practice. In this arena, coping with upper-class neurotics, psychiatrists might reasonably hope to dilute the ill-effects of institutional practice, especially the resulting overly close association with the poor, the stigmatized, and the unwanted, on the profession's public image and standing; and, in ministering to well-heeled 'nervous' cases, to establish its credentials with the elite as a doubly worthy enterprise. In the United States, this was indeed the most common outcome, and psychoanalysts during the middle third of the century came to occupy the commanding heights of the profession.[38]

In Britain, however, a similar psychoanalytic dominance never came to pass. The Maudsley Hospital under its first superintendent, Edward

35. Nathan G. Hale, Jr, *Freud and the Americans*, New York: Oxford University Press, 1971, p. 48.
36. James Jackson Putnam, 'Discussion of Edward Wyllys Taylor, "The Attitude of the Medical Profession Toward the Psychotherapeutic Movement"', *Journal of Nervous and Mental Diseases* 35, 1908, p. 411.
37. N.G. Hale, Jr, *Freud and the Americans*, p. 48. This was an ideological accomplishment of extraordinary significance and power. For madness is fundamentally behaviour too unintelligible to be accorded the status of human action, and psychoanalysis now provided accounts, constructable only by experts, which replaced commonsense judgements that something was 'irrational', literally did not make sense, with interpretations that were at once remarkably systematic, symbolically highly elaborated, and – once its premises were granted – both plausible and internally coherent.
38. Gerald Grob discusses the shift of American psychiatry's centre of gravity away from the dismal, despised, and depressing institutional sector in *Mental Illness and American Psychiatry, 1875–1940*, Princeton: Princeton University Press, 1983, esp. pp. 179–200, 234–322; and the increasing dominance of psychodynamic and psychoanalytically-oriented psychiatry from the 1940s until the late 1960s and early 1970s in *From Asylum to Community: Mental Health Policy in Modern America*, Princeton: Princeton University Press, 1991, pp. 292–301. Also useful are Andrew Abbott, 'The Emergence of American Psychiatry', unpublished Ph.D. dissertation, University of Chicago, 1982, esp. pp. 324–30; and idem., *The System of Professions: An Essay on the Division of Expert Labor*, Chicago: University of Chicago Press, 1988, pp. 280–314.

Mapother, rapidly emerged as the political centre of British psychiatry.[39] Quite deliberately, he used its political muscle to ensure that its chief potential rival and a major institutional focus of the emerging psycho-dynamic and psychoanalytically influenced community, the Tavistock Clinic, received no academic recognition, most especially no compet-ing affiliation with the University of London; and, as important, that it obtained no financial support from the public purse.[40] For public con-sumption, Mapother expressed an interest in undertaking an 'unprejudiced trial of every form of treatment'; but his confession in the same document that 'I find myself incapable of excepting [sic!] all the alleged facts of any school of psychoanalysis'[41] correctly suggests the rather different stance he and the institution he headed exhibited in practice.

To be sure, the traumatic impact of the mass epidemic of shell-shock cases had shaken the credibility and the self-confidence of the psychiatric establishment, so that the sort of open hostility and disdain common before the Great War[42] was now replaced by more soothing language and less transparently intemperate criticism. And certainly, the number of converts to some version of psychoanalysis had been swollen by the impact of the wartime experience, with its regiments of broken men apparently lacking any organic damage to their nervous systems. The mainstream of the profession, however, continued to keep its distance

39. Cf. Aubrey Lewis, 'Edward Mapother and the Making of the Maudsley Hospital', British Journal of Psychiatry 115, 1969, pp. 1344–66; Patricia Allderidge, 'The Foundation of the Maudsley Hospital', in G.E. Berrios and H. Freeman (eds), 150 Years of British Psychiatry 1841–1991, pp. 87–8.

40. I rely here on the accounts in H.V. Dicks, 50 Years of the Tavistock Clinic, esp. pp. 60–3, and in Aubrey Lewis, 'Edward Mapother and the Makings of the Maudsley Hospital'. The Maudsley, of course, enjoyed the enormous advantage of both this secure source of financial support and its monopolistic ties to the University.

41. Maudsley Hospital, unpublished annual report for 1923, quoted in Malcolm Pines, 'The Development of the Psychodynamic Movement', p. 225.

42. The resistance in these years was led by Allbutt and, more vociferously, by Mercier, both of whom objected to the psychoanalytic tendency to encourage 'men and women to wallow in the very miseries that obsessed them. It either dredged up recollections that were better left buried or allowed the doctor's potent suggestions to create alleged memories that tormented patients more cruelly than their own thoughts ever did.' Janet Oppenheim, 'Shattered Nerves', p. 307. See, for instance, T.C. Allbutt, 'Neurasthenia', in T.C. Allbutt and H.D. Rolleston (eds), A System of Medicine, 2nd edn, London: Macmillan, 1911, Vol. 8, pp. 727–91; and Charles Mercier, A Text-Book of Insanity and Other Mental Diseases, 2nd edn, London: Allen and Unwin, 1914. Compare also Sir James Crichton-Browne's contention that 'in a vast majority of cases it should be the aim of a rational psycho-therapy to withdraw the patient's mind from the contemplation of an objectionable and painful past and from ferreting out verminous reminiscences, and to occupy it with prospective duties and wholesome pursuits, and sure and certain hopes.' What the Doctor Thought, London: Benn, 1930, p. 228. Such attitudes were widespread in the medical profession as a whole, as was demonstrated most vividly in 1911, when David Eder and Ernest Jones addressed the British Medical Association on psychoanalysis. Before their papers could be discussed, the entire audience expressed their outrage by walking out. See J.B. Hobman, David Eder: Memoirs of a Modern Pioneer, London: Gollancz, 1945, p. 89; Ernest Jones, The Life and Work of Sigmund Freud, abridged edn, Harmondsworth: Penguin, 1974, p. 365.

from an approach which failed to correspond with what ordinarily passed for scientific medicine.[43] They preferred instead an eclecticism of a singularly atheoretical sort, justified, when and if such intellectual rationalizations were ultimately unavoidable, by reference to the almost wilfully obscure convolutions of Adolf Meyer's 'psychobiology'.[44]

3. Community Treatment

The state-supported network of mental hospitals, the second major legacy of the nineteenth-century reform movement, has met with a decidedly mixed fate in our own century. Until the 1950s, the institutional response remained the dominant approach to the problems posed by the mentally ill. The pattern of consistent year-by-year increases in the number of inmates confined in mental hospitals, so noticeable a feature of the nineteenth-century asylum system, persisted almost unchanged until 1954. And for most of the time since then, mental hospital admissions have continued to rise quite sharply, keeping the now decrepit nineteenth-century structures in constant use. Nevertheless, this latter period has witnessed a major departure from historical precedent, a reversal of the remorseless secular increase in the size of the mental hospital population. In the face of a century-and-a-half-old trend in precisely the opposite direction, the number of patients resident in English mental hospitals has fallen sharply, from 148,000 in 1954 to fewer than 60,000 three and a half decades later. Still more abrupt has been the mental hospitals' decline from official favour, to the point where they are now written off as 'doomed institutions', to be run down and closed within the foreseeable future. Under mounting attack because of their negative effects on those they treat, segregative techniques in their traditional form are now steadily losing ground to newer 'community-based' alternatives.

Madness seems to attract more than its share of myths. In the nineteenth century, the myth of the Noble Savage – free from the stress, the

---

43. On the roots of the persistent British suspicion of psychological accounts of mental disorder, cf. Michael Clark, 'The Rejection of Psychological Approaches to Mental Disorder', in A. Scull (ed.), *Madhouses, Mad-doctors and Madmen*, pp. 271–312. The sectarianism of psychoanalysis, as evident in Britain as elsewhere, cannot have helped its cause. Ernest Jones, for instance, used whatever authority he could muster to forbid 'orthodox' analysts to work at the Tavistock Clinic (see Malcolm Pines, 'The Development of the Psychodynamic Movement', p. 224), and the vicious infighting between the Kleinians and the Anna Freudians at times almost paralysed the British Psycho-Analytical Society in the 1930s and 1940s. For some less than disinterested commentary on the latter squabbles, see Judith Hughes, *Reshaping the Psycho-Analytic Domain: The Work of Melanie Klein, W.R.D. Fairbairn, and D.W. Winnicott*, Berkeley: University of California Press, 1989, esp. chapter 1; and Phyllis Grosskurth, *Melanie Klein: Her World and Her Work*, New York: Knopf, 1986, Parts 2, 3, and 4.
44. See Michael Gelder, 'Adolf Meyer and his Influence on British Psychiatry', in G.E. Berrios and H. Freeman (eds), *150 Years of British Psychiatry, 1841–1991*, pp. 419–35.

artificiality, the vices of modern life (and thus free from the insanity which was part of the price of civilization) – was given a widespread currency. The propagation of such a notion had obvious value for those bent on reforming the treatment of lunatics and bringing them the benefits of modern science; for only the adoption of their programme of a network of specially designed, medically run asylums could hope to stem the rising tide of madness with which the advance of civilization threatened Victorian England. The contemporary equivalent of the Noble Savage (in some intellectual circles at least) seems to be a mythical pre-institutional Golden Age, when the population at large enjoyed the blessings of living in 'communities' – an innocent rustic society, uncorrupted by the evils of bureaucracy, where neighbour helped neighbour and families gladly ministered to the needs of their own troublesome members, while a benevolent squirearchy looked on, always ready to lend a helping hand. Once again, a myth has had its uses for those bent on changing social policy, this time providing a counterpoint to a mass of social scientific research on the mental hospital which amounts to a full-blown assault on its therapeutic failings.[45] For such people, lunacy reform is seen as simply one colossal mistake.

Certainly, there is much in what I have said about the nineteenth-century asylum which can but serve as grist for their mill. But realism about the awfulness of asylum existence ought not to prompt us to opt for a blind faith in the virtues of its presumed antithesis. One can – indeed, I think must – be deeply sceptical about claims made on the mental hospital's behalf: yet one must not fall prey to equally groundless fantasies and illusions about the available alternatives. If one were to believe the devotees of the contemporary cult of the community, if we would only bring the mentally disturbed back into our midst, not only would we avoid the isolating and labelling effects of commitment to an institution, but 'by enlisting the good will and the desire to serve, the ability to understand which is found in every neighbourhood, we shall meet the challenge which such groups of persons present . . .'. Apparently, what is needed is a return to

> a simpler time not so very long ago . . . when the problems of the mentally retarded and disturbed, the aged and the troubled young, were dealt with in the communities where each of these people lived. A greater continuity or integration of the entire age spectrum seems

45. For example, Erving Goffman, *Asylums*, Garden City, New York: Doubleday, 1961 (London, Penguin, 1970); William Caudill, *The Psychiatric Hospital as a Small Society*, Cambridge, Massachusetts: Harvard University Press, 1958; Ivan Belknap, *Human Problems of a State Mental Hospital*, New York: McGraw Hill, 1956; Robert Perrucci, *Circle of Madness*.
46. B. Alper, foreword to Y. Bakal (ed.), *Closing Correctional Institutions*, Lexington, Massachusetts: Lexington Books, 1973, pp. vii–viii.

to have prevailed in those days:... and those who were deficient in intelligence or emotional balance were not only tolerated but accommodated.[46]

We may reasonably doubt whether such idylls existed in seventeenth- or eighteenth-century England, the Paradise presumably Lost when the insane were consigned to the asylum. The available evidence on the treatment accorded the insane in the community in this period is sketchy and inadequate, a situation complicated by the then prevalent failure to distinguish at all carefully between the mad and other deviant and dependent groups. Nevertheless, what we do know of the treatment either of the clearly frenzied or of problematic people in general lends little support to such romantic speculations. Nor should this come as a surprise, given what we know of the general tenor of eighteenth-century English social life, particularly, though not exclusively, among the lower orders. Even among their 'betters' the widespread credence given to the idea of the continuity of all forms of creation, including man, in the imperceptible gradations of a single great chain of being brought with it a ready acceptance of the notion that some men were indistinguishable from brutes – an easy equation between apes and savages, and between apes and men lacking in 'reason'.[47] And what we know of the treatment of brutes in this period scarcely inspires confidence about the treatment of human beings equated with them.[48]

Nor have recent experiences with 'community treatment' proved much of an advertisement for its virtues. Cutting through the clouds of rhetoric and wishful thinking with which the subject abounds, it is apparent that the whole policy was undertaken with little prior investigation of its likely effects, and that even now we lack 'substantiation that community care is advantageous for clients'.[49] While the acutely disturbed continue to receive some attention, frequently being dealt with through short-term hospitalization, this contrasts 'with a second class service, or no service at all, for the chronic patient'.[50] Many of those expelled from mental hospitals become lost in the interstices of social life, and turn into drifting inhabitants of those traditional resorts of the down and out, Salvation Army hostels, settlement houses, and so on. In those cases where families have attempted to deal with members discharged from mental hospitals,

47. See the discussion in W.F. Bynum, 'Time's Noblest Offspring: The Problem of Man in the British Natural Historical Sciences', unpublished Ph.D. dissertation, Cambridge University, 1974. The seminal work on this belief system is A.O. Lovejoy's *The Great Chain of Being*, New York: Harper, 1960.
48. On the treatment of animals, and the gradual development of heightened sensibilities about cruelty towards them, *cf.* Keith Thomas, *Man and the Natural World: Changing Attitudes in England 1500–1800*, London: Allen Lane, 1983, esp. chapters 3 and 4.
49. J. and E. Wolpert, 'The Relocation of Released Mental Hospital Patients into Residential Communities', *Policy Sciences*, Spring 1976. The following paragraphs draw upon my *Decarceration: Community Treatment and the Deviant – A Radical View*.
50. J.K. Wing, 'How Many Psychiatric Beds?' *Psychological Medicine* 1, 1971, p. 190.

they have frequently experienced severe difficulties in coping – indeed, they have only been induced to do so by the authorities' persistent refusal to accede to their requests for rehospitalization.[51]

In the United States, where the non-institutional approach has been pursued still more vigorously than in England, such outcomes would seem relatively benign. There, for thousands of the old already suffering from mental confusion and deterioration, the new policy has meant premature death.[52] For others, it has meant that they have been left to rot and decay, physically and otherwise, in broken-down welfare hostels or in what are termed, with Orwellian euphemism, 'personal-care' nursing homes. For thousands of younger psychotics discharged into the streets, it has meant a nightmare existence in blighted city centres, amidst neighbourhoods crowded with prostitutes, ex-felons, addicts, alcoholics, and the other human rejects now repressively tolerated by their society. Here they eke out a precarious existence, supported by welfare cheques they may not even know how to cash. They spend their days locked into or out of dilapidated 'community-based' boarding houses. And they find themselves alternatively the prey of street criminals, and a source of nuisance and alarm to those 'normal' residents of the neighbourhood too poverty-stricken to leave. All in all, it is difficult to avoid the conclusion that 'in the absence of aftercare and rehabilitation services, the term "community care" [remains] . . . merely an inflated catch phrase, which conceal[s] morbidity in the patients and distress in the relatives'.[53] And yet the massive reassignment of patients continues, apparently heedless of the predictable consequences.

4. The Therapeutic State?

Psychiatrists, and other social control experts for that matter, negotiate reality on behalf of the rest of society. Theirs is preeminently a moral enterprise, involved with the creation and application of social meanings to particular segments of everyday life. Just like physicians, they may be said to be engaged 'in the creation of illness as a social state which a human being may assume'.[54] Indeed, in view of the indefinite criteria employed to identify and define 'mental illness', its status as a socially constructed reality is, if anything, plainer than in the case of somatic illness, and the latitude granted the expert correspondingly wide. I would argue that for all the psychiatric professions's claims (and their complex verbal gymnastics notwithstanding), the boundary between the normal and the

51. G. Brown, M. Bone, B. Dalison, and J.K. Wing, *Schizophrenia and Social Care*, London: Oxford University Press, 1966, chapters 3 and 5, esp. pp. 51ff.
52. See R. Marlowe, 'When They Closed the Doors at Modesto', in *Where is my Home?* mimeo, Scottdale, Arizona: NTIS, 1974, pp. 110–24; J. and E. Wolpert, 'The Relocation of Released Mental Hospital Patients into Residential Communities'.
53. G. Brown, M. Bone, J. Dalison, and J.K. Wing, *Schizophrenia and Social Care*, p. 10.
54. E. Freidson, *Profession of Medicine*, New York: Dodd, Mead, 1970, p. 205.

pathological remains vague and indeterminate, and mental illness, partly as a consequence, an amorphous, all-embracing concept. Under such conditions, there exists no finite universe of 'crazy people', and the process of identifying who is and who is not to be defined as insane cannot, in the nature of things, be an activity governed by some objective, uniform, and unchanging standard.

I have suggested here how important this theoretical indeterminateness of the concept of insanity was in the nineteenth century, with the boundaries of mental disturbance stretched to encompass all manner of difficult, decrepit, socially inept, incompetent, and superfluous people, as well as victims of a whole spectrum of physical pathologies later assigned to a different ontological status (that of 'real' physical illness). It has proved equally significant in this century. As the psychiatric profession has advanced its social status and as it has succeeded in persuading a wider public to take seriously its claims to possess an expertise resting upon a scientific basis, so the psychiatric view of deviance has had a steadily growing influence on public policy. At least since the end of the Second World War, we have been moving to some degree away from a punitive and towards what Kittrie has termed a therapeutic state; that is, one which enshrines the psychiatric world view. Just as in 'the eighteenth and nineteenth centuries, a host of phenomena – never before conceptualized in medical terms – were renamed or reclassified as mental illness',[55] so in the present still other forms of deviance are being assimilated to a quasi-medical model, being relabelled as illness, and so 'treated' rather than punished.[56]

With sardonic wit and much insight, Peter Sedgwick has proclaimed that 'the future belongs to illness . . .', as the range of conditions subject to medical control and intervention is expanded, generating pressures to redefine various behaviours 'into medical (and thus controllable) pathologies'.[57] As I have demonstrated here at some length, such expansion is not necessarily tied to success; nor is the arena of medical action limited to those pathologies where its intervention is demonstrably efficacious. Those who benefit most from the existing social order are for obvious reasons attracted by an explanatory schema which locates the source of the pathology in intra-individual forces, and which allows the redefinition of all protest and deviation from the dominant social order in such individualistic and pathological terms. Not least, psychiatry is appealing because it masks the necessarily evaluative dimension of its activities behind a screen of scientific objectivity and neutrality. It was and is, therefore, of great potential value in legitimizing and depoliticizing

55. Thomas Szasz, *The Manufacture of Madness*, p. 137.
56. See Nicholas Kittrie, *The Right to be Different*, Baltimore: Johns Hopkins University Press, 1971; I.K. Zola, 'Medicine as an Institution of Social Control', *The Sociological Review* 20, 1972, pp. 487–504.
57. Peter Sedgwick, 'Mental Illness Is Illness', *Salmagundi* 20, 1972, p. 220.

efforts to regulate social life and to keep the recalcitrant and socially disruptive in line.

On the other hand, in stressing the substantial expansion that has taken place in psychiatry's jurisdiction, and the even greater potential for intervention in daily life that is implicit in the therapeutic approach, one must not get carried away. Strong countervailing forces exist, which to some extent hold these tendencies towards psychiatric imperialism in check. One obvious source of difficulty for psychiatry and its allied professions has been the continuing intellectual vulnerabilities of their cognitive claims, and the practical deficiencies of the remedies on offer. The opposite concern, however – the persistent disquiet aroused in many quarters on contemplating the implications of an approach which threatens to equate any deviation from conventional moral and social standards with illness, and to impose compulsory treatment – has also placed significant constraints on psychiatric expansionism.[58] Finally, psychiatry operates within a larger matrix of contending professions, each jealous of any attempt to seize portions of its jurisdiction.[59]

Thus, in the twilight of asylumdom, the profession to which these institutions gave birth still endures, constantly seeking to assure us of the benevolence and rationality of its interventions even as it attempts to lay claim to an ever-widening sphere of social life. Ironically enough, it has employed the 'miracles' of modern psychopharmacology – the phenothiazines, lithium, the anti-depressants – to reduce its involvement with the impoverished and clinically hopeless clientele which used to throng mental hospital wards to the occasional prescription of psycho-active drugs, preferably to be dispensed by others, a thin veneer of con-tinuing medical attention to the miseries of the mad in which profession and public can nevertheless take comfort. Simultaneously, however, and alongside the psychotherapeutic techniques which first allowed the spread

58. The polemical assaults of Thomas Szasz and Nicholas Kittrie are only the latest manifestations of a long history of spasms of public anxiety on this score. See, for nineteenth-century examples, Peter McCandless, 'Liberty and Lunacy: The Victorians and Wrongful Confinement', in A. Scull (ed.), *Madhouses, Mad-Doctors, and Madmen*, pp. 339–62; and Nicholas Hervey, 'Advocacy or Folly: The Alleged Lunatics' Friends Society', *Medical History* 30, 1986, pp. 254–75.

59. *Cf.* Andrew Abbott, *The System of Professions*. Lawyers, in particular, have a highly developed sense of turf, and the social power and cultural authority to offer a vigorous defense of their territory. Some psychiatrists, pushing their deterministic universe of discourse to its limits, have on occasion been rash enough to extend their imperial claims to encompass all forms of criminality, threatening to substitute pathology for sin, determinism for free will, treatment for punishment. Such efforts have tended to provoke sharply adversarial responses from the legal profession, whose traditional mandate to control crime has the distinct advantage of being rooted in a commonsense schema wherein will or intention and the voluntary basis of action assume a central place. Discretion being the better part of valour, and neither principle of social regulation being fully capable of vanquishing the other, both professions have more usually adopted a policy of conceding the other's heartland. Jurisdictional disputes thus only occur at the margin, where they take on a ritualized, if symbolically charged character.

of its jurisdiction beyond the asylum, the new drugs mean that psychiatry can now proffer a new treatment technology, adaptable without strain to the general hospital, the outpatient clinic, and the consulting room. And in modern psychopharmacology it has found a form of treatment which is unambiguously and indisputably the monopoly of the medically trained, thereby furnishing a decisive means of recementing the profession's jurisdictional claims to the value-free realm of medical science.

Bibliography

Manuscript Sources

Ashbrooke Hall Licensed House, Visitors' and Patients' Book, East Sussex Record Office, Lewes, QAL/1/5/E5.

Ashley, Lord (7th Earl of Shaftesbury), Diaries, SHA/PD/3–6, National Register of Archives.

Bedfordshire County Asylum Minute Books, 1812–22, 1822–35, 1835–44, 1844–9, Bedfordshire Record Office, LB 1/1, LB 1/2, LB 1/3, LB 1/4.

Bedfordshire County Asylum, Minutes of Visitors, Bedfordshire Record Office, LB 1/8.

Bedfordshire County Asylum, Miscellaneous Papers, 1812–30, Bedfordshire County Record Office, LBP 1.

Bedfordshire County Asylum, Reports of the Visitors and Chaplain, 1830–52, LB 2/1.

Brougham Papers, University College London Library.

Buckinghamshire County Asylum, Visitors' Book, 1853–1918, Hospital Archives, St. John's Hospital, Stone, Bucks.

Buckinghamshire County Asylum, Superintendent's Diary, 2 vols, 1853–6 and 1856–79, Hospital Archives, St. John's Hospital, Stone, Buckinghamshire.

Camberwell House Asylum, Casebooks 1845–6, Wellcome Institute for the History of Medicine, London.

Caterham Metropolitan District Asylum, Minutes, 1868–1886, MAB/243–252, Greater London Record Office.

Caterham Metropolitan District Asylum, Miscellaneous Correspondence and Papers, 1867–1905, MAB/284, Greater London Record Office.

Caterham Metropolitan District Asylum, Annual Reports of the Medical Superintendent, 1872–85, MAB/2281–2292, Greater London Record Office.

Colney Hatch County Asylum, Annual Reports of the Committee of Visitors and Superintendent, 1847–89, MA/RS/1/53–102, Greater London Record Office.

Colney Hatch County Asylum, Minute Book, 1847–85, H12/CH/A1.1–43, Greater London Record Office.

Hanwell County Asylum, Visiting Justices' Minutes for the Middlesex Lunatic Asylum, Volume 1, 1827–9, MA/A/J1; Volume 2, 1829–31, MA/A/J2, Greater London Record Office.

Hanwell County Asylum, Reports of the Visiting Justices, 1831–9, MJ/OC, Greater London Record Office.

Leavesden Metropolitan District Asylum, Annual Reports of the Medical Superintendent, 1876, 1879, 1882–5, MAB/2395–2400, Greater London Record Office.

Manor House Chiswick Male Casebook, 1884–91, Wellcome Institute for the History of Medicine, London.

Manor House Chiswick Female Case Book, 1884–93, Wellcome Institute for the History of Medicine, London.

Northampton County Lunatic Asylum, Minute Books of the Committee of Visitors, St. Crispin's Hospital Archives, Berrywood.

Northampton County Lunatic Asylum, Miscellaneous Documents, Letters, and Newspaper Clippings Relating to the History of St. Crispin's Hospital, Hospital Archives, Berrywood.

Parkes Weber, Frederick, Private Casebooks, Contemporary Medical Archives, Wellcome Institute for the History of Medicine, London.

Ringmer Asylum Visitors' Book, 1846–7, East Sussex Record Office, Lewes, QAL 1/4/3.

St. George's Retreat Asylum, Visitors' Reports, 1870–92, East Sussex Record Office, Lewes, QAL 1/5/2.

St. Luke's Hospital, Considerations upon the usefulness and necessity of establishing an Hospital as a further provision for poor Lunaticks, manuscript dated 1750, St. Luke's Woodside Hospital, London.

St. Luke's Hospital, General Committee Minutes, St. Luke's Hospital, Woodside, London.

St. Luke's Hospital, Visitors' Book 1829–94, St. Luke's Hospital, Woodside, London.

St. Luke's Hospital, House Committee Visiting Book, 1883–1900, St. Luke's Hospital, Woodside, London.

Society for the Diffusion of Useful Knowledge, Correspondence, University College London Library.

Sussex County Asylum, Correspondence between the Lunacy Commissioners and the Secretary of State, and the Quarter Sessions, East Sussex Record Office, Lewes (QAL 2/3/6).

Sussex County Asylum, Memorial from the Parish of Brighthelmston, Sussex, Concerning the Proposed County Asylum, 1845, East Sussex Record Office, Lewes, QAL 2/3/6.

Sussex County Asylum, Memorials Against the Establishment of a County Asylum, East Sussex Record Office, Lewes, QAL/2/6.

Ticehurst Asylum Visitors' Book, East Sussex Record Office, Lewes QAL 1/5/1, 2.

Ticehurst Asylum Miscellaneous Papers, 2 bundles, 1829–37, East Sussex Record Office, Lewes QAL 1/1/1.

Ticehurst Asylum Medical Journal and Visitors' Reports, 1843–65, East Sussex Record Office, Lewes QAL 1/2/2.

Ticehurst Asylum Registers of Patients Resident in 1830 and 1832, East Sussex Record Office, Lewes QAL 1/3/7.

Ticehurst Asylum Casebooks, 1845–1914, and Patients Bill Book, 1901–8, Contemporary Medical Archives, Wellcome Institute for the History of Medicine, London.

Warneford Asylum Ancient Book, Lunatic Asylum General and Special Meetings from 3 December 1812 to 10 April 1824, Warneford Hospital Archives.

Warneford Asylum, Memoranda Relating to the Origin, Progress and Completion of the Oxford Lunatic Asylum, 3 December 1812 to 28 June 1826, Warneford Hospital Archives.

Warneford Asylum, Building Committee Minutes, 2 July 1821–28 June 1826, Warneford Hospital Archives.

Warneford Asylum Patients' Book, 1845–1909, Warneford Hospital Archives.

Wiltshire County Asylum Visitors' Book, 1876–87, Roundway Mental Hospital Archives, Devizes.

Wiltshire County Asylum Case Books 1851–70, Roundway Mental Hospital Archives, Devizes.

York Retreat Visitors' Book, 1798–1822, Borthwick Institute of Historical Research, York, D/3/1.

Asylum Reports

Buckinghamshire County Asylum, *Annual Reports*, 1854–90.

Caterham Metropolitan Lunatic Asylum, *Annual Reports*, 1872–85.

Colney Hatch Asylum, *Annual Reports*, 1851–90.

Crichton Royal Asylum, *Annual Reports*, 1840–60.

Derby County Asylum, *Annual Reports*, 1852–70.

Hanwell Lunatic Asylum, *Annual Reports*, 1831–90.

Lancaster Lunatic Asylum, *Annual Reports*, 1841–5.

Leavesden Metropolitan Lunatic Asylum, *Annual Reports*, 1876–85.

Lincoln Lunatic Asylum, *Annual Reports*, 1845–50.

Littlemore County Asylum, *Annual Reports*, 1847–90.

Manchester Royal Lunatic Asylum, *Annual Reports*, 1860–3.

Middlesex County Asylum, Banstead, *Annual Reports*, 1877–90.

Northampton County Asylum, *Annual Reports*, 1870–90.

Northampton General Lunatic Asylum, *Annual Reports*, 1839–90.

St. Luke's Asylum, *Annual Reports*, 1830, 1851–90.

Suffolk County Asylum, *Annual Reports*, 1846–50.

Surrey County Asylum, *Annual Reports*, 1845–60.

Wakefield Lunatic Asylum, *Annual Reports*, 1817–45.

Warneford Asylum, *Annual Reports*, 1813–96.

Parliamentary Reports, Official Reports, Etc.

Commissioners in Lunacy, *Annual Reports*, 1846–98.

Commissioners in Lunacy, *Report of the Commissioners in Lunacy Relative to the Haydock Lodge Lunatic Asylum*, London, 1847.

Commissioners in Lunacy, *Report as to the State of Management of Bethlem Hospital, and of All Correspondence Thereon*, House of Commons Sessional Papers, 49, 1852–1853.

Hansard's *Parliamentary Debates*.

The History, Debates, and Proceedings of both Houses of Parliament of Great Britain from the Year 1743 to the Year 1774, London: Debrett, 1792.

House of Commons, *Report of the Select Committee on the State of Criminal and Pauper Lunatics,* 1807.

House of Commons, *Reports of the Select Committee on Madhouses,* 1815–16.

House of Commons, *Report from the Select Committee on Pauper Lunatics in the County of Middlesex, and on Lunatic Asylums,* 1827.

House of Commons, *Report from the Select Committee on Hereford Lunatic Asylum, with Minutes of Evidence,* 1839.

House of Commons, *Reports of the Select Committee on the Care and Treatment of Lunatics,* 1859–60.

House of Commons, *Report of the Select Committee on the Operation of the Lunacy Law, So Far as It Regards Security Afforded by It Against Violations of Personal Liberty,* 1877.

House of Lords, *Minutes of Evidence taken before the Select Committee of the House of Lords on the Bills Relating to Lunatics and Lunatic Asylums,* 1828.

Metropolitan Commissioners in Lunacy, *Reports for 1830, 1835–41.*

Metropolitan Commissioners in Lunacy, *Report of the Metropolitan Commissioners in Lunacy to the Lord Chancellor,* London: Bradbury and Evans, 1844.

Report of the Poor Law Commission of 1834, Harmondsworth: Penguin, 1971.

Books

Abbott, Andrew, *The System of Professions: An Essay on the Division of Expert Labor,* Chicago: University of Chicago Press, 1988.

Aikin, John, *Thoughts on Hospitals,* London: Johnson, 1771.

Allbutt, T.C. and H.D. Rolleston (eds) *A System of Medicine,* 2nd edition, London: Macmillan, 1905–11.

Allen, Matthew, *Essay on the Classification of the Insane,* London: Taylor, 1837.

Allen, Matthew, *Cases of Insanity, with Medical, Moral and Philosophical Observations Upon Them,* London: Swire, 1831.

Anderson, Michael, *Family Structure in Nineteenth Century Lancashire,* Cambridge: Cambridge University Press, 1971.

Anderson, Perry, *Lineages of the Absolutist State,* London: New Left Books, 1974.

Anonymous, *A Short Account of the Rise, Progress, and Present State of the Lunatic Asylum at Edinburgh,* Edinburgh: Neill, 1812.

Anonymous, *A Scheme of an Institution, and a Description of a Plan, for a General Lunatic Asylum, for the Western Counties, to Be Built in or Near the City of Glocester,* [Gloucester]: Raikes, 1794.

Anonymous, *Some Particulars of the Royal Indisposition of 1788 to 1789, and of Its Effects Upon Illustrious Personages and Opposite Parties Interested by It,* London: Taylor, 1804.

Anonymous, *Lunatick Asylums: An Essay,* Rugby: n.p., 1898.

Anonymous, *Life in a Lunatic Asylum: An Autobiographical Sketch,* London: Houlston and Wright, 1867.

Anonymous, *Views of Messrs. Newington's Private Asylum for the Cure of Insane Persons, Ticehurst, Sussex,* n.p., c. 1829.

Anonymous, *Some Thoughts Concerning the Maintenance of the Poor in a Letter to a Member of Parliament*, London: Goodwin, 1700.

Anonymous, *Insanity*, London: Underwood, 1817.

Anonymous, *On the Present State of Lunatic Asylums*, London: Drury, 1839.

Anonymous, *Proposals for Redressing Some Grievances Which Greatly Affect the Whole Nation*, London: Johnson, 1740.

Anonymous, *An Appendix to a Book Lately Published, Entitled, 'Incontestable Proofs, etc., etc.' (in which the Publications of Mr. Higgins and Others on the York Lunatic Asylum Are Not Sparingly Criticised)*, York: Storry, 1818.

Arlidge, John, *On the State of Lunacy and the Legal Provision for the Insane*, London: Churchill, 1859.

Arnold, Thomas, *Observations on the Nature, Kinds, Causes, and Prevention of Insanity*, 2 vols, Leicester: Robinson and Caddell, 1782–6.

Arnold, Thomas, *Observations on the Nature, Kinds, Causes and Prevention of Insanity*, 2nd edition, 2 vols, London: Phillips, 1806.

Ashley, W.J., *An Introduction to English Economic History and Theory Part II: The End of the Middle Ages*, New York: Putnam, 1893.

Bailey, William, *A Treatise on the Better Employment and More Comfortable Support of the Poor in Workhouses*, London: Dodsley, 1758.

Bakewell, Samuel Glover, *An Essay on Insanity*, Edinburgh: Neill, 1833.

Bakewell, Thomas, *A Letter Addressed to the Chairman of the Select Committee of the House of Commons, Appointed to Enquire into the State of Madhouses*, Stafford: for the author, 1815.

Bakewell, Thomas, *The Domestic Guide in Cases of Insanity*, Stafford: for the author, 1805.

Battie, William, *A Treatise on Madness*, London: Whiston and White, 1758.

Becher, Reverend J.T., *An Address to the Public on the Nature, Design, and Constitution of the General Lunatic Asylum Near Nottingham*, Newark: Ridge, 1811.

Becker, Howard, *Outsiders*, Glencoe: Free Press, 1963.

Beddoes, Thomas, *Hygeia*, Bristol: Mills, 1802.

Beier, Augustus Leon, *Masterless Men: The Vagrancy Problem in England 1560–1640*, London: Methuen, 1985.

Belcher, William, *An Address to Humanity, Containing a Letter to Dr. Thomas Monro; A Receipt to Make a Lunatic, and Seize his Estate; and a Sketch of a True Smiling Hyena*, London: for the author, 1796.

Belknap, Ivan, *Human Problems of a State Mental Hospital*, New York: McGraw Hill, 1956.

Bellers, John, *Proposals for Raising a College of Industry of All Useful Trades and Husbandry*, London: Sowle, 1696.

Bentham, Jeremy, *Panopticon; or, the Inspection House: Containing the Idea of a New Principle of Construction Applicable to Any Sort of Establishment, in which Persons of Any Description Are to be Kept Under Inspection*, London: Payne, 1791.

Bentham, Jeremy, *The Complete Works of Jeremy Bentham*, Volume X (ed. J. Bowring), Edinburgh: Tait, 1843.

Berrios, German E. and Hugh Freeman (eds), *150 Years of British Psychiatry 1841–1991*, London: Gaskell, 1991.

Bethlem Hospital, *Report from the Committee of Governors of Bethlem Hospital, to the General Court Appointed to Inquire into the Case of James Norris*, reprinted as an appendix of the *Report* of the Select Committee on Madhouses, 1815.

Bingham, Nathaniel, *Observations on the Religious Delusions of Insane Persons . . . with which are combined a copious practical description [. . .] of mental disease, and of its appropriate medical and moral treatment*, London: Hatchard, 1841.

Black, William, *A Dissertation on Insanity: Illustrated with Tables Extracted From Between Two and Three Thousand Cases in Bedlam*, London: Ridgway, 1810.

Blackmore, Sir Richard, *A Treatise of the Spleen or Vapours*, London: Pemberton, 1724.

Blagrave, Joseph, *Blagrave's Astrological Practice of Physick*, London: S.G.B.G. for Obad. Blagrave, 1671.

Boorde, Andrew, *The Breviary of Healthe: The Seconde Boke of the Brevyary of Health, Named the Extravagantes*, London: Powell, 1552.

Booth, William, *Darkest England and the Way Out*, London: Salvation Army, 1890.

Brewer, John, *The Sinews of Power: War, Money and the English State, 1699–1783*, Cambridge: Harvard University Press, 1990.

Briere de Boismont, Alexandre, *On Hallucinations: A History and Explanation*, London: Renshaw, 1859.

Briggs, Asa, *The Making of Modern England 1783–1867*, New York: Harper and Row, 1965.

Briggs, Asa, *The Age of Improvement*, London: Longmans, Green, 1959.

Bright, Timothie, *A Treatise of Melancholie*, London: Vautrollier, 1586.

Brook, Charles W., *Battling Surgeon*, Glasgow: Strickland, 1945.

Brougham, Henry, *The Life and Times of Henry Brougham by Himself*, London: Blackwood, 1871.

Brown, G., M. Bone, B. Dalison, and J.K. Wing, *Schizophrenia and Social Care*, London: Oxford University Press, 1966.

Browne, W.A.F., *The Moral Treatment of the Insane: A Lecture*, London: Adlard, 1864.

Browne, W.A.F., *What Asylums Were, Are, and Ought to Be*, Edinburgh: Black, 1837.

Brydall, John, *Non Compos Mentis: Or, the Law Relating to Natural Fools, Mad-Folks, and Lunatick Persons*, London: Cleave, 1700.

Bucknill, John Charles, *The Care of the Insane and their Legal Control*, London: Macmillan, 1880.

Bucknill, John Charles, and Daniel Hack Tuke, *A Manual of Psychological Medicine*, Philadelphia: Blanchard & Lee, 1858.

Bucknill, John Charles, and Daniel Hack Tuke, *A Manual of Psychological Medicine*, 2nd edition, London: Churchill, 1862.

Burdett, H.C. *Hospitals and Asylums of the World*, 4 vols, London: Churchill, 1891.

Burgh, James, *Political Disquisitions*, Vol. 3, London: Dilly, 1775.

Burnett, C.M., *Insanity Tested by Science, and Shown to Be a Disease Rarely Connected With Organic Lesion of the Brain, and on That Account Far More Susceptible of Cure Than Has Hitherto Been Supposed*, London: Highley, 1848.

Burrows, George Man, *Cursory Remarks on a Bill now in the House of Peers for Regulating of Madhouses, [...] With Observations on the Defects of the Present System*, London: Harding, 1817.

Burrows, George Man, *An Inquiry into Certain Errors Relative to Insanity*, London: Underwood, 1820.

Burrows, George Man, *Commentaries on the Causes, Forms, Symptoms, and Treatment, Moral and Medical, of Insanity*, London: Underwood, 1828.

Burton, Robert, *The Anatomy of Melancholy*, reprint edition (ed. Holbrook Jackson), London: Dent, 1932.

Bynum, W.F., Roy Porter, and Michael Shepherd (eds), *The Anatomy of Madness*, 2 vols, London: Tavistock, 1985.

Bynum, W.F., Roy Porter, and Michael Shepherd (eds), *The Anatomy of Madness*, Vol. 3, London: Routledge, 1988.

Byrd, Max, *Visits to Bedlam*, Columbia: University of South Carolina Press, 1974.

Cabanis, Pierre, *Rapports du physique et du moral de l'homme*, in *Œuvres complètes* (ed. P.J.G. Thurot), Paris: Bossange Frères, 1823–5 (original edition 1802).

Carkesse, James, *Lucida Intervalla: Containing Divers Miscellaneous Poems Written at Finsbury and Bethlem by the Doctors Patient Extraordinary*, Berkeley: University of California Press, 1979 (first edition, London, 1679).

Carter, Robert Brudenell, *On the Pathology and Treatment of Hysteria*, London: Churchill, 1853.

Castel, F., R. Castel, and A. Lovell, *La Société psychiatrique avancée*, Paris: Editions Grasset, 1979, translated as *The Psychiatric Society*, New York: Columbia University Press, 1982.

Castel, Robert, *The Regulation of Madness: The Origins of Incarceration in France*, Berkeley: University of California Press, 1988.

Caudill, William, *The Psychiatric Hospital as a Small Society*, Cambridge: Harvard University Press, 1958.

Chadwick, Edwin, *Report on the Sanitary Conditions of the Labouring Population of Great Britain*, London: Clowes, 1842.

Chambers, Robert, *The Vestiges of the Natural History of Creation*, London: Churchill, 1844.

Cheyne, George, *The English Malady: or, A Treatise of Nervous Diseases of All Kinds*, London: Wisk, Ewing, and Smith, 1733.

Clark, Sir James, *A Memoir of John Conolly, M.D., D.C.L.*, London: Murray, 1869.

Clarke, Basil, *Mental Disorder in Earlier Britain*, Cardiff: University of Wales Press, 1975.

Clarkson, L.A., *The Pre-Industrial Economy in England 1500–1750*, London: Batsford, 1971.

Clay, R.M., *The Mediaeval Hospitals of England*, London: Methuen, 1909.

Clouston, Thomas S., *Female Education from a Medical Point of View*, Edinburgh: Macniven and Wallace, 1882.

Clouston, Thomas, *Clinical Lectures on Mental Disease*, London: Churchill, 1887.

Clouston, Thomas S., *The Neuroses of Development: Being the Morison Lectures for 1890*, Edinburgh: Oliver and Boyd, 1891.

Clouston, Thomas S., *The Hygiene of Mind*, London: Methuen, 1906.

Cohen, Stanley, and Andrew Scull (eds) *Social Control and the State: Historical and Comparative Essays*, Oxford: Martin Robertson, 1983.

Collie, Michael, *Henry Maudsley: Victorian Psychiatrist – A Bibliographic Study*, Winchester: St. Paul's Bibliographies, 1988.

Combe, Andrew, *Observations on Mental Derangement: Being an Application of the Principles of Phrenology to the Elucidation of the Causes, Symptoms, Nature, and Treatment of Insanity*, Edinburgh: Anderson, 1831.

Combe, Andrew, *Phrenology: Its Nature and Uses*, Edinburgh: Maclachlan and Stewart, 1846.

[Combe, George], *Essays on Phrenology*, Edinburgh: Bell and Bradfute, 1819.

Combe, George, *The Life and Correspondence of Andrew Combe, M.D.*, Edinburgh: Maclachlan and Stewart, 1850.

Conolly, John, *An Inquiry Concerning the Indications of Insanity, With Suggestions for the Better Protection and Care of the Insane*, London: Taylor, 1830.

Conolly, John, *A Letter to Benjamin Rotch Esq., Chairman of the Committee of Visitors, On the Plan and Government of the Additional Lunatic Asylum for the County of Middlesex, About to Be Erected at Colney Hatch*, London: Churchill, 1847.

Conolly, John, *On the Construction and Government of Lunatic Asylums*, London: Churchill, 1847.

Conolly, John, *A Remonstrance with the Lord Chief Baron Touching the Case Nottidge v. Ripley*, London: Churchill, 1849.

Conolly, John, *The Treatment of the Insane Without Mechanical Restraint*, London: Smith, Elder, 1856.

Cooter, Roger, *The Cultural Meaning of Popular Science: Phrenology and the Organization of Consent in Nineteenth Century Britain*, Cambridge: Cambridge University Press, 1984.

Corbin, Alain, *Le miasme et la jonquille* Paris: Aubier Montaigne, 1982, translated as *The Foul and the Fragrant: Odor and the French Social Imagination*, New York: Berg, 1986.

Cotta, John, *A Short Discouerie of the Vnobserved Dangers of Seuerall Sorts of Ignorant and Vnconsidered Practisers of Physicke in England*, London: William Jones, 1612.

Cowper, William, *Memoir of the Early Life of William Cowper, Esq. Written by Himself*, London: Edwards, 1816.

Cox, Joseph Mason, *Practical Observations on Insanity: In Which Some Suggestions Are Offered Towards an Improved Mode of Treating Diseases of the Mind [. . .] to Which Are Subjoined, Remarks on Medical Jurisprudence as Connected with Diseased Intellect*, 1st edition, London: Baldwin and Murray, 1804.

Cox, Joseph Mason, *Practical Observations on Insanity*, 2nd edition, London: Baldwin and Murray, 1806.

Cox, Joseph Mason, *Practical Observations on Insanity*, 3rd edition, London: Baldwin and Underwood, 1813.

Crammer, John, *Asylum History: Buckinghamshire County Pauper Lunatic Asylum – St. John's*, London: Gaskell, 1990.

Crichton-Browne, Sir James, *What the Doctor Thought*, London: Benn, 1930.

Cruden, Alexander, *The London Citizen Exceedingly Injured: or, A British Inquisition Displayed*, London: Cooper and Dodd, 1739.

Cruden, Alexander, *The Adventures of Alexander the Corrector, With an Account of the Chelsea Academies, Or the Private Places of Such As Are Supposed to Be Deprived of the Exercise of Their Reason*, London: for the author, 1754.

Cullen, William, *First Lines of the Practice of Physic*, 4 vols, 4th edition, Edinburgh: Elliot, 1777–84.

Cullen, William, *First Lines of the Practice of Physic*, 2 vols, Edinburgh: Bell and Bradfute, 1808.

Dain, Norman, *Concepts of Insanity in the United States, 1786–1830*, New Brunswick: Rutgers University Press, 1964.

Darwin, Erasmus, *Zoonomia; or, The Laws of Organic Life*, 2 vols, London: Johnson, 1794–6.

Davey, J.G., *On the Nature, and Proximate Causes of Insanity*, London: Churchill, 1853.

Defoe, Daniel, *Augusta Triumphans*, London: Roberts, 1728.

De Giustino, David A., *The Conquest of Mind: Phrenology and Victorian Social Thought*, London: Croom Helm, 1975.

Deporte, Michael, *Nightmares and Hobbyhorses: Swift, Sterne, and Augustan Ideas of Madness*, San Marino: Huntington Library, 1974.

Dicks, H.V., *50 Years of the Tavistock Clinic*, London: Routledge and Kegan Paul, 1970.

Dickson, P.G.M., *The Financial Revolution in England: A Study of the Development of Public Credit, 1688–1756*, London: Macmillan, 1967.

Digby, Anne, *Madness, Morality and Medicine: A Study of the York Retreat 1796–1914*, Cambridge: Cambridge University Press, 1985.

Dobb, Maurice, *Studies in the Development of Capitalism*, New York: International Publishers, 1963.

Doerner, Klaus, *Madmen and the Bourgeoisie: A Social History of Insanity and Psychiatry*, Oxford: Blackwell, 1981.

Dowse, Thomas Stretch, *On Brain and Nerve Exhaustion: 'Neurasthenia,' Its Nature and Curative Treatment*, London: Baillière, Tindall, and Cox, 1880.

Dowse, Thomas Stretch, *Lectures on Massage and Electricity in the Treatment of Disease*, London: Hamilton, Adams, 1889.

Duncan, Andrew, *Observations on the Structure of Hospitals for the Treatment of Lunatics as a Branch of Medical Police*, Edinburgh: Ballantyne, 1809.

Dunn, Robert, *An Essay on Physiological Psychology*, London: Churchill, 1858.

Edsall, N.C., *The Anti-Poor Law Movement, 1834–44*, Manchester: University of Manchester Press, 1971.

Ellis, William Charles, *A Letter to Thomas Thompson, Esq., M.P., . . . on the Necessity of Proper Places Being Provided by the Legislature for the Reception of All Insane Persons*, Hull: Topping and Dawson, 1815.

Ellis, William Charles, *A Treatise on the Nature, Symptoms, Causes, and Treatment of Insanity, With Practical Observations on Lunatic Asylums, and a Description of the Pauper Lunatic Asylum for the County of Middlesex at Hanwell, With a Detailed Account of Its Management*, London: Holdsworth, 1838.

Esquirol, Jean Etienne Dominique, *Mental Maladies*, Philadelphia: Blanchard and Lee, 1845.

Evans, Robin, *The Fabrication of Virtue: English Prison Architecture 1750–1842*, Cambridge: Cambridge University Press, 1982.

Fairchilds, C.C., *Poverty and Charity in Aix-en-Provence 1640–1789*, Baltimore: Johns Hopkins University Press, 1976.

Falconer, William, *A Dissertation on the Influence of the Passions upon Disorders of the Body*, London: Dill, 1788.

Fallowes, Thomas, *The Best Method for the Cure of Lunaticks, With Some Account of the Incomparable Oleum Cephalicum Used in the Same, Prepared and Administered by Tho. Fallowes, at his House in Lambeth-Marsh*, London: for the author, 1705.

Ferriar, John, *Medical Histories and Reflections*, Vol. 2, London: Cadell and Davies, 1795.

Fielding, Henry, *An Enquiry into the Causes of the Late Increase of Robbers*, London: Millar, 1751.

Finnane, Mark, *Insanity and the Insane in Post-Famine Ireland*, London: Croom Helm, 1981.

Fletcher, R., *Sketches from the Casebook to Illustrate the Influence of the Mind on the Body, With the Treatment of Some of the More Important Brain and Nervous Disturbances*, London: Longman, 1833.

Forster, Nathaniel, *An Enquiry into the Causes of the Present High Price of Provisions*, London: Fletcher, 1767.

Forster, Thomas, *Observations on the Phenomena of Insanity*, London: Underwood, 1817.

Foucault, Michel, *Madness and Civilization*, New York: Pantheon, 1965.

Foucault, Michel, *Histoire de la folie*, new edition, Paris: Gallimard, 1972.

Foucault, Michel, *Mental Illness and Psychology*, Berkeley: University of California Press, 1987.

Foucault, Michel, *Discipline and Punish: The Birth of the Prison*, London: Allen Lane, 1977.

[Fox, E.L.], *Brislington House: An Asylum for Lunatics, Situate near Bristol, on the Road from Bath, and Lately Erected by Edward Long Fox M.D.*, Bristol: n.p., 1806.

Fox, Richard W., *So Far Disordered in Mind: Insanity in California, 1870–1930*, Berkeley: University of California Press, 1978.

Freidson, Eliot, *Professional Dominance*, New York: Atherton, 1970.

Freidson, Eliot, *Profession of Medicine*, New York: Dodd, Mead, 1970.

Furniss, Edgar S., *The Position of the Laborer in a System of Nationalism*, New York: Kelly, 1965 (original edition, New York: Houghton Mifflin, 1920).

Gay, Peter, *The Enlightenment: An Interpretation*, Vol. 2, *The Science of Freedom*, New York: Knopf, 1969.

George, M.D., *London Life in the Eighteenth Century*, Harmondsworth, Middlesex: Penguin, 1965.

Gilbert, Felix (ed.), *The Historical Essays of Otto Hintze*, New York: Oxford University Press, 1975.

Goffman, Erving, *Asylums: Essays on the Social Situation of Mental Patients and Other Inmates*, Garden City: Doubleday, 1961.

Goldstein, Jan, *Console and Classify: The French Psychiatric Profession in the Nineteenth Century*, Cambridge: Cambridge University Press, 1987.

Granville, Joseph Mortimer, *The Care and Cure of the Insane*, 2 vols, London: Hardwicke and Bogue, 1877.

Gray, Jonathan, *A History of the York Lunatic Asylum: with an Appendix, Containing the Minutes of Evidence on the Cases of Abuse Lately Inquired into by a Committee*, York: Hargrove, 1815.

Greg, Samuel, *A Layman's Legacy*, London: Macmillan, 1877.

Gregory, John, *A Comparative View of the State and Faculties of Man with Those of the Animal World*, London: Dodsley, 1765.

Greville, Robert Fulke, *The Diaries of Colonel the Hon. Robert Fulke Greville*, (ed. F.M. Bladon), London: John Lane, 1930.

Grob, Gerald, *Mental Institutions in America: Social Policy to 1875*, New York: Free Press, 1973.

Grob, Gerald, *Mental Illness and American Society, 1875–1940*, Princeton: Princeton University Press, 1983.

Grob, Gerald, *From Asylum to Community: Mental Health Policy in Modern America*, Princeton: Princeton University Press, 1991.

Grosley, Pierre, *A Tour of London, or New Observations on England and Its Inhabitants*, (trans. T. Nugent), Dublin: Ekshaw, Lynch, Williams, Montcrieffe, Walker, and Jenkin, 1722.

Grosskurth, Phyllis, *Melanie Klein: Her World and Her Work*, New York: Knopf, 1986.

Gruber, Howard E., and Paul H. Barrett, *Darwin on Man . . . Together with Darwin's Early and Unpublished Notebooks*, New York: Dutton, 1974.

Guislain, Joseph, *Traité sur l'aliénation mentale et sur les hospices des aliénés*, Amsterdam: Hey, 1826.

Guthrie, Leonard G., *Functional Nervous Disorders in Childhood*, London: Oxford University Press, 1907.

Hale, Nathan G. Jr, *Freud and the Americans*, New York: Oxford University Press, 1971.

Hall, Marshall, *Memoirs on the Nervous System*, London: Sherwood, Gilbert, and Piper, 1837.

Hallaran, William Saunders, *An Enquiry into the Causes Producing the Extraordinary Addition to the Number of the Insane*, Cork: Edwards and Savage, 1810.

Hallaran, William Saunders, *Practical Observations on the Causes and Cure of Insanity*, Cork: Hodges and M'Arthur, 1818.

Halliday, Andrew, *A Letter to the Magistrates of Middlesex on the Propriety of Erecting an Asylum for Pauper Lunatics*, London: Brettell, 1826.

Halliday, Andrew, *A General View of the Present State of Lunatics and Lunatic Asylums in Great Britain and Ireland*, London: Underwood, 1828.

Halliday, Andrew, *A Letter to Lord Robert Seymour: with a Report on the Number of Lunatics and Idiots in England and Wales*, London: Underwood, 1829.

Harper, Andrew, *A Treatise on the Real Cause and Cure of Insanity*, London: Stalker and Walter, 1789.

Harrison, J.F.C., *The Second Coming: Popular Millenarianism, 1780–1850*, New Brunswick: Rutgers University Press, 1979.

Hartley, David, *Observations on Man, His Frame, His Duties, and His Expectations*, London: Leake and Frederick, 1749.

Haslam, John, *Observations on Insanity: With Practical Remarks on the Disease and an Account of the Morbid Appearances on Dissection*, London: Rivington, 1798.

Haslam, John, *Observations on Madness and Melancholy*, 2nd edition, London: Callow, 1809.

Haslam, John, *Illustrations of Madness*, London: Routledge, 1989 (original edition 1810).

Haslam, John, *Observations of the Apothecary of Bethlem Hospital Upon the Evidence Taken Before the Committee of the Honourable House of Commons for Regulating Madhouses*, London: Bryer, 1816.

Haslam, John, *Medical Jurisprudence as it Relates to Insanity, According to the Law of England*, London: Hunter, 1817.

Hay, Douglas, Peter Linebaugh, and E.P. Thompson (eds), *Albion's Fatal Tree: Crime and Society in Eighteenth Century England*, New York: Pantheon, 1975.

Higgins, Godfrey, *A Letter to the Right Honourable Earl Fitzwilliam Respecting the Investigation Which Has Lately Taken Place into the Abuses at the York Lunatic Asylum*, Doncaster: Sheardown, 1814.

Higgins, Godfrey, *The Evidence Taken Before a Committee of the House of Commons Respecting the Asylum at York; With Observations and Notes*, Doncaster: Sheardown, 1816.

Hill, Christopher, *Reformation to Industrial Revolution: A Social and Economic History of Britain 1530–1780*, London: Weidenfeld and Nicolson, 1967.

Hill, George Nesse, *An Essay on the Prevention and Cure of Insanity*, London: Longman, Hurst, Rees, Orme, and Brown, 1814.

Hill, Robert Gardiner, *A Lecture on the Management of Lunatic Asylums and the Treatment of the Insane*, London: Simpkin, Marshall, 1839.

Hill, Robert Gardiner, *A Concise History of the Entire Abolition of Mechanical Restraint in the Treatment of the Insane*, London: Longman, Brown, Green, and Longman, 1857.

Hill, Robert Gardiner, *Lunacy: Its Past and Present*, London: Longman, Green, Reader and Dyer, 1870.

Hobman, J.B., *David Eder: Memoirs of a Modern Pioneer*, London: Gollancz, 1945.

Hobsbawm, Eric, *Industry and Empire*, Harmondsworth, Middlesex: Penguin, 1969.

Hobsbawm, Eric, and George Rudé, *Captain Swing*, Harmondsworth: Penguin, 1969.

Holland, Sir Henry, *Chapters on Mental Physiology*, 2nd edition, London: Longmans, 1858.

Hood, W.C., *The Statistics of Insanity*, London: Batten, 1862.

Howard, John, *The State of the Prisons*, Warrington: Egres, 1778.

Hughes, Judith, *Reshaping the Psycho-Analytic Domain: The Work of Melanie Klein, W.R.D. Fairbairn, and D.W. Winnicott*, Berkeley: University of California Press, 1989.

Hunter, Richard, and Ida MacAlpine, *Three Hundred Years of Psychiatry*, London: Oxford University Press, 1963.

Hunter, Richard, and Ida MacAlpine, *Psychiatry for the Poor. 1851 Colney Hatch Asylum: Friern Hospital 1973*, London: Dawsons, 1974.

Ignatieff, Michael, *A Just Measure of Pain: The Penitentiary in the Industrial Revolution in England*, New York: Pantheon, 1978.

Irish, David, *Levamen Infirmi, or: Cordial Counsel to the Sick and Diseased*, London: for the author, 1700.

Jackson, John Hughlings, *Selected Writings*, Vol. 1, London: Hodder and Stoughton, 1931.

Jacobi, Maximilian, *On the Construction and Management of Hospitals for the Insane* (trans. John Kitching), London: Churchill, 1841.

Jones, Ernest, *The Life and Work of Sigmund Freud*, abridged edition, Harmondsworth: Penguin, 1974.

Jones, Kathleen, *Lunacy, Law, and Conscience 1744–1845*, London: Routledge and Kegan Paul, 1955.

Jones, Kathleen, *Mental Health and Social Policy 1845–1955*, London: Routledge and Kegan Paul, 1960.

Jordan, W.K., *Philanthropy in England 1480–1660. A Study of the Changing Pattern of English Social Aspirations*, New York: Russell Sage, 1959.

Jordan, W.K., *The Charities of London 1480–1660*, New York: Russell Sage, 1960.

Jorden, Edward, *The Suffocation of the Mother*, London: Windet, 1603.

Kenealy, Arabella, *Feminism and Sex-Extinction*, London: Fisher Unwin, 1920.

Kittrie, Nicholas, *The Right to be Different: Deviance and Enforced Therapy*, Baltimore: Johns Hopkins University Press, 1972.

Knight, Paul Slade, *Observations on the Causes, Symptoms, and Treatment of Derangement of the Mind*, London: Longman, 1827.

Knox, R.A., *Enthusiasm*, London: Oxford University Press, 1950.

La Mettrie, Julian, *L'Homme machine*, Princeton: Princeton University Press, 1960 (original edition 1748).

Lawrence, William, *An Introduction to Comparative Anatomy and Physiology*, London: Callow, 1816.

Lawrence, William, *Lectures on Physiology, Zoology, and the Natural History of Man, Delivered at the Royal College of Surgeons*, London: Callow, 1819.

Laycock, Thomas, *A Treatise on the Nervous Diseases of Women*, London: Longman, Orme, Brown, Green, and Longmans, 1840.

Locke, John, *An Essay Concerning Human Understanding*, London: Everyman, 1965.

Locke, John, *Educational Writings*, Cambridge: Cambridge University Press, 1968.

Loudon, Irvine, *Medical Care and the General Practitioner, 1750–1850*, Oxford: Oxford University Press, 1986.

Lovejoy, A.O., *The Great Chain of Being*, New York: Harper, 1960.

Lubenow, William C., *The Politics of Government Growth: Early Victorian Attitudes Toward State Intervention 1833–1848*, Newton Abbot: David and Charles, 1971.

MacAlpine, Ida, and Richard Hunter, *George III and the Mad-Business*, London: Allen Lane, 1969.

MacBride, David, *A Methodical Introduction to the Theory and Practice of Physick*, London: Strahan, 1772.

MacDonald, Michael, *Mystical Bedlam: Madness, Anxiety, and Healing in Seventeenth Century England*, Cambridge: Cambridge University Press, 1981.

MacFarlan, John, *Inquiries Concerning the Poor*, Edinburgh: Longman and Dickson, 1782.

Macfarlane, Alan, *Origins of English Individualism*, Oxford: Blackwell, 1978.

MacGill, Stevenson, *On Lunatic Asylums*, Glasgow: for the Glasgow Asylum Committee, 1810.

MacKenzie, Henry, *The Man of Feeling*, London: Cadell, 1771.

Malthus, T.R., *An Essay on the Principle of Population*, London: Johnson, 1798.

Malthus, T.R., *An Essay on the Principle of Population*, 6th edition, London: Murray, 1826.

Mantoux, Pierre, *The Industrial Revolution in the Eighteenth Century*, London: Cape, 1928.

Marcus, Steven, *Engels, Manchester, and the Working Class*, New York: Vintage, 1974.

Marshall, Dorothy, *The English Poor in the Eighteenth Century*, London: Routledge, 1926.

Marx, Karl, *Capital*, 3 vols, New York: International Publishers, 1967.

Mason, W., *Animadversions on the Present Government of the York Lunatic Asylum*, York: Blanchard, 1788.

Matza, David, *Becoming Deviant*, Englewood Cliffs: Prentice-Hall, 1969.

Maudsley, Henry, *The Physiology and Pathology of Mind*, London: Macmillan, 1867.

Maudsley, Henry, *Body and Mind*, London: Macmillan, 1870.

Maudsley, Henry, *Responsibility in Mental Disease*, 2nd edition, London: Kegan Paul, 1874.

Maudsley, Henry, *The Pathology of Mind*, London: Macmillan, 1879.

Maudsley, Henry, *The Pathology of Mind: A Study of Its Distempers, Deformities, and Disorders*, London: Macmillan, 1895.

Mayne, Zachary, *Two Discourses Concerning Sense, and the Imagination, with an Essay on Consciousness*, London: Tonson, 1728.

Mayo, Herbert, *Anatomical and Physiological Commentaries*, Vol. 1, London: Underwood, 1822.

Mayo, Thomas, *Remarks on Insanity; Founded on the Practice of John Mayo, M.D.*, London: Underwood, 1817.

Mayo, Thomas, *An Essay on the Relation of the Theory of Morals to Insanity*, London: Fellowes, 1834.

Mayo, Thomas, *Medical Testimony and Evidence in Cases of Lunacy*, London: Parker, 1854.

McKendrick, Neil, John Brewer, and J.H. Plumb, *The Birth of a Consumer Society: The Commercialization of Eighteenth Century England*, Bloomington: Indiana University Press, 1982.

Mead, Richard, *Medical Precepts and Cautions*, London: Brindley, 1751.

Mead, Richard, *The Medical Works of Richard Mead*, London: Hitch and Hawes, 1762.

Mechanic, David, *Mental Health and Social Policy*, Englewood Cliffs: Prentice-Hall, 1969.

Mellett, D.J., *The Prerogative of Asylumdom: Social, Cultural, and Administrative Aspects of the Institutional Treatment of the Insane in Nineteenth Century Britain*, New York: Garland, 1982.

Mencher, Samuel, *Poor Law to Poverty Program: Economic Security Policy in Britain and the United States*, Pittsburgh: University of Pittsburgh Press, 1967.

Mercier, Charles, *Lunatic Asylums: Their Organization and Management*, London: Griffin, 1894.

Mercier, Charles, *A Text-Book of Insanity and Other Mental Diseases*, 2nd edition, London: Allen and Unwin, 1914.

Mercuriale, Girolamo, *De arte gymnastica*, Amsterdam: Frisii, 1672.

Metcalf, Urbane, *The Interior of Bethlehem Hospital, Humbly Addressed to His Royal Highness the Duke of Sussex and to the Other Governors*, London: for the author, 1818.

Millingen, J.G., *A Letter to the Ratepayers of Middlesex on the County of Middlesex Pauper Lunatic Asylum*, London: for the author, 1839.

Millingen, J.G., *Aphorisms on the Treatment and Management of the Insane, With Considerations on Public and Private Lunatic Asylums, Pointing Out the Errors in the Present System*, London: Churchill, 1840.

Mitchell, Silas Weir, *Wear and Tear, Or Hints for the Overworked*, Philadelphia: Lippincott, 1871.

Mitchell, Silas Weir, *Fat and Blood*, 3rd revised edition, Philadelphia: Lippincott, 1884.

Mitford, John, *The Crimes and Horrors of Warburton's Private Madhouses*, 2 vols, London: Benbow, 1825.

'Moderator,' *A Letter to the Right Honourable Lord Robert Seymour, On his Objectionable Proposals for Erecting County Lunatic Asylums for Paupers, With Remarks on the Present System of Private Madhouses*, London: Chapel, 1828.

Monro, Henry, *Remarks on Insanity: Its Nature and Treatment, and Articles on the Reform of Private Lunatic Asylums*, London: Churchill, 1850.

Monro, John, *Remarks on Dr. Battie's Treatise on Madness*, London: Clarke, 1758.

Monro, Thomas, *Observations of Dr. Monro Upon the Evidence Taken Before the Committee of the Honourable House of Commons for Regulating Madhouses*, London: Bryer, 1816.

More, Henry, *Enthusiasmus Triumphatus, or, A Discourse of the Nature, Causes, Kinds, and Cure, of Enthusiasme*, London: Morden, 1656.

More, Sir Thomas, *The Apologie of Syr T. More, Knyght*, London: Rastell, 1533.

Morel, Benedict Augustin, *Traité des dégénérescences physiques, intellectuelles, et morales de l'espèce humaine*, Paris: Masson, 1857.

Morison, Alexander, *Cases of Mental Disease, With Practical Observations on the Medical Treatment*, London: Longman and Highley, 1828.

Morison, Alexander, *Outlines of Lectures on the Nature, Causes, and Treatment of Insanity*, (ed. Thomas C. Morison), London: Longman, Green, Brown, and Longman, 1st edition, 1825, 4th edition, 1848.

Mott, F.W., *War Neuroses and Shell Shock*, London: Hodder and Stoughton, 1919.

Müller, Johannes, *Elements of Physiology*, 2 vols, London: Taylor and Walton, 1839–1842.

Myers, C.S., *Shell-Shock in France 1914–1918*, Cambridge: Cambridge University Press, 1940.

Namier, Sir Lewis, *England in the Age of the American Revolution*, 2nd edition, London: Macmillan, 1961.

Neville, William B., *On Insanity: Its Nature, Causes and Cure*, London: Longman, Rees, Orme, Brown, Green, and Longman, 1836.

[A New Governor], *A Vindication of Mr. Higgins from the Charges of Corrector: Including a Sketch of Recent Transactions at the York Asylum*, York: Hargrove, 1814.

Nicoll, Samuel William, *An Enquiry into the Present State of Visitation, in Asylums for the Reception of the Insane*, London: Harvey and Darton, 1828.

Nisbet, William, *Two Letters to the Right Honourable George Rose, M.P. on the Reports at Present before the Honourable House of Commons on the State of Madhouses*, London: Cox, 1815.

Noble, D. *Elements of Psychological Medicine: An Introduction to the Practical Study of Insanity*, London: Churchill, 1853.

Nye, Robert, *Crime, Madness, and Politics in Modern France*, Princeton: Princeton University Press, 1984.

Obelkevich, James, *Religion and Rural Society: South Lindsey, 1825–1875*, Oxford: Clarendon Press, 1976.

O'Donoghue, Edward Geoffrey, *The Story of Bethlehem Hospital from Its Foundation in 1247*, London: Unwin, 1914.

Oppenheim, Janet, *'Shattered Nerves': Doctors, Patients, and Depression in Victorian England*, New York: Oxford University Press, 1991.

Owen, Robert, *A New View of Society*, London: Cadell and Davies, 1813.

Pagan, J.M., *The Medical Jurisprudence of Insanity*, London: Ball, Arnold, and Company, 1840.

Pargeter, William, *Observations on Maniacal Disorders*, Reading: for the author, 1792.

Parkin, John, *On the Medical and Moral Treatment of Insanity, Including a Notice on the Establishment for the Treatment of Nervous and Mental Maladies: Manor Cottage, King's Road, Chelsea, Established in 1780*, London: Martin, [1843].

Parry-Jones, William Ll., *The Trade in Lunacy*, London: Routledge and Kegan Paul, 1972.

Pascal, Blaise, *Œuvres Complètes*, Paris: Gallimard, 1954.

Paul, Sir George Onesiphorus, *Address to Subscribers to the Gloucester Lunatic Asylum*, Gloucester: for the author, 1810.

Paul, Sir George Onesiphorus, *Observations on the Subject of Lunatic Asylums*, Gloucester: Walker, 1812.

Peers, Edgar A., *Elizabethan Drama and Its Mad Folk*, Cambridge: Heffer, 1914.

Perceval, John Thomas, *A Narrative of the Treatment Received by a Gentleman, During a State of Mental Derangement*, 2 vols, London: Effingham Wilson, 1838, 1840.

Percival, Thomas, *Medical Ethics*, Manchester: Johnson and Bickerstaff, 1803.

[Perfect, William], *Select Cases in the Different Species of Insanity, Lunacy or Madness, With the Modes of Practice as Adopted in the Treatment of Each*, Rochester: Gillman, 1787.

Perfect, William, *A Remarkable Case of Madness, with the Diet and Medicines used in the Cure*, Rochester: for the author, 1791.

Perkin, Harold, *The Origins of Modern English Society 1789–1880*, London: Routledge and Kegan Paul, 1969.

Perkin, Harold, *The Rise of Professional Society: England Since 1880*, London: Routledge, 1989.

Perrucci, Robert, *Circle of Madness*, Englewood Cliffs: Prentice-Hall, 1974.

Peterson, M.J., *The Medical Profession in Mid-Victorian England*, Berkeley: University of California Press, 1978.

Pinel, Philippe, *A Treatise on Insanity*, (trans. D.D. Davis), Sheffield: Cadell and Davies, 1806.

Playfair, W.S., *The Systematic Treatment of Nerve Prostration and Hysteria*, London: Smith, Elder, 1883.

Polanyi, Karl, *The Great Transformation*, Boston: Beacon, 1957.

Pollard, Sidney, *The Genesis of Modern Management*, Harmondsworth: Penguin, 1965.

Porter, Roy, *English Society in the Eighteenth Century*, Harmondsworth: Penguin, 1982.

Porter, Roy, *Mind Forg'd Manacles: A History of Madness in England from the Restoration to the Regency*, London: Athlone, 1987.

Porter, Roy, and Dorothy Porter, *In Sickness and in Health: The British Experience 1650–1850*, London: Fourth Estate, 1988.

Porter, Roy, and Dorothy Porter, *Patient's Progress: Doctors and Doctoring in Eighteenth Century England*, Oxford: Polity Press, 1989.

Powell, Richard, *Observations on the Comparative Prevalence of Insanity at Different Periods*, London: Woodfall, 1813.

Prichard, James Cowles, *A Treatise on Insanity and Other Disorders Affecting the Mind*, London: Sherwood, Gilbert, and Piper, 1835.

Prichard, James Cowles, *On the Different Forms of Insanity in Relation to Jurisprudence*, London: Baillière, 1842.

Reade, Charles, *Hard Cash: A Matter-of-Fact Romance*, London: Ward, Lock, 1864.

Reed, Robert R., *Bedlam on the Jacobean Stage*, Cambridge: Harvard University Press, 1952.

Reid, John, *Essays on Insanity, Hypochondriacal and other Nervous Affections*, London: Longman, Hurst, Rees, Orme, and Brown, 1816.

Reid, John, *Essays on Hypochondriasis and Other Nervous Affections*, 3rd edition, London: Longman, Hurst, Rees, Orme, and Brown, 1823.

Reynolds, F., *The Life and Times of F. Reynolds, Written by Himself*, Vol. 2, London: Colburn, 1826.

Rimlinger, Gaston, *Welfare Policy and Industrialization in Europe, American, and Russia*, New York: Wiley, 1971.

Roberts, David, *Victorian Origins of the British Welfare State*, New Haven: Yale University Press, 1960.

Robinson, Nicholas, *A New System of the Spleen, Vapours, and Hypochondriack Melancholy*, London: Bettesworth, Innys, and Rivington, 1729.

Rogers, J.W., *A Statement of the Cruelties, Abuses, and Frauds, Which Are Practised in Mad-Houses*, London: for the author, 2nd edition, 1816.

Rose, Michael, *The English Poor Law 1780–1930*, New York: Barnes and Noble, 1971.

Rose, Nikolas, *The Psychological Complex: Psychology, Politics, and Society in England, 1869–1939*, London: Routledge and Kegan Paul, 1985.

Rosenberg, Charles, *The Care of Strangers: The Rise of America's Hospital System*, New York: Basic Books, 1987.

Rothman, David, *The Discovery of the Asylum*, Boston: Little Brown, 1971.

Rowley, William, *Truth Vindicated: Or, the Specific Differences of Mental Diseases Ascertained, and Reasons for Declaring the Case of a Great Person to Have Been Only a Fever or a Symptomatic Delirium*, London: Wingrave, 1790.

Rusche, Georg and Otto Kirchheimer, *Punishment and Social Structure*, New York: Russell and Russell, 1968.

Rush, Benjamin, *Medical Inquiries and Observations Upon the Diseases of the Mind*, Philadelphia: Kimber and Richardson, 1812.

Rush, Benjamin, *The Letters of Benjamin Rush*, (ed. L.H. Butterfield), Princeton: Princeton University Press, 1951.

Ryle, Gilbert, *The Concept of Mind*, New York: Harper and Row, 1949.

Salmon, William, *System Medicinale: A Complete System of Physick, Theoretical and Practical*, London: for the author, 1686.

Savage, George Henry, and Edwin Goodall, *Insanity and its Allied Neuroses*, 4th edition, London: Cassell, 1907.

Savill, Thomas Dixon, *Clinical Lectures on Neurasthenia*, 3rd edition, London: Glaisher, 1906 (first edition 1899).

Scharlieb, Mary, *Womanhood and Race Regeneration*, New York: Moffat, Yard, 1912.

Scot, Reginald, *The Discoverie of Witchcraft*, London: Clark, 1665.

Scull, Andrew, (ed.), *Madhouses, Mad-doctors, and Madmen: The Social History of Psychiatry in the Victorian Era*, Philadelphia: University of Pennsyvlania Press, 1981.

Scull, Andrew, *Decarceration: Community Treatment and the Deviant: A Radical View*, 2nd edition, Oxford: Polity Press, 1984.

Scull, Andrew, *Social Order/Mental Disorder: Anglo-American Psychiatry in Historical Perspective*, Berkeley: University of California Press, 1989.

Scull, Andrew, *The Asylum as Utopia: W.A.F. Browne and the Mid-Nineteenth Century Consolidation of Psychiatry*, London: Routledge, 1990.

Sedgwick, Peter, *Psychopolitics*, London: Pluto Press, 1981.

Seymour, Edward J., *Observations on the Medical Treatment of Insanity*, London: Longman, Rees, Orme, and Brown, 1832.

Sheppard, Edgar, *Lectures on Madness in Its Medical, Legal, and Social Aspects*, London: Churchill, 1873.

Shorter, Edward, *From Paralysis to Fatigue: A History of Psychosomatic Illness in the Modern Era*, New York: Free Press, 1992.

Shortt, S.E.D., *Victorian Lunacy: Richard M. Bucke and the Practice of Late Nineteenth-Century Psychiatry*, Cambridge: Cambridge University Press, 1986.

Showalter, Elaine, *The Female Malady: Women, Madness and English Culture, 1830–1980*, New York: Pantheon, 1985.

Shyrock, Richard Harrison, *The Development of Modern Medicine*, Philadelphia: University of Pennsylvania Press, 1936.

Slack, Paul, *Poverty and Policy in Tudor and Stuart England*, London: Longman, 1988.

Smith, Adam, *The Wealth of Nations*, New York: Modern Library, 1937.

Smith, Roger, *Trial by Medicine: Insanity and Responsibility in Victorian Trials*, Edinburgh: Edinburgh University Press, 1981.

Smollett, Tobias, *The Adventures of Sir Launcelot Greaves*, London: Coote, 1762.

Snape, Andrew, *A Sermon Preach'd Before the Lord Mayor, the Aldermen, Sheriffs and Gouvenours of the Several Hospitals of the City of London*, London: Bowyer, 1718.

Solomon, Howard, *Public Welfare, Science, and Propaganda in Seventeenth Century France*, Princeton: Princeton University Press, 1972.

Southcomb, Lewis, *Peace of Mind and Health of Body United*, London: Cowper, 1750.

Sprigge, S.S., *The Life and Times of Thomas Wakley*, London: Longman, Green, 1899.

Spurzheim, Johann Gaspar, *Observations on the Deranged Manifestations of the Mind, or Insanity*, London: Baldwin, Craddock, and Joy, 1817.

Stafford, Richard, *Because to Many People, I have Seemed to Falsify My Word and Promise, Which I made Upon My Being Discharged Out of Bethlehem Hospital*, London: for the author, c. 1692.

Stark, William, *Remarks on the Construction of Public Asylums for the Cure of Mental Derangement*, 2nd edition, Glasgow: Hedderwick, 1810.

Steward, J.B., *Practical Notes on Insanity*, London: Churchill, 1845.

Strype, John, *A Survey of the Cities of London and Westminster Written at First in the Year MDXCVIII by John Stow, Corrected, Improved and Very Much Enlarged to the Present Time*, London: Churchill, 1720.

Swift, Jonathan, *A Tale of a Tub*, London: Everyman, 1975 (original edition, 1702).

Swift, Jonathan, *A Character, Panegyric, and Description of the Legion Club* Dublin, 1736, reprinted in Harold Williams (ed.) *The Poems of Jonathan Swift*, 2nd edition, Oxford: The Clarendon Press, 1966.

Synge, Edward, *Sober Thoughts for the Cure of Melancholy, Especially that which Is Religious*, London: Trye, 1742.

Szasz, Thomas, *The Myth of Mental Illness*, New York: Dell, 1961.

Szasz, Thomas, *The Manufacture of Madness*, New York: Dell, 1970.

Talbot, Matthew, *Affidavits Sworn Before Lord Ellenborough in Refutation of the Testimony of John Wilson Rogers and Mary Humieres, Given Before the Committee of the Honourable House of Commons, on the Madhouse Bill*, London: for the author, 1816.

Temple, William, *An Essay on Trade and Commerce*, London: Cunningham, 1770.

Thomas, Keith, *Religion and the Decline of Magic*, Harmondsworth: Penguin, 1973.

Thomas, Keith, *Man and the Natural World: Changing Attitudes in England 1500–1800*, London: Allen Lane, 1983.

Thompson, E.P., *The Making of the English Working Class*, Harmondsworth: Penguin, 1963.

Thompson, E.P., *Whigs and Hunters*, New York: Pantheon, 1975.

Thompson, F.M.L., *The Rise of Respectable Society: A Social History of Victorian Britain 1830–1900*, Cambridge: Harvard University Press, 1988.

Thompson, J.D., and G. Goldin, *The Hospital: A Social and Architectural History*, New Haven: Yale University Press, 1975.

Thurnam, John, *Observations and Essays on the Statistics of Insanity: Including an Inquiry into the Causes Influencing the Results of Treatment in Establishments for the Insane: To Which Are Added Statistics for the Retreat near York*, London: Simpkin Marshall, 1845.

[Townsend, Joseph], *A Dissertation on the Poor Laws by a Well Wisher of Mankind*, London: Dilly, 1786.

Trombley, Stephen, *All that Summer She was Mad: Virginia Woolf and her Doctors*, London: Junction Books, 1981.

Tryon, Thomas, *A Treatise of Dreams and Visions, to Which Is Added, a Discourse of the Causes, Nature, and Cure of Phrensie, Madness, or Distraction*, London: Sowle, 1689.

Tucker, Susie I., *Enthusiasm: A Study in Semantic Change*, Cambridge: Cambridge University Press, 1972.

Tuke, Daniel Hack, *Insanity in Ancient and Modern Life, with Chapters on its Prevention*, London: Macmillan, 1878.

Tuke, Daniel Hack, *Chapters in the History of the Insane in the British Isles*, London: Kegan Paul, and Trench, 1882.

Tuke, Daniel Hack, *Reform in the Treatment of the Insane: Early History of the Retreat, York; Its Objects and Influence*, London: Churchill, 1892.

Tuke, Samuel, *Description of the Retreat: An Institution Near York for Insane Persons of the Society of Friends*, York: Alexander, 1813.

Tuke, Samuel, *Practical Hints on the Construction and Economy of Pauper Lunatic Asylums*, York: Alexander, 1815.

Tuke, Samuel, *A Letter to Thomas Eddy of New York on Pauper Lunatic Asylums*, New York: Samuel Wood, 1815.

Upton, James, *A Letter to Sir Richard Carr Glynn, Bart., President of the Royal Hospitals of Bridewell and Bethlem, on the Treatment and Dismissal of the Late Medical Officers of Those Establishments*, London: Rivington, 1816.

Ure, Andrew, *The Philosophy of Manufactures*, London: Knight, 1835.

Uwins, David, *A Treatise on Those Disorders of the Brain and Nervous System, Which Are Usually Considered and Called Mental*, London: Renshaw and Rush, 1833.

Wallerstein, Immanuel, *The Modern World System*, New York: Academic Press, 1974.

Ward, Ned, *The London Spy (1698–1709)*, London: The Folio Society, 1955.

Warneford Asylum, *An Account of the Origin, Nature, and Objects of the Asylum on Headington Hill Near Oxford, Considered as a Benevolent Institution for the Reception, Relief, and Cure of the Insane*, Oxford: Munday and Son, 1827.

Warner, John Harley, *The Therapeutic Perspective: Medical Practice, Knowledge, and Identity in America, 1820–1885*, Cambridge: Harvard University Press, 1986.

Webb, Sidney, and Beatrice Webb, *English Poor Law History: Part I The Old Poor Law*, London: Longmans, Green, 1927.

Weber, Adna Ferrin, *The Growth of Cities in the Nineteenth Century*, New York: Columbia University Studies in History, Economics, and Public Law No. 11, 1899.

Weber, Max, *The Protestant Ethic and the Spirit of Capitalism*, London: Allen and Unwin, 1930.

Weber, Max, *From Max Weber: Essays in General Sociology*, London: Oxford University Press, 1946.

Weber, Max, *Economy and Society*, 2 vols, Totowa: Bedminister Press, 1968 (reprint edition, Berkeley: University of California Press, 1978).

Wesley, John, *Primitive Physick*, London: Trye, 1747.

Wesley, John, *The Journals of John Wesley*, 4 vols, (ed. Ernest Rhys), London: Everyman, 1906.

Willis, Francis, *A Treatise on Mental Derangement*, London: Longman, Hurst, Rees, Orme, and Brown, 1823, second edition, 1843.

Willis, Thomas, *Two Discourses Concerning the Soul of Brutes*, (trans. S. Pordage), London: Dring, Harper, and Leigh, 1683.

Willis, Thomas, *The Practice of Physick*, (trans. S. Pordage), London: Dring, Harper, and Leigh, 1684.

Wing, J.K., *Reasoning About Madness*, London: Oxford University Press, 1978.

Wing, J.K., and G.W. Brown, *Institutionalism and Schizophrenia*, Cambridge: Cambridge University Press, 1970.

Winslow, Forbes Benignus, *Principles of Phrenology as Applied to the Elucidation and Cure of Insanity*, London: Highley, 1832.

Winslow, Forbes Benignus, *Lettisomian Lectures on Insanity*, London: Churchill, 1854.

Winslow, Forbes Benignus, *On Obscure Diseases of the Brain, and Disorders of the Mind*, Philadelphia: Blanchard and Lee, 1860.

Woodroofe, Kathleen, *From Charity to Social Work in England and the United States*, London: Routledge and Kegan Paul, 1968.

Woolf, Leonard, *Beginning Again: An Autobiography of the Years 1911–1918*, New York: Harcourt Brace Jovanovich, 1972.

Wynter, Andrew, *The Borderlands of Insanity*, 1st edition, London: Hardwicke, 1875.

Wynter, Andrew, *The Borderlands of Insanity*, 2nd edition, London: Renshaw, 1877.

Yealland, L.R., *Hysterical Disorders of Warfare*, London: Macmillan, 1918.

York Asylum, *Observations on the Present State of the York Lunatic Asylum*, York: Richardson, 1809.

York Asylum, *Report of the Committee of Inquiry into the Rules and Management of the York Lunatic Asylum*, Doncaster: Sheardown, 1814.

Young, G.M., *Victorian England: Portrait of an Age*, 2nd edition, London: Oxford University Press, 1953.

Young, Robert M., *Mind, Brain, and Adaptation in the Nineteenth Century*, Oxford: Clarendon Press, 1970.

Zilboorg, Gregory, *History of Medical Psychology*, New York: Norton, 1941.

Articles

Allbutt, Thomas Clifford, 'Nervous Diseases and Modern Life', *Contemporary Review* 67, 1895, pp. 210–31.

Allderidge, Patricia, 'Bedlam: Fact or Fantasy?' in W.F. Bynum, Roy Porter, and Michael Shepherd (eds), *The Anatomy of Madness*, Vol. 2, London: Tavistock, 1985, pp. 17–33.

Allderidge, Patricia, 'The Foundation of the Maudsley Hospital', in G.E. Berrios and H. Freeman (eds), *150 Years of British Psychiatry 1841–1991*, London: Gaskell, 1991, pp. 89–102.

Anderson, Elizabeth Garrett, 'Sex in Mind and Education: A Reply', *Fortnightly Review* new series, 15, 1874, pp. 582–94.

Anderson, Michael, 'Smelser Revisted', *Social History* 1, 1976, pp. 317–34.

Andrews, Jonathan, 'A Respectable Mad-Doctor? Dr Richard Hale, F.R.S. (1670–1728)', *Notes and Records of the Royal Society of London* 44, 1990, pp. 169–203.

Andrews, Jonathan, '"In Her Vapours . . . [or] in her Madness"? Mrs Clerke's Case: An Early Eighteenth Century Psychiatric Controversy,' *History of Psychiatry* 1, 1990, pp. 125–43.

Anonymous, 'A Case Humbly Offered to the Consideration of Parliament', *Gentleman's Magazine* 33, 1763, 25–6.

Anonymous, 'Haslam, Arnold, and Others on Insanity', *Quarterly Review* 3, 1809, pp. 155–80.

Anonymous, 'Esquirol and the Treatment of the Insane', *Westminster Review* 18, 1833, pp. 129–38;

Anonymous, 'Review of *What Asylums Were, Are, and Ought to Be*', *Phrenological Journal* 10, 53, 1836–7.

Anonymous, 'Lunacy', *Westminster Review* 37, 1842, pp. 305–21.

Anonymous, 'Lunatic Asylums', *Westminster Review* 43, 1845, pp. 162–92.

Anonymous, 'Lunatic Asylums', *Quarterly Review* 101, 1857, pp. 353–93.

Anonymous, 'On the Degeneration of the Human Race', *Journal of Psychological Medicine* 10, 1857, pp. 159–208.

Anonymous, 'Commentary on S.A.K. Strahan, "The Propagation of Insanity and Allied Neuroses"', *Journal of Mental Science* 36, 1890, pp. 457–62.

Ardant, Gabriel, 'Financial Policy and Economic Infrastructure of Modern States and Nations', in Charles Tilly (ed.), *The Formation of National States in Western Europe*, Princeton, New Jersey: Princeton University Press, 1975, pp. 164–242.

Arlidge, John, 'Review of *An Examination of the Practice of Bloodletting in Mental Disorders* by Pliny Earle', *Journal of Mental Science* 2, 1856, pp. 165–75.

Armstrong, David, 'Madness and Coping', *Sociology of Health and Illness* 2, 1980, pp. 293–316.

Beier, A.L., 'Vagrants and the Social Order in Elizabethan England', *Past and Present* 64, 1974, pp. 3–29.

[Blackwell, J.], 'Report on the Treatment of Lunatics', *Quarterly Review* 74, 1844, pp. 416–47.

Blustein, Bonnie, 'New York Neurologists and the Specialization of American Medicine', *Bulletin of the History of Medicine* 53, 1979, pp. 170–83.

Blustein, Bonnie, '"A Hollow Square of Psychological Science": American Psychiatry and Neurology in Conflict', in A. Scull (ed.), *Madhouses, Mad-*

doctors, and Madmen, Philadelphia: University of Pennsylvania Press/London: Athlone, 1981, pp. 241–70.

Briggs, Asa, 'The Language of "Class" in Early Nineteenth Century England', pp. 43–73 in A. Briggs and J. Saville (eds), *Essays in Labour History*, London: Macmillan, 1960.

Browne, W.A.F., 'The Moral Treatment of the Insane: A Lecture', *Journal of Mental Science* 10, 1864, pp. 309–37.

Browne, W.A.F., 'On Medico-Psychology', *Journal of Mental Science*, 12, 1866, pp. 309–27.

[Bucknill, John Charles], 'Annual Reports of County Lunatic Asylums for 1856', *Journal of Mental Science* 3, 1857, pp. 477–8.

Bucknill, John Charles, 'Presidential Address', *Journal of Mental Science* 7, 1860, pp. 1–23.

[Bucknill, John Charles], 'Report from the Select Committee on Lunatics, July 1860', *Journal of Mental Science* 7, 1860, pp. 136–60.

Bucknill, John Charles, 'The Abolition of Proprietary Madhouses', *Nineteenth Century* 17, 1885, pp. 263–79.

Bynum, William F., 'Rationales for Therapy in British Psychiatry, 1780–1835', *Medical History* 18, 1974, pp. 317–34.

Bynum, William, 'Theory and Practice in British Psychiatry from J.C. Prichard (1786–1848) to Henry Maudsley (1835–1918)', in T. Ogawa (ed.), *History of Psychiatry*, Osaka: Taniguchi Foundation, 1982, pp. 196–216.

Bynum, William F., 'Physicians, Hospitals, and Career Structures in Eighteenth Century London', in W.F. Bynum and R. Porter (eds), *William Hunter and the Eighteenth Century Medical World*, Cambridge: Cambridge University Press, 1985, pp. 105–28.

Carswell, J., 'Some Sociological Considerations Bearing Upon the Occurrence, Prevention, and Treatment of Mental Disorders', *Journal of Mental Science* 70, 1924, pp. 347–62.

Checkland, G., and E.O.A. Checkland, eds, 'Introduction' to *The Poor Law Report of 1834*, Harmondsworth: Penguin, 1974.

Clark, Michael, 'The Rejection of Psychological Approaches to Mental Disorder', in A. Scull (ed.), *Madhouses, Mad-doctors and Madmen*, Philadelphia: University of Pennsylvania Press/London: Athlone, 1981, pp. 271–312.

Clark, Michael, '"A Plastic Power Ministering to Organization": Interpretations of the Mind-Body Relation in Late Nineteenth Century British Psychiatry', *Psychological Medicine* 13, 1983, pp. 487–97.

Clark, Michael, '"Morbid Introspection", Unsoundness of Mind, and British Psychological Medicine, *c.* 1830–*c.* 1900', in W.F. Bynum, R. Porter, and M. Shepherd (eds), *The Anatomy of Madness*, Vol. 3, London: Routledge, 1988, pp. 71–101.

Clouston, Thomas S., 'Puberty and Adolescence Medico-Psychologically Considered', *Edinburgh Medical Journal* 26, 1880, pp. 5–17.

Cochrane, David, '"Humane, Economical, and Medically Wise": The LCC as Administrators of Victorian Lunacy Policy', in W.F. Bynum, R. Porter, and M. Shepherd (eds), *The Anatomy of Madness*, Vol. 3, London: Routledge, 1988, pp. 265–6.

Conolly, John, 'On the Prospects of Physicians Engaged in Practice in Cases of Insanity', *Journal of Mental Science* 7, 1861, pp. 180–94.

Conolly, John, 'Presidential Address', *Journal of Mental Science*, 5, 1858, pp. 71–8.

Cooter, Roger, 'Phrenology and British Alienists, *ca*. 1825–1845', *Medical History* 20, 1976, pp. 1–21, 135–51, reprinted in A. Scull (ed.), *Madhouses, Mad-doctors, and Madmen*, Philadelphia: University of Pennsylvania Press/London: Athlone, 1981, pp. 58–104.

Crichton-Browne, James, 'Presidential Address', *Journal of Mental Science* 24, 1878, pp. 345–73.

Davey, J.G., 'On the Pathology of Insanity', *The Zooist* 1, 1944, pp. 111–19.

Dickens, Charles, and W.H. Wills, 'A Curious Dance Around a Curious Tree', 1852, reprinted in *Charles Dickens' Uncollected Writings from Household Words*, Bloomington: Indiana University Press, 1968, Vol. 2, pp. 381–91.

Digby, Anne, 'Changes in the Asylum: The Case of York, 1777–1815', *Economic History Review*, 2nd series, 36, 1983, pp. 218–39.

Dodds, Dr, Dr Strahan, and Dr Greenlees, 'Assistant Medical Officers in Asylums: Their Status in the Speciality', *Journal of Mental Science* 36, 1890, pp. 43–50.

Fears, Michael, 'Moral Treatment and British Psychiatry', paper presented at the conference of the British Sociological Association, 1975.

Fessler, A., 'The Management of Lunacy in Seventeenth Century England', *Proceedings of the Royal Society of Medicine, Historical Section* 49, 1956, pp. 901–7.

Fine, Bob, 'Objectification and the Bourgeois Contradictions of Consciousness', *Economy and Society 6*, 1977, pp. 408–35.

[Fitton, W.H.], 'Lunatic Asylums', *Edinburgh Review* 28, 1817, pp. 431–71.

Fitzgerald, Thomas, 'Bedlam', in *Poems on Several Occasions*, London: Watts, 1733.

Gairdner, W.T., 'Presidential Address', *Journal of Mental Science* 28, 1882, pp. 321–32.

Gelder, Michael, 'Adolf Meyer and his Influence on British Psychiatry', in G.E. Berrios and H. Freeman (eds), *150 Years of British Psychiatry, 1841–1991*, London: Gaskell, 1991, pp. 419–35.

Godlee, Fiona, 'Aspects of Non-Conformity: Quakers and the Lunatic Fringe', in W.F. Bynum, R. Porter, and M. Shepherd (eds), *The Anatomy of Madness*, Vol. 2, London: Tavistock, 1985, pp. 73–85.

Goodfield-Toulmin, June, 'Some Aspects of English Physiology, 1780–1840', *Journal of the History of Biology* 2, 1969, pp. 283–320.

Greene, Richard, 'The Care and Cure of the Insane', *Universal Review* July 1889, pp. 493–508.

Greene, Richard, 'Hospitals for the Insane and Clinical Instruction in Asylums', paper presented to the Hospitals Association, 1890, reprinted in H.C. Burdett, *Hospitals and Asylums of the World*, Vol. 2, pp. 248–64.

Grob, Gerald, 'Rediscovering Asylums: The Unhistorical History of the Mental Hospital', *Hastings Center Report* 7, 4, 1977, pp. 33–41.

Grob, Gerald, 'Marxian Analysis and Mental Illness', *History of Psychiatry* 1, 1990, 223–32.

Hare, Edward, 'Was Insanity on the Increase?' *British Journal of Psychiatry* 142, 1983, pp. 439–55.

Hervey, Nicholas, 'A Slavish Bowing Down: the Lunacy Commission and the Psychiatric Profession 1845–60', in W. Bynum, R. Porter, and M. Shepherd (eds), *The Anatomy of Madness*, Vol. 2, London: Tavistock, 1985, pp. 98–131.

Hervey, Nicholas, 'Advocacy or Folly? The Alleged Lunatics' Friend Society, 1845–63', *Medical History* 30, 1986, pp. 254–75.

Hinshelwood, R.D. 'Psychodynamic Psychiatry Before World War I', in G.E. Berrios and H. Freeman (eds), *150 Years of British Psychiatry 1841–1991*, London: Gaskell, 1991, pp. 197–205.

Howells, J.G., and M.L. Osborn, 'The History of Child Psychiatry in Britain', *Acta Paedopsychiatrica* 46, 1980, pp. 193–202.

Hunter, Richard, and Ida MacAlpine, 'Introduction' to Samuel Tuke, *Description of the Retreat*, facsimile edition, London: Dawsons, 1964.

Ignatieff, Michael, 'Prison and Factory Discipline, 1770–1800: The Origins of an Idea', unpublished paper presented at the Annual Meeting of the American Historical Association, 1976.

Ingleby, David, 'Mental Health and Social Order', in S. Cohen and A. Scull (eds), *Social Control and the State: Historical and Comparative Essays*, Oxford: Martin Robertson, 1983, pp. 141–88.

Jacyna, L.S., 'Somatic Theories of Mind and the Interests of Medicine in Britain, 1850–1879', *Medical History* 26, 1982, pp. 233–58.

Jarvis, Edward, 'On the Supposed Increase of Insanity', *American Journal of Insanity* 8, 1852, pp. 333–64.

Jarvis, Edward, 'The Influence of Distance From and Proximity to an Insane Hospital, on Its Use by Any People', *Boston Medical and Surgical Journal* 42, 17 April 1850, pp. 209–22.

Jarvis, Edward, 'The Influence of Distance and Nearness to an Insane Hospital on Its Use by the People', *American Journal of Insanity* 7, 1851, pp. 281–5.

Lalor, Joseph, 'Observations on the Size and Construction of Lunatic Asylums', *Journal of Mental Science* 7, 1860, pp. 104–11.

Laycock, Thomas, 'The Objects and Organization of the Medico-Psychological Association', *Journal of Mental Science* 15, 1869, pp. 327–43.

Laycock, Thomas, 'The Antagonism of Law and Medicine in Insanity, and its Consequences', *Journal of Mental Science* 8, 1863, pp. 593–7.

Laycock, Thomas, 'Reflex, Automatic, and Unconscious Cerebration: A History and Criticism', *Journal of Mental Science* 21, 1876, pp. 477–98 and 22, 1876, pp. 1–17.

Lewis, Aubrey, 'Henry Maudsley: His Work and Influence', *Journal of Mental Science* 97, 1951, pp. 259–77, reprinted in his *The State of Psychiatry: Essays and Addresses*, London: Routledge and Kegan Paul, 1967, pp. 29–48.

Lewis, Aubrey, 'Edward Mapother and the Making of the Maudsley Hospital', *British Journal of Psychiatry* 115, 1969, pp. 1344–66.

Linton, Eliza Lynn, 'The Higher Education of Women', *Fortnightly Review* new series, 40, 1886, pp. 498–510.

Lorber, Judith, 'Deviance as Performance: The Case of Illness', *Social Problems* 14, 1967, 302–10.

MacDonald, Michael 'Insanity and the Realities of History in Early Modern England', *Psychological Medicine* 11, 1981, pp. 11–25.

MacDonald, Michael, 'Religion, Social Change, and Psychological Healing in England, 1600–1800', in W.J. Sheils (ed.), *The Church and Healing*, Oxford: Blackwell, 1982, pp. 101–25.

MacDonald, Michael, 'Popular Beliefs About Mental Disorder in Early Modern England', in W. Eckhart and J. Geyer-Kordesch (eds), *Heilberufe und Kranke in 17 und 18 Jahrhundert*, Münster: Burgverlag, 1982, pp. 148–73.

MacDonald, Michael, 'Women and Madness in Tudor and Stuart England', *Social Research* 53, 2, 1986, pp. 261–81.

MacKenzie, Charlotte, 'Social Factors in the Admission, Discharge, and Continuing Stay of Patients at Ticehurst Asylum, 1845–1917', in W.F. Bynum, R. Porter, and M. Shepherd (eds), *The Anatomy of Madness*, Vol. 2, London: Tavistock, 1985, pp. 147–74.

Maher, W.B., and B. Maher, 'The Ship of Fools: *Stultifera Navis* or *Ignis Fatuus?*' *American Psychologist* 37, 1982, pp. 756–61.

Maudsley, Henry, 'Sex in Mind and Education', *Fortnightly Review* new series, 15, 1874, pp. 466–83.

Maudsley, Henry, 'Delusions', *Journal of Mental Science* 9, 1863, pp. 1–24.

Maudsley, Henry, 'Memoir of the Late John Conolly', *Journal of Mental Science* 12, 1866, pp. 151–74.

Maudsley, Henry, 'Considerations with Regard to Hereditary Influence', *Journal of Mental Science* 8, 1863, pp. 482–513.

Maudsley, Henry, 'Insanity and Its Treatment', *Journal of Mental Science* 17, 1871, pp. 311–34.

Maudsley, Henry, 'On the Alleged Increase of Insanity', *Journal of Mental Science* 23, 1877, pp. 45–54.

McCandless, Peter, ' "Build! Build!" The Controversy over the Care for the Chronically Insane in England, 1855–1870', *Bulletin of the History of Medicine* 53, 1979, pp. 553–74.

McCandless, Peter, 'Liberty and Lunacy: The Victorians and Wrongful Confinement', in A. Scull (ed.), *Madhouses, Mad-doctors, and Madmen*, Philadelphia: University of Pennsylvania Press/London: Athlone, 1981, pp. 339–62.

McKendrick, Neil, 'Josiah Wedgwood and Factory Discipline', *Historical Journal* 4, 1961, pp. 30–55.

Mellett, D.J., 'Bureaucracy and Mental Illness: The Commissioners in Lunacy 1845–90', *Medical History* 25, 1981, pp. 223–4.

Merksey, Harold, 'Shell-shock', in G.E. Berrios and H. Freeman (eds), *150 Years of British Psychiatry 1841–1991*, London: Gaskell, 1991, pp. 245–67.

Midelfort, Erik H.C., 'Madness and Civilization in Early Modern Europe', in B.C. Malament (ed.), *After the Reformation: Essays in Honor of J.H. Hexter*, Philadelphia: University of Pennsylvania Press, 1980, pp. 247–65.

Miller, Peter, 'The Territory of the Psychiatrist', *Ideology and Consciousness* 7, 1980, pp. 63–106.

Miller, Peter, and Nikolas Rose, 'The Tavistock Programme: The Government of Subjectivity and Social Life', *Sociology* 22, 1988, pp. 171–92.

Monro, Henry, 'On the Nomenclature of the Various Forms of Insanity', *Journal of Mental Science* 2, 1856, pp. 286–305.

Neugebauer, Richard, 'Treatment of the Mentally Ill in Medieval and Early Modern England: A Reappraisal', *Journal of the History of the Behavioral Sciences* 14, 1978, pp. 158–69.

Newington, Herbert Hayes, 'The Abolition of Private Asylums', *Journal of Mental Science* 31, 1885, pp. 138–47.

Newington, Herbert Hayes, 'Presidential Address', *Journal of Mental Science* 35, 1889, pp. 293–315.

Norman, Conolly, 'Presidential Address', *Journal of Mental Science* 40, 1894, pp. 487–99.

Parker, Geoffrey, 'The "Military Revolution", 1560–1660 – A Myth?' *Journal of Modern History* 48, 1976, pp. 195–214.

Parry-Jones, Brenda, 'A Calendar of the Eldon-Richards Correspondence *c.* 1809–1822', *Journal of the Merioneth Historical and Record Society* 1965, pp. 39–50.

Parry-Jones, William L., 'The Model of the Geel Lunatic Colony and Its Influence on the Nineteenth Century Asylum System in Britain', in A. Scull (ed.), *Madhouses, Mad-doctors, and Madmen*, Philadelphia: University of Pennsylvania Press/London: Athlone, 1981, pp. 201–17.

Paul, Sir George Onesiphorus, 'Suggestions on the Subject of Criminal and Pauper Lunatics Addressed to Earl Spencer,' reprinted in House of Commons, *Report of the Select Committee on Criminal and Pauper Lunatics*, 1807, pp. 14–20.

Pines, Malcolm, 'The Development of the Psychodynamic Movement', in G.E. Berrios and H. Freeman (eds), *150 Years of British Psychiatry 1841–1991*, London: Gaskell, 1991, pp. 206–31.

Playfair, W.S., 'Some Observations Concerning What Is Called Neurasthenia', *British Medical Journal* 6 November 1886, pp. 853–5.

Plumb, J.H., 'The New World of Children in Eighteenth Century England', *Past and Present* 67, 1975, pp. 64–95.

Porter, Roy, 'Was There a Moral Therapy in the Eighteenth Century?' *Lychnos* 1981–2, pp. 12–26.

Porter, Roy, 'The Rage of Party: A Glorious Revolution in English Psychiatry?' *Medical History* 27, 1983, pp. 35–50.

Porter, Roy, 'Introduction' to the reprint edition of John Haslam, *Illustrations of Madness*, London: Routledge, 1989.

Porter, Roy, 'Foucault's Great Confinement', *History of the Human Sciences* 3, 1990, pp. 47–54.

Porter, Roy, 'Anglicanism and Psychiatry: Robert Burton and Sir Thomas Browne', unpublished paper, Wellcome Institute for the History of Medicine.

Powell, Richard, 'Observations upon the Comparative Prevalence of Insanity at Different Periods', *Medical Transactions* 4, 1813, pp. 131–59.

Ray, Laurence, 'Models of Madness in Victorian Asylum Practice', *European Journal of Sociology* 22, 1981, pp. 229–64.

Reid, John, 'Report of Diseases', *The Monthly Magazine* 25, 1808, pp. 166–7, 374–5.

Renvoize, Edward, 'The Association of Medical Officers of Asylums and Hospitals for the Insane, the Medico-Psychological Association, and their Presidents', in G.E. Berrios and H. Freeman (eds), *150 Years of British Psychiatry 1841–1991*, London: Gaskell, 1991, pp. 29–78.

Robertson, G.M., 'The Prevention of Insanity: A Preliminary Survey of the Problem', *Journal of Mental Science* 72, 1926, pp. 454–91.

Rogers, T.L., 'Presidential Address', *Journal of Mental Science* 20, 1874, pp. 327–51.

Rollin, Henry, 'Whatever Happened to Henry Maudsley?' in G.E. Berrios and H. Freeman (eds), *150 Years of British Psychiatry 1841–1991*, London: Gaskell, 1991, pp. 351–8.

Rosen, George, 'Enthusiasm: "A Dark Lanthorn of the Spirit"', *Bulletin of the History of Medicine* 42, 1968, pp. 393–421.

Rosenberg, Charles, 'The Place of George M. Beard in Nineteenth-Century Psychiatry', *Bulletin of the History of Medicine* 36, 1962, pp. 245–59.

Rosenberg, Charles, 'The Bitter Fruit: Heredity, Disease, and Social Thought in Nineteenth Century America', *Perspectives in American History* 8, 1974, pp. 189–235.

Rosenberg, Charles, 'The Therapeutic Revolution: Medicine, Meaning, and Social Change in Nineteenth Century America', in Morris J. Vogel and Charles E. Rosenberg (eds), *The Therapeutic Revolution; Essays in the Social History of American Medicine*, Philadelphia: University of Pennsylvania Press, 1979, pp. 3–25.

Roth, Martin, 'Psychiatry and its Critics', *British Journal of Psychiatry* 122, 1973, pp. 374–402.

Rushton, P., 'Lunatics and Idiots: Mental Disability, the Community, and the Poor Law in North-East England, 1600–1800', *Medical History* 32, 1988, pp. 34–50.

Russell, Richard, 'The Lunacy Profession and its Staff in the Second Half of the Nineteenth Century, with Special Reference to the West Riding Lunatic Asylum', in W.F. Bynum, R. Porter, and M. Shepherd (eds), *The Anatomy of Madness*, Vol. 3, London: Routledge, 1988, pp. 297–315.

Sankey, W.H.O., 'Presidential Address', *Journal of Mental Science* 14, 1868, pp. 297–304.

Saunders, Janet, 'Quarantining the Weak-Minded: Psychiatric Definitions of Degeneracy and the Late-Victorian Asylum', in W.F. Bynum, R. Porter, and M. Shepherd (eds), *The Anatomy of Madness*, Vol. 3, London: Routledge, 1988, pp. 273–96.

Savage, George Henry, 'Hyoscyamine and its Uses', *Journal of Mental Science* 25, 1879, pp. 177–84.

Savage, George Henry, 'Uses and Abuses of Chloral Hydrate', *Journal of Mental Science* 25, 1879, pp. 4–8.

Savage, George Henry, 'A Lecture on Neurasthenia and Mental Disorders', *Medical Magazine* 20, 1911, 620–30.

Scull, Andrew, 'Madness and Segregative Control: The Rise of the Insane Asylum', *Social Problems* 24, 1977, pp. 337–51.

Scull, Andrew, 'The Social History of Psychiatry in the Victorian Era', in A. Scull (ed.), *Madhouses, Mad-doctors, and Madmen*, Philadelphia: University of Pennsylvania Press/London: Athlone, 1981, pp. 5–32.

Scull, Andrew, 'The Domestication of Madness', *Medical History* 27, 1983, pp. 233–48.

Scull, Andrew, 'Was Insanity Increasing? A Response to Edward Hare', *British Journal of Psychiatry* 144, 1984, pp. 432–6.

Scull, Andrew, 'The Theory and Practice of Civil Commitment', *Michigan Law Review* 82, 1984, pp. 793–809.

Scull, Andrew, 'A Failure to Communicate? On the Reception of Foucault's *Histoire de la folie* by Anglo-American Historians', in Arthur Still, and Irving Volody (eds), *Rewriting the History of Madness*, London: Routledge, 1992.

Scull, Andrew, and Diane Favreau, '"A Chance to Cut is a Chance to Cure": Sexual Surgery for Psychosis in Three Nineteenth Century Societies', in S. Spitzer and A. Scull (eds), *Research in Law, Deviance, and Social Control*, Vol. 8, Greenwich, Connecticut: JAI Press, 1986, pp. 3–39.

Sedgwick, Peter, 'Mental Illness Is Illness', *Salmagundi* 20, 1972, pp. 196–224.

Shapin, Steven, 'Phrenological Knowledge and the Social Structure of Nineteenth Century Edinburgh', *Annals of Science* 32, 1975, pp. 219–43.

Shapin, Steven, 'The Politics of Observation: Cerebral Anatomy and Social Interests in the Edinburgh Phrenology Disputes', in R. Wallis (ed.), *On the Margins of Science*, Keele, Staffordshire: Sociological Review Monograph 27, 1978, pp. 139–78.

Sheppard, Edgar, 'On Some of the Modern Teachings on Insanity', *Journal of Mental Science* 17, 1871, pp. 499–514.

Sicherman, Barbara, 'The Uses of a Diagnosis: Doctors, Patients, and Neurasthenia', *Journal of the History of Medicine and Allied Sciences* 32, 1977, pp. 33–54.

Skae, David, 'On the Legal Relations of Insanity', *Edinburgh Medical Journal* 12, 1867, pp. 811–29.

Slack, Paul, 'Vagrants and Vagrancy in England 1598–1664', *Economic History Review*, 2nd series, 27, 1974, pp. 360–79.

Smith, L.D., 'Eighteenth Century Madhouse Practice: The Prouds of Bilston', *History of Psychiatry* 3, 1992, pp. 45–52.

[Smith, Sydney], 'An Account of the Retreat', *Edinburgh Review* 23, 1814, pp. 189–98.

Smith-Rosenberg, Carroll, and Charles Rosenberg, 'The Female Animal: Medical and Biological Views of Woman and Her Role in Nineteenth Century America', *Journal of American History* 60, 1973, pp. 332–56.

Spitzer, Steven, and Andrew Scull, 'Social Control in Historical Perspective: From Private to Public Responses to Crime', in D.F. Greenberg (ed.), *Corrections and Punishment: Structure, Function, and Process*, Beverly Hills, California: Sage, 1977, pp. 281–302.

Steffan, Thomas, 'The Social Argument Against Enthusiasm (1650–1660)', *Studies in English* 21, 1941, pp. 39–63.

Stone, Martin, 'Shellshock and the Psychologists', in W.F. Bynum, R. Porter, and M. Shepherd (eds), *The Anatomy of Madness*, Vol. 2, London: Tavistock, 1985, pp. 242–71.

Strahan, S.A.K., 'The Propagation of Insanity and Allied Neuroses', *Journal of Mental Science* 36, 1890, pp. 325–38.

Suzuki, Akihito, 'Lunacy in Seventeenth and Eighteenth Century England: Analysis of Quarter Sessions Records, Part I', *History of Psychiatry* 2, 1991, pp. 437–56.

Suzuki, Akihito, 'Lunacy in Seventeenth and Eighteenth Century England: Analysis of Quarter Sessions Records, Part II', *History of Psychiatry* 3, 1992, pp. 29–44.

Thompson, F.M.L., 'Social Control in Victorian Britain', *Economic History Review* 34, 1981, pp. 189–208.

Todd, John, and Lawrence Ashworth, 'The West Riding Asylum and James Crichton-Browne, 1818–76', in G.E. Berrios and H. Freeman (eds), *150 Years of British Psychiatry 1841–1991*, London: Gaskell, 1991, pp. 389–418.

Tomes, Nancy, 'The Great Restraint Controversy: A Comparative Perspective on Anglo-American Psychiatry in the Nineteenth Century', in W.F. Bynum, R. Porter, and M. Shepherd (eds), *The Anatomy of Madness*, Vol. 3, London: Routledge, 1988, pp. 190–225.

Tomes, Nancy, 'The Anglo-American Asylum in Historical Perspective', in J. Giggs and C. Smith (eds), *Location and Stigma*, London: Unwin Hyman, 1988, pp. 3–20.

Tuke, Daniel Hack, 'On the Alleged Increase of Insanity', *Journal of Mental Science* 40, 1894, pp. 219–31.

Tuke, Samuel, 'Essay on the State of the Insane Poor', *The Philanthropist* 1, 1811, pp. 357–60.

Tuke, Samuel, 'Introductory Observations' to Maximilian Jacobi, *On the Construction and Management of Hospitals for the Insane*, London: Churchill, 1841.

Tuke, Thomas Harrington, 'On Warm and Cold Baths in the Treatment of Insanity', *Journal of Mental Science* 5, 1858, pp. 102–14.

Turner, Trevor, 'Henry Maudsley: Psychiatrist, Philosopher, and Entrepreneur', in W.F. Bynum, R. Porter, and M. Shepherd (eds), *The Anatomy of Madness*, Vol. 3, London: Routledge, 1988, pp. 151–89.

Turner, Trevor, 'Rich and Mad in Victorian England', *Psychological Medicine* 19, 1989, pp. 29–44.

[Uwins, David], 'Insanity and Madhouses', *Quarterly Review* 15, 1816, pp. 387–417.

[Uwins, David], 'Burrows on Insanity', *Quarterly Review* 24, 1821, pp. 169–94.

Viets, Henry R., 'West Riding, 1871–1876', *Bulletin of the History of Medicine* 6, 1938, pp. 477–87.

Wakefield, Edward, 'Plan for an Asylum for Lunatics', *The Philanthropist* 3, 1812, pp. 226–9.

[Wakefield, Edward], 'Extracts from the Report of the Committee Employed to Visit Houses and Hospitals for the Confinement of Insane Persons, With Remarks, By Philanthropus', *The Medical and Physical Journal* 32, August 1814, pp. 122–8.

Walton, John, 'Lunacy in the Industrial Revolution: A Study of Asylum Admissions in Lancashire, 1848–50', *Journal of Social History* 13, 1979, pp. 1–22.

Walton, John, 'The Treatment of Pauper Lunatics in Victorian England: The Case of Lancaster Asylum, 1816–1870', in Andrew Scull (ed.), *Madhouses, Mad-doctors, and Madmen*, Philadelphia: University of Pennsylvania Press/London: Athlone, 1981, pp. 166–97.

Walton, John, 'Casting Out and Bringing Back in Victorian England: Pauper Lunatics, 1840–70', in W.F. Bynum, R. Porter, and M. Shepherd (eds), *The Anatomy of Madness*, Vol. 2, London: Tavistock, 1985, pp. 132–46.

Warner, John Harley, 'The Edinburgh Bloodletting Controversy', *Medical History* 24, 1980, pp. 241–58.

Weatherly, Lionel A., 'Can We Instill Rational Ideas Regarding Insanity into the Public Mind?' *British Medical Journal* 16 September 1899, pp. 709–11.

Weiner, Dora, 'The Origins of Psychiatry: Pinel or the Zeitgeist?' in O. Baur and O. Glandien (eds), *Zusammenhang: Festschrift für Marielene Putscher*, Vol. 2, Köln: Wienand, 1984, pp. 617–31.

Williams, S.W.D., 'Our Over-Crowded Lunatic Asylums', *Journal of Mental Science* 17, 1871, pp. 515–18.

Williamson, George, 'The Restoration Revolt Against Enthusiasm', *Studies in Philology* 2, 1933, pp. 571–603.

Wing, J.K., 'Review of *Social Order/Mental Disorder*', *Times Literary Supplement* 7 July 1989, pp. 747–8.

Winslow, Forbes Benignus, 'Editorial', *Journal of Psychological Medicine and Mental Pathology* 5, 1852, pp. 399–401.

[Wynter, Andrew], 'Non-Restraint in the Treatment of the Insane', *Edinburgh Review* 131, 1870, 215–231.

Yellowlees, David, 'Presidential Address', *Journal of Mental Science* 36, 1890, pp. 473–489.

Zola, I.K., 'Medicine as an Institution of Social Control', *The Sociological Review* 20, 1972, pp. 487–504.

Unpublished Dissertations

Abbott, Andrew, 'The Emergence of American Psychiatry', unpublished Ph.D. dissertation, University of Chicago, 1982.

Andrews, Jonathan, 'Bedlam Revisited: A History of Bethlem Hospital *c.* 1634–*c.* 1770', unpublished Ph.D. dissertation, London University, 1991.

Bynum, William F., 'Time's Noblest Offspring: The Problem of Man in the British Natural Historical Sciences', unpublished Ph.D. dissertation, Cambridge University, 1974.

Clark, Michael, '"The Data of Alienism": Evolutionary Neurology, Physiological Psychology, and the Reconstruction of British Psychiatric Theory, *c.* 1850–*c.* 1900', unpublished D. Phil. dissertation, Oxford University, 1982.

Dowbiggin, Ian, 'The Professional, Sociopolitical, and Cultural Dimensions of Psychiatric Theory in France 1840–1900', unpublished Ph.D. dissertation, University of Rochester, 1987.

Evans, Robin, '"A Rational Plan for Softening the Mind": Prison Design, 1750–1842', unpublished Ph.D. dissertation, Essex University, 1974.

Fears, Michael, 'The "Moral Treatment" of Insanity: A Study in the Social Construction of Human Nature', unpublished Ph.D. dissertation, Edinburgh University, 1978.

Foster, J.D., 'Capitalism and Class Consciousness in Earlier Nineteenth Century Oldham', unpublished Ph.D. dissertation, Cambridge University, 1967.

Gatehouse, C.A., 'The West Riding Lunatic Asylum: The History of a Medical Research Laboratory', unpublished M.Sc. thesis, University of Manchester, 1981.

Goldstein, Jan Ellen, 'French Psychiatry in Social and Political Context: The Formation of a New Profession, 1820–1860', unpublished Ph.D. dissertation, Columbia University, 1978.

Hay, Michael, 'Understanding Madness: Eighteenth Century Approaches to Mental Illness', unpublished Ph.D. dissertation, York University, 1979.

Hervey, Nicholas, 'The Lunacy Commission 1845–60, with Special Reference to the Implementation of Policy in Kent and Surrey', unpublished Ph.D. dissertation, Bristol University, 1987.

Jacyna, L.S., 'Scientific Naturalism in Victorian Britain: An Essay in the Social History of Ideas', unpublished Ph.D. dissertation, Edinburgh University, 1980.

MacKenzie, Charlotte, 'A Family Asylum: A History of the Private Madhouse at Ticehurst in Sussex, 1792–1917', unpublished Ph.D. thesis, University of London, 1987.

McCandless, Peter, 'Insanity and Society: A Study of the English Lunacy Reform Movement 1815–70', unpublished Ph.D. dissertation, University of Wisconsin, 1974.

Moffett, John T., 'Bureaucracy and Social Control: A Study of the Progressive Regimentation of the Western Social Order', unpublished Ph.D. dissertation, Columbia University, 1971.

Phillips, H. Temple, 'The History of the Old Private Lunatic Asylum at Fishponds Bristol, 1740–1859', unpublished M.Sc. thesis, Bristol University, 1973.

Russell, Richard, 'Mental Physicians and Their Patients: Psychological Medicine in the English Pauper Lunatic Asylums of the Late Nineteenth Century', unpublished Ph.D. dissertation, Sheffield University, 1983.

Sicherman, Barbara, 'The Quest for Mental Health in America, 1880–1917', unpublished Ph.D. dissertation, Columbia University, 1967.

Smith, Roger, 'Physiological Psychology and the Philosophy of Nature in Mid-Nineteenth-Century Britain', unpublished Ph.D. dissertation, Cambridge University, 1970.

Stone, Martin, 'The Military and Industrial Roots of Clinical Psychology in Britain, 1900–1945', unpublished Ph.D. dissertation, London School of Economics and Political Science, 1985.

Thompson, Margaret Sorbie, 'The Mad, the Bad, and the Sad: Psychiatric Care in the Royal Edinburgh Asylum, Morningside, 1813–1894', unpublished Ph.D. dissertation, Boston University, 1984.

Tomes, Nancy, 'The Persuasive Institution: Thomas Story Kirkbride and the Art of Asylum Keeping, 1841–83', unpublished Ph.D. dissertation, University of Pennsylvania, 1978.

Index